Seymour Hersh is one of America's premier investigative
reporters. In 1969, as a freelance journalist, he wrote the first
account of the My Lai massacre in South Vietnam. In the 1970s,
he worked at the *New York Times* in Washington and New
York; he has rejoined the paper twice on special assignment. He
has won more than a dozen major journalism prizes, including
the 1970 Pulitzer Prize for International Reporting and four
George Polk Awards.

He is also the author of six books, including *The Price of
Power: Kissinger in the Nixon White House*, which won the
National Book Critics Circle Award and the Los Angeles Times
Book Award, *The Target is Destroyed: What Really Happened
to Flight 007 and What America Knew About It*, and *The
Samson Option: Israel's Nuclear Arsenal and America's
Foreign Policy*.

SEYMOUR HERSH

The Dark Side of Camelot

HarperCollins*Publishers*

HarperCollins*Publishers*
77–85 Fulham Palace Road,
Hammersmith, London W6 8JB

This paperback edition 1998
10

First published in Canada and the USA by
Little, Brown & Company 1997

ISBN 0 00 653077 X

Printed and bound in Great Britain by
Clays Ltd, St Ives plc

For Elizabeth,
Matthew, Melissa,
and Joshua

CONTENTS

AUTHOR'S NOTE

This is not a book about John Kennedy's brilliant moments, and his brilliant policies. Nor is it a book about the awful moment of his death and why he was shot.

John Kennedy's policies and his life contained many superb moments. After his death, his glamour and wit combined with his successes in foreign affairs and domestic policies — real and imagined — to create the myth of Camelot. But there was a dark side to Camelot, and to John Kennedy.

I began writing this book knowing that it would inevitably move into a sensitive area: When is it relevant to report on the private life of a public man? The central finding that emerged from five years of reporting, and more than a thousand interviews with people who knew and worked with John F. Kennedy, is that Kennedy's private life and personal obsessions — his character — affected the affairs of the nation and its foreign policy far more than has ever been known.

This is a book about a man whose personal weaknesses limited his ability to carry out his duties as president. It is also a book about the power of beauty. It tells of otherwise strong and self-reliant men and women who were awed and seduced by Kennedy's magnetism, and who competed with one another to please the most charismatic leader in our nation's history. Many are still blinded today.

In writing this book, my hope is that I have been able to help the nation reclaim some of its history.

Seymour M. Hersh

October 1997

THE DARK SIDE OF CAMELOT

1

NOVEMBER 22

It was America's blackest Friday.

President John F. Kennedy was gunned down on a Dallas street thirty minutes after noon on November 22, 1963. Vice President Lyndon B. Johnson, who had accompanied the president to Dallas, sped back to *Air Force One* and was sworn in with the bloodied widow of Jack Kennedy at his side. The presidential airplane soared away from murderous Texas to the safety of Washington.

Once *Air Force One* was airborne, some of the military and security men on duty were able to emerge from their despair and anger to begin asking necessary questions. Was Jack Kennedy's death the first move in an international conspiracy? Was Lyndon Johnson now the target? These concerns were shared in Washington, as the bureaucracy began the slow turn from one presidential orbit to another.

But it was the man closest to John F. Kennedy who needed to put aside his grief and begin immediately to hide all evidence of Kennedy's secret life from the nation — as well as from the new president, who could be sitting in the Oval Office by early evening. When word came of his brother's shooting, Attorney General Robert F. Kennedy, the second most powerful man in Washington, was at his Hickory Hill estate in suburban Virginia having a casual lunch of clam chowder and tuna fish sandwiches with, among others, Robert Morgenthau, the U.S. attorney for the Southern District of New York.*

In those first hours of horror, the president's remarkable younger brother lived up to his reputation for pragmatism and toughness, notifying members of the family, worrying about the return of his brother's body, answering legal queries from the new president, and, it seemed, losing himself in appropriate action. There would be time for mourning later. Now there was a state funeral to arrange and the president's widow and children to console. Among his many telephone calls early that afternoon was one to McGeorge Bundy, the dead president's national security adviser, who was told to protect Jack Kennedy's papers. Bundy, after checking with the State Department, ordered that the combinations to the president's locked files be changed at once — before Lyndon Johnson's men could begin rummaging through them.

Bobby Kennedy understood that public revelation of the materials in his brother's White House files would forever destroy Jack Kennedy's reputation as president, and his own as attorney general. He had spent nearly three years in a confounding situation — as guardian of the nation's laws, as his brother's secret operative in foreign crises, and as personal watchdog for an older brother who reveled in personal excess and recklessness.

The two brothers had lied in their denials to newspapermen and the public about Jack Kennedy's long-rumored first marriage to a Palm Beach socialite named Durie Malcolm. In 1947 Kennedy, then a first-term congressman, and Malcolm were married by a justice of the peace in an early-morning ceremony at Palm Beach. In an interview for this book, Charles Spalding, one of Kennedy's oldest friends, broke five decades of silence by family and friends and confirmed his personal knowledge of the marriage. "I remember saying to Jack at the time of the marriage," Spalding told me, "'You must be nuts. You're running for president and you're running around getting

---

* Morgenthau would not learn until he was interviewed for this book that Robert Kennedy had planned to tell him that afternoon that he was resigning his cabinet post and wanted Morgenthau to replace him as attorney general. Joseph F. Dolan, who was one of Kennedy's confidants in the Justice Department, said in a 1995 interview for this book that Kennedy "was going to run" his brother's 1964 reelection campaign.

married.'" The marriage flew apart. Spalding added that he and a local attorney visited the Palm Beach courthouse a few days later and
removed all of the wedding documents. "It was Jack," Spalding recalled, "who asked me if I'd go get the papers." No evidence of a divorce could be found during research for this book.

The president's files would reveal that Jack and Bobby Kennedy were more than merely informed about the CIA's assassination
plotting against Prime Minister Fidel Castro of Cuba: they were its
strongest advocates. The necessity of Castro's death became a presidential obsession after the disastrous failure of the Bay of Pigs invasion in April 1961, and remained an obsession to the end. White
House files also dealt with three foreign leaders who were murdered
during Kennedy's thousand days in the presidency — Patrice Lumumba, of the Congo; Rafael Trujillo, of the Dominican Republic;
and Ngo Dinh Diem, of South Vietnam. Jack Kennedy knew of and
endorsed the CIA's assassination plotting against Lumumba and Trujillo before his inauguration on January 20, 1961. He was much
more active in the fall of 1963, when a brutal coup d'état in Saigon resulted in Diem's murder. Two months before the coup, Kennedy
summoned air force general Edward G. Lansdale, a former CIA operative who had been involved in the administration's assassination
plotting against Fidel Castro, and asked whether he would return to
Saigon and help if the president decided he had to "get rid" of Diem.
"Mr. President," Lansdale responded, "I couldn't do that." The plot
went forward. None of this would be revealed until this book,
and none of it was shared with Lyndon Johnson, then the vice president.

The vice president also did not know that Jack Kennedy's ac-
claimed triumph in the Cuban missile crisis of October 1962 was far
from a victory. The world would emerge from fearful days of pending nuclear holocaust and be told that the president had stood firm
before a Soviet threat and forced Premier Nikita Khrushchev to back
down. Little of this was true, as Bobby Kennedy knew. Knowing that
their political futures were at stake, the brothers had been forced to
negotiate a secret last-minute compromise with the Soviets. The real
settlement — and the true import of the missile crisis — remained a
state secret for more than twenty-five years.

There were more secrets for Bobby Kennedy to hide.

In the last months of the Eisenhower administration, a notorious Chicago gangster named Sam Giancana had been brought into the Castro assassination effort, with Senator Jack Kennedy's knowledge. But Giancana was far more than just another mobster doing a favor for the government — and looking for a favor in return. Giancana and his fellow hoodlums in Chicago, one of the most powerful organized crime operations in the nation, had already been enlisted on behalf of Kennedy in the 1960 presidential campaign against Republican Richard M. Nixon, providing money and union support; mob support would help Kennedy win in Illinois and in at least four other states where the Kennedy plurality was narrow. Giancana's intervention had been arranged with the aid of both Frank Sinatra, who was close to the mob and the Kennedy family, and a prominent Chicago judge, who served as an intermediary for a meeting, not revealed until this book, between the gangster and Jack Kennedy's millionaire father, the relentlessly ambitious Joseph P. Kennedy. The meeting took place in the winter before the election in the judge's chambers. A few months after the election, allegations of vote fraud in Illinois were reported to Bobby Kennedy's Justice Department — and met with no response. The 1960 presidential election was stolen.

As Bobby Kennedy knew, President Kennedy and Sam Giancana shared not only a stolen election and assassination plotting; they also shared a close friendship with a glamorous Los Angeles divorcée and freelance artist named Judith Campbell Exner. Interviews for this book have bolstered the claims of Exner, who first met Kennedy in early 1960, that she was more than just the president's sex partner, that she carried documents from Jack and Bobby Kennedy to Giancana and his colleagues, along with at least two satchels full of cash. On one train trip from Washington to Chicago she was followed by a presidential advance man named Martin E. Underwood, who told in a 1996 interview of being ordered onto the train by Kenneth O'Donnell, Jack Kennedy's close aide. "Kenny suggested it might be a good idea," Underwood told me, "to go to Chicago by train. I said, 'What train?' It was the same train Judy took." He watched, he said, as Exner got off in Chicago and handed a satchel to a waiting Sam Giancana. Exner, in a series of interviews for this book, further admitted that she delivered money, lots of it, from California businessmen directly to the president. The businessmen were bidding on federal contracts.

There was further evidence of financial corruption in Kennedy's personal files. As the president's 1964 reelection campaign neared, Kennedy was put on notice by newspaperman Charles Bartlett, his good friend, that campaign contributions were sticking to the hands of some of his political operatives. "No books are kept," Bartlett wrote the president in July 1963, "everything is cash, and the potential for a rich harvest is clear. . . . I am fearful that unless you put a personal priority on learning more about what is going on, the thing may slip suddenly beyond your control."

Robert Kennedy understood, from his own investigations, that there was independent evidence for the Bartlett allegations: one of the attorney general's political confidants had assembled affidavits showing that money for JFK's reelection campaign was being diverted for personal use. The Bartlett letters could not be left for Lyndon Johnson.

Yet another group of documents that had to be removed dealt with Jack Kennedy's health. Kennedy had lied about his health throughout his political career, repeatedly denying that he suffered from Addison's disease. But as Kennedy and his doctors knew, the Addison's, which affects the body's ability to fight infection, was being effectively controlled — and had been since the late 1940s — by cortisone. Far more politically damaging was the fact that the slain president had suffered from venereal disease for more than thirty years, having repeatedly been treated with high doses of antibiotics and repeatedly reinfected because of his continual sexual activity. Those records would be hidden from public view for the next thirty years. There is no evidence he told any of his many partners. Kennedy also was a heavy user of what were euphemistically known as "feel-good" shots — consisting of high dosages of amphetamines — while in the White House. Dr. Max Jacobson, the New York physician who administered the shots, was a regular visitor to the White House and accompanied the president on many foreign trips; his name was all over the official logs. Jacobson and his shots were the source of constant friction between the president's personal aides and some members of his Secret Service detail, who persistently tried to keep the doctor, and his amphetamines, away from the White House. Jacobson's license to practice medicine was revoked in 1975.

* * *

Jack and Bobby Kennedy were even tougher than their most ardent admirers could imagine. They seemed to glide unerringly through the nearly three years of his presidency, with its constant domestic and foreign crises. But in reality they lived and worked on the edge of an abyss. The brothers understood, as the public did not, that they were just one news story away from cataclysmic political scandal.

How to keep secrets and carry on their activities was something they had learned from their father, a successful financier and controversial public official, who masked how much money he had and how he earned it, and from their maternal grandfather, John Francis "Honey Fitz" Fitzgerald, a corrupt Boston politician who simply ignored the unpleasant realities of his public life. Jack and Bobby Kennedy also learned from their father and grandfather that — as Kennedys — they could enjoy freedoms denied to other men; the consequences of their acts were for others to worry about.

The family's main antagonist was J. Edgar Hoover, director of the Federal Bureau of Investigation, who knew and was eager to take advantage — so the family was convinced — of the darkest Kennedy secrets, including the fact of Jack's marriage to Durie Malcolm. Hoover's biographers have told in compelling detail of Hoover's ability to collect damaging political and personal information about the men in the White House and use it as a weapon. The relentless FBI director had been keeping score on the Kennedys, father and sons, since the early 1940s and was appalled by their public and private excesses. But the Kennedys understood that Hoover, for all of his moralizing, was a firm believer in the institution of the presidency, and could be counted on in moments of crisis, even those involving angry women looking for a way to make trouble for the president.

Hoover's reappointment as FBI director was Jack Kennedy's first announcement as president-elect.

Jack Kennedy's embarrassing files were not the only materials removed from the White House on November 22. While *Air Force One* was still in the air, a senior Secret Service agent named Robert I. Bouck began disassembling yet another of the Kennedy brothers' deep secrets — Tandberg tape-recording systems in the Oval Office, Cabinet Room, and the president's living quarters on the second floor of the White House. There was also a separate Dictabelt recording system for use on the telephone lines in the president's office and his upstairs bedroom. In the summer of 1962, John Kennedy had summoned Bouck and instructed him to install the devices and be responsible for changing the tapes. Apparently Bouck told only two people of the system — his immediate superior, James J. Rowley, chief of the Secret Service, and a subordinate who helped him monitor the equipment. It was Bouck's understanding that only two others knew of the system while JFK was alive — Bobby Kennedy and Evelyn Lincoln, the president's longtime personal secretary.

The seemingly open and straightforward young president could activate the recording system when he chose, through a series of hidden switches that Bouck installed in the Oval Office and on the president's desk. "His desk had a block with two or three pens in it and a place for paper clips," Bouck said in a 1995 interview for this book. "I rigged one of those pen sockets so he could touch a gold button — it was very sensitive — and switch it [the tape recorder] on." Another secret switch was placed in a bookend that the president could reach while lounging in his chair. "All he had to do was lean on it," Bouck told me. A third was tucked away on a small table in front of the Oval Office desk, where Kennedy often met with aides and visitors. (Bouck would say of the tabletop switch only that it was placed "under something that was unlikely to be taken away.") Microphones were also hidden in the walls of the Cabinet Room and on the desk and coffee table in the president's office. Kennedy made little use of the devices in the family living quarters, Bouck said. The president could record telephone conversations by flicking a switch on his desk that activated a light in Evelyn Lincoln's office, alerting her to turn on the Dictabelt system. During its sixteen months of operation, Bouck said, the taping system produced "at least two hundred" reels of tapes. "They never told me why they wanted the tapes," Bouck said, "and I never had possession of any of the used tapes."

Bouck had no ambivalence as he tore his way through the office that now belonged to President Lyndon Johnson. Getting rid of the tapes and the taping system was something he did for Jack Kennedy: "I didn't want Lyndon Johnson to get to listen to them." The taping system was gone within hours, along with the reels of Oval Office and Cabinet Room recordings.*

By late afternoon it was getting crowded at Hickory Hill, as family friends, neighbors, and Justice Department aides — as if drawn by some survival instinct — made their way to the attorney general's side. Surrounded by sympathetic mourners, Robert Kennedy still found time to operate in secret, and he now turned away briefly from his need to protect his brother to seek out who might have gunned him down. His first suspect was Sam Giancana, the Kennedy family's secret helper in the 1960 election and in Cuba. He had been repeatedly heard on FBI wiretaps and bugs complaining about being the victim of a double cross since 1961: Bobby Kennedy had made the Chicago outfit a chief target of the Justice Department, and the mob's take was down.

Another target of Bobby's crime war was Jimmy Hoffa and his corrupt Teamsters Union; one of his most experienced operatives in that war was Julius Draznin, who was by 1963 a supervisor in Chicago for the National Labor Relations Board and responsible for liaison with the Justice Department. Bobby Kennedy had personally arranged for the installation of a secure telephone in Draznin's apartment on Chicago's South Side — one of many such telephones in what became an extraordinary and little-known communications system linking the attorney general with a select group of loyal government investigators across the nation. Draznin had spoken to Kennedy a few times on the secure telephone, but he talked most often with senior Kennedy aides such as Walter Sheridan, a Justice Department official closely involved with the Hoffa investigations. Draznin understood that such contacts were not to be reported to his labor board superiors. Nor, of course, were they to be mentioned to anyone from Hoover's FBI.

---

* The tape recordings remained in direct control of the Kennedy family until May 1976, when they were deeded to the John F. Kennedy Library in Boston. In a report issued in 1985, the library acknowledged that it was "impossible to establish with any certainty how much might have been removed" from the collection prior to 1975. "That at least some items were removed cannot be doubted." Some Dictabelt tapes of telephone conversations were also discovered to be in the possession of Evelyn Lincoln after her death in 1995.

Draznin's secure telephone rang twice on November 22. The first call came from Sheridan "four or five hours" after the assassination, Draznin told me in a series of interviews for this book. "Bobby is going to call you," Sheridan said. "He has some questions he wants you to help on — about the assassination." Kennedy's call came moments later. "We need all the help you can give. Can you open some doors for us in Chicago?" Kennedy made it clear, Draznin told me, that he suspected that Sam Giancana's mob might have been behind his brother's murder.

Moments after the call to Draznin, Kennedy dashed to the Pentagon, and with Secretary of Defense Robert S. McNamara and others flew by helicopter to Andrews Air Force Base, the home base for *Air Force One*, in suburban Maryland. A crowd of three thousand saddened Americans watched quietly as the presidential plane landed a few minutes after six o'clock. There was a sorrowful embrace between the president's brother and his widow. A small entourage, Bobby among them, then followed the body to Bethesda Naval Hospital, where an autopsy was to be performed.

Despite his grief, Kennedy continued to focus on the need to protect the Kennedy reputation. At the hospital, he took Evelyn Lincoln aside. "Bobby said to me that Lyndon's people were digging around in the president's desk," Lincoln told me in the most candid interview she ever gave, shortly before her death in 1995. She and her husband were at her desk packing her files of presidential papers by eight o'clock the next morning, she said, and were called into the Oval Office by President Johnson at eight-thirty. "He said, 'I need you more than you need me'" — a remark Johnson made to all of the Kennedy staff aides — "and then said, 'I'd like for you to move out of the office by nine A.M.'" Mrs. Lincoln immediately reported to Bobby Kennedy, who was waiting in a room nearby. "He couldn't believe it," Mrs. Lincoln said. "He got Johnson to agree to twelve noon." Johnson eventually decided to delay a few days before moving into JFK's office, but Bobby Kennedy was taking no chances; he had already ordered that his brother's Oval Office and National Security Council files be packed overnight and shipped to a sealed office by the crack of dawn on Saturday, November 23.

The president's personal papers and the White House tape recordings ended up in the top-secret offices of one of Jack Kennedy's most cherished units in the government — the Special Group for Counterinsurgency, whose mission was to battle communist-led wars of liberation in Latin America and Southeast Asia. The Special Group's third-floor corridor in the nearby Executive Office Building was the most secure area of the White House complex, with armed guards on patrol twenty-four hours a day. The president's papers and tape recordings were now safe.

One final act of cover-up occurred in the early-morning hours of Saturday, November 23, as Bobby Kennedy and an exhausted Jacqueline Kennedy returned to the White House, accompanying the body of the fallen president. There was a brief meeting between Kennedy and J. B. West, the chief White House usher, who turned over the Usher's Logs — the most detailed records that existed of the visitors, public and private, to the president's second-floor personal quarters. The logs provided what amounted to a daily scorecard of the president's sex partners, who were usually escorted by David Powers, JFK's longtime personal aide. The logs, traditionally considered to be the public records of the presidency, were never seen again by West, and are not among the documents on file at the Kennedy Library.

Bobby Kennedy knew, as did many of the men and women in the White House, that Jack Kennedy had been living a public lie as the attentive husband of Jacqueline, the glamorous and high-profile first lady. In private Kennedy was consumed with almost daily sexual liaisons and libertine partying, to a degree that shocked many members of his personal Secret Service detail. The sheer number of Kennedy's sexual partners, and the recklessness of his use of them, escalated throughout his presidency. The women — sometimes paid prostitutes located by Powers and other members of the so-called Irish Mafia, who embraced and protected the president — would be brought to Kennedy's office or his private quarters without any prior Secret Service knowledge or clearance. "Seventy to eighty percent of the agents thought it was nuts," recalled Tony Sherman, a former member of Kennedy's White House Secret Service detail, in a 1995 interview for this book. "Some of us were brought up the right way," Sherman added. "Our mothers and fathers didn't do it. We lived in another world. Suddenly, I'm Joe Agent here. I'm looking at the president of the United States and telling myself, 'This is the White House and we protect the White House.'"

Another Secret Service agent had the unceremonious chore of bringing sexually explicit photographs of a naked president with various paramours to the Mickelson Gallery, one of Washington's most distinguished art galleries, for framing. In a reluctantly granted interview in mid-1996, Sidney Mickelson, whose gallery framed pictures for the White House in the 1960s (and continued to do so for the next three decades), acknowledged that "over a number of years we framed a number of photographs of people — naked and often lying on beds — in the Lincoln Room. The women were always beautiful." In some cases the photographs included the president with, as Mickelson carefully described it, "a group of people with masks on." Another memorable photograph, Mickelson added, involved the president and two women, all wearing masks. "The Secret Service agent said it was Kennedy," Mickelson told me, "and I had no reason to doubt it." The photographs were always of high quality, Mickelson added, similar to those taken by official White House photographers.

Mickelson told me that the procedure for handling the extraordinary material was always the same. A Secret Service agent would arrive at his shop — ten blocks from the White House — early in the morning with a photograph. "I'd look at it, take the measurement, and then he'd take it back." The agent would return that evening, after the gallery closed, and wait once again in the same room with Mickelson until he completed the framing. He never had a chance, Mickelson told me, to make a copy of a photograph — something he thought about doing — because "the Secret Service agent was always with it."

Mickelson, who was seventy years old when we spoke, told me that he had remained especially troubled by the photographs, and his role in framing them, because at the time his shop was deeply involved in the restoration of the White House, managed by the first lady. "I had a very good relationship with Jackie and I respected her," Mickelson said. "But," he added with a shrug, "my feeling is whatever the White House sends me . . .

"No other White House did this."

* * *

John F. Kennedy's recklessness may finally have caught up with him in the last weeks of his life. One of his casual paramours in Washington, the wife of a military attaché at the West German Embassy, was believed by a group of Republican senators to be a possible agent of East German intelligence. In the ensuing panic, the woman and her husband were quickly flown out of Washington, and Robert Kennedy used all of his powers as attorney general, with the help of J. Edgar Hoover, to quash investigations by the Congress and the FBI. The potential damage of the presidential liaison was heightened, as the worried Kennedy brothers understood, by the ongoing sex scandal involving John Profumo, the British secretary of state for war, that was riveting London — and the British tabloids — throughout the summer of 1963. The government of Prime Minister Harold Macmillan barely survived the scandal.

Kennedy may have paid the ultimate price, nonetheless, for his sexual excesses and compulsiveness. He severely tore a groin muscle while frolicking poolside with one of his sexual partners during a West Coast trip in the last week of September 1963. The pain was so intense that the White House medical staff prescribed a stiff canvas shoulder-to-groin brace that locked his body in a rigid upright position. It was far more constraining than his usual back brace, which he also continued to wear. The two braces were meant to keep him as comfortable as possible during the strenuous days of campaigning, including that day in Dallas.

Those braces also made it impossible for the president to bend in reflex when he was struck in the neck by the bullet fired by Lee Harvey Oswald. Oswald's first successful shot was not necessarily fatal, but the president remained erect — and an excellent target for the second, fatal blow to the head. Kennedy's groin brace, which is now in the possession of the National Archives in Washington, was not mentioned in the public autopsy report, nor was the injury that had led to his need for it.

November 22, 1963, would remain a day of family secrets, carefully kept, for decades to come.

2

JACK

Jack Kennedy was a dazzling figure as an adult, with stunning good looks, an inquisitive mind, and a biting sense of humor that was often self-mocking. He throve on adoration and surrounded himself with starstruck friends and colleagues. Women swooned. Men stood in awe of his easy success with women, and were grateful for his attentions to them. Today, more than thirty years after his death, Kennedy's close friends remain enraptured. When JFK appeared at a party, Charles Spalding told me, "the temperature went up a hundred and fifty degrees."

His close friends knew that their joyful friend was invariably in acute pain, with chronic back problems. That, too, became a source of admiration. "He never talked about it," Jewel Reed, the former wife of James Reed, who served in the navy with Kennedy during World War II, said in an interview for this book. "He never complained, and that was one of the nice things about Jack."

Kennedy kept his pain to himself all of his life.

* * *

The most important fact of Kennedy's early years was his health. He suffered from a severe case of Addison's disease, an often-fatal disorder of the adrenal glands that eventually leaves the immune system unable to fight off ordinary infection. No successful cortisone treatment for the disease was available until the end of World War II. A gravely ill Kennedy, wracked by Addison's (it was undiagnosed until 1947), often seemed on the edge of death; he was stricken with fevers as high as 106 degrees and was given last rites four times. As a young adult he also suffered from acute back pain, the result of a college football injury that was aggravated by his World War II combat duty aboard *PT-109* in the South Pacific. Unsuccessful back surgery in 1944 and 1954 was complicated by the Addison's, which severely diminished his ability to heal and increased the overall risk of the procedures.

Kennedy and his family covered up the gravity of his illnesses throughout his life — and throughout his political career. Bobby Kennedy, two weeks after his brother's assassination, ordered that all White House files dealing with his brother's health "should be regarded as a privileged communication," never to be made public. Over the years, nonetheless, biographies and memoirs have revealed the extent of young Jack Kennedy's suffering. What has been less clear is the extent of the impact his early childhood illnesses had on his character, and how they shaped his attitudes as an adult and as the nation's thirty-fifth president.

Kennedy's fight for life began at birth. He had difficulty feeding as an infant and was often sick. At age two he was hospitalized with scarlet fever and, having survived that, was sent away to recuperate for three months at a sanatorium in Maine. It was there that Jack, torn from his parents and left in the care of strangers, demonstrated the first signs of what would be a lifelong ability to attract attention by charming others. He so captivated his nurse that it was reported that she begged to be allowed to stay with him. Poor health plagued Jack throughout his school years. At age four, he was able to attend nursery school for only ten weeks out of a thirty-week term. At a religious school in Connecticut when he was thirteen, he began losing weight and was diagnosed with appendicitis. The emergency operation — a family surgeon was flown in for the procedure — almost killed him; he never returned to the school. Serious illness continued to afflict Kennedy at prep school at Choate, and local physicians were unable to treat his chronic stomach distress and his "flu-like symptoms." He was diagnosed as suffering from, among other ailments, leukemia and hepatitis — afflictions that would magically clear up just as his doctors, and his family, were despairing. Once again, he made up for his sickliness with charm, good humor, and a winning zest for life that kept him beloved by his peers, as it would throughout his life.

His loyal friend K. LeMoyne Billings, who was a classmate at Choate, waited years before revealing how much Kennedy had suffered. "Jack never wanted us to talk about this," Billings said in an oral history for the John F. Kennedy Library in Boston, "but now that Bobby has gone and Jack is gone, I think it really should be told. . . . Jack Kennedy all during his life had few days when he wasn't in pain or sick in some way." Billings added that he seldom heard Kennedy complain. Another old friend, Henry James, who met Jack at Stanford University in 1940, eventually came to understand, he told a biographer, that Kennedy was not merely reluctant to complain about pain and his health but was psychologically unable to do so. "He was heartily ashamed" of his illnesses, James said. "They were a mark of effeminacy, of weakness, which he wouldn't acknowledge. I think all that macho stuff was compensation — all that chasing after women — compensation for something that he hadn't got." Kennedy was fanatic about maintaining a deep suntan — he would remain heavily tanned all of his adult life — and he once explained, James said, that "it gives me confidence. . . . It makes me feel strong, healthy, attractive." A deep bronzing of the skin when exposed to sunlight was, in fact, one of the symptoms of Addison's disease.

Kennedy had few options other than being strong and attractive; his father saw to that. Joseph Kennedy viewed his son's illness as a rite of passage. "I see him on TV, in rain and cold, bareheaded," Kennedy told the writer William Manchester in 1961, "and I don't worry. I know nothing can happen to him. I tell you, something's watching out for him. I've stood by his deathbed four times. Each time I said good-bye to him, and he always came back. . . . You can't put your finger on it, but there's that difference. When you've been through something like that back, and the Pacific, what can hurt you? Who's going to scare you?"

Jack was always striving to be strong for his father; to finish first, to shape his life in ways that would please Joe. Jack's elder brother, Joseph Jr., always in flourishing health, had been his father's favorite, the son destined for a successful political career in Washington. With Joe Jr.'s death in 1944 as a naval aviator, Jack became the focus of Joe Kennedy's aspirations. In Jack's eyes, his father could do little wrong. Many of Jack's friends thought otherwise, but learned to say nothing. "Jack was sick all the time," Charles Spalding told me in 1997, "and the old man could be an asshole around his kids." During a visit to the Kennedy home in Palm Beach, Florida, in the late 1940s, Spalding said, he and his wife, Betty, were preparing to go to a movie with Jack and his date, Charlotte MacDonald. Spalding went upstairs with Jack and Charlotte to say good night to Joe, who was shaving. The father turned to Charlotte and said scathingly, "Why don't you get a live one?" Spalding was appalled by the gratuitous comment about his best friend's chronic poor health and couldn't resist making a disparaging remark about Joe Kennedy to Jack. The son's defense of his father was instinctive: "Everybody wants to knock his jock off, but he made the whole thing possible."

Charles Bartlett, another old friend, saw both Joe Kennedy's toughness and his importance to his son. Bartlett, who became friends with Jack in Palm Beach after the war, declared that Joe Kennedy "was in it all the way. I don't think there was ever a moment that he didn't spend worrying how to push Jack's cause," especially as his son sought the presidency in 1960.

"He pushed them all," Bartlett, who later became the Washington bureau chief of the *Chattanooga Times,* told me in an interview for this book. "He pushed Bobby into the Justice Department, and he made Jack do things that Jack would probably rather not have done. He was very strong; he'd done things for the kids and wanted them to do some things for him. He didn't bend. Joe was tough." And yet, Bartlett added, "I just found that, in so many things, his judgment down the road was really enormous. You had to admire him."

Jewel Reed vividly recalled her first visit to a family gathering at Hyannis Port, Massachusetts, and the intense energy Joe Kennedy focused on his children. "The table was dynamic, and Mr. Kennedy was checking up on everybody about whether they had come in first or second or third in tennis or yachting or whatever," she said in an interview for this book. "And he wanted them to be number one. That stuck with me a long time. I remembered how intensely he had focused on their winning."

There was a high cost, Reed added. "His values that he imposed upon his children were difficult. His buying things. I hate to use the word bribery, but there was bribery in his agenda often." During Jack Kennedy's first Senate campaign, in 1952, Reed said, when he stunned the experts by defeating Republican Henry Cabot Lodge, Jr., "the billboards in Massachusetts came to about a quarter of a million dollars. That was a long, long time ago, and a quarter of a million was an awful lot of money." Reed also said that Joe Kennedy purchased thousands of copies of *Profiles in Courage,* Jack's Pulitzer Prize–winning bestseller, published in 1956, "to keep it on top of the bestseller list. I don't know what he did with all those books. That was bribery in a way. He was pushing, and if it cost money, he paid it. I'm sure that the children couldn't have felt comfortable about that."

The point, Reed added, was that Joe Kennedy "loved his family. It was very evident, and I remember Teddy [Edward M. Kennedy, Joe's youngest child] paying tribute to his father in saying that he was always there when they needed him. And that's saying a lot."

It was different with Rose Kennedy. As Jack's friends knew, he was full of misgivings about his mother. Kennedy once said to his aide Kenny O'Donnell that he could not recall his mother ever telling him, "I love you." Charles Spalding got a firsthand glimpse of a rare flash of Jack's hostility toward his mother. "I remember being down in Palm Beach and she [Rose Kennedy] came by in the middle of lunch and said to Jack, 'Oh, baby, I just hate the idea of your having to go back [to Washington].' Jack just blurted out, 'If you hadn't pushed me to be a success, I could stay here.'"

In an interview in 1990 with British biographer Nigel Hamilton, author of *JFK: Reckless Youth,* a definitive account of Kennedy's early years, Spalding speculated that Jack's craving for women and his compulsive need to shower, as often as five times a day, were linked to a lack of mothering. Kennedy, Spalding said, "hated physical touching — people taking physical liberties with him — which I assume must go back to his mother and the fact that she was so cold, so distant from the whole thing. . . . I doubt if she ever rumpled the kid's hair in his whole life. . . . It just didn't exist: the business of letting your son know you're close, that she's there. She wasn't."

"What *is* touch?" Spalding added. "It must come from some deeper maternal security — arms, warmth, kisses, hugs. . . . Maybe sex is the closest prize there is, that holds the whole thing together. I mean if you have sex with anybody you care about at all, you feel you've been touched. . . ."

In an extraordinary series of interviews, one of Jack Kennedy's lovers has candidly described his strengths and weaknesses as she saw them during a bittersweet relationship that spanned four years during which he campaigned for and won the presidency. The woman, who subsequently married and had a successful career, agreed to share her insights only upon a promise of anonymity. She had met Kennedy, then a U.S. senator, at a fund-raising dinner in Boston in the late 1950s; she was nineteen years old, a student at Radcliffe, and he began flirting with her.

"It was glamorous," she recalled. "It was supposed to be terrific. It was supposed to be just what anybody would want, what any woman would want. During that early time there would be looking at me. There would be nodding at me. There would be leaning across the table to say something just to me. There would be those signs of special attention. Yes, in public. And of course that was very flattering. I thought, 'Oh, gosh. I really must be quite something.'"

The affair deepened. She fell totally in love with the handsome Kennedy and spent hours, after making love with him, at dinner or in long conversations in bed. "I was absolutely thrilled to the gills," she told me. "Here I was, twenty years old, having dinner in the White House, the Abraham Lincoln bedroom. It seemed very amazing. There was a time when he needed to make a statement about a certain thing that happened in the world. And [he] went off and came back half an hour later and was really thrilled with the fact that he had come up with six declarative sentences that just laid it out." Their relationship, the woman said, "was supposed to be secret, and so I just went along and didn't talk about it." As for Kennedy's seemingly ideal marriage to Jackie, she said, "I did not have the foggiest idea of any consciousness of solidarity with other women. It just did not flicker. I cannot tell you how unevolved as a woman I was, and how it was assumed that women compete with each other for the best men. I just went right along with that. Somehow it didn't register with me at any deep level that what I was doing was absolutely immoral, absolutely atrocious behavior."

Kennedy, while attentive and engaging, rarely talked about his childhood in their time together, the woman told me. But she now understands that his ability to compartmentalize his life, to take the enormous risk — while seeking and occupying the presidency — of being so publicly married and so privately a womanizer, stemmed from his experiences as a child. He was "a boy who was sick frequently, who was frail, in a family where there was a tremendous premium on aggressive, competitive, succeeding, energizing activity. In the class that John Kennedy came from, there's a tremendous emphasis on appearance and how does it look? Well, it's not supposed to look like it's painful. It's not supposed to look like you feel like you don't know something or that you don't understand what's going on in your family or in the world. There's a tremendous premium on being smooth and in charge and in control — you aren't sweaty and nervous. You just sail effortlessly through the trials and tribulations that bring down other people, but not you."

The inevitable result, she explained, was that there were many times when Jack felt the pain of being excluded. "If you are a sickly child who spends a good deal of time in your bed at a young age in a house full of a lot of children, all of whom are in school or playing games or doing whatever they're doing, you could feel left out. It didn't sound like everybody then [in his family] took turns to come and sit with him and chat with him and draw pictures with him." Kennedy could have responded to the experience, the woman told me, by learning to "identify with others in the same situation. Or you can say 'I'm never going to have that feeling again.'" Kennedy chose to shut out the pain. "It was something he did not reflect [on] and didn't want to think about much and hoped would never happen and went out of his way to make sure it" — thinking about his childhood emotions — "didn't happen."

Kennedy spoke to the woman only once, she recalled, about being a trustworthy parent. If his daughter, Caroline, who was born in 1957, ever got into any kind of trouble, "he hoped that she would come to him and not feel that she had to hide it from him. His father had always wanted him to have that feeling about him, and that was a really important thing." The woman came to understand that Kennedy's relationship with his father was "the most vibrant relationship he'd ever had — love, fear, palpitations, trying to please him." Asked whether Kennedy felt he could turn to his mother for help, she answered, "I do not know. I never heard him speak about his mother. Never."

Jack Kennedy's delight in his children, and in all children, was profound, and recognized as such by staff aides who knew nothing of his early life. Marcus Raskin, who worked on nuclear disarmament issues for the National Security Council, recalled in an interview for this book that he and his colleagues would ask, in moments of international crisis, "Where are the children?" If Caroline and her younger brother, John, "were in Washington, then there wouldn't be a war. If the children were away, then you weren't sure." The question was not facetious, Raskin insisted. Jerome B. Wiesner, the president's science adviser, told McGeorge Bundy's national security staff, Raskin said, "to watch where the kids are. If they're here [in Washington], then there's going to be no war this week. If the kids aren't here, then we've got to be careful." Wiesner's remark was obviously tongue-in-cheek, Raskin said, but "many things are said ha-ha that have a grain of truth to them." He and his colleagues, Raskin said, looked in moments of crisis "for some sort of human affect to understand the momentous questions that they were dealing with."

If the president's national security advisers understood his love for children, so did the Secret Service. Larry Newman was one of the White House agents assigned to Kennedy on the evening in August 1963 when the president made a visit to his youngest child, Patrick, born prematurely and hospitalized with a lung ailment, who was fighting for his life in Children's Hospital in Boston. Newman, who was in the elevator with the president and Patrick's doctor, listened as Kennedy was told that his newborn son was unlikely to survive. The elevator stopped at the fifth floor, where the pediatric intensive care unit was. The floor had been cleared of all visitors for the presidential visit. The hallway was dark; the patient rooms were illuminated by night-lights. Newman recalled in an interview for this book that while walking with the president to intensive care, "we passed a room where there were two delightful-looking little girls who were sitting up in bed. They were probably about three or four years old, and they were talking and laughing together. The only problem — one girl was bandaged up to her chin. She had severe burns. And the other had burns down her arms and huge pods [of bandages] on the end of her hands. President Kennedy stopped and just looked at these two little girls. He asked the doctor, 'What's wrong with them?' And the doctor explained that one girl may lose the use of her hands. The president stood there. His son was down at the end of the hall in grave to critical condition. We just stood there with him; it was just a small party in the dark. He started feeling in his pockets — it was always a sign he wanted a pen. Someone gave him a pen. He said, 'I'd like to write a note to the children.' And nobody had any paper for the thirty-fifth president of the United States to write a note on. So the nurse scurries to the station and gets the name of the children and their family and Kennedy writes a note to each child. There was no fanfare, no photo-op. There was nothing. The nurse took the notes and said she would see that the family got it. And then we proceeded down the hall to see his son, who of course died the next day. It was something he didn't need to do, but he always seemed to come out of his reserved and Bostonish [ways] with children.

"Nothing was ever said about it. There was no press release or anything. He just went on to do what he had to do — to see his son. This was part of the dichotomy of the man — the rough-cut diamond. You could see so many qualities he had that just glowed; you couldn't see why he wanted to follow other roads that were so destructive. It was truly painful."

* * *

The women who knew Jack Kennedy, whether they were his lovers or not, invariably spoke, in interviews for this book, about his overwhelming attractiveness. The writer Gloria Emerson was an aspiring journalist when she was first introduced to Kennedy in the 1950s at a cocktail party. "I was almost hypnotized by the sight of this man," she told me in a 1997 interview. "He was such a stunning figure. He didn't have to lift a finger to attract women; they were drawn to him in the battalions, by the brigades. And the interesting thing was he didn't care if you made an effort to make him interested in you. He was perfectly cordial — but come and go, it didn't really matter to him."

Kennedy, Emerson added, "always seemed to be surrounded by men. And they were always talking about strategy or the moves of other people. And it was rather mysterious and exciting. You, of course, as a young girl were of no importance whatsoever. Jack always called you kid, because he couldn't remember women's names. It wasn't just the looks — it was the sense of mockery and that kind of fierce intelligence. He didn't like people who babbled. He was very impatient and often very tense. I didn't realize it then, but I think he must have been in pain a great deal of the time. Not just the stooped shoulders, but the shifting in chairs."

Emerson was dating one of Kennedy's classmates from Harvard when she and Jack first met. It was before his marriage to Jacqueline Bouvier. At the inevitable round of weekend parties, she said, "he was totally unselfconscious. He walked around half-naked, with just a towel wrapped around him — all bone, all rib, all shank. You have to have tremendous self-assurance to do that. I've never met anyone like that again. It was the audaciousness, the intensity, the impatience, even the brusqueness. Here was a man who wasn't going to wait; he was going to get what he wanted. He was going to go from the House to the Senate to the White House. And it was quite thrilling."

Another part of his charm, said Emerson, was young Jack Kennedy's total indifference "to his own beauty. He didn't care if a woman said yes or a woman said no. There would be another one. He was so absentminded about the women he was having affairs with. Once I had a roommate in New York and we were both very young. She was having a very pleasant affair with Jack and not taking it too seriously, which seemed very wise to me. But he could never remember her name. 'Hello, kid. How are you?' And he couldn't figure out how to get in touch with her, so he had to call up the doorman of the building and describe the woman, so the doorman could identify her."

Kennedy's longtime secret lover described, with some pain, the night before the inauguration in January 1961, when she slept with the president-elect in the Georgetown home he shared with his wife and two children. Her father, a prominent businessman, was then being considered for a high-level post in the new administration. "He [Kennedy] was getting dressed, in white tie, and he looked at me," the woman said, and he asked, "by any chance," whether she was related to the potential nominee. She and Kennedy had been lovers for two years by then, the woman said, and he did not know who she was.

Looking back at it, the woman added, she realized that her relationship with Kennedy was based solely on his need for "conquest." "I was somebody who happened to cross his radar screen, and so he said, 'Well, you. I'll take you.' Charge and send. I was young. I was pretty. I could talk along. I was just thrilled and said, 'Oh, wow, gosh. Here's this handsome older man. Here's this person, he's interested in me.' But in retrospect it's really sad. I was just another girl. There was a compartment for girls, and once you were in the sex compartment, you weren't a person anymore. I got declassed and depersonalized" by sleeping with Kennedy.

"He did not talk about his marriage to me," the woman added. "How do you settle within yourself a pattern of behavior that is a betrayal of someone else's trust? There are 'arrangements' and there's a whole rhetoric and a whole kind of nonsense that people talk, but the basic act is betrayal. It's hard to be a person who is trustworthy, when in your own family you are not. I think that somehow between his money, his position, his charm, his whatever, he was caught up in feeling that he was buffered. That people would take care of it. There is that feeling that you are not accountable; that the laws of the world do not apply to you. Laws had never been applied to his father and to him." Aiding in this was the fact that, "among other things, reporters also wanted to be his friends, wanted to have relationships with him, wanted to spend time with him. I don't know whether they did male bonding things about women, but the fact is a lot of reporters were very keen to spend time with him. And I think that he assumed they would not turn him in. And they didn't."

The woman came to understand that Kennedy's most significant attachments were not to women but to men. Jack Kennedy was a man's man. Men adored him, just as he adored his ever-demanding father. "He preferred the company of men," Gloria Emerson recalled. "They admired him and they wanted to be like him. And they wanted, as did women, to win his favor, but even more important, they seemed to love him. People wanted to please Jack." Schoolmates, navy buddies, political operatives, and those colleagues in the House and Senate with whom he chased women — all were attracted to Kennedy when they first met him, and had been ever since he was a gangly teenager. Charles Spalding vividly remembered his first glimpse of Kennedy at Hyannis Port in the early 1940s. Spalding, a navy aviator, had just published a bestselling memoir on flying entitled *Love at First Flight*. Kennedy, also in the navy, was lying down with no clothes on, except for a swimsuit casually draped across his loins. "He liked the fact that I'd written a book that had just come out," Spalding said. Kennedy's undergraduate thesis at Harvard, *Why England Slept*, had been published a few years earlier, and Spalding politely asked how it was going. "Going like hotcakes," replied Kennedy. "Dad's seeing to that."

"I never met anybody who felt that the minute was as important as it was [for him]," said Spalding. "He had to live for today. There was this inner pulse, and he could find it anywhere he went." Kennedy made things happen. "He was fun," newspaper editor Benjamin Bradlee recalled in an interview. "That's what you forget. He was fun to be with. He had a great sense of humor and surrounded himself with people with humor. He teased. He liked to be teased. I enjoyed being with him." But he made people feel that others had to live by his priorities. "He would ask you to go with him someplace a lot of times when it was inconvenient for you," George Smathers, a contemporary of Kennedy's in the Senate, told me. "He would say, 'Come on, go. Come on, go.' And he and I made several trips together. He was very wonderful, friendly and loyal."

Kennedy's impulsiveness was irresistible. Hugh Sidey, the White House correspondent for *Time* magazine, who drew close to Kennedy, had an Oval Office interview scheduled for what, he concluded, was the wrong time. When he walked in, the president was in a snit over a minor foreign policy dispute, Sidey recalled in an interview, "looking down at his desk and barking orders. And he looked up at me and says, 'Come on, Sidey. Let's go swimming.' I said, 'Mr. President, that's the one piece of equipment I have never thought to bring when I come over for an interview.' He said, 'Oh, in this pool you don't need a suit.'" Once at the pool, Sidey said, "I'm confronted with this problem of who removes his trousers first — the president or the guest?" Sidey laughed at the recollection. "Kennedy beat me. Obviously a man of practice. And we dove in."

Sidey got his clearest insight into Kennedy, he told me, when, while doing an article on the president's reading habits for *Life* magazine, he asked him to list his ten favorite books. "Without hesitating he said, '*Melbourne,*'" referring to the much-acclaimed 1939 biography of Lord Melbourne, Queen Victoria's prime minister and political adviser. Sidey immediately read the book. "It was the story," he said, "about the young aristocracy of Britain . . . who gave their lives in military campaigns, who held the ideal of empire and national honor above all else. But on the weekends, when they went to their country estates, it was broken-field running through the bedrooms. I mean they swapped wives, they slept with others. But the code of that period was nobody talked about it. And you didn't get divorced; otherwise, you were disgraced.

"I saw Kennedy," Sidey added, "and I said, 'Listen, now I know you better than anything. [*Melbourne*] tells me more about you than anything else.' He just laughed and said, 'Well, I'm fascinated with it. It was an interesting period in history.'" From then on, Sidey said, he and the president had a shared secret.

Kennedy was particularly energized by the West Coast. Joe Naar, an aspiring television producer, was a friend of the actor Peter Lawford, the president's brother-in-law, and spent weekends at the Lawfords' Santa Monica home, which was always crowded with show business celebrities. Naar remains enthralled today when he recalls Kennedy's vibrance and energy in their chance meetings over lunch in Santa Monica. "He would come in and sit down and go around the room,"

Naar recalled in an interview. "He knew everyone's business. He made you feel like he cared about you and about what you were doing with your life. I was like nobody — the least important person there. He knew I was trying to develop television series and he'd say, 'I've got an idea for a series I want to talk to you about.' He did that with everyone at the table, some significant and some more like me. He was just the best." Kennedy also had an unerring ability to put others at ease. Naar's home burned down in 1961 and the president sent a photograph of Smokey the Bear with a note wondering where the bear had been during the fire. There was a Los Angeles reception soon after, and Naar's wife was going to meet Kennedy for the first time. She was nervous about it and practiced shaking his hand and thanking him for the photograph. When the moment came, Naar recalled, his wife instead blurted, "Thank you, Mr. Picture." She was mortified, but Kennedy "just threw his arms all over her and hugged her and laughed. He knew what happened," Naar told me. "And I can't forget that."

Kennedy's sense of his own importance and his hold over his friends distressed some of their wives, who saw Jack in a far more ambivalent light than did their husbands. Charles Spalding's former wife, Betty, had met the Kennedys in the mid-1930s on Cape Cod and was especially friendly with Eunice, their third-eldest daughter. Her husband, she said, served one essential function for Jack Kennedy after his high-society wedding to Jacqueline Bouvier, as did all his male friends: escorting women in public who were really meant for Jack. "He bearded for him. That's what they were doing — even Bobby — cleaning up after or bearding for him." Like her husband, Betty Spalding found Jack Kennedy "charming and great fun to be with." But, she added, "you didn't know whether you were being manipulated."

Jewel Reed said that she eventually became very disturbed by Kennedy's "tremendous power over men — more than over women. Jack was more comfortable with men than with women. He didn't have any value for women, except for a particular purpose." Reed told me that Kennedy would often ask her husband to join him for a night of "male prowling," and leave her at home. Kennedy couldn't understand when his buddy Jim occasionally chose, at his wife's insistence, not to go. The Reeds' marriage, as did the Spaldings', broke up during Kennedy's days in the White House.

Gloria Emerson came to understand that the wives of Jack's friends "didn't like Jack at all because he had such a claim over their husbands." The women were "completely left out," Emerson said, "just put aside. It was another cultural climate. And I think they were jealous of JFK, because he could induce people to do things for him, and he was a great actor. He could make them believe that he really needed them to do these things for him — and why not? That's part of the role of a skillful politician."

Jack Kennedy's attitude toward marriage followed the pattern his father set: he and his sons were to get married, stay married, have lots of children, and sleep with any woman they could. Rose Kennedy embraced the Catholic church and ignored what was going on, with her sons as well as her husband, while the Kennedy daughters spent their lives embracing the infidelities of the men in their family, often helping to make it easier for their brothers to cheat on their wives.

Sometimes the daughters would do the same for their dad. The novelist Dominick Dunne, who was working in Hollywood as a television producer for a weekly dramatic series in the 1950s, recalled in an interview for this book that Patricia Lawford, Joe Kennedy's daughter, who was then married to actor Peter Lawford, routinely telephoned Dunne's wife when her father was in town to ask, "Who's on the show?" Lawford was told the names and telephone numbers of the female stars, Dunne said, and then relayed the information to the always eager Joe.*

---

* No outsider can fully comprehend the dynamics of another family's life, but outsiders were often shocked by what they encountered in the Kennedy household. In 1957 Lyndon Johnson, the Senate majority leader, was asked to make a speech in Palm Beach. It seemed only natural when Rose Kennedy telephoned and invited him to come to the family's beachfront home for lunch. Johnson, recovering from a serious heart attack, was accompanied on the trip by Lady Bird, his wife; Bobby Baker, his aide and confidant; and Senator George Smathers, of Florida. "So we went over for lunch," Baker recalled in an interview for this book. Rose Kennedy, gracious and charming, was alone. Suddenly, Baker said, "Old Man Joe comes in with a seventeen- or eighteen-year-old girl. Doesn't say boo. Walks right in and goes upstairs" and engages in what, clearly and noisily, is sexual intercourse. "Here you have the majority leader of the Senate and he and Jack had a great relationship," Baker told me. "I thought it was the rudest thing I've ever seen." The lunch went on as if nothing had happened. Baker learned later, he said, that the young woman was Joe Kennedy's caddy from the French Riviera, where the Kennedys maintained a vacation home.

The man most important to Kennedy, other than his father, was his brother Bobby; yet there were a few times early in the 1950s, Emerson said, when Jack hoodwinked even him. "Jack was having a liaison with one of my roommates in a hotel room and Bobby was at the door suddenly. And he made the woman stand in a closet while he talked to Bobby," Emerson remembered. "So there were some times he probably concealed, but less and less as time went by. The Kennedys have always felt themselves under siege and were distrustful of the outside world. And that's why so many men wanted JFK to believe that they could be trusted — it was a test they had to pass."

Hugh Sidey described the brothers' relationship as one of "almost total communication. It was almost osmosis. Almost every time I was in talking to Jack the phone would ring, once or twice, it would be Bobby. Muffled conversations back and forth about whatever it was. I don't think there were secrets of any significance they kept from each other."

Richard N. Goodwin, who wrote speeches for Kennedy during the 1960 campaign and accompanied him to the White House, described Robert Kennedy as "completely his brother's man. He was a guy whose basic purpose in life was to advance and protect the career of John Kennedy." In an interview for this book in 1997, Goodwin recalled one meeting between the president and a group of southern senators on the White House balcony. One of the senators "leaned forward and said, 'Well, Mr. President, I'm afraid I'm gonna have to attack you on civil rights.' And Kennedy says, 'Can't you attack Bobby instead?' Bobby played that role," Goodwin explained. The younger Kennedy "was always reflecting his brother's feelings." Goodwin was also present at a White House meeting after the Bay of Pigs when Bobby tore into a senior State Department official who, after the fact, had told a reporter that he was opposed to the invasion. "I watched Bobby just lash into him," Goodwin recalled. " 'You can't undermine my brother.' And John Kennedy just sat there quietly, never said a word throughout. But I have no doubt that Bobby was reflecting conversations that the two of them had."

Jewel Reed, whose husband had also commanded PT boats in the South Pacific, thought that Bobby was put at a disadvantage by his older sibling. "All Bobby wanted to do was to please his brother," Mrs. Reed said. "I felt Jack was more ruthless than Bobby."

After the 1960 election, Kennedy put his longtime lover, who came from a wealthy and socially prominent family, into a make-work White House job dealing with international affairs. She watched from the inside and grew extremely skeptical of the men around the president. "He was not surrounded by peers," she told me. "He was surrounded by intellectual associates, by show business cronies, by family, by old-time family retainers, by a lot of people who were acquaintances but were not friends of his heart." The woman recalled a private dinner in the White House with the president and one of his very old friends. "And basically what [the friend] wanted was some help in getting a discount on furniture at the Merchandise Mart," the huge Chicago wholesale furniture hub that was owned by the Kennedy family. "I was amazed. I mean, I was just staggered. It wasn't about being a friend. It wasn't about closeness."

Kennedy's male friends, she said, like many of his women friends, were attracted by his glamour. "Everyone kept stroking," she said. "'You're fine, it's great, everything is going well.' Real friends," she said, "wade in with you and say, 'Boy, this is difficult. This is painful.' I believe he was abandoned at some deep level by the people who thought they were trying to help by keeping things smooth, by saying it'll all be okay. 'How can I serve to make your life smoother?'"

Once in the White House, she said, aides such as McGeorge Bundy, the national security adviser, and Robert McNamara, the secretary of defense, "picked up from [Kennedy] not a sense of being Harvard eggheads and smart people, but a sense of being tough. There was part of Jack that rejoiced in knowing what you had to know, doing what had to be done," she said. "Bundy didn't know from dirty hands or what Jack knew from street fighting. These men were merely picking up the worst aspects of Jack; they felt they had to be more tough, more Catholic than the Pope."

All of Kennedy's aides wanted his acceptance, she said. "In some way I think he must have gotten the least [out] of all the brain power around, because of people's competition — 'How can we get more of

Daddy? How can we get more of his attention? How can we get more of his approval?' A lot of really radical thinking just went right out the window" on the part of the men who were supposedly giving the president their best advice. Men such as Bundy, McNamara, and Arthur M. Schlesinger, Jr., the Harvard historian who was a special adviser, "could have stretched their minds more if they hadn't gotten so tangled up in competing for his favor and his time. They wanted to hang out [with Kennedy], as well as to think about public policy. You wanted to be included at dinner, in rides on the boat, in going to movies."

Gloria Emerson saw the same behavior. The men working for him in the White House, she told me, "loved him too much. They wanted to please more than they wanted to enlighten, and that's very danger-ous, isn't it? Everyone wanted to see him smile."

Kennedy, with his glamour and quickness, seemed especially to bring out the insecurity of intellectuals. And no one was more eager to please than Ted Sorensen, Jack Kennedy's closest aide in the Senate and the White House. Ralph A. Dungan joined the Senate staff as a labor expert in the mid-1950s and was immediately put off by Sorensen, who was his office mate. "He was not the warmest human being that ever walked down the pike," Dungan told the Kennedy Li-brary in a 1967 oral history. "The one thing that bothered me the most was an incident that was very, very telling. The senator came roaring into that back office, yelling like hell about something, . . . directing his fire at me. And I didn't say anything. I hadn't touched the damned issue. It was Sorensen who had worked on it. He just sat right there and let me take the whole heat without ever saying, 'It wasn't him, it was me.' And I figured at that point whatever happened along the line, if it in any way impaired his relationship with the principal, Sorensen would pitch anybody over."

Kennedy's friends lived in terror of his boredom. "We relaxed him." That's what Ben Bradlee believed. "We made him laugh. We talked mostly about people and what was going on. . . . [Kennedy] loved gossip about what people are up to and what they're thinking about." You had to keep him interested, Bradlee said, but "if he were bored five minutes he'd get up and leave. He wasn't going to suffer that. I mean, when he was through he was through. He got up and left." Many others, even those considered to be old friends, had a sense that they, too, were disposable. Charles Bartlett, the journalist, was famed for having introduced Jack to Jackie at a dinner party; Bartlett profited, socially and professionally, from his closeness. But it came at a cost. "He was very spoiled," Bartlett told me. "One thing you couldn't do with Jack was bore him. It was one of his least attractive characteristics — how quickly he could turn off."

Gloria Emerson said that she thought Jack Kennedy became bored "when people talked too much — when they made their case at too great length. He liked movement and results. He had no sort of small talk. He wanted to talk strategy, politics, so one was totally excluded. Things had to have a point for him, and parties were a waste of time unless there was a political advantage to be gained."

Kennedy's lover experienced the same sense of impatience and the same anxiety about cutting through it. "It wasn't just the women going ga-ga," she said. "It's everybody trying to be good enough, smart enough, witty enough. I was trying to knock him out — to be terrific. It's much more criminal in the case of Bundy and McNamara."

Adding to her anxiety, she said, was Kennedy's constant "restlessness, a sense that there was something he wanted but it wasn't quite there. The tapping of the teeth, the tapping of the foot, the drumming of the fingers. A sense that it was hard work. You had to really work to keep his attention unless . . . he had something that he wanted from you. And then, boy, you were the object of extremely focused attention."

Her lover's goal, she said, was to fill his life "with adrenaline. 'What are we going to do that's exciting?' What will he do that will keep his attention from being pulled into darker events or darker feelings? When you want excitement, when you want to be occupied and pulled out of yourself, you're saying in some way that you don't have to mull over things that are painful, things that could be very uncomfortable. He was caught in a bind, and the people around him were caught. It was as if he was struggling to come out, but he struggled with people who were in the same dynamic as he was."

Kennedy ignored any problems in their relationship. When he could not perform sexually, it was simply not discussed, she said. "It was dealing with imperfection by just closing it down. 'Let's not think about this anymore.' But it was clear that he was thinking about it. What do you do? What do you say? I had no idea. Somehow I wasn't doing it right. I was sexually inexperienced, so I thought it was something I was doing or not doing. I didn't know what was going on."

Kennedy understood the extent of his power over men, and he used it. In the late 1950s, Jerry Bruno, who came from Wisconsin, was working in Washington for Senator William Proxmire, the Wisconsin Democrat. Bruno and Kennedy began a conversation in the underground shuttle linking the Senate office buildings to the Capitol. Kennedy invited him to come around his office for a chat. Bruno knew that Kennedy was going to run for president in 1960 and that Wisconsin would be a key primary election state. "I go there and Kennedy stands me up," Bruno said in a 1995 interview for this book. "I wait one and a half hours and then Evelyn [Lincoln, Kennedy's secretary] says he wants to see you at his home tomorrow morning at eight o'clock for breakfast. I go there, ring the bell, and the butler comes and puts me in the patio. I sit there and the butler gives me a newspaper." After a half hour, Kennedy came downstairs, sat at another table on the patio, ate breakfast, and read the newspaper. Caroline, his daughter, climbed on his knee for a moment to get a ride. "He knew I was there, but he didn't say anything," Bruno told me. Bruno continued to wait. Asked why he did so, Bruno explained, "Hey, listen, I'm a factory worker who only went to the ninth grade." He knew his place.

Finally, Kennedy turned to him, Bruno said, and "begins asking me a lot of questions about Wisconsin. He asks me to be his executive director for his campaign in Wisconsin. Later it dawned on me that he didn't know anything about me, but I had the identity of [having worked for] Bill Proxmire." Bruno took the job and, after the election, became a political advance man in the White House. He remains loyal to this day.

Kennedy's treatment of Bruno was that of a master to a servant, just as his father, Joe, would have dealt with the hired help. Kennedy's former lover talked at length in our interviews about what she termed his "tremendous acceptance of inequality." Kennedy did articulate the view that "things should be better, yes." He also "could do acts of personal kindness, yes." But, she said, deeply ingrained in him was "the acceptance of inequality at every level — that women were not equal with men, that African Americans were not equal with white people, that Jews were not equal to gentiles. That was absolutely acceptable, and that doesn't mean he was a horrible racist, anti-Semitic, classist, sexist person. He was a person of his time. And that involved a lot of limitations."

When discussing the poor, the blacks, the Jews, "he used to say, 'Poor bastards.' That was it. There were a lot of poor bastards in this world. There were people who either didn't get jobs they wanted or they didn't get programs they wanted. That phrase covered so many times when he would have turned someone down for a job, or would have turned down some legislation that was being pressed on him. You know, 'Poor bastard, they're going to feel terrible.'" Kennedy seemed to believe that "people who are different have different responses. The pain of poor people is different from 'our' pain."

Kennedy was aware of the disconnect. While interviewing candidate Kennedy for a *Time* magazine cover story in the late 1950s, Hugh Sidey suddenly asked if he had any memory of the Depression. Sidey had grown up in rural Iowa and vividly recalled the harshness of those days. "Kennedy had his feet on the desk, and he looked across at me and he said," Sidey said in a 1997 interview for this book, "'I have no memory of the Depression. We lived better than ever. We had bigger houses, more servants. I learned about the Depression at Harvard — from reading.'" Jack Kennedy, Sidey told me, with some consternation, "just hadn't encountered breadlines or bums that used to come to our doors and ask for handouts. He was the ambassador's son, and that was a very elegant existence. He was never in contact with the reality of the Depression."

Kennedy's former lover believed that it would have been difficult for Kennedy, given his comfortable family circumstances and the belief in his own destiny, to understand the aspirations of the people in Cuba and South Vietnam, the nations that became the object of presidential obsession, anger, and frustration. Kennedy, the woman said, "did a wonderful thing in trying to bring people into a sense of participation. But I feel most of it was on the basis of being special, and surrounding himself with the best and the brightest — with people whose accomplishments were their badge of worth." Thus, when "things got really troublesome," she said, the president and his immediate aides "reinforced each other's isolation. Those people, in their specialness, got separated from reality. It was as if Bundy, McNamara — all of these extraordinary men — in rising and shining, had cut off their ability to feel their own pain. I never did experience John Kennedy in a moment of reflection or pain or sadness," she told me.

The affair came to an end in late 1962, the woman said, but not before she learned of Kennedy's extensive womanizing. She was "crushed" by the news. "I thought, 'Gee, maybe I'm really special.' But no, I was one of many, many people. That was helpful in the long run, because I decided to leave Washington, and it was time to go."

The end was unsentimental. "It was very painful to be with someone who was everything and I was nothing," the woman said. "It was painful to have it called love. It was painful to be chosen and to have someone be interested in me for my class, my speech, my looks, my whatever — but not my heart." She was abroad, sitting by herself in a European café, when she learned of Kennedy's assassination. "It was sort of symbolic in the sense that I was alone with it," she said. "I'd been alone with myself during that relationship and I was alone" at Kennedy's death. "I read newspapers. I read magazines. I read every single thing I could read. I did not cry."

"What's the moral of the story?" Kennedy's former lover rhetorically asked during one interview. "That this grand man, this man of energy and intelligence and glamour and power, was to a certain extent dehumanized by the privileges that made him who and what he was. He allowed us to think that there are people who have it all. And that's a very dangerous illusion, because at some point they know they don't. Mythologizing this man did not help him and did not help us, because it allowed us to not take responsibility for our participation in the public life. We say, 'Oh well, let this wonderful leader do it.' But that is not inviting us to think."

The Kennedys' belief that they were extraordinary people who could make their own rules began long before Jack was born. It started with his grandfather.

3

HONEY FITZ

History has been kind to John F. "Honey Fitz" Fitzgerald, Jack Kennedy's maternal grandfather, who is invariably portrayed as an amiable longtime Boston pol famed for his energetic campaigning and singing "Sweet Adeline" at political events. The athletic, handsome Fitzgerald was said to be the first politician to campaign by automobile: dramatically speeding across Boston, he preached his antiboss, reformer message at twenty-eight rallies on the last night of his successful 1905 campaign for mayor. No one, it was said, shook more hands, danced more dances, talked more rapidly, or generated larger and more enthusiastic crowds than Honey Fitz.

It is that historical legacy that survives — and not the reality. Fitzgerald's contentious two terms as mayor of Boston, marked by sworn testimony of payoffs and cronyism, have been muted over the years into just another example of big-city political business as usual. His political alliance with his four brothers, who were provided with city jobs and other largesse, including valuable liquor licenses, was the beginning of the brother-to-brother family loyalty that would be repeated again and again in the next generation. And Fitzgerald's political humiliation in 1919, when he was investigated in the House of Representatives for eight months before being unseated for vote fraud, is written off in a sentence or two in most Kennedy family histories.

The incomplete historical record is partially the result of the Kennedys' purging of unsavory events from the family lore and the ability of family members to lie when necessary. The facts surrounding Fitzgerald's ouster from Congress were protected by the congressional rule dating back to 1880 that sealed all unpublished investigative materials for fifty years. More than three thousand pages of House Elections Committee depositions and files dealing with the challenge to the 1918 election were not available to the public until 1969, and were then left unexamined and unpublished until research began for this book.

Fitzgerald won the House seat on November 5, 1918, by defeating the incumbent, fellow Democrat Peter F. Tague, by 238 votes out of the 15,293 cast in Massachusetts's Tenth District. (Tague had been defeated by Fitzgerald in the Democratic primary election, amid charges of vote fraud, and ran again, as a write-in candidate, in the general election.) The newly examined elections committee files show that the Fitzgerald forces, who included his young son-in-law Joseph P. Kennedy, recruited immigrant Italians, then entering the United States in huge numbers, and sent them into election precincts with instructions to use threats and physical violence to prevent Tague supporters from casting their special ballots. A few professional boxers were also hired. The House investigators determined that at least one-third of the votes in three precincts in Boston's teeming Fifth Ward were fraudulent, so-called mattress votes cast by men who were falsely registered as living in the district in order to vote on election day. Other Fitzgerald votes were determined to have been cast by men who had been killed in combat or were still stationed overseas in World War I. Most of the illegal votes came from a strip of notorious bars and houses of prostitution in the Fifth Ward, and it was these votes, so the committee concluded, that enabled Fitzgerald to steal the election.

Fitzgerald offered little defense during the months of congressional inquiry, other than to insist that he had been "framed" and to deny that any fraud was involved in his election. The elections committee's report was debated for more than four hours on October 24,

1919. The House voted overwhelmingly to unseat Fitzgerald and swear in his opponent on the spot.

Fitzgerald's comment to newsmen outside the Capitol was almost jaunty: "Well, McKinley was unseated by the Congress and became a candidate and was elected president. See what's ahead of me?" In her bestselling biography *The Fitzgeralds and the Kennedys,* published in 1987, Doris Kearns Goodwin took brief note of the election of 1918 and its aftermath and observed that Fitzgerald, after being ousted from office, "remained as exuberant as ever, emerging once again from disgrace like a duck from water, and the local newspapers still considered him the leading citizen of Boston."

Why was Fitzgerald so exuberant?

One answer may be that he was successfully practicing what is known today as political spin control — putting on an act for the public and the press in an attempt to minimize the importance of the disaster that had befallen him.

Another possible answer revolves around Fitzgerald's lifelong ability to ignore the consequences of his actions. He had run for mayor of Boston in 1905 as a reformer but, once elected, presided over a regime that became infamous for patronage and graft. "From his earliest days in politics," Goodwin wrote, "Fitzgerald had been able to compartmentalize his actions so that he could hold on to an image of himself as a 'good' man and a 'reformist politician'" — even as he joined fully in the corruption of his administration. Fitzgerald's instinct for compartmentalization and tolerance for political dirty tricks would be passed along to his son-in-law Joe Kennedy and to Kennedy's second son, John.

Further, Fitzgerald might have understood how much more the House Elections Committee could have made public but did not. The unpublished hearings records of the committee depict Fitzgerald as a political leader who, like other corrupt big-city politicians of his time, relied heavily on alcohol, prostitution, and violence for financial and voter support.

The same files also demonstrate that Joe Kennedy was directly involved in many aspects of his father-in-law's public life, an involvement that has been generally overlooked by historians. Fitzgerald family patronage of Kennedy is revealed in documents such as long-forgotten 1918 campaign leaflets in which Tague released letters showing that Fitzgerald had urged him to recommend Kennedy as a director of the federal Farm Loan Board (a position Kennedy did not get). Other depositions and documents show that the elections committee suspected Kennedy of playing a major organizational role on election day in November 1918, when the Fitzgerald forces used fraud and intimidation to win Tague's seat. Some of the mattress voters from the shadiest hotels in the Fifth Ward were asked directly by suspicious House investigators whether Joe Kennedy had played a part in their illegal vote, but they provided no evidence. There was also a suggestion that Kennedy was involved in illicit campaign financing. A Fitzgerald supporter named Thomas Giblin told under oath of a secret $1,500 campaign account — roughly $50,000 in current dollars — in a small Boston bank then controlled by Kennedy, which was viewed by many of Fitzgerald's campaign workers as particularly dirty. "They are all running away from it," Giblin testified. He quoted Tague as telling Fitzgerald's campaigners that he "would have them prosecuted if they used [the Kennedy] money."

Fitzgerald, stung by his rejection in 1919 and later political failures, is described in family biographies as a happily doting grandfather who spent many afternoons in the 1920s catering to the needs of the children of his eldest daughter, Rose Kennedy, whose burgeoning family lived a few miles away until late in 1927. Fitzgerald became especially close to his two oldest grandsons, Joseph Jr. and John, taking them to the zoo, on boat rides in the Public Garden, and to cheer for the Boston Red Sox and the old Boston Braves.

Those accounts fail to emphasize the overriding toughness of the extended Fitzgerald family, a trait that was passed along to future generations and, eventually, into the presidency. Chester Cooper, a CIA official who served in the Kennedy White House, spent his summers in the 1920s a few blocks from the beach at Nantasket, south of Boston. The Fitzgerald summer house was directly on the beach. "I remember playing in front of the Fitzgerald house," Cooper told me in an interview. "A couple of burly guys came out of the house and said, 'Get off our beach.' I remember saying, 'This is a public beach.' I was violently hit for the first time in my life. They were [Fitzgerald] sons and uncles. They literally kicked us off the front of the beach."

The Fitzgeralds and the Kennedys always took care of their own. In the mid-1930s, Joe Kennedy risked his standing as an insider in the Roosevelt administration by urging the president to appoint one of Fitzgerald's brothers to a federal liquor position. President Kennedy, carrying on the family tradition, ignored talk of nepotism and appointed his brother attorney general; he ignored it again in 1962 by ensuring that Edward M. Kennedy, his youngest brother, was nominated and elected to the Senate from Massachusetts.

Fitzgerald's relationship with his often-absent son-in-law Joe was never close, according to the Kennedy family biographers. There was a crucial side to Honey Fitz, and his continued popularity among many Boston voters, that the constantly upward-striving Joe Kennedy could not comprehend: the mayor was an old-fashioned pol who was unapologetic about his humble beginnings and worked incessantly to present himself as a man of the people.

Joe Kennedy's political ambitions began at the top. He was ruthless, as we shall see, in his efforts while serving as President Roosevelt's ambassador to England to collect adverse information about the president, in a poorly conceived attempt in 1940 to force FDR from office — and position himself as a viable candidate. Joe Kennedy's political career was in ruins by the end of 1940, but he learned from his mistakes. His son Jack, emulating his grandfather, would develop a strong political base in Boston.

After his political disgrace, Honey Fitz remained loyal to the family, and did what his wealthy son-in-law told him to do. In 1942, at the age of seventy-nine, Fitzgerald served Joe's needs by running as a spoiler in the Democratic senatorial primary in Massachusetts against an attractive New Deal Democrat named Joseph E. Casey, one of FDR's favorites in the Congress. Fitzgerald, whose daily campaign activities were heavily subsidized by Kennedy — and carefully monitored by one of Joe's high-powered and well-paid speechwriters — took 80,000 votes away from Casey in the primary, and inflicted so much damage that Republican Henry Cabot Lodge, Jr., won the general election easily. The defeat, as expected, embarrassed the president and seriously hurt the career of Casey, who was viewed by Kennedy as a potential threat to the political ambitions of his first-born son, Joe Jr., ambitions Joe nurtured until his son's death in 1944. The Kennedys learned a vital lesson in 1942: even a very good candidate, like Joseph Casey, could be defeated with money.

Honey Fitz came into the limelight once again, in 1946, when Joe Kennedy turned to Jack, his eldest surviving son, as the family's political heir. Jack came out of the war as a decorated navy hero of torpedo boat skirmishes; it was decided that he would campaign for Fitzgerald's old seat in Congress* as one of ten candidates in the Democratic primary. The Kennedy public relations machine was turned loose again and the natural affinity between grandson and grandfather was put to work — with careful guidance from Joe, who remained in the background during the campaign, as he would throughout his son's political career. Dozens of favorable news stories appeared as the young man and old man campaigned together in the working-class districts of Boston's North End and West End, with the former mayor introducing his grandson to the city's elders. Honey Fitz seemed to play a significant role in the campaign.

Jack Kennedy and his campaign workers understood, however, that Fitzgerald was an anachronism whose politics had little to do with postwar America. Robert Kennedy, in an interview for the Kennedy Library four years after his brother's death, acknowledged that his grandfather's political "effectiveness . . . was not overwhelming. He had some important introductions and contacts which were significant. But the appeal that John Kennedy had was to an entirely different group." Kennedy added that his grandfather "felt very close to my brother."

Jack Kennedy's best friend, K. LeMoyne Billings, told interviewers after Kennedy's assassination that grandson and grandfather "were absolutely crazy about each other. Jack was undoubtedly the old man's favorite. He was a very attractive old man, full of the Irish blarney, full of mischief and full of life. . . . His humor was something

---

* Redistricting changed Honey Fitz's election district to the Eleventh by the time his grandson ran for office.

that Jack loved so much; he adored his grandfather's sense of humor."
As president, Jack would honor his grandfather's memory —
Fitzgerald died in 1950 — by naming the presidential yacht the
Honey Fitz.

Nonetheless, the family warmth was put aside at critical moments in
1946. Joe Kennedy, as usual, treated Honey Fitz contemptuously during his son's first campaign, and Jack Kennedy, never able to stand up
to his father, was unable to stand up for his beloved grandfather.

The chief adviser in the campaign, handpicked by Joe, was a hard-
nosed Boston political operative named Joseph L. Kane, who had
served as the political strategist for Peter Tague during his successful
fight to reclaim his House seat from Honey Fitz in 1919. Kane, who
was Joe Kennedy's first cousin and childhood friend, had done little
in subsequent years to hide his disdain for Honey Fitz, and did not
spare him in 1946.

In an interview in the late 1950s, published in *Front Runner, Dark
Horse,* a study of the 1960 campaign by journalists Ralph G. Martin
and Ed Plaut, Kane told of the tense moment, early in the primary
campaign, when Fitzgerald accidentally walked into a Kennedy strategy meeting. Kane yelled, "Get that son of a bitch out of here!" The
startled young Kennedy said, "Who? Grandpa?" Fitzgerald was ushered away and Jack, his political career on the line, stayed put. Young
Kennedy was learning to be as ruthless, if necessary, as his father. A
few days later, a pleased Joe Kennedy praised his son's ability to get
along with the difficult Kane: "I didn't think you'd last three hours
with him," Joe Kennedy said.

The famed Kennedy loyalty — father to sons, sons to father, and
brother to brother — did not always extend, at election time, to
grandfathers.

Joseph P. Kennedy, in his drive to elect Jack Kennedy in 1946, left
nothing to chance — an approach he would repeat in every one of
his son's political campaigns. Kane was deemed essential, because the
elder Kennedy was pouring hundreds of thousands of family dollars

into the campaign; Kane, who spent forty years as a backroom political operative in Boston, knew whom to pay off and how much to pay. Kane's political theory was very simple, as he told Martin and Plaut years later: "It takes three things to win: the first is money and the second is money and the third is money." One primary rival was paid $7,500 to "stay in or get out," depending on how the race was going. Yet another rival was neutralized when Kane paid to have someone with the same name enter the primary, inevitably confusing voters and splitting the vote. The Kennedy campaign bought up much of the available billboard space in the district, and advertised heavily on the radio. The campaign slogan, as devised by Kane, was appropriately vague: "The New Generation Offers a Leader."* Thousands of leaflets and pamphlets bearing those words were mailed, and many of the eligible women voters were personally invited by mail to join with Kennedy family members at a swanky hotel reception a few days before the election. The response was overwhelming. Kane said that Joe Kennedy was used to paying for what he got. "They paid a staggering sum in the Congressional race of 1946, but Jack could have gone to Congress like everyone else for ten cents."

John F. Kennedy campaigned vigorously and successfully for his grandfather's old seat in Congress, and with enormous charm, intelligence, and growing confidence. His first campaign invoked strategies that would bring him continued political success: an early start, effective use of volunteers, and a ferociously loyal organization made up of family members, old friends, former schoolmates, and shipmates from his combat days in World War II, when Kennedy commanded *PT-109* in the Pacific.

The essential lessons he learned in the 1946 campaign would stay

---

* Kennedy also was vague about his specific political views. In an interview during the 1946 campaign with Selig S. Harrison, then a staff reporter for the Harvard *Crimson*, Kennedy steadfastly refused to make any commitments. "Kennedy seems to feel honestly that he is not hedging, not playing politics," Harrison wrote, "by refusing to offer a positive specific platform. He feigns an ignorance of much in the affairs of government and tells you to look at his record in two years to see what he stands for." Recalling the interview in an essay for the *New Republic* in 1960, Harrison wrote, "It would be difficult to forget the irritation which Kennedy displayed when this reporter . . . peppered him with questions. . . ."

with Jack Kennedy for the next fourteen years, as he moved away from the local politics of his grandfather and began his long run for the presidency: Good looks, good organization, and hard work were not enough. Above all, he needed his father — and his father's no-holds-barred spending.

4

JOE

Money bought Joseph P. Kennedy enormous personal freedom, and bought his son the presidency.

At his death in 1969, Joe Kennedy's private estate and various trust holdings were estimated by the *New York Times* to be worth "perhaps $500 million." A complete accounting of what he owned, and how he got there, simply could not be obtained then, nor does one exist today. Joe Kennedy spent his life making money — and hiding it.

The Kennedy family biographers, relying on material supplied by Joe Kennedy, his wife, Rose, and other family members, have provided a familiar chronology of achievement that begins with Kennedy, a few years after his graduation from Harvard, becoming president of the Columbia Trust Company, a small Boston bank, and becoming known as the youngest bank president in the nation. Eager to avoid active duty in World War I, he left the bank in 1917 to become assistant general manager of Bethlehem Steel's huge Fore River shipbuilding plant in nearby Quincy. He left the shipyard after the war to join the brokerage firm of Hayden, Stone and Company in Boston, where he was an instant success. Within a year, he generated enough money by speculating in the stock market to buy a new twelve-room home in suburban Brookline — he and Rose then had four children — and also a new Rolls-Royce. Kennedy left Hayden, Stone in 1923 and, setting up shop as an independent banker, began speculating full-time in the stock market. By 1927, generally considered to have made millions, Kennedy had moved his burgeoning family to suburban New York and himself into the movie business, where he once again was said to have made millions. With his uncanny instinct for trends, he began pulling out of the high-flying stock market before the Wall Street crash of October 1929.

In 1931, no longer a movie magnate, Kennedy became a major contributor to and fund-raiser for Franklin D. Roosevelt's first successful campaign for the presidency. Roosevelt astonished Washington and Wall Street in mid-1934 by naming Kennedy, who was notorious as a stock market manipulator, chairman of the Securities and Exchange Commission (SEC), a New Deal agency set up to reform and regulate the financial markets. FDR was said to have explained the perplexing choice by citing, with a laugh, an old saw — "It takes a thief to catch a thief." There was a brief stint later as chairman of the Maritime Commission and a disastrous three years as U.S. ambassador to England, where by 1940 Kennedy's isolationism and vocal skepticism about England's ability to continue the war against Germany made him enormously unpopular abroad and at home. It was his last government post. Kennedy would spend the next twenty years shuttling between homes in Palm Beach, Florida, and Hyannis Port, Massachusetts, shepherding the careers of his nine photogenic children and making huge amounts of money in real estate and business. After his son's election to the presidency, Joe Kennedy served as a one-man kitchen cabinet until his severe stroke in December 1961. He remained an invalid, able to comprehend but unable to speak, until his death in 1969. He had outlived his daughter Kathleen and three sons — Joe, Jack, and Bobby.

Joe Kennedy was, by all accounts, a brilliant corporate predator and an expert manipulator of both Wall Street and his fellow investors. What is missing from the published accounts, and the public record, is an appreciation of how Kennedy was also able to profit from his understanding of the corruption that made American big-city politics work, knowledge that he acquired at the side of his father-in-law, Honey Fitz.

The House Elections Committee files make clear that Kennedy, at a minimum, served as a money man during Fitzgerald's campaign against Peter Tague; the committee generated evidence showing that Fitzgerald's decision to challenge Tague, a fellow Democrat, had been mandated by party bosses in Boston after Tague, while in the Congress, would not cooperate in a series of corrupt and highly profitable real estate schemes involving the Fore River Shipyard. Tague testified that he refused to help Fitzgerald and his cronies buy land adjacent to Fore River which was scheduled to be a future site for a large federal housing project. At the time, Joe Kennedy was assistant general manager of the shipyard, and the questioning by committee investigators strongly suggested that they believed Kennedy was involved in the profit-taking. Making money illicitly may well have been essential to Kennedy's early financial success — as important, perhaps, as his skill in Wall Street speculating.

As those who worked in politics with him came to understand, the seemingly straightforward Kennedy was, at best, extremely secretive and, at worst, an incessant liar on all matters involving his financial interests. Just how much money he made and how he made it always remained a secret, even from his wife and other members of the family, who learned never to ask questions. What is known, one biographer wrote, is that money began to "flood into the family" in the early 1920s, at the same time that federal agents, who knew nothing of Joe Kennedy, began to track huge shipments of illicit liquor into the United States, triggered by the insatiable American demand for liquor and the advent of Prohibition.

Kennedy was one of the first to seize a dominant position in the liquor importing business. He used medicinal permits to avoid the restrictions of Prohibition, gaining intimate knowledge of the industry that would place him ahead of his competitors for the legal trade when the moment arrived. He swept into London in the fall of 1933, when it was clear that Prohibition was about to end, and signed agreements making him the sole American distributor of two premium scotches and Gordon's gin.* Kennedy established Somerset

---

* Kennedy was accompanied on the high-profile London trip by James Roosevelt, the son of the newly elected president, who had star quality abroad. Kennedy, then forty-five years old, and Roosevelt, just twenty-seven, had become close friends during the 1932 presidential campaign. It was a friendship based on Roosevelt's weaknesses for liquor and women and Kennedy's ability to exploit weakness.

JOE   **47**

Importers Ltd., and operated it until its sudden sale, for $8 million, in 1946 (equivalent to about $55 million in 1997 dollars).

Kennedy's rapid and highly profitable shift into the liquor importing business helped trigger what would become an unverified national rumor by the time his son entered the White House: that Joe Kennedy had been deeply involved in the bootleg liquor business since the first days of Prohibition — a business that was dominated by such organized crime leaders as New York's Frank Costello, Newark's Abner "Longy" Zwillman, and Chicago's Al Capone. The rumors were made more plausible by Joe's shipbuilding experience at Fore River during World War I — most bootleg liquor came to America by boat — and by the sheer number of Kennedy and Fitzgerald family members who had been in the liquor business before Prohibition began in 1920. Joe Kennedy's father owned at least three taverns in Boston as well as a prosperous liquor importing business that handled shipments from Europe and South America. And two of Rose Kennedy's uncles, younger brothers of Honey Fitz, remained active in the bootleg liquor business during Prohibition.

The difficulty in attempting to evaluate the many reports of Joe Kennedy's participation in bootlegging is the remarkable lack of documentation in government files. The FBI, in the years since Joe Kennedy's death, has released hundreds of pages of Kennedy files in response to Freedom of Information Act (FOIA) requests, but those files — a compilation of security reviews and fawning letters between Hoover and Kennedy — make no mention of any link between Joseph Kennedy, organized crime, and the bootlegging industry. Yet, in scores of interviews for this book over four years, former high-level government officials of the 1950s and 1960s, including Justice Department prosecutors, CIA operatives, and FBI agents, insisted that they knew that Joe Kennedy had been a prominent bootlegger during Prohibition. "I do know that he had associates in organized crime who respected him," Cartha D. DeLoach, a deputy director of the FBI under J. Edgar Hoover, said in an interview for this book in 1997. But, added DeLoach, "I only knew him through Mr. Hoover. He had considerable experience in the bygone era of smuggling, and that's how he made his fortune, according to Mr. Hoover."

One uncontested fact is that Joe Kennedy, through his liquor importing activities, defied all the risks and all the gossip — a defiance his son Jack would emulate in later years — by doing retail liquor business with the most notorious organized crime families throughout the post-Prohibition 1930s and well into the 1940s.

The most direct assertion of Kennedy's involvement in bootlegging came from Frank Costello, the most powerful Mafia boss of the 1940s and 1950s, who sought in his later years to cast himself as a successful businessman. In February 1973, at the age of eighty-two, Costello decided to begin telling his life story to Peter Maas, the prize-winning New York journalist. Ten days after he began, he suffered a heart seizure and died, before Maas could fully explore the Kennedy-Costello relationship. Maas later told the *New York Times* that Costello had confided that he and Kennedy had been "partners" in the bootleg liquor business during Prohibition — a partnership that began, Costello said, after Kennedy sought him out and asked for his help. In an interview for this book, Maas said that Costello specifically recalled arranging for the delivery by sea of bootleg scotch to a Cape Cod beach party celebrating the tenth reunion of Joe Kennedy's Harvard class of 1912. "We were together in the liquor business," Costello told Maas, adding that Kennedy was responsible for the shipping of liquor to the United States from abroad.

Similarly, in his 1983 memoir, *A Man of Honor*, Joseph Bonanno, the retired New York Mafia boss, said that Costello always told him, "and I have no reason to doubt it, that during Prohibition he and Joe Kennedy of Boston were partners in the liquor business. . . . I would sometimes go to Sag Harbor, Long Island, in the summer. This was one of the coves, so I was told, that the Kennedy people used to transport whiskey during Prohibition."*

Some of Joe Kennedy's hired hands — those silent men whose

---

* Kennedy's recklessness in these years extended, not surprisingly, to his womanizing. Shortly after Prohibition ended in 1933, he began an affair with a Broadway showgirl named Evelyn Crowell, who was the widow of Larry Fay, a notorious and fashionable New York gangster who, at his height of power in the 1920s, maintained a lavish man-

names were appropriated for Kennedy's buying and selling of real estate and stock — also told me their secret stories about the Kennedy link to Costello. Harold E. Clancy of South Boston, one of the few Joe Kennedy employees still alive in the mid-1990s, said in an interview for this book that it was commonly supposed by the staff that Kennedy and Costello worked together during Prohibition. Kennedy "had trucks and he also had boats," Clancy said. "I heard anecdotes, rumors, and stories of bringing Haig & Haig scotch from Canada to Cape Cod and to Carson's Beach in South Boston." Another senior Kennedy aide once told him, Clancy recalled, that Costello, who made big money in the early 1930s running slot machines in New York and New Orleans, once "tried to interest the ambassador [Kennedy] in buying into the company that made the machines, but he was too smart." (The slot machines were manufactured in Chicago by a firm controlled by the Capone syndicate.)

Clancy was recruited by Kennedy for his personal staff in the late 1950s, after spending years as an investigative reporter and editor for the *Boston Traveler*. He told me that the more senior members of Kennedy's staff would share cryptic stories of Kennedy's derring-do. Many involved Kennedy's willingness to stand up to organized crime shakedowns in the years after Prohibition, when he was heavily involved in the legitimate sale and shipping of liquor. Kennedy, for example, was said to have hired "people from Murder, Incorporated" to

sion and gave lavish parties in Great Neck, New York. The dapper Fay, who began his career as a bootlegger but soon moved into extortion, became the model for the gangster in the F. Scott Fitzgerald classic *The Great Gatsby*. Fay was shot to death in 1932. Three years later, Kennedy's affair with Fay's widow made it as a blind item into Walter Winchell's widely read *New York Journal-American* gossip column: "A top New Dealer's mistress is a mobster's widow." Winchell's longtime assistant, Herman Klurfeld, who wrote most of Winchell's columns for thirty years, said in an interview for this book that Kennedy, who was an expert at dealing with the press, arranged a meeting with Winchell after publication of the item. The two men quickly became friends, Klurfeld said, and Kennedy eventually became one of Winchell's key sources. Although no such evidence exists in the case of Winchell, Kennedy's "friendship" with many journalists — such as Arthur Krock, the revered Washington bureau chief of the *New York Times* — was predicated on the fact that Kennedy provided them with the equivalent of money: lavish gifts and prepaid vacations and, in the case of Krock, women.

deal with gangster-led unions that were threatening labor trouble. "I knew," Clancy told me, "that Joe had hired some very hard cases to deal with these gangsters who were in control of unions and giving him a hard time." Clancy provided no further details.*

Yet another suggestion of an early Kennedy connection to bootlegging came from a 1996 interview with Q. Byrum Hurst, an attorney in Hot Springs, Arkansas, who for more than twenty years represented Owney Madden, the notorious gangster, until Madden's death in 1965. Madden, born in England, had in his youth been a sadistic killer in New York City, but he emerged in the 1920s as a sophisticated racketeer who moved as an equal among the crooked politicians and major crime figures along the East Coast. He ended his career as a Hot Springs casino operator, whose facilities — never challenged by local police — were always available for criminal leaders needing a quiet retreat. "Owney and Joe Kennedy were partners in the bootleg business for a number of years," said Hurst. "I discussed the Kennedy partnership with him many times. . . . Owney controlled all the nightclubs in New York then. He ran New York more than anyone in the 1920s, and Joe wanted the outlets for his liquor." Hurst, who served in the Arkansas state senate for more than twenty years, added that Madden "told me he valued Kennedy's business judgment. He recognized Kennedy's brains."

Another insider, Abraham Lincoln Marovitz of Chicago, who represented many leading organized crime figures before beginning a forty-year career as a local and federal court judge in Chicago, also insisted that Joe Kennedy had been a bootlegger. "I know about that era," the ninety-two-year-old Marovitz said in an interview for this book. "I represented some people. Kennedy was bootlegging out there in New England, and he knew all these guys. He had mob connections. Kennedy couldn't have operated the way he did without mob approval. They'd have knocked him off, too." Marovitz, a long-time associate of legendary Chicago mayor Richard J. Daley, was ap-

---

* Clancy said his job at first was to investigate various real estate properties and businesses for Kennedy, beginning with a Chicago company that was for sale. "I spent a week," Clancy said, before returning to report to Kennedy at his summer home in Hyannis. Kennedy began the meeting by telling his new employee what he was about to report: "For ten minutes he sat there and told me what I was going to tell him. He even had the sequence right. I thought this is the smartest son of a bitch I've ever met."

pointed a U.S. district court judge in 1963 by President John F. Kennedy.

There is further anecdotal evidence alleging that Kennedy was trying to profit, as were scores of other bootleggers, in the huge shipments of illicit scotch and gin that were off-loaded from ships anchored off the beaches of Massachusetts south of Boston. The liquor would then be trucked in convoys via nearby Brockton to New York City, where it could fetch higher prices than in Boston. The arrival of the first of the so-called rum fleets in 1923 was extensively reported by leading newspapers, including the *New York Times*.

In 1985 a New Jersey journalist, Mark A. Stuart, an assistant editor of the *Newark Record,* published a biography of Longy Zwillman in which he described Joe Kennedy's rage at Zwillman for Zwillman's involvement, so Kennedy believed, in the hijacking of a truck convoy of Kennedy-financed bootleg whiskey in 1923. The Stuart biography quoted Joseph Reinfeld, Zwillman's bootlegging partner, explaining that "I told Joe Kennedy that his shipment, the one that was hijacked outside of Brockton . . . couldn't have been done by one of our people. I don't think he believed me. . . . [Kennedy] said it must have been that punk kid Zwillman, making a deal to hijack his whiskey, . . . said he'd get Longy if it was the last thing he did."*

A description of the hijacking that suggested that Reinfeld was right in denying involvement was provided by Meyer Lansky to three Israeli journalists, Dennis Eisenberg, Uri Dan, and Eli Landau. They published a sympathetic biography of Lansky in 1979, based in part on extensive interviews. Lansky was then living quietly in Israel and trying to avoid extradition to the United States. In a chapter entitled "The Feud with Joseph Kennedy," Lansky and his longtime associate

---

* During Prohibition, Zwillman and Reinfeld operated out of Newark what the federal government later determined was the nation's largest bootlegging operation, responsible at its height for as much as 40 percent of illicit liquor sales. Reinfeld, who later changed his name to Renfield, went on after Prohibition to become a successful and legitimate liquor importer; Zwillman committed suicide in 1959, while facing a subpoena from the Senate Permanent Investigations Subcommittee, whose chief counsel was Bobby Kennedy. It was, as we will see, Zwillman and Reinfeld who bought Joseph Kennedy's Somerset Importers in 1946.

Joseph "Doc" Stacher claimed that their organization — and not Zwillman — was responsible for the hijacking, which they recalled as taking place four years later, in 1927. The subsequent shoot-out, they said, took the lives of eleven men. The whiskey had been shipped into New England from Ireland by Joe Kennedy, and Kennedy knew who was responsible for its diversion. "Kennedy lost a fortune in the hijack," the three Israelis wrote, "and for months afterward he was beset by pleas for financial help from the widows and relatives of the killed guards who were supposed to protect the cargo." Lansky and Stacher remained convinced, the Israeli authors wrote, that Kennedy "held his grudge" and passed on his hostility toward some organized crime bosses to his son Robert. "They were out to get us," Lansky said at his retirement home in Tel Aviv.

The most significant and yet least-noticed account of hard evidence tying Kennedy to business dealings with crime figures can be found among the many thousands of pages of testimony on organized crime generated in the early 1950s by the famed Senate hearings chaired by Estes Kefauver, a Democrat of Tennessee. During scores of public hearings across the nation, Senate investigators and local police officials focused on, among other things, the influx of gambling and racketeering in the Miami area prior to and during World War II. One of the most important front men for organized crime in that era was Thomas J. Cassara, a lawyer from New London, Connecticut, who first came to the attention of law enforcement officials in the late 1930s, when he signed a lease as co-owner of the newly constructed Raleigh Hotel in Miami Beach, which was known to have been financed by organized crime families led by Capone's successors in Chicago and Costello in New York. A few years later, just as World War II was breaking out in Europe, Cassara took over the leases of two nearby hotels, the Grand and the Wofford. Daniel P. Sullivan, a former FBI agent who became operating director of the Crime Commission of Greater Miami, told Kefauver's Special Committee to Investigate Organized Crime in Interstate Commerce that the area around the Cassara-operated hotels in Miami Beach "became nationally known as a meeting place probably for more nationally known racketeers and gangsters than any one local area in the United

States." The Wofford Hotel, in particular, became the hotel of choice for the criminal elite, Sullivan testified, including Costello, Joey Adonis, Longy Zwillman, and many senior members of the Miami-based organization of Meyer Lansky. This was an era, Sullivan added, when America's racketeers, hiding their ownership behind men such as Cassara, were pouring "difficult to trace" money into dozens of legitimate businesses, including hotels and nightclubs.

Cassara left Miami in 1941. By 1944, according to testimony before the Kefauver Committee, he was working full-time for Joe Kennedy's Somerset Importers. The testimony came from Joseph Charles "Joey" Fusco, a former bootlegger and strong-arm man for Al Capone in Chicago. In October of 1950, Fusco was subpoenaed to testify at a closed-door hearing and asked, among other things, about his dealings with Cassara. Fusco replied unhesitatingly: "When he first came to Chicago, I think [it] was in 1944, he was working for Kennedy, the Somerset Import Company. He was their representative here. He used to call on the trade as a missionary man [sic], and that is when I first met Tom Cassara in Chicago. He came into our office and introduced himself. From then on we knew Tom Cassara's working for Somerset in Chicago. Later on, he opened a company here called the Raleigh Distributing Company. He became one of the distributors with us. In other words, he came in and became a distributor for the Somerset line." The reference to Kennedy's company was fleeting, and although the committee understood who Fusco was talking about, Joseph P. Kennedy's name does not appear in the index to the hearings. Journalists plowing through the voluminous transcripts did not link Kennedy to Cassara or Fusco, and thus the important Fusco reference to Joe Kennedy's liquor importing business escaped public notice.*

In late January 1946, Cassara was shot in the head, gangland style, in front of a mob-dominated nightspot known as the Trade Winds on Chicago's trendy Rush Street, an area dominated by nightclubs, bars, and restaurants in the infamous East Chicago Avenue police

---

* Kefauver certainly understood the importance of Fusco's testimony. Kefauver's hand-written notes for the day of Fusco's testimony include references to Cassara and his ties to Somerset Importers. The senator, who took notes only on the testimony of key witnesses, filled six pages of his notebook with remarks and comments on Fusco. Kefauver's papers are on file at the University of Tennessee at Knoxville.

district, where the hoodlum "outfit" exercised near-total control over illegitimate — and legitimate — business activity. Chicago newspapers identified one of Cassara's business partners as Rocco De-Stefano, but did not report that DeStefano was a first cousin of Al Capone and Joey Fusco. Nor did the newspapers report that Cassara was an employee of Joe Kennedy's liquor importing business. Cassara survived the bullet wound, the case remained unsolved, and newspaper attention quickly turned elsewhere. Cassara left the liquor distribution business and moved to Los Angeles, where he once again operated as a front man for organized crime families in New York and Chicago.

Joe Kennedy began negotiating his exit from the liquor business within months of the Cassara shooting. On July 31, 1946, he formally sold Somerset to a New York firm controlled in part by New Jersey gangster Longy Zwillman and his longtime Prohibition partner, Joseph Reinfeld.

With that sale, Kennedy cut his last known tie to the liquor business. But few businessmen had his understanding of the intricate relationship between politicians, unions, and organized crime in the major American cities after World War II. Joe Kennedy's knowledge and contacts would play a major role in the 1960 presidential election, an election stolen, with the help of organized crime, from Richard Nixon.

In 1945 Kennedy bought the Merchandise Mart in Chicago, then the world's largest building, located just north of the Chicago River, in the East Chicago Avenue police district, and joined the long list of businessmen making monthly payoffs to stay in business. The Mart was famed for its block-long speakeasy, which swung into operation shortly after the building opened in 1930, with no interference by the local police. "The free lunch was magnificent," *New York Times* reporter Harrison E. Salisbury recalled in a memoir. "I never knew whether Old Joe owned the bar, but we thought he did and it made someone a lot of money." One of Kennedy's former employees, in interviews for this book, said he knew nothing of a Kennedy involvement in the Merchandise Mart speakeasy, but he did recall that Kennedy maintained ownership, at least into the late 1950s, of two old-fashioned Chicago saloons near the Mart that also were within the jurisdiction of the East Chicago Avenue police district.

The district was famed for having what senior police officials called "a solid set-up" of corruption. Organized crime controlled the bars, gambling, and prostitution that dominated the area's economics, just as it did in Boston's Fifth Ward. It was understood that any illicit business could operate without disruption, as long as two payoffs were made at the beginning of each month — one to the East Chicago Avenue police and one to the local ward committeeman, who represented Chicago's Democratic political bosses. Journalist Sandy Smith, who in the 1980s became the chief investigative reporter for *Time* magazine in Washington, was assigned to East Chicago Avenue as a police reporter for the *Chicago Tribune* in 1946. "The mob was so strong," Smith recalled in an interview for this book. "They had the police department and they had the politicians. If you paid at the beginning of the month, you had a month of immunity."

Only one FBI document showed a direct link between organized crime figures and Kennedy's liquor importing business, and it was not among the documents on Kennedy routinely released to journalists by the FBI. In this heavily censored document, part of a 1944 survey of "outstanding mobsters and racketeers" in the Miami area, the FBI reported that a gambler named Charlie Block was "the Southern representative of the Somerset Importers from New York City. He [Block] is known to be a big figure in the liquor industry." The FBI document added that Somerset was owned by Joseph Kennedy. Block later operated one of Miami Beach's most popular restaurants, the Park Avenue, in partnership with a professional gambler named Bert "Wingy" Grober, one of Joseph Kennedy's close friends, who was also heavily involved in Mafia-controlled casinos in Las Vegas. Joe Kennedy's love for Las Vegas, with its high life, beautiful women, and easy access to political cash, would be shared by his son Jack.

Joe Kennedy's decision in 1946 to sell Somerset to Longy Zwillman and Joe Reinfeld and get out of the liquor business has been interpreted by some historians as a result of Jack Kennedy's decision — made with his father's strong encouragement — to run for Congress that year. "He had enjoyed thirteen profitable years," wrote Richard J. Whalen, in *The Founding Father*, a bestselling 1964 biography of Joseph Kennedy, "but the whiskey trade was vaguely embarrassing and not at all in keeping with the public effect of dignity that Kennedy wished to achieve." And yet Joe Kennedy continued to flaunt his liquor connection after his sons moved to Washington, routinely sending gifts of high-priced scotch to the aides and colleagues of his sons. "Even when Bobby was attorney general," recalled Joseph F. Dolan, a top Kennedy deputy in the early 1960s, in a 1995 interview for this book, "every Christmas one of the black clerks would come around the Justice Department handing out bottles of Haig & Haig Pinch. If you got two bottles, the light shone on you."

Joe Kennedy's secret world also involved gambling. Harold Clancy, who began working for Kennedy in the late 1950s, recalled in an interview that Kennedy briefly considered buying into the mob-dominated company that manufactured the totalizer systems used by racetracks around the country to compute and transmit betting odds and race results. Kennedy decided against it. In 1943 he did buy 17 percent — a controlling interest — of the Hialeah Race Track in Miami, later selling it at a profit. Just how much and how seriously Kennedy gambled is not clear. His wife, Rose, in her memoir, wrote of visiting the track with her husband "a couple of times a week," adding that she "seldom ventured" from the two-dollar window. Kennedy also was a regular at the roulette tables in Miami Beach casinos during and immediately after World War II.

Joe Kennedy certainly understood that there was big money to be made from racetracks and gambling. In the mid-1940s he made a strenuous, and secret, effort to buy the Suffolk Downs Race Track near Boston at a fraction of its true value. Kennedy didn't get his way, but his hard-line tactics evoked the postwar tactics of organized crime families seeking to expand into legitimate businesses: threats, payoffs, and judicial corruption.

Suffolk Downs was the major asset of the Aldred Investment Trust (AIT), a nearly bankrupt Massachusetts firm that was registered with the SEC. During World War II the firm's trustees, in what was later determined to be a "gross abuse of trust," sold off many of its investments in order to buy the racetrack; some of the trustees then appointed themselves highly paid officers of the track. The SEC and an investor successfully sued AIT's management in federal court and forced the appointment of two outside receivers, who were instructed to reorganize or liquidate the trust. After the war, a group of independent investors, who included a financier named Richard Rosenthal, of Stamford, Connecticut, bought stock in AIT but found, to their dismay, that the court-appointed receivers were in the process of selling off the firm's control of Suffolk Downs for slightly more than $1 million — one-tenth the racetrack's value. The buyer, as all involved learned later, was Joe Kennedy, operating in his usual manner. The receivers' "idea of competitive bidding," Rosenthal recalled in an interview for this book, "was to get into a telephone booth with Joe Kennedy. They made a deal and brought it to court. We objected." Rosenthal retained his brother-in-law, the New York attorney Milton S. Gould (later of Shea and Gould), and others, and filed suit in federal court in Boston to stop the sale. "We argued that they [AIT management] had not followed common sense in having a private negotiation. The minimum is that you should have taken bids." What he and his lawyers did not know, Rosenthal added, with a laugh, "was that you couldn't beat Joe Kennedy in the Boston area."

Gould, who in 1997 was still practicing law in New York, recalled in an interview what happened next. The federal judge hearing the case, George C. Sweeney, who was named to the bench by President Roosevelt in 1935, summoned Gould and his cocounsel to an afternoon meeting in early 1946 in his chambers with the two AIT receivers, their lawyer, and the regional SEC director. Sweeney had a tough message for Gould and his clients: "You're sticking your nose where you don't belong. This is a local thing and we want local people involved." Gould later concluded that the judge was telling him that the AIT receivers did not want to sell the racetrack "to a bunch of Jews." Gould's cocounsel proposed to write a brief for the judge, summarizing the legal issues involved, to which Sweeney replied: "I don't need a brief. I may be wrong, but I'm never in doubt." Judge Sweeney, who died in 1965, then announced that he would deny the Rosenthal motion to intervene, with this sweetener: he would instruct the AIT receivers to buy back the stock held by Rosenthal and his colleagues for $250,000 more than they had initially paid; he also would grant Gould and his legal colleague a fee of $100,000.

The Rosenthal-Gould team rejected Judge Sweeney's offer and

filed suit in the U.S. Court of Appeals. Competitive bidding for the racetrack was eventually ordered, and Suffolk Downs was sold at auction to a Boston businessman for roughly $10 million. That businessman was not Joe Kennedy or even a proxy. Kennedy lost out, but not before one last, and typical, maneuver. Richard Rosenthal, while struggling unsuccessfully to put together a syndicate to bid on the track, received a telephone call and a visit from Joseph Timilty, the former police commissioner of Boston, who — as Rosenthal did not know at the time — was one of Joe Kennedy's most trusted operatives. "His entrée," recalled Rosenthal, "was that he'd been police commissioner and he could be helpful to me." Rosenthal also did not know that in March 1943, Timilty, then police commissioner, and six of his aides had been indicted by a grand jury in Boston and forced out of office for conspiring "to permit the operation of gaming houses and the registration of bets." The charges against Timilty never came to trial.*

At their meeting, Rosenthal told me, Timilty raised a disturbing issue: "He said you have to be careful how you handle this. This track is supported by people who drive out to it, and the roads are not in great shape. Suppose somebody decides to start repairing them during the [racetrack] meet. You'd be out of business." Rosenthal responded, simply, that "they wouldn't do that." "I wouldn't be too sure," answered Timilty. It was an obvious threat.

Rosenthal had few illusions, even then, about Joe Kennedy. In the years immediately before the war, as a young stock analyst in New

---

* Timilty and his senior aides in the police department were specifically accused of protecting in the early 1940s the vast gambling syndicate of Harry J. "Doc" Sagansky, the boss of New England's largest numbers racket. At his height, Sagansky, who lived in the Boston suburb of Brookline, employed an estimated three thousand people in his illicit rackets. He also owned numerous nightclubs and three racetracks, leading the Kefauver Committee to describe him as "perhaps the principal gambling racketeer in the New England area prior to . . . his conviction . . . in 1943." The committee also reported that Sagansky worked closely with Frank Costello and was in daily telephone communication with him through 1942, when Timilty's alleged protection of the racketeer was at its height. The initial indictment of Timilty was quashed in June 1943, but Timilty was reindicted. The second charge was dropped after a judge in Boston somehow ruled that Timilty only "administered" the police department and did not "enforce the law" or participate in arrests, as specified in the indictment. Timilty's term as police commissioner ended in November 1943.

York, he was assigned the shipbuilding industry. He wrote Kennedy, then chairman of the Maritime Commission, to arrange a face-to-face meeting. The airplane flight from New York to Washington was unforgettable — it was Rosenthal's first. He and Kennedy had "an informative conversation," recalled Rosenthal. "I was two years out of school and brash and young. I had a conviction that we were going to get into war." Kennedy asked whether Rosenthal had looked into a certain company, Todd Shipyards, and volunteered his view: "I think it's one of the best shipyards in the United States." Duly impressed, Rosenthal recommended Todd as a buy in his report. Years later, Rosenthal said, he learned that Kennedy, while chairman of the Maritime Commission, had maintained a large, and secret, personal investment in Todd. The stock was registered in the name of Edward E. Moore, Kennedy's longtime personal secretary.*

Ironically, Rosenthal maintained his financial interest in AIT and eventually became its sole owner. The firm is still being operated as a private investment company by Rosenthal, now an investor and philanthropist in Stamford. "When I was young," he said, "I thought intellect would win over everything. I honestly didn't believe that things got fixed, or that you could buy judges." He still does not un-

---

* Edward K. Linen of Rye, New York, who retired in 1979 as secretary of Todd Shipyards, confirmed in an interview for this book that Kennedy did hold a "sizable" amount of stock in the firm while serving as chairman of the Maritime Commission. "It was in Eddie Moore's name," Linen said. "I was assistant secretary of Todd at the time and Moore was a trustee for Joe Kennedy. Kennedy's name did not appear" on any document. Asked how he learned about the Moore-Kennedy connection, Linen recalled only that John D. Reilly, who was president of the shipyard in the 1930s, "was a friend of Joe Kennedy's and, at some point, I found out that Eddie Moore was Joe Kennedy." Kennedy's use of Moore to mask his stock purchases was made more insidious by the fact that he seemed to be completely aboveboard in disclosing his stock holdings to the White House and to Congress prior to his Senate confirmation to the Maritime Commission. In a series of March 1937 letters on file at the Roosevelt Library, Kennedy acknowledged that one of the family trusts, over which he had no control, owned 3,300 shares of stock in Todd. He also acknowledged personal ownership of an additional 1,100 shares in Todd, and proposed turning those shares over to his broker for sale within sixty days. In a letter to the Senate, Kennedy forthrightly promised to put the stock "beyond my control . . . before taking the oath of office. I think an understanding of these facts will clear my position much more satisfactorily, at least in my own mind." There is no evidence in the Roosevelt documents that Kennedy disclosed the stock he held in the name of Eddie Moore.

derstand, Rosenthal said, why Kennedy wanted the track and was willing to spend "a lot of political currency to get it." The financier shrugged and then offered an answer: "The track was a big cash handle business and he may have wanted it for other business."

Jack Kennedy once explained to Arthur Schlesinger, as Schlesinger recorded in *A Thousand Days,* that his father "held up standards for us, and he was very tough when we failed to meet those standards. The toughness was important." Kennedy brought his father's toughness and his history into the presidency, and with them he brought a sense that he, like his father, understood how the world really worked. It was an understanding that the earnest young businessmen, government officials, and academics in the Kennedy administration could never have — and it increased their awe and reverence for the president. Joe Kennedy's street-hardened past became, ironically, further proof of Jack Kennedy's qualifications for the Oval Office.

5

THE AMBASSADOR

Joe Kennedy played by his own rules both in running his personal life and in amassing his personal fortune. He employed the same ruthlessness and secrecy with all — his wife, fellow businessmen, organized crime leaders, newspapermen, and political figures. He served the Roosevelt administration with distinction as chairman of the Securities and Exchange Commission and, later, as chairman of the Maritime Commission, bringing the techniques and skills that worked so well in his business life to government service. His cherished ambition was to convince Franklin Roosevelt to nominate him as ambassador to Great Britain, the most socially prestigious post in the American government. "Being appointed ambassador to England," explained one Kennedy biographer, "would mean social preferment for the Kennedys and their offspring, and an opportunity to 'show' the Brahmins that he could 'get there' without their support. He would be their social superior — the social superior of Boston's snobbiest!" Kennedy spent months in 1937 lobbying for the appointment, with the continuing help of James Roosevelt, the president's son, whose presence had assured favored treatment when he accompanied Joe to seek British liquor contracts in 1933.

The president and his aides understood the cynicism of Joe Kennedy's friendship with Jimmy, but made no attempt to intervene. Kennedy's influence on the president's son remained enormous. Kennedy was rich and attractive to women, and the young Roosevelt wanted to be both. The two collaborated on business deals and vague promises of partnerships. Roosevelt, trading on his father's fame, was working as an insurance broker, and at Prohibition's end, Kennedy allowed him to write policies on overseas liquor shipments. There were always women. While ambassador to England, Kennedy told an embassy aide that Jimmy Roosevelt was "so crazy for women he would screw a snake going uphill."

In 1935, with Kennedy's help, Roosevelt was named president of the National Grain Yeast Corporation of Belleville, New Jersey, one of many companies that found themselves doing big business after the repeal of Prohibition. Yeast, of course, was essential for the mass production of beer, and it became one of the legitimate businesses that attracted former bootleggers. Roosevelt failed at the job and was out of work within six months.

James Roosevelt's business disappointments no doubt figured in his father's decision, despite opposition from his advisers, to name him his personal secretary at the beginning of his second term. Kennedy, not surprisingly, continued to lavish attention, affection, and, undoubtedly, women on the president's son. "You know as far as I am concerned," Kennedy wrote Roosevelt and his wife in a January 1937 letter on file in the FDR Library, "you are young people and struggling to get along and I am your foster-father."

Foster father was hyperbole, but James Roosevelt, as personal secretary to his father, played a major — and not fully known — role in assuring Kennedy's nomination as ambassador to England. The most extensive account of the machinations appeared in *Memoirs,* Arthur Krock's autobiography, published in 1968. Krock, then the columnist and Washington bureau chief of the *New York Times,* had a secret life. By the late 1930s he had become another of Kennedy's wholly owned subsidiaries — a journalist who vacationed at Kennedy's Florida home, shared in his lifestyle, and very often wrote whatever Kennedy wanted. It was a pattern that would be repeated again and again by the reporters covering Joe and, later, Jack Kennedy. In his autobiography, Krock told of a dinner with Kennedy, then chairman of the Maritime Commission, at which James Roosevelt arrived and took Kennedy into another room for an extended private conversation. Kennedy's nomination as ambassador was rumored at the time, and, Krock noted, there was sharp opposition inside the White House and from liberals in the Congress. After the meeting, a very angry Kennedy told Krock that young Roosevelt had proposed that he take an appointment as secretary of commerce. "Well, I'm not going to," Kennedy said. "FDR promised me London, and I told Jimmy to tell his father that's the job, and the only one, I'll accept."

Kennedy got his nomination in December 1937 and arrived in prewar London full of ambition.

Kennedy's rise and fall as ambassador in London has been often told: a brief honeymoon with the British press and public, much of it revolving around his highly social and photogenic children, and then a relentless fall from grace. Kennedy was reviled for his defeatism. His widely quoted belief was that Great Britain had neither the will nor the armaments to win a war against Nazi Germany. And he was ridiculed for his perceived cowardice during the intensified Luftwaffe bombing of London in 1940, when he chose to spend his nights at a country estate well away from the targeted city centers. German Foreign Ministry documents published after World War II show that Kennedy, without State Department approval, repeatedly sought a personal meeting with Hitler on the eve of the Nazi blitzkrieg, "to bring about a better understanding between the United States and Germany." His goal was to find a means to keep America out of a war that he was convinced would destroy capitalism.

There is no evidence that Ambassador Kennedy understood in the days before the war that stopping Hitler was a moral imperative. "Individual Jews are all right, Harvey," Kennedy told Harvey Klemmer, one of his few trusted aides in the American Embassy, "but as a race they stink. They spoil everything they touch. Look what they did to the movies." Klemmer, in an interview many years later made available for this book, recalled that Kennedy and his "entourage" generally referred to Jews as "kikes or sheenies."

Kennedy and his family would later emphatically deny allegations of anti-Semitism stemming from his years as ambassador, but the German diplomatic documents show that Kennedy consistently minimized the Jewish issue in his four-month attempt in the summer and fall of 1938 to obtain an audience with Hitler. On June 13, as the Nazi regime was systematically segregating Jews from German society, Kennedy advised Herbert von Dirksen, the German ambassador in London, as Dirksen reported to Berlin, that "it was not so much the fact that we wanted to get rid of the Jews that was so harmful to us, but rather the loud clamor with which we accompanied this purpose. He himself understood our Jewish policy completely." On October 13, 1938, a few weeks before *Kristallnacht,* with its Brown Shirt terror attacks on synagogues and Jewish businesses, Kennedy met again with Ambassador Dirksen, who subsequently informed his superiors that "today, too, as during former conversations, Kennedy mentioned that very strong anti-Semitic feelings existed in the United States and that a large portion of the population had an understanding of the German attitude toward the Jews."*

Kennedy knew little about the culture and history of Europe before his appointment as ambassador and made no effort to educate himself once in London. He made constant misjudgments. In the

---

* Kennedy remained insensitive, at best, about the Jewish issue through the later war years, when the existence of concentration camps was widely known. In a May 1944 interview with an old friend, Joe Dinneen of the *Boston Globe,* Kennedy acknowledged, when questioned about his alleged anti-Semitism: "It is true that I have a low opinion of some Jews in public office and in private life. That does not mean that I hate all Jews; that I believe they should be wiped off the face of the earth. . . . Other races have their own problems to solve. They're glad to give the Jews a lift and help them along the way toward tolerance, but they're not going to drop everything and solve the problems of the Jews for them. Jews who take an unfair advantage of the fact that theirs is a persecuted race do not help much. . . . Publicizing unjust attacks upon the Jews may help to cure the injustice, but continually publicizing the whole problem only serves to keep it alive in the public mind." Kennedy's discussion of anti-Semitism was withheld from publication at the time by the editors of the *Globe,* but in 1959 Dinneen sought to include a portion of it in a generally flattering precampaign family biography. Advance galleys of the Dinneen book, entitled *The Kennedy Family,* had been given to Jack Kennedy, who understood how inflammatory his father's comments would be and had no difficulty in successfully urging Dinneen to delete the offending paragraphs. The incident is described in Richard Whalen's biography of Joe Kennedy.

summer of 1938, for example, he blithely assured the president in a letter, described in the published diaries of Harold Ickes, FDR's secretary of the interior, that "he does not regard the European situation as so critical." Diplomats serving on the American Desk in the British Foreign Office quickly came to fear — and hate — Kennedy. They compiled a secret dossier on him, known as the "Kennediana" file, which would not be declassified until after the war. In those pages Sir Robert Vansittart, undersecretary of the Foreign Office, scrawled, as war was spreading throughout Europe in early 1940: "Mr. Kennedy is a very foul specimen of a double-crosser and defeatist. He thinks of nothing but his own pocket. I hope that this war will at least see the elimination of his type."

The Foreign Office notes also included many allegations of Kennedy's profiteering once the war began. Kennedy, still very much in control of Somerset Importers, was suspected of having commandeered valued transatlantic cargo space for the continued importation of British scotch and gin; it was further believed that he was abusing his position of trust as a high-level government insider to support his Wall Street trading. No proof of such business activity was then available to the British Foreign Office — officially, at least — but Kennedy was worried that he might be doing something illegal: in April 1941, shortly after his return to the United States, he telephoned the State Department and inquired whether there were rules governing private financial transactions of U.S. officials serving abroad. Kennedy was told that Congress had passed legislation in 1915 making any business dealings for profit illegal.

In 1992 Harvey Klemmer, an ex-newspaperman who served as Joe Kennedy's personal public relations aide at the Maritime Commission and had the same role in London, acknowledged in a British television interview that the Foreign Office suspicions more than fifty years before were valid: Kennedy, in fact, did continue to be a major investor and speculator on Wall Street, placing buy and sell orders by telephone through John J. Burns, a former justice of the Massachusetts State Supreme Court who was retained by Kennedy to run his New York office, a practice he continued into the 1950s. Klemmer, depicted by one British diplomatic reporter as Kennedy's "brains trust," remained silent about Joe Kennedy until a few months before his death, from cancer, in 1992, when he did a brief on-air interview with television producer Phillip Whitehead on Thames TV. Klemmer, who was severely disfigured from his cancer, also granted Whitehead an extraordinary interview on audiotape — much of it never made public until it was obtained for this book. The unedited transcripts of the two interviews provide a rare inside look at the Kennedy embassy. "Kennedy continued to do business as usual while in London," Klemmer told Whitehead. One night, while out at dinner, the ambassador left the table for a telephone call. "He was gone a long time. When he came back, he said, 'Well, the market's going to hell. I told Johnny [Burns] to sell everything.'" Also at the dinner, Klemmer recalled, was "a Jewish friend of his and mine. . . . In a little while [the friend] began to fidget and finally excused himself on the basis that he had something important to do and left. As soon as he had left, Kennedy said, 'Watch the son of a bitch go out and sell. Actually the market is doing very well and I told Johnny to buy.'"

Kennedy was equally unprincipled in his use of ambassadorial perquisites. Klemmer told Whitehead that one of his principal duties at the embassy was shipping Kennedy's liquor. "Using his name and the prestige of the embassy and also my connection with the Maritime Commission, I was able to get shipping space for up to, I think, around 200,000 cases of whiskey at a time when shipping space [from England to the United States] was very scarce." Kennedy's abuse of office on behalf of Somerset Importers was so extreme, Klemmer said, that "a British friend in the Ministry of Shipping came to see me one day and said, 'You'd better lay off with the ambassador's whiskey, because some of the other distillers, who can't get shipping space, are going to have the question raised in Parliament. He's using the influence of the American Embassy to preempt shipping space.' So," Klemmer concluded, "we kind of tapered off a little bit after that." Kennedy ignored the widespread gossip about his whiskey dealing, Klemmer added: "He just brushed it off. . . . His stock reply to any criticism was 'To hell with them.' . . . He didn't take things like that seriously."

London's concerns about the American ambassador went far beyond defeatism and profiteering. British policy, after the failure of Prime Minister Neville Chamberlain's appeasement of Hitler at Munich, was unstated but nonetheless clear: to somehow get the United States into the war against Germany. In May 1940, with France on the verge of defeat, Winston Churchill, who had been serving as first lord of the Admiralty, replaced the failed Chamberlain. A few days later, while shaving, Churchill announced to his son, Randolph: "I think I can see my way through." Randolph, recalling the conversation in a 1963 memoir, asked, "Do you mean we can avoid defeat or defeat the bastards?" His father, flinging his razor into a washbasin, proclaimed, "Of course I mean we can beat them." Asked how, the new prime minister simply said, "I shall drag the United States in."

It was clear even before Churchill became prime minister that Joe Kennedy, with his access to Roosevelt, his desire to meet personally with Adolf Hitler, and his eagerness to avoid American involvement in the war at all costs, had become a national security risk to England. Historians are in agreement that Kennedy was a priority target of Britain's famed MI5, its counterintelligence service, and was subjected to physical surveillance as well as extensive wiretapping. No such files have been declassified and released by the British government, despite repeated requests.

Harvey Klemmer knew firsthand, though, about MI5's close surveillance. Kennedy was seeing a wealthy English divorcée who was in touch with Sir Oswald Mosley, a leading British fascist. The woman, Klemmer said in his interview, "told me that Joe had asked her to initiate . . . contact with Mosley," in the mistaken belief that the fascists in England were more numerous than they were. "So one day [Kennedy] asked me to take her home and it was in one of her cars. So I did. And on the way back I was stopped by a man in uniform who said there was an air raid or invasion drill in progress. I would have to leave my car for a while and take refuge with them in a nearby country home. . . . I wondered if there was something going on, and so I arranged my gloves on the seat in a certain way, and I arranged some of the papers in the glove compartment." After an hour, when Klemmer was given the all-clear sign, "I looked and I could see the car had been searched. . . . I knew I was under suspicion" by British intelligence, Klemmer said, "because of my association with him. My files at the embassy were searched," as was, he believed, his London apartment. He and others at the embassy did learn later, Klemmer told Whitehead, that "the British had Kennedy's telephone tapped."

Given his precarious position in London, some of Kennedy's actions seem stupefying.

In the spring of 1939, shortly after Germany's occupation of Czechoslovakia, Kennedy — despite being instructed not to do so by Washington — encouraged a bizarre and little-known scheme being actively promoted by a naive American automobile executive who had been told in Berlin that the Nazi regime would agree to peace concessions and a general disarmament in return for an Anglo-American gold loan totaling between $500 million and $1 billion. The American, James D. Mooney, president of General Motors Overseas, flew to London to discuss the German proposal with an equally impressed Kennedy at the American Embassy. According to Mooney's unpublished memoir, made available for this book, Kennedy urged Mooney to return to Berlin and inform the Germans that he would "certainly like to have a talk with them, quietly and privately." Mooney's papers reveal that it was agreed that Kennedy would meet secretly in Paris with Dr. Helmut Wohltat, a high-level Nazi official who was a deputy to Field Marshal Hermann Göring. Only after Kennedy made the commitment to Mooney did he send a vaguely worded cable to the State Department, wondering whether there would be "any objections" to his flying to Paris to meet with Mooney and "a personal friend of Hitler." He was emphatically denied permission to make the trip by Secretary of State Cordell Hull. Mooney, still eager to involve Kennedy, returned to London and presented the ambassador with the list of the promised German concessions that would result from the gold loan. "What a wonderful speech could be built up from these points back home!" Kennedy exclaimed, according to Mooney's notes. Kennedy then took his case for a meeting directly to President Roosevelt, and was told once again to have nothing to do with the proposal.

Nonetheless, Kennedy met in secret with Mooney and Wohltat at a hotel in London on May 9, 1939. "Each man made an excellent impression on the other," Mooney recorded in his unpublished memoir. "It was heartening to sit there and witness the exertion of real effort to reach something constructive." Within days, London's *Daily Express* blew everyone's cover by reporting on its front page, under the headline "Goering's Mystery Man Is Here," that Wohltat had arrived in London "on a special mission." Neither Kennedy nor Mooney was named in the article, but a few days later Kennedy was singled out for censure in *The Week,* a radical weekly newsletter. Its editor, Claud Cockburn, wrote that Kennedy, in his talks with Germans, "uses language which is not merely defeatist, but anti-Rooseveltian. . . . Mr. Kennedy goes so far as to insinuate that the democratic policy of the United States is a Jewish production, but that Roosevelt will fall in 1940." The article was reprinted in the *New York Post* and eventually brought to Roosevelt's attention by Harold Ickes. In his diaries, Ickes noted that "the President read this and said to me: 'It is true.'"

Kennedy's indiscretion knew no limits. After Munich he had summoned a group of American journalists to the embassy and, among other things, briefed them off the record about a most secret plot by a group of dissident German generals to overthrow Hitler. James Reston of the *New York Times* summarized the briefing in *Deadline,* his 1991 memoir: "It was known in London on the eve of Munich that . . . a group of German officers led by Generals Halder and Beck had a plan to overthrow the Führer. Fearing war on three fronts, these conspirators informed officials in Westminster [the British Foreign Office] — so Ambassador Kennedy told us — that they would arrest Hitler if the British and French took military action to block the invasion of Czechoslovakia." It would not become publicly known until after the war that the plotters, General Ludwig Beck, then chief of the German General Staff, and his deputy, Franz Halder — their lives very much at stake — had approached the British Foreign Ministry. The Beck-Halder partnership was the most serious early resistance to Hitler and also involved, by some accounts, a plan to assassinate Hitler.*

It is impossible to assess what was in Kennedy's mind when he chose to casually brief American correspondents about the plot — and to provide the names of those involved. His blabbing can be seen most innocently as the actions of an ambitious man, eager to seem an insider, who would let nothing block his efforts to ingratiate himself

---

* Beck resigned as chief of staff in protest against Hitler's plan to invade Czechoslovakia, and was involved in a series of plots against Hitler for the next six years. He shot himself after the failure of Count Claus von Stauffenberg's final attempt to assassinate Hitler, by bomb, on July 20, 1944. Halder, who served as chief of staff until September 1942, was arrested in the Gestapo's widespread roundup after the 1944 bomb attempt and placed in a concentration camp. He survived the war.

with the press. But there is a far darker interpretation. The British Foreign Office's Kennediana files, which were made public after the war, show that Kennedy was opposed to any policy based on the assassination of Adolf Hitler, in fear that Hitler's death would leave Soviet communism unchecked. In late September of 1939, three weeks after Hitler's invasion of Poland, Kennedy directly raised his concerns in a conference with Lord Halifax, the British foreign secretary. Halifax quoted Kennedy as stating that he

> himself was disposed to deprecate perpetual reference to the personal elimination of Hitler. How could we be sure that it would not have precisely the opposite effect on German feeling? . . . According to Mr. Kennedy, United States opinion thought that Russia was a much greater potential disturber of world peace through Communist doctrine than was Germany. He thought that American opinion would inevitably be greatly disturbed if and when it came to think that the result of the present struggle was a greater extension of bolshevism in Europe. . . . He appreciated the strength of British opinion about Hitler and the Nazi system, but, if the end of it all was to be universal bankruptcy, the outlook was very black.

Halifax, according to his Foreign Office note, did not respond to Kennedy's comment about Hitler's assassination.*

During his years in London, Joe Kennedy compounded his political and personal problems with FDR and his senior advisers through his overriding presidential ambition and his clumsy attempts to mask it. "He thought he was about the most qualified individual on earth to

---

* Even Rose Kennedy knew something was up. In her gossipy memoir, *Times to Remember,* she described an early 1939 lunch at 10 Downing Street at which she asked Chamberlain "if Hitler died would he be more confident about peace, and he said he would." Rose defended her husband's contrary view in her memoir, published in 1974, insisting that "of course, no one knew then that Hitler was criminally insane and had no intention of living by humane standards except his own demented ones, and that his promises meant nothing to him." In Mrs. Kennedy's view, presumably, "no one" would not include the millions of Jews who were being systematically persecuted throughout Germany and German-occupied Central Europe by 1939.

be president," Klemmer said in his 1992 television interview. "He had supreme self-confidence, of course, as everybody knows, and he thought the monetary system in the United States needed revising and . . . one of his ambitions was to revise the whole monetary system." Kennedy spent much time masterminding a campaign — transparent to the men in the White House — for the Democratic presidential nomination in 1940. The Kennedy claque of newspaper sycophants, headed by Arthur Krock, repeatedly planted stories about a possible Kennedy candidacy. Krock's columns in the *New York Times* made the men in the White House gag. In a diary entry dated May 22, 1939, Treasury Secretary Henry Morgenthau described how Thomas G. Corcoran, one of Roosevelt's senior political advisers, "got really violent" while discussing Kennedy and Krock. "He said that Krock was running a campaign to put Joe Kennedy over for President."* Krock was further described as "the number one Poison at the White House." Harold Ickes had earlier expressed concern about Kennedy's qualifications, and his ambitions, in his diary: "At a time when we should be sending the best that we have to Great Britain, we have not done so. We have sent a rich man, untrained in diplomacy, unlearned in history and politics, who is a great publicity hound and who is apparently ambitious to be the first Catholic President of the United States."

Roosevelt, who had every intention of running for an unprecedented third term in 1940, was just as skilled as Kennedy at planting stories. Walter Trohan, the crusty bureau chief of the *Chicago Tribune,* who was known to be close to Kennedy, recalled being summoned to the White House by Steve Early, Roosevelt's press secretary, and given a challenge. " 'You're a friend of Joe Kennedy's, aren't you?' I said, 'Yes, I like Joe.' He said, 'You wouldn't criticize him?' I said, 'Oh

---

* In an interview in 1962 with Richard J. Whalen, Corcoran depicted Kennedy, with grudging admiration, as having staged a "remarkable coup d'état" in putting his son into the presidency. "You have to look at this piece of energy adapting itself to its time," Corcoran said. "A man not afraid to think in a daring way. He had imperial instinct. He knew what he wanted — money and status for his family. What other end is there but power?" Jack Kennedy's election in 1960 was a "long-shot risk," Corcoran added, into which Joe Kennedy "slammed money. . . . These are not the attributes of the philosopher, the humanitarian, educators or priests. These are the attributes of those in command."

yes, I would. I'd criticize any New Dealer. What's Joe done?'" Early then gave Trohan copies of two Kennedy letters. The first, Trohan told me in a 1997 interview for this book, was addressed to Arthur Krock and said, "We ought not to get into the war." The second, sent to the State Department, "was extremely pro-British and suggested getting along with Britain." Trohan wrote an account of Kennedy's gamesmanship for the *Tribune*. A few weeks later, Kennedy was called to Washington for a meeting. "He ran into me," Trohan said, "and drew his hand across his throat. Joe knew I got the information from the White House." The ambassador, Trohan added, "forgave me in the long run."

FDR reacted to the political and diplomatic dangers posed by Kennedy by keeping him in London and increasingly isolating him from the American public and from all important policy decisions. The president sent a series of personal representatives to Great Britain in mid-1940, after Hitler invaded Denmark and Norway and began his drive into the Netherlands and Belgium toward France, and instructed them to make on-the-scene surveys of British morale and military readiness. Men such as Colonel William J. "Wild Bill" Donovan, Colonel Carl Spaatz, General George Strong, and Admiral Robert L. Ghormley arrived in London, did their business, and returned to Washington — with little or no contact with the embassy, to Kennedy's embarrassment and rage. By that time, too, much more of America's business with England was being handled directly by the British Foreign Ministry, headed by Lord Halifax, including a highly sensitive proposal to swap long-term American leases on British overseas bases for fifty much-needed American destroyers. With war being waged throughout Europe, American diplomacy in Europe was made the primary responsibility of Ambassador William C. Bullitt in Paris, a Roosevelt confidant who shared FDR's contempt for Nazi Germany.*

Kennedy understood that Roosevelt, despite his many public

---

* Bullitt and the president were briefly put on the defensive in late March 1940, when the German Foreign Office released a series of diplomatic documents that had been found in Polish archives after the seizure of Warsaw the previous September. In a private conversation in November 1938, Bullitt was said by Count Jerzy Potocki, the Polish ambassador to Washington, to have expressed "great vehemence and strong

statements to the contrary, was intent on bringing America into the war. The president had begun an intermittent secret correspondence with Winston Churchill in the fall of 1939, nine months before Churchill was named prime minister. The two men were careful, even in their encrypted communications, not to talk openly about taking on Hitler together, but they did agree to work out procedures for sharing, among other intelligence, the location of German submarines and surface ships. Such exchanges would have provoked, at the least, an outcry among the isolationists in Congress and imperiled Roosevelt's reelection prospects. No copies of the sensitive communications were to be made available to the British Foreign Office; the two leaders communicated via the code room in the American Embassy — Joe Kennedy's embassy.

hatred about Germany and Chancellor Hitler. He said only strength, and that at the conclusion of a war, could make an end of the mad expansion of the Germans in the future." In a talk a few weeks later, Bullitt was said to have given the Poles "moral assurance that the United States will leave its isolationist policy and be prepared in the event of war to participate actively on the side of France and Britain." The White House quickly characterized the documents as propaganda and put out a statement, in Roosevelt's name, urging that they "be taken with several grains of salt." Over the next few days, however, reporters in Berlin were shown the documents in question and found them to have all the appearance of being genuine. One set of the Polish papers released by the Germans dealt with an interview with Joseph Kennedy, who, in a June 1939 talk with Jan Wszelaki, a Polish trade official, was quoted as boasting that his two eldest sons, Joseph and John, had recently traveled all over Europe and "intended to make a series of lectures on the European situation . . . after their return to the United States, at Harvard University. . . . 'You have no idea,'" Wszelaki further quoted Kennedy as telling him, "'to what extent my oldest boy . . . has the President's ear. I might say that the President believes him more than me.'"

6

TAKING ON FDR

By early October 1940, there was very bad blood between the president and his reluctant ambassador in England. Kennedy wanted out and he didn't care who knew it. On October 10, he took advantage of a farewell meeting in London with Foreign Minister Halifax to issue a warning to Roosevelt — correctly anticipating that the British Foreign Office would relay the threat to the State Department via the British Embassy in Washington. "His principal complaint," Halifax reported to the British ambassador, Lord Lothian, was that

> they had not kept him adequately informed of their policy and doings during the last two or three months. . . . He told me that he had sent an article to the United States to appear on November 1st, if by any accident he was not able to get there, which would be of considerable importance appearing five days before the Presidential election. When I asked him what would be the main burden of his song, he gave me to understand that it would be an indictment of President Roosevelt's administration for having talked a lot and done very little. He is plainly a very disappointed and rather embittered man.

Kennedy was more than embittered; he was in a rage. "I'm going back and tell the truth. I'm going home and tell the American people that that son of a bitch in the White House is going to kill their sons," he told Harvey Klemmer over lunch on the day before he left London, as Klemmer recounted in the television interview made available for this book.

Arthur Krock, Kennedy's faithful scribe, provided a detailed account of Kennedy's blackmail plottings in his *Memoirs:*

> On October 16 Kennedy sent a cablegram to the President insisting that he be allowed to come home. . . . That same day Kennedy telephoned . . . and said that if he did not get a favorable reply to his cablegram, he was coming home anyhow; . . . that he had written a full account of the facts to Edward Moore, his secretary in New York, with instructions to release the story to the press if the Ambassador were not back in New York by a certain date. A few hours after this conversation the cabled permission to return was received.

Kennedy's "full account" referred to the extensive exchange of cables between Roosevelt and Churchill that had been relayed through the American Embassy. Those secret cables had a secret history known to only a few in America and England in the spring of 1940. Kennedy had been shocked in May when a special unit of British counterintelligence staged a late-night raid on the apartment of Tyler Kent, an American Embassy code clerk, and uncovered a cache of more than 1,500 decoded diplomatic cables that Kent had taken home. Kennedy took the unusual step of immediately revoking Kent's diplomatic immunity — State Department immunity has never been revoked since — and Kent was secretly tried and convicted in a London court. He spent the war years in an isolated British prison on the Isle of Wight.

Kennedy's decisive action to keep Kent's betrayal of his nation — as well as the Roosevelt-Churchill correspondence — from becoming public has been credited by historians as high-minded and exemplary. Had this not been done, Kent could have been tried in America; his documents would become part of the court record, triggering anger and resentment in the Congress and among the many

Americans opposed to U.S. involvement in the war in Europe. The furor, the historian Michael Beschloss wrote in his *Kennedy and Roosevelt: The Uneasy Alliance,* published in 1980, "might have eliminated any chance of a third term for the president and made it nearly impossible for him to move public opinion so swiftly toward aid to the Allies. . . . [Kennedy] was unwilling to influence American policy at the cost of an act that seemed illegitimate and disloyal."

Kennedy had much more to gain, however, by making private use of the Tyler Kent materials in his war against FDR. American Embassy files show that on May 20, 1940, the day of Kent's arrest, Ambassador Kennedy arranged to ship a diplomatic pouch full of "personal mail and various packages" to Washington, in the care of a friend in the State Department. On May 23, three days after Kent's arrest, Kennedy sought and received authorization from the State Department for Edward Moore, his exceedingly faithful personal assistant, to return to New York with Rose Kennedy and their retarded daughter, Rosemary. Moore left London on May 28 and never went back.

Tyler Kent, obsessed with hatred for Kennedy, lived in obscurity after the war as a gentleman farmer in rural Maryland. The FBI files on his case remained secret until 1982, when the British journalist John Costello, an expert on World War II history, obtained them under the Freedom of Information Act. Costello, who died in 1995, also obtained scores of State Department documents on the Kent affair, including many of Ambassador Kennedy's cables to Washington. Costello approached Kent, who was intrigued by the newly released documents and agreed to a series of detailed interviews. In those interviews, Kent is quoted as explaining that his interest in the secret cables had been aroused only after Kennedy ordered him "to make copies of nonroutine messages that went in and out of the embassy for Kennedy's personal file." Kennedy also instructed Kent to retrieve all of Roosevelt's coded exchanges, dating back to the 1938 Munich accord, with Ambassador William C. Bullitt in Paris and with the other ambassador widely known to be avidly anti-Hitler, Anthony Drexel Biddle, in Warsaw.*

The Kent matter languished until later in the 1980s, when Robert

---

* Kent, after seeing Costello, kept on talking. In a separate interview later in 1982 with the BBC's *Newsnight* television show, he explained how easy it had been to smuggle

T. Crowley, a counterintelligence officer who specialized in Soviet penetrations of the West, retired from the Central Intelligence Agency. "There were a couple of guys left over when I retired, and one was Kent," Crowley recalled in an interview for this book. "I thought the guy was unstable" and a possible Soviet KGB agent. As a former CIA officer, Crowley had connections. Over the next few years he was able to obtain access to previously unavailable government files on Tyler Kent. The Kent-KGB spy story soon petered out, Crowley said: "Tyler never developed into anything we thought. We couldn't demonstrate that he was working for the Soviets, or the Germans, or the Italians. He was working for Tyler — and he's trying to save the United States from Roosevelt. He was everybody's tool. Just a kooky half-wit." But Crowley did find documentation, he told me, that convinced him that Kennedy had been assembling a political dossier on FDR, and was using Kent to get access to the potentially damaging Roosevelt-Churchill cables.

In Crowley's view, Kennedy's refusal of diplomatic immunity to Kent, thus assuring that he would be held without access to the American press, was a brilliant move. Kennedy made another brilliant move, Crowley said; he arranged to ship his copies of the sensitive and politically incriminating Churchill-Roosevelt cablegrams to America. Edward Moore, once in America, could retrieve the copies and prepare for the coming showdown with Roosevelt. The cablegrams, Crowley told me, "put Kennedy in a marvelous position with FDR. He had him in a spot and could possibly deny him his reelection. He had a knife."

Joe Kennedy declared war on the White House. Historians agree on what happened next: Kennedy arrived in Washington on the evening of October 26, amid much press speculation that he was planning to

---

the cable traffic out of the embassy code room. One source, he told the journalist Richard Harris, was to obtain cable copies that were "surplus and were to be incinerated . . . burnt in an incinerator. . . . Another source was that Ambassador Kennedy was having copies of important political documents made for his own private collection. Part of my function was to make these copies, and it was quite simple to slip in an extra carbon." The BBC show reported that Kent, described as an "amateur," had been followed for eight months by British counterintelligence before his arrest.

endorse Wendell Willkie, the Republican candidate. The election was only ten days away. Kennedy's flight from London had been delayed for days by poor weather, and en route he received a series of urgent and confidential messages from FDR inviting him to dinner at the White House. The two men talked early on the twenty-sixth — Kennedy was then in Bermuda, on the last leg of his Pan Am Clipper flight to New York — and Roosevelt's side of the conversation was overheard by Lyndon Baines Johnson, then an ambitious young congressman from Texas, who happened to be visiting the Oval Office. "Ah, Joe," the president said, "it is so good to hear your voice. Please come to the White House tonight for a little family dinner." Over the years, Johnson would dramatically tell many journalists what happened next: FDR slowly drew his hand across his throat and added, "I'm *dying* to talk to you."

Exactly what took place at the Kennedy-Roosevelt White House meeting may never be known. In Joe Kennedy's much-quoted version, as relayed by him to Arthur Krock, FDR was at his most charming with Kennedy and his wife, who had been personally invited by Roosevelt to join her husband at dinner. There was the inevitable praise for Kennedy's children and a presidential willingness to listen to Kennedy's complaints about the way he had been ignored and mistreated while in London. Roosevelt claimed, according to the account in Krock's memoir, that "he had known nothing about these matters; the fault lay with the State Department." FDR's sweet-talking prevailed, according to Krock. Temporarily smitten, Kennedy agreed to make a radio speech calling for Roosevelt's reelection.

That explanation, given the well-documented and high level of hostility between the president and his ambassador, is simply not believable. In later years, Kennedy provided at least two different reasons for his turnabout. He told the journalist Stewart Alsop that the president had held out the hope that a strong endorsement in the radio talk could lead to FDR's backing for a Kennedy presidential campaign in 1944. And Kennedy explained to Clare Boothe Luce, wife of his longtime friend Henry Luce, publisher of *Time* magazine, that "we agreed that if I endorsed him for president in 1940, then he would support my son Joe for governor of Massachusetts in 1942." Kennedy and Roosevelt viewed each other as consummate liars, so a presidential promise of future support — even if one was, in fact, proffered — would have meant little.

A far more compelling reason for Kennedy's decision to make the radio speech was provided by Winston Churchill's son, Randolph, who in 1960 privately told the *New York Times* columnist C. L. Sulzberger that MI5 had provided Roosevelt with a collection of intercepted Kennedy cables and telephone calls in which the ambassador was critical of the president. The cables were passed to Brendan Bracken, Winston Churchill's close friend and adviser, who, with Churchill's approval, passed them along to FDR's trusted aide Harry Hopkins. There is yet another version, which Joe Kennedy told Harvey Klemmer, who was surprised, as were many in London, at Kennedy's last-minute endorsement of the despised Roosevelt. In his Thames TV interview, Klemmer recalled a later conversation with Kennedy about the radio address. "I said the press was speculating that FDR had dragged out an old tax return and said, 'Joe, you wouldn't want me to show this to the public, would you?' And [Kennedy] said, 'That's a damn lie. I fixed that up long ago.' So," noted Klemmer, "there had been a tax mix-up at one time or another."

Whatever the truth, the president and his ambassador had become two scorpions in a bottle: Kennedy could damage and perhaps destroy Roosevelt's reelection chances by making public the Tyler Kent documents; Roosevelt, with Churchill's help, had assembled an equally lethal dossier of telephone and cable intercepts. The full story lies buried, perhaps forever, in classified U.S. and British archives.

Kennedy's half-hour radio speech on October 29 reassured Americans that the United States "must and will stay out of war." No secret commitments had been made to the British by the Roosevelt administration, Kennedy said. And as for the oft-stated charge that the president was attempting "to involve this country in world war . . . such a charge is false." The speech was jolting to those who knew what Kennedy really understood about Roosevelt's war policy. In his memoirs, Arthur Krock noted: "The speech was out of keeping, not only with the wholly opposite view he had been expressing privately (to me, among others), but with Kennedy's earned reputation as one of the most forthright men in public life."

Three days after the election, Kennedy self-destructed. In an interview with Louis Lyons of the *Boston Globe* and two other journalists, he essentially declared that Hitler had won the war in Europe. "Democracy is finished in England," Kennedy told Lyons. "Don't let anybody tell you you can get used to incessant bombing. There's nowhere in England they aren't getting it. . . . It's a question of how long England can hold out. . . . I'm willing to spend all I've got to keep us out of the war. There's no sense in our getting in. We'd just be holding the bag." The story made headlines. The American response was devastating for Kennedy: thousands of citizens wrote Roosevelt urging him to fire his defeatist ambassador. The British took it in stride, more astonished by Kennedy's suicidal indiscretion in granting the interview than by its substance. Kennedy's departure from London, during the Battle of Britain, with its nightly bombings and aerial dogfights, was seen by many as a cowardly retreat under fire. T. North Whitehead, one of the American specialists in the British Foreign Office, filed yet another caustic note in the office's Kennediana file: "It rather looks as though he was thoroughly frightened when in London and has gone to pieces in consequence."

The interview eroded Kennedy's public support and ended his dreams of being elected to high public office in 1940. It also gave his enemies the courage to be his enemies.

Roosevelt finally lashed out at Kennedy after a private meeting with him at Thanksgiving; Kennedy was to be a weekend guest of the president and his wife at their estate at Hyde Park. It is not known precisely what took place, but Roosevelt ordered Kennedy to leave. Eleanor Roosevelt later told the writer Gore Vidal that she had never seen her husband so angry. Kennedy had been alone with the president no longer than ten minutes, Mrs. Roosevelt related, when an aide informed her that she was to go immediately to her husband's office.

So I *rushed* into the office and there was Franklin, white as a sheet. He asked Mr. Kennedy to step outside and then he said, and his voice was *shaking*, "I never want to see that man again as long as I live. Get him out of here." I said, "But, dear, you've invited him for the weekend, and we've got guests for lunch and the train doesn't leave until two," and Franklin said, "Then you drive him around Hyde Park and put him on that train." And I did and it was the most dreadful four hours of my life.

Just what happened between the two men is not known, but Vidal, recounting the scene in a 1971 essay for the *New York Review of Books*, quoted Mrs. Roosevelt as wistfully adding, "I wonder if the true story of Joe Kennedy will ever be known." (Discussing the scene years later, in an interview for this book, Vidal said he thought at the time that Mrs. Roosevelt's real message was not only that the truth about Kennedy would not be known, but that it would be "too dangerous to tell.")

Kennedy's resignation as ambassador became official early in 1941. He would never serve in public office again.

Kennedy soon learned that having Roosevelt as an enemy meant having J. Edgar Hoover as an enemy, too. Published and private reports available to the White House and the British Foreign Ministry early in 1941 alleged that a notorious Wall Street speculator named Bernard E. "Ben" Smith had traveled to Vichy France in an attempt to revive an isolationist plan, favored by Kennedy, to provide Germany with a large gold loan in exchange for a pledge of peace. Kennedy, still intent on saving American capitalism from the ravages of war, was described in one British document as "doing everything in his power to try and bring this about." Smith, known as "Sell 'Em Ben" in his Wall Street heyday, was identified as Kennedy's emissary. In a confidential report to the Foreign Ministry dated February 4, Kennedy was reported to have sent Smith to visit senior officials of Vichy France in an effort to encourage "Hitler to try to find some formula for the reconstruction of Europe. . . . Having secured this, [Kennedy] hoped that, with the help of two prominent persons in England . . . [he could] start an agitation in England in favour of a negotiated peace." Roosevelt had learned of the Kennedy plan in advance, according to the Foreign Office report, and was able to abort it. Smith, a heavy contributor to Wendell Willkie's presidential campaign, did travel to Vichy France in late 1940, but the plan went nowhere. On

May 3, 1941, nonetheless, Hoover — getting his facts wrong — told Roosevelt that the FBI had learned from a "socially prominent" source that Kennedy and Smith had met secretly with Hermann Göring in Vichy, "and that thereafter Kennedy and Smith had donated a considerable amount of money to the German cause." There was no evidence that Kennedy went to Europe with Smith, and no evidence that a meeting with Göring took place; but Hoover clearly understood that the discredited Kennedy was fair game — at least inside FDR's White House.

By December 7, 1941, with Japan's surprise attack on Pearl Harbor and America finally in the war, it was over for Joe Kennedy. Caught up in his ambitions and his fears for the world economy, he had failed to see how Franklin Roosevelt connected to the American people. Kennedy, with his relentless social climbing and political scheming, had been on the wrong side of the greatest moral issue in his life — the need to stop Hitler's Germany. It was a mistake his son Jack would not make.

Joe Kennedy's political ambitions shifted, with a vengeance, to his two oldest sons, who would become his political surrogates, and would get the benefit of his money, intellect, and willingness to do anything. Joe Jr. was completing navy flight training in Jacksonville, Florida; Jack, a navy ensign, was assigned to the headquarters of the Office of Naval Intelligence in Washington, where he was put to work writing daily and weekly intelligence bulletins.

Even with the war on, Jack Kennedy still managed to find time for partying. Just before the end of the year he initiated a torrid affair with a married Danish journalist, Inga Marie Arvad, who was estranged from her husband, a Hungarian movie director named Paul Fejos. Arvad, a former beauty queen, had interviewed Hitler and briefly socialized with him and other leading Nazis in 1936, while covering the Olympics for a Danish newspaper. She had been spotted by Arthur Krock while attending the Columbia School of Journalism in 1941. Krock recommended her to Frank Waldrop, the editor of the isolationist *Washington Times-Herald,* and Waldrop hired her to write a fluffy human interest column that focused on new arrivals to wartime Washington. Jack Kennedy was among those she inter-viewed. The handsome twenty-four-year-old navy officer fell in love with the older, more experienced, and far more sophisticated former beauty queen.

The FBI, alerted to Arvad's meeting with Hitler by a jealous fellow reporter on the *Times-Herald*, marked her as a potential Nazi spy and began an investigation into her background. One early allegation, eventually discredited, was that Arvad's uncle was a chief of police in Berlin. By early 1942, J. Edgar Hoover, at the direct insistence of FDR, became personally involved in the Arvad investigation. The next step was classic Hoover. Walter Winchell, firmly established as the FBI director's favorite columnist, published the following item on January 12: "One of Ex-Ambassador Kennedy's eligible sons is the target of a Washington gal columnist's affections. So much so she has consulted her barrister about divorcing her exploring groom. Pa Ken-nedy no like." A few days later, Hoover personally relayed a warning to Joe Kennedy, as JFK told it, that "Jack was in big trouble and he should get him out of Washington immediately."

Eager to save his son's career, Joe Kennedy arranged for Jack's immediate transfer to a desk job at a base in Charleston, South Carolina. Jack continued, nonetheless, to meet with Arvad for the next two months, as the FBI — at Hoover's direction — maintained round-the-clock surveillance, wiretapping her in Charleston and at her apartment in Washington. Agents even broke into her apartment to plant eavesdropping devices and to search through her papers and other belongings. No evidence linking Arvad to any wrongdoing was found, but the FBI — and Hoover — accumulated a large file of explicit tape recordings of the lovers at play. Joe Kennedy was over-heard on the FBI wiretaps discussing politics with his son, who, the transcripts showed, was writing drafts of his father's speeches. One FBI summary, as reported in *JFK: Reckless Youth,* by the British biog-rapher Nigel Hamilton, showed that Joe Kennedy had political ambi-tions at an early stage not only for Joe Jr., as is widely known, but also for his second-born son. The FBI summary said Jack told Arvad that his father had stopped fully defending his very unpopular political positions in public "due to the fact that he believed it might hurt his two sons later in public." The FBI wiretaps further showed that

Arvad, while involved with Jack Kennedy, was also spending some nights with Bernard Baruch, the international financier and stock market speculator, who was close to the White House.*

Young Kennedy's involvement with Arvad dwindled by early March. Arvad got divorced in June 1942, moved to California, married the cowboy movie star Tim McCoy, and received her American citizenship. One of her references was Frank Waldrop, her former editor. In an unpublished essay written in 1978 and provided for this book, Waldrop, by then long retired, whimsically recalled how the much-ado-about-nothing FBI investigation had begun. A young female *Times-Herald* journalist who, wrote Waldrop, was Arvad's rival for the attentions of the handsome Jack Kennedy, breathlessly informed him in the office one day that Arvad had been photographed in Hitler's box during the 1936 Olympics. "That did it," Waldrop wrote. "There was a row. So I took Inga by the elbow on one side and the other girl on the other and marched the pair of them over to the Washington field office of the FBI and told the agent in charge: 'This young lady says that young lady is a German spy.'" At the time, Waldrop wrote, he did not know that a similar report by a fellow female student at the Columbia School of Journalism had been filed the previous year. "Nor did I guess what was going to happen next" — that a memorandum was sent by Roosevelt "directly to Hoover calling on him to have Inga 'specially watched.' How did FDR find out about Inga? Who broke in on his war planning to tell him about so trivial a

---

* Arvad's nickname for Baruch, Frank Waldrop told me, was "the old goat." Baruch could be very indiscreet, Waldrop wrote in an unpublished essay made available for this book, and the FBI agents assigned to wiretap the Arvad apartment gossiped about Baruch's many telephone conversations with her. During the early years of the war, Waldrop said, he often traded gossip with the old financier, sometimes over lunch on a bench in Lafayette Park, near the White House. "It was on just such a bench," Waldrop recalled, "that I heard about what was going on down at Oak Ridge, Tennessee — something about a bomb made of split atoms — for which Baruch was helping put together the labor force. He told me to keep mum and I did, but that should signify that Baruch was a very heavy carrier of important information in World War II. And he was tickled to have Inga come up to visit him, weekends, at his place on Long Island. He also carried on long palavers with her on the telephone which the FBI faithfully took down." It's not known whether Hoover, an expert on double standards, intervened with Baruch, as he did with Joe Kennedy.

matter, at the very time that the most critical moment of the war in the Pacific — the Battle of Midway — was in the making? I don't know, though I have tried to find out." In the end, Waldrop concluded, "Inga was no spy. Never had been. I have the official conclusions of the Department of Justice."*

Waldrop's assertions were confirmed in an interview with Cartha DeLoach, the FBI's deputy director who worked closely with Hoover for nearly thirty years. "The investigation on Inga Arvad never conclusively proved that she was a German espionage agent," DeLoach told me in 1997. "She had an amorous relationship with John F. Kennedy. And basically that's what the files contained. She was never indicted, never brought into court, never convicted."

Joe Kennedy understood what was going on. While some FBI field agents perhaps believed they were dealing with a true national secu-

---

* In an interview for this book in 1995, the ninety-year-old Waldrop, who first met Joe Kennedy, a fellow isolationist, in the 1930s, said that "the best way I know how to tell you how much smarter Franklin Roosevelt was than Joe Kennedy" was by citing a classic FDR story that had been relayed to him by Edward A. Tamm, a senior aide to Hoover who later became a highly respected judge on the U.S. Court of Appeals for the District of Columbia. Tamm began, Waldrop said, by asking whether Waldrop "knew the difference between an amateur and a pro." Waldrop said no. Tamm then told him the following: "FDR asked Hoover to come along to the White House. Hoover brought me along. He asked Hoover to get the goods on Jim Farley," the politically contentious postmaster general who was suspected by Roosevelt of leaking inside stories to an anti-Roosevelt newspaper columnist.

"Hoover said, 'I won't do it.'

"FDR outraged: 'What!'

"Hoover: 'I won't do it.'

"FDR: 'I'm ordering you to.'"

At this point, Tamm told Waldrop, Roosevelt was "quick enough to realize something was up. He asked Hoover: 'Why not?'

"Hoover: 'I'll put it on the other guy'" — the reporter — rather than wiretap a member of the cabinet.

"Roosevelt almost fell down laughing," Tamm told Waldrop, "and said, 'Edgar, I'm not going to tell you your business anymore.'"

Waldrop's point was that Roosevelt was tougher than Kennedy in ways Kennedy could not fathom: "Joe never understood how FDR could smile and smile and be a villain. Joe thought once he was dealing with a friend, they could make a crooked deal."

rity threat in the pretty Inga Arvad, the men at the top — Franklin Roosevelt and J. Edgar Hoover — were interested in payback, in reminding Joe Kennedy to stay in line and to remember that he was dealing with enemies who would be only too happy to hurt him. The FBI, as Joe Kennedy had to understand, had enough in its file on Jack Kennedy, complete with sound effects, to stop a future political career in its tracks.

Joe Kennedy knew what to do to safeguard his ambitions for his sons off at war. He had strayed from the church of Hoover and now sought redemption. In September 1943, Freedom of Information files show, Kennedy volunteered himself to the FBI bureau in Boston as a "Special Service Contact" and declared that "he would be glad to assist the Bureau in any way possible should his services be needed." In a letter to Hoover, Edward A. Soucy, the agent in charge of the Boston Bureau, added: "Mr. Kennedy speaks very highly of the Bureau and the director, and has indicated that if he were ever in a position to make any official recommendations there would be one Federal investigative unit and that would be headed by J. Edgar Hoover." A pleased Hoover accepted Kennedy's offer and outlined, in a subsequent letter to Soucy, some of the requirements: "Every effort should be made to provide him [Kennedy] with investigative assignments in keeping with his particular ability and the Bureau should be advised as to the nature of these assignments, together with the results obtained."

The full extent of Joe Kennedy's machinations will never be known, but he left little to chance. The investigation into Inga Arvad and her relationship with Ensign Jack Kennedy had been supervised inside the Justice Department by James M. McInerney, who in 1942 was chief of the department's national defense and internal security units. A former FBI agent, McInerney would remain in high policy positions in the Justice Department for the next ten years. In late 1952 McInerney successfully intervened to get Bobby Kennedy, just a year out of law school, a job as a staff attorney on the powerful Senate Permanent Subcommittee on Investigations. In 1953 McInerney went into the practice of law as a sole practitioner, opening up a small office on F Street in downtown Washington. Joe Kennedy and his three sons, Jack, Bobby, and Ted, were among his first clients, and they remained certainly his most important ones. Over the next decade, James McInerney would handle many sensitive matters on behalf of the Kennedy family and Jack Kennedy's presidential ambitions. Women were seen, bribes were offered, and cases were settled — all in secrecy.

7

NOMINATION FOR SALE

John F. Kennedy's rise is a story that has been told and retold in hundreds of biographies and histories. The senator, always suntanned, with his photogenic wife and daughter, was the subject of articles for national magazines month after month in the late 1950s. When he wasn't being interviewed, the senator, who relied on speechwriters on his staff and those in the pay of his father, published scores of newspaper and magazine articles as well as the bestselling *Profiles in Courage*, which won the 1957 Pulitzer Prize for biography.

Kennedy's political standing was given an enormous boost at the 1956 Democratic National Convention, when he narrowly lost a dramatic floor fight against Senator Estes Kefauver for the nomination as Adlai Stevenson's vice presidential running mate in the party's doomed campaign against Dwight D. Eisenhower. Kennedy's grace and seeming good humor in defeat, and his boyish good looks — viewed by millions of television watchers — overrode his lackluster record in the Senate and made him an early favorite for the party's nomination in 1960. Kennedy ran hard over the next four years, spending most weekends making speeches and paying political dues at fund-raising dinners across America.

He made his mark not in the Senate, where his legislative output remained undistinguished, but among the voters, who responded to Kennedy as they would to a famous athlete or popular movie star. From the start the campaign was orchestrated by Joe Kennedy, who as a one-time Hollywood mogul understood that his son should run for president as a star and not as just another politician. In an exceptionally candid interview in late 1959 at Hyannis Port with the journalist Ed Plaut, then writing a preelection biography of Jack, the elder Kennedy said that his son had become "the greatest attraction in the country today. I'll tell you how to sell more copies of your book," Kennedy told Plaut. "Put his picture on the cover." Plaut made a transcript of his interview available for this book.

"Why is it," Kennedy asked, "that when his picture is on the cover of *Life* or *Redbook* that they sell a record number of copies? You advertise the fact that he will be at a dinner and you will break all records for attendance. He will draw more people to a fund-raising dinner than Cary Grant or Jimmy Stewart and anyone else you can name. Why is that? He has the greatest universal appeal. I can't explain that. There is no answer to Jack's appeal. He is the biggest attraction in the country today. That is why the Democratic Party is going to nominate him. The party leaders realize that to win they have to nominate him.

"The nomination is a cinch," Joe Kennedy told the reporter. "I'm not a bit worried about the nomination."

By the summer of 1960, with brother Bobby serving as campaign manager and father Joe as a one-man political brain trust — as well as secret paymaster — Jack Kennedy arrived at the Democratic convention in Los Angeles as an unstoppable front-runner who apparently had earned the right to be the presidential candidate by running in, and winning, Democratic primary elections across America. He had conducted a brilliant campaign that would set the standard for future generations of ambitious politicians, especially in its relentless tracking and cataloguing of delegate votes. One of Kennedy's loyal aides, Ted Sorensen, would describe admiringly in *Kennedy,* his 1965 memoir, how Kennedy went over the heads of the backroom politicians and took his campaign to the people:

He had during 1960 alone traveled some 65,000 air miles in more than two dozen states — many of them in the midst of crucial primary fights, most of them with his wife — and he made some 350 speeches on every conceivable subject. He had voted, introduced bills or spoken on every current issue, without retractions or apologies. He had talked in person to state conventions, party leaders, delegates and tens of thousands of voters. He had used every spare moment on the telephone. He had made no promises he could not keep and promised no jobs to anyone.

What no outsider could imagine — and what Sorensen did not write about — was the obstacles overcome and the carefully hidden deals engineered as Kennedy achieved one political victory after another en route to Los Angeles.

Kennedy's most important primary victory came on May 10 in West Virginia. In his campaigning in the state, Kennedy directly confronted the religious issue, telling audiences, for example, that no one cared that he was a Catholic when he was asked to fight in World War II. He defeated Senator Hubert H. Humphrey of Minnesota by more than 84,000 votes. In his memoir, Sorensen quoted another of Kennedy's unsuccessful rivals for the nomination, Senator Stuart Symington of Missouri, as saying after the convention: "He had just a little more courage, . . . stamina, wisdom and character than any of the rest of us."

Sorensen's account, as with so much of the Kennedy history as told by Kennedy insiders, has many elements of truth but is far from the whole story. The Kennedys did not depend solely on hard work and stamina to win the primary elections en route to the Democratic nomination. They spent as never before in American political history. In West Virginia, the Kennedys spent at least $2 million (nearly $11 million in today's dollars), and possibly twice that amount — much of it in direct payoffs to state and local officials.

A far more complete account of the campaign emerges in the unpublished memoir of one of Kennedy's most trusted, and little-known, advisers during the 1960 campaign, Hyman B. Raskin, a Chicago lawyer who had helped manage Adlai Stevenson's presidential campaigns in 1952 and 1956. Raskin had been recruited in late

1957 by Joe Kennedy, and secretly paid, to help plan and organize his son's drive for the presidency. Raskin, who after the 1960 election retired to his law practice, died in comfortable obscurity in 1995 at the age of eighty-six in Rancho Mirage, California. His widow, Frances, later provided for this book a copy of his memoir, entitled *A Laborer in the Vineyards,* which contains a rare firsthand account of Joe Kennedy's direct, and powerful, intervention in national politics on behalf of his son — interventions that were always hidden from the press. In Raskin's account, the combination of unlimited campaign funding, Joe Kennedy's high-level political connections, and Jack Kennedy's strong showing in the Democratic primaries — especially his West Virginia victory — enabled the Kennedys to fly to Los Angeles knowing they had enough ironclad delegate commitments to win on the first ballot.

At the convention site, Raskin was entrusted with the all-important task of running communications. The Kennedys, in one of their political innovations, had leased a trailer and filled it with state-of-the-art communications gear that enabled the campaign's backroom operators to reach the leaders of state delegations instantly. In his memoir, Raskin depicted the convention as anticlimactic for the campaign insiders: "We were confident that the [delegate count] numbers which the state reports produced would closely approximate those we had before the initial [convention] meeting was held. . . . It appeared impossible for Kennedy to lose the nomination. The votes merely needed to be officially tabulated; therefore, in my opinion, if he failed, it would be the result of some uncontrollable event."

Texas senator Lyndon B. Johnson's last-minute declaration just days before the convention that he would, after all, be a candidate for the presidency — an announcement that created a flurry of press reports — was too little, too late, in Raskin's view. "The front-runner was unbeatable," he wrote. "For unknown reasons, some members of the press refused to concede the nomination of Kennedy, ignoring the arithmetic reported by their associates. . . . Johnson and his managers must have had access to the same information. Much of it was published and verifiable through Johnson connections in almost every state. Why then, I asked myself, did the anti-Kennedy forces continue their futile struggle?" Johnson stayed in the race until the presidential balloting and suffered an overwhelming defeat by Kennedy on the convention floor.

The fact that Kennedy had locked up the nomination weeks in advance of the convention was one of the campaign's secrets. There were other secrets far more damaging, any one of which, if exposed, could cost the handsome young candidate his otherwise assured presidential nomination.

The most dangerous problem confronting the Kennedys before the convention was the hardest to fix, for it was posed by a group of reporters from the *Wall Street Journal* who were raising questions about the huge sums of cash that had been spent by the Kennedys to assure victory in the West Virginia primary. Their story, triggered by the instincts of an on-the-scene journalist, never made it into print.

Alan L. Otten, the *Journal* correspondent who covered the campaign, had been stunned by the strong Kennedy showing. He had spent weeks walking through the cities and towns of the coal counties and concluded, as he wrote for the *Journal,* that Humphrey would capitalize on the pronounced anti-Catholicism in West Virginia and win the Democratic primary handily. "Every miner I talked to was going to vote for Humphrey," Otten recalled in a 1994 interview for this book. The reporter, who later became chief of the *Journal*'s news bureau in Washington, was suspicious when the votes were counted and urged his newspaper to undertake an extensive investigation into Kennedy vote buying. "We were fairly convinced that huge sums of money traded hands," Otten told me.

Buying votes was nothing new in West Virginia, where political control was tightly held by sheriffs or political committeemen in each of the state's fifty-five counties. Their control was abetted by the enormous number of candidates who competed for local office in the Democratic primary, resulting in huge paper ballots that made voting a potentially interminable process. In his Pulitzer Prize–winning account of the 1960 campaign, *The Making of the President, 1960,* the journalist Theodore H. White noted that the primary ballots for Kanawha County, largest in the state, filled three full pages when published the day before in the *Charleston Gazette.* Sheriffs and other political leaders in each county made the process less bewildering for voters by putting together lists, or slates, of approved party candidates for each office. Some candidates for statewide offices or for important local posts, such as sheriff or assessor, invariably ended up on two, three, or more slates passed out on election day by campaign workers. The unwieldy procedure continues today.

The sheriffs and party leaders were also responsible for hiring precinct workers and poll watchers for election day. Political tradition in the state called for the statewide candidates to pay some or all of the county's election expenses in return for being placed at the top of a political leader's slate. Paying a few dollars per vote on election day was widespread in some areas, as was the payment for "Lever Brothers" (named after the popular detergent maker) — election officers in various precincts who were instructed to actually walk into the ballot booth with voters and cast their ballots for them.

The *Journal*'s investigative team, which included Roscoe C. Born, of the Washington bureau, spent the next five weeks in May and June in West Virginia and learned that the Kennedys had turned what had historically been random election fraud into a statewide pattern of corruption, and had apparently stolen the election from Hubert Humphrey. The reporters concluded that huge sums of Kennedy money had been funneled into the state, much of it from Chicago, where R. Sargent Shriver, a Chicagoan who had married Jack's sister Eunice in 1953, represented the family's business interests. The reporters were told that much of the money had been delivered by a longtime Shriver friend named James B. McCahey, Jr., who was president of a Chicago coal company that held contracts for delivering coal to the city's public school system. As a coal buyer earlier in his career, McCahey had spent time traveling through West Virginia, whose mines routinely produced more than 100 million tons of coal a year. Roscoe Born and a colleague traveled to Chicago to interview McCahey "and he snowed us completely," Born recalled in a series of interviews for this book. Nonetheless, the reporter said, "there was no doubt in my mind that [Kennedy] money was dispensed to local machines where they controlled the votes."

Born, convinced that he and his colleagues had collected enough information to write a devastating exposé, moved with his typewriter into a hotel near the *Journal*'s office in downtown Washington. He was facing a stringent deadline — the Democratic convention was only a few weeks away — and also a great deal of unease among the newspaper's senior editors.

As with many investigative newspaper stories, there was no smoking gun: none of the newspaper's sources reported seeing a representative of the Kennedy campaign give money to a West Virginian. "We knew they were meeting," Otten recalled in our interview, "but we had nothing showing the actual handing over of money." The *Journal*'s top editors asked for affidavits from some of the sources who were to be quoted in the exposé; when the journalists could not obtain them, the editors ruled that the article could not be published. "The story could have been written, but we'd have to imply, rather than nail down, some elements," Born said. "I really wanted to do it, but I can see that the editors would be nervous about doing it practically on the eve of the convention." Other *Journal* reporters were told that Born and his colleagues had "gotten the goods," as one put it, on the Kennedy spending in West Virginia. The columnist Robert D. Novak, then a political reporter on the *Journal*, recalled in an interview for this book hearing that the newspaper's top management had concluded that the West Virginia money story could affect the proceedings in Los Angeles, and it was not "the place of the *Wall Street Journal* to determine the Democratic nominee for president."

The *Journal*'s reporting team was far closer to the truth than its editors could imagine. Jack Kennedy had wanted a clean sweep in the April 5 Democratic primary in Wisconsin, aiming to defeat Hubert Humphrey in all ten of the state's congressional districts, and he campaigned long hours to get one. He was bitterly disappointed when he won only six districts — and, most important, when his showing failed to discourage the equally hardworking Humphrey, who decided to continue his presidential campaigning in West Virginia. It was understood by professional politicians that Humphrey, too, would be putting in as much money as he could to meet the inevitable bribery demands of the county sheriffs. The Kennedy team also feared that other Democratic opponents for the nomination, Lyndon Johnson and Adlai Stevenson among them, would urge their backers to shove money into the state on Humphrey's behalf in an effort to stop Kennedy and deadlock the convention.*

West Virginia thus became the ultimate battleground for the Democratic nomination, and the Kennedys threw every family member and prominent friend they had, and many dollars, at defeating Humphrey. At stake was not only Jack's presidency, but Joe Kennedy's dream of a family dynasty: Bobby was to be his brother's successor.

In interviews for this book, many West Virginia county and state officials revealed that the Kennedy family spent upward of $2 million in bribes and other payoffs before the May 10, 1960, primary, with some sheriffs in key counties collecting more than $50,000 apiece in cash in return for placing Kennedy's name at the top of their election slate. Much of the money was distributed personally by Bobby and Teddy Kennedy. The Kennedy campaign would publicly claim after the convention that only $100,000 had been spent in West Virginia (out of a total of $912,500 in expenses for the entire campaign). But what went on in West Virginia was no secret to those on the inside. In his 1978 memoir, *In Search of History,* Theodore White wrote what he had not written in his book on the 1960 campaign — that both Humphrey and Kennedy were buying votes in West Virginia. White also acknowledged in the memoir that his strong affection for Kennedy had turned him, and many of his colleagues, from objective journalists to members of a loyal claque. White stayed in the claque to the end, claiming in his memoir, without any apparent evidence, that "Kennedy's vote-buyers were evenly matched with Humphrey's."

In later years, even the most loyal of the loyalists acknowledged what happened in the West Virginia primary. In one of her interviews in 1994, Evelyn Lincoln said, "I know they bought the election." And Jerry Bruno, who served as one of Kennedy's most dependable ad-

---

* Max Kampelman, Humphrey's longtime friend and political adviser, recalled warning Humphrey not to run against Kennedy in West Virginia. In an interview in 1994, Kampelman said he "knew" that the Kennedys would put big money into the state and "steal the election — and we had no money." An additional concern was Humphrey's political future: "I told Hubert, 'They'll [the Kennedys will] kill you in West Virginia, and you have to run for reelection [to the Senate] in Minnesota. They'll paint you as anti-Catholic, and there are a lot of Catholics in Minnesota.'" Humphrey nevertheless won reelection to the Senate in 1960.

vance men in the 1960 campaign, similarly said in an interview: "Every time I'd walk into a town [in West Virginia], they thought I was a bagman. They used to move polling places if you didn't give them the money. We didn't do it better, but we got the people who at least were half-honest. The Hubert people — they'd take the money and then come to see us."

The most compelling evidence was supplied by James McCahey, the Chicago coal buyer, who refused to cooperate with the *Wall Street Journal* in 1960. In a 1996 interview for this book, he revealed that the political payoffs in West Virginia had begun in October 1959, when young Teddy Kennedy traveled across the state distributing cash to the Democratic committeeman in each county. McCahey was told later that the payoffs amounted to $5,000 per committeeman, a total expenditure of roughly $275,000. McCahey, who left the coal business in Chicago for the railroad business (he retired in 1985 as a senior vice president of the Chessie System Railroads, in Cleveland), added that the *Wall Street Journal's* suspicions of him were wrong: his assignment in West Virginia had not been to make payoffs but to organize the teachers in each county "and help them get out the word about Kennedy." Through this assignment he was able to learn a great deal about what was going on in the state.

McCahey, a major fund-raiser in 1960 for Mayor Richard Daley of Chicago, was also a strong Kennedy supporter and had been assigned to direct the Kennedy campaign in the southern districts of Wisconsin. After the disappointing results there, McCahey told me, Sargent Shriver telephoned and invited him to an important insiders strategy meeting in Huntington, West Virginia, that had been put together by Jack and Bobby Kennedy, and included Jack's brother-in-law Stephen Smith, the campaign's finance director. New polling was showing a precipitous drop in support for Kennedy among West Virginians; the subject of the meeting was how to get the campaign back on track. It was then, McCahey said, that he learned about Teddy Kennedy's efforts the previous fall to pay for support from the county committeemen.

"It didn't work at all," McCahey told me. "You don't go into a primary [in West Virginia] and spread money around to committeemen. The local committeeman will take your money and do nothing. The sheriff is the important guy" in each county. "You give it to the sheriff. That's the name you see on the political banners when you go into a town." McCahey further recalled being told at the meeting that Joe Kennedy believed that the buying of sheriffs "was the way to do it."

The sheriffs, it was understood, had enormous discretion in the handling of the cash. Some would generously apportion the cash to their supporters; others would pocket most of the money.

McCahey recalled that his essential contribution was to tell the Kennedys "to forget what you've done and start again. I laid out a plan" — to organize teachers and other grassroots workers —"and they said go." He also worked closely with Shriver in visiting the major coal-producing companies in the state, all of which he knew well from his days as a buyer. "I'd drop into the local coal places and ask the fellows, 'What's going on?'" McCahey acknowledged passing out some cash to local political leaders while at work in West Virginia, paying as much as $2,000 for storefront rentals and for hiring cars to bring voters to the polls on primary day. He knew that far larger sums of money were paid to the sheriffs in the last weeks of the campaign. "If they did spend two million dollars," McCahey told me, with a laugh, in response to a question, "they figured, 'Hell, let McCahey go [with his plan to organize teachers and the like].' They had lots of angles."

There is evidence that Robert Kennedy was, as Teddy had been earlier, a paymaster in the hectic weeks before the May 10 primary. Victor Gabriel, of Clarksburg, a supervisor for the West Virginia Alcoholic Beverage Control Commission who ran the Kennedy campaign that spring in Harrison County, recalled in an interview for this book a meeting before the election with Bobby and the ever-loyal Charles Spalding. Gabriel told the two men that he needed only $5,000 in election-day expenses to win the county for them. The exceedingly low estimate, Gabriel told me, caused Spalding to exclaim, "You don't know what you're talking about."

Gabriel, eighty-two years old when interviewed in 1996, refused to take any more cash and delivered his county, as promised, on election night. Gabriel joined other Kennedy workers at a gala victory celebration at the Kanawha Hotel in Charleston. At some point during the party, he said, a grateful Bobby Kennedy ushered him into the privacy of a bathroom and pulled out a little black book. "You could have gotten this," Kennedy told him, as he pointed to a page in the book, "to get people on the bandwagon." Kennedy's notebook showed that as much as $40,000 had been given to Sid Christie, an attorney who was the top Democrat of McDowell County, in the heart of the state's coal belt in the south. The Kennedy notebook made it clear, Gabriel told me, that the campaign had "spent a bundle" to get the all-important support of all the sheriffs and political leaders in the south.

Gabriel told me that he had no second thoughts about the relatively small amount of Kennedy money he had requested. "I told [Bobby] what I needed and didn't take a damn dime more," Gabriel said. "All I had to do was tell him fifteen thousand or twenty thousand, instead of five thousand, and I'd have got it. But I don't operate that way. If you're going to be for a man, be for him." The sheriffs who took more than $5,000, Gabriel told me, were simply pocketing the money.

Two former state officials acknowledged during 1995 interviews for this book that they also knew of large-scale Kennedy spending.

Bonn Brown of Elkins was the personal attorney to W. W. "Wally" Barron, who was elected Democratic governor of West Virginia in 1960. He estimated the Kennedy outlay at between $3 million and $5 million, with some sheriffs being paid as much as $50,000. Asked how he knew, Brown told me curtly, "I know. If you don't get those guys"— the sheriffs —"they will really fight you." In his role as adviser to the Democratic gubernatorial candidate, Brown met with Robert Kennedy and other campaign officials "and told them who to see and what to do, but stayed clear of it myself. Bobby was smart and mean as a snake. I think he had more to do with West Virginia"— the victory there, and the payoffs —"than any other person. Bobby ran it; he was the one who set it up." Governor Barron was later convicted on bribery charges, and Brown was later convicted of the attempted bribery of a juror in the case.

Curtis B. Trent, of Charleston, who served as executive assistant to Governor Barron, also recalled that the Kennedys "were spreading it around pretty heavy. I thought they spent two million dollars." Trent, like Bonn Brown, insisted that he did not personally take any

Kennedy money. "They were trying to push it off on us," he recalled. "I'd explain to them that I was concerned with the governor's race and not the president's race." Kennedy reacted typically to Trent's refusal to help: "Bobby was so mad . . . just as angry as he could be." Trent, like more than a dozen officials of the Barron administration, the most corrupt in the history of the state, was convicted of income tax evasion and sentenced to a jail term in 1969.

The Gabriel, Brown, and Trent accounts are buttressed by Rein Vander Zee, a former FBI agent who had been working since early January 1960 in Humphrey's West Virginia campaign. Vander Zee was responsible for dealing with the sheriffs of West Virginia, and had — for a price — received their political commitments for Humphrey. "Four or five days before the primary," Vander Zee, now living in Bandera, Texas, told me in an interview in 1995, "I couldn't get some of my people on the phone. I said, 'Oh, my God,' and got in my car and started driving. They were laying out — the sheriffs — and I knew something was way wrong. The Humphrey signs were down and Kennedy signs were up. I met Sid Christie, who was supposed to be our man [in McDowell County] all the way. He was the absolute boss down there." Vander Zee arranged a meeting with Christie in the rural town of Keystone. "We sat in his car across from a deserted movie theater, like a scene from *The Last Picture Show*. I said, 'What can be done?'" Christie dryly responded: "It's too late. I didn't realize what a groundswell of support there'd be for this other fellow."

Vander Zee said he and Humphrey later held a last-ditch conference with Wally Barron, the governor-to-be: "We asked him what had to be done. I always liked Wally." Barron gave Humphrey the bad news: he was being vastly outspent by the Kennedys. "He said he had a figure [of Kennedy expenditures] that was something we couldn't meet," Vander Zee said. Years later, a West Virginia political professional told Vander Zee that he watched as Christie received a huge payoff from a Kennedy insider — at least $40,000, the professional said —"in green in a shoe box." Kennedy received 84 percent of the Democratic primary vote on May 10 in McDowell County.

In the years after Kennedy's assassination, many people would take credit for his strong showing in West Virginia.

In his autobiography, *The Education of a Public Man,* published in 1976, Hubert Humphrey told of a 1966 meeting with Richard Cardinal Cushing, the archbishop of Boston, in which Cushing expressed anger at what he called the self-aggrandizement of various Kennedy aides, such as Ted Sorensen. "I keep reading these books by the young men around Jack Kennedy and how they claim credit for electing him," Cushing told Humphrey. "I'll tell you who elected Jack Kennedy. It was his father, Joe, and me, *right here in this room.*" Humphrey and an aide sat in stunned silence as Cushing told how he and Joe Kennedy had agreed that West Virginia's anti-Catholicism could be countered by a series of cash contributions to Protestant churches, particularly in the black community. Cushing continued, Humphrey wrote: "We decided which church and preacher would get two hundred dollars or one hundred dollars or five hundred dollars."

The most widespread misinformation about the West Virginia election involves the role of organized crime, which, according to countless magazine articles and books over the past thirty years, supplied the cash that enabled Kennedy to win. The allegations center on Paul "Skinny" D'Amato, the New Jersey nightclub owner who in 1960 became general manager of a Nevada gambling lodge owned in part by Frank Sinatra and his good friend Sam Giancana of Chicago. D'Amato's account, as repeatedly published, is that he was approached by Joe Kennedy during the primary campaign and asked to raise money for West Virginia. D'Amato agreed to do so, with one demand: if Jack Kennedy was successful in gaining the White House, he would reverse a 1956 federal deportation order for Joey Adonis, the New Jersey gang leader. With Joe Kennedy's promise, D'Amato raised $50,000 for West Virginia from assorted gangsters. D'Amato, who died in 1984, has been quoted as telling a business associate that the $50,000 was used not for direct bribes but to purchase desks, chairs, and other supplies needed by local politicians. After Kennedy's election, D'Amato said, he reminded Joe Kennedy of his pledge. The father explained that the Adonis deal was fine with his son the president, but Bobby, the new attorney general, wouldn't hear of it. There is no basis for disbelieving D'Amato's account; but $50,000 in cash, when contrasted with what was really spent in West Virginia, was hardly enough to earn everlasting gratitude from the Kennedys.

D'Amato's big mouth got him in trouble. Soon after taking office, Bobby Kennedy was informed by the FBI that D'Amato had been overheard on a wiretap bragging about his role in moving cash from Las Vegas to help Jack Kennedy win the election. A few months later, D'Amato suddenly found himself facing federal indictment on income tax charges stemming from his failure to file a corporate tax return for his nightclub. The indictment was brought to the attention of Milton "Mickey" Rudin, a prominent Los Angeles lawyer who represented Frank Sinatra and other entertainment figures.

"Skinny [was] Frank's friend," Rudin told me in a series of interviews for this book. "Bobby [Kennedy] and the Old Man [Joe Kennedy] knew the relationship. When Skinny got indicted, I got pissed and called up Steve Smith. I tell him I want to see him. He meets me at the University Club in New York. I order my gin. 'What can I do for you?' Smith asks. I tell him, 'I'm unhappy about Skinny being indicted on the bullshit charges. It's unfair. No taxes were paid because there was no profit.'" Rudin said he did not raise the issue of D'Amato's political favors for the Kennedy campaign, but he did tell Smith, "This is a political act." Smith responded, "Well, you don't understand politics." Rudin then said, "Well, I'm glad I don't," drank his gin, and left.

Steve Smith delivered a clear message, Rudin said: D'Amato had been overheard on FBI wiretaps talking about Las Vegas cash going to the Kennedys, and the indictment neutralized any possible damage from such talk. "If some guy like Skinny had anything to do with moving money," Rudin concluded, "the way to handle him is to indict him so if he talked about it, it'd be [seen as] vengeance." Rudin told me that he returned to Los Angeles thinking — and saying as much to Sinatra and others — that the Kennedys were going to be much tougher than some had thought.

Organized crime, as we shall see, played a huge role in Kennedy's narrow victory over Richard Nixon in November. But Jack Kennedy had more than a few campaign promises to gangsters to worry about, both before and after the election.

8

THREATENED CANDIDACY

Jack Kennedy emerged from West Virginia as the man to beat, but there were still many dangers that threatened his drive for the presidency. At least four women could control his destiny. One of them was Marilyn Monroe, the American film goddess whose affair with Kennedy had begun sometime before the 1960 election and would continue after he went to the White House.

Like his father, Jack Kennedy had a special fondness for Hollywood celebrities. The celebrated and gifted Monroe, born Norma Jean Mortenson, emerged as a sex symbol in the early 1950s and worked her way through husbands, lovers, pills, liquor, and psychiatric hospitals until her death, apparently by accidental suicide, in August 1962. Some published accounts place the beginning of the Kennedy-Monroe relationship in the mid-1950s, as Monroe's second marriage, to the baseball star Joe DiMaggio, was unraveling and she was beginning a romance with the playwright Arthur Miller, who would become her third husband. Her affair with Kennedy was by all accounts in full bloom as the presidential campaign was getting under way. Many of their rendezvous were at the Santa Monica home of Peter and Patricia Lawford, Kennedy's brother-in-law and sister, who were Monroe's close friends. There has been published speculation that Monroe became pregnant by Kennedy and had an abortion in Mexico; the full story may never be known, but accounts of her affair and abortion have been published again and again since her suicide and his murder.

In interviews for this book, longtime friends and associates of Monroe and Kennedy acknowledged that the two stars, who both enjoyed living on the edge, shared a powerful, and high-risk, attraction to each other. "She was a beautiful actress," George Smathers, Kennedy's closest friend in the Senate, told me. "Probably as pretty a woman as ever lived. And Jack — everybody knew he liked pretty girls. When he had the opportunity to meet Marilyn Monroe, why, he took advantage of it, and got to know her a little bit." The attraction went beyond sex. Monroe had a quirky sense of humor and a tenacious desire to learn. "Marilyn made Jack laugh," Patricia Newcomb, who worked as a publicist for Monroe in the early 1960s, explained in an interview for this book. There was also a family connection that went beyond the Lawfords. Charles Spalding, who was a trusted intimate of Kennedy's by the late 1940s and remained so until the president's assassination, clearly recalled a private visit by Monroe to the family enclave at Hyannis Port, where she was welcomed enthusiastically as a friend of Jack's — even though he was married.

Monroe's repeated crack-ups did not diminish her looks or her ability to appeal to men. "Marilyn Monroe was the ultimate glamour girl," Vernon Scott, a longtime Hollywood reporter for United Press International, told me in an interview. "She was gorgeous and she was funny. She had more sex appeal than any woman I ever saw, and I've seen lots of them. She was probably every man's dream of the kind of woman he'd like to spend the rest of his life with on a desert island. She was much smarter than people gave her credit for. She never did or said anything by accident."

Monroe was said to be deeply in love with Kennedy. After her death, John Miner, head of the medical legal section of the Los Angeles district attorney's office, was given confidential access to a stream-of-consciousness tape recording Monroe made at the recommendation of her psychoanalyst, Dr. Ralph Greenson, a few weeks earlier; Miner put together what he considered to be a near-verbatim transcript of the tape. After obtaining permission from the Greenson family, Miner ended thirty-five years of silence by making the transcript available for this book in 1997. Many of Monroe's comments dealt with her sexuality; her extensive comments about her problems achieving orgasm — in very blunt language — were meant only for the analyst's couch, but her lavish admiration for Jack Kennedy could have been read from a podium:

> Marilyn Monroe is a soldier. Her commander-in-chief is the greatest and most powerful man in the world. The first duty of a soldier is to obey her commander-in-chief. He says do this, you do it. He says do that, you do it. This man is going to change our country. No child will go hungry, no person will sleep in the street and get his meals from garbage cans. People who can't afford it will get good medical care. Industrial products will be the best in the world. No, I'm not talking utopia — that's an illusion. But he will transform America today like Franklin Delano Roosevelt did in the Thirties. I tell you, Doctor, when he has finished his achievements he will take his place with Washington, Jefferson, Lincoln, and Franklin Roosevelt as one of our great presidents. I'm glad he has Bobby. It's like the Navy — the President is the captain and Bobby is his executive officer. Bobby would do absolutely anything for his brother and so would I. I will never embarrass him. As long as I have memory, I have John Fitzgerald Kennedy.

Show business people who worked behind the scenes with Monroe described a hard edge beneath the glamour. There were repeated breakdowns and repeated threats to tell the world about her relationship with Kennedy — threats that could have damaged his candidacy, and threats that only increased after he got to the White House. "What happened," George Smathers told me, "was that she, [like] naturally all women, would like to be close to the president. And then after he had been associated with her some, she began to ask for an opportunity to come to Washington and come to the White House and that sort of thing. That's when Jack asked me to see what I could do to help him in that respect by talking to her." Monroe, Smathers said without amplification, had "made some demands." Smathers said he arranged for a mutual friend to "go talk to Marilyn Monroe about putting a bridle on herself and on her mouth and not talking too much, because it was getting to be a story around the country." It had happened before. Charles Spalding recalled that at one point during the 1960 campaign, when Monroe was on a liquor and pill binge, Kennedy asked him to fly from New York to Los Angeles to make sure that she was okay — that is, to make sure that Monroe did not speak out of turn. "I got out there, and she was really sick," Spalding told me. With Lawford's help, "I got her to the hospital."

Monroe's instability posed a constant threat to Kennedy. Michael Selsman, one of Monroe's publicists in the early 1960s, depicted her as "a loose cannon" who toggled between high-spirited charm and mean-spirited cruelty. "Sometimes she had to put on this costume of Marilyn Monroe. Otherwise, she was this other person, Norma Jean, who felt abused, put-upon, and unintelligent. As Marilyn Monroe, she had enormous power. As Norma Jean, she was a drug addict who wasn't physically clean."

Vernon Scott told me that the other, insecure Monroe "made herself known to me one night" after he had concluded a newspaper interview with her at the Beverly Hills Hotel. Scott had a date with his wife-to-be and, as he and Monroe continued to chat over two bottles of champagne, he began looking at his watch. Monroe noticed and asked if he was going out. Scott said yes. "And she said," Scott recounted, "sniffling a little bit and feeling sorry for herself, that everybody had somebody else to go to, everybody had dates, except her. She said, 'I'm Marilyn Monroe. Everybody thinks the phone rings all the time with men asking me out. Well, everybody's afraid to date Marilyn Monroe or ask her for a date.' And she began crying, with mascara running down her face. And her eyes were red and she looked like kind of a clown. Her nose was red. She began sobbing. I tried to cheer her up and told her that I was sure most men would be delighted to take her out. She said, 'Well, they don't have the nerve to call me, not the right ones. And once in a while I meet a nice guy, a really nice guy, and I know it's going to work. He doesn't have to be from Hollywood; he doesn't have to be an actor. And we have a few drinks and we go to bed. Then I see his eyes glaze over and I can see it going through his mind: "Oh, my God. I'm going to fuck Marilyn Monroe," and he can't get it up.' Then she started howling with misery over this. I just bent over double laughing. And she began pounding on me —'It's not funny.'

"But," Scott told me, "this was not Marilyn Monroe. Norma Jean would never have allowed Marilyn to look like that, but she did this one time. So I saw [Norma Jean] as a frightened, insecure, young puppeteer that was running this machine known as Marilyn Monroe. It was very touching and somewhat sad. And I liked her all the more for it."

Monroe's affair with Kennedy was no secret in Hollywood. In early January 1961, before the inauguration, Michael Selsman was informed about the relationship. "It was the first thing I was told," Selsman said. "We had to be careful with this. We had to protect her, we had to keep her [private life] out of print. It'd be disastrous for me. It wasn't hard in those days. It was a different era. Today it would be impossible to keep anything resembling that a secret." Patricia Newcomb, who worked in the same public relations office with Selsman, also recalled knowing that her client "had been with the president," and added: "It never occurred to me to talk about it. I couldn't do it."

James Bacon, who spent much of his career covering Hollywood for the Associated Press, said in an interview for this book that Monroe, whom he had befriended early in her career, had given him a firsthand account of her relationship with Kennedy as early as the campaign. "She was very open about her affair with JFK," Bacon told me. "In fact, I think Marilyn was in love with JFK." Asked why he didn't file a story about the affair, Bacon said that in those days, "before Watergate, reporters just didn't go into that sort of thing. I'd have to have been under the bed in order to put it on the wire for the AP. There was no pact. It was just a matter of judgment on the part of the reporters."

Bacon added that he understood Kennedy's "fascination with Hollywood. This is where the beautiful girls are, you know, and that's why JFK loved it out here. He was a man who was addicted to sex, and if you want sex, this is the place to come."

Kennedy was placing his political well-being in the hands of a group of Hollywood actresses, reporters, and publicists. His confidence that the affair with Monroe would remain secret was all the more perplexing because he was, even before he declared his candidacy, the target of a letter-writing campaign by a middle-aged housewife named Florence M. Kater, who decided in 1959 that her mission in life would be to force the Washington press corps to deal with Kennedy's womanizing. Kater learned more than she wanted to know about the senator's personal life after renting an upstairs apartment in her Georgetown home to Pamela Turnure, an attractive aide in Kennedy's Senate office. Kennedy and Turnure were conducting an indiscreet affair that involved many late-night and early-morning comings and goings, to Kater's consternation. Turnure moved to another apartment a few blocks away. In late 1958 Kater ambushed Kennedy leaving the new apartment at three A.M. and took a photograph of the unhappy senator attempting to shield his face with a handkerchief.

The encounter rattled Kennedy, and he struck back. A few weeks later, Kater alleged, she and her husband were accosted on the street in front of her home by the angry Kennedy, who, waving his forefinger, warned her "to stop bothering me. If you do it again," Kater quoted Kennedy as saying, "or if either of you spread any lies about me, you will find yourself without a job." Kennedy eventually asked James McInerney, the former Justice Department attorney who had been retained in 1953 by Joe Kennedy, to try to muzzle Kater; the loyal McInerney spent dozens of hours in an attempt to convince her to stop her campaign.

McInerney met seven times with Kater, she later wrote, but for once the usual Kennedy mix of glamour, power, and money didn't work. In May of 1959, Kater mailed a copy of the photograph and an articulate letter describing her encounter with Kennedy to fifty prominent citizens in Washington and New York, including editors, syndicated columnists, and politicians. Her letter and photograph also ended up on the desk of J. Edgar Hoover, as similar letters would over the next four years. The FBI, of course, began keeping a file on Kater, one obtained under the Freedom of Information Act for this book. In the letter Kater explained that, as an Irish Catholic, she had been a "warm supporter" of Kennedy; she had taken the photograph in the belief that "shock treatment" was needed. "But Senator Kennedy thought his behavior was none of our business," Kater wrote. "We think he's wrong there; it's part of the package when you're a public figure running for the Presidency."

Kater became even more obsessed as Kennedy neared the Democratic nomination, and she continued sending out scores of letters complaining that the senator was a hypocritical womanizer who was morally unfit to be president. Kater was not taken seriously by the national press corps, but she came close to attracting media attention. On May 14, 1960, just four days after Kennedy won the West Virginia primary, she approached him at a political rally at the University of Maryland carrying a placard with an enlarged snapshot of the early-morning scene outside Pamela Turnure's apartment. Kennedy ignored her, but a photograph of the encounter was published in the next afternoon's *Washington Star,* along with a brief story describing her as a heckler. Kennedy's aides denounced the photograph on her placard as a fake, Kater later wrote, and no questions were ever asked of the candidate, although Kennedy's ongoing relationship with Turnure was no secret to the reporters covering his campaign or to campaign aides.

For all his apparent anger at Kater, Kennedy seemed to enjoy the added tension. Spalding told me of his concern at the time about the immense political liabilities posed by his friend's constant womanizing. "I used to think he was crazy to do this stuff." The risks were obvious: Kennedy's campaign stance as a practicing Catholic and a responsible husband and father would be fatally undercut by a sex scandal. Steeling his courage, Spalding raised the issue at one point with Kennedy. "Well, if you're worried about this," Kennedy responded, "let me show you these pictures." The candidate then pulled out a series of photographs — those mailed by Kater — showing him leaving the Turnure apartment.

Kennedy came much closer to exposure than he knew. Kater's photograph in the *Star* stimulated an editor's curiosity, and Bob Clark, a former White House reporter, was assigned to interview her. "I found her interesting and a little flaky," Clark, now with ABC News, said in a 1997 interview for this book. "I believed her story."

That story was complicated, Clark said, by the fact that Kater was a collector of Impressionist paintings and casually admitted that she had initially offered to drop her protests over Kennedy's involvement with Turnure if the Kennedy family would buy her a Modigliani. Jack Kennedy was a "good Catholic" and so was she, Kater told Clark, and she'd "let it go" for the art. It was that request, among others, Kater told Clark, that was being negotiated with James McInerney. "The family said no," Clark quoted Kater as saying, but only after protracted negotiations.

Kater's story was credible, Clark told me, because it was not just a question of her word against Kennedy's: Kater told Clark that she and her husband had secretly planted two tape recorders in the upstairs apartment while Turnure was spending nights there with Kennedy. The landlords overheard the senator in both the living room and the bedroom. Kater invited Clark to return later to listen to the recordings.

Despite her obvious eccentricity, Clark told me, he was persuaded that it was one hell of a story. He telephoned his editor, Charles Seib, and — as all reporters do — told him what he had, including the fact that Kater had been refused a painting. He was put on hold, while Seib checked with his superiors. A few moments later, Seib returned to the telephone and ordered him "to drop the story," Clark said. "He wouldn't even let me go back to listen to the tapes."

Clark did as instructed, but not without regret. "If the *Star,* a highly respected paper, had gone public with the [Kater] story," he said, "it could have blown Kennedy out of the water. There never would have been a President Kennedy. Today, with the same information, any of fifty newspapers would have gone after the story."

No responsible journalist touched the story. According to her FBI file, the outraged Kater carried her protest and her placard to the Democratic convention, and spent the final weeks of the 1960 campaign marching in front of the White House. She was not only ignored, as usual, by the press but also urged by passersby to go back "to the nuthouse." After his election Kennedy showed his disdain for Kater by appointing Pamela Turnure press secretary to his wife.

Kater, remarkably, picketed in front of the White House after Kennedy's inaugural, to no avail, and continued to send a stream of well-written protest letters to public officials and newspapers about the president's lack of morality, also to no avail. In one such letter, she wrote:

In 1960 the vast, vast majority of American women were hoaxed by the press, by television and by many influential people into believing that John Kennedy was the same clean-living man they read about or listened to on the air. That wasn't just everyday political cynicism; it was a brutal combination of power that could and did enforce total censorship of the truth about John Kennedy's well-known lecheries and his penchant to ruin anyone who dared criticize him for them. And I went out, all alone, to fight it with my little windbattered sign! But, far from being a fool, I was the one woman in America who wasn't fooled by John Kennedy.

The obsessed Georgetown housewife was a campaign-damaging bomb that did not explode. There were others, equally dangerous.

Senator Kennedy's scramble to protect his future presidential reputation began in earnest in late 1959, when a political opponent discovered that he was carrying on an affair with a nineteen-year-old student, the woman interviewed in Chapter Two. She was studying at Radcliffe College, the woman's college of Harvard University, on whose board of overseers Kennedy then served. His indiscretion was known to many: Kennedy's car and driver had been seen picking up and dropping off the student at her dormitory.

In this instance, Kennedy's biggest worries came not from Republicans but from his fellow Democrats, who were eager to find ways to discredit their competition. Word of the liaison reached Charles W. Engelhard, a South African diamond merchant and investor with corporate offices in New Jersey. Engelhard had endorsed Robert B. Meyner, the Democratic governor of New Jersey, who had presidential ambitions of his own; he and Meyner could not resist a chance to get rid of Kennedy. The two men arranged for one of Engelhard's aides to approach a former New York City policeman, then a private investigator, and offer him $10,000 to fly to Boston and take incriminating photographs of Kennedy with the Radcliffe student. However, the former policeman was a staunch Kennedy supporter. He turned down the job and, through a mutual friend, brought the plan to the attention of a politically connected Democratic lawyer in Washington. The lawyer, who had spent many years as a Senate aide, immediately arranged to see Jack Kennedy.

"Evelyn Lincoln shows me in," the lawyer, who did not wish to be identified, recalled in a 1996 interview for this book, "and I show him the name of the girl. He says, 'My God! They got her name.' He started to explain — some bullshit — and I said, 'I'm not really interested. I just wanted to let you know.' He was so appreciative that I'd tipped him off."

It was clear, the lawyer said, that "Charley Engelhard was trying to get the goods on Kennedy to knock him out of the running. They were going to set him up." Senator Kennedy, in the meeting, had exclaimed, "That goddamned Charley Engelhard. I'm going to give it to him up to there"— drawing his hand across his neck. Changing the subject, the lawyer asked Kennedy what he could do to help him win the Democratic nomination. He vividly recalled the answer: "I need money. I can't ask my father to pay for everything. Raise money."

Months later, during the campaign, the lawyer bumped into Kennedy and was thanked anew for his timely information. Kennedy told the lawyer he had assigned Carmine Bellino, one of his longtime assistants, to find out what was going on. Bellino, he said, had "put in a wire" on the Engelhard Industries official who had tried to hire the former New York City policeman. The lawyer raised an objection to the use of wiretaps and Kennedy reassured him, explaining, "We're not tapping his phone — just recording who he called."

In a meeting with the lawyer after the election, Kennedy reported that he was being urged by many ranking Democrat members of the Senate to name Engelhard ambassador to a high-profile embassy. "I'm going to fuck him," Kennedy said, with a laugh. "I'm going to send him to one of the boogie republics in Central Africa." Engelhard, who died in 1971 one of the world's richest men, never got his embassy, but the Kennedy administration did name him as the American representative to the Independence Day ceremonies in Gabon and Zambia. Kennedy, as we have seen, continued his relationship with the student. After his inauguration, he arranged for her to be named a special assistant to McGeorge Bundy, who had been dean of faculty at Harvard. She remained on Bundy's White House staff until late 1962. "It was very embarrassing," the woman recalled in one of our interviews. "It put McGeorge in a very creepy situation."

The fourth woman, and the one who, in the spring of 1960, posed the most direct threat to Kennedy's presidential aspirations, was a self-proclaimed artist named Barbara Maria Kopszynska, who had emigrated with her mother from Poland to Boston as a displaced person after World War II. According to heavily censored FBI files made public under the Freedom of Information Act in 1977, Kopszynska began telling reporters after the 1960 election that in 1951 she had become engaged to marry Jack Kennedy, then a member of the House, only to have the engagement broken up by Joe Kennedy because she was half Jewish. In March 1957 the blond and beautiful Kopszynska, who had changed her name to Alicia Darr, married Edmund Purdom, a British actor and playboy, and moved to Rome with him. The marriage quickly fell apart, and by early 1960 the Purdoms were in an Italian state court filing charges against each other.

Alicia Darr's FBI file created a brief stir when it was released in 1977. It included a summary of an interview in the issue dated January 31, 1961, of *Le Ore,* an Italian weekly magazine, in which Darr described her early relationship with Jack Kennedy and declared, according to a translation made for this book, that she "could have been the first lady." The FBI attaché in Rome told J. Edgar Hoover on January 30, ten days after Kennedy took office, that the article indicated that Darr "was considering the release of further information." The U.S. media paid no attention to the interview in 1961.

But a second FBI document in Darr's file, dated June 4, 1963, and sent at that time to Bobby Kennedy by J. Edgar Hoover (as the *Le Ore* summary had been two years earlier), made headlines in 1977, when America's newspapers, no longer in awe of the presidency after Watergate, were eager to publish any account of Kennedy's womanizing. Hoover warned the attorney general that the president's name had come up in connection with a disciplinary proceeding in New York against two Darr attorneys, Simon Metrik and Jacob W. Friedman. Metrik and Friedman, Hoover reported, had filed documents in court describing Kennedy's relationship with Darr and claiming that "just prior to the President's assuming office you"— Bobby Kennedy —"went to New York and arranged a settlement of the case out of court for $500,000." Reporters found Darr, by 1977 remarried and living in the Bahamas, and she denied having received any money from the Kennedys. The Hoover memoranda, even though heavily censored when released, produced the kind of stories that, if they had been published during JFK's days in office, would have seriously damaged his reputation and his chances for reelection. Most newspapers, citing the FBI documents, flatly reported that Kennedy had paid $500,000 to quash a lawsuit filed by Darr.

Those newspaper stories were wrong. The full story — that is, as much as could be obtained for this book — is far more dramatic.

The uncensored versions of Hoover's reports to Bobby Kennedy, made available in full for this book, reveal that Alicia Darr posed an extreme danger to Jack Kennedy in 1960, a danger that was hidden by deletions FBI censors made in the documents released in 1977. The uncensored versions reveal that Darr was well known to federal authorities and the New York police as a high-priced Manhattan prostitute and madam. The documents Hoover forwarded to Bobby Kennedy reported that in 1951, the year she first met Jack Kennedy, Darr was operating a "house of prostitution" in Boston. She moved to New York City a year later, where she turned again to prostitution, the FBI said, and also "was blackmailing people involved in the 'Jelke case'"— a highly publicized 1952 sex scandal involving New York's café society. The scandal led to a three-to-six-year jail term for Minot Frazier Jelke III, the twenty-three-year-old heir to an oleomargarine fortune, who was found guilty of procuring.* By 1953 Darr, described as a "talented prostitute," was operating "a call girl service" in midtown New York, the unexpurgated FBI report said. Another of the FBI documents depicted her as "a notorious, albeit high-class, 'hustler.'"

Darr's marriage to Purdom was in shambles by December of 1959, when she sued him in Rome for assault, battery, and nonmaintenance. She was out of money by early 1960 and, according to contemporary European newspaper accounts, began writing bad checks, for which she was eventually arrested and briefly jailed. In September 1961, a month after she was granted a divorce, in Mexico, Darr's

---

* The case attracted front-page attention even in the staid *New York Times*, which reported in August 1952 that Jelke, now deceased, had provided call girls to society figures and businessmen for fees ranging from $50 to $500. Alicia Darr's name did not show up in newspaper accounts; it is impossible to determine what role she had, if any, in the scandal, or how the FBI concluded that she had been blackmailing some of the participants.

finances improved dramatically: she married Alfred Corning Clark, a millionaire heir to the Singer sewing machine fortune. It was her second and his sixth marriage. Alfred Clark died of a heart attack in upstate New York thirteen days later, leaving her the bulk of his $10 million estate.

Alfred Clark's other surviving heirs quickly challenged his state of mind at the time he wrote the will. Simon Metrik, who had since 1958 been Alicia Darr's lawyer and media adviser, throughout her marriage to and divorce from Purdom, was retained on her behalf to handle the Clark family's protests. (He later said that he also twice kept her from getting arrested for prostitution, following two New York City vice raids.) Darr and Metrik eventually quarreled, according to court documents, and she dismissed him in December 1961, whereupon Metrik submitted a bill for $1.2 million. Darr, outraged, refused to pay. During the legal skirmishing over his fees, Metrik filed a bill of particulars against Darr, which described what a New York court would later characterize as "the commission of a contemplated crime." Darr's new attorneys argued that Metrik, in his papers, had violated the rules of attorney-client confidentiality; they asked the Appellate Division of the New York State Supreme Court to initiate disciplinary proceedings against him and against his partner, Jacob Friedman, who was acting for Metrik in the fee dispute with Darr.

The Appellate Division found in favor of Darr's new lawyers: Metrik and Friedman, it ruled, had breached the attorney-client privilege in their bill of particulars against Darr. On June 4, 1963, the two attorneys were publicly censured, and the file in the case was sealed. Metrik and Friedman were subsequently disciplined by the New York Bar Association. The two attorneys are deceased, and their firm disbanded; their file remains sealed today.* In its ruling, the Appellate Division noted that Metrik and Friedman's "disclosure here on the intended crime was not made to prevent the act or to protect

---

* In March 1996, the Supreme Court's Appellate Division denied my request to unseal the Metrik and Friedman file. The request was initially opposed by Richard M. Maltz, the deputy chief counsel to the disciplinary committee of the Appellate Division's First Judicial Department. In a memorandum dated April 11, 1995, Maltz noted that my argument had a "superficial appeal" because "there may very well be public interest in the type of information the applicant is seeking to uncover." However, Maltz

those against whom it was threatened. It was made long after the alleged occurrence" and was "not connected, even remotely," with issues arising out of the Clark inheritance. Alicia Darr Clark kept her inheritance, and Metrik did not receive his $1.2 million fee.

What was the "contemplated crime" cited by Metrik and Friedman? Hoover's memorandum to Bobby Kennedy — in the version released in 1977 — provided some clues; Kennedy received it on June 4, 1963, the same day the New York court announced its censure of Metrik and Friedman for their bill of particulars. Hoover reported that his sources had been told that Alicia Darr had in her possession letters signed by John F. Kennedy and photographs proving that the two had had a relationship. Hoover, as the press reported in 1977, wrote that Darr had initiated a lawsuit against Kennedy before the inauguration and that Bobby Kennedy had allegedly gone to New York and settled the matter for $500,000.

Hoover's information was apparently wrong. No record of a Darr lawsuit against Kennedy has been found, nor is there any evidence that the Kennedys paid anything to quash such a suit. A number of Jack and Robert Kennedy's former associates, contacted by reporters in 1977, denied any knowledge of a $500,000 payoff and expressed doubt about the accuracy of the FBI report. Hoover may have been wrong about the lawsuit, but there is much evidence that Darr tried for years to extort money from the Kennedy family.

Alicia Darr did have money problems in early 1960, at exactly the time the presidential campaign was in full bloom, and she did worry the candidate. On April 8, 1960, three days after the disappointing Wisconsin primary, Kennedy drafted in pencil a two-page memorandum for the record — made public for the first time in this book — summarizing a conversation with Bobby Baker, the secretary of the Democratic membership of the Senate and a protégé of Lyndon

---

said he could not determine from the available files why "the Court sealed a record that would otherwise, as a public censure, be public." Without such information, he added, the disciplinary committee had no choice but to oppose any proposed unsealing. As an alternative, he urged the justices of the Appellate Division to review the record, *in camera*, to determine whether the public interest would be served by unsealing. A year later, on March 8, 1996, the Appellate Division reviewed the files, deliberated on the issues, and denied my request in a one-page ruling.

Johnson. Baker met secretly with Kennedy and warned him that he had been approached by a New Jersey lawyer named Mickey Weiner and had been told that the wife of "a well-known movie actor"— Darr had not yet obtained her Mexican divorce — was willing to give Johnson an affidavit acknowledging an affair with Kennedy in return for $150,000. "Baker," Kennedy wrote, "said he thought it was blackmail, and did not inform Johnson of the matter." Baker may have been a Johnson protégé, but he was also a sometime playmate of Jack Kennedy; his loyalty to that part of Senate life and not to his mentor Johnson carried the day. Kennedy, obviously aware of the political danger posed by Alicia Darr, treated his memorandum as if it were a legal document; it was countersigned on the same day by Pierre Salinger, his press secretary, placed in an envelope, and sealed three days later by Salinger, as Salinger noted on the front of the envelope. The handwritten memorandum, still sealed, was found among the papers of Evelyn Lincoln, Kennedy's personal secretary, after her death in 1995.

In a 1995 interview for this book, Bobby Baker said he did not recall the blackmail threat or the conversation with Kennedy about it, but he did have a sharp memory of Mickey Weiner: "He was a whorehound, a percentager. He was trying to get defense contracts." Salinger said in an interview that he did not recall the document, or signing and sealing it.

Although there is no evidence of any blackmail payments to Alicia Darr, the Kennedy family did turn to Clark M. Clifford, the high-powered Washington lawyer, for help in a matter that may have been the same one Bobby Baker reported to Kennedy.* Clifford recalled in

---

* Clifford had performed valiantly for Kennedy in 1957, after questions were raised about the authorship of his *Profiles in Courage,* a series of case studies of senators who chose the greater good over narrow party interests. In an interview televised on ABC in December of that year, Kennedy was described by the columnist Drew Pearson as being "the only man in history that I know who won a Pulitzer Prize on a book which was ghostwritten for him, which indicates the kind of public relations buildup he's had." A few days later, a distraught Kennedy came to see him, Clifford wrote in his 1991 memoir, *Counsel to the President,* and sought his guidance. "I cannot let this stand," Clifford quoted Kennedy as saying. "It is a direct attack on my integrity and my honesty." At that point the telephone rang. It was Joe Kennedy. "Before I could even say hello," Clifford wrote, "Joe Kennedy said: 'I want you to sue the bastards for fifty million dollars. Get it started right away. It's dishonest and they know it. My boy

an interview for this book being asked by Kennedy to handle what he depicted as an "extraordinarily dangerous" situation in the spring of 1960, a few months before the Democratic convention. It involved a woman "who could destroy him," Clifford told me. "I had a conversation with Jack Kennedy that was so dramatic that if I could live to be a million years old, I could never forget it." The senator had gotten involved in a "very sensitive matter," Clifford said. "Public knowledge [of it] could have blown the Kennedy nomination out of the water."

At the time of Kennedy's request, Clifford was working for the presidential campaign of Stuart Symington, a fact he immediately mentioned to Kennedy. "I thought he'd say that I can't place you in the position of having this explosive information. He didn't say that. He said, 'I want you to go on representing me on this matter. Go ahead and work for Symington, but please continue on. If it becomes known, I've had it.'" Clifford added that he handled the incident until it got "to the point where I could turn it over to the Old Man [Joe Kennedy]." Clifford refused to say more about the matter, but did note that he made it a practice to have nothing to do with cash payoffs to women. "When it got into this area, I was never involved." The issue did arise in one case, the lawyer added: "I told Jack that I was not the right fellow to handle it. And they turned to [James] McInerney." Nothing more could be learned about the possible role of McInerney, who died in an automobile collision in 1963.

Further evidence of the threat posed by Alicia Darr emerged in yet another document in the FBI files, this one dated August 9, 1963, but not released in any form in 1977. Hoover warned Bobby Kennedy that

wrote the book. This is a plot against us.' 'Mr. Ambassador,' I said, 'I am preparing at this moment to go to New York and sit down with the people at ABC.' *'Sit down with them, hell! Sue them, that is what you have to do. Sue!'* he shouted in my ear. His son watched me with a faint air of amusement." Clifford eventually compelled an ABC vice president to state on the air that Pearson's charges were unfounded and that "the book in question was written by Senator Kennedy." In his diary, published years later, Pearson wrote that Kennedy "got a whale of a lot of help on his book" and expressed doubt that Kennedy "wrote too much of the final draft himself." But, he added, he met for an hour with Kennedy after their skirmish and concluded that he showed enough knowledge of the book to enable him to conclude that "basically it *is* his book."

some of the sealed documents in the Metrik disciplinary case were beginning to make the rounds of Kennedy enemies, who were depicting the documents as "dynamite" and an "H-bomb." In July, Hoover wrote, the documents were offered by a "private detective" going by the name "Robert Garden" to Senator John G. Tower of Texas, a Republican who was on the Armed Services Committee and a strong supporter of Barry Goldwater for the Republican presidential nomination in 1964; Tower was told that the materials dealt with a vital national security matter. Tower sent his administrative assistant, H. Edward Munden, to New York to visit Garden and take a look. Munden told the FBI in an interview soon afterward that the papers dealt with an affair in the 1950s between Kennedy and a woman named Clark who had become pregnant sometime before Kennedy's campaign for the presidency. There was also a letter from Clark to her attorney, the FBI summary said, that stated that "now that Mr. Kennedy had been elected President, 'their' position"— that is, Clark and Metrik's position —"was much better." Munden was told further during his New York visit to the private detective that there were additional documents and compromising pictures.

Munden, interviewed for this book in 1995, recalled that the subject of the meeting with Garden, which was obviously not his real name, was the 1964 election; the alleged detective, who made it clear that he wanted a large sum of money for the documents, was eager for Senator Tower's help in getting information to the Republican Party for use in the presidential campaign. The documents, Munden told me, included "legal papers concerning an illegitimate child of President Kennedy. The mother was one of the Singers." Munden, who had anticipated that the materials would deal with national defense or military issues, said he handed the materials back to Garden and told him that "it had nothing to do with the security of the United States." Munden returned to Washington and described the bizarre meeting to Tower, who immediately telephoned the attorney general. "He told him that we had nothing to do with the information," Munden told me. "Bobby thanked him and said he knew the rumor was out there." He heard nothing further, Munden recalled in our interview, but there was no question in his mind that somebody wanted Barry Goldwater "to buy this material to blackmail Kennedy" before he ran for reelection in 1964. There was also no doubt,

Munden told me, that Robert Garden, whoever he may have been, was convinced that his documents proved "that Kennedy had an illegitimate child" sometime in the late 1950s, although the documents he saw said nothing about a baby being born.

Alicia Darr Clark insisted in one of her interviews for this book that she had had no child out of wedlock by Jack Kennedy and would never have sought money from him. But in a 1997 telephone interview from Rome, Edmund Purdom, her former husband, said that the talk of a baby had a familiar ring. "She told me she was pregnant," he said. "That's why I married her [in 1957]. Of course," Purdom added, "she never had any children." Purdom, still involved in the entertainment business, was exceedingly bitter about his ex-wife, who is, he said, "a very dangerous woman" who has misrepresented many facts about her life and was always avaricious. He learned after their marriage, Purdom added, that his wife had been well known as a call girl among his friends in New York. Purdom said that in the early 1960s Simon Metrik told him, among other details, that he had "saved her from two police raids." At the time of the rescue, Metrik told Purdom, Darr was actively running a call-girl ring in partnership with a woman from West Germany. "I'm not out to get her," Purdom said, in concluding our conversation. "I'm out to forget her."

Alicia Darr, known today as Mrs. Alicia Clark, breezily refused to discuss her past in detail in interviews for this book in 1996 and 1997, but she remained eager to talk about her relationship with the "beautiful and charming" Jack Kennedy. "I was one of his pals," she said of John Kennedy, who was a congressman when they met. "I didn't want to be a first lady. Believe me, he loved me. He knew me as a kid and loved me to the day he died. But I preferred to be married to a movie star. Why marry Jack and be stuck with Old Joe, and having to please him? John Kennedy," she added, "was a spender. He'd buy you flowers, gifts. He told me he'd like to buy me diamonds, but he had trouble with his father, who was telling him he was spending too much money." Darr insisted that he was willing to marry her, but she said no. "He was looking for me," she told me. "I wasn't looking for him. He was calling Rome. He wanted to run away from it all with me — to Europe, just to skip town. But I'd say, 'Jack, you don't have enough money.'"

Once safely in the White House, the young president did seem to be more than ever intrigued by her — or by the danger of being with her. Maxwell Raab, a Boston attorney who was secretary of the cabinet in the Eisenhower administration, found himself dancing with Clark at a British Embassy party in the early 1960s. President Kennedy suddenly entered the room, and Clark whispered to Raab: "I'd like to see the president. Dance me over to him. I know him very well." Raab, recalling the incident in a 1995 interview, said he understood what "very well" meant.

The president was indeed delighted to see Clark, Raab said, and whisked her off. "I saw that I was not to be in this," Raab said, "and so I walked away."*

---

* Raab, who served with distinction as ambassador to Italy during the Reagan administration, had been used by Senator Kennedy during the 1960 campaign. He left the White House in 1959 and was working as an aide to Senator Kenneth Keating, Republican of New York, when Kennedy, very agitated, sought him out. The two men had known each other since the late 1940s, Raab told me in our interview. "I gotta talk to you," Kennedy said. "Nixon and the Republican National Committee are doing a job on me. They're trying to destroy me and they've got Jackie all upset. It's created havoc in my home. It's got to be stopped." Kennedy asked Raab to approach Nixon and his fellow Republicans and tell them "to stop spreading the word that I'm philandering." "It wasn't rage," Raab said of Kennedy's demeanor, but "the nearest thing." Raab dutifully brought up the matter with Leonard Hall, chairman of the Republican National Committee, and with Nixon. "Nixon said, 'I'm not doing it,' but he"— referring to Hall —"was." Raab, who admits he was very naive about Jack Kennedy at the time, subsequently reported back to the senator, assuring him that "there will be no more talk from the White House or Republican National Committee." Kennedy thanked him.

9

LYNDON

Jack Kennedy came to Los Angeles with more than enough delegates to assure a first-ballot nomination, and enough excess baggage — from the huge cash outlays in West Virginia and the womanizing — to threaten his certain victory. It is only with an understanding of the dark side of the Kennedy legacy — and who was aware of it at the time of the convention — that the surprise selection of Lyndon Johnson as the vice presidential candidate can be understood.

The public story is that for reasons of party unity Kennedy offered the vice presidency to Johnson fully expecting that the Texan, who was Senate majority leader, would turn it down. By this account, once Johnson accepted, Kennedy had no choice but to go along. Bobby Kennedy's profound dismay upon learning of Johnson's nomination was obvious to scores of politicians and journalists at the convention; the two men would remain bitter enemies for the next eight years. The word was put out after the convention that Joe Kennedy had been pushing all along for Johnson, who was seen as a more conservative political figure acceptable to the South, and able to deliver Texas. But the Kennedy brothers and their aides muddled the picture by providing political insiders and favored journalists with widely varying accounts of their thinking before, during, and after the convention, leaving a record of impossible-to-reconcile contradictions.

Hugh Sidey, of *Time* magazine, who covered Kennedy as a candidate and in the White House, vividly recalled in an interview for this book a conversation on the eve of the convention, as Kennedy was preparing to fly from New York to Los Angeles. Sidey had just spent a day with Johnson, and Kennedy "wanted to know his mood and all that. He told me that night in so many words, 'If I had my choice I would have Lyndon Johnson as my running mate. And I'm going to offer it to him, but he isn't going to take it.' So, right off," Sidey told me, "a lot of these stories about Bobby's anger and not knowing about this were nonsense."

Bobby Kennedy, in a 1965 oral history for the Kennedy Library, flatly contradicted his brother's words to Sidey. He said that any reports that "the president had the thought of Lyndon Johnson as vice president prior to his own nomination — that's not true. The idea that he'd go down and offer him the nomination in hopes that he'd take the nomination is not true." In an earlier interview for the library, Kennedy described the selection of Johnson as "the most indecisive time we ever had. . . . We changed and rechanged our minds probably seven times. The only people who were involved in the discussions were Jack and myself. Nobody else was involved in it."

Bobby Kennedy remained distraught after the convention. On the day after Jack's nomination, Charles Bartlett, the Chattanooga newspaper reporter and family friend, had been invited to join the family at a hideaway in Santa Monica. "Bobby told me that this was the worst day of his life," Bartlett said in an interview for this book. "He felt really badly about Lyndon Johnson going on the ticket. Jack seemed sort of stunned."

One reason for the dismay became clear in 1978, when Bobby Baker, Johnson's close aide, published his memoir, *Wheeling and Dealing*. Baker described a brutal breakfast meeting with Bobby Kennedy just as the convention was getting under way. After the usual banter over coffee, Baker complained mildly about Teddy Kennedy's suggestion in a speech in Texas that Johnson had not fully recovered from an earlier heart attack. Bobby Kennedy immediately reddened at the criticism of his younger brother, Baker wrote, and declared, "You've got your nerve. Lyndon Johnson has compared my father to the Nazis and [Johnson supporters] John Connally and India Edwards lied in saying my brother is dying of Addison's disease. You Johnson people are running a stinking damned campaign and you're gonna get yours when the time comes." Kennedy slammed a few dollars down on the table, Baker wrote, and stomped off.

Even Joe Kennedy found it necessary to console his sons. "There's a scene I'll never forget," Bartlett told me, recalling his day with the Kennedys in Santa Monica. "Old Joe was in a dinner jacket and velvet slippers, and he was standing with the setting sun glinting in his eyes. Old Joe said, 'Jack,' in that Boston accent, 'in two weeks they'll be saying this is the smartest thing you ever did.'"

Johnson's nomination pitted brother against brother, and as Kennedy's narrow plurality in the November election would show, did not ensure the success of the Democratic ticket. What made Johnson more attractive than the other candidates?

One account that has not been made public is the late Hyman Raskin's, as recorded in a chapter of his unpublished memoir, provided for this book, and buttressed by interviews with him in 1994 and 1995. In Raskin's account, Stuart Symington was always at the top of Kennedy's short list of running mates. That list was "precipitously and totally discarded," Raskin wrote, when Kennedy met early on the morning after his nomination with Johnson and Sam Rayburn, the Speaker of the House. At the meeting, Kennedy was "made an offer he could not refuse." In other words, Raskin assumed, Johnson blackmailed his way into the vice presidency. Raskin could not learn which aspect of the Kennedy history was cited by Johnson and Rayburn in making their threats, but he had no doubt that their morning meeting with Johnson disrupted months of careful planning and put the Kennedy campaign staff in an uproar.

Hy Raskin had been a major strategist and trusted campaign aide for more than two years by the time Kennedy won the nomination; he was much more of an insider than was publicly known. "It is a chronic weakness of all the books that have been written about the emergence of John F. Kennedy that the vital role played by Hyman B. Raskin is grossly underplayed or totally ignored," the Chicago television analyst Len O'Connor noted in his 1975 book, *Clout: Mayor*

Daley and His City. "It was Hy Raskin who had dropped in on old Democratic friends everywhere, using the soft sell that it would have to be Jack Kennedy at the convention or they would never make it in November, cashing in the chits he held for past favors, picking up a few delegates here, the promise of a few delegates there."

Once at the convention, Raskin was given the important task of running the campaign's communications center. It was natural for Bobby Kennedy to turn to him for confidential help in resolving the vice presidential issue. Moments after Kennedy's nomination was locked up on Wednesday, July 13, the third night of the convention — and before the decisive meeting — Bobby Kennedy ordered Raskin to make a series of discreet calls to arrange a late meeting with the candidate and a select group of Democratic party leaders. The session was to take place after Kennedy appeared before the convention delegates to make a short thank-you speech. The meeting's purpose, Raskin understood, was cosmetic:

> To assuage the feelings of a few ambitious men who were under the impression they were being seriously considered for the vice presidential nomination. In addition, the important leaders of the party who had not been consulted would have an opportunity to make their recommendations and then be the "first to know" the identity of the vice presidential candidate. This was the traditional method for giving comfort to political prima donnas.

Johnson and Rayburn were not on Bobby Kennedy's list of those who were to be called to the meeting, and Raskin, he later wrote, understood why: "Johnson was not being given the slightest bit of consideration by any of the Kennedys." The front-runner in all previous discussions inside the campaign, Raskin knew, was the attractive Symington, who had served as secretary of the air force during the Truman presidency. "On the stuff I saw," Raskin told me in an interview, "it was always Symington who was going to be the vice president. The Kennedy family had approved Symington." The Missouri senator's popularity in California was his most obvious asset, in Raskin's opinion; a Kennedy victory there would offset the expected losses in the South.

Raskin's recollection was supported by interviews for this book with Clark Clifford, who recalled a secret meeting on the evening of July 13 at which Jack Kennedy told Clifford, "We've talked it out — me, my dad, and Bobby — and we've selected Symington as the vice president." Kennedy asked Clifford to relay that message to Symington "and find out if he'd run." After a conference in Symington's suite, Clifford was authorized to tell Kennedy that Symington would accept the vice presidential nomination. "I and Stuart went to bed believing that we had a solid, unequivocal deal with Jack," Clifford told me.

In Raskin's account, the newly nominated Kennedy was expected to stop by the communications command post that night to shake hands with his loyal staff before proceeding to the convention hall, but he did not show up. It was said that he was running late. "When I was supplied with the facts and circumstances later," Raskin wrote, "it was clear that the reason Jack was 'running late' was a phone call from either Rayburn or Johnson. I know that his brother, Bob, was not with him" when the call came, because the younger Kennedy did not leave the command post until Jack Kennedy arrived to speak to the convention. A few hours later, after JFK's brief speech to the delegates, a distraught Bobby Kennedy telephoned Raskin and told him to cancel the meeting of party leaders. How should he answer the inevitable questions? Raskin asked. "Tell them the truth," Bobby responded. "You don't know." Raskin realized he was not going to learn anything more from Kennedy.

The party leaders, told that the meeting was off, began to gossip. "It was obvious to them that something extraordinary had taken place, as it was to me," Raskin wrote. "During my entire association with the Kennedys, I could not recall any situation where a decision of major significance had been reversed in such a short period of time. . . . Bob [Kennedy] had always been involved in every major decision; why not this one, I pondered." Raskin went to bed that night worrying that the decision to exclude Johnson and Rayburn from the Wednesday late-night meeting had backfired. "I slept little that night," he wrote. "I could hardly wait for the beginning of the next day."

By the next morning, Thursday, July 14, word was all over the convention that Johnson was to be Kennedy's running mate.

Clark Clifford recalled that he was summoned early the next morning — before his morning shave — to another meeting with a disconsolate Jack Kennedy, who said: "I must do something that I've never done before. I made a serious deal and I've now got to go back on it. I have no alternative." Symington was out and Johnson was in. Clifford recalled observing that Kennedy looked as if he'd been up all night.

Jack Kennedy was scheduled to host a luncheon later in the day for his immediate staff. He entered the dining room, followed by the usual horde of journalists and cameramen, spotted the avuncular, white-haired Raskin, and, as Raskin remembered it, dragged him to a window seat, saying: "Come with me. I have something to tell you." As they walked, Kennedy asked:

"Have you heard the news?"

"Yes."

"What do you think?"

Raskin shrugged, and Kennedy said: "You know we had never considered Lyndon, but I was left with no choice. He and Sam Rayburn made it damn clear to me that Lyndon had to be the candidate. Those bastards were trying to frame me. They threatened me with problems and I don't need more problems. I'm going to have enough problems with Nixon."

Raskin, as he wrote in his memoirs, remained haunted by the conversation: "The substance of this revelation was so astonishing that if it had been revealed to me by anyone other than Jack or Bob, I would have had trouble accepting it. Why he decided to tell me was still very mysterious, but flattering nonetheless."*

---

* Kennedy seemed to have a special softness toward the distinguished Raskin, who was twenty years his senior. After the election, Raskin recalled in a 1994 interview, he was invited to meet on December 2, 1960, with the president-elect at his home in Georgetown, the obvious issue being political payback — what job did Raskin want? Raskin entered the house via a side door; Kennedy had announced a major cabinet appointment that morning, and a large number of reporters were clustered in front. The two men had a pleasant chat, and Raskin told Kennedy that he wanted no job — his goal was to go back to his law practice and make money. It was left unsaid that his connections to the new administration would not hurt. At the end of their talk, Kennedy helped his longtime campaign colleague with his coat and, as he walked him to the front door, began recounting the following apocryphal story: "A Frenchman goes into

In an interview in 1995, Raskin acknowledged with a laugh that there have been literally dozens of published accounts, all described as authoritative versions, purporting to explain how Lyndon Johnson became the surprise choice. He maintained that Jack Kennedy "never wanted Lyndon on the ticket. The ideal guy was Symington. With Lyndon they lost California, but with Symington they would not have lost it."

Kennedy insiders, ever loyal, responded to Johnson's selection by immediately telling the press and the campaign staff that Kennedy had been as surprised as anyone when Johnson accepted his token offer of the vice presidency. That the story, thin as it was, worked was all the more amazing because Johnson, or someone close to him, wasted little time in telling his side to a favored journalist, John S. Knight, editor and publisher of the *Miami Herald*. Newspaper readers in Miami on the Friday morning of the convention woke to an eight-column banner headline in the *Herald* proclaiming: "The Exclusive Inside Story: How Johnson Demanded (and Got) 2nd Spot." Knight wrote that on Thursday morning — the story did not say when in the morning — Bobby Kennedy paid a courtesy call to Johnson to discuss various options for the vice presidency. To Kennedy's "amazement," Knight wrote, "Lyndon Johnson informed him that he and Sam Rayburn had been having a talk and had agreed that Johnson should be named for vice president." Johnson further said that he would put his name in nomination, with or without Kennedy's support, and make a floor fight, if necessary, at the convention. The can-

a Rothschild bank in Paris and waits in the lobby. After about fifteen minutes, out comes a Rothschild. 'Can I help you with anything? Your account? A loan?'" By this point in the story, Raskin told me, he and Kennedy were nearing the front door, and Raskin suddenly recalled the short walk he and Kennedy had taken at the Los Angeles convention when he learned of the Johnson-Rayburn threat. The president-elect continued his story: "'No,' says the man. 'Just put your arm around me and walk me around the lobby.'" The punch line was delivered just as the two men walked outside and were met by a multitude of microphones, flashbulbs, and television cameras. Kennedy wrapped an arm around Raskin and leaned his head close to him, talking animatedly, while the cameras clicked and reporters wondered. An AP wirephoto of Raskin and Kennedy appeared in hundreds of newspapers the next morning. Raskin's revived law practice was off to a roaring start. Raskin told the anecdote with obvious delight.

didate was informed and immediately visited Johnson, who repeated his threat. Kennedy then convened a meeting of party leaders, Knight wrote, all of whom had previously supported Symington, and eventually all present agreed that "they couldn't risk a fight with Johnson without endangering the party's chances in November. So, the capitulation was made."

The essential threat cited in the dispatch — that Johnson convinced Kennedy to make him his running mate by promising to stage a floor fight for the nomination — is ludicrous. Such a threat would give Johnson little leverage, as even a political novice would know: he would have been vilified for disrupting convention unity on the eve of the campaign, severely damaging his own standing in the party in the process. Nonetheless, the article flatly declared that Johnson had forced Kennedy to make him vice president. Bobby Kennedy ordered Pierre Salinger, the campaign's press secretary, to issue a public denial. Salinger described the events of that day in his 1966 memoir, *With Kennedy,* and noted that his denial, in turn, prompted an angry response from both Johnson and Rayburn. The two men, who clearly had much to do with getting the story to Knight, were aggressive in denying responsibility. They demanded, Salinger wrote, that Jack Kennedy himself telephone Knight, at his home, and tell him the story was false. Johnson wanted the story "nipped in the bud," Salinger wrote, before it got into wide circulation. Eventually Bobby Kennedy called Knight. Salinger noted, ingenuously, in his memoir: "Through this vigorous action that night, we were able to prevent spread of the story and I spent most of Friday (the 15th) backgrounding newspapermen on the facts of the vice-presidential nomination as they had been outlined by Bob Kennedy." The cover story — that Jack Kennedy had always wanted Johnson as his running mate — held, and Knight's page-one exclusive disappeared into obscurity.

A few days later, Salinger wrote, he asked Jack Kennedy whether he really expected Johnson to accept the vice presidential offer or whether he had been merely making a pro forma gesture. Kennedy began to respond, but suddenly stopped and said: "The whole story will never be known. And it's just as well that it won't be." Salinger added that he could not explain the cryptic remark. Similarly, Joseph

Dolan, who was Robert Kennedy's administrative assistant in the Senate in the mid-1960s, recalled in a 1995 interview for this book that Kennedy paused as he was leaving a meeting to say, about Lyndon Johnson, "Only two people alive know the whole story about 1960." Kennedy asked Dolan if he wanted to hear it. "I said," Dolan told me, "that it wouldn't be a secret if I knew." He'd been kicking himself since then, Dolan added, for not asking.

The only Kennedy insider to discuss the vice presidential nomination publicly over the next thirty-five years was Evelyn Lincoln, Kennedy's personal secretary, who told the British journalist Anthony Summers that she was convinced in mid-1960 that J. Edgar Hoover and Johnson had conspired. Hoover was known to be personally close to Johnson — they lived on the same street in northwest Washington — and had for years provided Johnson with information about Kennedy's private life. In *Official and Confidential,* Summers's biography of Hoover, published in 1993, Lincoln was quoted as saying that Johnson "had been using all the information Hoover could find on Kennedy — during the campaign, even before the Convention. And Hoover was in on the pressure on Kennedy at the Convention . . . about womanizing, and things in Joe Kennedy's background, and anything he could dig up. Johnson was using that as clout. Kennedy was angry, because they had boxed him into a corner. He was absolutely boxed in." In a later interview for this book, Lincoln told of finding Bobby and Jack deep in conversation early on the morning of July 15: "I went in and listened. They were very upset and trying to figure out how they could get around it, but they didn't know how they could do it." She did not hear any mention then of a specific threat from Johnson, Lincoln said. But, she added, "Jack knew that Hoover and LBJ would just fill the air with womanizing."

The principals are long dead, and the world may never know what threats Lyndon Johnson made to gain the vice presidency. Kennedy knew how much Hoover knew, and he knew that the information was more than enough to give Johnson whatever he needed as leverage. Kennedy's womanizing came at great cost: he could be subjected to blackmail not only by any number of his former lovers but also by anyone else who could accumulate enough specifics about his affairs — even an ambitious fellow senator. Kennedy found a way to make the best of it after the imbroglio over the vice presidency. He explained to Kenny O'Donnell, a longtime Johnson-hater, as O'Donnell wrote in his memoirs: "I'm forty-three years old. I'm not going to die in office. So the vice presidency doesn't mean anything. . . ."

10

THE STOLEN ELECTION

Joseph P. Kennedy did more than invest his time and money in his unrelenting drive in 1960 to elect his oldest surviving son president. He risked the family's reputation — and the political future of his sons Bobby and Teddy — by making a bargain with Sam Giancana and the powerful organized crime syndicate in Chicago. Joe Kennedy's goal was to ensure victory in Illinois and in other states where the syndicate had influence, and he achieved it, after arranging a dramatic and until now unrevealed summit meeting with Sam Giancana in the chambers of one of Chicago's most respected judges. The deal included an assurance that Giancana's men would get out the Kennedy vote among the rank and file in the mob-controlled unions in Chicago and elsewhere, and a commitment for campaign contributions from the corrupt Teamsters Union pension fund.

Jack Kennedy and his brother took office knowing that organized crime and Giancana had helped win the 1960 election. Just what Joe Kennedy promised Giancana in return is not known, but the gangster was convinced he had scored the ultimate coup by backing a presidential winner. The heat would now be off the Chicago syndicate.

* * *

The 1960 presidential election was a cliff-hanger in which John Kennedy defeated Richard Nixon by a final plurality of 118,000 out of more than 68 million votes. Since then, journalists and historians have raised questions about Kennedy's victory — by fewer than 9,400 votes — in Illinois, one of the last states to report and the one that gave Kennedy his dramatic early-morning triumph. The Illinois election was quickly mired in charges of vote fraud, with Republicans accusing Democrats, led by Mayor Richard Daley, of rigging the returns in Chicago. It was widely known that the mayor, since taking office in 1955, had been controlling returns in state and local elections in Chicago, and that in 1960 he had pressured his precinct captains to produce votes for Kennedy. The allegations of vote fraud did not faze Daley, the archetype of the big-city political boss. He stoically dismissed the charges, telling reporters, "This is a Republican conspiracy to deny the presidency to the man who was elected by the people."

Allegations of vote fraud were eventually filed against Democrats in eleven states. The Republican Party, after a series of high-level meetings in Washington, decided in late November to send officials on troubleshooting missions to seven of the eleven states — New Jersey, Texas, Missouri, New Mexico, Nevada, South Carolina, and Pennsylvania. Kennedy's margin in some of these states was so minute — he took Nevada and New Mexico by fewer than 2,500 votes — that any significant pattern of vote fraud could have changed victory to defeat. All the missions were futile.

It was the election in Illinois that captured the nation's attention. The turnout in Chicago was high, as usual: more than 89 percent of the eligible voters voted, or were recorded as having voted. The city's Democratic machine had turned out more than 80 percent of the voters in the 1952 and 1956 presidential elections. What was unusual in 1960 was Kennedy's huge plurality in Chicago, which enabled him to offset a wave of downstate Republican votes. He won Chicago by 456,312 votes, a margin nearly four times as great as his final plurality in the nation as a whole.

These statistics have been repeatedly cited in countless articles and books discussing the election in Illinois, with the assertion usually made that the Illinois vote was less essential, and therefore less dramatic, than was initially thought. Kennedy's narrow victories in

Texas, Michigan, New Jersey, and Missouri, the argument goes, gave him 303 electoral college votes — 34 more than he needed to claim the White House. But the fact is that Illinois was essential to Kennedy's victory. Without the state's 27 electoral votes, Kennedy would have had a plurality of only 7 votes over Nixon in the electoral college, with 26 unpledged Democratic electors in Mississippi, Georgia, and Alabama threatening to bolt unless they received significant concessions on federal civil rights policy from the Democratic Party. A loss in Illinois would have given those unpledged electors — fourteen of whom eventually did choose to cast their votes for Democratic senator Harry F. Byrd, of Virginia — a huge increase in leverage. They had the power, if Kennedy lost Illinois, to throw the election into the House of Representatives for the first time in the twentieth century.

At the time, Kennedy's huge Chicago margin was widely considered suspect, even by the newly elected president. "Mr. President," Kennedy quoted Mayor Daley as telling him on election night, "with a little bit of luck and the help of a few close friends, you're going to carry Illinois." That reported assurance caused a furor when it was made public in 1977 by the journalist Benjamin Bradlee, a close Kennedy friend who shared dinner with the newly elected president at Hyannis Port on the evening after the election. Bradlee would assert, lamely, in a later memoir that "Me, I don't know what the hell Daley meant." Two grand juries were convened in Chicago after the election, but they ended up indicting only five low-level Democratic Party officials for vote buying and vote fraud. The official investigations continued until July 1961, when a downstate Democratic county judge — in what one journalist subsequently described as "a gross display of partisanship"— dismissed the last of 677 contempt charges that alleged that Democratic precinct workers had intentionally erred in tallying votes. The judge ruled that there was "insufficient evidence" to prove that Democratic Party officials in Chicago had intentionally made errors in counting.

Richard Nixon had no illusions about what happened in Illinois, but he chose not to demand a recount, as some Republican leaders urged him to do. Many Americans considered Nixon's decision not to contest the legitimacy of the election one of his finest hours. In his memoir, *RN*, Nixon was candid in admitting that his decision was based on self-interest: "And what if I demanded a recount and it turned out that despite the vote fraud Kennedy had still won? Charges of 'sore loser' would follow me through history and remove any possibility of a further political career."

Nixon was right. The recount in Illinois was in the hands of the Democratic Party, and would not have come close to telling the real story of the election.

Joe Kennedy dealt with the mob out of necessity. As the owner of the Merchandise Mart, he understood as well as anyone the extent to which organized crime dominated the major unions in Chicago in the late 1950s. The Chicago "outfit," headed by Al Capone, had begun expanding into legitimate business and unions before World War II; by the late 1940s more than one hundred unions were controlled by the mob, providing millions of dollars annually in cash and — equally significant to Chicago's politicians — a huge manpower base that could be mobilized on demand. The outfit's labor expert was Murray "the Camel" Humphreys, who was credited in one biography with maintaining personal control over sixty-one unions at the height of the Capone empire.

The Kennedy patriarch's turn to Giancana for help was all the more risky because of Jack and Bobby's known antagonism to organized crime, stemming from their involvement in the late 1950s with the Senate special investigating committee on labor racketeering, officially known as the Select Committee on Improper Activities in the Labor or Management Field. Robert Kennedy had been especially aggressive and insulting in his first known encounter with Giancana, during the gangster's testimony before the committee in June 1959. Giancana took the Fifth Amendment and made a point of smiling at each of Kennedy's questions. "I thought only little girls giggled, Mr. Giancana," Kennedy remarked at one point. The exchange made huge news.

Joe Kennedy, according to the family biographers, bitterly objected to his sons' involvement with the Senate Rackets Committee. Senator John Kennedy was one of four Democrats on the committee, whose chairman was John L. McClellan, the Democrat from Arkansas. Robert Kennedy was the committee's chief counsel, and the driving force behind the high-profile investigations into labor racketeering, which placed special emphasis on the activities of James R. Hoffa, head of the Teamsters Union. In his 1978 biography, *Robert Kennedy and His Times,* Arthur Schlesinger described Joe Kennedy as being "deeply, emotionally opposed" to his sons' participation on the committee. Schlesinger described the senior Kennedy as believing that "an investigation . . . would not produce reform; it would only turn the labor movement against the Kennedys. . . . Father and son [Robert] had an unprecedentedly furious argument." Joe Kennedy then asked his good friend Supreme Court Justice William O. Douglas to intervene with Bobby. It didn't work, according to Schlesinger. Douglas told Joe that Bobby felt that the committee represented "too great an opportunity" to give up.

Joe Kennedy, fearful of losing union support in 1960, understood that labor unions, honest or not, could supply political campaigns with money and foot soldiers — and Jack, so his father believed, would need a great deal of both to win the presidency. Hoffa, as hardboiled as Bobby Kennedy, was sure to do all he could to stop JFK in 1960. Joe Kennedy was convinced that he had to make a deal in Chicago, and he turned for help to an old friend, William J. Tuohy, chief judge of the Circuit Court of Cook County (Chicago). Tuohy, who died in 1964, was given an assignment: to set up a clandestine meeting between Joe Kennedy and Sam Giancana, known as Mooney to his colleagues. Tuohy, who had served the state's attorney of Cook County before being elected to the bench in 1950, did not know Giancana. But a former protégé from his days in the state's attorney's office, Robert J. McDonnell, was then one of the mob's leading attorneys.

"Tuohy asked me to come to his chambers," the seventy-one-year-old McDonnell recalled in an interview for this book. The call came, McDonnell estimated, in the winter of 1959–60. "I went. We chatted. He said, 'I don't know how to pose this question. Do you know Mooney Giancana?' I said yes. He said, 'How do you suggest that I arrange a meeting between Mr. Giancana and Joseph Kennedy?'" McDonnell gave the judge the name of a local politician with close ties to the syndicate. A few days later, McDonnell was summoned to a meeting with Giancana at the Armory Lounge in suburban Forest Park, and was told that the meeting with Kennedy was going to happen in

Tuohy's courtroom. "Can you guarantee this will be a very, very private meeting?" Giancana asked, according to McDonnell.

The jittery Tuohy invited McDonnell to attend. "So," McDonnell continued, "I showed up about five o'clock. The courts were just getting out, and darkness was enveloping the courtroom. It's always melodramatic at that time of day." McDonnell entered the judge's chambers and was introduced to Joe Kennedy. After twenty minutes or so, McDonnell said, "we heard footsteps come into the courtroom, and in walked Mooney Giancana" and one of his associates. McDonnell made the introductions. "The three of them sat down. Judge Tuohy and I left the chambers. We went over to the jury box in the courtroom. I remember Judge Tuohy saying to me, 'I'm glad I'm not privy to this.' He was very dispirited. This was a man of the highest integrity, and he was asked to do a favor for Joe Kennedy. And I know that it repulsed him." McDonnell and Tuohy left the courthouse while the meeting between Kennedy and Giancana was still going on.

He later heard from his clients, McDonnell said, that Kennedy "was obsessed with the election of John Kennedy — absolutely obsessed with it. I don't know what deals were cut; I don't know what promises were made. But I can tell you, Mooney had so many assets in place. They were capable of putting drivers in every precinct to help out the precinct captains, to get the voters out. And they had the unions absolutely going for Kennedy. I realize that today the unions don't vote as they're told to vote, but in the days of 1960 they did. Mooney assisted in all of this.

"There was no ballot stuffing," McDonnell added. "I'm not suggesting that. They just worked — totally went all out. He [Kennedy] won it squarely, but he got the vote because of what Mooney had done. I'm convinced in my heart of hearts that Mooney carried the day for John F. Kennedy."

McDonnell, a Notre Dame graduate who was seriously wounded in World War II, was in financial trouble by the time of Tuohy's call for help. His success as a trial lawyer in the state's attorney's office was overwhelmed by his addictions to gambling and alcohol; by the early 1950s, he was constantly in debt and little more than a paid mouthpiece for the outfit. In 1966, he was found guilty of passing forged money orders; his license to practice law was suspended but not revoked. McDonnell renewed his legal practice in the early 1980s but lost his license after a second conviction for the attempted bribery of an electrical workers union official. In 1983 McDonnell married Antoinette Giancana, Sam Giancana's daughter; they were divorced in 1995.

McDonnell's account was buttressed by interviews for this book demonstrating that Joe Kennedy did have a long-standing, if little-known, friendship with Judge Tuohy. Tuohy's two sons, Patrick and John, both lawyers, told me that they knew nothing about a meeting involving their father and Sam Giancana, but they recalled Joe Kennedy — "the Ambassador," as he liked to be called — at casual dinners in their home after the war. John Tuohy told me that his father and Joe Kennedy attended a Chicago Bears football game together in 1947. Both Tuohys also said they knew McDonnell as a lawyer who, as Patrick put it, had fallen "off the normal track." Patrick added, "I'm pretty sure my father knew him."

Another witness to meetings between Kennedy and Tuohy was Thomas V. King, who was general manager of the Merchandise Mart in 1960, and worked directly under Kennedy. King said in an interview for this book that Kennedy and Tuohy "were very, very close." It was his understanding, King added, that "Joe took care of him, too — helped him out financially." King witnessed a number of meetings between Kennedy and Tuohy at the Merchandise Mart, he said, but did not hear their discussions. "I was an employee then, in the background," King explained.

Robert McDonnell's firsthand testimony is compelling, and evocative of a similar account of Joe Kennedy's insistence on a meeting with Giancana which appeared on national television in 1992, in a miniseries produced for CBS by Tina Sinatra, Frank's daughter. In the script for one episode of the dramatized series, the actor playing Joe Kennedy tells the actor playing Sinatra that "the best thing you can do for Jack" is to "go to those people" who "control the [Teamsters] union." Sinatra, in a subsequent scene, relays the request to Sam Giancana and gets his approval.

In a 1997 interview for this book, Tina Sinatra acknowledged that her father had provided the information for the scenes and had explicitly approved the script. Sinatra, in effect, broke faith with a long-held secret in an effort to provide some pizzazz for his daughter's show: he publicly admitted for the first time that he played a role in brokering Giancana's support for Jack Kennedy in 1960.

"What I understood," Tina Sinatra told me, "was that a meeting was called" late in 1959 at Hyannis Port. "Dad was more than willing to go. He hadn't been to the house before. Over lunch, Joe said, 'I think that you can help me in West Virginia and Illinois with our friends. You understand, Frank, I can't go. They're my friends, too, but I can't approach them. But you can.' I know that it gave Dad pause. But it still wasn't anything he felt he shouldn't do. So off to Sam Giancana he went." Her father arranged to meet Giancana on a golf course, Tina said, away from Giancana's seemingly constant FBI surveillance. Sinatra told him, Tina said, "I believe in this man and I think he's going to make us a good president. With your help, I think we can work this out."

Joe Kennedy's goal, Tina said, was "to assure the wins in Illinois and West Virginia — you know, getting the numbers out, getting the unions to vote."

Being a middleman seemed logical to her father, Tina said. "The notion that Joe would go to Sam Giancana was out of the question, for obvious reasons. Frank's affiliation with Sam Giancana and other mobsters — we all understand that. The Mafia was very smart. They knew that power and control would keep this country together. Now I don't think that they should have been out shooting each other, but they did. By the thirties and forties, when Dad was in the business, they were controlling the nightclubs. They were controlling the entertainment world. They were a motivated bunch. The power of an entertainer and the power of a mobster — it's all very much a part of America. They were all from the same neighborhoods. My dad grew up with gangsters next door. He was living with them. They were his personal friends, and he's not going to cast away a friend. The great vein through Frank Sinatra is loyalty. There is an absolute commitment to friends and family. It's very Italian and probably gave him a little more in common with the mob types."

Furthermore, Tina said, "these weren't people that Joe [Kennedy] didn't know. He had these relations as well. My grandmother called him 'that rum-running son of a bitch.' They did use the underworld to put their Golden Boy over the top — conduit, Frank Sinatra. They [didn't] hesitate to ask for favors; the Kennedys were very able to ask for anything they needed. And I think they were accustomed to getting it. Everybody was duped," she added, when Robert Kennedy, as attorney general, targeted organized crime as eagerly as he had done for the Senate Rackets Committee.

Frank Sinatra, Tina said, was enthusiastic about Jack Kennedy. "Dad felt that Jack Kennedy was a breath of fresh air. He said he hadn't been as excited about an election since Roosevelt, whom he also campaigned for." What is generally not known about her father, Tina Sinatra told me, is the extent to which politics was always a part of his life. "He was born into a family that was very politically motivated," she said, especially his mother, Dolly, who was a local Democratic campaign worker in Hoboken, New Jersey. "Dad says that he was carrying placards for candidates when he couldn't read what was on the signs. Politics were run out of the kitchens" in those days, Tina added. "I remember he taught me" about "potholder campaigns. They'd give gifts to the woman of the house, because she would be the one who would be making certain the voters voted."

Jack Kennedy was special, Tina said. Her father was strongly attracted to Kennedy's "lifestyle. And his power. I know they had a lot of fun together." Both before and after winning the presidency, Kennedy especially enjoyed weekend visits to Sinatra's home in Palm Springs, with its routine womanizing. "It's not as though the president and Dad would meet to play golf," Tina said. "Their small circle of friends would come together and have a good time. It was a place to escape to. I was never, ever there. That was not a weekend you brought the kids into."

Her father, Tina added, "was a happy bachelor-type guy. He was single. Jack Kennedy wasn't."

J. Edgar Hoover's FBI had picked up some hints of the preelection bargaining between Kennedy and the Chicago outfit, but it could not make them public because of the way the information was gathered. Beginning in the late 1950s, FBI agents had begun installing bugging devices in organized crime hangouts across the nation, without any specific court authorization to do so. Three bugs were put in place in Chicago. One of them produced many conversations — sometimes in Sicilian dialect — both before and after November 1960, in which Sam Giancana talked about an election deal with Joe Kennedy. In his 1989 memoir, *Man Against the Mob*, William F. Roemer, Jr., who was a special agent in the FBI's Chicago office in the early 1960s, revealed that Giancana had been overheard on a still-unreleased FBI wiretap discussing a straightforward election deal: mob support in return for a commitment from the Kennedy administration "to back off from the FBI investigation of Giancana." Transcripts of these conversations, with the source concealed, were circulated, in some cases during the campaign, on a need-to-know basis throughout the Justice Department.

Giancana also bragged, off microphone, about his influence. In *My Story*, a 1977 memoir by Judith Campbell Exner, the Los Angeles woman who was sexually involved with Kennedy in the early 1960s while also meeting with Giancana, the mob leader is quoted as telling her, "Listen, honey, if it wasn't for me your boyfriend wouldn't even be in the White House."

Giancana was not exaggerating. In a 1997 interview for this book, G. Robert Blakey, a former special prosecutor for the Justice Department, said that the FBI wiretaps, many of which have yet to be made public, confirmed that the Chicago syndicate used all its muscle to support Kennedy. "There has been a problem with vote fraud in Chicago really since the turn of the century," said Blakey, who obtained access to the wiretaps in the late 1970s while serving as chief counsel to the House Assassinations Committee. The FBI bugs in Chicago, he told me, demonstrated "beyond doubt, in my judgment, that enough votes were stolen — let me repeat that — stolen in Chicago to give Kennedy a sufficient margin that he carried the state of Illinois." The electronic surveillance also showed that organized crime's control of the voting was far more extensive than has been previously known, Blakey said: Giancana was overheard before one election discussing the specific number of votes a corrupt Illinois congressman was to receive.

"The surveillance in Chicago also establishes that money generated by the mob was put into the 1960 [national] election," Blakey told me. The funds traveled from the singer Frank Sinatra, who was a close friend of Sam Giancana's, "to Joe Kennedy. Can you say mob money made a difference?" Blakey asked. "My judgment is yes." In return, Giancana and his colleagues were convinced, Blakey told me, that "the Kennedys would do something for them"— reduce FBI pressure on their activities.

No two men could have emerged from backgrounds more different than those of Jack Kennedy of Hyannis Port and Palm Beach and Sam Giancana of Chicago. But the men had much in common. Each was obsessed with women; each was fascinated by Hollywood and was found fascinating in return; each learned how to operate in secrecy; and each could rigorously compartmentalize his life. Giancana was a foul-mouthed Mafia murderer who took on a top-secret mission for the CIA in 1960 and 1961 and never talked publicly about what he did. Kennedy was a brilliant politician who could openly espouse the idealism of a New Frontier and the Peace Corps while being deeply involved in a world of secret escapades that could destroy his career.

Giancana, born in 1908, began his criminal career as a hit man for Al Capone in the area known as Little Italy or The Patch, just west of downtown Chicago. By age twenty, Giancana had reportedly murdered dozens of men on his way to gaining control of the Chicago Mafia. His first conviction, for auto theft, came at the age of seventeen; he was arrested three times in connection with murder investigations by the time he was twenty. In all, Giancana was arrested sixty times during his career. By the late 1950s, his operation was skimming millions of dollars off mob-dominated gambling casinos in Las Vegas and in Havana, Cuba, and it had both political and economic control of at least six heavily populated wards in Chicago. The Chicago Mafia also exercised direct control over mobster and Teamsters Union activities in Cleveland, St. Louis, Kansas City, Las Vegas, and Los Angeles.

"Giancana was just a killer, that's all," Sandy Smith, the former chief investigative reporter for *Time* magazine who spent twenty years covering organized crime in Chicago, recalled in an interview for this book. "And he was proud of it. As a boss, if there was a problem, he'd listen to a very brief description and then say, 'Hit him! Hit him!' There were a lot of hits." The mob boss "couldn't really talk to you," Smith told me. "Giancana would curse and scream and howl and try to intimidate you. He was, in almost every respect, a savage."

Nonetheless, Giancana was immensely popular in Hollywood. His biographers usually date his ties there to the mid-1950s, a time when the Chicago mob was migrating to the West Coast. Yet Giancana's daughter, Antoinette, in her 1984 memoir, *Mafia Princess,* told of her 1949 trip to Hollywood as a teenager, during which a major producer fell all over himself giving her a guided tour of the Metro-Goldwyn-Mayer studio. "I was treated with as much respect as if I had been one of the studio's superstars," she wrote. By the late 1950s, Giancana, often identifying himself as Sam Flood, was openly socializing in Las Vegas with the entertainers, who were paid enormous sums to perform at hotels whose casinos he controlled. His close friend was Frank Sinatra, and Giancana became a fixture among Sinatra's famed Rat Pack, the group of singers and comedians who moved easily through Hollywood, Democratic politics, and organized crime. The actor Peter Lawford, who married Patricia Kennedy in 1954, was a charter member of the clique. In 1960 Giancana began what would become a long-term romance with Phyllis McGuire, one of the three singing McGuire Sisters, then at the top of their career. Bill Woodfield, a Hollywood photographer who was on full-time assignment for Frank Sinatra, recalled in a 1995 interview for this book that during the heyday of Rat Pack glamour, Giancana began showing up almost every day on the set of a movie in which McGuire and Sinatra were starring. Giancana sat next to Woodfield, who was to shoot still photographs of each scene. "I never photographed Sam," Woodfield told me, "although I took hundreds of Phyllis. A photographer knows what not to shoot."*

Further direct evidence about a deal between the Kennedy family and Sam Giancana was provided for this book by Jeanne Humphreys,

---

* Woodfield came to understand, he said, that Sinatra considered himself "to be the ambassador between the U.S. government and the mob." The photographer told of once being on assignment with Sinatra in Miami and accompanying him and some of his gangster friends to a dog track, where several scenes were to be shot. During a break for lunch, Sinatra called out, "Billy, put in a roll and take some pictures for me . . . just me." Woodfield then heard one of the gangsters tell another, "Come on. We're going to get our picture with Frank." The other responded: "Take a picture? I'm

the second wife of Murray Humphreys, a close colleague of Giancana's. Humphreys, a Welshman who died in 1965, was considered to be the brains and a dominant force behind the Chicago mob, but he was barred from formally becoming its leader because he was not Sicilian. Jeanne Humphreys, who now lives alone and under a different name in the suburbs of a major southern city, had been a teenage bar girl when she began an affair with her husband-to-be in the late 1940s. She was married to the dapper gang leader, who was famed among Chicago journalists for his style and intelligence, from 1957 until 1962. "Murray told me everything," Mrs. Humphreys said. "I was stuck in the middle of it all. He had to tell me.

"I know all about the Kennedys — the election," she told me. "It consumed our lives that year [1960]." In her account, Humphreys initially resisted Giancana's pleas for a political commitment to Kennedy, essentially because Humphreys had himself done bootlegging business with Joe Kennedy during Prohibition and did not trust him. "Murray called him a four-flusher and a double-crosser," Jeanne Humphreys told me. Kennedy was involved in smuggling liquor from Canada into the Detroit area, Humphreys told his wife, "and hijacked his own load that had already been paid for and took it and sold it somewhere else all over again. He [Humphreys] never stopped talking about what a jerk [Kennedy] was."

The question was finally put to a vote among Giancana, Humphreys, and three other Mafia leaders in Chicago — Paul Ricca, Anthony Accardo, and Frank Ferraro. Humphreys was the only one to vote against the commitment to Kennedy. "He hated having to go along with the outfit's vote to back Kennedy," Jeanne Humphreys recalled. "It was a constant source of aggravation for him. If he was outvoted on something, he was outvoted by the Italians. He'd say the spaghetti eaters and spaghetti benders stuck together. But he went along. The guarantee was that the investigators would lay off the outfit. That was the assurance [they] got from Joe Kennedy.

not supposed to be in the country." The exchange left Woodfield a little unnerved. Pete Hamill told me of once being asked by Sinatra to ghostwrite his autobiography. Hamill, aware that the book would be a bestseller, told the singer that he would consider doing so — but Sinatra would have to tell the truth about the women, the politicians, and the mob guys. Sinatra told Hamill he could live with the first two requirements, but not the third: "I don't want someone knocking on the fucking door."

"I was an airhead," Mrs. Humphreys added. "I didn't know then that a president could be elected on the whim of Chicago mobsters. In my ignorance, I thought majority ruled."

The reminiscences of Jeanne Humphreys were confirmed by a handwritten diary she compiled during her years with Humphreys. The diary, made available in part for this book, provides a seemingly candid and often droll account of her husband's role in the 1960 election. "It's ironic," one entry noted, "that most of the behind-the-scenes participants in the Kennedy campaign could not vote because they had criminal records." Electoral politics, Jeanne Humphreys wrote at another point, "was a bunch of crooks run by a bunch of crooks."

A previously unpublished FBI biography of Murray Humphreys covering the years 1957 to 1961 further supports her account. The FBI file, dated May 17, 1961, and also made available for this book, describes the little-known Humphreys as "being one of the prime leaders of the underworld in the Chicago area." By the mid-1950s, it adds, Humphreys, Giancana, and the voting mobsters were "members of what might be called the governing board of organized criminals in the Chicago area." Humphreys' areas of responsibility included "the maintenance of contact with politicians, attorneys, public officials, and labor union leaders in order to influence these people to act in behalf of the interests of the underworld." The FBI specifically noted Humphreys' close ties to the Teamsters Union and depicted him as "the go-between" for organized crime and the Teamsters in their joint effort to become entrenched in the lucrative Las Vegas hotel and gambling business.

Sandy Smith, who interviewed Humphreys several times while working for the *Chicago Sun-Times* in the early 1960s, described him as "the fixer" for the Chicago syndicate. "Humphreys had the ability to go into a judge's chambers and talk to a judge," Smith told me. "He could go into the Department of Justice and talk to lawyers there. He could talk to the Internal Revenue Service. Humphreys was a hard guy to dislike."

Humphreys had been one of attorney Abe Marovitz's clients in the years before Marovitz became a Chicago judge. "He was like a good businessman," Marovitz told me. "His talk was different than most hoodlums. He wasn't a vulgar guy. He controlled unions, lots of unions," and "they gave substantial money to folks in politics." But Humphreys' influence was not based on his appearance, the retired judge noted: "It was strictly muscle. Either you went along with him, or you found yourself shot in the head or someplace. It was just one of those tough things in those days."

Jeanne Humphreys' firsthand descriptions of her husband's attempts to corrupt the electoral process are consistent with Smith's view and the FBI file. In her account, the mob's endorsement of Jack Kennedy and its determination to get him elected led to two two-week meetings in Chicago: one in July, before the Democratic convention, and one in late October, before the election. During those meetings, Humphreys and his wife were sequestered in a suite at the Hilton Hotel, as Humphreys coordinated the politicking. "We weren't staying there," Mrs. Humphreys said of the Hilton. "We were stuck there — two weeks at a time. I was not allowed to go out, as we were sure we were being surveilled. This was very secret. Murray's phone rang off the hook. Always politicians and Teamsters.

"This was the whole country," she added. "The people coming to the hotel were Teamsters from all over. The Chicago outfit was coordinating the whole country — Kansas, St. Louis, Cleveland. They were coming in from everywhere, then fanning out across the country." The mob-dominated union officials were coming to the hotel suite, Mrs. Humphreys explained, "to get instructions from Murray. When we went back in October, it was just a follow-up, to see that everything went the right way. They got Kennedy elected."

A diary entry provided more detail of Humphreys' careful planning. "Lists were everywhere," Mrs. Humphreys wrote.

> Murray was arranging lists in categories of politicians, unions, lawyers and contacts. . . . I could see the list had at least thirty to forty names. . . . I didn't have time to think or care about the election. It was a foregone conclusion anyway and I didn't doubt that Murray's endeavors would succeed. He was so confident and low key about electing the president that I adopted the same attitude. . . . He didn't expect any accolades and was content to see Mooney [Giancana] bask in the glory and praise.

Government files released under the Freedom of Information Act show that the FBI learned almost immediately that Humphreys had registered, under the name of Fishman, at the Hilton Hotel in Chicago in late October 1960, just as Jeanne Humphreys recounted. Humphreys, aware that he was constantly being monitored, seemed to go out of his way to be misleading. In one telephone call intercepted while he was at the Hilton, the FBI quoted Humphreys as casually telling an associate, "Since I heard all the Irish are voting for Kennedy, I'm voting for Nixon, the Protestant." Nothing in the FBI documents, as made public, linked Humphreys with the Kennedy campaign.

Jeanne Humphreys, who was in her late sixties when she spoke to me and being treated for cancer, said she first learned of the Kennedy connection when she accused her husband of "partying with the celebrities" while on a trip to the West Coast. He told her, "No, we're working. Sam is golfing with Joe Kennedy. They're doing business." Frank Sinatra had been the "middleman" in arranging the Kennedy-Giancana golf dates. Humphreys told her that Joe Kennedy had promised "to lay off the mob" in exchange for political support from the Giancana outfit.

Mrs. Humphreys recalled that various locals belonging to the Teamsters Union, headed by Jimmy Hoffa, were under pressure to help get out the vote for Kennedy, legally and otherwise. At the time, Hoffa had been instrumental in putting the huge assets of the Teamsters pension fund behind the Chicago outfit's expansion into the gambling and hotel business in Las Vegas: millions of dollars had been lent to organized crime front men, with millions more in the pipeline. But Hoffa, who became an avid supporter of Richard Nixon, posed a special problem for Humphreys during the election campaign because he became convinced that "by loaning union money to the outfit . . . he was contributing" to the election efforts of the hated Kennedys. Mrs. Humphreys overheard Hoffa indignantly complaining to her husband after one meeting in Florida that "my members' money is . . . going to get that son of a bitch elected." Humphreys later told her that Hoffa "is a hard man to sell. I have to sell that Robert Kennedy to Hoffa."

*   *   *

As the mob did its politicking, J. Edgar Hoover was sifting through his agents' reports and keeping up-to-date files. Joe and Jack Kennedy were careful with Hoover as they were with few other men; Hoover, they knew, did not approve of the candidate's personal life.

By the late 1950s, according to Cartha DeLoach, one of Hoover's deputies, Joe Kennedy and the FBI director had become friends. "Two big men who felt it necessary to know each other," DeLoach told me in an interview. "They both had the same conservative politics. Hoover catered to him, to some extent, and Joe Kennedy catered to Mr. Hoover, knowing of the FBI's capabilities insofar as getting information. Not using it for blackmail purposes," DeLoach insisted, "but getting it and having it in files. Strange as it may seem to some people today, who constantly castigate Hoover as an individual who leaked information, who extorted in order to save his job and to protect the FBI, he had a deep sense of loyalty to the presidency."

Hoover, for reasons not clear, chose to pretend early in 1960 that he knew little about Jack Kennedy when he ordered DeLoach to review the files. "He called in the following day," DeLoach told me, "and I told him Jack had quite a relationship with Inga Arvad and other sexual escapades. And that, frankly, while he was somewhat of a bright individual, he had a very immoral background. Hoover told me, 'That is not right. You have misinterpreted the files. You're talking about the older brother of John F. Kennedy. Go back and recheck those files.' When he called back, I was able to tell him, 'I am not wrong. This is the man who is a candidate for the presidency.' That was the first that Hoover knew about him. Hoover knew nothing about the sexual background until we checked the files." Hoover was troubled by the files, DeLoach said, because "he did feel that the presidency should be a very dignified office, representing the people of the United States, the strongest nation in the world. Jack Kennedy and his constant acts of immorality certainly offended Hoover."

By 1960 the FBI director had become a genius at intimidating politicians. He was born in 1895 in segregated Washington, the youngest of four children, and grew up in a solidly middle-class Protestant environment. A stutterer in his youth, Hoover went into adulthood with a series of idiosyncrasies and obsessions that tormented those who worked under him. FBI agents had to meet Hoover's standards of dress and physical appearance; sweaty palms or a colored shirt could lead to a dismissal. The agents learned not to tell the director what he did not want to know. Hoover sought to control those above him — the presidents and members of Congress to whom he reported — through the secret dossiers he kept in his office. Many of those files were reportedly destroyed after his death, in 1972.

After working his way through law school, Hoover found his first significant job in the Alien Enemy Bureau of the Justice Department, where he dealt with foreigners accused of disloyalty. By 1919 he was the Justice Department's expert on radicalism and aliens, and in 1920 he took part in the infamous Palmer Raids against suspected communists, which led to more than four thousand arrests. Throughout his career, Hoover remained obsessed with rooting out communists, socialists, and other suspected subversives from American society; his concern was not only for what the radicals did but for what they thought.

In 1924 Hoover was appointed head of the Bureau of Investigation, which later became the FBI, and he moved brilliantly to increase the size, skill, and morale of the agency. He was one of the first to push for the establishment of a national fingerprint center, which revolutionized crime fighting. He also understood the value of public relations. By the mid-1930s, Hoover was constantly striving to personify himself, and *his* FBI, as being in the forefront of the war against crime, stopping such killers — amid front-page fanfare — as Machine Gun Kelly and John Dillinger. He began in those years what would become three decades of close cooperation with Hollywood, leading to a series of wildly popular "G-man" movies: one, starring James Cagney, fixed Hoover's public image as the nation's foremost crime fighter. In 1936, with World War II looming, President Roosevelt authorized Hoover to investigate Nazi and communist subversion in the United States, giving the FBI the right to become entrenched in all areas of domestic surveillance. Hoover expanded the FBI's use of bugging devices and wiretaps — and also expanded his personal intelligence-gathering on politicians, public figures, and journalists.

Hoover's hypocrisies and insecurities became more pronounced as his prestige and authority grew. For more than thirty years he took vacations with Clyde Tolson, the FBI's assistant director, who maintained an apartment close to Hoover's home. The two men went on at least two extensive vacations a year — never publicly depicted as such — to swanky resorts in Florida and California, where Hoover indulged his fondness for racetrack betting. Hoover's favorite key lime pie was regularly flown at government expense from Florida to Washington. Rumors about the two bachelors and their personal relationship have persisted until today. Visitors to the Hoover home were astonished to find that the prudish FBI director, who constantly inveighed against what he called the decline of public morality among America's youth, had installed a gallery of nude photographs in the basement rec room, including one of Marilyn Monroe. Over the years, FBI agents spent thousands of hours maintaining and improving his home. By 1960, as Kennedy campaigned for the presidency, Hoover was insisting that when outside Washington he be driven only in new black Cadillac sedans, which had to be immaculately clean. The drivers were instructed to plan their routes with no left turns — a Hoover edict issued after his car was struck while turning left. When on the road, agents were required to reserve suites only in Hoover-approved hotels, which provided the specified bed, mattress, and down pillows.

Like Jack Kennedy, Hoover knew few limits.

Joe Kennedy learned all about Hoover's power, and his obsessions, during his disastrous prewar opposition to FDR's determination to wage war against Nazi Germany. Kennedy had worked hard since then at buttering up the FBI director. His role as a special service contact for the FBI ended when the program was suspended after the war; he was reinstated in 1950 by Hoover as one of two such agents in Boston. At the time, an FBI letter described Kennedy as having "innumerable contacts in the international diplomatic set" and added that he "has expressed a willingness to use his entree into those circles for any advantage the Bureau might desire. . . ."

No amount of flattery was too much, as Joe Kennedy realized. Kennedy's FBI files, released under the Freedom of Information Act, are full of praise for Hoover in letters and statements from father, sons, and daughters. One postwar FBI report quoted Eunice Kennedy as telling colleagues at a Conference on Citizenship in Boston that her father had recently met with Hoover and "was very much impressed with the administrative organization and the operation of the bureau." Jack Kennedy, after his election to the Senate, was quoted in a confidential FBI report to Hoover that said he believed "the FBI to be the only real Government agency worthy of its salt and expressed his admiration for your accomplishments." In 1953 Joe Kennedy was appointed to serve as a member of a federal commission on government efficiency, which, while accomplishing little, did complete a study on defense spending. The elder Kennedy, according to FBI files, managed to relay word to Hoover expressing "shock" at the extent of Pentagon waste and mismanagement. "The deeper he delves into the matter, the more he appreciates your work," Hoover was told.

Joe Kennedy's courting of Hoover paid off in 1956, when he was nominated by Eisenhower to serve on a high-powered new advisory group known as the President's Board of Consultants on Foreign Intelligence Activities.* An FBI security check ignored the extensive allegations about Kennedy's involvement in bootlegging during Prohibition and glossed over his dubious record as ambassador to England. A synopsis of the report ended with these words about Kennedy: "He has frequently expressed admiration for the Director and the work of the Bureau." Kennedy spent six months on the intelligence review panel, and made at least one secret trip overseas to review CIA operations. His mission created mayhem in the CIA station in Rome when Kennedy demanded — and got — access to the names of the agency's undercover field agents inside the Italian government and the Vatican. Thomas F. McCoy, then a CIA operations officer in Rome, said in an interview for this book, "All he was doing was pushing the view of his right-wing friends in the Vatican — the aging monsignors who were out of things and wishing for the good old days." McCoy added, "Joe had his own point of view, which many

---

* The committee, which exists today as the President's Foreign Intelligence Advisory Board (PFIAB), was headed by Dr. James R. Killian, Jr., president of the Massachusetts Institute of Technology, who played a major role in developing America's satellite intelligence capability. Others on the board included retired general James H. Doolittle; Edward L. Ryerson, retired chairman of Inland Steel; and the Wall Street lawyer Robert A. Lovett. Kennedy resigned from the committee on July 25, 1956, explaining in a letter to President Eisenhower that he was becoming "deeply involved" in political activities on behalf of his son, then seeking the vice presidential nomination.

people were supporting" in the aftermath of Senator Joseph Mc-Carthy's loyalty investigations. "He didn't want us to support anybody who was mildly left: 'If they weren't communists, why were they acting like communists?'"*

Joseph Kennedy was thus no outsider when it came to the good — and the bad — of the American intelligence community. He undoubtedly shared his understanding of the CIA's clandestine world with his sons Jack and Bobby, and perhaps with J. Edgar Hoover.

In declassified files there is a strong suggestion that Kennedy may have privately briefed Hoover on what he was learning about the CIA, a conversation, if it took place, that would surely have delighted the bureaucratic-minded FBI director, who was often at war with the CIA and other government intelligence agencies. FBI files show that on February 16, 1956, Hoover told his key deputies about a visit the day before with Kennedy, who informed him that he planned to analyze the issue of "duplication of coverage abroad by the military, CIA and the State Department. . . . I discussed with Mr. Kennedy generally some of the weaknesses which we have observed in the operations of CIA, particularly as to the organizational set-up and the compartmentation that exists within that Agency." There is no evidence in the publicly released files of any further contact between Kennedy and Hoover about the CIA, but the files do show that Kennedy continued to send flattering personal letters to Hoover as his son began his presidential campaign.

Joe Kennedy's fawning relationship with Hoover was not the only thing the Kennedys had going for them. The FBI director was then just five years away from reaching the federal government's compulsory retirement age of seventy, and his overriding interest was to remain in power. Hoover, and Jack Kennedy, understood that only the president of the United States, whatever his private morality, had the

---

* Somebody in Washington obviously had qualms about Kennedy's visit. William L. Colby, who would become director of the CIA, was a senior officer in the Rome station in 1956. Prior to Kennedy's arrival there, Colby recalled in an interview for this book, he had been given secret instructions from CIA headquarters that he and others in the station were to cooperate with Kennedy about covert operations but were not to provide him with the names of any agents. Kennedy got his way, nonetheless, Colby said, by telling the station: "Either you're going to give me the names or I'm going to go to the president and quit this job."

authority to keep Hoover on the job. Hoover's reappointment was assured — but Kennedy first had to win the election.

There was at least one known backup plan in case the Kennedy campaign's mixture of hard work, charm, money, and gangster connections failed and left Jack Kennedy on election night with only a small plurality of electoral college votes. The campaign feared that the twenty-six unpledged electors in Mississippi, Alabama, and Georgia — fourteen of whom would shortly announce they would vote for Senator Harry Byrd, amid reports that the others might join their revolt — could take away the presidency. The plan was centered, not surprisingly, on money.

Oscar Wyatt, a wealthy oilman, banker, and Democratic Party fund-raiser in Corpus Christi, Texas, spent election night anxiously watching returns at home, as did the rest of the nation. "We didn't know whether Jack won," Wyatt recalled in an interview for this book. "If Illinois went against Jack, we'd have to get the Mississippi vote"— the eight unpledged electors in that state. Wyatt was telephoned at home late in the evening by Clifton Carter, one of Lyndon Johnson's most trusted political lieutenants, and told: "You've got to get one hundred thousand dollars to Mississippi tonight." Wyatt was further told that each of the delegates would cost $10,000. "I owned a substantial interest in a bank in Corpus Christi and got the bank opened up and got the money," Wyatt told me, adding that getting a bank president to open up in the middle of the night was no easy chore. Wyatt arranged for his private plane to be fueled and readied for an immediate flight to Jackson, Mississippi. It was now eleven P.M., and Wyatt decided to stay at the airport.

At two A.M. Carter telephoned again and told him to hold the plane. "Don't leave." A third call came at four A.M. "Don't leave." Finally, at six-thirty A.M., Wyatt, asleep on a couch in his hangar, was called a last time by Carter and told, "Daley brought it in. Go to sleep." The plane returned to its hangar. When interviewed in 1995, Wyatt was chairman of the board and chief executive officer of the Coastal Corporation, in Houston.

The Mississippi electors, without any $10,000 inducements, duly cast their ballots for Senator Byrd on December 19, 1960. Their vote was little more than a gesture; Kennedy defeated Richard Nixon by a total of 300 to 219 in the electoral college (Hawaii's 3 votes were added later) and was ratified as the thirty-fifth president of the United States.

Hoover, with his access to the secrets of electronic surveillance, knew that the election corruption went far beyond Illinois. But he did not act on what he knew. The day after the election — the day Jack Kennedy announced he would reappoint Hoover as FBI director — Hoover summoned Philip Hochstein, editorial director of the Newhouse newspaper group. "When I got to his office," Hochstein later told the British journalist Anthony Summers, "I offered my congratulations on the announcement of his appointment by the President-elect. He replied in a surly manner, 'Kennedy isn't the President-elect.' He said the election had been stolen in a number of states, including New Jersey, where my office was, and Missouri, where Newhouse had recently bought a paper. . . . It was quite a harangue, and I think Hoover wanted me to be part of a crusade to undo the election. . . . I didn't tell anyone at the time."

Sometime shortly after Jack Kennedy took office, the FBI in Chicago forwarded a report on the Illinois election to the Justice Department. "I can tell you," Robert Blakey, then in Justice, said in an interview for this book, "that the fact that it was stolen was brought to Robert Kennedy's attention." Nothing happened.

The lack of action was precisely why Joe Kennedy had insisted after the election that Bobby be nominated as attorney general. Jack, always reluctant to take on his father, at first waffled. "I don't know what to do with Bobby," he told George Smathers. "He busted his tail for me." The two men were talking, Smathers recalled in an interview for this book, while dangling their feet in the water at the shallow end of the pool at Palm Beach. Joe Kennedy was reading the morning papers at the other end. "The Old Man," Kennedy said, "wants him to be attorney general." Smathers, a former U.S. attorney who was not an admirer of Bobby's, was stunned. "He never had a case in his life," he recalled telling Kennedy. "He never argued in a courtroom. If you make him an assistant secretary of defense, he'll have a lot of power. It's an appropriate job for a guy who has never done a damn thing."

Jack Kennedy's response was intimidating, Smathers recalled: "Why don't you tell the Old Man?"

Smathers accepted the challenge and walked to the other end of the pool. "'Excuse me, Mr. Ambassador. Jack and I have just been talking about Bobby. He wants to do something with Bobby. I thought he could be assistant secretary of defense, and then in a year or two he could move up.' Joe said, 'Jack! Come here.' Jack walked over. [Joe] said, 'I want to tell you, your brother Bobby gave you his life blood. You know it and I know it. By God, he deserves to be attorney general and by God, that's what he's going to be. Do you understand that?' Jack said, 'Yes sir.' And so Bobby became attorney general."

The Republicans quickly learned all they needed to know about Kennedy loyalty. Everett Dirksen, the ranking Republican senator from Illinois, later telephoned Cartha DeLoach and requested a full-scale FBI investigation of the election; he had evidence, he said, that the election had been stolen. "I told him the FBI had received considerable information and we sent that information to the Department [of Justice]," DeLoach recalled. "We'd be glad to receive his information, or any other information, and refer [it] to the attorney general. But Senator Dirksen said, 'You say turn it over to the attorney general?' I said, 'That's the only recourse we have.' And he said, 'Thanks a hell of a lot,' and slammed the phone down. He knew that Bobby Kennedy was the attorney general.

"And," DeLoach added, Dirksen "probably knew that the Department of Justice had already advised the FBI not to conduct any further investigation."

11

CAMPAIGN SECRET

Jack Kennedy and Richard Nixon campaigned in the fall of 1960 as security-conscious Cold Warriors, with few substantive disagreements on foreign policy. The crucial difference, as had been foreseen and carefully orchestrated by Jack's father, was Kennedy's celebrity status, and his confidence and ease before television cameras.

Kennedy's good looks also gave him an enormous advantage over the jowly and sweaty Richard Nixon in the unprecedented series of national televised debates that were the most dramatic events of the campaign. Public opinion polls later revealed that it was Kennedy's appearance, and not what he said, that carried the day in the first, and most heavily watched, of the four debates. Those who heard the first debate on radio were more inclined to vote for the deep-voiced Nixon.

Nixon's main asset was the fact of his service under Eisenhower, the avuncular leader whose presidency brought the nation to new heights of prosperity. Kennedy sought to undercut that advantage by proclaiming that America was suffering from a "missile gap," having fallen behind the Soviet Union in the production of intercontinental ballistic missiles (ICBMs). The charge was preposterous, as Kennedy had been privately told by many officials in the Eisenhower administration; America's secret U-2 spy planes had been recording the laggard pace of Soviet missile production since 1956. But the "gap" provided Kennedy with a strong political issue. As the election neared, public opinion polls showed that Americans were more concerned about short-range missiles from Cuba than about nuclear blockbusters from Russia. Fidel Castro's actions were making his anti-American policies a campaign issue: on October 14 he announced the nationalization of 382 U.S.-owned businesses in Cuba, including all banks and industries.

On the surface, Jack Kennedy and Fidel Castro had much in common. They were young, dynamic leaders who were physically attractive, articulate, and athletic; both lived on the edge and had enormous appetites for women. Both had come from families of means and attended elite schools, but Castro did what Kennedy could not conceive of doing — he turned on his father, a landowner in Oriente Province, and accused him of abusing his workers. In the mid-1950s, the increasingly radical Castro had organized the 26th of July Movement, a tiny guerrilla army in the Sierra Maestra, to campaign for land reform, free elections, public housing, and profit sharing — and an end to the corrupt presidency of Fulgencio Batista. Castro's movement gathered popular support from poorly paid factory workers and farmers, and eventually forced Batista to flee for his safety on New Year's Day, 1959.

Senator Kennedy, however, saw Cuba through his father's eyes; an island that had been safe for American investment before Castro — and where gambling and prostitution were legal. Under Batista, American corporations owned 40 percent of Cuba's sugar industry, 80 percent of its utilities, and 90 percent of mining. Havana's flourishing gambling casinos, nightclubs, and brothels, all of which Jack Kennedy had enjoyed during private visits in 1957 and 1958,*

---

* There were the usual sexual shenanigans. Commander Lionel Krisel, a former American naval attaché in Havana, recalled in a 1995 interview for this book being told that the U.S. Embassy had been visited by the Cuban police and military intelligence officials during one of Kennedy's stays in the late fifties and put on notice that the senator was of concern to them "for security reasons." The Cubans reported, Krisel told

were under the direct control of the leading organized crime families, who had spent untold millions in payoffs to the Batista regime.

Kennedy and Nixon campaigned relentlessly throughout the fall as vigorous foes of Fidel Castro. But Kennedy went much further than did Nixon, speaking emotionally of the need for the United States to help unleash those exile "freedom fighters" whose dream was to overthrow the Castro government. Kennedy's attacks on the communist "menace" off the shores of Florida struck a last-minute chord with the voters, who had no way of knowing that the handsome young senator was relying on briefings he had been given about the Eisenhower administration's top-secret invasion planning — and on his awareness that Nixon could say nothing in public that would reveal or disrupt those plans.

Jack Kennedy's successful election strategy had its beginnings not in 1960 but in 1952, when Richard Nixon's famous "Checkers" speech, named after a reference he made to the family dog, soured the men running the CIA on the young candidate for vice president. Nixon, a hard-line anticommunist who had been elected to the U.S. Senate from California, had emerged at the Republican National Convention as a surprise choice for the vice presidency on a ticket headed by General Dwight Eisenhower. The campaign was disrupted when newspapers began reporting on a private slush fund, said to total $18,000, that had been raised for the young senator by a group of seventy-six conservative California businessmen. The "fund" soon mushroomed into a major scandal that threatened both the Republican ticket and Nixon's future. On September 23, 1952, Nixon defended himself in a half-hour television speech, denying that any money had been spent for his personal use. He told the audience that

me, that Kennedy had been "going to bed with the wife of the Italian ambassador and 'You know those Italians.' They would hate" to have the young senator shot while on a visit to Havana. An embassy representative was assigned to tell Kennedy "to cut it out." Kennedy was staying at the home of Earl Smith, the American ambassador to Cuba, who was a social friend of the Kennedys and a strong Batista supporter. Many historians have said that Kennedy had a long-standing romance with Smith's wife, Florence. Krisel retired in 1975 from the navy as a captain and was living in Bel Air, California, when interviewed.

his wife, Patricia, did not have a mink coat but "a respectable Republican cloth coat," and confessed that his family had received a gift: "a little cocker spaniel — and our little girl — Tricia, the six-year-old — named it Checkers." He added that "the kids love the dog and . . . we're gonna keep it." The Checkers speech was a national sensation and solidified, forever, the nation into two groups: those who worshipped Nixon and those who hated him. The outpouring of support for Nixon overwhelmed Eisenhower's strong inclination to dump his running mate, and the two men went on to overwhelm Democrats Adlai Stevenson and John Sparkman in the November election.*

Nixon was far more vulnerable, in 1952 and in 1960, than anyone knew, except for a few officials of the Central Intelligence Agency. At the time of the Checkers speech, the top men at the CIA had unassailable evidence of a Nixon bribe: a copy of a check for $100,000, made out to Nixon, that he had deposited in his checking account at the Bank of California. The CIA's information was all the more dramatic, and politically damaging, because the bribe had been given to Nixon by Nicolae Malaxa, a controversial Romanian industrialist and metallurgist who had, during World War II, been a business partner of Albert Göring, brother of Field Marshal Hermann Göring. Malaxa had been a financial supporter of the pro-Nazi Romanian Iron Guard in early 1941, when the Guard's storm troopers were responsible for a vicious pogrom involving the murder of an estimated seven thousand Jews in Bucharest. After the war, Malaxa served the Communist leadership in Romania and was rewarded with the return of some $2.4 million in personal funds that had been seized by the party. Malaxa, suddenly wealthy, came to the United States on a trade mission in 1946 and stayed, despite repeated efforts by the Immigration and Naturalization Service to deport him. At the time of his death, in 1972, he was living on Fifth Avenue in New York City, still without citizenship.

Malaxa survived in America because of his money. In 1951, at the height of the Korean War, Malaxa organized a solely owned company

---

* In his memoir, *RN*, published in 1978, Nixon described the 1952 political crisis over the fund in full, but did not mention the two elements for which his televised speech remains famous: his wife's cloth coat and the dog, Checkers.

known as the Western Tube Corporation, whose stated purpose was to manufacture tubing for oil drilling. The company announced plans to build a factory in Whittier, California — Nixon's hometown. Nixon, as senator from California, signed a letter in September 1951 urging the federal government to give the firm a "certificate of necessity" and Malaxa a "first preference quota" for permanent residence in the United States, on the grounds that he was essential to the construction of the plant. At the time, Western Tube had the same address and telephone number in Whittier as Nixon's former law firm, Bewley, Knoop & Nixon. Western Tube never got beyond the paper stage and was later determined to be nothing more than a dummy corporation set up to help Malaxa's citizenship efforts. In 1952 Nixon proposed a bill in the Senate granting Malaxa the right to remain in the United States, but the legislation was quashed by Representative Emanuel Celler of New York, the Democratic chairman of the House Judiciary Committee, who later explained that he saw "something rather suspicious" about it.

Nixon denied any wrongdoing in his efforts on behalf of Malaxa, and the issue attracted little press attention in the 1952 campaign; the focus was on the Nixon fund. But Malaxa was a source of enduring interest to the Romanian émigré community in the United States. Its leaders, Constantin Visoianu and Alexandre Cretzianu, were doing all they could to get Malaxa out of the country, fearing that his ties to the fascist Iron Guard would taint every Romanian exile. The dispute appeared to be just another tedious postwar argument among exiles jostling for position in America, but Visoianu and Cretzianu had far more influence than it seemed: they were secretly on the payroll of the CIA, as were the leaders of many anticommunist exile groups in America. Both were especially close to an officer named Gordon B. Mason, who had served undercover in the CIA station in Bucharest from 1947 to 1951 and had then returned to run the CIA's Romanian operations desk in Washington.

After Nixon's nomination as vice president, Visoianu, a former Romanian foreign minister, and Cretzianu, a former Romanian ambassador to Turkey, approached Mason and told him that Malaxa had bribed Nixon as part of his effort to remain in the United States. Their evidence was explicit, Mason reluctantly acknowledged in an interview for this book in 1996: they had a photographic copy of

Malaxa's check for $100,000 deposited by Nixon in his bank in Whittier. The money was apparently Malaxa's payoff to Nixon for his support in the Congress. One of the tellers in the bank was a Romanian exile, Mason told me, and had been paid by Visoianu and Cretzianu after turning over the copy of the check.

Mason wrote a report on the transaction, which quickly moved up the CIA's chain of command from Frank Wisner, who was director of clandestine and covert operations, to Allen Dulles, the deputy director, and finally to Walter Bedell "Beedle" Smith, who had been the CIA's director since October 1950. Smith, a retired army lieutenant general, had served loyally as Eisenhower's chief of staff during World War II — in Eisenhower's phrase, he had been "general manager of the war." Everyone knew that Smith would not be pleased by the information, which might well devastate the Eisenhower campaign. Mason was especially nervous. "I was the junior member of the clan," he recalled. "I handed the file to Beedle Smith. 'You son of a bitch,' he yells. 'What are you trying to do? Destroy Eisenhower?'" The CIA director was "purple-faced" with anger. "Where'd you get information like this? I'm not going to have it . . . scuttling Eisenhower." He ordered Mason and a colleague to bring to his office "every goddamned scrap" of paper on the affair. Mason did so, and Smith told him: "Just leave everything here. I'll take care of everything . . . everything."

After a week of silence, Smith summoned Mason and his superiors to another meeting and announced that he had "just had a call" from President Harry S. Truman "asking about the report. Which one of you sons of bitches leaked it?" Mason said nothing, but he was reasonably sure that the Romanian exile leaders, having heard no more from him, had taken their spectacular information to the White House. Smith told his subordinates at the meeting that he had told the president, in essence, "If you want this report, you'll have it with my resignation." The CIA director further said that he had told President Truman, misleadingly, that the report was a "two-edged sword"; Malaxa had been involved with Democrats as well as with Nixon. In fact, Malaxa had done nothing more than hire a number of Democrats as his attorneys.

Beedle Smith, Mason quickly realized, had no intention of permitting his agency — or the truth about Richard Nixon — to get in

the way of Eisenhower's election. Ever loyal to his former commanding general, Smith undoubtedly relayed what he knew about Nixon
to Eisenhower. That information, nowhere on the record to this day,
may have played a role in Eisenhower's initial decision to drop Nixon
from the ticket, which was reversed by the outpouring of public support after the Checkers speech. Whether or not Eisenhower ever discussed the Malaxa payment with Nixon, he remained ambivalent
about his vice president throughout his two terms in the presidency.
And Nixon came away from the Malaxa incident with a lifelong distrust of the CIA.

Smith may have stopped his associates from acting, but the men
in the upper echelon of the CIA knew that the vice presidential candidate was lying when he denied taking any bribes while in the Senate. Richard Nixon was not, in the CIA's phrase, "an honorable man."
This attitude, George Mason told me, explains why eight years later
some top leaders of the CIA, no longer ruled by Beedle Smith's iron
fist, strongly favored the election of Kennedy.

The election was going to be very close, and Nixon's chance of becoming president could hinge on the Eisenhower administration's
Cuba policy — which could succeed only if the CIA and the mob
murdered Fidel Castro before November.

The Eisenhower administration watched with increasing anxiety as
Castro, while talking about human rights and democracy, seized control of the press, rigged elections, nationalized industry, shut down
the gambling casinos, and moved increasingly close to the Soviet
Union. Five years earlier, another left-leaning Latin American leader,
President Jacobo Arbenz Guzman of Guatemala, had been successfully overthrown by the CIA in a bloodless coup d'état; inevitably,
there was talk in Washington of another coup. But Castro was far
more menacing to American interests than Arbenz, and this time
blood would be shed. In the late summer of 1959, Kenneth M. Crosby,
a stockbroker who was one of the leaders of the American business
community in Havana, was invited to Washington to give Allen
Dulles (the CIA's director since 1953) and two of his aides a secret
briefing on Castro. Crosby was no amateur in the intelligence business: he had spent five years with the FBI during World War II and

was working closely with James Noel, the CIA's current station chief in Havana. Crosby did not mince words, he recalled in a 1996 interview for this book; he told the CIA director that he and many of his business associates in Havana were convinced that "the only way to get rid of [Castro] was to kill him. He was such a powerful, powerful presence, and an evil influence." Crosby remembered describing Castro as "another Hitler. We already knew he was a communist." He told Dulles about Castro's "tremendous influence over the people" and compared his power to that of Rasputin.

The plotting against Castro intensified in early 1960, when Anastas Mikoyan, the Soviet deputy premier, negotiated a Soviet-Cuban trade pact during a visit to Havana. Within a few weeks, according to the 1975 report of the Senate Select Committee on Intelligence Activities (known as the Church Report, after the committee's chairman, Idaho Democrat Frank Church), there was agreement at the top of the Eisenhower administration that the Castro regime could only "be overthrown by the use of force." Further, "unless Fidel and Raul Castro and Che Guevara could be eliminated in one package," any covert action against the Cuban government "would be a long, drawn-out affair." The Soviet shootdown of the American U-2 piloted by Francis Gary Powers on May 1, 1960, and Eisenhower's subsequent lying about it, destroyed a planned summit meeting with Nikita Khrushchev and ended any chance of easing Cold War tensions. Castro did not help matters by pronouncing in July that the Monroe Doctrine was dead. "The only thing you can do with anything dead," he said, "is to bury it so that it will not poison the air."

According to the Church Report, the CIA made its first overt move to bring the Mafia into the assassination plotting against Castro in late August of 1960. Richard M. Bissell, Jr. — the CIA's deputy director of plans — was the man in charge of dirty tricks. Bissell, a former economics professor at Yale University and the Massachusetts Institute of Technology, was a golden boy inside the agency, famed for his intellect and his suffer-no-fools attitude. There was no question about Bissell's ability to get things done: working in intense secrecy, he had masterminded the development of the U-2, whose dramatic high-flying missions over the Soviet Union opened up what had been a closed society. Without hint of publicity, the U-2 went from the drawing board in 1954 to successful flight two years later. It was delivered ahead of schedule and under budget. Now Bissell had been given the task of getting rid of the Castro regime, and he turned to Sheffield Edwards, director of the CIA's office of security, for fresh ideas. Bissell authorized a cash payment of $150,000 for the operation. What happened next has been the subject of congressional reports, books, and television documentaries over the past two decades.

The CIA was convinced that the Mafia had access to reliable gunmen in Cuba, but someone was needed to serve as a middleman — to broker the deal. Edwards and his deputy, James O'Connell, agreed that the man for the job was a former FBI agent named Robert A. Maheu, a private investigator who was known for his extensive contacts in Los Angeles and in Las Vegas, where he lived. Maheu, in a 1994 interview for this book, recalled that O'Connell asked him to get in touch with Johnny Rosselli, who had been involved with gambling, extortion, and other syndicate operations since the 1930s. "They asked if I'd help 'dispose' of Castro," Maheu recalled. He was reluctant. "It was not an easy decision for me. I'd be the cutout between the Mafia and the CIA — now I've got a big army on each side of me." Maheu decided that killing Castro fell within the parameters of a "just war," and arranged a lunch in Los Angeles with Rosselli to tell him what the mission was and that the CIA was behind it. Rosselli told Maheu "he'd have to check it with someone in Chicago."

By 1960 the handsome and well-spoken Rosselli had become the representative of the Chicago mob on the West Coast. His gangster credentials gave him a special cachet and status; he moved easily among the social set in Los Angeles, and in the late 1940s even dabbled briefly as a film producer. It was through those connections that he had met Maheu; through Maheu he had been introduced to the CIA's James O'Connell at a cocktail party. The CIA saw Rosselli in a less sinister light than the FBI did: the FBI knew him as a mobster believed to be personally involved in no fewer than thirteen Mafia murders — a top man, directly responsible to Sam Giancana.

*　*　*

In September 1960 events in Cuba heightened the Eisenhower administration's feeling of urgency. On the evening of September 14, Cuban counterintelligence agents seized three CIA operatives as they were attempting to bug the New China News Agency, in downtown Havana. The men, who claimed that they were tourists (travel to Cuba was not yet illegal), were arrested while drilling into a ceiling, with electronic gear scattered around them. They were tried a few months later in Havana, found guilty of espionage, and slammed into a Cuban prison, where they remained until April 21, 1963, when the Kennedy administration negotiated their release.

Everything about the case has remained highly secret, until this book. One of the three agents, David L. Christ, was perhaps the CIA's most sophisticated electronic eavesdropper. He worked for a top-secret unit in the agency — the D branch of foreign intelligence (FI-D). One of the essential missions of D branch was to penetrate foreign embassies — those friendly to the United States or otherwise — and obtain up-to-date codebooks. Christ was the best break-in man the CIA had; by some accounts, he had successfully penetrated dozens of European and Asian embassies. In a CIA internal critique of the New China News Agency mission, prepared in the fall of 1960, Christ was described as "probably the most knowledge-able officer in the Agency of world-wide audio operations"; he had been briefed on the Eisenhower administration's invasion planning for Cuba. If the Cubans learned who he was and, as was feared, compelled him to talk, the agent could provide Castro with extremely damaging information. David Christ was as potentially lethal to American interests as Francis Gary Powers had been after he was shot down over Russia, displayed on television, and tried for espionage. No one in Washington wanted to see David Christ put on public trial or displayed by Castro's side at a public rally.* To the CIA's relief, no one ever did.

---

* In its after-action assessment, the CIA depicted Christ's mission as full of ineptness and miscalculations. Most significantly, Christ had been in Cuba in August 1960, under cover as a tourist, and went home for a week before beginning his fateful mission. While at home, he told a colleague that he "believed he had been under surveillance during the first trip." Nonetheless, he returned to Havana once again as a "tourist," at a time, the CIA report noted, when "few genuine tourists were traveling." There were

The arrests increased the CIA's sense of purpose. "There was such hatred for Castro," one senior CIA official told me. "Word kept on filtering down that the honorable thing for an intelligence officer to do was to think of ways to get rid of Castro."

Ten days after the September arrests of the CIA operatives in Havana, Maheu flew to Miami, where he met Giancana for the first time and discussed the ground rules for working with him and Rosselli. "I made an agreement with them," Maheu told me. "This was a one-shot deal, and I would not discuss anything [about their organized crime business] that I happened to overhear." Giancana's assignment was to find someone close to Castro who could do the killing.

In interviews in 1995 and 1996, Maheu insisted that the recruitment of Rosselli — and the subsequent involvement of Sam Giancana — was sheer happenstance triggered by the chance meeting of Rosselli and O'Connell, the CIA's security officer, at a cocktail party. "It was so logical," he explained to me. "I'm having a party. Johnny is in town. I invite him over. I know Jim O'Connell was there. It was soon afterward that Shef [Edwards, O'Connell's boss] got in touch with me." Maheu, Giancana, and Rosselli ended up working closely together for the next eight months — both before and after the presidential election — until the failure at the Bay of Pigs. In all that time, Maheu told me, Giancana gave no hint that he knew Joe and Jack Kennedy.

But the FBI wiretap logs and the recollections of Robert McDonnell, Jeanne Humphreys, and Frank Sinatra through his daughter Tina provide indisputable evidence that since mid-1960 Giancana

---

many other mistakes. Christ and his colleagues, Thornton J. Anderson, Jr., and Walter E. Szuminski, all of whom were assigned to the agency's technical services division, had not coordinated plans for a story to be used in case of arrest and interrogation; they failed to provide a lookout during the critical phase of the break-in; they did not adequately coordinate the operation with the CIA station in Havana; and the operation, in general, "did not receive the careful analysis and thorough action that an activity of this sensitivity requires." After their release from prison in 1963, the three men, who insisted to the Cubans throughout that they were merely tourists, quietly returned to their CIA careers. There was no evidence that the Cuban government learned of the immense importance of Christ, who died in 1970.

had been secretly working on behalf of Kennedy's election. By early fall, when the CIA's plotting with the Mafia was intense, Giancana was also playing a major role in persuading his organized crime and Teamsters Union associates in Chicago to campaign, legally and illegally, for Jack Kennedy against Richard Nixon.

Giancana was thus theoretically in position to affect, perhaps irrevocably, the outcome of the 1960 election. Did Giancana do everything in his power to murder Castro before the election in November, which would have given a boost to Richard Nixon in the very close presidential campaign? This question is crucial.

Giancana certainly seemed to understand what the Republicans wanted him to do — and when they wanted him to do it. In early October of 1960, according to the Church Report, Giancana bragged over dinner with some mob associates in a New York restaurant, according to an FBI informant, that he had already met three times with Castro's would-be assassin, and the Cuban leader would be "done away with . . . in November." But nothing happened before the November 8 election, despite the boasting.

As the election neared, Nixon was frantic about Cuba. Getting rid of Castro, by overthrow or murder, he thought, would give him the presidency. The CIA's planning for Cuba, which had begun with the idea of training and infiltrating a few dozen guerrilla cadres who would spark an overthrow, had evolved into the landing of a six-hundred-man force that would hit the beaches at the town of Trinidad and move inland to the Escabray Mountains, to be supplied by airdrop. In an interview years later, the vice president's national security aide, Marine Corps general Robert E. Cushman, Jr., told the author Peter Wyden that Nixon had repeatedly nagged President Eisenhower to get the job done in Cuba. "The Vice President regarded the operation as a major political asset," Wyden wrote in *Bay of Pigs: The Untold Story,* published in 1979. "He was eager for the Republican administration to get credit for toppling Castro before the election. 'How are the boys doing at the Institute?' he asked Cushman, always careful not to discuss sensitive matters openly, even in the office. 'Are they falling dead over there? What in the world are they doing that takes months?'"

By November 1960 CIA operations in Guatemala, where the invasion force was being trained, were behind schedule, and the method for killing Castro was undecided. Giancana and his gang weren't doing much — at least not in the weeks before the election, according to the reports of the only two official investigations into the Castro plotting. Both the 1975 Church Report and a top-secret study prepared in 1967 by the CIA's inspector general (the IG Report) said that the assassination plotting was barely in the planning stage by the late fall of 1960. There were some false starts. The CIA's internal report, made public in 1993 under the Freedom of Information Act, noted that in the summer a batch of poisoned cigars, obviously meant for Castro, a heavy smoker, had been concocted by the agency's office of medical services and was ready for delivery by October 7, 1960. But the cigars were not actually delivered for operational use, according to the report, until February 13, 1961 — three weeks after Kennedy's inauguration — and were never sent into Cuba. According to the IG Report, there was also talk in the fall of 1960 — before the elections —"of a typical, gangland-style killing in which Castro would be gunned down. Giancana was flatly opposed to the use of firearms," the report continued. "He said that no one could be recruited to do the job, because the chance of survival and escape would be negligible. Giancana stated a preference for a lethal pill that could be put into Castro's food or drink."

It took months of trial and error before the CIA's scientific experts could develop a lethal pill that would dissolve in either cold or hot water with the same efficacy. One early batch of pills had been rejected; according to the Church Report, it was "probably" not until the February after the elections that a suitable assassination product was given to Rosselli. "The record clearly establishes that the pills were given to a Cuban for delivery to the island some time prior to the Bay of Pigs invasion in mid-April, 1961," the Church Report stated. By then, Giancana and a colleague, Santos Trafficante, a Florida Mafia boss who controlled much of the casino activity in Havana, had found a Cuban official who agreed to drop the poison in Castro's drink.

The record thus is clear that Giancana made no attempt to assassinate Castro before the election and, in fact, did nothing until Kennedy was in the White House. His failure to move quickly raises a second crucial question: Did Giancana tip off the Kennedys about what the Republicans were trying to do in Cuba in the fall of 1960?

No published evidence definitively proves that Jack Kennedy knew from Giancana about the planning for Castro's overthrow and assassination. But the fact is that a warning from Giancana wasn't needed. As interviews for this book reveal, the candidate was told before the election about the activities against Castro by at least three other involved sources — including Richard Bissell, who originated and led them.

It must have been reassuring for the young senator to learn that his presidential campaign, with its reliance on secret family money and assistance from organized crime, had met its moral equivalent in the Republicans, who were seeking to murder a foreign political leader before the election and using the very same Chicago mobsters in the effort. America's Cuba policy became the most important, yet most secret, issue of the Kennedy-Nixon campaign.

12

TRAPPING NIXON

Richard Bissell never told it all.

The patrician Bissell, with his academic background and his passion for sailing, was the prototypical CIA man in the early 1960s, as America began its love affair with the novels of Ian Fleming and his dashing British spy hero, James Bond, the martini-sipping Agent 007. Bissell, handsome and tall, was the man in charge of the CIA's get-Castro planning. He also helped elect John F. Kennedy by meeting with him before the 1960 election and briefing him about the CIA's ever-expanding plans for the overthrow of the Castro regime.

The original covert CIA schedule, as endorsed by Eisenhower, called for military action: the training of exile guerrilla teams was to be completed before the November elections. By midsummer of 1960, with training falling behind schedule, and with Castro becoming more entrenched in power and more hostile to Washington, Bissell and his CIA colleagues escalated to invasion and assassination. Knowing the CIA's plans was essential to Kennedy's political well-being.

No preelection Kennedy-Bissell meeting appears in the official records. CIA files released in 1995 show that Allen Dulles, following the common practice during presidential campaigns, gave Senator

Kennedy top-secret briefings in the summer and fall. On July 23, 1960, Dulles flew to Hyannis Port for a meeting of more than two hours with Kennedy. The Cold War dominated the session, according to the CIA file reports; Dulles described Soviet progress in strategic missile capabilities. The agency's files show that the second briefing took place, on short notice, on September 19, when Dulles gave Kennedy a thirty-minute update on world trouble spots. General Charles P. Cabell, the deputy CIA director, provided Kennedy with a third briefing, on November 2 — less than a week before the election — which was officially said to have focused on world tensions. A CIA internal review of the available records, made public in 1995, concluded that there was no evidence that either Dulles or Cabell specifically briefed Kennedy on the Cuban invasion planning.

But Clarence B. Sprouse, an army sergeant who was recruited by the CIA in mid-1960 to help train the Cuban exile forces, vividly recalled in a 1995 interview for this book that he helped Bissell arrange a private briefing on the Cuba plans for Senator Kennedy months before the election. Sprouse, who retired near San Antonio, Texas, after a thirty-year army career, was the command sergeant major for the Eighty-second Airborne Division in 1960 — the division's highest-ranking enlisted man — when he was reassigned to the exile training camp, in Guatemala. Late that summer he was sent to CIA headquarters in Washington, where he did nothing "but hang around ops" — the headquarters of Bissell's invasion force, which was focused on training small-unit guerrilla teams. There was a flurry of activity, Sprouse recalled, over scheduled briefings for both Vice President Nixon and, a day later, Senator Kennedy. Sprouse specifically recalled preparing charts for a "very detailed briefing" for Kennedy on the Cuba planning, which took place in a safe house in northwest Washington, near CIA headquarters. "I went over and set it up," he told me. "The briefing was on the Trinidad landing. The initial thing was to go in, like Castro had gone, and fight his guerrillas in the mountains." Sprouse said he was not allowed to attend the briefing and did not actually see Kennedy at the safe house, but he was told that Bissell personally briefed the senator. There is no official record of the meeting in the CIA files. Such a briefing, if it did take place, would have caused an uproar in the Eisenhower White House.

Sprouse's account is made more credible by Bissell's acknowledgment, in his posthumous memoir, *Reflections of a Cold Warrior,* published in 1996, that he had met informally with Kennedy during the campaign. "About a month before the election," Bissell wrote,

> I received a call from an intermediary of Kennedy's who said that the senator would like to talk to me about general issues raised during the campaign. It was probably Joe Alsop who suggested to Kennedy that as a well-informed Washington insider I was someone he should get in touch with. I am sure I told Dulles about the planned meeting, and I probably reported to him about it afterward. I found Kennedy to be bright, and he raised a number of topics on which I had something to say. I made it clear to him, however, that I was still working for Eisenhower and therefore could not do anything of an active nature for him.

Bissell gave a different and probably misleading account of his initial campaign meeting with John Kennedy in his oral interview for the John F. Kennedy Library. In that interview, conducted in April 1967, at the height of reverence for the memory of Camelot, Bissell told of being summoned by Senator Kennedy to his office on Capitol Hill not a month before the election but "at a fairly early stage in his campaign." The meeting had nothing to do with CIA business, Bissell insisted. Kennedy "invited me to contribute, in writing, any ideas that I might have that could be fed into the campaign that would be valuable to him in the campaign. I was eager to do so," Bissell added, "but the press of business kept me fairly busy, and I think, as it turned out, I never did make such contributions. I may have seen him once or twice more during the campaign." Asked why Kennedy had sought the meeting, Bissell responded vaguely that "I'm inclined to think he was more interested in economic policy [than in the CIA], but we didn't really bring it to the point of sharply defining a field." What the two men really discussed is, of course, impossible to determine, but there is no reason to believe the conversation focused on economic policy. Significantly, there is no record that Bissell officially reported to the CIA the astonishing fact that a presidential candidate had asked him — the CIA's director of clandestine and covert operations — to contribute ideas to his campaign while Bissell was still serving the rival party's administration.

Bissell's varying accounts in his memoir and his oral history for the Kennedy Library were at best incomplete. Until his death in 1994 he provided journalists, academics, former colleagues, and others who sought him out in retirement with a seemingly unending maze of conflicting descriptions of his role in the Bay of Pigs. Eventually Bissell began acknowledging that he and Jack Kennedy had begun meeting secretly early in 1960, when it was clear that the young senator had a strong chance to win the Democratic nomination. In an interview in the 1970s with R. Harris Smith, a former CIA analyst who in 1972 published a well-researched history of the Office of Strategic Services (OSS), Bissell said that he "was meeting as far back as February of 1960" with Kennedy. In an interview for this book, Smith said that Bissell had described those meetings as social.* In the year before his death, Bissell told a former CIA colleague from the Bay of Pigs, Grayston Lynch, that he and Kennedy were "friends from before"— as Lynch recalled in a 1997 interview for this book. Bissell made it very clear, Lynch said, that the personal relationship had existed long before Kennedy got to the White House.

Bissell's implication in his memoir, therefore, that he or Jack Kennedy needed the services of a third party in the late fall of 1960, in the person of columnist Joseph Alsop, to get "in touch" with each other is ludicrous. Bissell and Alsop had been friends since childhood, and stayed close as their careers in Washington progressed. Alsop had also been an intimate of the Kennedys — one biographer said he was "smitten" with the family — since the end of World War II. He would become one of JFK's confidants after the election, a reporter who understood that the friendship depended on knowing what to write and what not to write. Kennedy surely did not need Joe Alsop to tell him in mid-1960 that Bissell was important.

The Kennedy connections to the CIA were long-standing. In 1956,

---

* Smith's seminal work was OSS: The Secret History of America's First Central Intelligence Agency, published by the University of California. The book was the stepping-stone to a planned biography of Allen Dulles. After years of interviewing, and even more years of inactivity, however, Smith turned over his notes and other data to Peter Grose, a former New York Times reporter, who published a Dulles biography, Gentleman Spy, in 1994. Grose, apparently relying on the Smith materials, reported that Bissell had also made "discreet" contact with Adlai Stevenson early in 1960, suggesting that he would be willing to leave the CIA, if need be, to work on a Stevenson campaign for the presidency.

as noted in an earlier chapter, Joe Kennedy had served on a high-level CIA review panel and had been entrusted to conduct on-site inspection visits to CIA stations abroad. Allen Dulles was an acquaintance from Palm Beach who shared the Kennedy passion for womanizing; he was a regular visitor to the Kennedy compound there. Dulles had known since the flap over Nicolae Malaxa in 1952 that Richard Nixon was not "an honorable man," as the CIA would put it.

The early relationship between Dulles and Jack Kennedy was much closer than is generally known. In his little-noted oral history for the Kennedy Library, recorded in late 1964, Dulles revealed that he and JFK had "fairly continuous" contact, beginning in the early 1950s, when he was deputy director of the CIA, "because my trips to Palm Beach were quite frequent. He [JFK] was often there, and whenever he was there we always got together. I respected his views. I thought he had a very keen appreciation of foreign problems, and being in the intelligence business, I pumped him as much as I could to get his views on things and his reaction to things, and continued on during these days until the days when I served under him for a short time as director." Dulles became CIA director in 1953 and continued talking foreign policy with Kennedy. While in Palm Beach, Dulles usually stayed at the home of Charles B. Wrightsman, a Kennedy neighbor. He specifically recalled one dinner after the overthrow of Prime Minister Mohammed Mossadegh of Iran, a coup engineered in 1953 by the CIA. "Charles Wrightsman was an oilman and he was interested and we were all deeply interested in the developments of the Middle East at the time." Jack Kennedy, Dulles added, "was always trying to get information. I don't mean secrets or things of that kind particularly, but to get himself informed. He wanted to get my views . . . and we had many, many talks together. As I say, very often Joe [Kennedy] was there at the same time."

Jack Kennedy had another tie to Richard Bissell and Allen Dulles — a tie that was unavailable to Richard Nixon — stemming from Kennedy's acceptance in the upper reaches of Washington society. One anecdote repeatedly published in the Kennedy literature, involving a March 1960 dinner party at JFK's Georgetown home, tells much about the senator's social ease with top-level CIA officers. The guest of honor was author Ian Fleming; other guests included Joe Alsop and his brother and fellow columnist, Stewart. John Bross, a CIA official who had successfully run covert operations in Central and Eastern Europe in the 1950s and was one of Bissell's closest personal friends, was also present, and the talk turned to Cuba. Fleming, at Kennedy's urging, described how he would use "ridicule" to force Castro out of office. Since the Cubans cared only about money, religion, and sex, Fleming said, fake dollar bills should be dropped on the island, to destabilize the currency, as well as leaflets declaring Castro to be impotent. At the time, as Fleming may or may not have known, the CIA's covert action planners were seriously contemplating a series of similarly childish operations, including the use of a depilatory powder that would make Castro's beard fall out. Allen Dulles learned of the dinner-table conversation the next morning and, according to one published account, unsuccessfully sought an immediate meeting with Fleming.*

There were few secrets in Georgetown. The socially prominent journalists, politicians, and intelligence officials shared the same dinner tables and the same fear of international communism. It would be naive to think that at the height of a close presidential campaign, a private meeting between Bissell and Kennedy — such as the one Clarence Sprouse described to me, concerning the Trinidad landing — would not deal with substantive matters. All that Jack Kennedy and his father had strived for, and paid handsomely for, during the past four years would be at stake in a few weeks, and a sudden Republican success against Castro was simply not acceptable. The Kennedy campaign had to find some way to stall the invasion.

Kennedy did not need Richard Bissell to tell him about the Republican administration's operation against Fidel Castro. He had several other sources who were only too willing, even if it meant betraying

---

* In *The Very Best Men* (Simon and Schuster, 1995), a biographical account of four CIA officials, including Bissell, author Evan Thomas quoted one guest at the Kennedy dinner party as reporting that Dulles telephoned her early the next morning "desperate to find Ian." Dulles had heard, Thomas wrote, that Fleming had discussed some "interesting ideas of how to deal with Castro" and wanted a personal briefing. But Fleming, it turned out, had already left for London.

their primary loyalties. Not only was there Sam Giancana, who by September was recruited into the CIA assassination planning, but there was also Allen Dulles, who became one of two appointments (J. Edgar Hoover was the other) announced by Kennedy on the day after the election. Both were deeply involved with candidate Kennedy in ways not fully understood before now. Arthur Schlesinger, in his memoir, would call the two sudden reappointment announcements part of the president-elect's "strategy of reassurance."* As we now know in the case of Hoover, reassurance of the electorate had nothing to do with it. Was the Dulles reappointment also a reward for past confidences? While there is no explicit evidence that during the campaign Dulles told Kennedy, or arranged for Kennedy to learn, the essentials of the Cuba operation, the fact is that Kennedy did know before the election of the Eisenhower administration's secret planning for Cuba. If Kennedy knew that Dulles, his old family friend, had chosen to keep make-or-break information from him, why would the pragmatic and tough-minded president-elect honor that disloyalty by immediately reappointing him?

Any lingering public doubt about what Kennedy knew or did not know before the election about the Cuban invasion planning should have ended with a revelation six years after the Bay of Pigs from a little-known political insider, John M. Patterson, the Democratic governor of Alabama. In 1967 Patterson was asked to give an oral history to the Kennedy Library. He chose that occasion to tell, for the first time, how he became involved in the early planning in the summer of 1960 for Castro's overthrow and how he directly relayed what he knew to candidate Kennedy weeks before the election. At the time,

---

* Schlesinger's colleague Ted Sorensen failed to mention J. Edgar Hoover at all in *Kennedy*, his 860-page book published in 1965, which included a long chapter on President-elect Kennedy's appointments. Two other Kennedy insiders, Kenneth O'Donnell and David Powers, also failed to mention Hoover in their 1970 bestseller, *"Johnny, We Hardly Knew Ye."* O'Donnell and Powers went even further than Sorensen in their denial: they wrote about the early reappointment of Allen Dulles while ignoring Hoover's reappointment.

Patterson's account was suppressed by the library, which continues to suppress it today.

In a series of interviews for this book, Patterson, who served thirteen years as a state judge in Alabama before retiring in 1997, told me the story. He first met Kennedy in 1955, when the senator came to Montgomery to make a speech, and Patterson, then an ardent segregationist, was the crime-busting attorney general of Alabama. On later visits to Kennedy's home and office in Washington, "he and I became friends," Patterson told me. In 1959, a newly elected governor, Patterson broke ranks with fellow Democrats and publicly endorsed the senator before he officially announced for the presidency. Patterson went on to lead the Alabama delegation at the 1960 convention. "I felt he was going to win," he said, "and I was happy to have access" to the White House.

That summer the CIA decided, with Eisenhower's approval, that it needed the help of the Alabama Air National Guard to train exile pilots in Nicaragua for what was initially planned to be the insertion of small guerrilla teams into Cuba. Sometime in mid-1960, Patterson recalled, Major General George R. Doster, commander of the state air national guard, telephoned him and said that a "very hush hush" meeting had to be arranged immediately — at the governor's mansion, not Doster's office. Doster arrived with a senior CIA official, who explained the mission and requested the governor's authorization. Patterson had been a young lieutenant in Eisenhower's headquarters in London during World War II; that experience, the governor reasoned, had led the CIA to him and his air national guard. "I had a high regard for Eisenhower and asked if the Old Man knew about it. They said yes. 'Is he for it?' 'Oh, yeah.' I was patriotic and agreed to let them" use the national guard.

By the fall of 1960, Patterson continued, as the CIA's Cuba planners began turning from small-unit guerrilla activity toward a full-scale ground invasion, hundreds of national guard members — including pilots, cooks, and administrative officials — were needed in Nicaragua to train Cuban flight crews. "Every time Doster came home" from Nicaragua, Patterson added, "he'd stop by and give me a report." Sometime in early or mid-October Doster visited again and said, "Any morning now you're going to read in the morning newspaper when you wake up where we've invaded Cuba."

Patterson was active at that time in the Kennedy campaign in Alabama, and immediately realized that Castro's overthrow would have deadly political implications for the Democrats. "After some thought," he told me, "I called Steve Smith [Kennedy's brother-in-law and campaign finance manager] and said it was important for me to see Kennedy. I'd meet him anywhere, anytime." He was told to fly to New York and check into the Barclay Hotel. Kennedy showed up at nine o'clock on the night Patterson arrived. "I made him promise," Patterson recalled, "that he wouldn't breathe a word, and I told him what was going on . . . that the invasion was imminent and if it occurred before the election, I believed Nixon would win. I recall watching him very closely. I couldn't read him. He heard me out and thanked me." Kennedy showed no emotion throughout, Patterson said, and gave no sign that he had received significant information. "I made him promise never to tell" that he had supplied Kennedy with such confidential — and vital — information. "I made a serious breach of security."

There was yet another business matter at hand. "I had ten thousand dollars in cash," Patterson continued. "Contributions. In a paper bag. And I gave it to him. Kennedy said good-bye and left. That's the way we did things then," the former governor said with a nervous laugh. Patterson acknowledged, in response to a question, that he "frequently made contributions" in cash during the 1960 campaign, either directly to Kennedy or, if he was not readily available, to Steve Smith. Neither Patterson nor Kennedy spoke to the other about Cuba during the campaign.

Patterson decided in 1967 to include a full account of his preelection trip to New York in the oral history he recorded for the Kennedy Library. He had answered all of the usual questions and was asked, as were all interviewees, whether he had anything to add. It was at that moment that he decided to spill the beans. Months later, Patterson told me, he was mailed the typed transcript of his interview for review. All was intact "except that portion pertaining to Cuba. It was just cut out. No reference to it. I called and asked why they did that. They said it was classified." Patterson laughed anew at the thought: "They classified my own stuff." He dropped the issue for the next fifteen years, he said, but suddenly decided to tell the story while being interviewed in October 1982, on the twentieth anniversary of the

Cuban missile crisis, by his local newspaper, the *Birmingham News*. No one paid much attention.

Kennedy now had a secret weapon in the 1960 campaign — Cuba. His polling showed that the Republicans, and Richard Nixon, scored high when foreign policy issues were defined in "tough versus soft" terms. Voters who wanted to do something about communists usually favored Nixon. Kennedy could publicly swing away at Cuba knowing that there would be no response in kind. In *Six Crises*, his 1962 memoir, Nixon explained why: "The [anti-Castro] program had been in operation for six months before the 1960 campaign got under way. It was a program, however, that I could say not one word about. The operation was covert. Under no circumstances could it be disclosed or even alluded to. Consequently, under Kennedy's attacks and his new demands for 'militant' policies, I was in the position of a fighter with one hand tied behind his back."

Kennedy swung away. In late September 1960, even before the Patterson visit, he had begun moving away from public restraint in his comments, strongly suggesting that someone — perhaps Giancana, Bissell, or Dulles — had already told him what was going on in Guatemala. Asked about Cuba by the Scripps-Howard newspapers, Kennedy, in a written response released on September 23, emphasized the failure of the Eisenhower administration to address the abuses of the Batista regime. He then suggested, apparently for the first time in the campaign, that there should be an active American role inside Cuba, saying that "the forces fighting for freedom in exile and in the mountains of Cuba should be sustained and assisted." If the next president "can help create the conditions in Latin America under which freedom can flourish," he said, "then Castro and his government will soon be isolated from the rest of the Americas — and the desire of the Cuban people for freedom will ultimately bring Communist rule to an end."

Nixon was trapped. There was no turning back on the Cuba policy, even with his election at stake. Getting rid of Fidel Castro was one of Dwight Eisenhower's highest priorities, and considered vital to national security. Nixon's response to Kennedy's hard line was to begin desperately urging the CIA to get Castro out of power before the election. His fear was that Americans who wanted to act against Castro would vote for Kennedy, when it was the Eisenhower White House that had made the crucial decisions. There were ironies all around: if Castro was not ousted before election day, Nixon would get the peace vote from Americans who disapproved of Kennedy's demands for violent overthrow.

By early October, with Nixon still pressuring the CIA to act against Castro and with the Sam Giancana assassination plotting now under way, Kennedy became much more strident. On October 6, in Cincinnati, he evoked the worst fears of the Cold War in a harsh speech that egregiously exaggerated Castro's regional ambitions, denigrated the Eisenhower administration's handling of Cuba, and provoked fear about the Cuban leader's plans to spread his political views to Latin America:

"I want to talk with you tonight about the most glaring failure of American foreign policy today — about a disaster that threatens the security of the whole Western Hemisphere — about a Communist menace that has been permitted to arise under our very noses. . . .

"Castro is not just another Latin American dictator — a petty tyrant bent merely on personal power and gain. His ambitions extend far beyond his own shores. He has transformed the island of Cuba into a hostile and militant Communist satellite — a base from which to carry Communist infiltration and subversion throughout the Americas. With guidance, support and arms from Moscow and Peking, he has . . . rattled red rockets at the United States, which can hardly close its eyes to a potential enemy missile or submarine base only ninety miles from our shores. . . . The American people want to know how this was permitted to happen — how the iron curtain could have advanced almost to our front yard. They want to know the truth. . . ."

Two weeks later, well after his meeting at the Barclay Hotel with John Patterson, the Kennedy rhetoric escalated once again. Late on October 19, two days before the fourth — and final — television debate with Nixon, the Kennedy campaign issued a dramatic press statement that, in effect, envisioned the Bay of Pigs invasion: "We must attempt to strengthen the non-Batista democratic anti-Castro forces in exile, and in Cuba itself, who offer eventual hope of overthrowing Castro. Thus far these fighters for freedom have had virtually no support from our government." The statement led to a headline at the top of the *New York Times* on October 21: "Kennedy Asks Aid for Cuban Rebels to Defeat Castro: Urges Support of Exiles and 'Fighters for Freedom' Already on Island." The lead of the dispatch, written by veteran reporter Peter Kihss, was unambiguous: "Senator John F. Kennedy called last night for United States aid to 'fighters for freedom' in exile and inside Cuba who are seeking to overthrow Premier Fidel Castro's regime."

The sensational play in the press ensured that Cuba would become a major topic of the next evening's debate and put Nixon on the defensive. In *RN,* Nixon recalled his assumption that Kennedy had been briefed by Allen Dulles about Cuba and had chosen to take political advantage of that information. Kennedy's statement, he said, "jeopardized the project, which could succeed only if it were supported and implemented secretly. . . . I had no choice but to take a completely opposite stand and attack Kennedy's advocacy of open intervention in Cuba. This was the most uncomfortable and ironic duty I have had to perform in any political campaign."

Dulles, and Kennedy, would insist after the election that no information about covert operations against Castro had been discussed in the preelection briefings of the candidate, a position upheld by the CIA's official records. But Nixon was convinced that his opponent knew otherwise, and was enraged at Dulles for his presumed indiscretion in telling Kennedy anything at all about Cuba. Nixon was reported by his biographer Stephen E. Ambrose to have "exploded" at Dulles during a National Security Council meeting at the White House shortly before the final television debate with Kennedy, insisting, as another biographer wrote, "You never should have told him! Never!"

During the debate, Nixon, who had since mid-1959 campaigned in secret for the overthrow of the Castro regime, was forced to argue on national television that the United States was barred by international law from providing any assistance to Cuban exile groups. He depicted Kennedy's proposal as "probably the most dangerously irresponsible recommendation that he's made during the course of the campaign," adding that any assistance to the anti-Castro rebels would violate treaties, cause the United States to "lose all our friends in Latin America," and invite "Mr. Khrushchev . . . to come into Latin America."

Ironically, Nixon received rare kudos from liberals in the American press corps for what seemed to be his principled stand against violence in Cuba. James Reston, in the *New York Times*, reported from Washington that Nixon's criticism of the Kennedy plan "for assisting the anti-Castro forces to regain power in Cuba was approved by well-informed people here tonight." Walter Lippmann, the preeminent syndicated columnist, rebuked Kennedy for "making so much of a campaign issue of Cuba," especially because the Eisenhower administration's handling of Castro was "about the best that was possible." The acidic Murray Kempton declared in the *New York Post* that "I really don't know what further demagoguery is possible from Kennedy on this subject, short of announcing that, if elected, he will send Bobby and Teddy and Eunice to Oriente Province to clean Castro out."

Nixon complained bitterly about his untenable public posture in *Six Crises:* "For the first and only time in the campaign, I got mad at Kennedy *personally.* I thought that Kennedy, with full knowledge of the facts, was jeopardizing the security of a United States foreign policy operation. And my rage was greater because I could do nothing about it."

As the presidential campaign neared its end, the morning newspapers and nightly television news broadcasts provided extensive coverage, but the real story was known to only a few. Sometime in 1960 the Eisenhower administration had lost control of its most important secret, and it was being used to defeat the Republican candidate. Allen Dulles and Richard Bissell, the two men running the CIA's operations against Cuba, had apparently decided to break ranks and do what they could to elect Kennedy. Candidate Kennedy had no quarrel with the means, or the ends, of the CIA's anti-Castro activity, as he would demonstrate in the months ahead. For now his overriding goal was to get elected, and he did not hesitate to take advantage of the nation's most sensitive secrets to do so.

Dulles and Bissell, with their secrets, thus joined ranks with Kennedy's father and the Irish Mafia — serving the greater good of Jack Kennedy.

Fidel Castro got the message while Kennedy and Nixon slugged it out over the future of Cuba. By October 19 his spokesmen were predicting that the United States would launch "a large-scale invasion." On October 25, four days after the final debate, the Cuban government nationalized a final batch of American-owned industries in Cuba and again claimed, this time in the United Nations, that it had proof of American invasion plans that would be triggered by a "manufactured provocation" at Guantanamo Naval Base. A few days later Castro talked publicly about mercenaries who were being trained by Americans. The *New York Times* considered Castro's complaints ludicrous. "Dr. Castro and his friends," the paper editorialized, "cannot for a moment think that the United States would be wicked enough or foolish enough to attempt an armed conquest of Cuba."

Meanwhile, Nixon was pushing, until the end, for Castro's ouster. His campaign press secretary, Herbert G. Klein, later told the author Peter Wyden that until the end of October he had expected "our Nicaraguan friends" to engineer the overthrow of Castro. It would have been "a major plus" and "a real trump card" for the Republicans, Klein said, as the neck-and-neck campaign came to its end.

The Kennedy campaign got one late scare on October 25, when an anonymous caller warned campaign manager Bobby Kennedy that "most of the Cuban exiles [in Miami] are saying that there is an invasion fever in Guatemala but they are being rushed into it and they are not yet equipped for it." The candidate reminded himself in a note that day, on file at the Kennedy Library, to "talk to Allen Dulles to make sure nothing being done Cuba." The *Washington Post* reported a few days later that the Kennedy campaign staff was worried that a final "foreign crisis" might help Nixon in the last days of the campaign. It was this fear that apparently prompted deputy CIA director Charles Cabell's flight to California on November 2, six days before the election, and his last-minute briefing for candidate Kennedy, a briefing officially recorded as being on world tensions.* The world tension that worried Kennedy at the time was Cuba, and the possibility that the CIA would precipitously move against Castro.

Nixon, the ultimate political pragmatist, had met his match in 1960, but only he and a few of his close aides knew it. The public, fascinated with his opponent's charm and style, would see very little of the real John F. Kennedy, and would never fully sense the Kennedy cynicism and toughness. "I had been through some pretty rough campaigns in the past," Nixon wrote in *RN*,

> but compared to the others, going into the 1960 campaign was like moving from the minor to the major leagues. I had an efficient, totally dedicated, well-financed and highly motivated organization. But we were faced by an organization that had equal dedication and unlimited money that was led by the most ruthless group of political operators ever mobilized for a political campaign. Kennedy's organization approached campaign dirty tricks with a roguish relish and carried them off with an insouciance that captivated many politicians and overcame the critical faculties of many reporters.

Nixon eventually came to believe that it was Kennedy's manipulations on Cuba that defeated him, and not the impact of Kennedy's sleeker appearance during the television debates. Of that fourth debate, Nixon wrote, "Kennedy conveyed the image — to 60 million people — that he was tougher on Castro and communism than I

---

* A compendium of CIA presidential campaign briefings, published in 1995 by the Center for the Study of Intelligence at the CIA, reported only that Robert Kennedy had sought the final briefing on possible trouble spots. Cabell flew out to deliver a memorandum, the CIA study said, dealing with the Soviet Union, the Middle East, Southeast Asia, and "possible action by Cuba against Guantanamo Naval Base," the American naval station located on the eastern tip of Cuba. The only newspaper known to have reported on the Cabell-Kennedy meeting was the *San Diego Union*, which published two paragraphs about it on November 3. A Kennedy spokesman told the newspaper that Cabell had briefly come aboard the senator's campaign plane to inform Kennedy "if there is anything important that he needed to know to fulfill his responsibility as a nominee for President."

was." He cited Gallup polls showing that Kennedy's two-percentage-point lead after the first debate dwindled seven weeks later, after all four debates, to a one-point lead. By election day, the polls showed a dead heat. "Those who claim that the 'great debates' were the decisive turning point in the 1960 campaign overstate the case," Nixon concluded.

The losing Republican candidate had learned a lesson that he would act on in future campaigns: "From this point on I had the wisdom and wariness of someone who had been burned by the power of the Kennedys and their money and by the license they were given by the media. I vowed that I would never again enter an election at a disadvantage by being vulnerable to them — or anyone — on the level of political tactics."

The lessons learned would lead Nixon to the presidency in 1968 and to the disgrace of a forced resignation, with impeachment pending, in August 1974. Jack Kennedy, once elected to the White House in 1960, got on with the business of assassinating Fidel Castro.

13

EXECUTIVE ACTION

Murder was in the air at the CIA and at the White House as the new administration was taking office. A few senior men in the CIA learned in January that the incoming president was going to be much tougher than any outsider could imagine; sometime just before his inauguration, President-elect Kennedy asked Richard Bissell, the CIA's director of clandestine and covert operations, to create inside the agency a formal capacity for political assassination.

In the last few months of the Eisenhower administration, three foreign leaders — Fidel Castro; Patrice Lumumba, of the Congo; and Rafael Trujillo, of the Dominican Republic — had already been selected as potential targets of political assassination. The planning, under the aegis of Allen Dulles and Richard Bissell, continued without interruption after the November election and throughout the presidential transition period. Political assassination, Dulles and Bissell knew, was not a new concept for the Eisenhower government. In 1953, according to declassified files, the CIA, while plotting the overthrow of President Jacobo Arbenz Guzman of Guatemala, drew up a "disposal list" of fifty-eight Guatemalans suspected of communist leanings, and trained assassins for their murder. The assassinations were not carried out, but the released files show that the CIA's plans were discussed in detail at the highest levels of the State Department.*

Candidate Kennedy, as we have seen, utilized his close relationship with Dulles and Bissell, among others, to learn what he needed to know about the planned invasion of Cuba by CIA-trained exiles, facts that helped him defeat Richard Nixon. Now, as the president-elect, he continued to meet officially and unofficially with Bissell.

Bissell, with his lucidity and arrogant wit, seemed a perfect match for the new president and the energetic New Frontier; he was said to have wowed Kennedy and his senior aides in the White House by introducing himself at a get-acquainted staff dinner as "your basic man-eating shark." As a professional intelligence officer, he was dedicated to "plausible deniability"— the CIA's sacrosanct procedure for insulating the president from any responsibility for a failed, or exposed, intelligence operation of dubious morality or legality, such as the murder of a foreign leader.

From the outset Bissell had Kennedy's trust; Secret Service logs list Bissell at thirteen off-the-record Oval Office meetings with Kennedy and others in the first three months of 1961, as planning intensified for the invasion of Cuba. "He was there all the time," his secretary, Doris Mirage, recalled in an interview for this book. "If he wanted to see [Kennedy], I'd call Evelyn Lincoln." It was understood that Bissell was the heir apparent as CIA director; it was just a matter of time before the aging Allen Dulles would retire.

Of course, there is no written record of any discussion of assassination by Kennedy or any other president. But the CIA's plotting against the three foreign leaders did more than continue under Kennedy. It was formalized at the time of Kennedy's inauguration as a highly secret program known as executive action — given the code

---

* The CIA files, made public in May 1997 by the National Security Archives, a public interest group in Washington, included no evidence that President Eisenhower approved the assassinations. But the files also included a twenty-two-page CIA training manual, entitled *A Study of Assassination,* that amounted to a how-to murder kit. The manual included this caution: "No assassination instruction should ever be written or recorded." Other sections discussed various murder techniques, appropriate weapons, and advice on how to make a political murder seem to be an accident.

name ZR/RIFLE. William K. Harvey, one of the agency's most success-ful and flamboyant operatives, was put in charge.

Bill Harvey, who died in 1976, was a larger-than-life figure inside the CIA. He was short and fat, with bulging eyes, a raspy voice, and a serious drinking problem — in his heyday, two double martinis and then a single were his norm at lunch. He often walked around with two pearl-handled pistols tucked into his belt and bragged inces-santly about his success with women. Harvey was by all accounts brilliant, dedicated, a gifted writer of memoranda, and not afraid to tell the truth to a superior. He was also a devout keeper of secrets, sometimes to the distress of his colleagues: a generally laudatory CIA "fitness report" for the years 1960–62 described him as being "less than outgiving of information about operational matters in which he is engaged." It was Harvey, a former FBI agent who joined the CIA af-ter the war, who looked beyond Harold "Kim" Philby's social connec-tions in Washington and concluded in the early 1950s that the British intelligence attaché was a most valuable Soviet agent. And it was Harvey who provided the CIA with an early Cold War success by masterminding construction of a tunnel into East Berlin that gave the CIA access to underground East German and Soviet telephone lines. Harvey's achievement made his assignment in the late 1950s as head of the D branch of foreign intelligence — the elite group responsible for CIA communications intelligence and the theft of codebooks from foreign embassies — a natural. It also made him the inevitable choice to set up and operate ZR/RIFLE.

Despite the secrecy surrounding ZR/RIFLE, and the protection of "plausible deniability," the evidence linking Jack Kennedy and Mc-George Bundy to ZR/RIFLE and to the murder plots is overwhelming. Much of it was known in 1975 to the Senate investigating committee headed by Frank Church, whose Democratic members chose — for political reasons — not to confront it. Much more remained for me to disclose.

In late January 1961, as the new administration was settling in, Richard Bissell summoned William Harvey and ordered him to de-velop an "executive action" program for the murder of foreign leaders. Harvey was a careful note taker, and his notes of the meeting, as provided to the CIA's inspector general in 1967, quoted Bissell as saying that "the [Kennedy] White House had twice urged me to create such a capability." The new young, aggressive president wanted results. Harvey's notes and other documents were left on file with the inspector general's office in 1967, but by 1975, when the Church Committee began its post-Watergate investigation, the notes of his conversations with Bissell about White House pressure had been destroyed.* Harvey, however, had made other notes from his early days as head of ZR/RIFLE, and those notes, provided by Harvey to the Senate in 1975 but not published at the time — and obtained, without deletions, for this book — gave Senate investigators the first clear evidence that ZR/RIFLE's targets were Castro, Trujillo, and Lumumba. Harvey further told the committee, according to Senate files, that specific "approval by President" was one of the CIA's three requirements for the authorization of what he called "assassination as a tool."†

Bissell, asked by the Church Committee about Harvey's supplementary notes and his explanatory testimony about them, did what was unthinkable to Kennedy loyalists — he brought the White House into the concept of political assassination. Rather than challenging the Harvey material, Bissell volunteered the extraordinary fact that he had talked about executive action with McGeorge Bundy, the president's national security adviser. But Bissell quickly added that he and Bundy had discussed "an untargeted 'capability' rather than the plan or approval for an assassination operation." Bissell further supported Harvey's account by testifying that although he did not

---

* Richard Helms, the CIA director at the time of the IG Report, ordered the destruction of all notes and working papers dealing with the CIA's Castro assassination efforts. An internal CIA memorandum for the record written in May 1967, one month after the IG Report was completed, noted that Helms returned his copy of the report to the inspector general's office with orders that it was the only copy to be kept on file. All other copies of the 133-page document were to be destroyed.

† The other requirements cited by Harvey, according to the Church Committee files, were the existence of "a real threat" and the possibility that the assassination could "be done successfully."

have a specific recollection, he "might have" mentioned Castro, Lumumba, and Trujillo to Harvey in the course of a discussion of executive action, "because these were the sorts of individuals at that moment in history against whom such a capability might possibly have been deployed."

The relatively honest, if far from complete, 1975 testimony from Harvey and Bissell put McGeorge Bundy on the spot. The former national security adviser was afraid — far more than was publicly known — of a perjury charge. Even prior to his midsummer appearance before the Church Committee, Bundy felt compelled to revise sworn testimony given to a presidential commission.

The Church Committee's investigation was triggered by a *New York Times* article (written by me) in December 1974, which described a series of illegal domestic activities by the CIA. President Gerald R. Ford, obviously hoping to avoid congressional hearings, responded to public outcry over the disclosures by establishing a presidential commission, headed by Vice President Nelson Rockefeller, to investigate the CIA. Ford's hopes were dashed when the Senate voted to begin its far-ranging independent investigation.

In his first day of Rockefeller Commission testimony, on April 7, 1975, the former national security adviser categorically denied any knowledge of "an actual decision" to assassinate a foreign leader. He also testified that he had "no recollection" of an executive action program. The next day, obviously fearing perjury, Bundy held a private meeting with David W. Belin, the executive director of the Rockefeller Commission, "to make some additions to the record." Bundy claimed, according to the record of the meeting, declassified in 1996, that "as I reflected overnight about my answers to certain questions, my recollection was refreshed." Asked anew about executive action, he said, "I recall the words 'executive action capability' more clearly today than I did yesterday. . . . I think it was something like . . . a plan to have some kind of standby capability for actions against individuals." Having taken care of any worrisome legal liabilities, Bundy continued to obfuscate: "But I do not have any recollection as to when I knew about that or who requested it or how much was done under it."

Bundy's two days of testimony angered Belin, a former lawyer on the Warren Commission, which had investigated John Kennedy's assassination. In an interview in 1997 for this book, Belin, still angry, said what he would not say earlier: "There is no doubt that Bundy lied to me." Belin, now practicing law in Des Moines, Iowa, added that he came away from the 1975 hearing believing that President Kennedy "knew" about the CIA's assassination plotting. "Bobby Kennedy [also] knew about it. The Kennedys were out to get Castro."

Some witnesses "lied," Belin said. "Some did not." Among those who told the truth, in his view, was William Harvey.

Bundy appeared before the Church Committee in July 1975, after the committee had interviewed Bissell and Harvey. His memory once again suddenly improved. Most important, Bundy, like Bissell, broke with Camelot and its fourteen years of lies and cover-ups, confirming Bissell's account of their conversation. He acknowledged that there was talk of murder in the White House, and that the men of the CIA had not been on their own in the assassination plotting.

The president's man did include a series of caveats in his testimony. He reiterated that he and Bissell were talking only about what the Senate report called "an untargeted capability, rather than an assassination operation." It was his impression, Bundy said, that Bissell was "testing my reaction" and not "seeking authority" for ZR/RIFLE. "I am sure I gave no instruction. But it is only fair to add that I do not recall that I offered any impediment either." He took no steps to halt the CIA's executive action program or investigate it further, because it had been set up in the abstract and would not become "operational" until a specific individual was targeted. Asked if he had discussed the CIA's new program with the president, Bundy said that as far as "I can recall," he did not.

Thus John F. Kennedy's national security adviser, a former Harvard dean of faculty, acknowledged that shortly after taking office he had discussed expanding the CIA's capability for political assassination with the CIA's director of covert operations, who was then, as reported by the committee, in charge of a major clandestine effort to assassinate three unwanted foreign leaders. Yet this extraordinary admission attracted no significant attention when made public by the Senate in November 1975. Bundy's testimony might have been given more importance if the Washington press corps had known that Bundy had a long-standing tie to the Central Intelligence Agency —

a tie that suggested he was far more of an insider than was generally assumed.

Bundy's name came up in surprising fashion in 1994, during an interview for this book with Lawrence Devlin, a former CIA station chief in the Congo, who retired from the agency in 1974. "Do you know who tapped me on the shoulder for the agency?" Devlin asked. "Bundy. He was a secretary of the Council on Foreign Relations [in New York City]. He flew in to see me." Devlin, a World War II veteran, was attending Harvard on the GI Bill when he was approached in 1949 by a professor who asked "if I was looking for a job." Devlin and three other candidates were invited to the professor's office to discuss working for the newly formed CIA. "And then," Devlin remembered, "McGeorge Bundy showed up, giving each of us a pep talk. He offered me a job, and negotiated the level of entry." Years later, Devlin said, during a policy argument at the White House in the Johnson administration, Bundy plaintively asked Devlin, "How did you get recruited in the agency?" His reply, Devlin said, made the national security adviser laugh: "You recruited me."

After his meeting with Bissell in early January 1961, Bill Harvey had no illusions about what ZR/RIFLE and executive action were supposed to accomplish. He immediately scheduled a meeting with Bissell's scientific adviser, Dr. Sidney Gottlieb, who could produce a lethal virus or poison on demand. In an interview for this book in 1994, Gottlieb told me that Harvey said, "I've been asked to form this group to assassinate people and I need to know what you can do for me." Harvey kept notes of that meeting, too — notes he did not turn over to the CIA's inspector general in 1967 — and they indicate that the meeting with Gottlieb took place on January 25, 1961, five days after Kennedy's inauguration. The two men specifically discussed Castro, Lumumba, and Trujillo as potential targets. Harvey's notes show that he and Gottlieb talked of assassination as a "last resort" and as "a confession of weakness." On the next day, Harvey met with Arnold Silver, the CIA's experienced station chief in Luxembourg, with whom he had worked closely in previous operations. Harvey's notes show that he and Silver talked about recruiting agents for the ZR/RIFLE program — men who could be trusted to kill and say nothing. There was much talk of security and the need not to put anything in writing: "No other agencies. No project on paper. . . . Never mention word assassination."

The intense secrecy inside the American government did not prevent word of the Bissell-Harvey enterprise from traveling throughout organized crime circles. Sometime that winter, Joe Bonanno, the retired Mafia boss of New York City, volunteered his services to the CIA. Doris Mirage, Bissell's secretary, recalled in an interview for this book that Bonanno "was always calling on the outside line" in Bissell's office. "Bissell wouldn't take the call and I had to deal with the guy myself." At one point, Mirage said, Bonanno managed to get a handwritten letter delivered directly into Bissell's office, presumably with the help of someone working at the agency. "I got the letter from Bissell's out file," Mirage said. "He was a terrible writer. The letter said that he'd do what [Bissell] wanted him to do." She understood, Mirage said, that Bonanno was offering "to kill Castro." She didn't know where to file the letter, she added. "So I kept it."*

In the fall of 1961, Harvey was assigned to what became known as Task Force W, the CIA component in a get-Castro squad that was assembled by the White House. He spent much of the next year and a half plotting to overthrow and kill the Cuban leader — and growing increasingly frustrated about the constant pressure to do so from Robert Kennedy. Harvey's animosity toward the attorney general grew with each failed assassination attempt. It was Harvey's frustration, apparently, that led to a breach of his rules about never talking out of turn. At some point he told a valued colleague, Samuel Halpern, the executive officer of Task Force W, what no one in the CIA would ever tell Congress: that Jack Kennedy had personally authorized Richard Bissell to set up ZR/RIFLE before his inauguration. "After the election," Halpern recalled in one of his many interviews for this book, "Kennedy asked Bissell to create a capacity for political assassination. That's why Harvey set up ZR/RIFLE."

*   *   *

* Years later, Mirage said, she destroyed the Bonanno note.

As Kennedy entered office, the Third World — such countries as Cuba, the Dominican Republic, and the Congo — was the new Cold War battleground. "Now the trumpet summons us again," Kennedy declared in his famed inaugural address, "not as a call to bear arms, though arms we need; not as a call to battle, though embattled we are; but a call to bear the burden of a long twilight struggle year in and year out." The president's new twilight war against Soviet communism was being waged through surrogates all over the world. A few days earlier, Soviet officials had made available the text of a January 6 secret speech by Nikita Khrushchev in which the Soviet premier described the importance of "just wars" of national liberation; it was must reading for the president-elect. "These wars, which began as uprisings of colonial peoples against their oppressors, developed into guerrilla wars," Khrushchev said. "The Communists support just war of this kind wholeheartedly and without reservation." With nuclear war no longer acceptable, support for guerrilla war was now the only "way of bringing imperialism to heel."

Historian Michael Beschloss noted in *The Crisis Years*, his 1991 study of the Khrushchev-Kennedy relationship, that much of what Khrushchev said on January 6 had been said by him before, and was intended as a rejection of hard-liners in Moscow and Peking, with their hotheaded talk of all-out nuclear war. Eisenhower was unruffled by the speech, Beschloss wrote, because he had come to understand that with Khrushchev "tough talk usually substituted for action." Khrushchev undoubtedly thought he was reassuring the West by renouncing nuclear armageddon, Beschloss added, but "he did not realize the extent to which Kennedy might take the timing and content of his address as a provocation and test of a new young President."

To Kennedy, the speech was a challenge. Once in office, he sent copies to key members of his administration with a memorandum stating, "Read, mark, learn, and inwardly digest. . . . Our actions, our steps should be tailored to meet these kinds of problems." Robert S. McNamara, the secretary of defense, told an interviewer years later that the speech was "a significant event in our lives."

* * *

The hottest surrogate war at the time Kennedy took office was in the newly independent Congo. Belgium had left its colony poorly prepared for self-rule, with fewer than twenty college graduates in the entire country and the army still controlled by white officers. When Congolese soldiers mutinied and violence broke out, reports reached the West of white civilians killed and nuns raped. Belgium flew in paratroopers to protect its citizens. Prime Minister Patrice Lumumba requested and received intervention by the United Nations to drive out the Belgians, then accepted Soviet military aid to retain the breakaway province of Katanga. Officials in the Eisenhower administration were convinced the Congolese premier was a dangerous radical who would be difficult to dislodge. He was all the more threatening to Washington because he had wide popular backing: in May 1960 his political party, the Mouvement National Congolais, won more seats in the nation's new parliament than any other party. The U.S. response, as Kennedy was well aware, had been to order the CIA to assassinate Lumumba.

The focal point of the American effort was the CIA's technical services division (TSD), whose scientists were asked to produce a lethal virus or poison that could be put into Lumumba's food, or perhaps his toothpaste. The men running the TSD did not flinch; it was not their first such assignment.

Earlier in 1960, the TSD had created a poisoned handkerchief that was mailed with the approval of the agency's top management to the home of General Abdul Karim Kassem, the military strongman of Iraq. Kassem had seized power in a bloody coup and, to the dismay of the United States, immediately restored diplomatic relations with the Soviet Union and lifted a ban on the Communist Party in Iraq. Sidney Gottlieb came up with the idea of infecting a handkerchief and mailing it to Iraq via the CIA station in New Delhi, India. "It was not an assassination," Gottlieb told me in an interview. "They [the CIA's Near East division] just wanted him to get sick for a long time. I went to Bissell and he said go ahead." Others in the agency saw it differently. One senior officer, in an interview for this book, revealed that the men running the Near East division were interested in getting rid of General Kassem permanently. "Why else would we authorize such a drastic action?" It is not known whether the handkerchief ever reached Kassem, or anyone in his immediate family who chanced to open the package. The general was executed by a firing squad in Baghdad, in 1963.

The trusted Dr. Gottlieb also played a major role in creating a CIA assassination kit, containing needles, rubber gloves, gauze masks, and lethal biological materials. In mid-September of 1960, Richard Bissell ordered Gottlieb to the Congo, with his kit, and authorized him to tell Lawrence Devlin, the station chief in Kinshasa (then Léopoldville), that he was to use the poison or any other feasible means to murder Lumumba. Before leaving Washington, Gottlieb told me, "I did ask Bissell, 'Was this our idea?' The answer was that it came from 'the highest source'"— President Eisenhower. Devlin acknowledged in a 1994 interview for this book that there were enormous risks in plotting to murder Lumumba. "Had I been caught [in such planning], every white person in Kinshasa would have died." Gottlieb, Devlin added, "was just a mule in the affair, as was I."

Lumumba, aware of the price on his head and pursued by rival Congolese factions, shrewdly placed himself in the protective custody of the United Nations forces. The CIA's goal, contrary to the high-flowing rhetoric from Washington about the sanctity of UN involvement, became to flush Lumumba out of his UN sanctuary somehow and leave him at the mercy of his political opponents in Katanga Province, who were funded by Belgian mining companies seeking return of their colonial holdings.

The official American policy in the Congo did not change with Kennedy's election. "From the start," Arthur Schlesinger wrote in *A Thousand Days,* "the new President had a simple and constant view: that, unless the United Nations filled the vacuum in the Congo, there would be no alternative but a direct Soviet-American confrontation." The same point was made in *Kennedy,* by Ted Sorensen, who described the United Nations as the "chief channel" of JFK's policy for restoring an independent, peaceful, and noncommunist Congo. "The Kennedy Congo policy was largely an extension of the Eisenhower policy," added Sorensen.

The unofficial American policy — the bloody one being attempted by the CIA — was not changed after Kennedy's victory at the polls, and was made official after his inauguration. Bill Harvey and his colleagues had every reason to believe that the authorization for ZR/RIFLE signaled Kennedy's endorsement of the policy of murdering foreign leaders.

In mid-January 1961, Lumumba was persuaded to leave United Nations protection. He was seized by opposition troops, taken to Katanga Province, and murdered sometime between January 17 and early February. The precise role of the CIA in his demise is not known, but cables made available to the Church Committee conclusively showed that the CIA's men in Africa understood that Lumumba would be murdered once he left his UN sanctuary. President Kennedy was not asked a single question about Lumumba's death in his televised news conferences in 1961.

The efforts to assassinate Trujillo were far less complicated. The Dominican leader was a brutal and repressive dictator; the Church Committee concluded in 1975 that both the Eisenhower and Kennedy administrations had repeatedly "encouraged the overthrow of his regime by Dominican dissidents." Trujillo was seen throughout Latin America as an American protégé — which, indeed, he had been during the 1940s and early 1950s — and the fear was that if his inevitable overthrow was not orchestrated by Washington, the country might fall into the hands of pro-Castro, procommunist radicals.

In August 1960 the Eisenhower administration formally broke diplomatic relations with the Trujillo regime, withdrew most of its diplomatic personnel, including the CIA station chief, and closed its embassy. Henry Dearborn, an American foreign service officer, stayed behind as consul general and de facto CIA station chief. Dearborn met with dissident groups and became increasingly outspoken in his view that no effort to overthrow the regime could be successful unless accompanied by the assassination of Trujillo; he filed cables expressing that view to the State Department, for distribution to government offices throughout Washington. Dearborn was explicitly talking about murder, and he was not reproved for doing so; he was merely urged to confine his reporting — and his recommendations — to more secure CIA communication channels. In December 1960, amid intense plotting for the murder of Fidel Castro and Patrice Lumumba, the Eisenhower administration approved a plan put forward by Richard Bissell, which called for supplying anti-Trujillo forces with weapons and bombs with electronic detonators.

The policy did not change with Kennedy's inauguration on January 20; Henry Dearborn stayed on the job and continued to file cables full of assassination talk.

At this point Joe Kennedy and the Palm Beach social circuit intervened. Joe Kennedy was friendly, in the way that rich men have friendships with journalists, with a gossip columnist named Igor Cassini, whose brother, Oleg, a New York fashion designer, was supplying Jacqueline Kennedy with couturier evening wear at no cost. Igor Cassini, who wrote under the name Cholly Knickerbocker, was an excellent golfer who shared the Kennedy interest in beautiful women; he also was married to a daughter of Kennedy neighbor Charles Wrightsman. In February 1961, according to documents made available to the *New York Times* a year later in the Dominican Republic, Cassini approached Joe Kennedy and proposed that the two of them work to open a line of communication between the new president and Trujillo. At the time, Cassini had been offered a public relations contract for $150,000 a year by the Trujillo regime. Cassini, in an interview for this book in 1996, claimed that he discussed the pending contract with Joe Kennedy and was told, "It might be a mistake for you." Cassini took the contract anyway.

Just what Joe Kennedy sought — or got — for his role in the affair will never be known, but his son the president subsequently approved a secret meeting between Trujillo and, on behalf of the administration, Robert D. Murphy, a former Eisenhower administration official. Cassini accompanied Murphy on the trip, which took place just as the Bay of Pigs invasion collapsed. Trujillo agreed to Murphy's visit, according to documents published in 1962 by the *Times,* in the hope that it would lead to a meeting at sea or in Florida with either Joe or Jack Kennedy. One of the documents reported that Murphy and Cassini knew "from confidential talks with the eldest Kennedy that the President had already decided to act favorably in the Dominican case, even going over the heads of the adverse opinion in the Department of State." The White House, embarrassed after the *Times* account by the clear evidence that Joe Kennedy could insert himself at will into the administration's foreign policy, issued a statement denying that the president had any plans to meet with Trujillo. The press took the denials at face value, and the incident blew over within a few days with no serious questions raised about Joe

Kennedy's involvement. The mess was left for Bobby Kennedy to clean up, and he employed the same tactic that was used to neutralize Skinny D'Amato of Las Vegas after he was overheard on an FBI bug bragging about his help in West Virginia. Igor Cassini was indicted in 1963 by the Justice Department for failing to register as a foreign agent.*

In the spring of 1961, Jack Kennedy made his own secret attempt to intervene with Trujillo. Senator George Smathers of Florida, Kennedy's pal from his days in Congress, told the Church Committee in 1975 testimony that Kennedy asked him to see Trujillo and raise "the possibility of his relinquishing his power and moving out." Smathers made his case, failed to move Trujillo, and spent two pleasant days visiting with the dictator. "He was a very, very interesting character," Smathers testified. "He pulled out a .45 pistol and he laid it right out on the desk, pointed right at [me], and we started talking. . . . The next thing I knew he was assassinated." There is nothing in the record to indicate the president's purpose in agreeing to the Murphy and Smathers missions, but the obvious question is this: Were Jack Kennedy and his father giving Trujillo a chance to get out before it was too late?

Trujillo continued on the executive action assassination list. In early April 1961, with the approval of Bissell and the White House, authorization was granted for a second set of weapons and ammunition — a first set had gone in February — to be sent by diplomatic pouch to the Dominican Republic, for relay to the dissidents.

Washington's attitude, not surprisingly, underwent a dramatic

---

* In interviews for this book and in his memoir, *I'd Do It All Over Again,* Igor Cassini insisted that his ruinous indictment (to which he eventually pleaded *nolo contendere,* resulting in a $10,000 fine and a six-month suspended prison sentence) came about because of his role in bringing Joe Kennedy into the public eye. Cassini acknowledged accepting a public relations contract for $150,000 from the Trujillo regime in early 1961 and not disclosing it, as required by federal law, but claimed that he had not done so because he did not want to reveal his participation in the secret negotiations involving Trujillo, Robert Murphy, and the Kennedys. "I know for a fact," Cassini insisted in an interview in 1996, "that neither Jack nor Bobby wanted to prosecute me, but when it came to their being embarrassed [over their father's involvement], they let me go to the wolves."

change following the failed Bay of Pigs invasion on April 17; three days afterward, Dearborn was admonished to keep tight control of the matériel. One CIA cable cited by the Senate committee noted that the decision to keep the weapons from the dissidents was "based on judgment that filling a vacuum created by assassination now bigger question than ever view unsettled conditions in Caribbean area." Trujillo was murdered, nonetheless, on May 30, 1961, by a group of dissidents who, a later CIA study determined, had received American weapons earlier in the year. The White House, eager to avoid any taint of involvement, ordered all intelligence personnel immediately withdrawn from the Dominican Republic. The State Department, according to the Senate committee, "cabled the CIA station . . . to destroy all records concerning contacts with dissidents."

Two days after Trujillo's murder, Robert Kennedy dictated a four-page memorandum for the files summarizing his involvement, reprinted in part in the final report of the Church Committee. Kennedy complained about the lack of reliable intelligence after the slaying, but expressed no upset about the direct American involvement in shipping weapons to Trujillo's assassins. "Nor is there any record," the committee noted, "that anyone took steps following Trujillo's assassination to reprimand or censure any of the American officials involved either on the scene or in Washington, or to otherwise make known any objections or displeasure to the degree of United States involvement." In later documents, the committee added, the CIA described the Kennedy administration's action in the Dominican Republic "as a 'success' in that it assisted in moving the Dominican Republic from a totalitarian dictatorship to a Western-style democracy."*

* * *

---

* The Church Committee, in its summary of Robert Kennedy's June 1 memorandum, avoided making what seemed to be an obvious judgment. It "is uncertain," the committee said, whether Kennedy's failure to express concern about the American role in Trujillo's murder "was due to the press of other matters, including concern over Trujillo's successor and the future government of the Dominican Republic, or whether it represented a condonation or ratification of the known United States involvement."

In his thousand days in office, President Kennedy showed no official curiosity about the many allegations of American involvement in the assassination of foreign leaders.

One hint of Kennedy's real attitude was provided by Smathers in a March 1964 oral history for the Kennedy Library. He was talking with the president about the consequences of Fidel Castro's assassination, a subject the two men had discussed previously. JFK's concern, Smathers noted, was not about the morality of political murder but about the pragmatic difficulty of getting it done without leaving any evidence. "We had further conversation of assassination of Fidel Castro," Smathers said, "what would be the reaction, how would the people react, would the people be gratified. . . . As I recollect, he was just throwing out a great barrage of questions. He was certain it could be accomplished — I remember that. It would be no problem. But the question was . . . whether or not the reaction throughout South America would be good or bad. And I talked with him about it and, frankly, at this particular time I felt that [he] wasn't so much for the idea of assassination, particularly where it could be pinned on the United States."

The president did have one explicit conversation about the murder of Castro with Hans Tofte, a socially prominent CIA operative who was an old Asia hand and something of a dandy. One CIA colleague described him as a "swashbuckling guy who dressed well and had a lovely house in Georgetown." He looked like a CIA agent should, and apparently began a social acquaintance with "Jack"— as Tofte referred to Kennedy in conversations with his friends — when the president served in the Senate. The swaggering Tofte got in trouble with the agency in the mid-1950s for keeping classified materials at home; his travails were described in *The Man Who Kept the Secrets,* the journalist Thomas Powers's definitive 1979 book on former CIA director Richard Helms. Tofte, angered by some of the materials in the book, asked after its publication to meet with Powers. The conversation turned to Kennedy, Powers recalled in a 1994 interview for this book.

Tofte told Powers of an extraordinary meeting he had with the president in March 1961. Tofte had just returned from a CIA assignment in Colombia, where he had conducted an extensive study of the government's attempt to stop La Violencia, the long-running guerrilla insurgency in the countryside. Research had begun under the Eisenhower administration, but Tofte's three-volume report was not completed until the first weeks of the Kennedy administration. How to combat communist movements was of paramount concern to the new president, and Kennedy, always willing to be briefed by working-level officials, summoned Tofte to the White House. Tofte told Powers that he personally handed JFK a copy of his report and described what was going on in Colombia. He also had the audacity to raise the Cuban invasion with the president. Like many CIA men throughout Latin America, Tofte had heard a great deal about the pending exile invasion of Cuba and, as Powers put it, he "seized the moment to urge Castro's assassination as a prelude to invasion, saying nothing would be achieved so long as Castro was in power. But the Cuban government would evaporate if he were killed."

Kennedy listened intently and then said, "That is already in hand. You don't have to concern yourself about that." Tofte understood precisely what the president meant, he told Powers, and was later astonished to hear that the invasion took place with Castro still in power. He had assumed, as Powers put it, "that the deed would be done."*

---

* A Kennedy Library official reported that the library's classified holdings include volumes two and three of Tofte's report on the insurgency in Colombia. Suzanne Forbes, a national security archivist at the library, said that one of the volumes has a note attached stating that it had been received from presidential aide Ted Sorensen in February 1964, three months after Kennedy's assassination. Ms. Forbes said in an interview for this book that it would be fair to conclude that Tofte, as he told Thomas Powers, did give a copy of his report to the White House. The Eisenhower administration left virtually none of its national security files behind, Ms. Forbes said, as is usually the case with outgoing governments, when it vacated the White House and Executive Office Building on January 20, 1961. Tofte died in 1987.

14

BAY OF PIGS

In the early spring of 1961, Marcus Raskin, a bright young congressional aide, got an irresistible offer: Would he be interested in joining the Kennedy administration's National Security Council staff as an assistant to McGeorge Bundy for arms control? Raskin said yes and in early April arrived at the Executive Office Building for a meeting with Bundy, a few days before a planned exile invasion of Cuba at an obscure beach known as the Bay of Pigs. Raskin knew nothing officially of the invasion, but he had heard, as had many in Washington, that something was up. The government of Brazil had publicly proposed brokering a settlement between the United States and Cuba; Raskin, never afraid to speak his mind, suggested that the White House consider the offer. "Oh, no," Bundy said. "It'll take just one detachment and he'll be out of there."

The few Kennedy insiders who knew about the invasion in advance shared Bundy's confidence about its success; doubts, if any, were overcome by the president's mystique — and the prevailing sense that Kennedy could do no wrong. Richard N. Goodwin was a speechwriter who became a trusted presidential assistant after the campaign. "I remember saying at one point," he recalled in an interview for this book, "'You know, the problem with the Cubans is they'll fight and they'll die. And we can end up killing a lot of people in Cuba.' But Kennedy felt he was on a roll. He had won the nomination; he had won the election. He figured things were going his way, and so he tossed the dice one more time."

Bundy knew what Raskin and Goodwin did not: the dice were loaded. The Mafia's men in Havana were on the job. Fidel Castro, the Cuban prime minister, was to be assassinated by the Mafia on or before the day the invasion force landed at the Bay of Pigs. It looked like a sure thing.

Though he was only one of three prospective targets of political assassination as the new administration was being formed, Castro was the most important. His death, so the planners thought, would precipitate a widespread revolt.

"Taking out Castro was part of the invasion plan," Robert Maheu, the CIA's liaison to the Mafia, told me during one of our interviews for this book. Castro's murder was to take place "before — but preferably at the time of — the invasion," Maheu said. "We'd get word that something had happened. And we were waiting to hear" if "poison had made it into his food." Maheu spent much of the winter and spring of 1961 plotting Castro's murder while holed up in hotels in Miami with Sam Giancana and two of his fellow mobsters, Johnny Rosselli and Santos Trafficante.

The link between the invasion and Castro's assassination was publicly acknowledged by Richard Bissell. But he waited more than twenty years to do so, and chose an obscure journal in which to reveal his ultimate Bay of Pigs secret. "Assassination was intended to reinforce the plan," Bissell explained to Lucien S. Vandenbroucke, a foreign service officer who interviewed him in 1984 for a scholarly article published that fall in *Diplomatic History,* an academic quarterly. "There was the thought that Castro would be dead before the landing. Very few, however, knew of this aspect of the plan."*

---

* Vandenbroucke interviewed Bissell in May 1984, after discovering an unpublished essay dealing with the Bay of Pigs among the papers of Allen Dulles, which were donated after Dulles's death to Princeton University. In his essay, entitled "The 'Confessions' of Allen Dulles: New Evidence on the Bay of Pigs," Vandenbroucke de-

The Cubans and Soviets certainly knew. Cuban intelligence, working closely with the Soviet KGB, had captured a huge cache of weapons in January 1961, including pistols with silencers, in what was determined to be a CIA undercover center in Havana. Soviet intelligence files provided in the mid-1990s to two academics, Aleksandr Fursenko and Timothy Naftali, showed that Cuban security and the KGB concluded that the pistols were for "the murder of Fidel Castro." Fursenko and Naftali, in *"One Hell of a Gamble": Khrushchev, Castro, and Kennedy, 1958–1964,* their 1997 study of the Cuban missile crisis, concluded that the pistols "make some sense" in the planning for the Bay of Pigs: "The Kennedy administration had expected Castro to die before he could rally support for destroying the invasion." Cuban and Soviet intelligence would claim later to have uncovered a total of more than two dozen assassination plots against Castro.*

In his biography of Castro, *Fidel,* journalist Tad Szulc quoted Ramiro Valdés, who set up Cuba's security service after the 1959 revolution, as claiming that his operatives were able to track the CIA's planning for the Bay of Pigs step by step, from the first days of training in Guatemala. So much information was pouring out of Miami, Valdés said, that it was difficult to sort out truth from rumor.

The story — as told in the 1975 Church Committee's report and the top-secret 1967 report by the CIA's inspector general — begins with Santos Trafficante, a longtime associate of Sam Giancana and the former Mafia boss of Cuba, who was eager to get rid of Castro and go

---

scribed how Dulles had written a number of drafts of the essay before he abandoned his effort to explain away the failed invasion. But Vandenbroucke buried the lead. Bissell's admission linking the assassination plotting to the Bay of Pigs was relegated to a footnote in the last paragraph of the article. In his posthumous memoir, published in 1996, Bissell was far more circumspect about the link between Castro's murder and the Bay of Pigs: "No doubt as I moved forward with plans for the brigade, I hoped the Mafia would achieve success."

* The documents supplied to Fursenko and Naftali show that the Soviet leadership took the intelligence seriously and believed, correctly, that Washington wanted Castro dead. The Cuban state security service was continually arresting alleged counter-revolutionaries and extracting "confessions" of their plotting, on behalf of the CIA, to assassinate Castro.

back into the gambling business in Havana. Trafficante was instrumental in putting the Giancana team in touch with two disaffected Cubans who — upon being promised as much as $50,000 by the CIA — were prepared to murder Castro.

The first was Juan Orta Cordova, whose official title was director general of the office of the prime minister; he was, in effect, Castro's private secretary, with daily access to him, and therefore able, so he told the Giancana team, to slip a poisoned pill into one of Castro's drinks. After much trial and error, the agency had prepared a lethal pill dissolvable in cold water; by early February 1961 at least six of the pills had been provided to Giancana's team for relay to Orta in Cuba. But Orta had already lost his direct access to Castro, or was in the process of losing it. A CIA analysis later quoted the Mafia leaders as complaining that he got "cold feet." Eventually he took refuge in the Venezuelan Embassy in Havana a few days before the Bay of Pigs; he remained under embassy protection, a de facto political prisoner, until October 1964, when Castro permitted him to flee to Mexico City.

Giancana and Trafficante also had a backup plan. Through Rosselli they had made contact early in 1961 with Tony Varona (Dr. Manuel Antonio de Varona y Loredo), a dissident who had worked closely but unsuccessfully with the gambling elements in Havana to oust Castro and was now living in Miami. Varona, a leader of the anti-Castro coalition known as the Democratic Revolutionary Front, was heavily involved in the CIA's planning for the Bay of Pigs; if Orta failed to slip Castro the pill, Varona would somehow find the people inside Cuba to get it done. Varona and the Mafia, in their Miami hotel rooms, knew more about what was planned for Cuba, and for Fidel Castro, than did most of the CIA officers engaged in the day-to-day training of the Cuban exile force in Guatemala.

One CIA operative chose not to know. Jacob B. Esterline, a CIA career man, was named director of operations for the Cuban task force in the summer of 1960, working under Richard Bissell. Getting the exiles ready to hit the beach was his most important assignment yet, and Jake Esterline recalled in a series of interviews for this book that he was gung ho. He was convinced that the exile force, once in Cuba, would take over the government. Sometime that winter, just before Kennedy's inauguration, Esterline was summoned to a meeting with Sheffield Edwards, the CIA's director of security, and got, he said, "one of the big shocks of my life. All of a sudden I was to make a payment of fifty thousand dollars [for the assassins in Cuba] through a blank check." Esterline, who had studied accounting in college, took his fiduciary responsibility as director of operations seriously, and he refused to authorize the funds without a complete briefing. "I was told it was for a mobster. They said the White House wanted this done." Esterline signed two, or perhaps three more vouchers, equally large, over the next few months; sometime shortly before the planned invasion, he learned that the money was going to Johnny Rosselli for assassination plotting. Esterline was told not to write memoranda about the payments. "I didn't tell anybody on my staff," Esterline said, "not even my deputy."

Esterline, who had served as a behind-the-lines commando in Burma during World War II, knew about tough times, he told me; while in Burma, he had paid his operatives in raw opium. But now he was appalled. "Fooling around with the Mafia really got me on edge," he said. "There's a world of difference between facing some guy in combat and setting out to kill him behind his back." Esterline kept his mouth shut, made the payments, and continued training the Cubans for the invasion. He was never formally told by Bissell or Edwards that Castro's death was an integral part of the plan, and, as Esterline ruefully acknowledged in our interview, he resisted facing the truth. "The two [assassination and invasion] were supposed to be contiguous, but I didn't want to believe that," Esterline said. "How do I tell people to get ready for mortal combat when there's some quick and easy solution? They were being so ruthless. I guess I did put it together, but I was trapped. Was I supposed to blow a whistle?"

There was no office in the Kennedy administration prepared to handle such a complaint. Even before being sworn in, the president himself had told the CIA to be ready to kill, and the attorney general, his brother, would become his ally in political assassination after the Bay of Pigs, continually pressuring the CIA's men to get on with their lethal plans, instructions long suspected and assumed but not confirmed until this book. Bobby Kennedy's role was two-edged, as usual: he was the president's surrogate, demanding that the CIA do more, and he was the president's protector, making sure that the FBI and other federal police agencies were unable to derail the assassination operations.

Jack Kennedy had every reason to believe in April 1961 that Sam Giancana and his men in Miami and Havana would do the deed. Giancana had delivered, as promised, on the 1960 election. And, as Kennedy surely knew, no one was more adept at murder.

That confidence perhaps made it easier for Kennedy and the men who ran the CIA to ignore their friends in the agency, the press, and elsewhere who sought to warn the administration that the secret of the Cuban training in Guatemala and planned invasion was no secret — not in America, and most certainly not in Cuba. In late 1960 Thomas Polgar, the CIA station chief in Hamburg, Germany, was informed by Axel Springer, the conservative and influential German publisher, that he wished to see Allen Dulles. A meeting was quickly arranged. Once in Washington, Polgar recalled in a 1994 interview for this book, Springer told Dulles that "he and his reporters were picking up stories about [exile] training in Guatemala" for an invasion of Cuba. Springer added that he had "no problems with that, ideologically, but if my reporters can pick it up, surely Castro's people can pick it up, too." Dulles laughed away the warning, telling the German, "It's true that we're training Cubans, but it's better to train them than to put them on relief."*

That winter Ernest Betancourt, a onetime Castro supporter who defected after Castro seized power, ran into arrogance and hostility

---

* Polgar also got a firsthand glimpse into the acute tensions inside the CIA over Bissell's operation. The clandestine service was essentially divided into two camps in 1960 and 1961 — those agents who followed Bissell's leadership and supported the exile invasion, and those who were loyal to Richard Helms, the deputy chief of operations, who was convinced that large-scale maneuvers like the Bay of Pigs would destroy the CIA. Late in 1960, Polgar recalled, he was offered a Cuba-related job by Bissell and asked Helms for advice. "Remember, I didn't offer that job to you," Helms said. Polgar understood, he said, that Helms was warning him to "stay away." A few months later Polgar, again in Washington, was given an unofficial briefing about the planned invasion and was "appalled. I went to see Helms and said it was a terrible mistake. Helms's response was, 'No one's asked for your opinion. Don't touch it with a ten-foot pole.'"

when he attempted to warn the White House about the folly of the exile invasion. In an interview for this book, Betancourt said that he approached the journalist Charles Bartlett, a Kennedy confidant, and cautioned that the administration was viewing Cuba only in terms of the Cold War and ignoring the bases of Castro's legitimate popularity there. "My judgment was that the operation was antihistorical," Betancourt told me. "There was a total lack of understanding [in Washington] of what Fidel had done." Betancourt, one of the few Cubans in the anti-Castro movement to oppose an exile invasion, had gone to Bartlett with his concerns, he said, because he knew that "talking to him was like talking to Kennedy." A few days later Bartlett called "and warned me about the [anti-invasion] group I was associating with." The implication was clear: Betancourt's complaint about the pending invasion had endangered his political standing in the United States. Bartlett, in a subsequent interview for this book, acknowledged that Betancourt had warned him that "everybody in Havana knows an invasion is coming." But, he said, "I didn't want to burden Jack," and he chose to relay Betancourt's complaints instead to Allen Dulles. Weeks later, as the invasion was getting under way, Bartlett said, Dulles telephoned to say that "he'd checked out my story and it wasn't true that the operation was out of control." He also assured Bartlett that the planned invasion "had not leaked to the Cubans."

Disaster struck on April 17. Fidel Castro's army and militia routed the CIA-recruited and trained brigade of 1,400 Cuban exiles which attempted an amphibious landing at the Bay of Pigs, on Cuba's south coast. President Kennedy had been told that the landing would trigger a widespread revolt against the regime. But the only resistance was against the exile brigade, which in two days of fierce fighting suffered devastating losses of 114 dead and nearly 1,200 captured. Castro claimed victory in a four-hour televised speech, mocking the Kennedy administration for its misreading of the Cuban people.

At the time, it remained a White House secret that on the eve of the invasion Kennedy personally canceled a second air strike that was considered crucial to the success of the landings. Eight air sorties had left from Nicaragua two days before the landing, but the exile pilots, flying unmarked B-26 bombers of World War II vintage, failed to wipe out the small but effective Cuban air force. A ninth B-26 flew directly from Nicaragua to Miami, where the pilot proclaimed that he was part of a group of Cuban air force defectors who had spontaneously carried out the bombings as part of a revolt against the Castro regime. The cover story fooled no one, and Kennedy, fearful that his administration would become even more closely linked to the invasion, refused to let the second bombing take place — with the inevitable deadly consequences for the exile army already approaching Cuba's beaches. The young president's direct role in the failed operation, and his indecision, would become public over the next fifteen years, but both would remain secret during the spring of 1961.

Kennedy eliminated much of the controversy over who ordered what when he told a news conference on April 21 that "there's an old saying that victory has a hundred fathers and defeat is an orphan. . . . I'm the responsible officer of the government and that is quite obvious."* His seeming willingness to take the heat won him enormous support from the public, who shared Kennedy's fear and hatred of Castro, and his public approval rating soared. In private, however, Kennedy complained to all, including many reporters, that he had done little more than follow the recommendations of the CIA and the Joint Chiefs of Staff. "I just took their advice," he insisted a few days later, during a meeting with Dwight Eisenhower, whose administration had initiated the invasion planning a year earlier and had also recruited Giancana and Rosselli to assassinate Castro. At the time, none of the journalists reported Kennedy's private eagerness to have it both ways, but at least one did in a later memoir. Hedley Donovan, onetime editor in chief of Time Inc., wrote in 1987 that the

---

* Kennedy opened his news conference by flatly declaring a moratorium on any questions about Cuba: "I do not think that any useful national purpose would be served by my going further into the Cuban question this morning." It was a device, after the travails of Vietnam and Watergate, that would be denied to future presidents. When one journalist dared to bring up the subject, Kennedy merely repeated his view that talking about Cuba would not "benefit us during the present difficult situation." He suggested, however, that what the reporters were hearing — presumably from Castro and his supporters around the world — was not true and added, without any evident irony: "One of the problems of a free society, a problem not met by a dictatorship, is this problem of information."

president "was getting preposterous praise — and amazingly high ratings in the polls — for simply stating the inescapable constitutional fact that he was 'responsible.' Which did not stop him from telling scores of friends, senators, journalists, only slightly privately, that his mistake was to pay any attention to the CIA and the military brass."

The portrait of a young president victimized by subordinates was reprised in *Kennedy,* Ted Sorensen's memoir, a huge bestseller when published in 1965. "John Kennedy," Sorensen wrote, "was capable of choosing a wrong course but never a stupid one; and to understand how he came to make this decision requires a review not merely of the facts but of *the facts and assumptions that were presented to him*" (emphasis in original). Sorensen argued that Kennedy had been misinformed by the CIA and the military, because the president's doubts and questions were being answered by those experts "most committed to supporting the plan." Arthur Schlesinger, in *A Thousand Days,* also published in 1965, theorized that Kennedy's mistake in authorizing the invasion stemmed from his inexperience, having been in office only seventy-seven days. "He could not know which of his advisers were competent and which were not," Schlesinger wrote. He told of a lunch after the debacle in which Kennedy acknowledged that "I probably made a mistake in keeping Allen Dulles on" as CIA director.

Kennedy had many doubts about the feasibility of the Bay of Pigs invasion, Schlesinger noted. But he was also concerned — as was Dulles — about the "disposal problem" if the operation was called off before it began and the Cuban exiles went back, unbloodied, to Florida, where they would surely tell their story of frustration and disappointment to every journalist they could find. Schlesinger quoted Kennedy as saying of the Cuban exile brigade, "If we have to get rid of these . . . men, it is much better to dump them in Cuba than in the United States, especially if that is where they want to go." It was a rare glimpse into Kennedy's instinct for self-preservation. He understood that the political price of canceling the invasion would be great, far greater than if it were to go forward and collapse in failure. By canceling, he would appear weak and indecisive, and give the Republicans an opportunity to accuse him of being soft on communism. But Schlesinger's account depicted Kennedy's dilemma in far loftier terms. If the president canceled, he "would forever be haunted by the feeling that his scruples had preserved Castro in power." In going forward, the historian added, Kennedy was motivated "by the commitment of the Cuban patriots" and "saw no obligation to protect the Castro regime from democratic Cubans."

Sorensen and Schlesinger apparently did not know the critical truths about Cuba. They did not know that candidate Kennedy had been privately informed by CIA officials and some participants before the election that the island would soon be invaded by the secret exile army — information he used to great effect against Richard Nixon. And they were not privy to one of the major reasons for President Kennedy's last-minute ambivalence about the Bay of Pigs operation: Sam Giancana's henchmen inside Cuba had been unable to murder Castro in the days immediately before the invasion.

One of Kennedy's most controversial and least-understood decisions during the Bay of Pigs was the cancellation of the second bombing mission. There has been an outpouring of declassified White House documents in recent years on the invasion, none of them dealing with assassination. But the assumption that Castro would be dead when the first Cuban exiles went ashore, and the fact that he was not, may explain Kennedy's decision to cut his losses. The Mafia had failed and a very much alive Castro was rallying his troops.

The White House documents that have been declassified make it clear that Kennedy, Bundy, and others on the president's staff were intimately involved with the day-to-day planning and decision-making for the invasion. One especially significant memorandum from Bundy to Kennedy, dated March 15, 1961, one month prior to the invasion, shows that Kennedy's subsequent cancellation of the second B-26 bombing strike — a decision not publicly disclosed at the time — was done with full knowledge of the consequences. "I think," Bundy told the president, "there is unanimous agreement that at some stage the Castro Air Force must be removed. . . . My own belief is that this air battle has to come sooner or later, and that the longer we put it off, the harder it will be. . . . Even the revised landing plan depends strongly upon prompt action against Castro's air." Bundy was recommending that one air strike, involving six or eight B-26s, should come "some time *before* the invasion" (emphasis in original). The final invasion plans, as approved by Kennedy, doubled the number of B-26 strikes to two — one on April 15 and the second two days later, on the morning of the Bay of Pigs landings, to ensure the destruction of Castro's air force. The first strike failed to do the job — and it also led to immediate Cuban and Soviet protests in the United Nations and elsewhere.

Kennedy's refusal to go forward with the essential second bombing mission — or, for that matter, simply to call off the exile invasion — was not a military but a political decision. As Kennedy had to know, his decision amounted to a death sentence for the Cuban exiles fighting on the ground. But he and Nikita Khrushchev had just agreed, after weeks of secret back-and-forth, to an early June summit meeting in Europe. A second bombing attack was sure to focus attention on American involvement; it would jeopardize Kennedy's face-to-face meeting with the Soviet premier and his chances for an early foreign-policy triumph. In terms of domestic politics, the president understood that a failure at the Bay of Pigs was preferable to the political heat he would take from Republicans and conservative Democrats if he did not go forward with the invasion. He would be considered just another liberal, like the much-maligned Adlai Stevenson. Nothing — not even the death and capture of hundreds of Cuban patriots — was worth that.

Robert Maheu, still working in Miami to enlist the Mafia's help, knew that Castro's assassination was integral to the invasion plan. But that fact was so sensitive he had not been authorized by James O'Connell, Maheu's liaison with the CIA, to share it with his Mafia contacts. Giancana and his men had no need to know, Maheu told me in an interview: "Their job was to get rid of Castro."

Over the winter and spring of 1961, Maheu told me, O'Connell, chief of the operational support division in the CIA's office of security, met privately with him and kept him up to date on the progress of the exile army's readiness in Guatemala. The two men understood that if the Mafia failed to assassinate Castro, the invasion of Cuba would go forward — but only as long as President Kennedy authorized air cover and the bombing of Cuban military targets. "Everyone involved to our knowledge had said that this invasion could not be a success unless the air raid took place and the adequate air cover was carried out," Maheu told me. On the eve of the landings, Maheu was told that Kennedy had canceled the second raid and air cover. "I asked if as a consequence of those decisions the invasion had been called off," he recalled. "We could not get an answer. Finally we did get an answer — that it had not been called off. And I tried to reach the president at the White House." Maheu could not get past the White House switchboard and turned to a friend and former client, David J. McDonald, president of the United Steelworkers of America, a Kennedy favorite whose union had funneled untold millions of dollars into the 1960 campaign. "I begged him to try to get the president to call off the invasion," Maheu told me. "Dave reported to me that he had been unable to reach the president."

At that point, Maheu recalled thinking, "I'm finished." He returned to Las Vegas and his job as a security consultant and said nothing in public about Cuba and the CIA until his 1975 testimony before the Church Committee. "I didn't want anything more to do with it. I never talked to Sam [Giancana] again."

Maheu believes today that the Kennedy administration was criminally irresponsible in permitting the Cuban exiles to land at the Bay of Pigs without the support necessary for survival. "When we called off the [second] air raid and the adequate air cover, we inherited the responsibility of calling off the invasion," he told me. "We could not allow those kids to hit those beaches and be destroyed by hardware that should have been destroyed by us hours before. And as far as I'm concerned, we thereby indulged in mass murder."

As the "kids" of the exile brigade fell, Castro was noisily leading the successful defense of his nation. Sam Giancana's assassination efforts had failed: Juan Orta fled to the safety of sanctuary in the Venezuelan Embassy, and Tony Varona's gangster friends in Cuba were not able to pull the trigger.

Kennedy continued to cut his diplomatic and political losses while the invasion turned to disaster. As he had warned the Pentagon brass beforehand, he refused to permit American jet fighters and warships to come to the aid of the Cuban exiles. A navy task force, warplanes and ships at the ready, sat in international waters off Cuba and watched Castro's military destroy the exile force. The military's frustration was heightened by the fact, not widely known at the time, that the White House — and not the Pentagon — was running the show in the waters and airspace near Cuba; the president's men, not generals and admirals, were deciding where to dispatch each ship and each warplane.

Kennedy's fear, which would return in future crises, seemed to be that he would lose control of the military as the invasion floundered. An important oral interview — one overlooked by historians — was recorded in the early 1970s at the U.S. Naval Institute. Admiral Robert L. Dennison, commander in chief of the U.S. Navy forces in the Atlantic, told of being ordered by the Pentagon to have his destroyers set up a safe haven fifteen miles off the coast of the Bay of Pigs and wait there for possible survivors of the debacle. The orders, as relayed by General Lyman L. Lemnitzer, chairman of the Joint Chiefs of Staff, not only instructed Dennison what to do but how to do it. "It was really a tactical order," Dennison recounted. "I wouldn't have sent the thing to a captain. . . . So I called up Lemnitzer on the scrambler phone and said, 'I've gotten a good many orders in my life, but this is a strange one. . . . This is the first order I ever got from somebody who found it necessary to interpret his own orders.' [Lemnitzer] said, 'Where did you get this directive?' And I said, 'I got it from you.' He said, 'Who do you think wrote it?' I said, 'You did.' He said, 'No, I didn't. That order was written at 1600 Pennsylvania Avenue.' "

Dennison, who died in 1980, was no amateur in the ways of political Washington; he spent five years as the naval aide to President Truman before returning to combat assignments. In his view, he said in his Naval Institute interview, many of the orders emanating from the Joint Chiefs of Staff during the crisis "came from the White House or from CIA, with very little understanding of what the situation requires. . . . I hope somebody, like Lemnitzer, has some diaries or something, but there's too much of value in this whole story to just have it disappear. But, so far as I know, the record that I have is the only one extant."

Lemnitzer did not write a memoir, and none of the reportage and histories of the Bay of Pigs and its aftermath has revealed the precise extent to which Jack Kennedy's White House directly controlled events.

As the Cuban operation, with its negative political ramifications, was failing, Jack Kennedy turned to his brother Bobby, who would remain his only real confidant over the next thirty months, a presidential protector not afraid of anyone in the American government. After the Bay of Pigs, it was Bobby Kennedy who took the hard line or delivered the bad news, while the president said nothing. The two brothers moved to minimize the political fallout from Cuba, and their hardheaded zeal in so doing led to a final humiliation for Bissell, whose sure thing as the next director of the CIA dissolved with the failure in Cuba.

Sometime on April 19 the Kennedys received the unsettling news that four American pilots, members of the Alabama Air National Guard who were in Nicaragua secretly training the Cubans, had ignored the president's refusal to authorize a second strike and had taken off on their own, in two B-26s, to go to war against Castro. The two bombers inflicted heavy damage to the Cuban forces before being shot down. It was not immediately known whether the pilots survived. The possibility existed that an Alabama pilot, if one survived, would be put on display by Castro on Havana television — as Francis Gary Powers had been shown off a year earlier by Khrushchev in Moscow. The White House's repeated public insistence — in Washington and in the United Nations — that no Americans were involved inside Cuba would be in shambles.

On the afternoon of April 19, with the fate of the rogue pilots still unclear, Bissell was summoned to an Oval Office meeting with John and Robert Kennedy. It took Bissell thirty-two years to reveal to Janet Weininger, the daughter of one of the dead pilots, what happened at the meeting. "When everything was over," Bissell told Weininger in 1993, as she recounted to me in a 1995 interview, "I went to brief the president. Bobby met me when I entered [the president's office]. He was short but got right in my face as best he could. The first words out of his mouth were 'Those American pilots had better goddamned well be dead.' All he could see was another Francis Gary Powers. . . . Bobby's only concern was the image of his brother and what the pilots could do if they were captured. For once I stood as tall as possible, glad to be well over his height," the elderly Bissell told Weininger, according to her notes, which she made available for this book. "Bobby was like a wounded animal, while the president just sat back and let him attack." The Central Intelligence Agency, Bobby Kennedy said, "had better keep the [pilot] families quiet." The attorney general insisted that a cover story be devised for the disappearance of the four Alabama pilots, all of whom were determined to have died. Weininger described Bissell to me as someone who "had been waiting a long time to share the pain" of the scene in the White House. At the time of the Bay of Pigs, Bissell told her, he "didn't know the real Jack Kennedy."

In a subsequent interview for this book, Jake Esterline, Bissell's deputy, confirmed that he, too, knew of Bissell's meeting with the two Kennedys. Esterline said that Bissell, obviously distressed, began a conversation with him shortly after the failed invasion by saying, "I don't like to tell you this." He then said, "Bobby wanted them dead," Esterline continued. "Bissell did tell me that."

Robert Kennedy, worried about the political fallout from a leak about the Alabamans' deaths, sought to delay or deny military pensions for the men. The wife of one of the pilots got in touch with Oscar Wyatt, the wealthy Texas oilman who was a strong supporter of the Kennedy-Johnson ticket in 1960. "I went up to see Jack," Wyatt said in an interview for this book in 1995. "Bobby was there. I said, 'The woman has kids.' Bobby said, 'The hell with this foolishness' "—making the point that if the pilots were paid, word of their link to the Kennedy White House would be known. "I said," Wyatt continued, " 'Look, if you don't do this, I'll walk over to the *New York Times* and the *Washington Post* and tell them the whole story about the pilots.' " The president finally ended the dispute by saying, "We'll do it. We'll pay the pensions." The CIA eventually retained a Miami attorney named Alex Carlson to serve as a financial buffer between the U.S. government payments and the families of the four pilots.* The fam-

* "I was hired by the CIA [after the Bay of Pigs] to handle the families," Carlson readily acknowledged in a telephone interview in 1995. Kennedy "really screwed them [the pilots]," he added. "It would have been so easy to let the navy come in." The attorney added that, at the time of his involvement, the fact that four Americans had been shot

ilies were paid, but did not receive the full value of the military pensions.

Bissell paid the inevitable price for his failure: he was cast out of the White House loop and permitted to resign in early 1962. There were a few quiet years at a Washington think tank, but his government career was over. He held no more high-level jobs before moving back to a life of yachting, reading, and reflection in his hometown of Hartford, Connecticut.

Bissell remained loyal to the presidents he had served, or to the presidency, throughout the tense months of 1975, when the Church Committee was seeking to find out whether Eisenhower and Kennedy had known of and authorized assassination plotting against Castro. The senators on the committee never seemed to comprehend the obvious: the whole point of covert action is to provide the president with a secret channel for carrying out foreign policy without accountability. The men running the agency, when called to testify before the Senate, viewed it as their duty to blur any authorization by Eisenhower or Kennedy. Even in secret testimony, telling the truth would be a breach of faith with the presidency, and would turn the CIA into just another finger-pointing federal bureaucracy.*

down over Cuba was considered a vital national security secret. Janet Weininger, who was in first grade when her father was killed in Cuba, recalled receiving $1,000 per month in government funds until she finished her college education. Her mother, Mrs. Margaret Ray, received a stipend of $225 a month until she remarried in 1965, when the funds were cut off.

* Telling the truth about who had ordered what, as a few journalists understood, also would have made the truth teller a pariah inside his community. In his perceptive study of Richard Helms, *The Man Who Kept the Secrets,* Thomas Powers noted that Helms's impossibly vague testimony before the Church Committee was based on two factors: his promise not to tell the secrets and the fact that "there would not be one single piece of paper to support anyone who had the temerity to tell the truth." The truth was, Powers concluded, that the Kennedy brothers had ordered Castro's assassination. "If Helms had said that," wrote Powers, "(which in my opinion he could have), he not only would have been the target of some extremely caustic comment, but from that day forward he would have lunched alone."

Bissell gave the senators a primer on plausible deniability, explaining that the goal was to indicate "the general objective of the operation that was contemplated," thus giving the president the option of terminating the operation while also providing "just as little information . . . as possible beyond an understanding of its general purpose." Thus, Bissell added, the president would be able "to deny knowledge of the operation if it should surface."

Plausible deniability meant that those who briefed the president could not testify honestly about having done so. At one point, a frustrated Senator Church expressed surprise that Bissell and Dulles would admit to briefing President-elect Kennedy about the planned invasion of Cuba but also claim that they had not told him of the Castro assassination plans: "It just seems too strange . . . that you would tell Mr. Kennedy about one matter and not the other." Bissell's answer was double-talk: "It is quite possible that Mr. Dulles did say something about an attempt to or the possibility of making use of syndicate characters for this purpose. I do not remember his doing so at that briefing. My belief is that had he done so, he probably would have done so in rather general terms and that neither of us was in a position to go into detail on the matter."

In their memoirs, both Schlesinger and Sorensen sought to depict Jack Kennedy as a victim of the CIA's ambitions, a leader who inherited an invasion plan from his predecessor and reluctantly let it unfold. "The whole project seemed to move mysteriously and inexorably toward execution," wrote Sorensen, "without the President able either to obtain a firm grip on it or reverse it. . . . In later months, he would be grateful that he had learned so many major lessons . . . at so relatively small and temporary a cost." Schlesinger described Kennedy as "wondering" for months after the Bay of Pigs "how a rational and responsible government could ever have become involved in so ill-starred an adventure."

Marcus Raskin had one answer. His first day on the job, as a disarmament expert for McGeorge Bundy, had been the fateful Monday of the Bay of Pigs landings. A few days later he was invited to attend a staff postmortem on the invasion in the office of Walter W. Rostow, a hard-line political economist from the Massachusetts Institute of Technology who was Bundy's deputy. Many of the White House staff were there, including Schlesinger, Richard Goodwin, and Bromley Smith, the administrator of Bundy's staff. "Walt always had a large bowl of fruit in his office," Raskin recalled, "and so a dozen of us sat around eating the fruit, much the way, I suppose, the Roman emperor's assistants would sit around eating fruit and talking about the outlying provinces and the outlying wars. Mac Bundy then walks into the room and says, 'Well, I guess Che learned more from Guatemala than we did.'" Ernesto "Che" Guevara, the radical Latin American leader, was widely seen in Washington as the intellectual guru of Castro's revolution. Guevara had been in Guatemala in 1954, when the CIA, successfully using air cover, overthrew the Arbenz regime.

Raskin asked, "Well, Mac, it's very interesting that Che learned something from Guatemala. What have we learned from Cuba?" There was a moment of silence, and Bromley Smith then remarked, "There should be no recriminations. There must be loyalty." Later that day, or perhaps the next morning, Raskin got a telephone call from one of Bundy's aides, who told him, "Mac would appreciate it very much if you did not go to any more staff meetings." If he had something to say, Raskin was told, he could see Bundy personally in his office. Raskin remained on Bundy's staff until June of 1962, but he understood that in terms of effectiveness, as he recalled with a laugh, "I was done after two days."

President Kennedy, devastated, turned to his father for solace. Rose Kennedy, in her memoir, wrote of telephoning her husband late on April 19 and learning that "Jack had been on the phone with him much of the day, also Bobby. I asked how [Jack] was feeling and he said 'dying'— [the] result of trying to bring up Jack's morale after the Cuban debacle. . . . Jackie walked upstairs with me and said he'd been so upset all day. Had practically been in tears, felt he had been misinformed by CIA and others. . . . Said she had never seen him so depressed except at time of his operation [in 1954]."

Kennedy called in Clark Clifford, who had advised Democratic presidents since Harry Truman, and asked him to reconstitute Eisenhower's Board of Consultants on intelligence activities; the advisory board had been disbanded, along with many others, when Kennedy took office. Clifford, who had been shunted aside during the 1960 campaign by the Irish Mafia, was obviously still aggrieved during a 1994 interview for this book. "My God," he told me of his post–Bay of Pigs visit to the White House, "you never saw such a whipped bunch. [Kennedy] was at the bottom of the barrel — totally, totally discouraged." Clifford, the political veteran, said he saw it coming. He had listened to Kennedy aides Kenny O'Donnell and Lawrence O'Brien after the election and thought to himself: "Oh boy, they think they're going to change politics and change government — like a road sign that says, 'Brilliance ahead.'

"Three months later," Clifford said, "I saw the roof fall in."

The Bay of Pigs was the first political defeat of Jack Kennedy's life and he sought revenge — but not on the advisers and the government agencies that, so he told everyone, had misled him. His target was Fidel Castro, and he spent his remaining days in office determined to make Castro pay — with his life, preferably — for staining the Kennedy honor.

But there were other, more immediate, concerns in the world, and not all of them were on America's doorstep. On April 21, Walt Rostow sent the president a memorandum arguing that "the greatest problem we face is not to have the whole of our foreign policy thrown off balance by what we feel and what we do about Cuba itself." Rostow informed the president that he had urged caution to Bobby Kennedy, whose instinct was to deal immediately, and brutally, with Castro's Cuba. "As I said to the Attorney General the other day, when you are in a fight and knocked off your feet, the most dangerous thing to do is to come out swinging wildly. Clearly we must cope with Castro in the next several years. . . . But let us do some fresh homework."

America needed to learn how to deal with communist aggression, Rostow said, and he had a recommended learning ground: "Vietnam is the place where — in the Attorney General's phrase — we must prove that we are not a paper tiger. . . . We have to prove that Vietnam and Southeast Asia can be held."

At a National Security Council meeting on April 29, according to the Pentagon Papers, the U.S. government's secret history of the Vietnam War, the president approved a series of clandestine actions to escalate the war. Within a few weeks four hundred members of the army's Special Forces were on their way to South Vietnam, where they were to begin training agents for operations against the North. The Americans were to help the South Vietnamese "form networks of resistance, covert bases and teams for sabotage and light harassment." The quagmire was forming.

John F. Kennedy turned again to the world of stealth and secret armies to solve a foreign policy problem. He had learned a valuable lesson from the Bay of Pigs. In South Vietnam there would be far more presidential control and far more secrecy. He and his brother would handle it themselves.

15

SECRET SERVICE

Image saved Jack Kennedy and his White House from the political consequences of the Bay of Pigs. There was no political bloodletting — no demand for congressional hearings, no exhaustive analyses by the *New York Times* or *Washington Post*. Americans rallied around their attractive and contemporary leader, and his approval rating rose to a remarkable 83 percent. Kennedy's glamour made him the 1961 equivalent of a Teflon president, someone to whom no bad news could stick.

The manipulation was extraordinary. The president was living a public lie as an attentive husband and hardworking chief executive, a speed reader who spent hours each night poring over bulky government files. But the Secret Service agents assigned to the White House presidential detail saw Jack Kennedy in a different light: as someone obsessed with sex, and willing to take enormous risks to gratify that obsession. They saw a president who came late many mornings to the Oval Office, and was not readily available for hours during the day to his immediate staff and his national security aides; a president, some thought, whose behavior was demeaning to the office. In a series of unusual on-the-record interviews for this book, four of these men agreed to tell what they saw.

The mythmaking and media wooing began soon after Kennedy took office. Newspapers and magazines were filled with articles and photographs, usually touted as exclusive, of family life in the White House or a day in the life of the president. Even the most earnest publications fell prey. In March 1961 the deadly serious *U.S. News & World Report* devoted ten pages to photographs of JFK at work. In April a *Washington Star* photographer who had been granted access to the Oval Office in order to capture the president at his desk came away with a winsome series of photos of Caroline, then three years old, chatting on her father's telephone with her grandfather Joe. The photos were syndicated to newspapers around the nation.

That month *Life* magazine published a glowing account of Kennedy's "voracious" reading habits, depicting — undoubtedly with accuracy — the president's absorption with newspaper stories about his administration. The article, written by Hugh Sidey, was accompanied by a photograph of Kennedy poring over a morning paper. Sidey's story noted that the rate at which Kennedy read "has not been precisely determined, but his speed is at least 1,200 words per minute and sometimes more than that (the average person reads 250 words per minute)." One Kennedy adviser told Sidey that he watched as the president read a dense twenty-six-page memorandum on economics in ten minutes and then "asked 25 questions about it — intelligent questions."*

A professional photographer named Jacques Lowe was hired by

---

* Years later, in his oral history for the Kennedy Library, Sidey told of telephoning a reading institute in Baltimore where, he had been told, Senator Kennedy had taken a speed-reading course. No one there could confirm such a high rate of speed. "They suggested that he probably read about seven or eight hundred words a minute, which was twice normal," Sidey recalled. "The president didn't like that one bit." After some back-and-forth, Sidey recalled, he and the president agreed on a reading speed of 1,200 words per minute, and that was the statistic published in *Life* magazine. "I noted for months and years after," Sidey told the library, that "this became the real gospel on his reading speed."

the family itself and given carte blanche to roam through the White House, taking photos at will. The major American television networks were also given unprecedented access. In February 1961 CBS presented a half-hour taped telecast, narrated by Walter Cronkite, that purported to be the first time television was permitted to show "the actual conduct of official business" in the Oval Office. Two months later CBS was invited to film a documentary about presidential family life in the second-floor living quarters of the White House, known to the staff as the Mansion. Jacqueline Kennedy told the cameras, without any apparent irony, that she wanted her daughter, Caroline, to have a "normal" life. John F. Kennedy, Jr., was then five months old.

Kennedy was the first president to hold televised news conferences, averaging one every two weeks in his thousand days. An estimated 65 million Americans tuned in to the first conference, five days after the inauguration, and saw the president at his informative best, answering questions — especially tough ones — with charm and wit. The news conferences and TV specials furthered the image, enunciated by Joe Kennedy years earlier, of John Kennedy as a celebrity politician, a leader whose presence inspired confidence and loyalty as it sold magazines and attracted huge television audiences.

There was nothing accidental about JFK's decision to use television as a White House bully pulpit, just as Franklin Delano Roosevelt had used radio for his fireside chats. Before his inauguration, Kennedy met privately in Palm Beach with Blair Clark, a classmate from Harvard who was a reporter for CBS News. There was talk of an ambassadorial appointment for Clark but, more important, much talk about how to use television. "I don't think he had anything but an instinct about television," Clark recalled in a 1997 interview for this book. "He knew newspapers were less important. He instinctively knew that it was absolutely vital that he use it right." The president-elect understood that he was a good performer, Clark added. "Jack Kennedy never forgot that he was an actor in a public drama. He had a quip and a smile — he was an actor about that. And that's what you should be. Roosevelt was too, of course."

Clark, who became a vice president of CBS News, said he helped persuade Jackie Kennedy to conduct the televised tour of the White House, and overrode her husband's worry that he would be criticized politically for exploiting his wife. It wasn't a hard sell. "He and she were so charming and young — the new generation," Clark told me. "And the kiddies. There was a young couple struggling with problems — not household problems, but the problems of state. That was appealing. Never mind the serious business of government."

The White House, like its leader, seemed to be more open and more accessible. "What impressed people was how candid he was," recalled Fred Holborn, a Senate aide who moved with Kennedy to the White House. "He wouldn't be nervous if you were in the room while he was taking telephone calls." One surprise, Holborn added in a 1995 interview for this book, was the absence of Joseph Kennedy at the White House: "It was amazing how infrequently he called, and he'd only appear personally once a year." Holborn, for all of his years with JFK, didn't understand how it worked. Evelyn Lincoln explained in one of her interviews for this book that the Kennedy family had leased a private telephone line that ran from Joe Kennedy's office in New York directly to the Oval Office and to the president's living quarters. JFK also had a telephone installed in his private hideaway off the Oval Office. "It was a little office with a couch and telephone where [the president] could go and rest," Lincoln told me. "It was called the prayer room. When anyone he'd rather talk to in his private way called, he'd say [on the intercom] to me, 'Line five,' and he'd go take it." When his father called on his leased telephone line, Lincoln added, she would walk into the Oval Office and give him a card saying, "Your dad," and the president would move to his hideaway — especially if there were others present — to take the call.

The discrepancy between the public perception and the reality deepened after the president's murder. Arthur Schlesinger and Ted Sorensen followed the script in their Kennedy books, depicting the president's daily routine in the White House as one of constant work and constant action. "It was always an exhaustingly full and long day," Sorensen wrote, "as he remained in the office until 7:30, 8:00 or even 8:30 P.M., sometimes returning after his customarily late dinner, and usually reading reports and memoranda in the Mansion until midnight." Even when he and his wife were socializing with friends at dinner followed by a movie in the White House screening room, the president "would often slip away after fifteen minutes of the film to work, and then rejoin them when it was over." One of the president's few moments of relaxation, wrote Sorensen, came in the early afternoon, when he took fifteen-minute swims, accompanied by Dave Powers, his personal aide, in the White House heated pool.

Schlesinger, in his version, wrote that the president worked through the morning and then took a relaxing swim in the White House pool before lunching in the Mansion alone or with his wife. "When his family was away," the historian added, "the President used to have his afternoon appointments on the second floor. But generally he returned to the West Wing [Oval Office] after his nap, where he worked until seven-thirty or eight at night." In the evenings, there were small dinner parties, depicted by Schlesinger as "the most agreeable occasions in the world." Weekends were preserved "as much as possible for themselves and the children."

There is certainly a core of truth to the idyllic Sorensen and Schlesinger accounts. But they are far from the whole story, and far from the reality of life inside the Kennedy White House. The most dispassionate observers were the Secret Service agents assigned to the president's personal detail, the men whose responsibility was to be consistently at Kennedy's side ready to take a bullet meant for him. Their account of Kennedy's daily routine in the White House bears little resemblance to what is known. The accounts also share a crucial starting point: none of the agents, before they were assigned to the White House — the most prestigious job in the Secret Service — had any idea of what was going on. They have kept their silence, until now.

Larry Newman, the first college graduate in his family, proudly joined the Secret Service in 1960, and in the fall of 1961 was quickly promoted to the presidential detail. His first major assignment was to provide security for a presidential speech in Seattle in November. Newman and Clint Hill, a senior agent, flew to Washington ten days before Kennedy's visit. "We had excellent cooperation with the Seattle police department," Newman recalled in a 1995 interview for this book, and the president made his speech and returned without incident to the safety of his suite in the Olympic Hotel. The floor of the hotel had been sealed; as Secret Service protocol dictated, access was limited to those with special clearance. That night Newman got what he called "my baptism by fire."

Sometime after Kennedy was back, Newman heard "a commotion up at the elevator." A local Democratic sheriff "had come out of the elevator with two hookers and was bringing them down toward the president's suite. I stopped the man, and he was loudly proclaiming that the two girls were for the president's suite." The sheriff's party included a group of local policemen who had helped to provide security for Kennedy's speech. It was clear, Newman told me, that the sheriff and the policemen knew the women and knew they were "high-class call girls." Before long, Dave Powers came out of the suite. The sheriff tried to walk inside with the two women, but Powers "cut him off," Newman recalled, "thanked him for bringing the girls up, and took them into the suite."

Newman was embarrassed, and at one point threatened to arrest the sheriff for interfering with the activities of federal officers. "He only wanted the thrill of letting the president know what a great favor he'd done for him, but what he wanted to do" — personally deliver the prostitutes — "was impossible." Before leaving the floor, the sheriff officiously warned the two women that "if any word of this night gets out, I'll see that you both go to Stillicoom [a state mental hospital] and never get out."

"I couldn't believe he said this, but he did," Newman recalled. "One of the policemen, a lieutenant, asked me, 'Does this go on all the time?' I just didn't know what to say and said, 'Well, we travel during the day. This only happens at night.' The cops, the firemen, and everybody else" involved with presidential security had been "alerted that these girls were going in and meeting with the president," Newman said. "There was no question about that."

Later that evening, Newman made what should have been a routine check of security along the corridors of the U-shaped hotel. The presidential party had booked all the rooms on the floor, and the suites for the president and his senior aides, Powers and Kenny O'Donnell, were located on one end of the corridor. At least six Seattle police officers had been assigned to guard the fire escape exits on the floor, but Newman found their posts unmanned. Instead the officers were all bunched together in a fire escape well directly across from the presidential suites. In a room next to the president's, two young women on the White House staff could be seen having a three-way sexual encounter with O'Donnell. The president's chief of staff had drawn the window's gauze curtains but not the heavier blinds. The policemen were passing a pair of binoculars back and forth — binoculars that were supposed to be used to survey the streets outside. "They were waiting in turn so they could watch," Newman told me. "The sergeant apologized to me and they reposted themselves, and that was it for me for the day. I didn't know what to do or say.

"What I saw in Seattle became commonplace to me and the other agents when we were on the road. Dave Powers was the interface on these occasions, and he would find the women or bring the women along." The women would be brought out of the president's suite after three or four hours. "This became a matter of great concern," Newman told me, "because we didn't know who these people were and we didn't know what they had on their person. You would just look up and see Dave Powers mincing down the hall and saying 'Hi pal,' and we had no way to stop it. We were told to just not interfere with it. We didn't know if the president that next morning would be dead or alive."

Newman, now living in Fort Collins, Colorado, is quick to say that he and his fellow agents loved Kennedy and loved the fact that he made an effort to learn the names of the agents and some personal details about them. "It was highly frustrating, because we thought so much of the guy," Newman told me. "We really didn't like seeing him think so little of himself, if that's the right word." One solution was to blame Powers, O'Donnell, and other Kennedy hangers-on who supplied the women. "They could have been better friends, in my opinion," Newman said. "And also they could have had more respect for the security. They've written many books about how much they loved him. They were really running a hard risk on this."

One of the risks involved the attempts to assassinate Fidel Castro, and the possibility, in case of success, of a retaliatory attack by Castro's agents on Kennedy. Even a botched murder attempt posed danger. Newman told of a dramatic off-the-record briefing for the Secret Service late in 1961, given by an army colonel who, so Newman and his fellow agents assumed, was on assignment with the Central Intelligence Agency. Newman could not recall the colonel's name. "He gave us a protective briefing at the EOB [Executive Office Building]," Newman told me. "The ties between the Pentagon and the CIA were stronger then than they are now. He told us that they had Castro's lunch at a shipyard in Cuba"; Castro had been fired on while attending a noisy party for the launching of a new ship, but the bullets instead struck the ship's propeller. "We just missed him," the colonel told the agents. The point was obvious, Newman said: "This was serious business and there was a possibility of retaliation against our leader. So he wanted to let us know how sharp we had to be and how tight we had to keep security at that particular time."

Even under such circumstances, Newman told me, he and other agents did not have the authority to tighten presidential protection. "They [the president and his close aides] were the ones that were well aware of it"— the increased danger from assassination attempts — "and aware of more things than we were. And the tighter we made [the loop] . . . we couldn't believe it . . . it got more riddled. What we learned from the people we had talked to was enough to literally scare us into [believing] that this was serious business. And if the administration knew that, [we thought] they would want to assist us in making the security as tight as possible."

The president's womanizing was his business, Newman said: "It didn't really bother us from a point of morality." But the Secret Service, he added, did not respect Powers, because he prevented the agents from conducting even a quick security check of the women's purses. "He knew we were trying to protect the president. We didn't know if these women were carrying listening devices, if they had syringes that carried some type of poison, or if they had Pentax cameras that would photograph the president for blackmail. Your security is only [as good] as its weakest link, and the weak link was Powers in bringing these girls in."

In one typical case, he said, "I saw Dave Powers bring in two starlets who were easily recognizable. He had one [of the women] put a scarf over her head. They had a White House car go out and pick her up at the airport, and Powers met her at the car and walked her up to the second floor." It was Powers who arranged for the ambitious Hollywood starlets to fly into Washington to service the president. "It might be their career if they told their [theatrical] agent in Hollywood they didn't want to play," Newman said. "A lot of agents felt sorry for a lot of the girls . . . that they were used this way. There wasn't a thank you — not like an affair. It was just being used. It was like a function." Afterward, while driving the women back to the airport, Powers would "counsel" the women, essentially warning them, Newman said, that "if this ever gets out in any way, your career is through." The Secret Service agents on duty at the time were often unsure of a visiting actress's identity, as they were about the identities of most of the women who came in and out. "If she wasn't a starlet, we didn't know who she was."

Of course, Newman added, the agents understood that Powers "was doing the president's bidding. You'd have to say it starts at the top and works its way down. It caused a lot of morale problems with the Secret Service. You were on the most elite assignment in the Secret Service, and you were there watching an elevator or a door because the president was inside with two hookers. It just didn't compute. Your neighbors and everybody thought you were risking your life, and you were actually out there to see that he's not disturbed while he's having an interlude in the shower with two gals from Twelfth Avenue. . . . Other times when we were in hotels around the country and Powers would bring these girls that we didn't know, we often said we would draw the black bean to see who got to testify before the House subcommittee [on the annual Secret Service budget] if the president received harm or was killed in the room by these two women. This was the president of the United States, and you felt impotent and you couldn't do your job. It was frustrating."

"We often joked," Newman told me, that "we couldn't even protect the president from getting a venereal disease."

Newman and his fellow agents did not know that it was far too late to protect the president from venereal disease. Kennedy suffered much of his adult life from nongonorrheal urethritis, a painful venereal infection; despite repeated treatment, he went to his death with it. The navy pathologists who conducted the Kennedy autopsy on the night of November 22 found evidence of chlamydia, a high-ranking military officer told me in an interview for this book. Those autopsy notes were not published, the officer added, at the request of the Kennedy family.

The long-suppressed medical records describing Kennedy's condition were uncovered in the Kennedy Library by the journalist Nigel Hamilton, and mentioned briefly in *JFK: Reckless Youth*, initially projected to be the first of a two-volume biography. (Hamilton chose not to continue the project.) The medical file, made available for this book, reveals that Kennedy had been treated since 1940 for a series of venereal diseases, and often experienced acute pain while urinating. In 1953 he was referred to the late Dr. William P. Herbst, Jr., a prominent Washington urologist, who treated Kennedy until the end of his life. Herbst's incomplete handwritten notes, as released by the Kennedy Library, show that Kennedy was being repeatedly reinfected — and, presumably, infecting his partners. Kennedy's most often repeated complaint, as noted by Herbst, was "burning" and "prostate tenderness." Treatment included a massive dose of antibiotics and gentle massaging of the prostate gland. The documents indicate that his condition continued after Kennedy was placed under the primary care of Dr. Janet Travell, his hand-picked White House physician. Travell and Herbst apparently worked together closely in the treatment of the president.

Kennedy was aware of at least some of the implications of his disease. In a source note for the 1993 biography *President Kennedy: Profile of Power*, the writer Richard Reeves anonymously quoted a family doctor saying that Kennedy, anxious about the effect of his disease on his ability to father children, had his sperm count tested after his marriage.

The Herbst documents raise questions about Kennedy's health and well-being at moments of international crisis. On April 14, 1961, for example, as Kennedy neared a final decision to authorize the Bay of Pigs, Herbst was summoned to the White House by Travell, and he treated Kennedy for "burning" and "occasional mucus" while urinating. The president had suffered a similar flare-up three weeks earlier, according to Herbst's notes, and "responded rapidly" to penicillin. After an examination, Herbst ordered that Kennedy, if he did not improve within a few days, be treated with 600,000 units of penicillin. He received a shot with that dosage on April 17, as the Cuban invasion was getting under way.

Dr. Sidney Wolfe, director of health research for Public Citizen, a public interest medical group in Washington, D.C., reviewed Herbst's notes for this book in 1995 and described the April 17 dosage as "high then"— although, he added, such large dosages are more common today. "If he was having sex all the time," Wolfe told me, "he'd get re-infected all the time." Kennedy's infection presented symptoms similar to gonorrhea, Wolfe added, but it was not that disease, because Herbst's notes show that there were no gonorrheal bacteria in Kennedy's urine. The president was successfully treated with a variety of antibiotics that include erythromycin, nitrofuran, and tetracycline.*

In his opinion, Wolfe added, the Herbst files show that Kennedy "clearly was suffering from a sexually transmitted bacterial disease called nongonorrheal urethritis." Kennedy's venereal disease was not formally diagnosed by the medical community until the late 1960s, Wolfe said, and is known today as a chlamydial infection. "Initially it was considered more of a nuisance than a serious disease," Wolfe added, "especially by doctors who did not have it." The disease is easily transmitted to women, and creates special risks for them; chlamydia can damage a woman's reproductive tract and make her unable to bear children, while producing only mild physical symptoms. By 1997, untreated chlamydia was believed to be the cause of 35 percent of infertility among American women.

Six days after Kennedy's death, according to notes Herbst made, Janet Travell telephoned and asked him to turn over his Kennedy file to her for safekeeping. In his notes, Herbst quoted her as saying that the file "'does not belong to me but to the country.' This I do not agree with," Herbst wrote, "but [I] am sending it to her for what is considered appropriate disposition." Kennedy, Herbst wrote on the last page of his file, one week after the assassination, was "reading constantly" and was "always considerate, courteous, friendly."

The doctor obviously did not feel the same about Janet Travell. The Kennedy Library files show that Herbst apparently changed his mind and instead forwarded his notes to Bobby Kennedy. On December 6, 1963, Herbst wrote the attorney general and said he was including "a copy of the records" of Jack Kennedy's clinical treatment. On that date, too, according to the library's files, Travell, in a

---

* The cortisone injections that Kennedy needed to control his Addison's disease may have heightened his sex drive. The side effects of the steroid include, for many users, an enhanced sense of confidence and personal power, and a marked increase in libido.

memorandum for the record, reported Bobby Kennedy's "ruling" that the president's medical records would be regarded as "privileged communication" and not be kept in a federal archive.*

The data about Kennedy's venereal disease have come into public view only because Herbst hedged his bets and sent a copy of the file he gave Robert Kennedy, including handwritten notes, to the archives of the National Library of Medicine in Washington. The file was found in a locked drawer in 1982 by archivists at the library and brought to the attention of Dr. Manfred Wasserman, head of the library's history of medicine division. Wasserman did not keep the file at his library, as Herbst had obviously intended, but in early 1983 instead sent it to the Kennedy Library with a note explaining that Herbst had hoped the file "would at some reasonable future time become available to researchers." Wasserman wrote that Herbst had an "esteemed" reputation among the medical profession in Washington, and had been the physician to Presidents Harry Truman and Lyndon Johnson. Herbst had wanted the files kept "for posterity."

Wasserman, in a 1995 interview for this book, said that he and his colleagues agreed at the time that such "delicate records" were "much more in the scope of the Kennedy Library than the National Library of Medicine. Without any question," he said, "something like that belongs in the presidential library." Asked what he thought of the Herbst file, Wasserman said, "You wonder if it [Kennedy's venereal disease] was transmitted." Thus Kennedy's risk taking was as dangerous, at least to his health, as some of the Secret Service agents thought. There was also an obvious risk to his wife, and to his other sexual partners.

---

* Travell said nothing about Kennedy's venereal disease in an oral history for the Kennedy Library recorded in 1966. In describing her treatment for a high fever Kennedy suffered in June 1961 — his sickest day in the White House, she said — Travell explained that she had to treat the infection with "large doses of penicillin on the basis of the history that we had that he was extremely tolerant of penicillin." Kennedy's fever spiked at 105 degrees that night, Travell said, adding that it went down to 101 degrees after treatment. She chose to tell the press corps that Kennedy's fever had reached only 101 degrees, explaining that "I skipped the whole intermediate period of the night" when his temperature soared. Travell played a similar role during the 1960 campaign in denying, as Kennedy's physician, that he was suffering from Addison's disease. She was interviewed for the library by a not-very-probing Ted Sorensen, who had drafted many of the misleading 1960 campaign press releases describing the candidate's state of health.

Another source of tension over the president's well-being was Dr. Max Jacobson, the New York physician who was the doctor of choice in the early 1960s for many in fast New York society. Jacobson made more than thirty visits to the White House, according to gate logs, and attended to the president and the first lady, who was also his patient, in Palm Beach and Hyannis Port. "Miracle Max" Jacobson supplied the president, as he did so many of his patients, with vials of specially prepared drugs and hypodermic needles for self-administration.

Jacobson, who died in 1979, would come under investigation by federal authorities in 1968 for suspected misuse of amphetamines; his license to practice medicine was revoked in 1975 by the New York State Board of Regents. But many of the Secret Service agents had questions in early 1961 about Jacobson and his "medicines."

"He was the bat wing and chicken blood doctor," Larry Newman told me. He and other agents knew nothing about Jacobson's medical credentials, Newman added — he was known to them as "Dr. Feelgood"— but they knew what the shots did to the president. "After lunch," Newman told me, "he was done for the day if he didn't have a boost."

The physician, carrying his bag of drugs and needles, "came and went" in and out of the White House without challenge, Newman said, as Kennedy's women did. He was part of "the inner circle, with Dave Powers, and nobody got in there." One of the senior agents, Newman added, "knew what the guy [Jacobson] was doing, and tried to keep him away" from the president and first lady. "We didn't see them [shots] administered or know the schedule" of when Kennedy gave himself other shots, the agent said, "but I was aware that during the waking hours . . . it was every six hours."

George Smathers learned how necessary the shots were while playing golf with the president in Palm Beach. "We played about seven or eight holes," he said in a 1996 interview for this book, "and then Jack said to me, 'I'm just hurting so bad that I can't believe it. I got to get a shot of painkiller,' or whatever. But it was something in addition, some medicine he had. So we go back to his house, and Jack lies down and says to me or Frank, my brother, 'Somebody's got to give me a shot.' He told us where the medicine was, and Frank went and got it. It had a big needle, at least two and a half, three inches long. Jack was lying down and he said, 'Now, Frank, here's what you got to do. Get this tall bottle and take the syringe,' . . . and so on. 'And then I'm going to lie down and pull down my britches, and stick this needle in my butt and shoot it in there.' Frank did just that — got it out, put it in, and whooo, stuck it right in his butt. That's what [Kennedy] had to do. And he had to do that about once every six hours at that time."

Kennedy was introduced to Jacobson and the magic of his shots during the 1960 campaign by Charles Spalding. In an interview, Spalding said that he had himself been referred to Jacobson by Stanislaus Radziwill, the exiled Polish prince, known as Stash to his friends, who was the brother-in-law of Jacqueline Kennedy.* "I picked up Jacobson from Radziwill," Spalding told me. "I'd see Stash jumping around town and went to see Max. I guess it was speed or whatever he gave us." After taking a shot, Spalding said, he visited with the Kennedys. "I was hopping around," he told me. "They said, 'Jesus! Where do you get all this energy?' After seeing Max, you could jump over a fence." Spalding's former wife, Betty, recalled Jacobson with

---

* Jack Kennedy liked Radziwill and especially liked his hard work on his behalf in 1960 as an effective vote-getter for the Kennedy-Johnson ticket in Polish communities in the Midwest. Gore Vidal, who had the same stepfather, Hugh D. Auchincloss, as Jacqueline Kennedy (his half-sister and half-brother were her stepsister and stepbrother), recalled in a 1995 interview for this book that Kennedy wanted to give Radziwill a job in his upcoming administration. But Radziwill had been accused of fiscal improprieties while working with the Red Cross in London, Vidal said, and his FBI file, Jack Kennedy later told him, "weighs ten pounds." Kennedy then repeated to Vidal his dialogue with the FBI about the Radziwill report: "Do I have to read all this?" "Oh no, just don't appoint him."

The president found another way to take care of Radziwill in late 1960, which tells much about the Kennedys' belief that normal standards of conduct did not apply to them. The family's vehicle for rewarding Radziwill turned out to be the General Aniline & Film Corporation, an American chemical company once owned by Germany's I. G. Farben that had been seized by the Justice Department, under the Alien Property Act, after the outbreak of World War II. By war's end, the firm's ownership had been shifted to a Swiss holding company known as Interhandel, and the Swiss wanted their profitable American company back. There were intense negotiations in the late 1950s; Interhandel retained Charles E. Wilson, the former president of General Electric, as its American lobbyist. But the Eisenhower administration refused to return General Aniline to Interhandel, arguing that the Swiss firm was merely a front for General Aniline's original Nazi owners. The issue remained moot until Jack Kennedy's election and his nomination, on December 16, 1960, of his brother Robert as attorney general. Documents made available for this book show that on the day of his

less fondness. "Chuck used to shoot himself," she told me in an interview. "The doctor would give him the needles for use in the house. I don't think [Chuck] knew what he was giving him." Spalding would "take a shot," his former wife said, and "get flushed in the face. His eyes would get a glazed look — the whites would look full of mucus and be fixed — and his mouth would get dry." She did not want to know, Betty Spalding added, what it was her husband was taking.

Jacobson, in an unpublished memoir, wrote that he first treated Kennedy with a shot shortly before one of the televised debates with Richard Nixon in the fall of 1960. He traveled with Kennedy and gave him repeated shots during the president's June 1961 visit to Paris and Vienna. One shot was given moments before Khrushchev was scheduled to arrive for a summit meeting, Jacobson wrote. The doctor was listed on the official White House staff manifest for the trip. Jacobson also treated the president, he said, during the tense moments of the

---

nomination, Robert Kennedy was given a briefing on the case by an official of Interhandel. In mid-1961, court records show, Interhandel decided to dismiss Charles Wilson as its American lobbyist and replace him with an unskilled but well-placed new lobbyist — Stanislaus Radziwill. A lawsuit was eventually filed, with Interhandel sued for $7.5 million by one of the American agents displaced by Radziwill. It could not be learned how much Radziwill was paid for his services. A senior official of Interhandel testified in the case that Radziwill had visited him in mid-1961 "for a quarter of an hour" in his office in Zurich and told him that, "as a favor . . . he would be willing to introduce me to the Attorney General, but only if I could declare for him solemnly that there was no German taint in this, and that there was really the moral basis for a talk." By this time, court records showed, two of Jack Kennedy's associates, childhood friend LeMoyne Billings and family accountant Carmine Bellino, had been appointed to high-level management jobs in General Aniline, and two of Joe Kennedy's longtime cronies, Harold Clancy of Boston and New York attorney William P. Marin, were members of the GAF board. There is no evidence that Bobby Kennedy intervened in any inappropriate manner in the subsequent negotiations, which resulted in a compromise: General Aniline would not be returned to the Swiss, but its stock would be offered on the New York Stock Exchange, with profits to be distributed between the U.S. Treasury and Interhandel. The stock sale in 1963 returned $207 million — about $67 million more than anticipated — to the U.S. Treasury. William Orrick, one of the Justice Department officials who handled the General Aniline case, said in a 1996 interview for this book that he had not been told by Bobby Kennedy that Radziwill received a lobbying fee from Interhandel. "I didn't know he was in the picture," added Orrick, who is now a U.S. district court judge in San Francisco. If he had known, he added, "I certainly would have raised questions." The eventual settlement, he said, was a good one, nonetheless.

October 1962 missile crisis. FBI records made available under the Freedom of Information Act show that in June 1962 one of Bobby Kennedy's aides in the Justice Department sought to have a vial of Jacobson's drugs analyzed by the FBI's laboratory. The laboratory could not do so, the FBI reported, because the sample supplied was insufficient. In his memoir, Jacobson claimed that the president "hesitantly" told him that his brother Bobby "had demanded a sample of all my medications for testing by the FDA [Food and Drug Administration]." The doctor said he sent fifteen vials of medicine to the attorney general's office, but heard nothing further. Jack Kennedy, Jacobson wrote, had no intention of stopping treatment. "I don't care if it's horse piss," Jacobson quoted Kennedy as saying. "It's the only thing that works."

The president's womanizing, like his questionable reliance on Jacobson's "feel-good" shots, was widely known to members of the White House staff, Larry Newman said. Kennedy's daily swims in the White House pool were not merely to soothe his back, as the Schlesinger and Sorensen memoirs depicted them, but a focal point for sexual activity. "It was common knowledge in the White House," Newman said, "that when the president took lunch in the pool with Fiddle and Faddle, nobody goes in there." These were two young female staff aides who would be "scooped up by Dave Powers and taken into the pool at noon with JFK. They would go skinny-dipping with Jack." The president's brothers, Bobby and Teddy, often joined in.

During those moments, Newman added, the pool was completely off-limits, even for staff members of the National Security Council who were dealing with international crises. "We had one occasion when one of the military aides came up from the Situation Room," Newman told me, carrying a cable that needed immediate attention from the president. "He came around the corner and he was moving fast — and stopped and cursed when he saw me standing up, away from the [pool] door, and just said, 'How long has he been in there?' I didn't answer him at first. Then I said, 'Oh, about half an hour.' And he said, 'What's your best guess?' And I said, 'Another half hour. Take your best shot if you want to go in. It's up to you.' So he swore again and said, 'I'll wait.' He stood there awhile and shuffled his feet. And he said, 'I got to get an answer on this.' And then turned around and went in by the Oval Office and then paced back out. Eventually Kennedy came out, in about half an hour. This guy was a ranking officer in the military and he wasn't going in that room at all."

An added complication was the affection and respect the agents had for Jacqueline Kennedy. "We thought a lot of her, and it sort of pulled you and pushed you both ways," Newman told me. "You thought, 'Well, I'm really proud because I'm with a popular guy and the public loves him and he's good to the Secret Service.'"

The president did not carry on when his wife was in the White House, Newman said, but the first lady spent much of her time, especially on weekends, with their children at the rented family retreat at Glen Ora, near Middleburg, in Virginia's horse country. Clint Hill, the Secret Service agent in charge of her protection, usually went with her. "When Jackie left with Clint for Glen Ora," Newman told me, Kennedy "was out of there [the Oval Office], had his bowl of soup, and hit the pool with Fiddle and Faddle. When she was there, it was no fun. He just had headaches. You really saw him droop because he wasn't getting laid. He was like a rooster getting hit with a water hose." Despite the president's womanizing, Newman said, he and the other Secret Service agents on the detail were convinced that Mrs. Kennedy "really loved him."

There were obvious tensions in the marriage, however. One Secret Service agent said he came away from a two-year assignment on the presidential detail feeling "sorry for Jackie. She was real lonesome." He recalled driving her home by herself from parties. "She seemed sad — just a sad lady," he said in an interview. At times, according to Mary Gallagher, the first lady's personal secretary, "the president was so busy that Jackie occasionally had to make a date to get to see him in the evening." In her 1969 memoir, *My Life with Jacqueline Kennedy,* Gallagher described the procedure: "I would call Evelyn [Lincoln] and ask, 'Has the President anything to do Thursday night?' And another time, 'Has the President anything on his schedule for Saturday night? Would he like to go to a dinner dance?'"

The White House pool was an especially important area for sexual partying in the Kennedy years and, not surprisingly, it was Joe Kennedy who paid for the pool to be redecorated and repainted in the spring of 1961. A new sound system was installed, enabling swimmers — and partygoers — to listen to music while in the water. Most important, the one wall in the pool area with windows was redesigned; workmen covered the glass with a large mural depicting the sunset over St. Croix, in the Virgin Islands. A private passageway also was constructed that enabled the president and his guests to have direct access from the pool area to an elevator leading to the second-floor living quarters. In her 1966 oral history for the Kennedy Library, Dr. Janet Travell praised the setup: "He would have his swim just before lunch and put on a beach robe and beach slippers and walk from the pool directly to the elevator and upstairs, not meet anybody, and rest and have his lunch."

A few days after arriving at the White House, Newman caused near panic among a group of Secret Service supervisors by casually wandering after duty hours into the sacrosanct pool area, which contained exercise machines, and treating himself to a workout and a swim. "I told my supervisor that was a pretty nice thing they had, and I thought the man was going to have a baby. He was very nice and patient with me, but he said, 'Never, never do that again.' And I didn't." Newman, the new guy on the job, was mystified. He came to understand that the supervisors knew what Kennedy was doing in the pool, "but they didn't want to tell the agents. Nobody wanted to talk about it because . . . they didn't want to end their careers. You [the newly assigned agents] just learned by doing. It gave new definition to on-the-job training."

Newman said he agreed to talk to me on the record about what he saw in an attempt to balance history. "It irks me that some of the people who worked with him are historically incorrect about how he ran his presidency, how he ran his life, and what a picnic the whole thing was. There were things that went bump in the night," Newman added. "It was also our time with him," referring to the Secret Service, "and we loved the man. By the same token, we grieve that he would conduct himself in such a way as to make us so vulnerable and make the country so vulnerable."

Newman left the presidential detail in 1963, not long before the president's assassination, and was reassigned to the Secret Service office in San Francisco. He worked in Secret Service field offices on the

West Coast for the next twenty years, pursuing counterfeiters among others, and became chief of security for Western Union after retiring.

William T. McIntyre, of Phoenix, Arizona, arrived at the presidential detail in the fall of 1963, just as Newman was leaving, from a two-man Secret Service office in Spokane, Washington. He came with high expectations. "How often does a twenty-eight-year-old guy get a chance to participate in anything in and around the center of government?" McIntyre asked in a 1995 interview for this book. "You expect to see a lot of professionalism, a lot of integrity." He, too, was given no warning of what was to come. The new arrival was briefed by Jerry Behn, head of the White House detail, and immediately assigned to the midnight shift. McIntyre got his first hint on the first or second night on duty. His shift supervisor, the highly respected Emory Roberts, took him aside and warned, McIntyre told me, that "you're going to see a lot of shit around here. Stuff with the president. Just forget about it. Keep it to yourself. Don't even talk to your wife." Over the next few days, McIntyre said, he saw "girls coming in — hookers." Roberts was nervous about it. "Emory would say," McIntyre recalled with a laugh, "'How in the hell do you know what's going on? He could be hurt in there. What if one bites him'" in a sensitive area? Roberts "talked about it a lot," McIntyre said. "Bites." Despite such fears, McIntyre said, "we would never stop them from going in if Powers or O'Donnell was with them. We wouldn't check them over."

McIntyre, too, had a pool story. He was on duty when Jacqueline Kennedy decided, on short notice, that she wanted to take a swim. Her husband, as Mrs. Kennedy undoubtedly suspected, "was in the pool with a couple of bimbos." The agent on duty refused to let her in, and an angry first lady summoned Clint Hill, the senior agent on her detail. "By the time Clint got there," McIntyre recalled, "the president had gotten the word somehow" and fled the pool. "You could see one big pair and two smaller pair of wet footprints leading to the Oval Office." In McIntyre's view, a public scandal about Kennedy's incessant womanizing was inevitable. "It would have had to come out in the next year or so. In the [1964 presidential] campaign, maybe."

McIntyre said he and some of his colleagues on the White House detail felt abused by their service on behalf of President Kennedy. "Each agent is, after all, a sworn law enforcement officer," he told me. "When you see some type of criminal offense, whether it's a misdemeanor or a felony, occurring in your presence, blatantly, that makes you feel a little bit used" — especially if it's done by the president. "A procurement is illegal," McIntyre added. "And if you have a procurer with prostitutes paraded in front of you, then as a sworn law enforcement officer you're asking yourself, 'Well, what do they think of us?' When that occurs, the agent would feel that his authority and his reason for being there is nullified." McIntyre said he eventually realized that he had compromised his law enforcement beliefs to the point where he wondered whether it was "time to get out of there. I was disappointed by what I saw."

Tony Sherman, of Salt Lake City, served two years on the Kennedy presidential detail before returning to Secret Service field work on the West Coast and in Salt Lake City. "It was just not once every six months, not every New Year's Eve, but was a regular thing," Sherman said of the presidential womanizing in interviews in 1995 and 1997 for this book. "I'm serious in my job. I didn't want a part of it. It's difficult to talk morally about other people, but we aren't talking about other people. We're talking about the president of the United States. We're talking about my country. And we're talking about people my age with wives and children who were willing to give their lives."

"It took me a week to learn what was going on," Sherman said. He learned the hard way. Within a week or so of being assigned to the president's personal detail, Sherman flew with Kennedy for a weekend at his father's home in Palm Beach. Sherman was assigned to the midnight to eight A.M. watch. At around two in the morning he heard noises at the pool, and he investigated, gun at the ready. To his dismay, he found the president and a prominent European socialite, both naked, at play in the water.

"We had bosses who'd been around a long time," Sherman told me. "Their attitude was different: 'This is a family. We not only protect the family, we protect the ability of him to do whatever he wants inside the family.' We got to the point where we'd say, 'What else is new?' When you see nude bodies going down the hall. . . . Were we bothered by it? It didn't matter. There were women everywhere. Very often, depending on what shift you were on, you'd either see them going up, or you'd see them coming out in the morning [from the president's family quarters]. People were vacuuming and the ushers were around. And we were there. There were several of them that were regular visitors. Not when Jackie was there, however. We'd say good morning."

There were many days, Sherman told me, when Kennedy "didn't work at all. He'd come down late, go to his office. There were meetings — the usual things — and then he had pool time before his nap and lunch. He is president, but it's so regular and so often that we didn't know what to think. If the president is happy and doing his job, we're doing our job. But I wanted out." He left the White House detail shortly before Kennedy's assassination.

Sherman also told me that one of the Secret Service's jobs was to prevent Kennedy from being caught in the act by his wife. Jackie would "visit New York and things would go on in the White House pool," Sherman said. "We would receive word that the first lady was landing, and we would notify the president, and his friends would leave. I never figured for the two years I was there that she really didn't know what was going on. It would have been impossible" to keep her eyes shut. There was one very tense moment when the warning didn't come until Mrs. Kennedy was en route from the airport, Sherman told me. The agent in charge screwed up his courage and ran into the pool to tell the president that his wife would arrive within fifteen minutes. Bobby and Ted Kennedy were also in the pool. "The door opened," Sherman recalled, "and people scattered. And as [the president] ran out, he was holding a bloody mary in his hand. I happened to be on the post and he said, 'Here. Take this.' He didn't know what to do with it. He went and everybody left, none the wiser. Another day on the beat. It got to the point where we didn't worry about [the president's pool time], particularly when both brothers were around. How safe can you be in the White House, in the swimming pool . . . both your brothers with you?" Bobby and Ted would do anything, the agents knew, to protect their brother. "We felt secure," Sherman said.

Sherman's worst moment came during a presidential trip to Honolulu, where Kennedy attended a Pearl Harbor memorial ceremony. The president stayed in the residence of Admiral Harry Felt, commander in chief of the Pacific Fleet; Sherman's job was to secure the premises, with the help of a marine colonel. Hot towels and the president's favorite foods and drinks were ordered and in place when Kennedy arrived, said his hellos, and disappeared into a bedroom. "Within ten minutes," Sherman said, "a [White House] staff member arrived in a car escorting two ladies who were not on the guest list. They were unknown to me but were in the company of a staff member — therefore they were allowed in the house. I knew what they were there for, I guess. This was sort of the usual routine in many stops. And the colonel turned to me and said, 'Uh, who are they?' And I turned to him and I said, 'Well, they're secretaries, and I assume there's some work the president wants done this evening.'

"I got mad. This is not what the president of the United States should be doing. There was no regard for who was there. The marine colonel — he knew what was going on. Other people were there. Navy people were in the house. Cooks were in the house. There were police on the streets. What can you say? I got angry at any president who doesn't treat the White House like I think he should. You're dealing with people who are in intimate contact with the president and may have been sent there by other people, if you want to get really spooky about it. The possibility of blackmail and things like that are astounding. I never knew the name of the outsiders, where they came from, where they were, or anything. I opened the door and said good evening and they said good evening. And in they went and the door shut. And when I reported for my next shift the next day, the president was still alive."

Joseph Paolella, of Los Angeles, remains proud of the fact that he was the first Secret Service agent of Italian descent to be assigned to the presidential detail. Paolella loved the assignment and adored Kennedy, but he shared the agents' constant concern that the president would end up being a blackmail victim. "The worry was that one of these women could be a spy . . . might be working for the Russians or Communist Party," Paolella told me in a 1997 interview. Sometimes the agents were upset about the president's women for a different reason — they weren't very attractive. In one case, a prominent

California Democrat came for a meeting with Kennedy and brought along "these real skinny-looking broads," Paolella told me. "You'd say, 'Geez, what's the president doing with something like that?' We might think he could do better than that. But not from a protective standpoint."

Paolella left the Secret Service in 1964, after six years on the job, because of his dislike of President Johnson. Protecting Jack Kennedy had been far more exciting, and Paolella, a bachelor, had enjoyed being near a president who attracted women at every stop. Some of the agents and military aides who traveled with Kennedy, surfeited with available women, soon found themselves doing what the president was doing. Drinking and partying became a constant feature of presidential travel, especially on the weekend trips to Hyannis Port and Palm Beach. After leaving the Secret Service, Paolella told me, he talked to no one about what he witnessed in the Kennedy White House. "In those days," he explained, "no one would have believed it."

Agents acknowledged that the Secret Service's socializing intensified each year of the Kennedy administration, to a point where, by late 1963, a few members of the presidential detail were regularly remaining in bars until the early morning hours. Larry Newman said in one of his interviews with me that an "honest snapshot" of the Secret Service's partying in the months before the president's death would have triggered much public anger. The irony, Newman added, was that the fault may have been Jack Kennedy's. "It's not like he ruined you [as an agent]," Newman said, "but you get the tone of the way the detail works from the top. It was loose."

The looseness extended beyond the president. At least three female Kennedy family members propositioned various Secret Service agents, according to Newman, Paolella, and their colleagues. One Kennedy relative was particularly forward, and was eventually given a colorful sobriquet by the agents — "rancid ass." Peter Lawford, the president's brother-in-law, was seen by the agents as a contemptible buffoon who drank too much, was too aggressive with women, and, on presidential trips, was constantly trying to push himself into the Secret Service's backup car. There was one occasion, during a raucous party in December 1962, at Bing Crosby's huge estate in Palm Springs, California, when, Paolella told me, agents literally rescued a young airline stewardess from Lawford's drunken advances, and left him sprawled in the desert.

The Crosby party was the high point — or low point — of presidential partying, Paolella said. Some of the women at the pool, the agents knew, were stewardesses from a European airline; their names, as usual, were not known to the Secret Service. The party was so noisy that a group of California state policemen on duty at the front of the estate, which bordered on a desert wilderness area, assumed that the shouts and shrieks of the partygoers were the nighttime calls of coyotes.

Paolella was reluctant to provide further details, but Larry Newman, who also was on duty that night, was not. He and Paolella "thought we were going to have a quiet tour of duty around the house," Newman told me. "But as the evening got darker, the state police were calling us on the radio and asking us if there were coyotes up around the house bothering the president." The two agents were posted in front of the home, and they agreed, after some discussion, that they had to intrude on the president's privacy by going poolside for a look. What they saw, Newman told me, was Powers "banging a girl on the edge of the pool. The president is sitting across the pool, having a drink and talking to some broads. Everybody was buckass naked." At a later point in the party, Newman said, Powers moved to the edge of the pool, bent over, made an obscene gesture, and said, apparently to the president, "Hey, pal. Look at this." As always, Powers became increasingly frantic in his efforts to amuse the president. He began running in and out of the Crosby house with armfuls of Crosby's suits and diving with the clothes into the pool. "The president thought that was pretty funny — laughed and about fell out of the chair," Newman told me. "The only difficulty was Bing Crosby didn't think it was funny." The White House later had to pay for the ruined clothes, Newman said.

He and Paolella were just doing their job, Newman said, by checking out the private party. "It may sound a bit perverted," he said, "but some of the girls had foreign accents . . . and you have to keep an eye on him to see he doesn't get lost or somebody doesn't come out of the desert. We also had to keep the California state patrol on the checkpoint at the main highway and not [have them] come up and check the coyotes and see if we were all right. We didn't want them to see that the president was swimming with all these ladies and they were all nude. So we had to lie to them, and we just agreed with them that there are coyotes running like hell all over the place and we couldn't stop them. We'd let them know if it got too thick."

Newman said he and Paolella subsequently discussed what they had seen with their supervisors, and were told to ignore the events — "just act like nothing was happening." A fellow agent later remarked, to the displeasure of his supervisors, that "nothing's happening out there, but one coyote is sitting on top of another one."

"You had to have some kind of a police squadroom humor about the thing," Newman said, "because here you are. You've got the Cold War going on. You're protecting the leader of the free world. And the highway patrol is going to come up and you're protecting him from getting caught naked. And you're carrying guns and you have all kinds of automatic weapons and you can't see in the desert, and the only thing you find is Peter Lawford out there, moaning in his beer because he can't get with a girl that he's just met that night."

16

CRISIS IN BERLIN

Henry A. Kissinger was left behind in Cambridge on January 20, 1961, when McGeorge Bundy and other colleagues on the Harvard faculty moved to top jobs in the Kennedy administration. Kissinger, a German-born professor of government, was named a consultant on European affairs to the National Security Council, and in the early summer of 1961 he was invited to a Cabinet Room meeting on the Berlin crisis. It was his first inside look at the Kennedy administration, and the A team, including Robert Kennedy, was there, seated around a conference table. The president's men all stood, as is the custom, when he arrived to open the meeting. Within a few moments, a White House steward entered the room with a tureen of clam chowder. He served soup and crackers to the president and then moved around the room to Bobby Kennedy, who also got a bowl of soup. No one else was served.

When Kissinger returned to Harvard, he described the scene to Morton Halperin, one of his teaching fellows, speaking, Halperin recalled in an interview for this book, of the king and his duke and their misguided "sense of entitlement."

In fact, Robert Kennedy became, after the Bay of Pigs, not a duke but his brother's prime minister — the second most powerful man in the United States. The attorney general, through a Soviet intelligence officer in Washington, and with the president's approval, began back-channel communications with Nikita Khrushchev, the Soviet premier. The two Kennedys spent the next eighteen months negotiating foreign policy with Khrushchev through a secret intermediary. They did so despite opposition from their Soviet experts, who were aware of the back channel but rarely knew what was being discussed or agreed to. Bobby Kennedy's portfolio by the middle of 1961 was staggering: he was the president's legal adviser, his political adviser, his protector, his best friend, and his most influential foreign affairs adviser.

The history of the Kennedy administration and its dealings in the Cold War is incomplete without a full understanding of the president-to-premier agreements reached in Washington and Moscow. And yet not one official document dealing with the Kennedy-Khrushchev relationship through the back channel has been made public by the John F. Kennedy Library; the most detailed information has come from Soviet archives opened after the fall of communism. Robert Kennedy, in a 1964 interview with the Kennedy Library — published in part by family biographer and historian Arthur Schlesinger, Jr., in 1978 — revealed that the Soviet he met with in Washington was Georgi N. Bolshakov, an intelligence officer posing as a journalist. Kennedy added, almost casually, "Most of the major matters dealing with the Soviet Union and the United States were discussed and arrangements were made between Georgi Bolshakov and myself. . . . We used to meet maybe once every two weeks."

Georgi Bolshakov was a professional intelligence agent whose résumé dated back to World War II service with GRU, the intelligence branch of the Soviet army. His fluent command of English led him to an assignment in Washington in 1951, ostensibly serving as an editor for TASS, the Soviet news agency. In 1955 he was transferred to the staff of General Georgi Zhukov, the war hero who was the Soviet minister of defense. In 1959 he was sent again to Washington, where he maintained a long-standing Soviet relationship with Frank Holeman, a reporter for the *New York Daily News,* who was one of the few journalists unafraid to have occasional lunches with Soviet diplo-

mats. Holeman was friendly with Edwin O. Guthman, a former reporter who was Bobby Kennedy's press secretary at the Justice Department. It was on Holeman's recommendation that Kennedy and
the seemingly moderate and understanding Bolshakov first met,
three weeks after the Bay of Pigs.*

Over the next eighteen months, Bolshakov became a central figure
for the president and his brother, as the middleman in the most intense confrontations of the Kennedy administration: the Vienna
summit, the Berlin crisis, and the Cuban missile crisis. The full story
of Georgi Bolshakov's contacts with Bobby Kennedy during those
crucial days may never be known. "I don't know why they [the Sovi-
ets] wanted to proceed in that fashion," Kennedy told the library,
"but they didn't want to go through their ambassador" in Washington. The Soviet ambassador, Mikhail Menshikov, "handled the regular routine matters, and he — Bolshakov — handled other things. . . .
I met with him about all kinds of things."

The American bureaucracy was also cut out, Kennedy acknowledged, and knew little of what was being said by the president and his
brother to the Soviet leadership. "Unfortunately, stupidly," Robert
Kennedy told the library, "I didn't write many of the things down. I
just delivered the messages verbally to my brother, and he'd act on
them. I think sometimes he'd tell the State Department — and sometimes he didn't." Kennedy was, once again, being less than candid
about a vital matter: in fact, he did document some of the meetings

---

* There is some evidence that the GRU and the KGB, the main Soviet intelligence service, might have been skeptical about Robert Kennedy as a secret conduit. The skepticism was linked to a 1955 visit to the Soviet Union that Robert Kennedy made at
the invitation of Supreme Court Justice William O. Douglas, who was one of Joe
Kennedy's close friends. During their research for *"One Hell of a Gamble,"* Fursenko
and Naftali were given access to the KGB's files on the Kennedy-Douglas trip. The
KGB concluded, in a report to Khrushchev, that Kennedy was a provocateur who had
a "negative opinion of the Soviet Union" and constantly sought to uncover secret intelligence. He expressed an interest "in the techniques of tapping telephone conversations, secret censorship of mail, Soviet intelligence activities abroad, the system of
repression, including the means of punishing captured foreign spies." Kennedy also
displayed the family weakness, Fursenko and Naftali wrote, by cavalierly requesting
his Soviet Intourist guide to "send a woman of loose morals" to his hotel room. In
1961, with the ascent of the Kennedy administration, the attorney general was as-
sessed as a "troublemaker" by the Soviets.

with Bolshakov, but those papers, if they still exist, remain locked away in his personal files in the Kennedy Library.

Bolshakov was well known to the Washington press corps in the early 1960s and known to be friendly with the Kennedys. But no reporter realized his importance. In his 1975 memoir *Conversations with Kennedy,* Ben Bradlee, then with *Newsweek* magazine, wrote about an evening he and his wife spent with the president and the first lady in her bedroom at the White House, watching a television special on the Kremlin. "While the President walked around in his underdrawers and wondered what life must be like in that mausoleum," Bradlee wrote,

> Jackie told us about the day that Bobby Kennedy had called the Kremlin in a rage about something, a story that had been kicking around town for some time and had been denied often. He was apparently calling Georgi N. Bolshakov, the Washington press corps' and the New Frontier's favorite Soviet diplomat [presumably then in Moscow], who was carried on the Soviet embassy's rolls as a journalist but who was felt by all of us to be a spy, like all Soviet diplomats. If so, he was a gregarious spy, could drink up a storm, and liked to arm wrestle. Anyway, Jackie was now confirming that story that had been so often denied. But, she reported, there had been no answer at the Kremlin when the United States attorney general had called late at night.

Schlesinger was given unprecedented access to Bobby Kennedy's oral history, and to a few of his personal notes, while researching his authorized biography, *Robert Kennedy and His Times,* published in 1978. But he was unable to deal substantively with the possibility that Jack and Robert Kennedy, two men Schlesinger dearly admired, had been talking with the Kremlin behind the backs of all who were serving in the government. He trivialized Bolshakov as being "full of chaff and badinage," and said that one of Bobby Kennedy's aides, who could not have known of Bolshakov's secret role, depicted Bolshakov as full of "self-deprecating nods, smiles, and circus English" and benefiting from "Bobby's predilection for harmless buffoons."

The need for secrecy was great because the risks of the Kennedy-Khrushchev back channel were high. The president was making strategic decisions without the informed advice of the men and women in the State Department, Defense Department, and CIA who had served in the Soviet Union and who knew the language, people, and history. "Jack was his own secretary of state," Bobby Kennedy told the library.

Jack and Bobby Kennedy defied the experts and nay-sayers in their government — some of the same experts, the president had come to believe, who had assured him that the invasion at the Bay of Pigs would work. With their daring, the Kennedys seized control of America's Cold War policy; it was a heady time for two brothers who were inexperienced in the workings of the foreign policy establishment.

The back channel, and Bobby Kennedy's ascendancy, had their beginnings in the disastrous spring of 1961. On May 9, according to Soviet files summarized in *"One Hell of a Gamble,"* by the historians Aleksandr Fursenko and Timothy Naftali, Bobby Kennedy and Bolshakov had their first exploratory meeting in Washington: the issue was the pending summit in Vienna, about which Jack Kennedy was justifiably very nervous. Kennedy and Bolshakov met and telephoned each other at least six times before the summit in early June, but failed to resolve any of the outstanding issues. A precedent was set, however, and an important message communicated, according to Fursenko and Naftali: Robert Kennedy told the Soviets that the tough language his brother was using in public did not indicate "any lessening of commitment to a constructive meeting with Khrushchev." The Soviets were being told to watch what Kennedy did and not to listen to what he said.

The summit was brutal. Khrushchev bullied and threatened the unprepared Kennedy over the question of allowing the Western Allies continued access to West Berlin. After World War II, Germany was divided into zones of occupation, and Berlin, deep inside the Soviet zone, was itself divided. Thousands of East Germans, including many intellectuals and scientists, were fleeing from communism by walking across the checkpoints between East and West Berlin; the brain drain was humiliating to the East German government and deleterious to the state's long-term economic well-being. Khrushchev gave

Kennedy an ultimatum: the United States, Britain, and France had six months to negotiate, in consultation with the Soviet Union, a postwar peace treaty that would resolve the status of Germany and confirm East German control over traffic into West Berlin. The United States was reluctant to agree, since that would amount to de facto recognition of the division of the country. If the Allies did not consent, Khrushchev threatened, the Soviets would go it alone and sign a separate treaty with East Germany. Without a settlement, Khrushchev said, there could be nuclear war. Kennedy, badly shaken, told his longtime friend LeMoyne Billings that he had "never come face to face with such evil before." He fumed to his aide Kenny O'Donnell that Khrushchev was a "bastard" and a "son of a bitch."

Kennedy linked the dispute to the failure in Cuba. "The Russians thought they could kick [the president] around," Robert Kennedy explained in his interviews for the Kennedy Library. "Khrushchev got the idea . . . that he was dealing with a rather weak figure because [JFK] didn't do what Khrushchev would have done in Cuba, in not going and taking Cuba . . . that he was dealing with a young figure who perhaps had no confidence. It was a shock to [Jack] that somebody would be as harsh and definitive, definite, as this."

A few favored members of the Washington press corps learned how thoroughly rattled President Kennedy had been by his confrontation with Khrushchev at Vienna, but they did not share that information with their readers — as Kennedy knew they would not. In *Deadline,* his memoir, James Reston told how he had been smuggled into the American Embassy in Vienna on a Saturday morning for an exclusive interview with Kennedy after one of the summit meetings. The president, wearing a hat pulled over his forehead, arrived

over an hour late, shaken and angry, . . . sat down on a couch beside me, and sighed. I said it must have been a rough session. Much rougher than he had expected, he said. Khrushchev had threatened him over Berlin. . . . He felt sure Khrushchev thought that anybody who had made such a mess of the Cuban invasion had no judgment, and any president who had made such a blunder but then didn't see it through had no guts. . . . He had tried to convince Khrushchev of U.S. determination but had failed. It was now essential to demonstrate our firmness, and the place to do it, he remarked to my astonishment, was Vietnam! I don't think I swallowed his hat but I was speechless. . . . Khrushchev had treated Kennedy with contempt, and . . . he felt he had to act.

Reston's reports made headline news in the *New York Times* during the summit, but Reston wrote nothing in his dispatches about the Khrushchev ultimatum or Kennedy's tough talk on Vietnam.* The columnist did share what he learned with at least one colleague. In an interview with a group of academics in 1978, Joseph Alsop described seeing a "very gray" Kennedy at a diplomatic reception in London a day after the summit. "I really didn't know what had happened in Vienna," Alsop recalled. "Scotty Reston did, but naturally it horrified him so that he didn't write about it properly. The president backed me against the wall and said, 'I just want you to know, Joe, I don't care what happens, I won't give way, I won't give up, and I'll do whatever's necessary.' It was a little chilling. . . . I hadn't the vaguest idea that there was anything to give way or to give up about. I knew there was pressure on Berlin, but I didn't know there had been an ultimatum." Alsop, like Reston, did not write about the encounter.

In an interview for this book, Hugh Sidey recalled a private chat with Kennedy after his return from Vienna. "I asked him, 'What's Khrushchev like? Tell me.' And he said, 'I never met a man like this. [I] talked about how a nuclear exchange would kill seventy million people in ten minutes and he just looked at me as if to say, "So what?" My impression was that he just didn't give a damn if it came to that.'" Sidey later described the president's distress to Robert Kennedy and asked, "Did you talk to him about that?" Bobby, in his response, seemed eager to convince Sidey that he and the president were one. "Oh yes, we talk all the time, about everything," the attorney general said, adding that he had never known Jack to be "so upset. I've never

---

* On Sunday, June 4, Reston described the atmosphere of the Kennedy-Khrushchev talks as "apparently more cordial than had been expected after the rising controversies of the last few months." In his dispatch published Monday, Reston reported that the summit had ended with "hard controversy," but added that "there were no ultimatums and few bitter or menacing exchanges." Khrushchev was quoted as saying that the meetings were a "very good beginning." Kennedy was not directly quoted in either Reston article.

seen my brother cry before about something like this. I was up in the bedroom with him and he looked at me and said, 'Bobby, if nuclear exchange comes, it doesn't matter about us. We've had a good life, we're adults. We bring these things on ourselves. The thought, though, of women and children perishing in a nuclear exchange. I can't adjust to that.'" Tears ran down the president's cheeks, Bobby Kennedy told Sidey.*

Just when and how Georgi Bolshakov and Robert Kennedy linked up again after the summit is not known; no Soviet documents dealing with the period have been made public, and Kennedy did not say in his library interviews. The Kennedy brothers allowed other government officials only a glimpse of the give-and-take of the Bolshakov back channel; not surprisingly, the few officials who knew of it thought it was — as one said — a "dangerous game." An obvious pitfall was the huge discrepancy in status between Kennedy and Bolshakov. Robert Kennedy was indispensable to the running of his government; Bolshakov was not. Any disinformation relayed by Kennedy would immediately taint the president; Bolshakov, if caught lying, could be accused of having gotten the story wrong and be recalled to Moscow, if necessary, or reassigned. The most outspoken critic of the Bolshakov channel was Llewellyn E. Thompson, Jr., the ambassador to the Soviet Union, who after his return from Moscow in mid-1962 was named Kennedy's special assistant on Soviet affairs. "This was a great mistake," Thompson, who died in 1972, told the Kennedy Library in an oral history. The Kennedy brothers, he said, "tried to sell the idea, 'Well, the State Department is so biased against us that we can't get anywhere. If we could just get direct contact, why, we could do this.' This way, they hoped to avoid any staff and to avoid having all the facts known." Thompson worried that Jack or Bobby Kennedy would not be precise in conversations with Bolshakov, to be relayed to Khrushchev, and the Soviet "might attach great importance to careless remarks."

---

* Sidey did not include the Bobby Kennedy anecdote in his 1963 biography, *John F. Kennedy, President*, published by Atheneum.

Thompson's interview was done after Jack Kennedy's assassination; it's not known what, if anything, he said earlier to the president or his brother. But there is little reason to believe that any complaints would have been heeded. Bobby Kennedy made it clear in his Kennedy Library interviews that he cared little for the opinions and expertise of the American ambassador in Moscow. Asked whether the ambassador there made any difference, Kennedy said, "I don't know whether he does. I think that [the Soviets] had some confidence in Thompson. I don't know whether he becomes just a messenger. Perhaps for the first two or three months [the American ambassador] has some effect, when they think he's in touch with the president." Asked specifically whether the ambassador was bypassed by the Bolshakov back channel, Kennedy responded tersely, "I suppose he was."

Another State Department concern, surely, was the fact that the Kennedys simply did not know as much as they thought they did about communism and international affairs. In early 1962 David Herbert Donald, a Harvard historian widely respected for his scholarly research and writings on the Lincoln presidency, was invited to give an informal talk at a meeting in the private quarters of the White House with the president, first lady, and a small group of friends and administration officials. Donald spoke about Reconstruction for forty minutes and then took questions, half of which came from an attentive president. Donald afterward had a private meeting with Kennedy and came away with grave reservations, as he wrote a friend a few weeks later. His letter, made available for this book, was caustic: "I did not think his mastery of American history particularly impressive; not surprisingly, it reflected a sort of general textbook knowledge of about twenty-five years ago and not much familiarity with recent literature or findings. His view of history, it is clear, is very largely in personal terms — great men and their influence. This is a man," Donald wrote, "determined to go down in our history books as a great President, and he wants to know the secret."

In a 1996 interview for this book, Donald recalled his disquiet after the talk. The president was fascinated with Lincoln and Franklin Delano Roosevelt, because "he thought to be a great president you had to be a wartime president. That was scary to me," Donald said. "I came away feeling that this is a young man who doesn't understand history."

But the young president, even in serene settings — as with Professor Donald — was careful to muffle his real strategy. Kennedy understood that Berlin was not the place to make his stand against Khrushchev. The president and his brother evolved a pattern during the crisis there in mid-1961 that would be essential to superpower negotiations over the next eighteen months — talk tough in public and compromise in private to keep from going to war.

A flaw in Kennedy's approach was that the adoring men who served JFK as national security advisers saw only his toughness and unwillingness to yield. Being as tough in a crisis as the president became a mantra in the administration; senior officials who advocated compromise and conciliation — such as Adlai Stevenson, the ambassador to the UN, and Chester Bowles, the liberal undersecretary of state — soon found themselves isolated, their advice disregarded. In the summer and fall of 1961, the president's advisers gave him a list of options to resolve foreign policy issues in Germany, Cuba, and South Vietnam. The options were all tough.

The embattled Kennedy seemed to be heroic and unyielding in public in the weeks after the Vienna summit, as he struggled to regain his poise and as his administration wrestled over the appropriate response to what was seen as Khrushchev's challenge to the postwar status of Berlin. Khrushchev renewed his threat to limit the movement of American troops into and out of West Berlin, and the unrelenting president dealt in kind. There was an atmosphere of crisis. On July 25, 1961, Kennedy, in a televised speech to the nation that echoed the themes of his inaugural address, called the nation to arms in defense of West Berlin, which he depicted as "the great testing place of Western courage and will. . . . We are clear about what must be done — and we intend to do it."

America, the young president said, must "have a wider choice than humiliation or all-out nuclear action." He announced a dramatic series of military escalations. He tripled draft calls, added more than 200,000 personnel to the army, navy, and air force, and gave the Pentagon new authorization to call up reservists and extend tours of duty. If more military manpower and higher taxes were needed, he said, "I shall not hesitate to ask for them." He also announced a $3.25 billion increase in defense spending and urged Americans to prepare for the worst by constructing nuclear fallout shelters in basements and backyards. More than $200 million was added to the defense budget for civil defense, triggering what would become a bitter national debate over the morality of digging a shelter and then arming family members against those less-prudent neighbors who in moments of nuclear peril found themselves without their own shelters.

The imminent Soviet threats to freedom and peace were depicted in the president's speech as being not only in Berlin but — echoing the post–Bay of Pigs view of Walt Rostow — in South Vietnam. "There is also a challenge in Southeast Asia," the president said, "where the borders are less guarded, the enemy harder to find, and the dangers of communism less apparent to those who have so little. . . . We will at all times be ready to talk, if talk will help. But we must also be ready to resist with force, if force is used upon us."

Other moves, not made public, were designed to signal American seriousness to the Soviet high command. Robert Kennedy, in his interview with the Kennedy Library, revealed that the American submarine fleet had been redeployed in the North Atlantic that August and elements of the Strategic Air Command placed on heightened alert. Military leaves were canceled and shipments to Europe of military hardware and munitions stepped up.

Kennedy's speech was a spectacular public relations success. A vast majority of Americans rallied around their handsome young president, as they had after the Bay of Pigs. White House mail ran better than 100 to 1 in support of the president's firm stand in the threat of crisis; there also was a quick response from Congress, which overwhelmingly voted to authorize the increased defense spending. A Gallup poll showed that more than 85 percent of those polled expressed a willingness to keep American troops in West Berlin; 67 percent favored sending troops to fight their way into the city if the Soviets dared block access. In an editorial the *New York Times* described Kennedy as "at once solemn, determined, and conciliatory." The president, it added, "last night reasserted American leadership of the free world. . . . We are confident that the American people and free men everywhere will support him."

Khrushchev's solution was to permanently isolate East from West. Early on the morning of August 13, East German state police began laying wire along the twenty-seven-mile border dividing East and West Germany — the first step in erecting what was to become the Berlin Wall. The Kennedy administration did nothing to stop construction of the wall, provoking enormous anxiety — and much anti-American sentiment — among West Berliners. Kennedy reaffirmed the U.S. commitment within days by sending a battle group of fifteen hundred Americans through East German corridors into West Berlin; on August 30 he announced the appointment of General Lucius Clay, the retired army hero of the 1948 Berlin blockade, as his special envoy. Clay was a hard-line anticommunist who was openly skeptical of Kennedy's decision to accept the wall. But the wall remained.

Historians today have obtained access to documents in Washington and Moscow that demonstrate what was not known for more than two decades: the Kennedy White House had concluded well before August 1961 that the United States could not and would not do anything to prevent the erection of a physical barrier. The president correctly understood, as history has shown, that Nikita Khrushchev and his colleagues needed a peaceful way to prevent the hemorrhaging of East Germany's best and brightest to the West. The wall, odious as it was to many Americans — especially those who responded to the rhetoric of the president — could defuse the Berlin crisis. Some in his administration viewed the wall as a provocation, and the beginning of what could be an all-out Soviet push into West Berlin. But not the president. "Why would Khrushchev put up a wall if he really intended to seize West Berlin?" Kennedy rhetorically asked Kenny O'Donnell, according to O'Donnell's memoir. "This is his way out of his predicament. It's not a very nice solution, but a wall is a hell of a lot better than a war." There was family agreement on the president's caution. Joseph Kennedy told the writer William Manchester, then doing a book on the Kennedy White House, that trying to hold Berlin would be "a bloody mistake."

Did John Kennedy use the back channel to let Khrushchev know that the United States would do nothing about the wall? In his Kennedy Library interview Robert Kennedy said only that he had repeatedly warned Bolshakov before the wall was put up that the United States "would go to war on Berlin," and quoted Bolshakov as responding that he was "sending back that message." Kennedy added that he cut off relations with Bolshakov "for a while" after the Soviets built the wall "because I was disgusted with the fact that they had done so." But the breach, if there was one, was brief. The back channel played a key role two months later in resolving a contretemps between Soviet and American tanks at Berlin's Checkpoint Charlie.

Robert Kennedy's account of his "disgust" over the wall may have been fabricated, or exaggerated, to hide the White House's secret dealings with Khrushchev. It is not known what, if anything, Khrushchev communicated to Kennedy before the wall went up; one Berlin expert, David E. Murphy, who was in charge of the CIA's intelligence operations in Berlin in 1961, believes that there was no need for Kennedy and Khrushchev to discuss the wall specifically in their back-channel exchanges. Kennedy "was sending message after message" in public and private to Khrushchev in the summer of 1961, Murphy said in a 1997 interview for this book. "No one used the term *wall*. What Kennedy did make clear was that they [the Soviets] had the right to control movement through their sector." Murphy was formally assigned in August 1961 as chief of the Berlin operations base, the focal point for the CIA's intelligence and espionage efforts in East Berlin and East Germany. In his view the Kennedy administration conveyed all it needed to convey on July 30, 1961, when Senator J. William Fulbright of Arkansas, chairman of the Senate Foreign Relations Committee, publicly declared in a television interview, "I don't understand why the East Germans don't close their border, because I think they have the right to close it." That statement, Murphy said, could not have been made without advance presidential approval. It was understood inside the CIA station, he added, that Kennedy "never had any intention of challenging the wall. Everybody knew that."

As a senior intelligence officer, Murphy was aware that Kennedy's options in Berlin were extremely limited. In March 1961 Henry Kissinger, as the National Security Council's consultant on Germany, asked the CIA to review possible clandestine action that "could be undertaken in support of the U.S. position on Berlin." The answer, reported by Murphy in his 1997 book, *Battleground Berlin*, written in collaboration with Sergei A. Kondrashev, his KGB counterpart, was disappointing. Some propaganda activities would perhaps be useful, the CIA replied. But open insurrection against the government — as was being urged for Cuba — was "not a feasible clandestine action" in East Berlin. Three months later, Murphy wrote, the CIA's William Harvey, who had directed clandestine operations in Berlin for seven years in the 1950s, told a meeting at CIA headquarters in Washington that it would be "unrealistic" for America's policymakers to conclude that the agency could be effective in organizing resistance groups inside East Germany. "Our abilities are not equal to this task," Murphy quoted Harvey as explaining, "when balanced against the defensive capability" of the East German security services. Murphy, who published little about his intelligence work prior to *Battleground Berlin*, also reported that the Kennedy administration informed the American Embassy in Bonn in a cable in late July that "there is not much the United States could do" if the East German government tightened controls in Berlin.

The president's technique in superpower confrontations would become ingrained by the Cuban missile crisis in late 1962. The president would speak with resolve to his aides and in public, but privately do everything — using Georgi Bolshakov, if he was available — to settle the dispute. He used this technique again in late October 1961, when American and Soviet tanks squared off against each other at Checkpoint Charlie, a highly publicized gate in the Berlin Wall formally known as the Friedrichstrasse crossing. The tanks were armed and had authority to fire.

The dispute began when East German border guards stopped the automobile of Allan Lightner, the senior American diplomat in Berlin, who with his wife was going into East Berlin to attend an opera. The guards asked to see Lightner's passport. He refused, since to show it would have suggested American recognition of the authority of East Germany, and not the Soviet Union, in East Berlin, a concession the United States did not wish to make. Lightner was refused access to the East, and returned with a squad of American soldiers, backed up by four tanks. The border guards stepped aside and Lightner and

President and Mrs. John F. Kennedy

John F. "Honey Fitz" Fitzgerald

Hy Raskin with President-elect Kennedy

John F. Kennedy, J. Edgar Hoover, and Robert F. Kennedy

Robert F. Kennedy, John F. Kennedy, and Joseph P. Kennedy

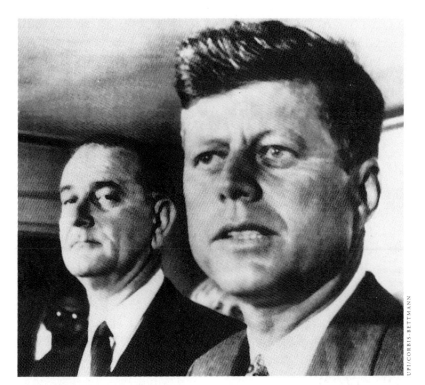

Lyndon Johnson and John F. Kennedy

Murray and Jeanne Humphreys

Sam Giancana and Phyllis McGuire

Johnny Rosselli

Judith Campbell Exner

Durie Malcolm

Alicia Darr Clark

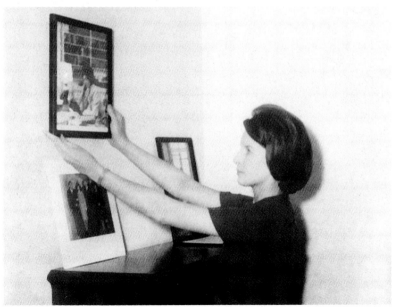

Pamela Turnure

Marilyn Monroe

Ellen Rometsch

Fidel Castro

Robert A. Maheu and Richard Bissell

Larry Newman

Tony Sherman

William T. McIntyre

Joseph Paolella

Allen V. Dulles

Ted Sorensen

Clark Clifford

Sam Halpern

Kenny O'Donnell

Dave Powers

Bill Thompson (in sunglasses), George Smathers, John F. Kennedy

Dr. Max Jacobson

Bobby Baker

John F. Kennedy

his wife were allowed to drive through. General Clay telephoned the president and won approval to escalate the issue. American civilians, ignoring the border guards, thus began to drive into East Berlin, accompanied by ever-increasing numbers of American troops. On October 26, a battalion of thirty-three Soviet tanks entered East Berlin, precisely matching the number of American tanks in reserve on the other side. The formal standoff began a day later, when ten Soviet tanks moved up to the East German side of the checkpoint, facing ten American tanks, which also moved forward.

Publicly, as Clay told his biographer Jean Edward Smith, Kennedy backed him all the way. The president telephoned during the crisis and urged him to not "lose your nerve." Clay responded, he said, "Mr. President, we're not worried about losing our nerve over here. What we're worried about is whether you people in Washington are losing yours." Kennedy said, "I've got a lot of people here that have, but I haven't." In private, of course, Kennedy was agitated by the dispute, telling an aide, "We didn't send him [Allan Lightner] over there to go to the opera in East Berlin." The president and his brother turned once again to Georgi Bolshakov. In his interview with the Kennedy Library, Robert Kennedy said, "I got in touch with Bolshakov and said the president would like them to take their tanks out of there in twenty-four hours. He said he'd speak to Khrushchev, and they took their tanks out in twenty-four hours. He delivered effectively when it was a matter that was important."

In a little-noted analysis published thirty years later in *Foreign Policy* magazine, Raymond L. Garthoff, a former CIA and State Department official who has written widely on U.S.-USSR affairs, wrote about the Checkpoint Charlie incident from the Soviet point of view. In Soviet archives and through interviews in Moscow, Garthoff discovered that — apparently unknown to the Kennedy brothers — General Clay had that fall secretly replicated a section of the wall in a secluded area of West Berlin and was practicing, with army combat engineers, effective ways to tear it down. The Soviet high command learned of Clay's activities, which it assumed had been approved by the Kennedy White House, and concluded that an American military invasion of East Berlin was being considered. Garthoff interviewed a senior Communist Party official, Valentin Falin, then part of Khrushchev's brain trust, who told him that Soviet intelligence agents had documented Clay's training activities with photographs and had presented their evidence to the Soviet leadership by October 21.

On that day, too, Roswell Gilpatric, the deputy secretary of defense, gave a speech, personally reviewed by the president, in which he revealed more than had ever been said publicly before about America's nuclear superiority over the Soviet Union. Citing specific numbers, and referring directly to Berlin, Gilpatric declared that America "has a nuclear retaliatory force of such lethal power that an enemy move which brought it into play would be an act of self-destruction on his part. . . . Therefore, we are confident that the Soviets will not provoke a major nuclear conflict. . . . The United States does not intend to be defeated." Gilpatric's jingoistic speech, which put an end to any concern about an American "missile gap," had been planned long in advance, but Moscow didn't know that. The Soviets' Twenty-second Party Congress was in session at the time, and the party leaders were struggling over dissent in Albania and China. They feared, Garthoff was told years later in Moscow, that the United States might seek to open a "second front" in Europe while the Soviet leadership was distracted. There was an added reason for concern: four days earlier, in his opening speech to the Party Congress, Khrushchev had publicly withdrawn his ultimatum that America negotiate a postwar peace treaty with Germany by the end of 1961 — the ultimatum that had caused Kennedy so much distress at Vienna. The Gilpatric speech seemed to be Kennedy's response to the Soviet retreat.

These factors led Khrushchev and his advisers to conclude, Valentin Falin told Garthoff, that Clay's decision a few days later to begin moving American tanks up "seemed deliberate and sinister." Were the Americans going to breach the wall and being pouring troops and tanks into East Berlin? It was at this point, Falin said, that the Kennedy-Bolshakov back channel got active. The exchange was far more complex — and more important — than that described by Robert Kennedy.

"President Kennedy," Garthoff reported in *Foreign Policy*, "did ask Khrushchev to remove the Soviet tanks — but only to do so first in the context of a mutual disengagement. Kennedy promised that if Khrushchev did so, the American tanks would withdraw in turn."

The back-channel message, far from seeking a unilateral Soviet withdrawal, as depicted by Robert Kennedy, "was a plea from the president for mutual restraint and deescalation, asking Khrushchev to take the initial step." Khrushchev, in his memoirs, did not mention his back channel to Kennedy, but he said that he instructed his commanders in Berlin to withdraw their tanks first. He quoted himself as saying, of the Americans, "They're looking for a way out, I'm sure, so let's give them one. We'll remove our tanks, and they'll follow our example." Khrushchev's published claim, Garthoff added, that he removed his tanks confident of a reciprocal U.S. response "had heretofore been considered a belated invention or a lucky gamble. Now it is clear that Khrushchev had Kennedy's prior assurance."

It was also clear, Garthoff wrote, "why some Soviets, including Falin, regarded this as perhaps the most dangerous confrontation of the Cold War. Such claims now make sense — a U.S. breach of the Berlin Wall would have violated a vital Soviet interest."

The flare-up at Checkpoint Charlie, Garthoff concluded, was "the last serious challenge of the Berlin crisis." The city remained divided for the next three decades.

John Kennedy had exercised restraint, in secret, to head off potentially devastating confrontations over Berlin with the Soviet Union. The men in charge of the Kremlin understood Kennedy's instinctive caution, but the men around the president, who knew little or nothing of the back channel, saw Khrushchev's "retreat" in Berlin as validation of the president's toughness. That fall Bobby Kennedy had declared during an appearance on *Meet the Press,* the Sunday morning TV interview show, that there "is no question" his brother would order the use of nuclear weapons if he considered it essential to safeguard freedom in West Berlin. Reporters were later told that Kennedy's statement was "no accident," as the *New York Times* put it the next day. Echoing the public theme, Arthur Schlesinger declared in *A Thousand Days:* "Kennedy's determination to rebuild the military power of the West had shown Khrushchev that he could not obtain his maximum objectives by bluff."

The president was getting a lot of hard-line advice that fall. In South Vietnam he had been urged by every senior adviser, with the exception of Secretary of State Dean Rusk, to escalate the American commitment dramatically by stationing at least eight thousand American soldiers there. The president's newly named military adviser, General Maxwell Taylor, a disciple of counterinsurgency warfare, had traveled to Vietnam in October and provided a very aggressive recommendation that, as the future would show, was wrong in every detail. In urging the deployment of troops, Taylor depicted South Vietnam as "not an excessively difficult or unpleasant place to operate" for American soldiers. Much of the terrain, he said, "is comparable to parts of Korea where U.S. troops learned to live and work without too much effort." Taylor further assured Kennedy that North Vietnam "is extremely vulnerable to conventional bombing."

Presidential notes from one key meeting show that Kennedy expressed fears about a "two-front war," asking if the commitment of American troops in South Vietnam would jeopardize the tenuous Berlin stalemate that he and Khrushchev had worked out. Kennedy eventually rejected Taylor's call for troops, but agreed to a steady, and secret, incremental increase in American support for the South Vietnamese government. Two fully operational American helicopter companies were quietly transferred to South Vietnam, and the president allowed air force "trainers" to begin flying combat operations in the South. By the end of 1961, at Kennedy's direction, there were 2,200 American advisers assigned to South Vietnamese combat units, a nearly 300 percent increase since January. Americans were beginning to die in combat — with no public announcement of the deaths — and so were many more Vietnamese, combatants and noncombatants alike. The president, despite his hesitancy about a manpower commitment to the Saigon regime, had no objection to what amounted to a continuous increase in covert operations, including the use, as of January 1962, of U.S. aircraft to spray virulent herbicide defoliants in areas where the Viet Cong guerrillas were concentrated. The goal of the operation, code-named Ranch Hand, was to deny the enemy jungle cover and deny him food. The American activities were in direct violation of the 1954 Geneva Accords, partitioning North and South Vietnam, to which the United States was a signatory.

Kennedy's low-profile approach to the expanding war in South Vietnam masked the extent of his commitment. The policy debate on Vietnam, as captured in the Pentagon Papers, was not about whether to save the nation from communism, but how to do it. After one early meeting, General Lionel McGarr, chief of the military advisory group in Saigon, informed his superiors in the Pacific Command that President Kennedy and General Lyman Lemnitzer, chairman of the Joint Chiefs of Staff, "have repeatedly stated Vietnam is not to go behind [the] Bamboo Curtain under any circumstances, and we must do all that is necessary to prevent this from happening." McGarr was told that the president believed this was "a primarily military problem," and that the American officials in Saigon should not be restricted by the Geneva Accords.

Kennedy had a chance in 1961 to disengage from an American involvement in South Vietnam. He instead chose, quietly and indirectly, to go to war, with the vast majority of his senior advisers solidly in front of him, urging him to send in American troops and confront Soviet expansionism in Southeast Asia.

Kennedy's instinctive caution in Berlin and fear of Soviet reprisal did not play a part in his thinking about South Vietnam — or even about Fidel Castro. The Cuban leader continued to be targeted, and so did his potential allies.

On October 25, 1961, as American and Soviet tanks were jousting for position near Checkpoint Charlie, President Kennedy held what seemed a routine morning meeting with Dr. Cheddi Jagan, the first native-born prime minister of British Guiana, whose socialist People's Progressive Party had swept into power in elections the month before. The tiny Latin American nation of 600,000 citizens, divided between East Indians and blacks, was still a British colony, but was soon to obtain independence (as Guyana); Jagan came to Washington to plead for American foreign aid.

Jagan's financial needs, Arthur Schlesinger noted in *A Thousand Days*, were viewed in the White House in Cold War terms: How much foreign aid would it take to keep Jagan from turning, as many thought was his predilection, to the Soviet Union? During the meeting with Kennedy, Schlesinger wrote, Jagan "turned out to be a personable and fluent East Indian but endowed, it seemed to those of us present, with an unconquerable romanticism or naïveté." Jagan's mistake, apparently, was to tell the president that, as a committed socialist, he believed in state planning. Kennedy's response, according to Schlesinger, was gracious: "We have often helped countries which have little personal freedom, like Yugoslavia, if they maintain their national independence. That is the basic thing. So long as you do that, we don't care if you are socialist, capitalist, pragmatist or whatever."

Jagan didn't get his money. Within months race riots and labor unrest broke out, with the loss of more than one hundred lives. The center of downtown Georgetown, British Guiana's capital, burned down in February 1962, in the aftermath of a riot. British troops were called in to maintain law and order. New radio stations went on the air and newspapers began printing false stories. Jagan clung to power until late 1964, when a coalition government under Forbes Burnham, a black who was strongly anticommunist, was elected.

Thirty-three years after Cheddi Jagan's visit to Washington, the *New York Times* reported what had happened in the hours after he left Kennedy's office. "Kennedy met in secret with his top national security officers," the *Times*'s Tim Weiner wrote. "A pragmatic plan took shape. Still-classified documents depict in unusual detail a direct order from the President to unseat Dr. Jagan." The *Times,* quoting unnamed government officials said to be "familiar with the secret documents," reported that the CIA's classified files on the Jagan operation "are a rare smoking gun: a clear written record, without veiled words or plausible denials, of the President's command to depose a Prime Minister."*

The CIA's men inside the Guianan labor movement triggered the riots, the CIA's money financed the new radio stations, and the CIA's propaganda experts produced the phony newspaper stories that heightened the unrest.

Arthur Schlesinger, asked to comment in 1994, blamed the CIA, as

---

* The thrust of Weiner's story was that the CIA and State Department were refusing to declassify the file on the anti-Jagan operations in British Guiana, and other potentially embarrassing activities, despite a law mandating the declassification of government papers after thirty years unless the release would compromise national security secrets. The release of a historical volume on Guyana had been prepared, but later withheld, Weiner was told, because of a reluctance to declassify the Jagan papers. Someone involved in the process provided the gist of the embarrassing material to Weiner.

he had done after the Bay of Pigs, and not the president. Jagan "wasn't a communist," he told the *Times*. "The CIA decided this was some great menace, and they got the bit between their teeth. . . . We misunderstood the whole struggle down there."*

Jack Kennedy, as Schlesinger perhaps did not know or could not acknowledge, had behaved in the Oval Office like a bully at the beach, flinging sand in the face of a weaker man. The president was sending no diplomatic signal in the destruction of Cheddi Jagan, no implicit warning to Nikita Khrushchev about further restrictions of access to West Berlin. Cheddi Jagan was a surrogate for the real target of presidential obsession — Fidel Castro. In Cuba, the president could meet his need to live on the edge without jeopardizing all of mankind.

---

* Robert Kennedy, in one of his 1964 interviews for the Kennedy Library, was once again glib, in concealing what really happened to Cheddi Jagan. The interviewer, John Barlow Martin, who served in the Kennedy administration as ambassador to the Dominican Republic, cited Jack Kennedy's private meeting with Jagan and commented, "The president seems to have gone to a good deal of trouble to be nice to him." Martin apparently did not know of the CIA operations in British Guiana. Bobby Kennedy explained that the meeting took place because his brother had been "concerned" about the spread of communism in the Western Hemisphere and was "convinced that Jagan was probably a communist." But, added Kennedy, the president wanted to "see whether we could work something out with him. . . . There were various plans we went through . . . of trying to get the British to come up with something. . . . I think there was an election coming on [in British Guiana]. . . . Most of our efforts were to try to get the British to recognize the concern that we had and ask them to take action to control the situation. They were reluctant." Asked why, Kennedy explained that the British "were not as concerned about him and about the situation." At that point, Martin noted, "But it's a very small country." Kennedy responded: "Well, I suppose Cuba is too. It's caused us a lot of trouble." Nothing more about Jagan was said.

17

TARGET CASTRO

Robert Kennedy, fresh from his crucial back-channel role in the Berlin crisis, took on yet another assignment in the fall of 1961: he became the driving force in a renewed American effort to murder Fidel Castro and overthrow his government. His enthusiasm for the assignment and his insistence on getting it done made the thirty-five-year-old attorney general the most feared, and despised, official in the government — especially at the Central Intelligence Agency. But everyone involved understood that Bobby Kennedy was doing his brother's bidding.

"The Kennedys were on our back constantly to do more damage to Cuba, to cause an uprising, to get rid of Castro and the Castro regime," the CIA's Samuel Halpern, who served as the executive assistant to three deputy directors for clandestine operations, told me in one of our interviews for this book. "They were just absolutely obsessed with getting rid of Castro. . . . I don't know of any senior officer that I talked to who felt, aside from the pressure from the Kennedys, that Castro had to go. Me and my buddies kept asking over and over again, 'Why are we doing this? We're not getting anywhere.' We didn't know why we were doing what we were doing, but we were told to do it, so we did it. We were good soldiers."

Halpern, who began his intelligence career with the OSS in 1943, was brought to Washington from the Far East in the fall of 1961 and was eventually designated executive officer for the Cuba task force, as the CIA's bureaucracy grew in response to the White House's demand to oust Castro. Within months what soon became the largest CIA station in the world was in operation on the campus at the University of Miami, with six hundred American case officers monitoring the activities of an estimated three thousand Cuban exiles on the payroll. Scores of guerrilla teams infiltrated Cuba by boat, collecting intelligence and attempting to carry out hit-and-run sabotage. The Kennedy administration had changed its approach. The Bay of Pigs had called for a military invasion by a large and well-armed exile force and the murder of Castro, provoking an uprising on the island. The new plan, which became known as Operation Mongoose, relied on propaganda, economic sabotage, and the infiltration of small-unit exile teams to create the conditions for an internal revolt. To run the operation, Jack Kennedy sought out Edward G. Lansdale, an air force general famed for his exploits as a covert operator in the Philippines and South Vietnam (he was said to be the model for *The Quiet American,* Graham Greene's 1955 novel about Saigon). William Harvey, still responsible for executive action (ZR/RIFLE), was the CIA's point man on Mongoose — and the revived assassination plotting against Castro. Johnny Rosselli and his friends in the Mafia would now be working directly for Harvey and once again trying to get poison pills into Havana.

The pressure was on at the CIA, whose anti-Castro operatives the Kennedys held in contempt after the failure at the Bay of Pigs. Bobby made plain his feelings about the agency in a 1964 interview with the Kennedy Library: "The people the CIA had originally were not very good. . . . I was trying to do things, mostly trying to get them to come up with some ideas about things to be done."

The people in the CIA saw it differently. "You don't know what pressure is until you get those two sons of bitches laying it on you," Halpern told me. "We felt we were doing things in Cuba because of a family vendetta and not because of the good of the United States." The Kennedys were taking on Castro "for personal reasons — because the family name was besmirched by the Bay of Pigs. Cuba stained the Kennedy escutcheon. It wasn't national security. It was like their father always said: 'Don't get mad; get even.' We knew we were in a political operation inside the city of Washington."

Even as the Mongoose project was taking form, the CIA's Richard Bissell, soon to leave the agency's payroll, was given his marching orders: get on with eliminating Castro. There was a brutal meeting in the White House, Bissell later confided to Halpern. "Bissell said he had been called over to the White House and met with the president and his brother," Halpern told me. "He was chewed out and told to get off his ass and do something about the Castro regime — and Castro. What they said was, in effect, that he hadn't done anything since the Bay of Pigs and it was time to get back into action. They expected him to continue to do the same kinds of things that the Bay of Pigs was supposed to do — to get rid of Castro."

Halpern, the new man on the team, asked Bissell what the words "get rid of" meant. "He said, 'Use your imagination.' There were no holds barred." Of course, Halpern added, no one talked about murdering Castro "in so many words, and nobody was about to in those kinds of operations. It just doesn't happen that way. I'll bet even the Mafia doesn't have pieces of paper on that kind of stuff. We knew what we were doing, because that's what they wanted."

Bill Harvey certainly understood his orders. A few weeks after Bissell's meeting at the White House, he attended a five-day conference on a British breakthrough in code-breaking in a secure room at the National Security Agency's headquarters, in suburban Maryland. Also at the conference was Peter Wright, one of Britain's most experienced intelligence operatives and an advocate of using intelligence, rather than force, to combat political insurgencies. During a break, Wright wrote in his 1987 memoir, *Spycatcher*, Harvey sought him out and asked what "the Brits" would do about Castro. Wright was apprehensive about being drawn into "the Cuban business," he wrote, because he and his colleagues were convinced that "the CIA [was] blundering in the Caribbean."

"Would you hit him?" Harvey asked. "We're not in it anymore, Bill," Wright responded. "We got out a couple of years ago." Harvey, dropping his voice and speaking very slowly, explained, Wright said, that "we're developing a new capability in the Company to handle these kinds of problems, and we're in the market for the requisite expertise." The agency needed "deniable personnel and improved 'delivery mechanisms,'" he said. The conversation was unnerving, Wright added: "I began to feel I had told them more than enough. . . . They seemed so determined, so convinced that this was the way to handle Castro, and slightly put out that I could not help them more."

Bill Harvey, as a professional intelligence officer, had not told Wright about the pressure from the Kennedy brothers. But he did tell all he knew to the Church Committee fourteen years later. In an interview with a committee aide, unpublished until this book, Harvey was asked about the White House pressure on the agency. Was it possible that the Kennedys, in their tough talk with Bissell, merely wanted to topple Castro's government? "Harvey said, 'No,'" according to the previously secret committee summary of the interview. "Bissell," the summary paraphrased, "clearly said that the White House had reiterated its interest in executive action capability." Harvey added, when questioned further, that it "was possible" that the president and his brother had approved Castro's assassination again that fall without being told any details. "It would not have been good form," a committee summary quoted Harvey as explaining, for the agency to give the president and his brother "the actual specifics of the plot, or the day-by-day account of its going forward."

Jack and Bobby Kennedy were not being subtle about what they wanted done to Castro. On January 19, 1962, with Operation Mongoose finally in place, Bobby Kennedy convened what he called a "How it all got started" meeting. Careful notes, later declassified, were taken by the CIA's Richard Helms, soon to be named to replace Bissell as deputy director for plans, in charge of clandestine operations. Kennedy was quoted as saying that Cuba carried "the top priority in the U.S. government. All else is secondary. No time, money, effort, or manpower is to be spared. Just the day before," Bobby added, according to Helms's notes, the president had told him that "the final chapter [on Castro] has not been written. It's got to be done and will be done." In his carefully hedged Senate testimony Helms told the Church Committee that Kennedy's impassioned talk reflected the "kind of atmosphere" in which Helms perceived that assassination was authorized.

There is evidence that Operation Mongoose had its own assassination component, separate from the ongoing CIA effort. One of the CIA men who worked with Lansdale told me in an interview for this book that Lansdale's planning documents initially included the concept that Castro would "die during fighting for the island." At President Kennedy's request, the former intelligence operative said, such language was removed from all future Mongoose papers. The operative, who did not wish to be named, shrugged at the memory: "Would Castro be killed in the overthrow? Yes. He wasn't going to accept a golden invitation to leave the island." This understanding about Castro's fate helps explain a handwritten note later in 1962 from Lansdale to Bobby Kennedy, made public by the Church Committee, in which Lansdale told the attorney general that a packet of enclosed documents "does not include the sensitive work I have reported to you; I felt that you preferred informing the President privately." A few days later, Lansdale alerted Kennedy to the possibility that "we might uncork the touchdown play."

Bill Harvey formally took over the CIA's Cuba task force in February 1962, renamed it Task Force W, and began running what he always thought, he told the Church Committee, was a continuation of the ongoing Castro assassination operation that had started before the Bay of Pigs. In early April, Harvey met with Johnny Rosselli in New York and gave him CIA-produced poison pills intended for Castro. Rosselli told the committee he informed Harvey at the meeting that the Cuban exile operatives had expanded the hit list to include Che Guevara and Castro's brother, Raul. Rosselli testified that Harvey approved the targets, saying, "Everything is all right." The CIA also arranged for a shipment of long-range rifles with night scopes and other equipment, including radios and ship radar, to be delivered in May to the Cuban hit team in Miami. The murder plotting continued unabated until February 1963, Harvey testified, although he had grave doubts by September whether the assassination would ever take place. The Mafia's delivery man, once again, was Tony Varona. And, once again, the mob did not deliver.

"Bill Harvey was a rough and tough SOB," Sam Halpern told me, "but when push came to shove, he couldn't deliver either. He had no more expertise than you and I in eliminating anybody. We never killed anyone," Halpern added, "but not for lack of trying."

Until his death in 1968, Robert Kennedy repeatedly denied that he or his brother had anything to do with the Castro assassination attempts. The most explicit denials came during his taped interviews in April and May 1964 at the Kennedy Library. Asked whether there had been any direct attempts on Castro's life during his brother's administration, Kennedy said, "No."

"No one tried?"

"No."

"Contemplated?"

"No."

By mid-1961 the president and his brother had gained complete control of military operations and foreign policy. The military chiefs were mute; Robert McNamara, the defense secretary, was loyal, almost slavish, in his admiration for the president. The Kennedy brothers terrorized the CIA.

Bobby Kennedy had gotten his first insight into the clandestine world of the CIA while spending two months on the four-man study group to investigate the disaster at the Bay of Pigs, headed by the retired Maxwell Taylor. The dapper and well-spoken Taylor, a former army chief of staff, had won the president's admiration by breaking with his fellow generals in the Eisenhower administration and advocating "flexible response": the ability to fight communist insurgencies locally instead of relying on massive retaliation to deter Nikita Khrushchev's support for wars of liberation.

The other two members of the study group were Allen Dulles, at that time still director of the CIA, and Admiral Arleigh Burke, chief of naval operations. There is evidence that Taylor quickly learned what Kennedy and Dulles already knew — that assassination plotting had been an integral part of the failed invasion.

The evidence came in a memorandum from the ever-methodical J. Edgar Hoover. On May 22, 1961, while the Taylor panel was still interviewing witnesses, Hoover sent Bobby Kennedy a memo putting on record, among other things, the fact that the FBI had received a briefing on Richard Bissell's testimony before the panel. The disgraced Bissell, still in charge of the assassination plotting, had been permitted to testify, so Hoover learned, before only two members of the panel, Taylor and Bobby Kennedy. Bissell subsequently described his testimony to Sheffield Edwards, of the CIA's office of security (it was Edwards who talked to the FBI, Hoover said), and claimed to have told Taylor and Kennedy about "the use of Giancana and the underworld" in the agency's "dirty business" against Castro.*

Max Taylor, like many men instinctively loyal to the president, included no hint of assassination plotting against Castro in his final report. He also did not tell what he knew to Admiral Burke, who was suspected of being more loyal to the truth than to Jack Kennedy.† But Hoover's memorandum about Bissell's revelatory testimony remained in Justice Department files — yet another problem for the Kennedys.

Taylor's highly classified report on the Bay of Pigs, whose conclusions were leaked in part to the press in the summer of 1961, was everything Jack Kennedy could have wanted. It was unrelenting on the threat posed by Castro. "There can be no long-term living with

---

* As noted earlier, the attorney general's files included the October 18, 1960, memorandum from Hoover reporting that Sam Giancana had been overheard bragging in a suburban Chicago bar that Castro would be "done away with . . . in November." That document was uncovered in 1975 by the Church Committee.

† In his oral history for the Kennedy Library, Bobby Kennedy constantly confused loyalty with competence. He praised the faithful Taylor as being one of the "two people who have made the greatest difference as far as the government is concerned"— the other was Robert McNamara. Once Taylor officially joined the White House in mid-1961 as JFK's military adviser, Kennedy added, "every decision that the president made on foreign policy" was cleared through him. "I was really terribly impressed with him," Kennedy said, "his intellectual ability, his judgment, his ideas." Taylor's fellow generals were less impressed. Air force general Nathan Twining, who served from 1957 to 1960 as chairman of the Joint Chiefs of Staff, was especially bitter, and would later claim that Taylor's rise to prominence in the Kennedy administration was a turning point in Vietnam policy. In an oral history interview with Columbia University, Twining said he and his fellow officers "couldn't understand" how Kennedy and Taylor "were putting so many troops" into Vietnam. "We used to fight with him all the time," Twining said, but "got euchered" into intervention because of Taylor's optimistic assessments about the progress of the war. "I've always felt sorry for him," Twining said in the oral history interview. "He must have a hard time living with himself. He always goes over there [to Vietnam] and says they're doing fine. Well, sure . . . but my God, how long does it go on?" Twining's interview was cited in *Masters of War*, a 1996 study of military politics in the Vietnam era by Robert Buzzanco, a history professor at the University of Houston. Buzzanco noted that Twining's charges about Taylor's decisive role in policy, while "exaggerated," accurately reflected the deep divisions inside the military about the war during the Kennedy administration.

Castro as a neighbor," the report concluded. "His continued presence within the hemispheric community as a dangerously effective exponent of communism and anti-Americanism constitutes a real menace capable of eventually overthrowing the elected governments in any one or more of the weak Latin American republics." The report, which was not declassified for two decades, criticized the CIA for not making the need for two air strikes before the landing at the Bay of Pigs "entirely clear in advance" to the president; it also criticized the Joint Chiefs of Staff for not making clear their overall doubts about the invasion. "By acquiescing," the report said, the Joint Chiefs "gave the impression to others of approving it."

The report was a cover-up, and known to be one by many in the CIA and the military. Grayston Lynch, a CIA operative who went ashore at the Bay of Pigs with the first wave of Cuban exiles, waited more than thirty years before writing a memoir recounting the testimony he gave the Taylor panel. In his manuscript, made available for this book, Lynch reported that Taylor had seemed to be seeking the facts; during his questioning, the retired general allowed Lynch to complain that the collapse of the invasion "goes back to the planes"— the failure to destroy the Cuban air force. Bobby Kennedy was not interested in testimony about his brother's decision-making, Lynch wrote. The attorney general posed questions that were narrowly focused, he noted, and meant "to show that the invasion would have failed, even with the air strikes. This was something that was impossible to prove." Lynch, like many in the CIA, was convinced that the president had doomed the Cuban freedom fighters by his last-minute cancellation of the second air strike. After Bobby Kennedy's questioning, Lynch asked permission to make a statement and told the panel that, in his opinion, "had the Castro planes been destroyed on the ground, as planned," the operation would have succeeded. Lynch was quickly excused and was not surprised, he wrote, when the Taylor Report not only deflected "the blame" for canceling the air strike from the president but placed it "on the shoulders of the very persons [in the CIA] who had warned them against canceling the air strikes."

Admiral Burke also kept his distress at the Taylor Report to himself. Burke was a strong believer in the presidency, and had been stunned by the aftermath of the Bay of Pigs. "When the news started coming in that it was a disaster," Gerry M. McCabe, a navy officer who was one of Kennedy's military aides, said in a 1995 interview for this book, "all the civilians"— including McGeorge Bundy —"folded up their desks and went home by four-thirty [P.M.]. The president stayed in his office until six. Nobody was around." Burke arrived at the White House Situation Room moments later, "slammed down his briefcase and"— with McCabe's help — began coordinating rescue efforts for the remnants of the defeated Cuban exile army. McCabe recalled his astonishment at how thoroughly Burke knew the waters: "He was able to tell those guys [the captains] how close to come offshore. Those who got out got out because of him." A week or so later, McCabe told me, Burke gathered his top admirals and ordered them not to talk about what had really happened in Cuba. He also wrote a private letter to Kennedy, telling him, in essence, that "the navy and the military had broad shoulders" and would accept the blame for the invasion "for the good of the presidency and the good of the country."

Kennedy distrusted the outspoken Burke. In his memoir, *A Thousand Days*, Arthur Schlesinger provided one reason why: Burke "pushed his black-and-white views of international affairs with bluff naval persistence . . . and he took every opportunity to advocate full support for all anti-communist regimes, whatever their internal character." But Burke had also been one of the very few to directly challenge the president when, during a panic-filled meeting on the second day of the Bay of Pigs invasion, Kennedy refused to authorize a navy counterattack on Cuba, saying, "I don't want the U.S. to get involved." "Hell, Mr. President," Burke responded. "We are involved."

Burke remained troubled by the Bay of Pigs. After retiring from the navy, in 1962, he conducted a private inquiry into the president's decision-making, a study he never published. Burke's documentation included a transcript of a telephone call he made in June 1961, as the Taylor Report was being written, to General Lyman Lemnitzer, chairman of the Joint Chiefs of Staff. The transcript, never published until now, shows that Lemnitzer was enraged because Taylor was planning to conclude in his report that "the Joint Chiefs of Staff approved the plan" for the Bay of Pigs. "I've got a bone to pick with him," Lemnitzer told Burke. "I don't agree with that statement . . . and he insists on putting it in his report." Burke reminded Lemnitzer that he had told President Kennedy that the plan "had a fifty-fifty chance."

Lemnitzer: "Damned right and he just put it out loud and clear that we approved it. We didn't do any such thing."

Burke: "Did I ever tell you why I went along with it finally? . . . This is the reasoning. I went as far as I could until Bobby said, 'We will put out the whole thing about the alternative landing sites [to the Bay of Pigs] mentioned earlier . . . that the Joint Chiefs considered these three alternatives for twenty minutes.'"

Lemnitzer: "That's not correct. He's wrong. . . . I, individually, considered them longer than that."

Burke: ". . . He said he would spread it out [in the press] and if he does do that, we are in worse shape because these things — although they aren't true — are hard to refute."

Lemnitzer: "But he had no business in stating it the way he does — that the Joint Chiefs gave de facto approval [for the invasion]. That is a damned erroneous statement."

Burke: "Yes, that is right. But they said, why did you not object to it?"

Lemnitzer: "Well, to hell with that."*

Like Burke, Lemnitzer remained silent. The Taylor Report came out the way the Kennedys wanted it to. No one in the military dared cross the popular president, even in private.

In September 1961 Kennedy announced that Allen Dulles would be replaced as CIA director by John A. McCone, a rich California Republican known as a rigid Cold Warrior. McCone shared the Kennedys' hatred for the Cuban premier. In 1975 he told the Church

---

* Jack Kennedy, nonetheless, added Burke to his list of military officers who had assured him in advance that the Bay of Pigs would work. Jack L. Bell, who covered the White House in 1961 for the Associated Press, told the Kennedy Library in 1966 that he had asked the president, in the "gloomy" days after the Bay of Pigs, "How did you get yourself in this mess?" Kennedy blamed everyone else. "I had believed those things I'd read in the magazines about all these people in government," he told Bell. "I didn't really know them. I didn't know how good they were, but everything I read said they were tremendous. Arleigh Burke came in, sat down by my desk. I said, 'Will this thing work?' He said, 'As far as we have been able to check it out, this is fine. The plan is good.' Hell," Bell quoted Kennedy as adding, "I'd been reading about 'Thirty Knot' Burke for a long time. I thought he was tremendous."

Committee that Castro was "a man who had spent a couple of years abusing our country, our government, our people in the most violent and incredible and unfair way. . . . [H]e turned over the sacred soil of Cuba to plant missiles."* But when it came to Cuba, Walter N. Elder, McCone's executive assistant at the CIA, recalled in an interview for this book, even McCone "always regarded Bobby as looking over his shoulder." Robert Kennedy, Elder added, "decided that Castro had rendered a personal insult to the Kennedy family by the action of the Bay of Pigs and so Bobby led the charge. And he was the spirit behind the founding of Mongoose and he went into the agency, through back channels. It was really almost an act of revenge for the humiliation, not only to the United States but to the Kennedy family. That was sacred to Bobby."

By late fall, after his success with the Taylor Report and in Berlin, Bobby Kennedy was more assertive than ever. "We had the impression," Walter Elder told me, "that Bobby was simply Jack's ruffian. Jack could sit above it. Bobby was the one who wanted action. There was an intense dislike in CIA for Bobby."

"Bobby, in my view, was an unprincipled sinister little bastard," Thomas A. Parrott, a CIA official who worked on intelligence matters in the office of Maxwell Taylor, recalled in a 1995 interview for this book. In early 1962 Taylor, whose advocacy of counterinsurgency was viewed with disdain by his four-star peers in the Pentagon, was made chairman of what would become the most important foreign policy entity in the Kennedy administration — the Special Group for Counterinsurgency (CI). "Both brothers got enamored of counterinsurgency," Parrott told me. "Everything had to be CI. I was the secretary." Bobby Kennedy was also a member of Special Group (CI). The attorney general, Parrott said, would invariably arrive late at the

---

* There is no evidence that McCone, a devout Catholic, knew — or wanted to know — about the long-standing assassination plotting against Castro. The murder attempts, prodded by Bobby Kennedy, probably went on behind his back. Sam Halpern, asked in a 1993 interview for this book whether McCone had a "need to know" about the assassination plotting, said scathingly: "Need to know? Who knew what he needed to know? McCone was an outsider and he didn't know and nobody would tell him." Halpern added that at the time he thought "McCone was a tough son of a bitch and I didn't want to work with him." Years later, Halpern said, he changed his mind and concluded that McCone, who died in 1991, was "one of the best [Directors of Central Intelligence] ever."

highly classified meetings and put his feet up on the table "so others had to look at the soles of his shoes." At one point, Parrott told me, Kennedy was adamant that Arthur Goldberg, the secretary of labor, be allowed to join the counterinsurgency group. Goldberg had attended an earlier meeting and, Taylor and Parrott thought, talked too much. Taylor said no. Kennedy then said, in essence, "I'll have to take this up with my brother." To Parrott's chagrin, the members of the group — who included McGeorge Bundy, of the White House; Roswell Gilpatric, of the Pentagon; General Lyman Lemnitzer, of the Joint Chiefs; General Charles Cabell, of the CIA; and Edward R. Murrow, the former CBS correspondent who was director of the United States Information Agency — backed down one at a time, saying, in effect, Parrott recalled, "'Yes, maybe you have a point there.' Even Ed Murrow went along. Cabell ducked it, saying he had not been at the earlier meeting. Every one of them folded after Bobby made his threat. It got back to Taylor and he said, 'Well, we're not going to have him.' Whereupon Bobby pushed his notebook closed, said, 'Oh shit, the second most important man in the country loses another one,' and flounced out of the room, like a child, slamming the door."*

The concept for Operation Mongoose, which became the focal point of the Kennedy brothers' war against Castro, originated not in the Oval Office or during a Situation Room meeting but in the fertile imagination of Tad Szulc, the *New York Times* reporter who in January 1961 had published an early account of the plans for an exile invasion of Cuba. Szulc was considered an expert on Latin America and known to be close to the anti-Castro Cuban community in Miami; appropriately, he made it his business to be close to senior officials in the Kennedy administration. Szulc was perhaps closer than many of his colleagues at the *Times* knew; in fact, he had turned down an offer from Murrow, the USIA director, to be one of his

* Special Group (CI) had a broad mandate from the president to ensure that the U.S. armed forces and all U.S. agencies abroad were trained to combat subversion and "wars of liberation" around the world. Some members of the group were asked to leave when the discussion turned to covert operations in Cuba. The pared-down committee, including Taylor and the attorney general, then became Special Group (Augmented), responsible for Operation Mongoose.

assistants. In October 1961 Szulc paid a late-night visit to the home of Robert A. Hurwitch, the deputy director of the office of Cuban affairs in the State Department. As Hurwitch recalled in interviews and in a privately published memoir he made available for this book, Szulc said that he had been "thinking about the Cuban situation. 'If the communists could successfully launch wars of national liberation, why couldn't we, the U.S?'"

Hurwitch dismissed the idea, telling Szulc that successful wars of national liberation "require highly motivated, well-organized armed opposition from within, which was not the case in Cuba." Szulc insisted that his Cuban exile contacts "believed that the time was ripe." He told Hurwitch that he had tried the thought out on several people, including Richard Goodwin, who had been named White House coordinator of Cuban affairs after the Bay of Pigs. A few days later, Szulc visited Hurwitch again and reported that he "was making good progress with his project, and might even have a meeting" with President Kennedy on the subject. "Foolishly," Hurwitch wrote in his memoir, "I thought he was boasting."

Goodwin, as Szulc and Hurwitch did not know, had fallen out of favor and was soon to be reassigned from Kennedy's personal staff in the White House to the State Department. With his unkempt hair, gleaming eyes, and swarthy complexion, Goodwin was an anomaly among the buttoned-down Kennedy men. His brilliance as a speechwriter was widely recognized: Goodwin had been editor of the *Harvard Law Review* and a law clerk to Supreme Court Justice Felix Frankfurter. But in the eyes of those close to the president, this did not compensate for his independence, ambition, and lack of reverence for those above him. Goodwin understood that Jack Kennedy did not stand on protocol when it came to plotting against Fidel Castro; he also understood the power of careful flattery. His praise, in a series of job-enhancing memoranda to Kennedy, was aimed not at the president but at his brother. On November 1, in an "eyes only" memorandum released years later under the Freedom of Information Act, the young aide appropriated Szulc's ideas as his own, endorsing the concept of a "command operation" to handle an "all-out attack on the Cuban problem. . . . I believe that the Attorney General would be the most effective commander of such an operation. Either I or someone else should be assigned to him as Deputy for this activity." On the next day Goodwin tried again in a second memorandum, and dropped the name of Tad Szulc. "As for propaganda, I thought we might ask Tad Szulc to take a leave of absence from the *Times* and work on this one," Goodwin wrote. A week later Szulc met with Bobby Kennedy at the Justice Department and spent more than an hour afterward with the president and Goodwin in the Oval Office.

Szulc's typed notes of the meeting, provided by him to the Church Committee and published in scores of books, say nothing of a job offer from Jack Kennedy. The president was discussing the general need to control the CIA, Szulc wrote, when he suddenly "leaned forward and asked me, 'What would you think if I ordered Castro to be assassinated?' I said this would be a terrible idea because a) it probably wouldn't do away with the regime . . . and b) I felt personally the U.S. had no business in assassination. JFK then said he was testing me — that he felt the same way — he added, 'I'm glad you feel the same way'— because indeed U.S. morally must not be part [of] assassinations." Kennedy said he had raised the question because he was "under terrific pressure from" — Szulc was unsure whether he said advisers or intelligence people —"to okay a Castro murder. Said he was resisting pressures."

In a 1994 interview for this book, Goodwin asserted that "Tad was auditioning for a job, and Kennedy was recruiting him." Goodwin added that the president trusted Szulc "well enough to bring up" the subject of political murder; Goodwin also conceded that the president, as was much more likely, "may have been laying down a disclaimer." Goodwin told me that he had no knowledge of Jack Kennedy's involvement in the murder plots against Castro. "The only explanation" for the president's bringing up the subject with Szulc, Goodwin added, "is that he didn't want Tad to think he was involved"— if the president did know of the assassination planning. In other words, JFK was setting Szulc up to write in case of Castro's death an authoritative account of a president who had not wanted the murder to take place.*

* In a 1994 interview for this book, Szulc acknowledged that Goodwin told him after the meeting with Kennedy that the White House was "trying to put together some kind of a task force." There was a subsequent meeting with an official at the State Department, Szulc said, but nothing came of it: "I said, 'I'm really not interested.'" A year later, however, according to declassified CIA files, Szulc was the linchpin of a long-

Neither Goodwin nor Szulc got a job with Mongoose. In November 1961, shortly after his second visit from Szulc, Hurwitch told me, there was a top-secret conference at the White House and Jack Kennedy began it by saying, "I've just had a meeting with a well-known journalist." The president then gave the group what amounted to a summary of Szulc's project to initiate an insurgency against Castro, and told them that a task force would be established under Bobby Kennedy. Daily supervision of the task force would be the responsibility of General Lansdale. "I was speechless," Hurwitch wrote in his unpublished memoirs, "and regrettably failed to object to what had seemed to me to be a doomed, romantic adventure." In an interview, Hurwitch said what he chose not to write: "What the hell do you do with the brother of the president of the United States? I've got four kids." Hurwitch understood that anyone who objected to any aspect of the secret war on Cuba would be deemed "soft" and would suffer professionally. He was assigned as the State Department's representative to what became Operation Mongoose. "After the first meeting," he wrote in his memoir, "I regretted more than ever not having objected at the White House meeting. . . . Cutting a dashing Air Force figure, very clever about imagery including his own, Lansdale became the darling of many who became 'experts' in foreign affairs vicariously. . . . He had sufficient support to obtain

---

running CIA operation, code-named Operation Leonardo, that was aimed at an attempt to create dissent inside Castro's military. A CIA summary, released under the Freedom of Information Act, described the Leonardo plan as resulting from pressure "by Higher Authority [State Department and the White House] to consider a proposal for an on-island operation to split the Castro regime. The proposal was presented to Hurwitch, the State Department Cuban Coordinator, by Tad Szulc of the *New York Times*." Szulc was quoted as saying he "first thought of bringing the plan to the attention of President Kennedy, as he had had a standing invitation, since November 1961, for direct contact." The CIA document depicted Szulc as attending meetings at agency safe houses in Washington with a clandestine officer from Task Force W. In the interview with me, Szulc dismissed the meetings as the routine workings of a Washington newspaperman, and said he had cleared his participation in advance with the late Emanuel Freedman, then an assistant managing editor of the *Times*. In interviews for this book, James Reston, chief Washington correspondent in 1962, and Clifton Daniel, then assistant managing editor, told me that they had no knowledge of Szulc's contact with the CIA.

this assignment despite his total lack of experience in Latin America, in general, and Cuba, in particular."*

At his death in 1987, Edward Geary Lansdale was eulogized as "one of the greatest spies in history" by William Colby, the retired CIA director. Walter Rostow, the Kennedy administration aide, depicted Lansdale in a 1972 book as a "unique national asset" who "knew more about guerrilla warfare on the Asian scene than any other American." The journalist David Halberstam similarly saw Lansdale, who returned to Saigon after Kennedy's assassination, as "the classic Good Guy, modern, just what Kennedy was looking for."

During his year as head of Operation Mongoose, Lansdale would work to turn the Cuban exile community into a political force that could mobilize widespread opposition to Castro. But the widespread opposition never materialized — what there was of it languished in Cuban jails or lived comfortably on CIA stipends in Miami. The operation failed to spark an internal political movement against Castro, but it succeeded, with its propaganda and sabotage raids, in creating a siege mentality among the population of Cuba and helped to drive the nation into the arms of the Soviet Union. In April 1962 Castro

---

* One of Lansdale's early schemes, Hurwitch wrote, was to have someone write a stirring song to Cuban rhythms which would be smuggled into Cuba and adopted by the Cuban opposition. Hurwitch claimed that he "longed for a way" to "turn off Mongoose." In 1975 Tom Parrott, the CIA official, told the Church Committee of another bizarre Lansdale scheme: "He had a wonderful plan for getting rid of Castro. This plan consisted of spreading the word that the Second Coming of Christ was imminent and that Christ was against Castro [who] was anti-Christ. And you would spread this word around Cuba and then on whatever date it was, there would be a manifestation. . . . At that time — this is absolutely true — . . . just over the horizon there would be an American submarine which would surface off Cuba and send up some starshells. And this would be the manifestation of the Second Coming and Castro would be overthrown. . . . Somebody dubbed this 'Elimination by Illumination.'" In a January 1976 letter to Frank Church, the committee chairman, Lansdale, who had been linked in the committee's published report to political assassination and sabotage, chose to heatedly deny only the Parrott allegation. "I never had such a plan nor proposed such a plan," he wrote. Lansdale added, however, that "it is possible that such a plan was submitted to me . . . and was tabled by me. It is possible, also, that I mentioned the plan to Parrott as an example of unrealistic proposals given to me." Lansdale's letter is on file with his archived papers at the Hoover Institution on War, Revolution, and Peace in Stanford, California.

overcame the final remnants of political opposition to his leadership — much of it from old-line communists — and signed a $750 million trade agreement with the Soviet Union.

In interviews for this book, former CIA officials were emphatic in saying they knew of no national security basis for Mongoose. "None of us that I know of," Sam Halpern told me in 1997, "thought that Cuba was all that important in terms of the national security of this country. We've lived now for thirty-five or more years with Castro in charge. We're still here; he's still there. The only thing I can figure is they [the Kennedys] probably felt some remorse that they cut the air support" at the Bay of Pigs. "I guess they felt that they had to go after it and show their manhood. I have no plausible explanation other than that." Walter Elder recalled that John McCone's private view "was that this whole thing [Mongoose] was doomed from the beginning." There is no evidence that the usually outspoken McCone said as much to the president. CIA files made public in 1996 show that even McCone chose to be upbeat when he was asked by Bobby Kennedy in January 1962 for his "frank and personal" opinion of Lansdale and the Cuban effort. He assured Kennedy that his agency was giving "every effort and all-out support" to Operation Mongoose, although such an operation "has never been attempted before" and would be "extremely difficult to accomplish."

Halpern, Elder, and other former operations officers who voiced their private complaints about Mongoose in 1962 were powerless when it came to conveying their views to the White House. None of their superiors had the courage to tell the president or his brother that the operation was nearly certain to fail. Not even Lansdale, who had his own doubts.

In an interview Richard Goodwin revealed that he and Lansdale had discussed the difficulty of invoking counterinsurgency in Cuba. Lansdale was delighted to be working for the Kennedy administration; but, as he explained to the less-experienced Goodwin, "there were no guerrillas in the hills, no rebel force. Not even any underground movement of any substance. Without that, you wouldn't hope to do anything through counterinsurgency." Lansdale, Goodwin told me, "was Lansdale. He wasn't in charge. He just had an opinion."

Operation Mongoose was a monumental failure. Its ambitions, outlined by Lansdale in a series of top-secret documents in early 1962, were simply unachievable. There were to be six phases to the elimination of Castro and his regime, moving from guerrilla operations by midsummer to open revolt in the first two weeks of October. In one paper Lansdale set a target date of October 20, 1962, for the installation of a new Cuban government. "It was nonsensical," Sam Halpern told me. "We were supposed to be able to plan for a victory march down the streets of Havana the last week of October of 1962. And if you look at the calendar, you'll notice that there was a congressional election coming up. In the clandestine intelligence business," Halpern told me, "you don't set up a plan which says you're going to recruit three by Wednesday, five by Friday, and ten by Sunday. How the heck can you do something like that? Some of his directives were laughable. But those were the kind of orders we got from Ed. My lord, Ed was nothing more than a man in a gray flannel suit off Madison Avenue. I think he could sell refrigerators to Eskimos. I personally didn't have much faith or belief in his ability. We tried a lot of stuff but nothing worked. We used to hold meetings about how many leaflets we'd dropped, how many ships we'd tampered with."

There was no correlation between Lansdale's ambitious plans and what the CIA could actually do in Cuba. "I told Helms," Halpern recalled, "'Dick, we haven't got a pot to piss in in Cuba. Everybody we know was rolled up when Castro came in. We need a year to build up a base.' We didn't know what was going on. We had no intelligence. Dick didn't believe me, saying, 'It can't be that bad.' Helms's problem was that he's got to handle the White House. The Kennedys were sold a bill of goods by Lansdale. We [in Task Force W] would refer to Lansdale on the telephone as the FM — for field marshal."

Mongoose, including Task Force W, cost American taxpayers at least $100 million. The operation did nothing to jeopardize the security of Fidel Castro or his standing with the Cuban population. Many Mongoose operations defied common sense. After a Soviet freighter malfunctioned and was forced to pull into a Caribbean port to off-load its cargo of Cuban sugar, a CIA scientist broke into a warehouse and injected the sugar with a chemical to ruin the taste. "It was childish," Halpern says now. "But we were doing something under the pressure."

There was further humiliation for the men of Task Force W. Bobby Kennedy, increasingly impatient with the lack of progress in Cuba, decided in the early spring of 1962 to run his own operation. He once again moved into the back channel, as he had done with the Soviets, this time working with the Mafia. On his orders an experienced clandestine CIA operative named Charles Ford was assigned as the attorney general's personal agent. Kennedy's unprecedented request went up the chain of command to General Marshall Carter, the new deputy CIA director, for approval. Ford spent the next eighteen months, until the assassination of President Kennedy, making secret trips, at Bobby Kennedy's direction, to Mafia chieftains in the United States and Canada, while continuing to serve with Harvey and Halpern on Task Force W. "Bobby was absolutely convinced," Halpern told me, "that the mob had a stay-behind system in Cuba since they had so many assets left there. There were the casinos and gambling dens and prostitution rings and God knows what else. Kennedy thought that by tapping into those stay-behind units we could get some decent intelligence on what's going on in Cuba. The concept was crazy. The Mafia couldn't have set up a stay-behind system; it's too hard. Also, Castro had a great internal security system and you couldn't work contacts in the cities. That's why we"— in Task Force W —"operated in the countryside."

It was also possible, Halpern said, that Bobby Kennedy's primary purpose in dealing with Charles Ford was to do what Bill Harvey was not doing — find someone to assassinate Fidel Castro. "Charlie saw Kennedy in his office and of course talked to him on the phone quite regularly," Halpern told me. "Charlie was a good officer, and Bobby was his case officer. Charlie never reported that kind of information to me. He may never have reported it to anybody. He was Bobby's man. Nobody's going to touch him."

Kennedy initiated some of the telephone calls to Ford, Halpern said, but they were usually made on his behalf by Angie Novello, his longtime personal secretary. Novello, interviewed for this book briefly by telephone in 1994, said she remembered Halpern but had

"no memory" of ever calling CIA operatives, including Ford.*
Halpern told me that Ford would make it a point to stop by his cu-
bicle in the Task Force W offices and say, "See you again, Sam.
I'm off again." Ford averaged two trips a month for the attorney general, and would dictate reports for Kennedy upon his return. "I
know," Halpern said, "he went to places like Chicago, San Francisco,
Miami — wherever Bobby sent him — including one trip to Canada."
Ford, obviously following instructions from Kennedy, relayed nothing to his nominal superiors in Task Force W. "We never got a single
solitary piece of [written] information," Halpern said. Charlie Ford's
reports, if they still exist, presumably are among the millions of pages
of Robert F. Kennedy papers that have yet to be released by the John
F. Kennedy Library.†

Halpern said he and his colleagues had an ongoing concern for
Ford's security. "We like to control our meeting places," he explained.
"We don't like to walk into an unknown place." The husky and dark-
skinned Ford, who had served in Japan and knew a great deal about
the CIA's extensive operations there, was given identity papers and a
careful cover story in the hope that his identity as a clandestine CIA
officer would not become known to the Mafia.

"I don't know how Bobby Kennedy squared that in his own
mind," Halpern said. "On the one hand, he allegedly was going after

---

* Halpern's recollection of conversations between Kennedy and Ford is supported in
part by Robert Kennedy's telephone logs and appointment book for 1962, as made
public by the Kennedy Library in 1994. They show that Kennedy met twice with Ford
in September and also received a telephone call that month from Ford. In his 1993
memoir *CIA and the Cold War*, Scott D. Breckinridge, who was one of the authors of
the CIA inspector general's 1967 report on assassination plotting, cryptically described the Ford assignment. As part of Mongoose, the CIA "was directed to provide
an operations officer to meet with Mafia figures identified by Kennedy under circumstances over which CIA had no control." Breckinridge acknowledged in an interview for this book that he had been told the story by Halpern, and others, during the
1967 inquiry. Breckinridge did not identify Ford in his book, even after Ford's death,
in keeping with the CIA practice of not naming previously unidentified clandestine
agents. Halpern himself did not confirm Ford's involvement for this book until he
was shown Ford's name and title on the attorney general's office logs.

† In a 1993 compilation, the Kennedy Library reported that its collection of RFK papers
totaled 1,541 linear feet, of which 440 feet have been released for research. Few of
Kennedy's working papers from his days as attorney general have been made available.

the Mafia to destroy them; on the other hand, he was using them for information about Cuba. Maybe it was a deal he made with them. Who knows?" Ford, who died in the late 1980s, never discussed — even years later — his missions for Kennedy, Halpern said.

Bobby Kennedy was doing more than "allegedly" going after the Mafia. Within days of taking office in January 1961, the attorney general had announced what the *Wall Street Journal* approvingly depicted as the "most sweeping campaign against gangsters, labor racketeers and vice overlords that the country has ever seen." His goal, Kennedy said, was to jail top criminals by bringing them up on whatever charges could be proven in a court of law. Kennedy backed up his words by invigorating the Justice Department's organized crime division and decreeing that he would make war on crime his priority as attorney general. He took the fight to Congress and won legislation making it a federal crime to transmit gambling information from state to state by telephone or telegraph, cutting deeply into the main profit center of organized crime. In his speeches and congressional testimony, Kennedy repeatedly insisted that fighting crime was a moral issue that could not be successful without fundamental changes in society. "The paramount interest in self, in material wealth, in security must be replaced by an actual, not just a vocal, interest in our country, by a spirit of adventure, a will to fight what is evil, and a desire to serve," he had said in *The Enemy Within* (1960), his account of the McClellan Committee investigation. "It is up to us as citizens to take the initiative as it has been taken before in our history, to reach out boldly but with honesty to do the things that need to be done."

Robert Kennedy's previously unrevealed involvement with Charles Ford provides new insight into a May 1962 meeting in the Justice Department. Arthur Schlesinger and other Kennedy admirers have repeatedly cited the meeting as evidence of both the attorney general's innocence of the CIA's assassination plotting and his adamant disapproval of any collaboration with organized crime.

At issue was a year-old dispute between the CIA and the FBI over the FBI's insistence on prosecuting Sam Giancana on wiretap charges that stemmed from Giancana's jealousy. The incident took place in

October 1960, when Giancana and Robert Maheu, the private investigator who was then serving as a CIA cutout, were sharing a hotel suite in Miami while trying to find a way to assassinate Castro. Giancana became convinced that his girlfriend, the singer Phyllis McGuire, was having an affair in Las Vegas with Dan Rowan, of the comedy team of Rowan and Martin. Maheu, eager to keep Giancana in Miami — and perhaps seeking to ingratiate himself with his Mafia collaborator — got approval from his CIA handlers, along with some necessary cash, and arranged to have Rowan's hotel room bugged and wiretapped. Maheu's man, a private investigator named Arthur J. Balletti, gained entrance to the room and, believing Rowan would not be back soon, left his wiretap equipment in it, unattended. A maid discovered the equipment and called the local sheriff, who arrested Balletti.

The case was turned over to the FBI, whose agents were told in late April 1961 that the CIA was working with Sam Giancana and the mob. Their informant was none other than Maheu, who — distressed at what he perceived as President Kennedy's cowardice at the Bay of Pigs — began talking to his former FBI colleagues. The FBI was "madder than hell," according to Sam J. Papich, a Hoover aide who handled liaison between the FBI and CIA, one of the most sensitive jobs in the American intelligence community. Papich told investigators for the Church Committee in 1975, according to a summary made available under the Freedom of Information Act, that the CIA's involvement posed a huge stumbling block to any possible prosecution of Giancana for illegal wiretapping. Papich, who was a reluctant witness, further told the committee that Bobby Kennedy "was concerned that this operation would become known, and didn't want it to get out." The flap went to the top of both agencies. Sheffield Edwards, director of the CIA's office of security, spent the winter and spring of 1961–62 trying to convince the FBI and Justice Department to drop the case and keep what they knew secret.

Nothing was resolved until April 1962, when Lawrence Houston, the CIA's general counsel, met with Herbert J. Miller, the assistant attorney general in charge of the Justice Department's criminal division. Miller told him, Houston recorded in a memorandum obtained by the Church Committee, that he envisioned "no major difficulty in stopping action for prosecution," thus protecting the secrecy of the

CIA's use of the Mafia. Three weeks later, on May 7, Houston and Sheffield Edwards, representing the CIA, met with Bobby Kennedy in his office and — as Edwards told investigators for the CIA inspector general's 1967 assassinations report — "briefed" the attorney general "all the way."

Houston, who was also questioned for the IG Report, described Bobby Kennedy as saying that "he could see the problem and that he would not proceed against those [Giancana et al.] involved in the wiretapping case." Kennedy added, speaking "quite firmly, 'I trust that if you ever try to do business with organized crime again — with gangsters — you will let the Attorney General know before you do it.'" At the time, of course, as Houston and Edwards apparently did not know, Kennedy — aided by Charles Ford — was himself trying to do business in Cuba with organized crime. Kennedy also was goading the agency to get on with getting rid of Castro and knew, as did his brother, that a pretty California woman named Judith Campbell was carrying messages to that effect between the president, Sam Giancana, and Johnny Rosselli. In the meeting with Edwards and Houston, the IG Report noted, Bobby Kennedy brought up the subject of Johnny Rosselli and his motivation: "The Attorney General had thought that Rosselli was doing the job (the attempt at assassination of Castro) for money. Edwards corrected that impression; he was not." Four days later, Kennedy asked Houston and Edwards for a memorandum of the meeting. That summary, delivered on May 14, gave Kennedy an invaluable document for the record, stating that he had been angered upon hearing — presumably for the first time — of the Mafia's use in activities against Castro and had ordered the CIA to check with him before dealing again with criminals. It made no mention of Castro assassination planning — past, present, or future. Such actions, as Kennedy surely was aware, were never to be put in writing.

Thus, the 1967 CIA report, made public in 1993, concluded that although Houston and Edwards had fully briefed Kennedy on the CIA's use of the Mafia in the fall of 1960 and spring of 1961, they had left the impression that the operation "presumably was terminated following the Bay of Pigs fiasco." What Houston and Edwards did not do, the IG Report added, was tell the attorney general that the assassination plotting was continuing, even as their meeting took place. "As far as we know," the IG Report added, Kennedy was never told that the CIA "had a continuing involvement with U.S. gangster elements."

Both the IG Report and Church Committee report eight years later concluded that Edwards knew about the continuing assassination operation and had deliberately misled Kennedy at their meeting and in his follow-up written report.* They may have been wrong. By the fall of 1961 — several months before Edwards's meeting with Kennedy — the Castro assassination effort was in the hands of Bill Harvey's task force. Harvey, as many witnesses testified, was well known for keeping his operations to himself. In 1975 Edwards, then seriously ill, had it both ways when he testified before the Church Committee. He told the senators that he "did not know" when he met with Kennedy that the plotting against Castro had been revived. But he also said, "I thought Mr. Harvey was pretty foolish to continue this thing." The retired CIA officer was candid about his reluctance to discuss the assassination plotting before the committee, saying, "I am not prepared to testify to that under oath. Please understand me. I am not trying to fight the battle, see." Frank Church, the committee chairman, tried to be helpful: "I think if you say it [assassination] once you will get over the difficulty." Edwards replied, "Well, what do you want me to say, Senator? What do you think I should say?" Edwards clearly intended to take his secrets to the grave with him.

The gist of the IG Report and Church Committee testimony is this: On May 7, 1962, the attorney general, having learned for the first time that the CIA had retained Giancana and Rosselli to murder Castro before the Bay of Pigs, did nothing more than tell the agency not to use the Mafia without clearing it with him first. He took no names, began no inquiry, and did nothing to make sure that such efforts never took place again. The incomplete and possibly false Edwards-Houston account of their meeting with Kennedy became the basis for Schlesinger's conclusion, in *Robert Kennedy and His Times*, that "the Kennedys did not know about the Castro assassination plots

---

* William Harvey, in his 1975 testimony before the committee, said that Edwards's suggestion that the assassination plotting had ended "was not true, and Colonel Edwards knew it was not true." He explained that Edwards chose to "falsify" the record to insulate himself from any possible damage and from prosecution. "If this ever came up," Harvey said, "the file would show that on such and such a date . . . he was no longer chargeable with this."

before the Bay of Pigs or about the pursuit of those plots by the CIA after the Bay of Pigs."

There was another consideration, Schlesinger wrote: "No one who knew John and Robert Kennedy well believed they would conceivably countenance a program of assassination. Like McCone, they were Catholics."

Sam Halpern believes that he understands the import of the May 7 meeting: "Bobby was not telling us to stop, but [was telling us] not to do it again without checking with him." If that interpretation is correct, Kennedy's goal in the meeting with Houston and Edwards was twofold: to get on the record a statement that the CIA had ended its assassination plotting and, much more important, to ensure that the agency did not authorize a future clandestine operation that could compromise or endanger Charles Ford's continued meetings with the Mafia.

The most effective participant in Operation Mongoose was the Pentagon, whose planners had been instructed to prepare for a pitched battle in Cuba in the fall of 1962, in the event Lansdale's schemes paid off and Cuba was in revolt. As part of that planning, hundreds of thousands of American soldiers and sailors took part in military exercises in the Caribbean, under the watchful eye of Cuban intelligence. In August more than 65,000 men participated in Operation Swift Strike II, obviously meant to simulate an attack on an island like Cuba. Later, 7,500 U.S. Marines conducted a mock invasion of an island near Puerto Rico named "Ortsac"— Castro spelled backwards. In the fall of 1962 the Pentagon was ordered to begin prepositioning troops and matériel for a massive invasion of Cuba. If the president so ordered, an estimated 100,000 troops in military bases along the East Coast could hit the beaches of Cuba in eight days.

The military planning was being led by Admiral Robert Dennison, commander in chief of the Atlantic Fleet, and he took his mission seriously. "I had five army divisions and the Second Marine Division, reinforced by elements of the First Marine Division," Dennison said in a 1973 oral history for the U.S. Naval Institute. "And there were operations planned for the use of these forces against various landing areas in Cuba. All these would require naval and air force support. . . . My plans were approved by the Joint Chiefs of Staff and, of course, were known to the president. He had to know what we could do, and how we were going to do it. We were up against some pretty strong ground forces, so some very drastic preparation would have to be made in the way of our bombing, gunfire. A great many people would have been killed. It would have been quite a bloody affair. And then, once having captured Cuba and occupied it, the United States would have had a terrible problem in rehabilitation, establishing a government. We would have been in there for years."

All of this — the helter-skelter sabotage, the continued assassination efforts, and the military planning and exercising — was seen and fully noted by the Cubans and their benefactors in the Soviet Union. The American aggression played a role in Nikita Khrushchev's decision to move Soviet nuclear missiles and launchers into Cuba, triggering the missile crisis of October 1962. It "now seems likely," the renowned Cold War historian John Lewis Gaddis of Yale University wrote in 1997, that "Khrushchev's chief purpose had not been to shift the strategic balance," as the White House claimed it was at the time,

> but rather to save the Cuban revolution. . . . There has long been ample evidence that the Kennedy administration was trying to get rid of Castro *by all means short of an invasion*. Given the unprecedented level of American military activity in the Caribbean in the months and particularly the weeks before the crisis broke, it seems foolish to claim that the next step would never have been taken — especially if one of the CIA's many assassination plots against Castro had actually succeeded.

18

JUDY

Judith Campbell had never heard of John F. Kennedy until she was introduced to him by Frank Sinatra on February 7, 1960, at the Sands Hotel in Las Vegas. She did not know he was a U.S. senator. She did not know he was a presidential candidate. She did not know he was married.

What she did know was that he was gorgeous. By the next day, she was falling in love. It was a relationship that ruined her life — and, she says sadly, a mistake she would make again.

Campbell burst onto the national scene when the Church Committee, in its November 1975 report on CIA assassination attempts, discreetly noted that it had received evidence that "a close friend of President Kennedy had frequent contact with the President from the end of 1960 through mid-1962. FBI reports and testimony indicate that the President's friend was also a close friend of John Rosselli and Sam Giancana and saw them often during this same period." Those two sentences created a firestorm. Reporters soon learned what the committee had tried to hide: the "close friend" of the president was a young woman named Judith Campbell Exner (she was then married to a professional golfer named Dan Exner), who had testified under subpoena two months earlier. Exner told the committee that her relationship with President Kennedy was only personal and that she had no knowledge of any relationship between Kennedy and Giancana.

Exner made the same denials in a December 1975 news conference in San Diego. She accused the press of "wild-eyed speculation" in suggesting that she was a go-between for the president and Giancana and was having simultaneous affairs with the two men. Two years later Exner published a memoir, *My Story,* written with Ovid Demaris, that listed the times and places of her many rendezvous with Kennedy. In a series of interviews for this book, Exner acknowledged that she did not tell the truth to the Church Committee or at her news conference about her service as a conduit between the president and the mob leader. Sam Giancana had been brutally murdered in his home on June 19, 1975, the night before he was to meet with a lawyer for the Church Committee, and she had been too frightened, Exner explained, to tell the whole story to the committee — or in her book. Furthermore, Exner told me, the committee lawyers made it easy for her to shade the truth by asking the wrong question during her deposition: whether she had been a conduit between Sam Giancana and the president. She very narrowly answered no. They did not ask whether the document flow originated with Jack Kennedy.

My Story contained many distortions and inconsistencies, especially about her relationship with Giancana, but it also included impossible-to-refute details about her meetings with Kennedy, including his private telephone numbers. After years of rumors about his liaisons, she was the first woman to come forward and admit to an affair with the president while he was in the White House. Kennedy's recklessness in the affair, once it was public knowledge, was a blow to his image and to the image of Camelot. And while the affair was taking place, it was also far more serious: a relationship that exposed the president to blackmail by the mob and friends of the mob.

In August 1962, with the FBI watching, Judith Campbell Exner's apartment in Los Angeles was broken into by two brothers whose getaway car was rented by their father — the chief of security of the General Dynamics Corporation, one of America's largest defense contractors. Three months later, General Dynamics — everyone's second choice — was awarded a $6.5 billion contract for the experimental TFX jet fighter. The controversial award, for what was then the largest U.S. military aircraft contract in history, was investigated for months by a Senate committee, which failed to find collusion between General Dynamics and any senior official in the government. But the committee was not told what the FBI knew. The Senate shut down its investigation after Jack Kennedy's assassination, and billions of the American taxpayers' dollars were spent on a navy version of the aircraft that became renowned as a failure.

Judith Exner, as she is now known, was born in 1934 and grew up in a strict Catholic family in Los Angeles, one of five children. There was money. Her father, Frederick Immoor, was an architect and an expert in hospital design; in the late 1930s the family lived in a four-story, twenty-four-room Mediterranean villa in Pacific Palisades, with a view of the ocean. The home was later bought by actor Joseph Cotten. Her parents often socialized with Hollywood celebrities, including the comedian Bob Hope. Judith's older sister Jacqueline, whose stage name was Susan Morrow, was a budding star. "I grew up thinking," Exner said in one of her interviews for this book, "that these people were no different than anyone else." Timid and unsure of herself, Judith had a troubled childhood — she was terrified of the dark and of loud noises, and too shy even to raise her hand in class. She was very close to her mother, Katherine, and was traumatized as a young teenager when Katherine was severely injured in an automobile accident. Her father decreed that Judith was to be taken out of a Catholic girls school, to her shame, and taught at home, by a tutor. There was no thought of her attending college.

At sixteen, her schooling ended, she sometimes spent afternoons at the office of her sister's publicist in Hollywood, answering the telephone and doing typing. Johnny Grant, a retired television broadcaster when interviewed for this book, worked in the office as an aspiring press agent in 1950. He recalled Exner as "one of the most beautiful young women I ever saw in my life, and one of the nicest. She came from a well-to-do family, was well dressed, had a wonderful smile and no desire to be a model or an actress. I used to sit and talk to her," Grant said. "I just liked her." She was a strict Catholic, Grant added, and "wide-eyed."

Men were captivated by her striking beauty. "I'd say she was in the Elizabeth Taylor category," the reporter James Bacon, who covered

Hollywood for the Associated Press, told me in an interview for this book. "She was a gorgeous, gorgeous girl." While still sixteen, she met an actor named William Campbell; two years later, in 1952, over her parents' protests, she and Campbell got married. She was now a Los Angeles housewife.

Billy Campbell was never a box-office star but worked steadily in the 1950s, under contract to Warner Brothers, MGM, and Universal Studios. "When you were a contract player in those days," Exner told me, "you had to go to every premiere, every social event. You had to do movie magazine layouts; you were forced to be in the public eye as much as possible." More beautiful than ever as a young woman, Exner became the 1950s equivalent of a Valley Girl — preoccupied with clothes and her appearance. Bathing, putting on makeup, and picking out her wardrobe for another Hollywood party would take as long as four hours. Bill Campbell's career reached a high point when he starred in *Cell 2455, Death Row,* the life story of Caryl Chessman. But the marriage soured, Exner said, and they divorced in 1958.

She discovered that dating was fun, and her life began to revolve around men, and how they viewed her. "For the first time in my life," she wrote in *My Story,*

> I began dating the way most girls date when they're in high school. Life became so good. I slept until nine, sometimes ten if I was up very late, and tried to paint at least two hours every morning. I lunched with friends or went to the studio and had lunch with Jackie [her sister]. I painted some more in the afternoon, or went shopping. I didn't have dinner at home one night a month. And I never went out to dinner in a restaurant alone or with just other women. To this day I don't like the picture [that not dining with a man] presents. When I travel alone on a train, I never leave my compartment. The same applies to hotels. When I'm alone, I live on room service.

In the fall of 1959, Exner began dating Frank Sinatra; the affair was brief. In her memoir she told of her horror when Sinatra invited a second woman to join them one night in bed. "I just absolutely froze," she wrote. "I went rigid; no one could have moved my arms or legs." Sinatra apologized. In an interview for this book, Exner did not deal with her naïveté and her ignorance of Sinatra's reputation as a swinger, but said only that Sinatra "really wasn't for me. You might say he wasn't the ideal escort." But, she added, "he was a very good friend to have."

She and Sinatra stayed in touch, and she readily accepted Sinatra's invitation to see him and other members of the famed Hollywood Rat Pack — including Dean Martin, Sammy Davis, Jr., and Peter Lawford — perform at the Sands Hotel in Las Vegas on February 7, 1960. Jack Kennedy showed up at the hotel that night. There is no evidence that Kennedy's meeting with Exner was prearranged. He had been campaigning in New Mexico that morning and was en route in the family plane to another appearance in Oregon, with two reporters on board, when it was announced that there would be a stop in Las Vegas. The two reporters, Blair Clark of CBS Radio and Mary Mc-Grory of the *Washington Star,* ended up, as did Kennedy, at the Sands. "The telephone rings," Clark recalled for this book. "Frank Sinatra's on the phone saying, 'Jack wants you and Mary to come down for a drink at five o'clock.' So we went down . . . and there we met a famous character in Kennedy's life — Judith Exner."

In Exner's telling, Sinatra introduced her to Jack Kennedy and his brother Teddy, who was Jack's campaign manager for Nevada and the other Rocky Mountain states. It was Teddy who ended up walking her back to her room after a night of shows and partying. There was a moment of awkwardness, Exner told me, when she rebuffed the over-attentive Teddy. Then — early the next morning — Jack telephoned. They agreed to meet poolside for lunch. "When I arrived he was having a press conference," Exner told me, with a dozen or so reporters. "And he called over to me and said, 'Judith, I'll be right with you.'" The reporters turned to stare, but Kennedy "just went right on with the press conference," Exner said. "I didn't think about it then, because I didn't really know his situation — that he was running for the presidency. I was not politically inclined at all, and so it meant nothing to me. And also coming from California, a senator from Massachusetts just would not be high on my list of knowing."*

---

* In *My Story,* Exner gave a different account, indicating that she knew about Kennedy's aspirations before she met him. She described a December 1959 dinner in Palm Springs with Sinatra and Peter and Pat Lawford at which Pat Lawford analyzed her brother's chances in the coming primaries. "This was the first time I remember the name of Jack Kennedy coming up in the conversation," Exner wrote. In interviews for

There was a long lunch. "He was very interested in the fact that I was from a large family and that I was Catholic," Exner told me. "We talked about everything — the same things that you'd talk about to anyone that you find attractive. He was an amazing man. When you talked to him, you felt you were the only person on the planet, much less just in the room. He never forgot anything you said — good or bad. He didn't just pretend to be listening to you — he listened to you. He absorbed everything." They had another date that evening, and another Rat Pack show. By this time he was "very interested," Exner told me. "I didn't know he was married. It didn't even enter my mind to ask. Nobody said anything."

Kennedy went back on the campaign trail, but telephoned constantly. "He kept asking if I would fly up and meet him," Exner said. "That was all a little too soon for me. I was being a little cautious, as much as I wanted to see him. He was calling almost every day." It was during this period, she told me, that she learned Kennedy was married. "I knew this was something I should stay away from," she said, "but my heart started ruling my head. I can't make any excuses for it." She and Kennedy finally became lovers, she said, in her Plaza Hotel room in New York on March 7, the eve of Kennedy's lightly contested victory in the New Hampshire primary. Three weeks later, while Kennedy was campaigning in Wisconsin, Exner flew to Miami Beach for another Sinatra show, at the Fontainebleau Hotel. At the show's closing party, Sinatra called her over and said, "I want you to meet Sam Flood." It was Sam Giancana, who used as many as nineteen aliases in his career, according to the FBI. Exner said she had no idea who Sam Flood really was — many people in Hollywood used fake names when traveling. But the meeting stood out because Sam teased her about a favorite piece of costume jewelry on her dress. " 'A woman like you should be wearing real jewels,' he said. He thought I'd take that as a compliment, and I was highly insulted, because I loved that

this book, Exner acknowledged that many of the specific incidents and dates in the memoir are not correct. Some details were deliberately fudged, she said, out of fear; other mistakes were the inevitable result of collaboration. The book was written by Demaris, she said, who relied solely on her memory and her recollection. When she first met Jack Kennedy in Las Vegas in early 1960, she said, "I knew him as Pat's brother rather than as a senator."

piece of jewelry. I just looked at him and said, 'A woman like me often does.'" Sam Flood laughed.

There was the usual late-night telephone call from Kennedy. "Jack always wanted to know where I was at all times," Exner said. "He wanted to know who I was seeing, who I was having dinner with. He loved gossip, just thrived on gossip. I used to tell him, 'Go out and buy a movie magazine.' He always used to ask a lot about Frank, what Frank was doing, who Frank was seeing. I now think he may have been interested in some of the women he asked about." She told Kennedy about the odd encounter with "this man and how annoyed I was about what he said about my jewelry. It was just a little story to tell. And when I said, 'Frank introduced me to Sam Flood,' he said, 'Oh yes, I know. Sam Giancana.' And I said, 'Oh, is that his real name?' And he said, 'Yeah.' The name Giancana didn't mean any more to me than the name Flood would have meant to me. You have to remember that back in the sixties people were not familiar with the name of Giancana."

But the Kennedys were. Joseph Kennedy and Giancana had reached an extraordinary understanding months earlier about Mafia help in the 1960 presidential election.

On April 6, 1960, Exner was again intimate with Jack Kennedy, at the Georgetown house he shared in Washington with his wife and daughter. Jacqueline Kennedy, pregnant with their second child, had just left for Florida. The day before, Kennedy had defeated Hubert Humphrey in the Wisconsin primary. Victory had come at high cost, however; Kennedy won by a smaller plurality than expected, and would now have to take his campaign into West Virginia. The primary there would be won, Kennedy knew, not with speeches but with millions of dollars in cash. The problem was not getting the money but getting it to the right people without being observed. None of this was on Exner's mind. "You can't imagine how I felt," she told me. "I guess only a woman in my position would know what it feels like to be in his wife's home. There was another man there. That night, after dinner, they had been talking about the primaries and it was mostly political conversation the whole evening." Kennedy told the man of his desire to fire Hoover and also discussed "whether or not to keep Evelyn Lincoln." By this point, Exner noted, she and Kennedy's secretary had become "old telephone friends. . . . She never failed to give

Jack my messages and Jack never failed to return my calls." She butted in on the conversation to tell her lover that she thought Lincoln "should stay on the job."

Judith Exner initially remembered only that the other guest was a large man named Bill who worked, so Kennedy told her, as a railroad lobbyist.

Bill Thompson's special relationship to Kennedy was kept carefully hidden from the White House press corps. The only known newspaper photographs of Kennedy and Thompson together were published by the *Miami Herald* in March 1962, when a photographer caught the vacationing president enjoying an obviously animated dockside conversation with Thompson, then president of the Florida East Coast Railway, and Senator George Smathers, who had introduced Kennedy to the tall, handsome Thompson in the mid-1950s. Kennedy served as best man when Thompson remarried in 1958, and the three men jokingly referred to themselves as "the Three Musketeers." Women were for the taking.* A few of Kennedy's close friends and aides knew about Thompson, who was a notorious ladies' man, and didn't like what they knew. "He was a pimp for Jack," Charles Bartlett, Kennedy's longtime friend, said in an interview for this book. "He was the dark side of Jack Kennedy," Jerry Bruno, who worked for Kennedy in the Senate, told me.

He was also a lot of fun, and unafraid to make a joke at Kennedy's expense. Hyman Raskin, the Kennedy campaign official, recalled the time in the late 1950s when Thompson prevailed on Evelyn Lincoln to slip him a book of blank bank checks from Kennedy's account. The

---

* Another member of the gang was Torbert Macdonald, a Kennedy college roommate who was a congressman from Massachusetts. On one occasion at least, in the 1950s, the presence of a buddy seemed to provoke Kennedy to rare coarseness. A former Senate secretary told of a distressing encounter with the two men in front of a Senate office building. Kennedy, while crossing the street with Macdonald, flagged down her automobile as she drove past and asked her to "come out" with him and Macdonald. "I was scared," the secretary (who did not wish to be named) recalled in an interview for this book. But she did not want to risk offending Kennedy by flatly rejecting the offer. She made a weak joke, but Kennedy persisted. At that point, the secretary realized that the new edition of *Life* magazine was on the car seat next to her, with a photograph of Jacqueline Kennedy on the cover. She showed Kennedy the magazine and remarked that his wife looked beautiful. Kennedy "got angry," the secretary said, "slammed his hand on the car fender, and walked away."

senator was a notorious penny-pincher who never carried cash — a habit he would keep in the presidency — and, thus, was never able to pay his share of a restaurant or bar bill. When the bill came, Raskin told me, Thompson would "pull out a blank check and toss it to Jack, saying, 'Here. Sign it.'" Kennedy adored it.

Thompson also had fun with Kennedy, Raskin recounted, when he bought an exotic new car. When the car, shipped from Europe, arrived dockside in New Jersey, Thompson figured, he told Raskin, "What's the sense of having rich friends?" He telephoned Kennedy's Senate office and explained to Evelyn Lincoln that he needed a check for "thirty-five" to pay for the car. She telephoned later to say that the senator had left the check in his office. Thompson picked up the envelope, took the train to New Jersey, and once at the shipping company found out that the check was for $35,000 — ten times more than he needed. It got worked out, Thompson told Raskin; he got his car and a check for $31,500 from the shipper to Kennedy. Raskin, laughing hard in the telling, said Thompson chided the senator about his mistake. Kennedy responded, "How the hell do I know what a foreign car costs?"

Thompson remained close after Kennedy won the presidency. "He was flying wing for Jack," George Smathers told me in a 1994 interview for this book. "When we went on the *Honey Fitz* [the presidential yacht], Bill would go and get three or four girls and meet Jack twenty or so miles downriver." Thompson's daughter, Gail Laird, of Miami, his only surviving relative, recalled answering the telephone in the family's suburban Virginia home as a teenager and being greeted by the president, who placed the call himself. Her father, a skilled cook, often made dinner at home, put it in a huge pot of the kind used by railroad cooks, and drove it to the White House. During the Cuban missile crisis, in October 1962, Laird told me in interviews for this book, her father spent "days on end" at the White House as the president's guest. "He was over there all the time," Laird said. She understood one source of her father's appeal to the president: the two men "liked women. That was one of their common bonds." Her father, she added, "kept his mouth shut. He never talked about Kennedy — never. He always told me, 'You never kiss and tell.'"

Bobby Baker, Lyndon Johnson's man in the Senate, depicted Thompson as a lobbyist who parlayed his personal relationship into the presidency of the Florida East Coast Railway, although "he didn't know a thing about railroads. He wasn't the classiest guy," Baker told me. "Thompson could fix things, and the main shareholder of the railroad was always in trouble in Washington." Thompson had one other asset that Jack Kennedy appreciated, Baker said: "He was one of the few guys who didn't have an enemy." Thompson was loyal to the end: he died in obscurity in 1970 without leaving a clue about his important relationship with the president — a relationship that never bored Jack Kennedy.

As her dinner with Kennedy and Thompson came to an end, Exner told me, "Jack asked, would I set up a meeting with Sam Giancana for him. I was a little surprised and I said, 'Well, yes. I'd be happy to. Why, or should I ask?' He said, 'Well, I think he can help me with the campaign.' And we talked about that. He said, 'When you leave here, call Sam.' He told me where he was going to be over the next five days and said, 'We'll arrange a convenient time for the both of us.' He had this large satchel and he asked would I mind taking this to Sam. I said, 'Not at all.' He said, 'But I want you to know what's in it.' He opened it and it was money."

Kennedy made it clear, she said, that she was free to say no. Exner, as Kennedy obviously sensed, was eager to help. "I assumed it was for the campaign," she said. "I didn't think there was anything strange going on. He was asking me to do something that I felt was very important to him. He was bringing me into his life, and that was very important to me." Exner told me that when she saw the money — perhaps as much as $250,000 in hundred-dollar bills — she asked if it would be safe. "He said, 'Yes, someone will be looking out for you on the train.'" Kennedy would not tell her more, explaining that "you're better off without knowing." At the time, she told me, she only knew that the money was "for the campaign." Exner was far more interested, she acknowledged, in showing off a new mink coat she had bought. Kennedy offered to pay for the coat. "I said, 'Absolutely not.' And he said, 'There isn't anything I can do for you. We can't go out. I can't take you to restaurants. Please let me do this for you.' I refused." Kennedy later gave her an envelope and urged her, she wrote in *My Story*, not to open it until he left. It contained two one-thousand dollar bills and a note urging her to use the money to buy "something special." She decided to keep the money. "Everyone tries to make something so sinister out of it," Exner told me, "like I was being paid for setting up the meeting. He wanted to do something nice for me."

The overnight train ride to Chicago was uneventful, Exner continued. She was met by Giancana, who "just took [the satchel] from my hand. Not a word was said. This was expected," she added; it was clear that "the plans all had been made without me, way ahead of time." The next few days were spent with Giancana, Exner recorded in her memoir, as he gave her a tour of his Chicago — including a visit to the Armory Lounge. "He conducted a lot of business at our booth in the bar right in front of me," Exner wrote. "But it was in Sicilian." Even then, she claimed, she wasn't sure "who he was. . . . Perhaps he always looked like a hoodlum to the police or to the public at large. All I can say is that he was different when he was with me. . . . That, I know, was terribly naive," Exner wrote. "There are times when I wonder who or what I was in those days." She and Giancana were not sexually involved at the time, Exner wrote: "It was almost a year and a half before we became intimate.* Being a normal male, Sam tried to change that situation, but after I told him about my feelings for Jack, he didn't push it beyond the teasing stage for at least a year. His patience so impressed me at the time that I actually felt guilty. . . . As I look back, it's possible that Sam got exactly what he wanted from our relationship"— leverage, or what he thought would be leverage, with Jack Kennedy.

Judith Exner's story about delivering money to Chicago was buttressed during research for this book by Martin E. Underwood, a political operative for Richard Daley, the Chicago mayor, who lent Underwood to the Kennedy campaign in 1960. Underwood worked closely with Kenny O'Donnell, who told him in April 1960 to take the overnight train from Washington to Chicago and keep an eye on Exner. Underwood dutifully spent the night on the train and, he told

---

* But see below, page 323.

me in a 1997 interview for this book, watched Exner early the next morning give the satchel to the waiting Sam Giancana. Underwood assumed that Giancana "was going to take care of somebody," but he asked no questions of anyone. (Underwood also recalled that O'Donnell once told him that Teddy Kennedy had "picked out" Exner at their first meeting in Las Vegas, but Jack, who was always competitive with his brothers, "went out for her." Throughout their relationship, Exner wrote in her memoir, Kennedy joked about Teddy's early interest and gloated one time, while in bed with her, "Boy, if Teddy only knew, he'd be eating his heart out.")

Once in Chicago with Sam, Exner told me, she had no qualms about serving as the message carrier when Kennedy and Giancana agreed on the time and place for their secret meeting — probably the Fontainebleau Hotel in Miami Beach on April 12. Her goal was to keep her man happy. "I asked Jack," she said, "'Do you want me there?' He said, 'Yes. Absolutely.'" Exner insisted in her interviews with me that she did not know in April 1960 that Sam Giancana was a Mafia boss, only that "he was an important man. He was with Frank and he was at Frank's table. When you grow up around people who are of great importance," she told me, "you can gauge just how important they are by the way other people treat them. It wasn't that early that I found out exactly who Sam was, but I did know that he was someone of importance, someone with power."

By this time, too, she liked Sam Giancana. "I really thought he was a gentleman; he was funny," she said. "We started to become friends. I'm always amused when I read that someone characterized him as a 'dese, dem, and dose' kind of flashy dresser. Someone said he had a pink Cadillac or something like that. I've never met anyone who was so the opposite. He was well spoken. He was very conservative. I don't think we ever drove in anything more than a Ford. He was just a very charming friend."

Exner did not see Giancana and Kennedy together in Miami, and Kennedy, during a disappointingly short visit with her, said that the appointment with Giancana had gone well. Kennedy said nothing more about the meeting, but did talk, for the first time, Exner told me, about his marriage: "He told me that they had come to an agreement that if he didn't get the nomination, they were parting." He wanted Exner to know, she remembered him saying, that "this was a decision they had made before he ever met me. He didn't want me to think I was the reason for it."

In early August of 1960, a few weeks after his triumph at the Democratic convention in Los Angeles, Kennedy asked Exner to help him move a second satchel of money to Giancana. Exner had sublet an apartment in New York, and Kennedy was in and out of the city. On one visit, she said, he left the satchel, explaining that "this is for the campaign." Giancana stopped by later to pick it up. Exner said she asked no questions of either Kennedy or Giancana: "I have never been one to question people," she told me. "It has a great deal to do with my upbringing. I was taught that people will volunteer what they want you to know. And that it's very rude for you to pry." A few days later — as the Eisenhower administration was gearing up its assassination planning for Castro — Exner set up a meeting at her apartment for Kennedy and Giancana. "I went into the bedroom, into my bedroom," she told me, "and waited until they were finished talking."

By this point, Exner acknowledged in her book, she understood who Sam Giancana was: "the Godfather of the Chicago mafia." She somehow managed to rationalize the implications. "What difference did it make that his name was Giancana instead of Flood?" she wrote. "Both names meant absolutely nothing to me. Unless you're a celebrity, what's in a name? Outside of Chicago, in 1960 how many people had ever heard his name?"

Exner told me some of the techniques she used to arrange contacts between Kennedy and Giancana. "As a rule I would just call Sam," she said. "I learned to almost speak in a kind of code. I would usually say, 'Have him call the girl from the West.' And if something was happening in Florida, it was, 'Can you meet him in the South?' Sam always knew that 'him' was Jack. I really became very adept. I think that I was having a little bit of fun with this also. It was intriguing to have a conversation with someone and as far as anyone else was concerned, you didn't say anything, but you had just arranged a meeting between Sam Giancana and Jack Kennedy."

In one of her interviews for this book, Exner said she was convinced it was Kennedy, and not Giancana, who "made the decision that I was the perfect person" to be a conduit. "I was the one person around him who didn't need anything from him or want anything," she said. "He trusted me. I had money from my grandmother." The next stage in her deepening involvement came after the election, and before the inauguration. It dealt with murdering Fidel Castro.

Sometime just before the inauguration, Exner told me, Kennedy asked her "to take some information to Sam. We had a conversation much like the conversation regarding the money. He explained to me what it was about and he wanted me to be able to say no if I wasn't comfortable doing it." What the documents in the envelope were about, she was told, was getting rid of Castro. "I knew what they [the documents] dealt with. I knew they dealt with the 'elimination' of Castro and that Sam and Johnny [Rosselli] had been hired by the CIA. That's what Jack explained to me in the very beginning.

"I have to emphasize," Exner told me, "that he didn't say anything about assassination. I use that word now because I know more about it now than I did then. I was aware of 'elimination,' which in my mind just meant removing him from office. Had I realized it was assassination, I'd have been much more frightened."

Over the next year, as the Kennedy brothers settled in at the White House, Exner made ten or more trips to Sam Giancana and Johnny Rosselli with envelopes from Jack Kennedy. "I wasn't thinking it's high-level government activity," Exner said. "I was doing something for someone I loved dearly. It was as if my husband had asked me to do something for him, to carry some papers — if I had a lawyer for a husband and he wanted me to take some papers to a client. I never had the sense of just how serious all of it was. I was far too wrapped up in the fact that he trusted me. It just didn't register."

John F. Kennedy was, after all, the president of the United States. "Was I supposed to have better sense and more judgment," Exner asked rhetorically, "than the president?"

At some point, too, after Kennedy was in the White House, Exner said, the attorney general also became "very much a part of all of this." After making love, she and the president usually had dinner in the second-floor Mansion. "Bobby would come in and bring the information in a manila envelope to Jack," she told me. "And they would discuss a little bit about it. And Bobby often would put his hand on my shoulder and ask, 'Are you still comfortable doing this? We want you to let us know if you don't want to.'"

The Kennedy brothers "were very smart in the way they handled this," Exner told me. "I was this little bauble." The brothers "seemed at ease" as they discussed the contents of the papers in front of her, she said, "almost like this was not a great coup. This was the way business was done."

"I remember one trip," Exner said, "where I left the White House and went to Chicago and just stayed at the airport for one hour. Sam looked at the documents, put them in the envelope, and gave them back to me. I flew to Las Vegas, gave them to Johnny Rosselli. I left them there and went to California. But very quickly I was back on a plane to Washington. Very often that's the way it was." Exner said she tried to be scrupulous about noting her comings and goings in her diary, her lifelong practice, and about keeping all travel receipts. There were occasions when she left the White House documents with Giancana or Rosselli; other times the men quickly scanned the papers and returned them to her, for delivery back to Kennedy.

The envelopes were not always sealed, but she never went through the documents, she told me. She did recall hearing names bandied about as the Kennedy brothers talked between themselves, but they meant nothing to her. She always understood, she said, that the papers handed her for delivery did not originate in the FBI and assumed that they came from the CIA. She delivered her final envelope, she said, sometime late in 1961.

In the president's first year in office, Exner said, she arranged two more meetings for him with Sam Giancana.

On April 28, 1961, less than two weeks after the Bay of Pigs, Kennedy attended a political dinner at McCormick Place in Chicago to celebrate his election.* Exner had arrived in Chicago the day be-

---

* Kennedy, still reeling from the disaster in Cuba, began his speech at the dinner by taking note of the strong support he got from the Democratic Party faithful. He added, "I do not know whether to thank you or not, but I am here and I expect to do my duty." He added that "if all of you had voted the other way — there's about 5,500 of you here tonight — I would not be the president of the United States." The remark, given what really happened on election day in Chicago, might have been tongue-in-cheek.

fore, and took a room at the Ambassador East Hotel, about ten minutes away. A few hours before the speech, Exner told me, "Sam came to my room. And then, in a short while, Jack came." The president, Exner said, shook hands with Giancana, who called him Jack — and not Mr. President. "He was there for a very short period of time and I asked him, 'Do you want me to leave?' He said, 'No. Don't go out in the hall,'" where the Secret Service stood on guard. "So," Exner continued, "I went into the powder room and sat on the edge of the tub while they met for a few moments. And then [Kennedy] knocked on the door and I came out. He apologized. I knew that he wasn't going to be able to spend any time with me."

The last Kennedy-Giancana meeting she knew of took place in Washington on August 8, 1961, Exner told me, as the issue of access to West Berlin was nearing the crisis stage. The White House log for that day shows nothing on the president's official schedule between one and four o'clock. In her 1977 memoir, Exner described a tense lunch with the president and Dave Powers, his longtime aide. Things began badly when Kennedy, perhaps unaware of the many hours it took Exner to get ready for their meeting, unsuccessfully tried to get her to join him in the pool for a swim. Over lunch, and in front of Powers, the president brought up an occasion when Exner had become upset, once again, when a man — this time it was Jack Kennedy — brought a second woman into the bedroom with them. Kennedy told Exner he knew she had been complaining to others about the unsuccessful ménage à trois. Exner denied it — a lie, she noted in her memoirs, one she justified by explaining that she was angered because Kennedy's phrasing and tone of voice "implied that I was lending credence to a malicious story someone had invented." She also was appalled, she said, that Kennedy would discuss such matters in front of Powers. That evening, Sam Giancana stopped by her hotel room in Washington and told her he had just come from a meeting with Kennedy. It is not known where the meeting took place, if it did, but Exner's recollection was buttressed by the discovery thirty years later that Giancana was in Washington on that date and applied for a passport at the passport office there. A copy of his application, obtained under the Freedom of Information Act, shows that Giancana described his occupation as the "motel business." On that date, too, according to government records, FBI agents broke into Giancana's main hangout, the Armory Lounge in suburban Forest Park, to install yet another listening device.

Throughout her years with Jack Kennedy, Exner was under intense FBI surveillance. In her account, she learned of the federal scrutiny on November 4, 1960, four days before the presidential election, when two agents, from the FBI and Internal Revenue Service, came to her apartment in Los Angeles and interrogated her about Sam Giancana. "It was terrible," she said in an interview for this book. "They treated me with such disrespect. I gladly let them come into my home. And the way they were acting, I finally just told them to leave." In her memoir, she told how the agents had described Giancana to her in vivid terms and said, "He's not the kind of man a nice girl should be running around with." Had the FBI approached her earlier, Exner wrote, "the idea of associating with an underworld boss might have frightened me. But now that I *knew* Sam . . . I wouldn't have told them anything about Sam if my life depended on it. . . . I kept thinking, 'So this is how they treat innocent people.' I thought of myself as innocent, which I suppose was open to debate." From then on, Exner wrote, she was aware of a steadily increasing FBI presence. "The FBI not only questioned all my friends, but I think they questioned anyone who had the misfortune of riding in an elevator with me. And they were such hypocrites." One of Johnny Rosselli's girlfriends responded to a question about her by telling the agent, "I know she just came back from the White House. Why don't you go ask the president?" The agent said nothing.

The president wasn't much help. After the first FBI visit in the fall of 1960, Exner told me, "I, of course, called Jack right away. He always had the same pat answer for me. He'd always say, 'Don't worry about them.' Even after they were harassing me so terribly, following me everywhere, questioning all my friends, he would always say, 'You have nothing to be afraid of. You've never done anything wrong in your life. You know Sam works for us.'"

The FBI's view of Exner was more than a little disrespectful. She was invariably described in FBI reports, made available to her under the Freedom of Information Act, as a "very good-looking blonde girl" who was "a friend of Rosselli and Giancana." One retired FBI agent, in a 1997 interview for this book, said that he and his colleagues considered Exner to be "a high-class whore" who was doing business with both mobsters. The former agent, William R. Carter, now a private investigator in Oklahoma City, worked undercover investigating Rosselli and Exner in Los Angeles. Exner was identified as a Giancana-Rosselli girl in early 1960, Carter told me. He and his colleagues "definitely thought she was selling her favors. We believed she was bedding both of them. Someone obviously was giving her big money." (Carter offered no proof for his assertion, and Exner's FBI file, released in its entirety under the Freedom of Information Act, contains no evidence linking Exner to prostitution, despite years of surveillance.) Giancana and Rosselli were both considered "bad news," Carter added. Giancana was "a degenerate, as bad as they came," and Rosselli was believed to be responsible for "as many as thirteen murders."

The heavy surveillance of Exner led to a shocking discovery during the July 1960 Democratic convention, Carter said: Exner and John F. Kennedy, the newly nominated candidate, were found to be "having a tryst." That explosive information, Carter said, which may have come from a bug in Exner's apartment, was "very tightly held" by his superiors, though it undoubtedly was forwarded to J. Edgar Hoover. "The agents wanted to throw up" after they discovered the Exner-Kennedy liaison, Carter said. "They could not understand that type of behavior of a top official of the United States. It's demoralizing, really." Much of the agents' anger was directed at Exner. "Here's a person who's no better than a common street slut" consorting with a presidential candidate, Carter told me, "when we're trying to do our job" by going after organized crime. "We considered Kennedy to be no better than Giancana or Rosselli."

During the Kennedy years, Carter said, he and other agents in Los Angeles talked often about the apparent contradiction between what they knew and Bobby Kennedy's highly publicized campaign against organized crime. "We attributed it to political ambition," Carter told me. "Figured it was the way several people have become famous. Fighting crime means you're a good guy." There was little chance that J. Edgar Hoover or any other law enforcement official would publicly use the information about Kennedy and Exner, Carter said, because the source of some of it was electronic surveillance. The extent of the buggings, he added, if known to the public, would create "a furor" and damage the FBI's reputation, "so Hoover had no choice."

By early 1962, however, the FBI's intensive monitoring of Giancana, Rosselli, and Exner had produced an impossible-to-refute link to the White House: Exner had repeatedly telephoned the White House office of Jack Kennedy. On February 27, 1962, Hoover, always the bureaucrat, sent a memorandum to Bobby Kennedy officially notifying him that Judith Campbell (Exner), known to be in contact with Johnny Rosselli and Sam Giancana, had made two telephone calls within a week to Evelyn Lincoln. "The relationship between Campbell and Mrs. Lincoln or the purpose of these calls is not known," Hoover wrote. Copies of the memorandum were sent to Kenny O'Donnell, in the White House, and to two of Bobby Kennedy's aides in the Justice Department — Nicholas Katzenbach, the deputy attorney general, and Herbert J. Miller, the assistant attorney general in charge of the criminal division.

Bobby Kennedy, of course, knew of Exner and the role she was playing as his brother's lover and as a conduit to Giancana and Rosselli. He also had his own sources, in the FBI, on the status of the inquiry into Exner. In a 1995 interview for this book, Jane Leahy, one of Kennedy's secretaries in the Justice Department, told of seeing a photograph of Exner among Kennedy's files. "I kept all of his personal papers," Leahy told me. When an unclassified envelope came over from the FBI, she didn't hesitate to look. "It was a picture of Judy Exner — just a picture, not with the president," Leahy said. "She was just walking on the street." The photograph clearly was one of the dozens of FBI surveillance photos taken of Exner in the early 1960s.

Hoover's memorandum meant that the president's affair with Exner — and connection to Giancana — could soon be known to dozens of FBI agents and Justice Department officials. Like his brother, Bobby Kennedy needed cover: he had to isolate his role as the nation's leading law enforcement official from his involvement with the anti-Castro activities of the Chicago mob. Bobby turned to Joseph Dolan, an assistant attorney general and one of his closest associates. In a 1995 interview for this book, Dolan — still flattered by

Kennedy's trust in his judgment — told of being summoned to the attorney general's office at the end of February 1962 and shown a copy of the Hoover memorandum and the FBI file on Exner. Exner's person-to-person calls to Evelyn Lincoln were beyond challenge; even more disconcerting were Exner's ties to Giancana and Rosselli. "An hour later I have to see him on something else," Dolan told me, "and Kennedy brought it up again. I said to myself, 'Oh shit, he's afraid to tell his brother.' Bobby asked me what do I think? I looked him right in the eye and said, 'Mrs. Lincoln shouldn't take calls from her.' He looked at me like I came from the moon. 'What would you do?' he asked." Dolan said he told the attorney general that he would "write a memo to Mrs. Lincoln saying that she shouldn't take the calls." Kennedy responded, "Do it." As Dolan walked out of the office, Kennedy added, in typical fashion, "Today." Dolan then made a visit to Mrs. Lincoln at the White House. "It's terrible," he quoted Mrs. Lincoln as saying. "I didn't know she was like that."

John Kennedy was the president and it seemed clear to Dolan that no one, not even his brother, was eager to tell him that he had to stop seeing a woman who gave him pleasure. The official Justice Department records, made available in 1975 to the Church Committee, show that it was left to Hoover to give the president the bad news. On March 22, Hoover went to lunch at the White House with the president, for only the second time since Inauguration Day.

Both men had hidden agendas. Hoover was going to tell the president about a dangerous sexual relationship, but not tell him that the FBI had known since the summer of 1960 — before Kennedy got to the White House — of his affair with Exner and her ties to Giancana and Rosselli. Jack Kennedy knew from his brother what was on Hoover's mind, and how he was going to respond.

The Kennedy-Hoover lunch became the basis for a good deal of fiction over the next three decades, much of it originating in the Church Committee. "According to White House logs," the Church Committee reported, "the last telephone contact between the White House and the President's friend occurred a few hours after the luncheon." (In fact, Exner told me that she and the president talked repeatedly in the next few months. White House logs uncovered in 1975 by committee investigators showed that as many as ten of the eighty calls from Exner to Kennedy's office took place after March

1962.) The committee accepted at face value Exner's lies about not knowing of the plotting against Castro and not serving as a conduit between Giancana and the president. Therefore, the committee concluded, the president's lunch with Hoover merely provided Hoover with a chance "to fulfill his duty" and tell the president that there was evidence that Giancana "had been involved in a CIA operation that included 'dirty business.'" In the committee's view, Judith Exner had nothing to do with such matters; the president's affair with her was seen as little more than a very indiscreet sexual romp.

The committee's failure to closely quiz Exner on the Kennedy-Hoover lunch and its aftermath was its biggest mistake. The only account of the lunch is Exner's, as told to her by an angry Jack Kennedy. He telephoned Exner after the meeting. "I called him back," Exner told me, "and he said, 'Go to your mother's and call me.'" Exner did and Kennedy warned her that her home phone was not safe from an FBI wiretap. "He said he'd just had this meeting with Hoover and Hoover told Jack," Exner said, "that he knew, first of all, about Jack's relationship with me. And he also knew that I was carrying documents regarding the Castro assassination plot to Sam Giancana and John Rosselli for Jack. And he knew that they worked for the CIA." Hoover certainly knew that Giancana and Rosselli were working for the CIA — and thus for the White House — in their assassination efforts, and he, of course, knew of Exner's relationship with Kennedy. Some Church Committee investigators came to believe in 1975 that Hoover was aware of Exner's role as a conduit. But evidence of this, if any exists, was not available to the committee.

The president was angered, Exner told me, over the fact that "Hoover would have the audacity to come into his office and confront him with this information. He called him an SOB and said, 'He tried to use, you know, this information as leverage.' [Kennedy's] attitude was 'the gall of the man' to try to intimidate *him*. He was absolutely livid." The president, Exner added, "was well aware that Hoover knew every move that he made, and he did not care. That's the reckless side of Jack — that he would allow himself to be in that position. I mean, he never should have been involved with me. They wanted to get rid of Hoover and they couldn't, because of the information that Hoover had on the Kennedys — not just Jack."

Exner was referring, perhaps, to another facet of her relationship with Kennedy, one that she discussed with great reluctance in our interviews: in 1962 she had begun serving as a conduit for payoffs to the president from a group of California businessmen interested in obtaining defense contracts. She became involved, Exner told me, through her close friendship with Richard Ellwood, a neighbor who was vice president of a small electronics company in Culver City. Through Ellwood, who died in 1966, Exner was introduced to two senior Pentagon procurement officials and began socializing with them on her many trips to Washington. The two officials are dead, but the widow of one, who knew little of her husband's business affairs, confirmed in an interview in 1996 for this book that she and her husband had shared a drink with Exner in the Mayflower Hotel during the Kennedy administration. She will never forget the meeting, the widow said, because "we were all over there having a drink and [Exner] told the group that 'If a White House car comes to pick me up, just go on and party.' Sure enough, the car came for her." Everyone understood, the widow said, that Exner was having an affair with the president.

There was also much socializing with the two Pentagon officials when they visited California. At one point, Exner said, she discussed with the president her plan to make "a substantial investment"— more than $10,000, she acknowledged later — in one of Ellwood's research companies. "Jack advised me to invest," Exner said. "Jack said it'd be a good idea."

Eventually, Exner told me, "what was going on was there were payoffs. I took payoffs" from the California businessmen to Kennedy in the White House. "I didn't want to go to Jack" with the payoff money, she told me. "I asked Jack about it and he thought it was a good idea." She recalled three contract proposals for which she took payoffs into the White House. "One envelope was for an unmanned vehicle on land," Exner said. "It was one of the first of its kind — unmanned robotics." She remembered, she said, that the vehicle was "massive. The size of a tank." The second project, she said, involved a new procedure for desalinization, an area that was being heavily researched by the government in the early 1960s. The final contract proposal dealt with avionics for a fighter plane. Asked who initiated the process of sending payoffs to the president, Exner told me, "It came from both sides. I know everybody was working together. I saw when there were transfers of cash. They were all in it." She personally delivered the money, Exner told me, along with envelopes containing technical data, to Kennedy.

Exner said she had never before discussed her role in bringing bribes to the president because she had no receipts for the money or other evidence, and she was convinced no one would believe her account — just as few initially believed her testimony in 1975 about Kennedy's ties through her to Sam Giancana. But she did know, she said, that the FBI was aware of her relationship with Ellwood and knew that she had invested money in one of his businesses. The FBI, she told me, "used to go to Dick [Ellwood] when they were going to everybody, asking questions about me." Ellwood tried to "protect me," he said, by telling the agents that he loaned her the funds she used to invest in his company. Ellwood's apparent concern, Exner said, was that she might not have reported the money she invested to the Internal Revenue Service.

Asked if Kennedy had perhaps been frightened of Hoover's knowledge, Exner told me, "I really don't think so, because Jack didn't alter his behavior one iota." She and Kennedy continued to meet, she said, although the once-passionate affair was fading fast. Over the winter of 1961–62, she wrote in *My Story,* "slowly I began to feel that he expected me to come into bed and just perform. . . . I understood about the position he had to assume in lovemaking when his back was troubling him, but slowly he began excluding all other positions, until finally our lovemaking was reduced to this one position. . . . The feeling that I was there to service him began to really trouble me." One of the problems, she wrote, was the presidency. "The weight of his office was getting heavier on his shoulders, and he was changing. He wasn't as happy-go-lucky, not as relaxed and cheerful. . . . By early 1962, I dreaded going to the White House. I wanted to see Jack, but not in that place."

Jack Kennedy's womanizing had repeatedly put his career at risk, but until now the potential loss had always been his. The affair with

Exner posed a much broader danger: to the well-being of the nation's security. The Kennedy-Exner relationship apparently became known in the late summer of 1962 to the General Dynamics Corporation, one of two defense firms intensely competing for the right to manufacture a new generation of air force and navy combat plane known as the TFX (Tactical Fighter Experimental). General Dynamics may have used that knowledge to win the contract and force the government to spend billions of dollars to build a navy version of TFX that many in the military knew would not work.

J. Edgar Hoover's lunch in March 1962 with Jack Kennedy had not left the FBI director reassured enough to stop the Los Angeles field office from continuing its round-the-clock surveillance of Exner's apartment from a nearby undercover observation post. Hoover's hunch paid off in an unexpected way late on August 7, 1962, when the FBI's William Carter watched as two young men climbed onto a balcony at Exner's apartment on Fontaine Avenue, in west Los Angeles; one man watched as the other slid open a glass door and entered. After fifteen minutes or so — more than enough time to sort through records or install a wiretap — the pair fled. Carter and his FBI colleagues had been patiently watching the apartment since Exner had moved there in early March, before the Hoover meeting with Kennedy, and had not seen any disturbances. "We were absolutely stunned," Carter told me. But his supervisors decided not to report the illegal entry to the Los Angeles Police Department, as would have been routine procedure when FBI agents observed illegal behavior. To be collegial in this instance, Carter was told, "would have jeopardized our operation."

Carter's role in the Exner break-in ended at that point. His supervisors did not tell him that within three days they tracked the break-in team to a getaway car rented by a former FBI special agent named I. B. Hale, of Fort Worth, Texas. The two men who entered Exner's apartment were identified by the FBI as Hale's twin sons, Bobby and Billy, twenty-one years old. I. B. Hale, who died in 1971, was in charge of security for General Dynamics.

At the time of the break-in, the company's chances of winning the immensely lucrative TFX contract were precarious, as the men running General Dynamics were only too aware. To improve the company's odds, nothing could be ruled out in the summer of 1962, including the utilization of a high-priced former FBI agent who might be in a position to accumulate information on the Kennedy administration. The Hale family's criminal entry into Judith Campbell Exner's apartment, which has never been reported before, raises an obvious question: Was Jack Kennedy blackmailed by a desperate corporation?

General Dynamics was in bad shape in 1962. The company had lost more than $400 million in the previous two years, and the $6.5 billion TFX contract was essential for its survival. The prospects were not favorable. Its main competitor, the Boeing aircraft company, of Seattle, was without question the favorite of the military men who ran the air force and navy. "When we got to the endgame," George A. Spangenberg, who was then chief of the navy's technical evaluation division, said in a 1997 interview for this book, "Boeing was always better than General Dynamics." The navy was desperate to deny the contract to General Dynamics, Spangenberg said. "You couldn't get there from here" with the General Dynamics design. "Our game was how do we keep from getting a useless aircraft."

The bidding process was complicated by Defense Secretary McNamara's insistence, for economic reasons, that the new fighter have "commonality"— that is, be capable of simultaneously meeting the needs of both the air force and the navy. The navy bitterly resisted his approach, arguing that its requirement for a fighter light enough to land on an aircraft carrier was incompatible with the air force's need for long-range flight capability. At the time, the Pentagon's unwieldy procurement process called for six levels of review, with the final recommendation — before going to McNamara — being the responsibility of the secretaries of the navy and the air force. The procedure to decide who would build the new jet fighter was repeated four times in 1961 and 1962, with untold thousands of man-hours spent evaluating the competing proposals. Boeing was recommended every time.

Thus, the Pentagon and the military committees in the Congress were flabbergasted in November 1962 when McNamara chose General Dynamics. Contentious Senate hearings the next year about the last-minute change, headed by Senator John McClellan of Arkansas, shed little light on the decision. The issue was seen then and is still seen today as a dispute over McNamara's right to impose his standards on military procurement. President Kennedy's public role was limited to repeatedly endorsing McNamara's decisions, while at the same time distancing himself from them. "My judgment is that the decision reached by Secretary McNamara," Kennedy told a press conference during the McClellan hearings, "was the right one, sound one, and any fair and objective hearing will bring that out. . . . Everything I have read about the TFX and seen about it confirms my impression that Mr. McNamara was right."

But McNamara was not right. And the president, as Senate investigators discovered almost immediately, had been involved in the decision, despite McNamara's denials. The committee's high-powered chief investigator, Jerome S. Alderman, who worked on the Senate Rackets Committee with Bobby Kennedy, learned in an early meeting with Roswell Gilpatric, the deputy secretary of defense, that the president knew in advance that the award would go to General Dynamics. Gilpatric's admission troubled David McGiffert, a McNamara aide who sat in, as a lawyer, on the committee's interview with Gilpatric. Gilpatric, McGiffert knew, had violated the first commandment of dealing with congressional investigators: to protect the president. McGiffert later told the journalist Deborah Shapley, author of *Promise and Power*, a 1993 biography of McNamara, that Gilpatric, known for his loyalty to the White House, undoubtedly thought "dropping the bombshell" of presidential involvement would help Kennedy. McClellan, a fellow Democrat, might look the other way if he knew the president was involved. McGiffert had the feeling, he told Shapley, that Gilpatric's admission "would only make things worse."

The Senate hearings were suspended by Kennedy's death, and never resumed. The TFX, later renamed the F-111, became one of the most criticized defense projects in modern history, and a bellwether for those military men who complained about unnecessary civilian interference. After Kennedy's assassination, McNamara continued to insist that the F-111 go forward, although the costs per plane had tripled by mid-1966. In the end, the navy, which had once planned to buy 1,700 F-111s, took delivery of seven prototype models, none of which saw combat use. By that time, the navy's version of the F-111 was 1,600 pounds overweight, far too heavy to land on an aircraft carrier. The navy canceled its contract with General Dynamics in 1968.

The air force, which had planned to buy 2,400 F-111s, took delivery on fewer than 600. The average cost per plane had climbed from the $2.8 million estimated in 1962 to more than $22 million by 1970.

The uncensored FBI reports and cables on the August break-in at Exner's Los Angeles apartment, made available for this book under the Freedom of Information Act, were urgently forwarded, in code, to J. Edgar Hoover. An FBI summary from the Los Angeles bureau, dated August 17, 1962, told Hoover something he already knew, even if some of his California agents didn't realize it. The summary described Exner as being in contact with Giancana and Rosselli and with Evelyn Lincoln. It also told Hoover something he didn't know: the Hale family and General Dynamics were linked to the break-in. "A man answering the description of the individual who entered [Exner's] apartment was observed leaving the area in an automobile registered to former Special Agent I. B. Hale who resides in Fort Worth, Texas," the summary said. "Our Dallas office has advised that . . . Hale is employed by General Dynamics . . . in charge of security." The summary noted that the crime its agents witnessed "is not being disseminated to the Los Angeles Police Department at this time."

One FBI cable to Hoover, dated August 14 and marked "urgent," summarized I. B. Hale's association with the FBI and depicted him as "cooperative" in the past with Dallas agents. Hale, a prewar football star at Texas Christian University, was described as "well known in Fort Worth and . . . active in many community affairs. It is the opinion of [the FBI bureau in] Dallas [that] any additional inquiry" by the FBI into the Los Angeles break-in "would come to Hale's attention. It is also the opinion of Dallas that Hale would be completely cooperative in any interview. However, in view of the sensitive nature of Los Angeles investigation, no additional action [is] being taken by Dallas." In other words, the FBI bureau in Los Angeles was more interested in keeping up its surveillance on Judith Exner's apartment than in prosecuting a crime or trying to find out what I. B. Hale and his sons were doing there.

William Carter, in his interview for this book, said he and his

FBI colleagues assumed at the time that the entry into Exner's apartment was "to install a bug" or a wiretap. According to available documents, no one in the FBI even considered alerting Exner to the break-in. If a bug was installed, the FBI did nothing to prevent I. B. Hale and his superiors at General Dynamics from eavesdropping on Exner. A warning to Exner also might have prevented the FBI from continuing its own electronic surveillance of her apartment.

The trail ended in Fort Worth three decades ago. During the five years of research for this book, I tried unsuccessfully to find out how General Dynamics learned of Judith Exner's ties to Jack Kennedy. I was unable to make contact with Billy or Bobby Hale despite repeated efforts. Billy, trained as a veterinarian, left his Fort Worth practice and his family in the early 1990s and disappeared into the Central Plains states. The twins' younger brother, Tommy Hale, of Fort Worth, said in a series of telephone interviews that Billy "told us he was going to live his life for Jesus. He gave it up for Jesus."* Bobby Hale, as of mid-1997, was living in isolation with his family on a commune in rural Mora County, New Mexico; he is in constant trouble with authorities there, according to the Moro County sheriff.

I. B. Hale and his wife divorced in 1960, Tommy Hale told me. Tommy stayed with his mother, and his older brothers moved in with their father. His father, Tommy said, was "a good secret keeper" who maintained a respect for J. Edgar Hoover "all through his life. He admired Hoover."

The break-in at Exner's apartment was never investigated by the FBI, nor did it evoke a sudden rush of curiosity that fall, when the Kennedy administration's surprise selection of General Dynamics to build the TFX triggered outcries in the press and the Congress. What happened was not a cover-up, but something much more mundane. I. B. Hale, as a prominent college football star, had been one of Hoover's favorites while he was in the FBI; it would be almost reflexive for his former colleagues to find some reason not to investigate him. Most important, Judith Exner's relationship with the president

---

* I mailed Tommy Hale some of the FBI documentation dealing with the 1962 break-in; he did get a chance, he told me, to show it to his brother Billy when Billy made a brief visit to Fort Worth in mid-1997. Billy looked at the materials, Tommy said, but "wouldn't talk to me about it. He wasn't interested."

and the FBI's surveillance of her were deemed state secrets that had to be kept, even if crimes were ignored in the process.

Judith Exner did not learn about the break-in at her apartment until fifteen years later, when she won a Freedom of Information Act lawsuit and obtained her heavily censored FBI files. The documents, as released and still censored, said nothing about I. B. Hale, nor did they mention General Dynamics. By August 1962 her involvement with Kennedy and his brother had ended. Bobby Kennedy had replaced Exner with Charles Ford as a liaison to organized crime, and for Jack Kennedy there were dozens of women who would replace her in other ways.

By that fall, Exner said in *My Story*, she was deeply involved with Sam Giancana. "Love with Sam was not as exciting as it had been with Jack," she wrote, "but . . . it left me with a comfortable feeling instead of a gnawing emptiness. I felt like I really knew how to handle Sam. Once we became intimate, Sam did not change with me, he didn't revert to some unreasonably possessive creature." In an interview for this book, Exner acknowledged what she had not in her memoir: Sam Giancana had his own reasons for maintaining the relationship with her. "I'm not so naive that I don't think that his friendship with me and continued friendship wasn't very beneficial," she told me. "He could use it to his advantage if need be."

Jack Kennedy, she said, also used "Sam for his own purpose. And Sam would naturally expect something for it. I don't like to think of friendship being used that way." But, Exner added, "Jack didn't play by our rules; Jack had his own rules. I believe that all of the Kennedys play by their own rules. I don't think they conduct themselves the way we do. I think that's very sad."

In the late summer of 1962, Exner said, "I was very troubled, again, about the FBI surveillance and [Kennedy's] treating it lightly. He did say a couple of times that he would talk to Bobby and see what they could do about it. But it never seemed to me that anything was done. We had been having difficulties because I wouldn't move back to Washington. After we more or less broke up, he convinced me to go back and see him one more time."

In recent years, Judith Exner has been waging a furious battle against a pervasive cancer; she was told ten years ago that she had only a few more years to live. In interviews for this book and for a 1996 profile in *Vanity Fair* magazine, she has added another new element to her story — Jack Kennedy made her pregnant on their last visit. It was that pregnancy, she now says, that drove her into the arms of Sam Giancana.

Exner, in her interview for this book, said that she and Kennedy agreed in late summer 1962, after she told him about the pregnancy, that she could not keep the baby. "In our next conversation," Exner said, "he asked, 'Would Sam help us?' I spoke to Sam and he said yes. Sam was angry at Jack, but it took the two of us for me to be in that position." In Sam's eyes, Exner insisted, "he was helping me. You know, a lot of people can say, 'Oh boy, this is just something else he [Giancana] could hold over Jack's head.' I don't care what they say, I know what he did for me." She wasn't angry at Kennedy, she said. "I was heartbroken."

It was at this point, Exner told me, that she became intimate with Sam Giancana. He had responded to news of her pregnancy by asking her to marry him. "I told him, 'Sam, you don't want to marry me.' I knew he was in love with Phyllis [McGuire]. And he just said, 'You deserve to be asked.' It was the one time with Sam and it was an emotional response to his loving-kindness and caring for what I was going through. But I would hardly say that that was having a simultaneous affair with two men."

Exner's most recent account of her faithfulness to Jack Kennedy conflicts with the chronology in *My Story*. She may have indeed been faithful to Jack Kennedy for much of their time together, as she has steadfastly insisted, or she may have been making love to both men at the same time. The issue of when she became intimate with Sam Giancana, however important to Exner today, does not affect the importance of her story.

Exner, in her interviews for this book, told me that despite all, she remains convinced that "Jack loved me, to the extent that he could love someone. A lot of people think that I'm kidding myself, but I knew him. I was the one who was with him. He had a place for everything in his life, and he gave only so much of himself to whatever that was — whether it be love, work, or play." In that regard, she said, "he emulated his father. I think all the boys in the family have emulated their father. He had to have great trust and faith in me," she said, to permit her to serve as a conduit for the mob.

Judith Exner was out of Jack Kennedy's personal life by the fall of 1962, but the FBI was keeping up its pressure on her. There was talk of compelling her to appear before a Los Angeles federal grand jury that was looking into organized crime. Exner's attorney, who had been recommended by Johnny Rosselli, "had me going from hotel to hotel so the FBI couldn't subpoena me. I sensed I was in terrible danger" from organized crime or the U.S. government. In her view, they were moral equivalents: "There is no good and bad," she told me. "No black hats, no white hats. They were all out for themselves."

During this panicky period, Exner ran into Johnny Grant, the former press agent who befriended her as a teenager, while in Palm Springs in March of 1963. Grant was now a reporter for the NBC television and radio affiliates in Los Angeles. The two began talking and, Exner told me, "I did tell him what had been going on. Johnny just happened to be there, luckily for me — not lucky for Johnny, because I think I scared him to death — but it was good to have a friend to confide in."

Grant, when interviewed for this book, clearly recalled the meeting. "I hardly recognized her," he told me. "Her happy eyes were dull — like she'd been abused. I knew something was very wrong." They agreed to meet again that evening. Over a drink, Grant recalled, "she told me that she'd been seeing Jack Kennedy and Sam Giancana. I called the waiter over and got the check." He assumed, he said, that she was sleeping with both men.

They drove out into the desert, and parked. Exner told him of carrying a satchel of money from Jack Kennedy to Sam Giancana in Chicago. She told of carrying messages between organized crime and the White House. She told of her love for Jack Kennedy. She told of taking documents after the election that dealt with Castro's elimination. "I asked her," Grant said, " 'What do you mean, assassination or elimination?' And she said, 'Jack's word was elimination.' By then I was ready to leave. 'My God, here you are,' " he told her, " 'talking about the great symbol of justice and freedom — the office of the president of the United States. On the other hand, you're talking about the most negative thing in America at the time — the underworld. And they are communicating, and passing money.'"

"I did not ever think she was bullshitting me," Grant said. "I just thought to myself, 'You son of a bitch. You fell into something you didn't want to know.' I was overwhelmed and frightened — in terror. In those times, if they didn't want somebody around, they could disappear you quick." His last words to Exner, Grant recalled, were, "Please don't tell anybody you talked to me."

He never thought of writing the story. Instead, he told me, he returned to his home in Los Angeles and told his business manager, "'If anything ever happens to me, it'll be the Mafia or the CIA.' I didn't talk to a lawyer. I got drunk." For years afterward, he said, "if an acorn fell on the roof, I got up fast."

Judith Exner would have understood his fear. She is, she says, still sleeping with a gun under her pillow.

19

FIRST MARRIAGE

President Kennedy's involvement with Judith Exner and Sam Giancana was the most dangerous issue that he and Bobby had to deal with in mid-1962, but that potential scandal wasn't the one that got their attention. The biggest family worry that summer had nothing to do with organized crime or getting rid of troublesome leaders, but was just as politically deadly: the revival of long-standing rumors that Jack Kennedy had been secretly married to a Palm Beach socialite named Durie Malcolm before his high-society wedding to Jacqueline Bouvier in 1953.

Charles Spalding, a retired New York stockbroker who had been a Kennedy intimate since World War II, was the first to acknowledge for this book that he and other insiders had known for many years that the rumors were true: Kennedy and Malcolm were married, albeit very briefly, in early 1947. Spalding knew Durie Malcolm from her childhood days at the Winter Club in Lake Forest, Illinois, a wealthy suburb north of Chicago. She was a sensational athlete, Spalding said: "She'd play ice hockey in the winter and basketball with the guys." Malcolm was special in other ways, he added; she was as adventurous in romance as in sports. "She got into men in a big way," Spalding told me. "She had plenty of men hanging around." By the winter of 1946–47, when Kennedy first became infatuated with her, Malcolm had been twice married and was in the process of getting her second divorce. (The final decree for her second divorce was filed on January 24, 1947.)

Spalding loyally sought to describe Kennedy's marriage as little more than a lark —"a high school prank, a bit of daring that went too far." Getting married with no advance notice, he told me, "was the kind of joke that Durie would go for"— a spur-of-the-moment event that lasted "just twenty-four hours. They went down and went through the motions. It was like Halloween. I remember saying to Jack," Spalding told me, "'You must be nuts. You're running for president and you're running around getting married.'"

But there is evidence that the relationship was more serious. The *New York World-Telegram*'s society writer, Charles Ventura, in his column, "Society Today," reported on January 20, 1947, that young John F. Kennedy was on the verge of being given Palm Beach's "annual Oscar for achievement in the field of romance." Kennedy, pictured in the column, was cited for giving Malcolm "the season's outstanding rush. . . . Only the fact that duty called him to Washington as a Congressman from Massachusetts kept Jack from staying around to receive his Oscar in person, so it may be awarded to Durie. The two were inseparable at all social functions and sports events. They even drove down to Miami to hold hands at football games and wager on the horses." Durie was described by Ventura as beautiful and funny.

Even in early 1947, Spalding said, it was clear that Jack was being groomed and financed for the White House by his father. Joe Kennedy had "a hemorrhage" when he learned about the marriage, Spalding told me. Malcolm, besides being twice divorced, was Episcopalian. "He demanded that it be taken care of," Spalding recalled. "They [the family] were afraid the whole thing was going to come out.

"I went out there and removed the [marriage] papers," Spalding told me, presumably from the Palm Beach County courthouse. "It was Jack who asked me if I'd go get the papers." Spalding said he "got" the marriage documents with the help of a lawyer in Palm Beach.

Florida law requires no blood test before a couple can apply for a marriage license. Prior to 1983, however, couples making application had to wait three days for a license to be issued. If Jack Kennedy and Durie Malcolm followed the law, their wedding was planned at least three days in advance and thus was more than a spur-of-the-moment "prank," as Charles Spalding claimed.

Palm Beach County officials, queried for this book, were unable to find documentary evidence of a Kennedy-Malcolm wedding in 1947. But one city attorney explained in an interview that the county's marriage records were recorded by hand in those days, and were not filed in alphabetical order. It was "impossible to determine if something was missing," the attorney told me, after she personally researched the county records. "The whole point of expunging," the attorney said, "is to leave no record at all." It is possible the couple applied for a marriage license but changed their minds. It is also possible that Kennedy, who married in 1953, and Malcolm, who married twice more, were bigamists. No evidence of a divorce was found during research for this book.

It was the issue of bigamy that prompted the wife of one of Jack Kennedy's friends from the high-society days in Palm Beach to urge that this book say nothing about the Kennedy-Malcolm marriage, which she was convinced had taken place. "You sit down and think hard about it," the woman said to me in a 1997 telephone interview granted only after I promised her anonymity. "Jack was never married legally to Jackie, and all that's left of Jack are his two children and his grandchildren." Telling about the marriage "makes them [Caroline and John Jr.] not legal. That's a very disruptive thing to do. Those children had a hard enough time as it is — they lost their father."

In recent years, gossip and allegations about Kennedy's suspected first marriage have been fodder for tabloid newspapers and television entertainment news shows in the United States and England. A typical article in London's *Daily Mail* on January 24, 1997, included an enlarged photograph of a young Durie Malcolm, wearing a wedding dress, with a caption asking, "Was she JFK's secret first bride?" Malcolm, now over eighty years of age and a widow — her fourth husband, Frank Appleton, died in 1996 — has consistently denied the story. "I wouldn't have married Jack Kennedy for all the tea in China," she told London's *Sunday Times* in 1996. "I'll tell you why, if you want to know the truth. I didn't care for those Irish micks, and old Joe was a terrible man." Malcolm has issued similar denials since the story first became public, in 1961. Her only child, a daughter also named Durie Malcolm, who lives in London, has never spoken publicly about her mother.

Durie Malcolm, contacted in the fall of 1997 by a close friend on behalf of the author, was categorical in refusing to be interviewed. "Tell him one thing," she told her friend. "I've never been married to John Kennedy and there's nothing to discuss. Just call him up and say we were never married."

An extensive search for family members and friends who might be willing to talk proved disappointing: Malcolm outlived many members of her immediate family, and none of her old friends from the 1940s, as reported in the Palm Beach society pages from that era, could be located.

Charles Spalding was seventy-nine years old when interviewed, and suffering from impairment of his short-term memory. However, his account of Jack Kennedy's early marriage was directly supported in subsequent interviews with me and indirectly confirmed by the late Richard Cardinal Cushing, the archbishop of Boston, who functioned as a parish priest to the Kennedy family. Cushing, committed to social action, in 1958 founded the St. James Society, a Boston-based group of young priests dedicated to missionary work among the poor in Latin America. In 1964, during a visit to Bolivia, the cardinal stayed up late one night, sharing a bottle of scotch with a dozen or so missionaries, including Father James J. O'Rourke. The young priests were eager "for a taste of things back home," O'Rourke told me in a 1997 interview for this book. "What's going on in the diocese. What's here, what's there. Somebody said, 'Your Eminence, if Jack Kennedy had run for reelection, would he have been reelected?' I think most of us just figured the question would give an automatic, 'Sure.' But he didn't. He said, 'Well, you've got to remember the Republicans would have put up [Nelson] Rockefeller, and Rockefeller's very popular, . . . the only guy with the image who could go against Kennedy. The Democrats would have tried to make political hay out of Rockefeller's divorce. And divorce was a strong issue. But then again,' [the cardinal] said, 'the Republicans would have used Jack Kennedy's first marriage. They would have brought that up.'

"I don't think one of us in that room had ever heard a whisper of that," O'Rourke told me. "We kind of hung in space. And he said, 'Well, they won't find anything [or] any mention of it. The pages are torn out of the register.' And he chuckled and that was it," O'Rourke said. Cushing noticed the stunned reaction of the young missionaries, O'Rourke recalled, and added, "Yeah, Kennedy was married before, but it got taken care of."

Father O'Rourke, who was pastor of a parish church in Brighton, Massachusetts, in Boston, when interviewed, also explained that if Kennedy's marriage to Malcolm did not take place in a Catholic church, as it apparently did not, he would not need a formal annulment from the authorities in Rome. Instead, Kennedy would need only a Declaration of Nullity from a local church marriage court before being free to marry again in a church ceremony. "An annulment only comes into play when a Catholic is involved and the marriage has taken place in the Catholic church," O'Rourke told me. "It's less complicated" to get a nullity declaration, he said. "One still has to go through the local marriage court. You present them with evidence and they have to say, 'Yes, we concur that so and so is free to get married.' But that wouldn't take a great deal of time. If the Kennedys wanted something done," O'Rourke added, "I assume they would have called" Archbishop Cushing. "I doubt if they'd have bothered with the middleman"— a parish priest — "when they could talk to the boss."

In a separate interview, Spalding's former wife, Betty, also supported her former husband's recollections. Eunice Kennedy, Jack's younger sister, told the then–Mrs. Spalding that "there was a drunken party and they [Jack and Durie Malcolm] went off to a justice of the peace to get married" at two o'clock in the morning. Eunice Kennedy's account laid the blame on Malcolm. Betty Spalding quoted Eunice as claiming that Malcolm "wouldn't sleep" with her brother "unless he married her." Afteward, Betty Spalding recalled hearing, "the Old Man had a shitfit and got it nullified." The presumed marriage took place in the years after World War II, Betty Spalding said, when she and her then-husband were living with his parents at their home in Palm Beach. Betty Spalding remembered Durie Malcolm as "tiny, blond, and very pretty."

Joe Kennedy got his way with his son, as he always did, and on July 11, 1947, Durie Malcolm married another wealthy Palm Beach socialite named Thomas Shevlin. It was her third (acknowledged) marriage, and his second, but it lasted until Shevlin's death, in 1973. Durie's secret marriage to Kennedy was widely known inside the Shevlin family, according to Frances Howe of Greenville, South Carolina, who was married for thirteen years to Deering Howe, Jr., Thomas Shevlin's nephew. (Deering Howe's mother was Shevlin's only sibling.) "I knew all the players in Palm Beach well," Frances Howe said in a 1997 interview for this book. Information about Durie Malcolm's brief marriage to Jack Kennedy "was all over the family."

Shortly after marrying Deering Howe, Frances told me, she ran into Durie Malcolm at a party. "She tapped her finger on my cheek and said, 'You poor child. Shouldn't have married into the family.'" Frances said she immediately took a liking to Durie and, after getting "up to speed" on the Shevlin family history, asked Durie at a polo match "whether it"— the marriage to Jack Kennedy —"was true. She said 'Yes.'" It was her understanding, Frances Howe added, that "Joe went ballistic and got everything eradicated — all the records wiped out." Shevlin family history had it, Frances Howe told me, that "Jack really loved [Malcolm] and wanted to be with her." But "young Joe [Kennedy] had died and Jack would be running for president."

Kennedy's marriage was known to at least a few of the phalanx of friends who could be found on any summer weekend at the Kennedy compound at Hyannis Port. Morton Downey, Jr., whose father was close to Joseph Kennedy, recalled hearing as a teenager all about Jack Kennedy's stupidity in getting married and Joe Kennedy's anger at his son. "Dad told me, 'I hope you have enough sense not to do this'— run off and get married," Downey said in a 1997 interview for this book. Morton Downey was a popular radio and television singer in the 1950s.

Kennedy's first marriage remained a family secret until 1957, when Louis L. Blauvelt, an amateur genealogist, privately printed three hundred leather-bound copies of a Blauvelt family tree. Blauvelt, a retired toolmaker who lived in East Orange, New Jersey, spent thirty years compiling entries for each generation of the family, beginning with Gerri Hendricksen Blauvelt, who came to America in 1638. Entry number 12,427, the eleventh generation, listed Durie Malcolm (her name was misspelled) and said that her third marriage was to "John F. Kennedy, son of Joseph P. Kennedy, one time Ambassador to England." Blauvelt was careless in his handling of the Durie Malcolm entry; he did not cite her later marriage to Shevlin, and he also reversed the names of her first two husbands. The Blauvelt book attracted no attention until mid-1961, when its entry on Jack Kennedy began being circulated by his political opponents. The word soon passed to newspapermen.

In his memoir *Conversations with Kennedy,* Benjamin Bradlee, who, like the journalist Charles Bartlett, was a social friend of the Kennedys, recalled first hearing of Kennedy's "other wife" in August 1961, as the crisis over the Berlin Wall was unfolding. "Some D.A.R. type had walked into the city room of the [*Washington*] *Post,* announcing that she had documentary proof of an earlier Kennedy marriage," Bradlee wrote. "She had offered the story to the *Chicago Tribune,* which had refused to print it." The woman told the *Post* about the Blauvelt genealogy, which was on the shelves at the Library of Congress. Bradlee, then covering the White House for *Newsweek* magazine, immediately telephoned the library, he said, "only to be told pointedly that the book was out, and that the waiting list included ten members of Congress."

Kennedy turned once again to Clark Clifford, the Washington lawyer who had helped him weather other crises. In his memoir, *Counsel to the President,* Clifford recounted how "Kennedy and his staff had tried to deal with the matter by ignoring it; but when the rumor continued to circulate and then surfaced in a few minor periodicals, the President called me. 'All I know is that some years ago, I knew very briefly a young woman named Durie Malcolm. I think I had two dates with her. One may have been a dinner date in which we went dancing. The other, to my recollection, was a football game.'" Clifford telephoned Malcolm, whom he had met when she was married to her second husband, Firmin V. Desloge of St. Louis; she told a very similar story in denying the marriage. "My recollection," Clifford quoted Malcolm as saying, "is that we had two dates. We may have had dinner in New York and the other time we went to a football game." She agreed to sign an affidavit stating that she had not been married to John F. Kennedy, according to Clifford's memoir. She took her telephone off the hook.

Ben Bradlee reentered the scene at that point. He met with the president and was told by Kennedy and Pierre Salinger, the White House press secretary, that Durie Malcolm had "executed an affidavit, swearing she had never been married to John F. Kennedy." Malcolm's sworn affidavit, if it existed, has never been made public. "Kennedy later confirmed to me," Bradlee wrote in his memoir, "that he had dated her once, but that she had been a girlfriend of his brother, Joe." Bradlee was unable to reach Durie Malcolm by telephone; he also discovered the discrepancies in the Blauvelt genealogy. Louis Blauvelt had died, at age seventy-nine, in 1959, and there was nothing in his files, Bradlee was told, proving that the Kennedy-Malcolm marriage took place. All of this was reported to the president, who, Bradlee wrote, breezily told him, "You haven't got it, Benjy. You're all looking to tag me with some girl, and none of you can do it, because it just isn't there." The first lady listened to her husband "with a smile on her face," Bradlee wrote.

Neither Bradlee nor any other White House reporter wrote a story on the marriage that summer. But Kennedy remained unnerved, and told differing stories about the number of times he went on dates with Malcolm. A few journalists were still snooping around, including a young reporter in the Washington bureau of Cowles Publications, owners of *Look* magazine, who flew to St. Louis to ask questions of the Desloge family. Kennedy, giving an interview that summer to Laura Bergquist, a *Look* reporter who enjoyed special access to the president and his children, suddenly brought up the magazine's continuing investigation. "I heard that somebody from *Look* magazine . . . has been doing some snooping around about my secret marriage," he said to Bergquist, according to her 1977 oral history for the Kennedy Library. Bergquist put it directly to the president: "Were you ever secretly married?" Kennedy said, "No. I knew her and I took her to a football game, and that was about it." The president seemed "edgy," Bergquist told the library, and said that his brother Bobby had told him that someone on the magazine "was digging on this story" in St. Louis. Kennedy then warned: "You print that story and I'll wind up owning *Look* magazine." Bergquist tried to make light of this remark, saying, "That sounds to me like a threat." Describing the exchange to the library, Bergquist recalled Kennedy's intensity. "He was kidding, but he wasn't kidding," she said. Bergquist's interview was made available by the library in the fall of 1997.

Gossip about Kennedy's marriage, though not published in any major newspaper, would not go away. That fall, J. Edgar Hoover received three reports from FBI bureaus within a few weeks reporting that they had received letters describing "rumors" of an early Kennedy marriage; the letters all cited the Blauvelt genealogy. On November 22, 1961, Hoover raised the issue with Bobby Kennedy, who acknowledged, according to Hoover's declassified FBI memorandum, made public under the Freedom of Information Act, that "a number of newspapermen have spoken to him about it." The attorney general, Hoover noted, said that "he hopes" the reporters would print stories about the Blauvelt allegations, "because then 'we'"— the Kennedy family —"could all retire for life on what 'we' collect" in libel awards.

The tough talk did not hide the fact that Jack Kennedy was a newspaper story away from political embarrassment — if Durie Malcolm or one of his close friends, such as Charles Spalding, began to talk. His reelection in 1964 would be impossible if the American public, and the voting Catholics, believed that he had been secretly married outside the church and had lied about it.

His fear of the truth must have explained the president's sensitivity to seemingly innocuous newspaper gossip about his personal life. *Time* magazine's Hugh Sidey recalled his surprise when Kennedy "got furious" after *Time* published a brief account in late 1961 of the president's doing the twist on a patio during a society party in Palm Beach. "These little personal items began to eat away at him," Sidey told me in an interview. "They bothered him more than [published] discussions of the Bay of Pigs or what he was going to do in Berlin." On another occasion, in February 1962, Kennedy tore into Sidey after *Time* published a gossipy item stating — incorrectly — that the president had modeled a "trimly tailored dark gray suit" for a cover photo of *Gentlemen's Quarterly* magazine. Sidey, who knew nothing about the item, never had a chance to defend himself. "He picked up *Time* magazine," Sidey told me, "threw it on the desk, came around, shook his fist in my face and said, 'You SOBs are out to get me. You do this stuff — this personal stuff — as much as you can. You're out to discredit me. Why do you do this to me?' On and on.

"I took the heat," Sidey told me, "but I never did anything about it. I mean, it just disappeared. Kennedy passed on to other issues. He just had to blow his stack at that moment. There obviously was something else bugging him, but it came out in that bizarre way."

A few months later the Kennedy brothers were upset when they were leaked a copy of an internal *Time* memorandum in which Sidey described, in unsparing terms, a wild New Year's Eve party at the end of 1961 in Palm Beach. Sidey was in town, traveling with the White House press corps, and needed an official answer that evening to a foreign policy question. He sought out Pierre Salinger and his deputy, Andrew Hatcher. "Salinger was off someplace with a girl who was not related in any way by law or by blood to him," Sidey told me. "Hatcher had gone to Jamaica with a bunch of models. I went around. There was nobody. Everybody [was] partying. I have to say that I did sense it was excessive and probably not the way to run a presidency. He was the leader of the free world and this was the height of the Cold War." Sidey wrote nothing for publication, but did forward a note to his editors in New York for a weekly interoffice newsletter known as *The Washington Memo;* his note included lines, he told me, like "Not since the fall of Rome, et cetera." At another point in his note, Sidey quoted a caustic remark about the president's mother that was being passed around the bar before the New Year's Eve party by the White House press corps: Who was going to be Rose Kennedy's gigolo that night? Sidey thought the *Memo* was circulated only to employees of *Time,* but he learned later that the document, with its insider's gossip, was routinely provided to the magazine's advertisers.

Sometime in April, Sidey said, he was summoned to the Justice Department to meet with an angry Bobby Kennedy. "He had that memo I had written" over the New Year's holidays, Sidey said. "I made the mistake of making a little joke. It wasn't funny. He said, 'If this were Britain or someplace, we'd sue you for slander. This is the worst thing I've ever read, Sidey. I thought you were fair up till now.' I said, 'Bobby, I'm just reporting the feeling down there — what reporters are telling me.' It turned out that he was more upset about his mother than anything." The attorney general was more than a little distressed, Sidey told me: "He was shaking like a leaf." Sidey eventually apologized in a letter to Bobby Kennedy for bringing in Rose Kennedy's name. Sidey told me he later heard from John Seigenthaler, one of Bobby Kennedy's close aides, that "he'd never seen [Kennedy] so furious over anything, and he never thought he'd forgive me for it. And maybe he didn't."*

In May 1962 *The Thunderbolt,* a racist Alabama newsletter that called itself "The White Man's Viewpoint," published an account of the Kennedy-Malcolm marriage, based on Blauvelt's genealogy. Another racist publication, *The Winrod Letter,* printed in Arkansas, picked up the story a month later. In September the rumor reached the mainstream press. *Parade* magazine, a Sunday newspaper supplement with a huge audience, recycled the Blauvelt story in its widely read letters column, "Walter Scott's Personality Parade," written by Lloyd Shearer. The Shearer account cited Blauvelt's errors and stated that Kennedy and Malcolm were never married. But it also put the rumor into wide circulation.

The president turned to Ben Bradlee, who was in JFK's doghouse. Bradlee had made the mistake of being quoted in a *Look* magazine

---

* The minicrisis did not prevent the Kennedy brothers from going all out to get Marilyn Monroe to appear at a May 1962 Madison Square Garden rally in honor of the president's forty-fifth birthday. Monroe was then shooting *Something's Got to Give* for 20th Century–Fox; the film was over budget and far behind schedule, essentially because she repeatedly showed up late and unprepared. Milton Gould, by 1962 a highly regarded New York attorney, was asked that year to serve on the board of 20th Century–Fox and, he recalled in a 1995 interview for this book, "clean up the company." Gould decided the president would not get his way: he ordered Monroe to continue working on the film in Hollywood. Bobby Kennedy telephoned and asked Gould to waive his objections. "I said, 'Look, General, in no way can we do this. The lady has caused all kinds of trouble. We're way behind budget. I just can't.' 'Come on,' Bobby said." Gould continued to say no. At some point, Gould recounted, Kennedy "got very abusive. I said, 'Forget it, we're just not going to do it.' He called me 'a Jew bastard' and hung up the phone on me." Bobby Kennedy "never apologized" for his outburst, Gould said. Monroe defied Gould and flew to New York; her breathless rendition of "Happy Birthday" to her lover became one of the most widely remembered events of the Kennedy presidency. Hugh Sidey was assigned to the White House press pool that night and had a close-up look. "It was quite a sight to behold, and if I ever saw an appreciation of feminine beauty in the eyes of a man," Sidey told me, "it was in John F. Kennedy's eyes at that moment."

article, published in August, suggesting that Kennedy's relationship with the press was beginning to erode. It was "almost impossible to write a story they [Jack and Bobby] like," Bradlee told *Look*. "Even if a story is quite favorable to their side, they'll find one paragraph to quibble with." In a 1996 interview for this book, Bradlee said he was "dumb" to have spoken to the magazine — and to have told the truth. The president was in a snit. "God," Bradlee quoted him as exclaiming, "You guys! You get more out of this White House than anybody did and this is how you express your thanks." After that, Bradlee told me, "I didn't see him for two or three months. Didn't answer a phone call."

The impasse ended in September 1962 when Bradlee agreed, as Kennedy surely knew he would, to collaborate with the White House to debunk the Durie Malcolm marriage story once and for all. In *Conversations with Kennedy,* Bradlee depicted the renewed determination to prove the story false as his idea: "I felt *Newsweek* could be first with the story if we backed into it by writing about the hate sheets themselves. . . . I approached Salinger with the idea, but told him I would need some solid FBI documentation about the character of the organization and the people involved in spreading the Blauvelt story." Clark Clifford, in his memoir, had a contradictory account: "In order to 'control' the story, he invited his closest friend in the press corps, Benjamin Bradlee, . . . to print the story in the form of a false rumor revealed, denied, and hopefully buried. At the President's request, I recounted to Ben my involvement in the story."*

---

* Bradlee, who went on to fame as the *Washington Post* editor in charge of the paper's brilliant Watergate coverage in 1972, always seemed unclear about the crossover point between journalist, friend, and campaign adviser when it came to Jack Kennedy. In May 1959 Bradlee covered an early campaign speech by Lyndon Johnson in Harrisburg, Pennsylvania, and later wrote a personal letter to Kennedy about it. The letter is on file at the Kennedy Library. "My own response to Johnson is that . . . he could never make it," Bradlee wrote. "The image is poor. The accent hurts. Even if we assume many people would say they have no prejudice against a southerner, the fact is that in this country the Texan is partly a comic, partly a horse opera figure. . . . Johnson really does not have the requisite dignity. His personal mannerisms are destructive of the dignified image. He's somebody's gabby cousin from Fort Worth. . . . None of it adds up to President. . . . Having seen him, I'm more convinced than ever that he's engaged in a hopeless effort from the viewpoint of advancing himself. That, for you, is not the real danger. . . . What is to be feared is that he will come to Los Angeles with a block

Bradlee, in his memoir, said that Pierre Salinger telephoned a few days later with "the following proposition: If I agreed to show the president the finished story, and if I got my tail up to Newport where he was vacationing, he would deliver a package of the relevant FBI documents to a Newport motel and let me have them. . . . I was not to indicate in any way that I had been given access to FBI files." After checking with the magazine's senior editors, Bradlee said, "we decided to go ahead, despite a reluctance to give anyone, even the president of the United States, the right of approval of anything we wrote."

There was another reason, as Bradlee also wrote: "I wanted to be friends again. I missed the access, of course, but I missed the laughter and the warmth just as much." In his interview with me, Bradlee described the FBI file as disappointing. "There were a couple of classified documents, not that many, but a couple," he said. "Mostly they were [newspaper] clips." He and a colleague "went up to some motel in Newport and we were given the documents at five o'clock and we gave them back at nine o'clock the next morning. I hadn't seen the president for a long time. And I walked in to show him the story at Newport and he said, 'Oh, hello.' Like that. He looked at the story and just gave it back to me."

Bradlee's story, published September 24, 1962, in *Newsweek*, debunked the rumors as well as the hate groups and gossip columnists who were continuing to spread them. There was praise for the newspapers and magazines that had refused to publish anything. "Scores of reporters, working independently before the story was ever publicly printed, have found no evidence to support Blauvelt's statement" as published in his genealogy, Bradlee wrote. "But irresponsi-

of 300 or more delegates and hold them off the market for three or four ballots. . . . If at the outset you are in a commanding position, this tactic will avail him nothing. . . . He's to be feared not as a potential winner but as a game-player who might try to maneuver you right out of the contest in Los Angeles." At the time, Jack Kennedy had not yet announced his candidacy for the White House. Bradlee himself recognized his ethical dilemma. "At issue, then and later," Bradlee added honestly in the opening chapter of his memoir, "was the question that plagued us both: What, in fact, was I? A friend, or a journalist? I wanted to be both. And whereas I think Kennedy valued my friendship — I made him laugh, I brought him the fruits of contact with an outside world from which he was now shut out — he valued my journalism most when it carried his water."

ble groups keep printing it to this day, thus putting the President into a position where he is damned if he denies the story and damned if he doesn't."

The Bradlee account quoted one of Blauvelt's relatives, not by name, as saying that the Malcolm entry was "just one colossal mistake. It was likely that the old man formed the idea in his head" after seeing a gossip column about the Kennedy-Malcolm friendship. "The family hadn't seen anyone famous for a long time." In a 1996 interview for this book, Sue Waite, Louis Blauvelt's granddaughter, took issue with the notion that Blauvelt, who died before Kennedy's election, was a sloppy researcher. "He was a history buff, and a member of the Genealogical Society of New York and the New York Historical Society," she said. He also was a veteran of the Spanish-American War who had a great respect for the presidency and "never would have wanted this to happen." The family had been contacted in 1961 by Pierre Salinger, she said, who asked them to review her grandfather's files. The fact that they found no evidence of the marriage in his files, as Salinger was told, did not mean that the family considered Louis Blauvelt to be wrong. Her own personal view, Waite said, was that Louis Blauvelt was probably right. But his evidence, whatever it was, no longer exists.

Bradlee's *Newsweek* story was reprinted in full by the *Washington Post* and cited in newspapers around the world. *Time,* in its account, added a categorical denial, her first, from the elusive Durie Malcolm; she was found vacationing with her husband, Thomas Shevlin, in Italy. "It's absolutely false and ridiculous," Mrs. Shevlin was quoted as saying. "I know the President's family well and have known him for a long time, and saw him years ago at Palm Beach and once went with him and his family to an Orange Bowl game in Miami. I've rarely seen him since."

The Bradlee story did its job, Clark Clifford noted in his memoir: "As the Kennedys had hoped, . . . once the falsehood had been exposed to public light, it was reduced to a curious footnote to the Kennedy legend. I remain to this day convinced that the entire affair was nothing more than the result of an error made by an old man who was not careful in checking his facts."

Ben Bradlee found himself in good standing once again at the White House. His ostracism had been painful. "From regular contact," he wrote in *Conversations with Kennedy*, "— dinner at the White House once and sometimes twice a week, and telephone calls as needed in either direction — to no contact." "Maybe the exile is ending," he noted in an entry dated November 6, 1962. "Jackie invited Tony [Bradlee's wife] over to the White House to play tennis today, and then invited the children over for movies and supper. Just before leaving, the whole clan . . . trooped down to the president's office, shouting, screaming, and licking lollipops." Three days later the Bradlees were invited to a dance and the president had a long discussion with Tony, Bradlee wrote, "about the difficulties of being friends with someone who is always putting everything he knows into a magazine. Everybody loves everybody again."

Jack and Jacqueline Kennedy had become close friends in the 1950s with a Georgetown neighbor, John Sherman Cooper, the distinguished Republican senator from Kentucky; the Kennedys enjoyed going to dinner and movies with Cooper and his second wife, Lorraine. The relationship continued into the White House, and Cooper, though a Republican, remained a trusted confidant. Lorraine Cooper, as few in Washington knew, was Thomas Shevlin's first wife. One evening, years after the assassination of Jack Kennedy, Maxine Cheshire, than a society reporter for the *Washington Post*, was at dinner at the Coopers'. "We were eating soft-shell crabs in her dining room in Georgetown," Cheshire said in a 1995 interview for this book, "and Lorraine told how Jack would laugh [at a dinner party] and say, 'Lorraine and I are related by marriage.' And then the two of them would die laughing, and nobody else knew what they were talking about."

20

MISSILE CRISIS

John F. Kennedy's greatest triumph as president came in the missile crisis of October 1962, when, as the world watched in fear, the United States and the Soviet Union moved to the edge of nuclear war. Nikita Khrushchev had been caught in the act of arming Fidel Castro with Soviet nuclear missiles and, confronted by the steely young American president, backed down and agreed to take them out. "We're eyeball to eyeball," Secretary of State Dean Rusk said at a meeting to deal with the crisis, "and I think the other fellow just blinked." The quotation, cited all over the world, seemed to summarize the American victory. Jack Kennedy, in discussing Khrushchev with his friends, had his own summary: "I cut his balls off."

At the height of the crisis, Kennedy mobilized a vast army of men and matériel that stood poised to attack Cuba and perhaps trigger a nuclear holocaust. The invasion plan called for the largest drop of paratroopers since the battle for Normandy in 1944; the Pentagon estimated that 18,500 Americans would be killed or wounded in the first ten days of battle. The Strategic Air Command's fleet of 1,436 B-52 and B-47 bombers and 172 intercontinental ballistic missiles was moved to DEFCON 2, the highest military alert short of all-out war. One-eighth of the bombers were in the air at all times during the next thirty days, prepared to drop devastating nuclear weapons on targets in Cuba and the Soviet Union. The 579 fighters of the air force's Tactical Air Command were programmed to fly 1,190 combat sorties in the invasion's first twenty-four hours; aviation fuel and other essential supplies were positioned throughout southern Florida and on a British base in the Bahamas. More than 100,000 combat-ready army infantrymen had deployed to ports along the East Coast, a few hours from Cuba. A huge navy fleet, backed up by 40,000 marines, was steaming, moments away from battle stations, through international waters in the Caribbean and the South Atlantic. The American war machine was at its "highest state of readiness," according to military documents made public years later, and awaited only a go signal from the White House. The president's determination, and his show of force, seemingly won the day.

Kennedy earned plaudits and admiration not only for his clear triumph but for his cool style and confident demeanor between the discovery of medium-range missiles on Cuba on October 15 and Khrushchev's public capitulation on October 28. "It was this combination of toughness and restraint," Arthur Schlesinger wrote in *A Thousand Days,* "of will, nerve and wisdom, so brilliantly controlled, so matchlessly calibrated, that dazzled the world. . . . The thirteen days gave the world — even the Soviet Union — a sense of American determination and responsibility in the use of power which, if sustained, might indeed become a turning point in the history of the relations between east and west."

Over the next thirty-five years a vast assortment of evidence — including published memoirs, interviews, and documents released from Soviet archives — has revealed that much of what the Kennedy administration said about the crisis at the time, publicly and privately, was not true. The overriding deceit — one that still distorts the history of those thirteen days — was the absolute determination of Jack and Bobby Kennedy to conceal their campaign to assassinate Fidel Castro and destroy his regime. The American public was not told what the KGB and Nikita Khrushchev knew. Even more disturbing, many of the American government officials on the ad hoc crisis committee, known as Ex Comm, who served the president as councillors of war, had no knowledge — no "need to know"— of Edward Lansdale's Operation Mongoose and Bill Harvey's Task Force W. Kennedy did not dare tell the full story of the Soviet missiles in Cuba, because it was his policies that brought the weapons there.

Historians and journalists have debated for years whether Khrushchev, in sneaking his missiles into Cuba, was primarily concerned with protecting Cuba, as he claimed, or simply attempting to alter the strategic balance of power, as Kennedy claimed. But Khrushchev's ultimate motive aside, the Kennedy brothers surely understood that the administration's policy of relentless pressure against Castro had given the Soviet premier the opening and the political rationale for his gamble in Cuba. With his missile deployment, Khrushchev was asserting his country's status as a superpower. The Soviet Union had submarines that were capable of launching nuclear missiles on New York, Washington, and other major American cities; it was the threat from a missile that was of interest to American policymakers, not whether it was fired at sea or from an island ninety miles offshore. Few in Washington seriously believed that a few dozen ballistic missiles in Cuba could change the essential fact of the strategic balance of power: the Soviet Union was hopelessly outgunned. By the fall of 1962, America's arsenal contained 3,000 nuclear warheads and nearly 300 missile launchers — far more than the Soviet Union's 250 warheads (including those in Cuba) and estimated 24 to 44 missile launchers.

The attention given the administration's highly publicized state of readiness masked another important fact: the Soviet Union made no military moves at all on its home territory during the crisis. Its fleet of liquid-fueled ICBM launchers, which required hours to be ready for a launch, was not put on alert. Soviet reserve forces were not called up. There were no threats against Berlin.

Yet there was a crisis, and it was provoked by Khrushchev, at least publicly. In putting missiles into Cuba, the Soviet premier was even more daring than the record showed. He used Georgi Bolshakov and other back-channel messengers in the summer and fall of 1962 to repeatedly assure Kennedy, who was continually receiving intelligence reports of a Soviet buildup on Cuban soil, that missiles were not being shipped to Cuba.

Jack Kennedy, confronted with political and personal difficulties that fall, chose to believe Khrushchev's assurances over his own intelligence services. His administration had accomplished little in Congress in its first two years, and he wanted to get more Democrats elected in the midterm congressional elections, scheduled for November 6. More Democrats would mean a better legislative record for the all-important presidential reelection campaign in 1964. Another crisis in Cuba would evoke the Bay of Pigs and give the Republicans a vibrant foreign policy issue.

The Republicans already had civil rights. In late September the reluctant president, urged on by his brother, fought his way through yet another bloody black-white confrontation in the South, and put the full weight of the federal government behind the ultimately successful attempt of one black, James Meredith, to register at the University of Mississippi. Most Americans, sickened by the violence of southern sheriffs, seemed to be supporting their president, Kennedy was privately told by his pollsters. But no one could predict whether that support would translate into votes for Democrats.

The president also continued to maneuver through a succession of potentially career-ending personal crises, all revolving around women. Marilyn Monroe's suicide in early August triggered a wave of conspiracy theories, but no journalist had — yet — publicly reported what many in Hollywood knew: that she and the president had been lovers. His liaison with Judith Campbell Exner was still a secret from the public, although J. Edgar Hoover and dozens of FBI agents now knew of Kennedy's involvement with her and that she met regularly with Sam Giancana and Johnny Rosselli. Hoover also knew that a senior employee of General Dynamics, one of two bidders for the $6.5 billion TFX aircraft contract, had been part of a team that in August broke into Exner's apartment in Los Angeles. Rumors about his first marriage to Durie Malcolm were still afloat, despite Ben Bradlee's seemingly definitive story.

On the morning of October 16, when the president learned that Khrushchev had been systematically lying to him about the missiles in Cuba, his ambitious hopes for the 1962 and 1964 elections were directly put at risk. Once again, Kennedy was facing the prospect of being undone by Cuba, and humiliated, as he had been in the Vienna summit, by Nikita Khrushchev. One possible solution was diplomatic: the president could privately confront the Soviet premier with evidence of his treachery, and negotiate the quiet withdrawal of the missiles.

But Kennedy remained obsessed with Cuba, and so it became Khrushchev's turn to be humiliated. Over the next thirteen days, the president eschewed diplomacy and played a terrifying game of nuclear chicken, without knowing all of the facts. For the first time in his presidency, Kennedy publicly brought his personal recklessness, and his belief that the normal rules of conduct did not apply to him, to his foreign policy. On October 27, at the height of the crisis, when the downing of an American spy plane threatened to move events beyond his control, Kennedy was forced to seek a compromise and to rely on Khrushchev's common sense and dread of nuclear war to keep the superpowers apart. Once again, at a moment of high risk the president turned to Bobby Kennedy, his protector, to bail him out.

Jack Kennedy's deceits about his personal life and the corruption of the 1960 presidential election pale beside the false legacy he and his brother manufactured in the days and weeks after the missile crisis. Kennedy brought the world to the edge of nuclear war to gain a political victory: to humble an adversary who had humbled him before. But the public would be told, and would believe, that the valiant young president had *won* the missile crisis, by negotiating from strength. The lessons seemingly learned in the missile crisis would haunt American policymakers during the peace negotiations with North Vietnam, and would have made it more difficult for Presidents Lyndon Johnson and Richard Nixon to accept a compromise had they chosen to do so, thus perpetuating a war that claimed the lives of thousands of Americans and millions of Asians.

This, then, is a new history of the missile crisis, centered on the two most powerful men in Washington in the fall of 1962, the two men who knew all the secrets.

In May 1962 Nikita Khrushchev decided to make the boldest gamble of his career: he would station Soviet nuclear weapons in Cuba — the first deployment of such weapons outside of Eurasia — and do it in secret.

One factor, certainly, was strategic. A year earlier, President Kennedy had overridden objections from Khrushchev and some of his own advisers and approved operational status for fifteen medium-range Jupiter nuclear missiles in Turkey, across the Black Sea from Russia. The weapons had been ordered to Turkey in 1959 by President Eisenhower, but were not ready to fire until the Kennedy administration was in office. Khrushchev, who had a seaside summer home in Soviet Georgia, was incensed by the deployment, and often asked guests, especially Americans, to peer with binoculars across the water. When they asked what they were looking at, he said, "U.S. missiles in Turkey, aimed at my dacha." Soviet missiles in Cuba might not change the balance of power, but they would put dozens of major American cities more directly in harm's way and remind the young president that the Soviet Union insisted on being treated as a superpower equal. There were many troubling international issues still to be resolved between Washington and Moscow: the American insistence on unfettered access to West Berlin; the deepening American commitment in South Vietnam; and the White House's decision in March to respond to renewed Soviet nuclear testing by beginning its own atmospheric tests.

A second factor was the U.S. threat to Cuba. Operation Mongoose and the continued secret American attempts to assassinate Castro had driven the Cuban government more firmly into the protective grasp of Moscow, which had provided some $250 million in arms and matériel since mid-1960. The White House responded with public intimidation. In April 1962 the president lent the prestige of his office to the anti-Cuba effort by flying to Norfolk, Virginia, to watch a huge military exercise; some 40,000 men conducted amphibious landings at beaches in North Carolina and off Vieques Island, Puerto Rico, less than fifty miles from Cuba. In their 1997 study of the missile crisis, *One Hell of a Gamble,* Aleksandr Fursenko and Timothy Naftali, who had access to Soviet archives, concluded that Khrushchev "came to believe" in the first few months of 1962 — as the president wanted him to believe — that "John F. Kennedy was prepared to invade Cuba." In his memoirs, published in 1970, Khrushchev wrote, "I'm not saying we had any documentary proof that the Americans were preparing a second invasion [after the Bay of Pigs]. We didn't need documentary proof. We knew the class affiliation, the class blindness, of the United States, and that was enough to make us expect the worst."

To ensure the secrecy of the missile deployment, Khrushchev relied on Georgi Bolshakov and the fascination of the Kennedy brothers with back-channel negotiations. Bolshakov and Bobby Kennedy met at least six times in July 1962, according to Fursenko and Naftali, with Bolshakov suggesting at one point that Washington would have better relations with Moscow if it stopped aerial monitoring of Soviet shipping in international waters. Such overflights constituted "harassment," Bolshakov told the unsuspecting Kennedys, who continued to be worried about a flare-up in Berlin. In late July, Bolshakov was invited to a private meeting in the Oval Office with the Kennedy brothers, and the president seemingly agreed — so the Soviets thought — to limit U.S. surveillance of Soviet shipping if Khrushchev would put the Berlin issue "on ice." Soviet files show that in early August Bolshakov was authorized to tell John Kennedy that Khrushchev was "satisfied with the president's order to curtail U.S. planes' inspections of Soviet ships in open waters." There is no evidence that surveillance was significantly cut back, however. The American intelligence community was able to report in late August 1962 that fifty-five Soviet ships docked in Cuba that month — four times more than in August 1961.

By late summer the first intelligence reports of Soviet surface-to-air missiles in Cuba began circulating in Washington, and Khrushchev escalated his back-channel manipulations to deceive the Kennedy brothers. On September 6, Anatoly Dobrynin, the new Soviet ambassador to Washington, forwarded Khrushchev's assurances to the brothers that "nothing will be undertaken before the American Congressional elections that would complicate the international situation or aggravate the tension in the relations between our two countries." A similar message was passed to Charles Bartlett, Kennedy's newspaper friend, by Aleksandr Zinchuk, the Soviet minister in Washington. The message presented on behalf of Khrushchev was warm, Bartlett recalled in an interview for this book: "Khrushchev wants the president to know that he understands he is busy with the elections coming up and he will not in any way interfere with the election." The Soviet reassurances could not have come at a better time. The president was being lambasted in public by Senator Kenneth Keating of New York, a prominent liberal Republican, who claimed that "our do-nothing president" was suppressing intelligence about the extent of a Soviet missile buildup in Cuba. Georgi Bolshakov, on home leave in Moscow, was summoned to see Khrushchev and instructed to tell the president, through Bobby Kennedy, that the Soviet Union was providing Cuba only with weapons that were "defensive in character."

Khrushchev was unquestionably being deceptive in his use of the back channel throughout the summer and fall, but he was apparently careful to avoid an explicit lie. Throughout the crisis, and for years afterward, he insisted the Soviet missiles in Cuba were defensive — just as American policymakers called the Jupiters in Turkey "deterrent/defensive."

Cuba was once again front-page news, and the White House was forced to put out a statement declaring that there was no evidence of ballistic missiles in Cuba or "of other significant offensive capability either in Cuban hands or under Soviet direction and guidance." At a news conference on September 13, the president put his credibility on the line, saying that if the Soviet Union was shown to have provided Cuba with offensive weapons, "this country will do whatever must be done to protect its own security and that of its allies."

By this point, the president was getting a steady stream of cables and reports from John McCone, the CIA director, warning that Soviet offensive missiles, capable of delivering a nuclear warhead, were coming into Cuba. The direct warnings began on August 22, when McCone told Kennedy what he had been saying for two weeks at Operation Mongoose meetings: the CIA had learned from its sources inside Cuba that Soviet SAMs were being shipped to the island. In his opinion, McCone said, according to a CIA summary declassified in 1996, there was a probability that medium-range ballistic missiles would be the next step in the Soviet buildup. McCone's memorandum of the meeting, published in 1992 by the CIA, showed that Kennedy specifically raised the question "of what we could do against Soviet missile sites in Cuba." The linkage between the Jupiter missiles in Turkey and the Soviet missiles was also discussed, according to the memorandum: "McCone questioned value of Jupiter missiles. . . . McNamara agreed they were useless but difficult politically to remove them." McCone coupled his aggressive intelligence reporting with aggressive recommendations for an immediate American invasion of Cuba in sufficient force "to occupy the country, destroy the regime, free the people, and establish in Cuba a peaceful country."

In September, McCone renewed his reporting, sending a series of "eyes only" messages to the president and other senior officials warning that "an offensive Soviet Cuban base will provide Soviets with most important and effective trading position with all other critical areas and hence they might take an unexpected risk to establish such a position." The CIA director began to insist on a U-2 overflight of mainland Cuba; direct flights over the island had been limited since August for fear of a shootdown.

McCone's intelligence, and his insistence on pushing his view on the national security leaders of the administration, posed a dilemma for Jack Kennedy and his brother. In early October, with the congressional elections a month away, Bolshakov once again told Bobby Kennedy that the weapons going into Cuba were of "a defensive character." The president chose to believe Georgi Bolshakov over his CIA director, and did not authorize a direct U-2 flight over Cuba until October 9. It was the president's mistake, but McCone ultimately paid for it.

In *Thirteen Days*, his posthumous 1969 memoir of the missile crisis, Bobby Kennedy dealt with McCone's intelligence by pretending that it did not exist. When the book was published, none of McCone's reporting on the missiles had been made public. "We had been deceived by Khrushchev, but we had also fooled ourselves," Kennedy wrote. Ignoring Senator Keating's public assertions, Kennedy added that "no official within the government had ever suggested to President Kennedy that the Russian buildup in Cuba would include missiles." In his oral history for the Kennedy Library, which was not made public in full until 1988, Kennedy again insisted that McCone had not warned his brother about the Soviet missiles, and accused the CIA director of the most grievous offense in the White House — disloyalty. "He has not the loyalty that, for instance, Bob McNamara has," Kennedy said. "He is very careful of his own position. That's how he's been able to survive so many years in Washington. . . . I think he liked the president very much. But he liked one person more — and that was John McCone. . . . We all knew that John McCone was moving among senators and congressmen peddling this idea [that he had warned the president about the missiles] because it got him off the hook. Who was primarily responsible for not knowing there were missiles in Cuba earlier? The CIA. He wasn't going to have that on his back."

The first U-2 flight was a success and, on the evening of October 15, the intelligence community notified McGeorge Bundy that it now had photographic evidence of a Soviet ballistic missile site in Cuba. The president was briefed the next morning, and immediately spread the bad news.* Bobby Kennedy had an appointment with Richard Helms of the CIA a few moments later. "Dick, is it true? Dick, is it true?" he asked. Helms, describing the scene years later to the journalist Richard Reeves, said yes. "Shit!" said the attorney general.

He and his brother were convinced they had been duped in the back channel by Khrushchev. There are no notes or available records in the Kennedy Library to provide any insight into the president's thinking, but his actions over the next few days seem to have been brilliantly conceived. There would be an angry series of I-told-you-so's from John McCone and the military men in the Pentagon, who would — predictably — call for immediate air strikes or a ground invasion to destroy the missile sites. Being tough and advocating military action had never damaged the career, or the reputation, of anyone in the Kennedy White House. The president would have to act quickly to keep control of his staff and head off any Republican calls for a congressional investigation into the Cuban intelligence failure. Jack Kennedy did not want the Republicans to begin asking about what the president knew and when he knew it.

---

* Bundy, in his repeated telling of the missile crisis over the next few months, explained that he did not immediately give the intelligence to Kennedy because the president had spent the day before campaigning and seemed worn out. "I decided that a quiet evening and a night of sleep were the best preparation you could have," he later told Kennedy in writing, "in light of what you would face in the days ahead." Bundy made the explanation to the president after a magazine raised questions in early 1963 about the legality of his unilateral decision not to immediately inform the president of so significant a matter. Bundy was obviously going through the motions in his written explanation. As we have seen in this book, there were many times in the Kennedy White House, according to the Secret Service, when the president could not be disturbed, even for the most urgent of matters.

Kennedy's first move was to organize the Ex Comm (for Executive Committee of the National Security Council), staff it with insiders and outsiders, and insist that its deliberations remain totally secret. He gave the Ex Comm members one goal: the Soviet missiles in Cuba had to go, either by a blockade of Soviet shipping or something more drastic. In one move, Kennedy isolated those men who could lead a public charge against his stewardship of state and left them to debate in private, while he and his brother struggled to reap political gain from a mess that had been triggered by their obsession with Cuba. The Ex Comm members, who included cabinet secretaries and establishment figures such as Dean Acheson, the hard-line former secretary of state, and Robert A. Lovett, the New York lawyer and financier, were kept busy plotting air strikes and planning invasions.* But the real decision-making was done elsewhere.† The American public would not be informed of the missile crisis until the president decided to inform them, six days hence; until then, barring a leak, the Soviet Union would also not know that its missiles had been discov-

---

* Lovett, a wealthy New York lawyer whose father was president of the Union Pacific Railroad, had served as defense secretary in the Truman administration. He also served in the mid-1950s with Joseph Kennedy on the Eisenhower administration's intelligence advisory board; Jack Kennedy was eager to bring him into the inner circle during the missile crisis. Lovett arrived for a meeting in the Oval Office while the president was getting yet another briefing on the Soviet missiles. The CIA's Dino A. Brugioni, one of the briefers, described what happened next in a later memoir, *Eyeball to Eyeball,* published in 1991: "The president . . . asked Bobby to do the honors [escort Lovett to the Oval Office]. Bobby stuck his head out of the office door and called out to the waiting guest, 'Hey, you!' Lovett, calm, dignified, and reserved, did not respond. 'Hey, you,' Bobby called out a second time, and Lovett quizzically pointed to himself. 'Yes, you!' Bobby said with some irritation. 'Come here!' The president slammed his pen to the desk, ran his hand across his brow and, thoroughly disgusted, screamed out, 'Goddamn, Bobby!' To us," Brugioni noted, "it wasn't evidence of a brotherly feud or family infighting. It was simply the president dressing down a younger sibling who just happened to be the attorney general of the United States. We hastily packed our briefing materials and left."

† Some of the Ex Comm meetings were tape-recorded by Kennedy, who — under the recording system set up a few months earlier by the Secret Service — had to manually push a button to do so. The president and his brother were the only persons involved in the deliberations who knew that there could be a record for posterity. By the late 1980s, the Kennedy Library began making public many of the transcribed proceedings of the Ex Comm; their historical value can only be diminished by the fact that the two key players of the crisis knew they were being recorded.

ered. Jack Kennedy had time to consider, in secret conversations with his brother, the next step.

There was one quick casualty of Khrushchev's daring in Cuba — Ed Lansdale's White House career as a covert operative. On the afternoon of October 16, Bobby Kennedy managed to find the time to go through with a previously arranged meeting in his office with Lansdale and the Special Group (Augmented). It was a cathartic session, as summarized in a memorandum that day by Richard Helms, with the attorney general venting anger and frustration over Mongoose's inability "to influence significantly the course of events in Cuba." Kennedy said, according to Helms, that "the operation has been under way for a year" with no significant acts of successful sabotage. Helms's memorandum, written with ominous understatement, noted that the attorney general, after expressing the "general dissatisfaction" of the president, "traced the history of General Lansdale's personal appointment by the president a year ago." Mongoose was shut down after the missile crisis, and the disgraced Lansdale was shuffled over to a job in the Pentagon.

President Kennedy, skeptical about the ability of Lansdale and Harvey, had begun worrying months earlier about what to do if, as the intelligence community was predicting, Soviet missiles did arrive in Havana. Documents released in the early 1990s under the Freedom of Information Act show that on August 23 Kennedy had asked the Pentagon for a list of possible responses in case of a Cuban capacity to launch a nuclear strike against the United States. On October 3, Admiral Robert Dennison, commander in chief of the Atlantic Fleet, was ordered to plan for a blockade of Cuba; those plans were ready, according to a later Pentagon history, before the first public announcement of the missile crisis.

The missiles were politically toxic. Later in the crisis, after the blockade was under way, Bobby Kennedy reassured his brother by telling him, he wrote in *Thirteen Days*, "I just don't think there was any choice, and not only that, if you hadn't acted, you would have been impeached." The president thought for a moment, and said, "That's what I think — I would have been impeached."

*   *   *

On October 18, as the Ex Comm debated whether to bomb Cuba, invade Cuba, or blockade Soviet shipping, the president went ahead with a previously scheduled meeting with Andrei Gromyko, the Soviet foreign minister, who had come to the United States for the opening of the fall session of the UN General Assembly. In *Thirteen Days,* Robert Kennedy quoted the dutiful Soviet official as repeating the party line: "All Cuba wanted was peaceful coexistence; . . . she was not interested in exporting her system to other Latin American countries." Gromyko said nothing about the ballistic missiles his country was installing in Cuba, and insisted that the USSR had simply sent some specialists "to train Cubans to handle certain kinds of armament, which were only defensive." Kennedy quoted Gromyko as saying that his country's sole objective was to "give bread to Cuba in order to prevent hunger in that country." His brother, Bobby Kennedy wryly concluded, "was displeased with the spokesman of the Soviet Union."

"It was incredible," Jack Kennedy later told Kenny O'Donnell, "to sit there and watch the lies coming out of his mouth." The foreign minister's lies became a major component in the newspaper and magazine telling and retelling of the missile crisis, with a State Department official permitting a *New York Times* reporter to take verbatim notes of the transcript to demonstrate the Russian's "perfidy."

It was a setup, and Gromyko fell right into the trap. The president had anticipated, an approving Ted Sorensen reported in *Kennedy,* that Gromyko would say nothing about the missiles in Cuba. "Kennedy had hoped for this," wrote Sorensen, "believing it would strengthen our case with world opinion."

But Jack Kennedy participated in the lie, too. Why didn't he come clean with Gromyko and share the U-2 evidence of the Soviet missiles in Cuba, and thus give Khrushchev a chance to privately withdraw them? Bobby Kennedy explained in *Thirteen Days* that his brother, after some debate, decided against any revelations, since "he had not yet determined a final course of action and the disclosure of our knowledge might give the Russians the initiative."

There is a better answer. Even before his meeting with Gromyko, Jack Kennedy had decided there would be no diplomacy but instead a blockade and an ultimatum about what would happen if the Soviets defied it. He would seem to be willing to force Khrushchev to his knees — at any cost. The possibility exists, too, that Kennedy decided early on in the crisis that if his threats failed, and Khrushchev remained steadfast, he would compromise in secret, as he had done in Berlin a year earlier.

Only one Washington journalist seemed to understand the danger of Kennedy's policy as it was publicly stated, and was not afraid to write about it. "By confronting Mr. Gromyko privately," the columnist Walter Lippmann, who had visited Khrushchev in 1961 at his Black Sea dacha, wrote in the *New York Herald Tribune*, "the President would have given Mr. Khrushchev what all wise statesmen give their adversaries — the chance to save face." Kennedy's subsequent speech on the missiles would then have been more effective, Lippmann added, "for it would not have been subject to the criticism that a great power had issued an ultimatum to another great power without first attempting to save face."* There is no evidence that those in the government who knew about it took issue with Kennedy's decision to entrap Gromyko amidst a nuclear crisis.

The Soviet version of the Kennedy-Gromyko meeting, published in the winter 1996–97 *Cold War International History Project Bulletin*, added an essential detail: Kennedy went out of his way to offer an explicit agreement, as the foreign minister reported to Moscow, not to attack Cuba in return for a reduction in Soviet arms shipments. "If Mr. Khrushchev addressed me on this issue," Kennedy said, "we could give him corresponding assurances" not to invade Cuba. Gromyko quoted Kennedy as stating at another point that he had already told Khrushchev that the 1961 Bay of Pigs invasion "was a mistake." The president then repeated his offer to give the Soviet premier "assurances that an invasion would not be repeated neither on the part of Cuban refugees, nor on the part of the USA armed forces."

If Kennedy's soft words were designed to lull Gromyko and his Politburo colleagues to complacency, they were a success; Gromyko reported to Moscow, according to the *Bulletin*'s newly released Soviet

---

* Kennedy was confounded by Lippmann, who seemed unmoved by his charms. "You have lunch with Lippmann or Reston and they go back and knock the shit out of you to prove their integrity," Kennedy told Charles Bartlett. "The hell with them." Bartlett told the anecdote to Richard Reeves.

documents, that all was well. "Everything which we know about the position of the USA government on the Cuban question," Gromyko smugly told Khrushchev, "allows us to conclude that the overall situation is completely satisfactory. . . . There is reason to believe that the USA is not preparing an intervention in Cuba and has put its money on obstructing Cuba's economic relations with the USSR and other countries. . . . In these conditions a USA military adventure against Cuba is almost impossible to imagine."

What Gromyko and Khrushchev knew — and the Kennedy brothers did not — was that, according to declassified intelligence files in Moscow, the Soviets had secretly shipped at least 134 nuclear warheads, and perhaps more, into Cuba. Within hours, in case of invasion or all-out air attack, the 42,000 Soviet troops in Cuba — twice as many as American intelligence reported — would be able to mount the warheads on Soviet missiles and aircraft.* The Soviet commander in Cuba, General Issa Pliyev, was a battle-hardened veteran who had fought at Stalingrad and had commanded a division that beat back the Germans in defense of Moscow. Pliyev had direct operational control of twelve short-range tactical nuclear missiles, known as Lunas, with two-kiloton warheads. There is every reason to believe that Pliyev would have used every weapon in his arsenal if American marines and army paratroopers began an invasion. The possibility that a Soviet commander in Cuba could respond to American invasion by launching nuclear weapons was never considered in the missile crisis deliberations by the president, his brother, or any member of the Ex Comm. "We never had any positive evidence" that Soviet nuclear warheads were in Cuba, Deputy Secretary of Defense Roswell Gilpatric told the Kennedy Library in a 1970 interview. "If you ask my own belief, I don't think that there were," he added. "I think there were plans for flying them in, but I don't think they were actually matched up . . . with the launchers." Even eight years after the event, Gilpatric was wrong.

* * *

* One of the ironies of the missile crisis, Sam Halpern told me, was that the huge CIA station in Miami, relying on defector reports and other data, estimated the Soviet troop level in Cuba at slightly more than 42,000 by the fall of 1962. But that estimate was rejected as far too high by the intelligence community in Washington. "The president didn't know the numbers that our people in Florida were using," Halpern said.

Gromyko's assurances to Moscow came as America's military machine, unchecked by the increasingly confident president, was flexing its might, moving aircraft, ships, men, and matériel to jumping-off positions for what many generals and admirals were urging: a full-fledged invasion of Cuba. On Monday, October 22, six days after learning of the Soviet missiles in Cuba, Kennedy finally shared what he knew with the American people — and with Nikita Khrushchev. It was an aggressive and chilling crisis address, in which the president compared Castro's revolution to the Third Reich and depicted the Soviet missiles in Cuba as posing the gravest of national security threats to the United States. "The 1930s taught us a clear lesson," Kennedy said. "Aggressive conduct, if allowed to grow unchecked and unchallenged, ultimately leads to war." He announced a blockade on all Soviet military equipment being shipped to Cuba and described that action as "the one most consistent with our character and courage as a nation. . . . The cost of freedom is always high — but Americans have always paid it. And one path we shall never choose, and that is the path of surrender or submission."

"It shall be the policy of this nation," Kennedy declared, "to regard any nuclear missile launched from Cuba against any nation in the Western Hemisphere as an attack by the Soviet Union on the United States, requiring a full retaliatory response upon the Soviet Union." The president had staked out his position: the fate of the world now rested with Khrushchev.

Kennedy's audience, of course, was not only Moscow but his political critics in the Republican Party. "Who lost Cuba?" would not be a theme of the 1962 congressional elections.

Earlier in the day, Kennedy had telephoned Dwight Eisenhower at his retirement farm in Gettysburg, Pennsylvania, to give him advance word of the blockade. The call was recorded by Evelyn Lincoln, at Kennedy's direction, on the White House's standard Dictaphone system. (Lincoln removed fourteen Dictabelts containing the president's telephone conversations from the National Archives after Kennedy's assassination; the Dictabelts, never before made public, were transcribed for this book.)

Kennedy was resolute and fatalistic in his talk with Eisenhower. He assured his predecessor that "we will continue" the U-2 surveillance of Cuba, although, Kennedy said, "I would anticipate . . . Khrushchev will make a statement that any attack upon Cuba will be regarded as an attack upon the Soviet Union. We have to assume," Kennedy added, "that as this surveillance continues with the U-2s, these SAM sites may shoot one down." He and his advisers were considering what steps to take if that did happen, Kennedy added. "I don't know, we may get into the invasion business before many days are out, but we just have to."

Eisenhower was approving of the tough talk, and the two men then casually discussed the possibility of all-out nuclear war.

Eisenhower: "Of course, from a military standpoint, [invading Cuba is] a clean-cut thing to do now."

Kennedy: "That's right."

Eisenhower: "Because you've made up your mind you've got to get rid of this thing. The only real way to get rid of it, of course, is the other thing. But having to be concerned with world opinion . . ."

Kennedy: "And Berlin . . . I suppose that may be what they're going to try to trade off."

Eisenhower: "My idea is this: the damn Soviets will do whatever they want, what they figure is good for them. . . . I could be all wrong, but my own conviction is that you will not find a great deal of relationship between these things [Cuba and Berlin]. . . ."

Kennedy: "General, what if Khrushchev announced tomorrow, which I think he will, that if we attack Cuba, it's going to be nuclear war? What's your judgment as to the chances they'll fire these things off if we invade Cuba?"

Eisenhower: "Oh, I don't believe they will."

Kennedy: "In other words, you would take that risk if the situation seems desirable?"

Eisenhower: "What can you do? If this thing is such a serious thing here on our flank . . . you've got to use something. Something may make these people [the Soviets] shoot them off. I just don't believe this will. . . . I'll say this: I'd want to keep my own people very alert."

Eisenhower and Kennedy shared a laugh at that point.

Kennedy: "Well, hang on tight."

America was bristling and ready for war. At seven o'clock that evening, as the president began his speech, the Pentagon placed the American military establishment on increased alert, to DEFCON 3, beginning the greatest mobilization since World War II. The Strategic Air Command (SAC), which would unilaterally move to DEFCON 2 two days later, began deploying its bomber fleet to more than thirty predesignated civilian airfields across the United States. Nuclear weapons were loaded aboard bombers on SAC bases in Spain, Morocco, and England. Fighter-bombers at American bases throughout Europe and Asia also went on alert and many were armed with tactical nuclear weapons and assigned targets in the Soviet Union and Eastern Europe. Several Polaris missile submarines, the heart of the American underwater attack force, left their bases in Scotland and began patrols in the North Atlantic. The submarines had enough nuclear ordnance to destroy every major city in Russia.*

There was a final, contemptuous contact with Bolshakov, whose loyalty to his government had, not surprisingly, been greater than his loyalty to the Kennedys. After the president's Monday-night speech, Charles Bartlett was instructed by Bobby Kennedy to telephone Bolshakov and let him know that he and the president were enraged at his manipulations. The attorney general, Bartlett said in an interview for this book, "wanted me to tell [Bolshakov] how mad he was." It was, Kennedy told Bartlett, "a slimy thing [for Bolshakov] to do." (Moments after making the call to Bolshakov, Bartlett was telephoned by the attorney general, who chided him for not being very subtle. It was clear, Bartlett told me, that Kennedy had wiretapped either his or Bolshakov's telephone.) There was more payback: Bol-

---

* In April 1962 Kennedy had visited the navy's Atlantic Fleet headquarters, and was given a briefing by Admiral Robert Dennison on the command-and-control procedures for firing a Polaris nuclear missile. "I gave President Kennedy my chair at my desk, where he could see everything," Dennison recounted in his oral history for the U.S. Naval Institute. "I told [him] what was going to happen, because things happen so fast . . . just a lot of bang, bang, bang, and it's all over. I gave the command to start the exercise. Of course, all hell broke loose. Bells and buzzers and everything else started going, . . . getting the necessary instructions . . . and giving the order to shoot." After the exercise, Dennison said, he asked Kennedy if he had any questions. "He didn't say anything, and there was quite an appreciable pause, which seemed like a long time but was probably maybe six or seven or eight seconds. Finally, he said, 'Can these missiles be stopped?' I said, 'No, sir.' . . . I've wondered often what he was thinking about; what could happen in a matter of a few seconds — not half an hour or fifteen minutes — for him to think about countermanding an order to shoot." Kennedy's question — asking, in effect, whether he could reverse his decision once a nuclear weapon was launched — is indicative of his constant concern with maintaining personal control over events.

shakov's role as a purveyor of misleading information soon surfaced in the Washington press, ending his usefulness. He was recalled to Moscow.

With Bolshakov no longer in the picture, Robert Kennedy turned to Dobrynin, the new ambassador. Soviet documents show that the two men met at the Soviet Embassy late on Tuesday, October 23. Kennedy's message seemed to be that his big brother wasn't kidding. Dobrynin's account, summarized in a cable sent that night to Moscow, described an "obviously excited" Kennedy explaining that the president understood "the seriousness of the situation" and "what sort of dangerous consequences" could arise if the Soviet ships did not respond to the American blockade —"quarantine" was the word now being used — in the Caribbean. Nonetheless, Kennedy said, his brother "cannot act in any other way." The president, Kennedy added, had been deliberately misled by Khrushchev in the back channel. "The personal relations between the president and the Soviet premier have suffered heavy damage," Kennedy told the ambassador. "The president believed everything which was said from the Soviet side, and in essence staked on that card his own political fate, having publicly announced to the USA that the arms deliveries to Cuba carry a purely defensive character, although a number of Republicans have asserted to the contrary. . . . President Kennedy felt himself deceived, and deceived intentionally" by Khrushchev, who "the president has always trusted on a personal level . . . despite the big disagreements and frequent aggravations in relations."

Having made his case, Kennedy stood at the door of the embassy, Dobrynin reported, and asked, "as if by-the-way . . . what sort of orders the captains of the Soviet ships bound for Cuba have, in light of President Kennedy's speech yesterday." Dobrynin told the attorney general what he knew: that the Soviet captains had been instructed not "to stop or be searched on the open sea." At that point, Bobby Kennedy, "having waved his hand, said, 'I don't know how all this will end, but we intend to stop your ships.'"

In his 1995 memoir, *In Confidence,* Dobrynin, who as a forty-two-year-old was the youngest man ever to serve as Soviet ambassador to the United States, acknowledged that at the time of Kennedy's visit he had been told nothing about the Soviet missiles in Cuba. Years later, in Moscow, Dobrynin added, a high Soviet official explained that the lack of instructions and explicit information at the height of the crisis reflected "the sense of total bewilderment that enveloped Khrushchev and his colleagues after their plot [to install the missiles in Cuba] had taken such an unexpected turn."

Dobrynin was ordered to keep on talking in private with the attorney general; it turned out to be one of the most important decisions of the crisis. The Tuesday-night conversation with Kennedy led to a subsequent series of confidential meetings, usually after midnight, throughout the crisis. "We met either at my embassy or in his office at the Department of Justice," Dobrynin wrote.

> When he visited me, I used to meet him at the entrance, and we ascended to the third floor to my sitting room where we proceeded to talk in the perfect silence of the night. Never was anyone else present at those meetings. . . . All this made the ambiance somewhat mysterious and at the same time reflected the tense atmosphere of Washington in those days. This tension was accentuated by the fact that Robert Kennedy was far from being a sociable person and lacked a proper sense of humor. . . . He was impulsive and excitable.

On Wednesday the nation was riveted to television sets as the first of twenty Soviet merchant ships approached the navy blockade. Jack Kennedy was unflappable, as usual. As the tension grew, Charles Bartlett and his wife were dining in the White House with the president and his wife. "That's when I admired him the most," Bartlett told me in a 1997 interview, "the night that the Russian ships were approaching the blockade. He was very cool and yet very sensitive to the implications of what was going on. It was scary. He literally did not know what the Russian reaction was going to be when they reached that blockade. We went home early and he hadn't heard. And he called me about ten-thirty and said, 'Well, we've got the word they turned around.' He'd been perfectly normal all night."

Nikita Khrushchev backed off. The Soviet ships either stopped dead in the water or turned back toward the Soviet Union. Jack Kennedy kept up the pressure. He had Ex Comm under firm control, with its members lined up in unanimous support of the blockade. He had the nation's armed forces on alert and ready to pounce. America's

newspapers and television networks were called in for a briefing by
Dean Rusk and warned that tensions had not eased, despite the Soviet
capitulation on the high seas. Overflights of Cuba showed that construction at the missile sites was proceeding at breakneck pace. Newspapermen depicted Bobby Kennedy, McGeorge Bundy, and Robert
McNamara as among those advocating an invasion of Cuba, if necessary, to get the missiles out. Local newspapers published articles on
the status of food reserves, civil defense systems, and bomb shelters,
as much of America — and the world — continued to be terrified.
The Soviet Embassy in Washington warned Moscow, Dobrynin wrote
in his memoirs, that Jack Kennedy, "like a gambler, actually was stak-
ing his reputation as a statesman, and his chances for reelection in
1964, on the outcome of this crisis. That was why," Dobrynin added,
"we could not rule out — especially given the more aggressive members of his entourage — the possibility of a reckless reaction."

A crucial piece of information in Washington was withheld from
the public: the American intelligence community found no evidence
of an increase in military readiness or alerts in the Soviet Union.
Samuel Halpern and his colleagues in Task Force W were closely
monitoring the crisis and finding no sign of a Soviet mobilization, although the Soviet troops in Cuba continued to work round-
the-clock assembling medium-range ballistic missile sites. "By the
twenty-sixth [of October]," Halpern told me, "we're saying,
'What's going on?' There's no Soviet reaction. Nobody is getting
ready to shoot at us. We're asking, 'Have we won already?'" The
Strategic Air Command had gone to DEFCON 2, the stage just short of
war, while the Soviets, Halpern said, "did not do a damn thing, even
though they had nukes [in Cuba] that we didn't know they had."
Most significant, the Soviets did nothing to upgrade the readiness of
their nuclear missile fleet.

There was another crucial player in the crisis: Fidel Castro, whose
importance was, astonishingly, discounted by the White House. Castro was convinced that the Americans were coming — he knew the
Kennedys wanted him dead — and was increasingly agitated by the
refusal of General Pliyev to fire at American intelligence planes. By
Friday, October 26, American reconnaissance aircraft were crisscross-
ing the island at treetop level with impunity, and presumed to be
gathering the intelligence needed for a ground invasion. Castro

began urging Pliyev to get authority to begin knocking the Americans out of the sky with surface-to-air missiles. Pliyev agreed and, according to the Soviet documents obtained by Fursenko and Naftali, permission was received a day later.

Castro panicked early on the morning of October 27, according to *"One Hell of a Gamble,"* and began telling his Soviet counterparts that "under certain circumstances"— the possible loss of Cuba — a nuclear first strike against an American target was justified. If the Americans "actually carry out the brutal act of invading Cuba," Castro wrote in a letter to Khrushchev, "that would be the moment to eliminate such danger forever through an act of legitimate defense, however harsh and terrible the solution would be." "We must not wait to experience the perfidy of the imperialists," Castro told a Soviet diplomat in Havana, "letting them initiate the first strike and deciding that Cuba should be wiped off the face of the earth."

Khrushchev was losing control.

Confronted with fanaticism from both Fidel Castro and John Kennedy, Khrushchev brought the superpower game of chicken to an end. He sent Kennedy a long, rambling letter that offered a way out. "It is . . . no secret to anyone that the threat of armed attack, aggression, has constantly hung and continues to hang over Cuba," Khrushchev wrote. "It was only this that impelled us to respond to the Cuban government's request to give it aid to strengthen its defensive capacity. If the President and the government of the United States were to give assurance that the USA itself would not participate in an attack on Cuba and would restrain others from this kind of action, if you would recall your fleet, this would immediately change everything." The Soviet premier was accepting the offer that the president had made to Andrei Gromyko a week earlier, before there was any public mention of the missiles in Cuba.

In *"One Hell of a Gamble,"* Fursenko and Naftali reported that by this time, according to Soviet documentation, twenty-four medium-range ballistic missiles were operational and could be loaded with nuclear warheads within hours. Why didn't Khrushchev, who had overridden the opposition of many in the Politburo to put the missiles in Cuba, now announce their readiness and challenge Kennedy to war? "In the heat of the crisis," the authors wrote, "Khrushchev backed away. . . . Time and again between 1956 and 1961, he had threatened nuclear retaliation as a bargaining chip to further his political objectives. But Khrushchev did not have the desire to threaten nuclear war when [the threat] might actually lead to one."

On the next morning, however, Khrushchev, under pressure from the Politburo, made a last-minute attempt to strengthen his position — and save his political standing in Moscow. The White House received a second proposal from him, advocating a public trade of the missiles in Turkey for the missiles in Cuba. The American Jupiters in Turkey were known to be strategically insignificant and vulnerable to Soviet attack, and Khrushchev's offer put the president in a dilemma. "He obviously did not wish to order the withdrawal of the missiles from Turkey under threat from the Soviet Union," Bobby Kennedy explained in *Thirteen Days*. "On the other hand, he did not want to involve the U.S. and mankind in a catastrophic war over missile sites in Turkey that were antiquated and useless." McGeorge Bundy and Ted Sorensen, always tough in front of their boss, argued against the trade, telling Kennedy that American credibility in NATO as a nuclear defender of Europe would be undermined by withdrawal of the Jupiters. The president was on the verge of a knockout punch of Khrushchev, they said, and his political standing among the Republicans would be jeopardized if he resolved the crisis by trading off America's nuclear arsenal, strategically relevant or not.

But there was more bad news from Cuba that morning. The CIA's photo interpreters, whose analyses turned out to be correct, concluded that construction work at all twenty-four medium-range missile sites was now complete. The missiles, with a range of 1,020 nautical miles — enough to strike Washington — could be fueled, armed, targeted, and ready to launch in six to eight hours. The FBI reported that Soviet diplomats were behaving as if war was imminent: they had begun burning files and archives at their embassy in Washington and at their UN enclave on Long Island.

The crisis worsened later that afternoon, when it was learned that a Soviet surface-to-air missile had shot down an American U-2 spy plane during an intelligence-gathering overflight of the island. The Joint Chiefs had agitated since the crisis began for a massive air strike unless the Soviets began to dismantle their missiles. It had been agreed in Ex Comm, without serious debate or known dissension, that if a reconnaissance plane was shot down, the air force could retaliate by destroying a Soviet surface-to-air site. Maxwell Taylor, the Kennedy's favorite general, who had recently been named chairman of the Joint Chiefs, recommended with the support of his four-star colleagues that the air strike be followed by an all-out invasion. "There was the knowledge that we had to take military action to protect our pilots," Bobby Kennedy wrote. "There was the realization that the Soviet Union and Cuba apparently were preparing to do battle. And there was the feeling that the noose was tightening on all of us, on Americans, on mankind, and that the bridges to escape were crumbling."

Kennedy was losing control.

At the suggestion of Bundy, the president agreed that he would respond to Khrushchev's first letter and ignore the second, which insisted on a missile trade. In *Kennedy*, his 1965 insider's memoir, Ted Sorensen described what happened next. "At the private request of the President, a copy of [a] letter was delivered to the Soviet Ambassador by Robert Kennedy with a strong verbal message: The point of escalation was at hand; the United States could proceed toward peace and disarmament, or, as the Attorney General later described it, we could take 'strong and overwhelming retaliatory action . . . unless [the President] received immediate notice that the missiles would be withdrawn.'" On the next morning, Sorensen wrote, the Kremlin announced that "Kennedy's terms were being accepted. . . . I [was] hardly able to believe it." Later, at a cabinet meeting, Sorensen wrote, "John F. Kennedy entered and we all stood up." The president, he added, had "earned his place in history by this one act alone. . . . Cuba had been the site of his greatest failure and now of his greatest success."

Sorensen's published account was a half-truth. As he knew, and would not reveal for twenty-seven years, the crisis was resolved when Bobby Kennedy, on behalf of his brother, held a last-minute meeting with Dobrynin and made a secret arrangement to give Nikita Khrushchev the trade he wanted — Jupiter missiles removed from Turkey in exchange for withdrawal of Soviet missiles from Cuba.

Dobrynin's secret cable to Moscow about the meeting, published with little fanfare in 1995 by the *Cold War International History Project Bulletin,* reported that Kennedy arrived with a compromise offer as well as a warning: time was of the essence, because, Kennedy said, "there are many unreasonable heads among the [American] generals, and not only among the generals, who are 'itching' for a fight. The situation might get out of control, with irreversible consequences." His brother, Robert Kennedy told the Soviet ambassador, was under "strong pressure" to permit the air force to retaliate against Cuban targets if American reconnaissance planes were fired upon. "The USA can't stop these flights," Kennedy said, "because this is the only way we can quickly get information about the state of construction of the missile bases in Cuba." If the American bombing took place, the president's brother said, the result could be nuclear war between the United States and the Soviet Union. "In response to the bombing of these bases," Dobrynin quoted the distraught Kennedy as saying, "the Soviet government will undoubtedly respond with the same against us, somewhere in Europe. A real war will begin, in which millions of Americans and Russians will die. We want to avoid that any way we can."*

---

* Bobby Kennedy seemed unaware that his statement about the danger of escalation in Europe could be construed as undercutting the American bargaining position in the crisis. The American goal was to use the threat of bombing, or worse, to compel the Soviets to withdraw their missiles from Cuba. If Bobby Kennedy and his brother believed that an American bombing would lead to Soviet retaliation in Europe, the cost to America of hitting Cuba would be much higher — weakening the credibility of the American threat of force. In their 1994 study of the missile crisis, *We All Lost the Cold War,* published by Princeton University Press, Richard Ned Lebow and Janice Stein noted that "to maintain or enhance that credibility, [President] Kennedy would have had to discount the probability of Soviet retaliation to Dobrynin." There is another, more disturbing, analysis. Bobby Kennedy was reminding Khrushchev, through Dobrynin, that *events could get out of control* unless they made a private deal right away. He was warning that pressure from the Joint Chiefs might force the president to take steps he didn't want — the bombing of Cuba — and reminding Khrushchev that the same thing could happen to him within hours in the Soviet Union.

"During our meeting," Dobrynin wrote in his cable home, "R. Kennedy was very upset; in any case, I've never seen him like this before. . . . He didn't even try to get into fights on various subjects, as he usually does, and only persistently returned to one topic: time is of the essence and we shouldn't miss the chance."

The brothers had lost control because of the downing of one American spy plane. What began as payback for the Bay of Pigs was beginning to evolve into a world war. The Kennedys, fanatical about being tough and resolute in front of their peers, could not turn to the government they controlled to extricate themselves from disaster. They turned for help, instead, to Nikita Khrushchev.

With a missile trade on the table, Bobby Kennedy asked Dobrynin and Khrushchev for secrecy, explaining that only two or three people in Washington were aware of the behind-the-scenes bargaining. "The president can't say anything public in this regard," Kennedy added. The missiles in Turkey were nominally under NATO command, and to order their removal unilaterally "would seriously tear apart NATO. However," Dobrynin's cable quoted Kennedy as saying, "President Kennedy is ready to come to agreement on that question with N.S. Khrushchev, too. I think that in order to withdraw these bases from Turkey, we need four–five months." If Khrushchev agreed, Kennedy added, he and the president could continue to work together, with Dobrynin serving as the middleman in a new back channel.

In his memoirs Dobrynin described three further meetings with Bobby Kennedy over the missile issue. On Sunday, October 28, the ambassador was instructed by cable from Moscow to tell the attorney general that Khrushchev accepted the agreement. The relieved Kennedy smiled and said, according to Dobrynin, "At last, I'm going to see the kids. Why, I've almost forgotten my way home." On the next day Khrushchev told Kennedy, through Dobrynin, that he agreed to keep the missile trade secret and to continue the new back-channel discussions. In a cable sent on the thirtieth to Moscow, published in the *Cold War International History Project Bulletin*, Dobrynin quoted the attorney general as saying that he and the president "are not prepared to formulate such an understanding in the form of letters, even the most confidential letters, between the president and the head of the Soviet government when it concerns such a delicate issue."

Kennedy was referring to a private letter Khrushchev had sent to the president the day before; the Soviet premier had explicitly stated that he accepted Kennedy's commitment to eliminate the Jupiters at a future date. The letter could not stand, Bobby Kennedy told Dobrynin, because it was a political liability.

"Speaking in all candor," Kennedy added, according to the Dobrynin cable, "I, myself, for example, do not want to risk getting involved in the transmission of this sort of letter, since who knows where and when such letters can surface or be somehow published — not now, but in the future — and any changes in the course of events are possible. The appearance of such a document could cause irreparable harm to my political career in the future. This is why we request that you take this letter back."

The top stratum of the Soviet government was getting a lesson in cover-up from the Americans. "As a guarantee," Dobrynin quoted Kennedy as saying, "I can only give you my word. Moreover I can tell you that two other people besides the president know about the existing understanding"— Dean Rusk and Llewellyn Thompson, the former U.S. ambassador to the Soviet Union. There was a carrot for the ambitious Dobrynin. Kennedy told the ambassador, Dobrynin cabled, that "on the Turkish [missile] issue and other highly confidential issues he was prepared to maintain a direct contact with me. . . . I answered," Dobrynin said, "that I was prepared to maintain contact with him on highly important issues in the future, passing over the heads, as he himself suggested, of all intermediaries."

The Dobrynin cable did not include Kennedy's most remarkable statement — saved, no doubt, for his 1995 memoir. "Very privately," Dobrynin wrote, "Robert Kennedy added that someday — who knows? — he might run for president, and his prospects could be damaged if the secret deal about the missiles in Turkey were to come out."

Jack Kennedy was planning to stay in office six more years, and to be followed by his brother for two four-year terms. For perhaps the next fourteen years, therefore, the men running the Soviet Union, with or without a formal letter, would have the means to publicly devastate the Kennedys by putting the lie to their inspiring victory in

the missile crisis. The president and his brother were true existential-
ists at that moment, bargaining their way out of an immediate crisis
by putting their future credibility in the hands of the Soviet leadership.

The American people, knowing none of this, cheered the victori-
ous end of the crisis and their hero-president, Jack Kennedy. Those
few who doubted or criticized his negotiating tactics ate crow, like
Nikita Khrushchev, in public. Walter Lippmann, who had complained in writing about Kennedy's reckless handling of Andrei
Gromyko, lauded the president for having shown "not only the
courage of a warrior, which is to take the risks that are necessary, but
also . . . the wisdom of the statesman, which is to use power with
restraint." A few days later Lippmann had lunch at the White House
with the president and was shown some of the top-secret correspondence between Kennedy and Premier Khrushchev. The correspondence did not deal, of course, with Kennedy's secret concession on
the Jupiter missiles.

Kennedy also did not tell Dwight Eisenhower, his new telephone
confidant, the real story, although Eisenhower shrewdly asked the
right questions. A transcript of the call, from the Evelyn Lincoln
Dictabelts, shows that the president claimed victory over the Soviets
and told Eisenhower that he had rejected Khrushchev's public
demand that the Jupiters be withdrawn. "We couldn't get into that
deal," Kennedy said, disingenuously.

Eisenhower: "Of course, but Mr. President, does [Khrushchev]
put any conditions on?"

Kennedy: "No, except that we're not going to invade Cuba. . . .
That's the only one we've got now. But we don't plan to invade Cuba
under these conditions anyway, so if we can get them out, we're better off by now."

Eisenhower: "I quite agree. I just wondered whether he would try
to engage us in any kind of statement or commitments that would
finally one day be very embarrassing."

Kennedy: "I don't think the Cuban story can be over yet. . . . If
they engage in subversion, if they attempt to do any aggressive acts
and so on, then all bets are off. In addition, my guess is that by the end
of next month we're going to be toe-to-toe in Berlin anyway, so I

think this is important for the time being because it requires quite a step-down for Khrushchev."*

Not everyone cheered Kennedy's agreement, as it was publicly stated — trading the Soviet missiles in Cuba for an explicit American commitment never to invade. "We now have a U.S.-protected Soviet base in the Western Hemisphere," Sam Halpern recalled telling one of his colleagues on Task Force W at the time. As Halpern anticipated, the president's attitude toward Castro did not change after the missile crisis; the CIA would still be asked to get rid of him.

The Kennedy brothers brought the world to the edge of war in their attempts to turn the dispute into a political asset. They survived by making private entreaties to a Soviet premier they had sought only days earlier to humiliate before the world. Jack Kennedy was willing to trust the Soviet leadership with information that, if made public, would destroy his presidency. Robert Kennedy was also willing to hold his future presidency hostage to the vagaries of a foreign government that could choose, at any time, to make public the terms of the missile trade.

Robert Kennedy could not bring himself to tell the truth, either in his memoir or in his oral interviews with his brother's library. Jack Kennedy accepted the nation's adulation as a peacekeeper, while remaining eager to tell his friends that he'd "cut off Khrushchev's

---

* Kennedy also telephoned former president Harry Truman in Independence, Missouri, and once again misrepresented the agreement. A transcript of that call shows the following exchange:

Truman: "I'm just pleased to death the way these things came out."

Kennedy: "Well, we'll just stay at it. I just wanted to bring you up to date on it. We got a letter from [Khrushchev] on Friday night which was rather conciliatory on these withdrawals. Then on Saturday morning . . . we got this entirely different letter about the missile bases in Turkey."

Truman: "That's the way they do things."

Kennedy: "Well, then we rejected that. Then they came back and accepted the earlier proposal so . . . we're making some progress about getting these missiles out of there. In addition, Khrushchev's had some difficulties in maintaining his position."

"Truman: "You're on the right track. You just keep after them. That's the language they understand, just what you gave them."

balls." Members of the Ex Comm were also hailed by the public and the media for their role in repeatedly encouraging the president to be tough. The president's public approval ratings shot up to 77 percent — almost as high as in the weeks following the Bay of Pigs. Kennedy arranged for Tiffany's, the posh New York jeweler, to design a silver calendar, mounted in walnut, that depicted the month of October 1962, with the thirteen days of crisis etched more deeply. He presented the desktop mementos to each member of the Ex Comm and other aides who participated in the crisis.

The public was touched by his display of affection for the men who had helped him make the tough decisions. Kennedy kept up the pretense of toughness after the crisis by helping to smear the dovish Adlai Stevenson, his ambassador to the United Nations, who had been the only member of the Ex Comm to have the courage to suggest trading the missiles in Cuba for the Jupiters in Turkey — the precise agreement that was secretly worked out. Stevenson's suggestion was criticized by his peers at the time; six weeks later the ambassador was anonymously accused of having "wanted a Munich" in an article coauthored by Charles Bartlett and Stewart Alsop. Jack Kennedy denied any role in the mud-slinging, but Stevenson later learned, according to his public papers, that Bartlett and Alsop presented a draft of the article to the president in advance. "It is true," Alsop later acknowledged, "that Kennedy read the piece for accuracy, and proposed a couple of minor changes."*

The few men who knew part or all of the story said nothing, and the missile crisis continued to be the most misunderstood and poorly reported event of the Cold War. McNamara has never talked about what he knew. And Dean Rusk waited until 1987 before he finally

---

* Evelyn Lincoln's Dictabelt tapes show that Kennedy was privately doubtful of Stevenson during the crisis. At one point early in the crisis, he telephoned the conservative John McCloy, a banker who was his special adviser on disarmament, and urged him to cut short a European business trip to fly to Stevenson's side at the United Nations. "I think we need somebody up there to sort of sustain Adlai, and stiffen him, and support him," the president said. McCloy, who was one of the architects of America's postwar reconstruction policies, wasn't eager to return, but did so when Kennedy arranged for a special flight. The president later informed Dwight Eisenhower that he had sent McCloy to the United Nations "to assist Adlai, so that we get somebody who's had some experience."

acknowledged that the president, after dispatching his brother to see Dobrynin on the night of October 27, desperately sought a further compromise, although not the one that was actually negotiated. Kennedy authorized Rusk to draft a statement calling on U Thant, the United Nations secretary-general, to propose a public trade of Soviet missiles for American Jupiters. The president would then publicly accept the offer.*

Anything was better, in Jack Kennedy's world, than being compelled to admit to his admirers in the government — and to the hard-nosed generals and admirals who ran the armed forces — that their heroic young president had compromised to avoid war.

---

* Ted Sorensen waited until 1989, and some public complaints by Dobrynin about the distortion of history, before revealing at an international conference on the missile crisis that he had deleted from *Thirteen Days* the essential fact that Jack and Robert Kennedy had decided to approach Khrushchev secretly — that is, behind the back of the Ex Comm — and explicitly agreed to withdraw the missiles in Turkey. Sorensen spent much of his professional life as a ghostwriter for Jack Kennedy and did the same for his brother's posthumous book. *Thirteen Days* was based on Bobby Kennedy's personal diaries, Sorensen said in a note published on the last page of the text, and written by Kennedy, in draft, in the summer and fall of 1967. As the editor of Robert Kennedy's book, Sorensen explained in 1989, he chose to delete the reference to the back-channel bargaining with Khrushchev, through Ambassador Dobrynin, "because at the time it was still a secret even to the American side." Sorensen's revelation left the impression that Bobby Kennedy, had he lived, would have described the secret agreement in his book. There is nothing in the record, or in Kennedy's oral history, that suggests that he would have done so.

21

DECEPTIONS

Jack Kennedy's shining moment in Cuba immediately paid off in the midterm election on November 6, nine days after the missile crisis ended. The Democratic Party gained four seats in the Senate and lost four seats in the House — the best midterm showing by a party in the White House since 1934, in FDR's first term. One of the winners was Teddy Kennedy, who became the junior senator from Massachusetts; one of the losers was Senator Homer Capehart, of Indiana, a Republican who had spent the fall attacking Kennedy for being too soft on Castro.

On December 17, 1962, the three major television networks simultaneously broadcast an hour-long interview with Kennedy, who handled the starstruck correspondents' questions with ease. Asked how he went about the decision-making in the missile crisis, Kennedy repeated the agreed-upon history by explaining that decisions were "hammered out" by the Ex Comm members over "five or six days. . . . After all alternatives were examined . . . a general consensus developed . . . that the course of action that we finally adopted was the right one." The president wanted no one to know that the Ex Comm had been excluded from the final bargaining with Nikita Khrushchev, and from the secret agreement to withdraw American missiles in Turkey in return for the removal of the Soviet missiles in Cuba.

Meanwhile, a few administration officials and members of Congress were asking the president more pointed questions than the reporters: Why had the American government given orders for the withdrawal of all fifteen Jupiter missiles from Turkey? In early 1963 Alexander M. Haig, Jr., an army lieutenant colonel assigned to the Pentagon, was ordered by the Joint Chiefs of Staff to write an analytical study of the missile crisis from a military point of view. Haig, who in ten years would be President Richard Nixon's chief of staff, wrote in his 1992 memoir, *Inner Circles,* that he and his colleagues were troubled both by the order to pull the Jupiters out and by its timing: the withdrawal order was issued by Secretary of Defense McNamara the day after Khrushchev's public capitulation. "It certainly looked as though there had been a secret deal," Haig wrote in his memoir. "Soviet missiles out of Cuba in return for the removal of American missiles from Turkey." The final report to the Joint Chiefs, he wrote, "mentioned the possibility that what was being described as a coincidence could easily be interpreted as a secret arrangement." JCS chairman Maxwell Taylor "flushed angrily" when he read the paper, Haig recounted, "slammed it down on the table and said that he would never approve it for transmittal to the President. Our paper disappeared."

The president's men handled questions from Congress by lying. In January 1963 Secretary of State Rusk was asked by Senator Bourke B. Hickenlooper of Iowa, the second-ranking Republican on the Senate Foreign Relations Committee, to confirm that the removal of the Jupiters "was in no way, shape or form, directly or indirectly connected" with the missile crisis settlement. "That is correct, sir," Rusk responded. One month later, Senator John C. Stennis of Mississippi, chairman of a Senate defense appropriations committee, asked Robert McNamara whether the two were related. "Absolutely not," the defense secretary responded. McNamara apparently could not resist a bit of embellishment: "The Soviet government did raise the issue, [but the] President absolutely refused even to discuss it. He wouldn't even reply other than that he would not discuss the issue at all." At another hearing in February, McNamara, who, like Dean

Rusk, knew all about the secret trade with Khrushchev, provided more false history. Khrushchev backed down, he said, because Ex Comm "faced . . . the possibility of launching nuclear weapons and Khrushchev knew it, and that [was] the reason, and the only reason, why he withdrew [his] weapons."*

In the spring, McGeorge Bundy, Kennedy's national security adviser, responded to rumors from Europe of a Jupiter deal by writing Raymond Aron, the French political scientist, in a letter that those "who would spread rumors" about the Jupiter trade, "of course, must be pretty far gone in their mistrust of the United States to start with." The Pentagon's annual report for 1963 described Turkey as being among a group of nations that had "announced their decision to phase out" their intermediate-range missiles.

Kennedy's high public standing gave him renewed freedom to go after Fidel Castro in secret. "We started up all over again after the missile crisis, to try to unseat the Castro government," the CIA's Samuel Halpern told me in an interview. The Kennedy brothers pressed the

---

*Bobby Kennedy made essentially the same claim in an interview with Elie Abel, a correspondent for NBC News, who in 1966 published *The Missile Crisis,* considered at the time to be a definitive study. Kennedy "told me himself," Abel said in a 1970 interview with the Kennedy Library, that he had warned Anatoly Dobrynin, the Soviet ambassador, at the height of the crisis that if the missiles in Cuba were not withdrawn "we would have to take direct military action early in the week. I think that's the way he put it." In a widely quoted portion of his book, Abel authoritatively described President Kennedy as being enraged to learn, after Khrushchev proposed the Jupiter trade, that the missiles were still in Turkey. "He distinctly remembered having given instruction," Abel wrote, "long before the Cuban missile crisis, that the Jupiters must be removed." Following his conversation with the president, Abel wrote, he checked with an official of the National Security Council who "was able to confirm the President's recollection. Kennedy had, indeed, issued instructions for the removal of Jupiters from Turkey in the third week of August, 1962, two months before the crisis." No such orders were given; all that Kennedy did, according to *The Other Missiles of October,* published in 1997 by historian Philip Nash, was to request that the Defense Department on August 23, 1962, study the question of how to remove the Jupiters. No action was taken on the president's request before the missile crisis, Nash wrote. Elie Abel's mistake, one that any reporter would have made, was to believe what his sources in the White House were telling him.

CIA for more sabotage operations inside Cuba — one list had nine targets, including the Texaco oil refineries in Havana and Santiago.

Bill Harvey, the career operative who ran Task Force W, the agency's anti-Castro operation, remained a skeptic who was unafraid to speak his mind; by the end of 1962, he and Bobby Kennedy had been in undeclared war for months. In Harvey's view, Kennedy was an amateur who had no understanding of covert intelligence. And the attorney general was not shy about expressing his unhappiness at the failure of Harvey's task force. A few weeks before the missile crisis, Kennedy had stunned a White House meeting by ripping into Harvey after he began dozing, as he usually did, after lunch. It was the "damnedest tirade," General Charles E. Johnson III, the army representative to Special Group (Augmented), told investigators for the Church Committee in 1975. Kennedy's personal attack went on for "quite a while, eight to ten minutes," Johnson related, with John McCone, the CIA director, saying nothing in defense of his man. "It couldn't have been a tirade for just a failure to make Mongoose succeed, I don't think," the general said. "It seemed to be something beyond that — a failure beyond that." What Johnson probably did not know when he was interviewed was that Harvey and his Mafia collaborators had been unable to pull the trigger on Castro.

Harvey struck back during one of the early meetings on the missile crisis, Halpern told me, saying directly to the president and his brother, in essence, "'We wouldn't be in such trouble now if you guys had had some balls in the Bay of Pigs.' Everybody was thunderstruck," Halpern said. "You don't say that to the president in his own office, but Harvey was the only guy who had the guts to do it." John McCone, who was at the meeting, wanted to fire Harvey immediately, Halpern said. But Richard Helms "saved" Harvey by suggesting that he be reassigned as CIA chief of station in Rome. In late 1962, before leaving Task Force W, Harvey wrote a final memorandum to McCone on Cuba, obtained for this book under the Freedom of Information Act. Harvey argued that the president's pledge of noninvasion — Kennedy's only public retreat in the missile crisis — had put the CIA in an impossible position. Jack Kennedy still wanted the Castro government overthrown, but he had taken away his best asset — the possible use of the American military. Kennedy's pledge also vitiated another favored plan, Harvey wrote, that of "invading Cuba on the pretext of a contrived provocation such as an attack on Guantanamo," the American navy base on Cuba.

The administration's long-standing goal of provoking "a revolt inside Cuba" was now meaningless, Harvey wrote, because "such a revolt if provoked would be totally destroyed by Cuban counteraction in a matter of hours or, at the most, a few days unless supported by a major United States military commitment." It was unnecessary for Harvey to remind McCone that Edward Lansdale's pie-in-the-sky scheming during Operation Mongoose had, at its core, the use of American forces inside Cuba in case of a full-scale revolt.

There was a parting shot at Bobby Kennedy's renewed push for Cuban sabotage: "Commando and sabotage operations, except in rare selective instances, will serve little purpose," Harvey wrote.

Just before Christmas 1962, Bobby Kennedy put together a privately funded ransom of $53 million in pharmaceuticals and farm machinery and paid it to Castro in return for the release of the members of Cuban Brigade 2506, who had been captured and imprisoned during the April 1961 invasion. On December 27, the returned exiles held an emotional meeting in Miami with a contrite John Kennedy, who told them he was sorry for what had happened at the Bay of Pigs. He also asked, according to published accounts, if the exiles had really expected American air support. The answer, given by Pepe San Román, the brigade commander, was yes. In his 1964 book on the Cuban invasion, *The Bay of Pigs,* Haynes Johnson quoted San Román as telling Kennedy that "naturally we expected it because we had been told the sky would be ours and we knew the B-26s were not enough." The president, wrote Johnson, "looked serious." He did not tell the men that it was his decision to call off the crucial second air strike. Two days later, Kennedy and the first lady attended a tumultuous mass rally at the Orange Bowl in Miami, and the president, as if to make amends, waded into the men of the brigade, shaking hands and exchanging greetings. Some members of the White House press corps told Haynes Johnson, as he wrote, "they had never seen the President act so informally and with such enthusiasm." Kennedy's speech was exuberant. "I can assure you," he said, amidst flag waving and cheering, "that it is the strongest wish of the people of this country, as well as the people of this hemisphere, that Cuba shall one day be free again, and when it is, this brigade will deserve to march at the head of the free column." Those words were as heartfelt as any the president uttered while in office.

Bill Harvey's replacement as head of Task Force W was Desmond FitzGerald, a CIA veteran who had made his reputation in the late 1950s as a clandestine operator in the Far East. FitzGerald was everything Harvey was not: a New York socialite who went to all the right schools and belonged to all the right clubs. His first wife was Marietta Tree, the granddaughter of Endicott Peabody, the very proper rector of Groton. He had a house in Georgetown and a country place among the horsey set in The Plains, Virginia, where the first lady often rode. He also had the dashing good looks and athletic mien, as did Max Taylor and Ed Lansdale, that attracted the Kennedy brothers; many in the CIA thought, incorrectly, that FitzGerald was a distant relative of the Kennedys.

FitzGerald, who died in 1967, was eager to do what the president and his brother wanted, to get rid of what he thought was the bad taste left by the truculent Harvey. In *The Very Best Men,* published in 1995, FitzGerald's biographer, Evan Thomas, quoted a letter FitzGerald wrote to his daughter, the writer Frances FitzGerald, explaining that "my first job was to convince the Administration that anyone from my firm dealing with the Cuban situation is not necessarily a Yahoo bent on disaster." His goal, he added, was "to make the Agency's operations acceptable as respectable, which they obviously haven't been since the Bay of Pigs."

FitzGerald's problem was Bobby Kennedy. Frances FitzGerald told Evan Thomas that her father initially thought the attorney general was "a young punk." However, Barbara Lawrence, Desmond FitzGerald's stepdaughter, told Thomas that FitzGerald "was scared of Bobby's power. He felt threatened by him. He felt Bobby was just there because he was the president's brother. He thought he was an amateur, and he didn't really like him." FitzGerald, asked in early 1963 by an old colleague whether he was having fun as Harvey's replacement, responded, wrote Thomas, "All I know is that I have to hate Castro."

Under FitzGerald's supervision the CIA began providing funds, arms, and intelligence in 1963 to rabidly anti-Castro exile groups, operating on their own — not under the control of the large CIA station in Miami. The activities of the rogue exile groups were publicly condemned at the time by the Cuban and the Soviet governments, and the Kennedy administration repeatedly denied any involvement with them. The full story of the direct role of the CIA and Bobby Kennedy in support of the ad hoc raids has remained untold until this book.

The CIA's concept, Sam Halpern told me, was "to let the exiles go on their own and give them money for arms and ammunition. We did it under Des [FitzGerald]." Knowledge of the support activity was limited to a very few in the government, Halpern said: "Only one guy was working on it, who had good Spanish, and he reported to Des. Des reported to Bobby."

The White House was explicitly warned, Halpern told me, that "we couldn't control them and they might not hit what we wanted them to hit. We were fighting an undeclared war and people were dying on both sides." There were at least twenty-five exile deaths among the groups fighting in Cuba in 1963, Halpern told me, with many more deaths among Cuban civilians as well as soldiers battling the rogue attackers. The agency did more than merely supply the funds for weapons, Halpern said. "We told them where to buy arms, so they wouldn't get rooked." The weapons were usually bought from foreign arms dealers. The CIA also provided the exile groups with intelligence support, Halpern said, on the rare occasions when the groups "told us what they were doing" in advance.

A major problem, Halpern said, was Bobby Kennedy's penchant for getting involved directly in what was considered to be the CIA's business. One of the groups was led by newly liberated Manuel Artime, the fanatical founder of Brigade 2506, who had been jailed for eight months by Castro in 1959 for opposing the revolution. Artime's escape led him to the Bay of Pigs and more time in jail. In newspaper interviews before his death in 1977, Artime claimed that in 1963 he met repeatedly with Bobby Kennedy at his office and at his home at Hickory Hill, as he and his men were staging violent and seemingly independent hit-and-run attacks on targets through-out Cuba.*

Evan Thomas, in his biography, described FitzGerald's rage upon learning that Bobby Kennedy had been privately socializing with Cuban exile leaders, presumably including Artime, at suburban Hickory Hill, and also meeting with them in a Washington hotel, where they were guests of the CIA. Ad hoc exile operations were being agreed to in advance with the attorney general, undermining the basic purpose of the rogue missions — to isolate the U.S. government from any possible link to the exiles' indiscriminate strikes in Cuba. One of FitzGerald's nephews, Albert Francke, told Thomas of overhearing his uncle on a Sunday afternoon in 1963 telling Bobby Kennedy, firmly and loudly, on the telephone, "No, Bobby, we can't do that. We cannot do that." When FitzGerald, face red, emerged from his study, Francke asked him what was going on. "Oh, nothing," the CIA man said. What was going on, Sam Halpern explained in one of his interviews for this book, was clear. The Cuban exiles "were getting different orders from Bobby. We never knew what was going on."

FitzGerald, with his desire to please, was in an untenable position, Halpern told me: "He was working his heart out to try and do what they wanted, and it couldn't work." In a letter to his daughter, Frances, cited in the Thomas biography, FitzGerald expressed dismay at his situation: "I have dealt with a fairly rich assortment of exiles in the past, but none can compare with the Cuban group for genuine stupidity and militant childishness. At times I feel sorry for Castro — a sculptor in silly putty."

By mid-1963, with the rogue exile groups becoming increasingly active, the president and his brother were directing a two-track operation. The CIA was still being asked to plan and mount propaganda and sabotage operations against the Castro regime, using CIA-paid operatives under the control of the Miami station, while the real campaign

---

* Robert Kennedy's Justice Department office diaries for 1963 have not been located by the Kennedy Library. In its finding aid for researchers, the library reports: "The desk diaries for 1963 are not in the custody of the Kennedy Library. Their whereabouts are unknown to the library staff."

was being run, with little paperwork and some unwanted help from Bobby Kennedy, out of FitzGerald's back pocket. There was no national security reason for keeping up the pressure and supporting the fighting, as even the president acknowledged — privately. In *Conversations with Kennedy,* Ben Bradlee related how Kennedy explained, after a private dinner in February 1963, that

> the presence of 17,000 Soviet troops in Cuba . . . was one thing viewed by itself, but it was something else again when you knew there were 27,000 U.S. troops stationed in Turkey, right on the Soviet border, and they had been there some years. He warned me against releasing this information. Obviously, it is classified, and just as obviously it would be politically suicidal for him publicly to equate the two. "It isn't wise politically, to understand Khrushchev's problems in quite this way," he said, quietly.

The Kennedys' support for the concept of the ad hoc exile raids was telegraphed at a bizarre final meeting of the Ex Comm on March 29, 1963, in which Jack Kennedy, just as during the missile crisis, did not speak candidly to the men who were supposedly his most trusted advisers. Declassified notes, prepared by Bromley Smith of the National Security Council and published in 1996 by the State Department, show that the president began the meeting by announcing that he wanted the group to "talk about" a recent series of hit-and-run raids staged by Cuban exiles. Two days earlier, an exile raiding team had severely damaged a Soviet vessel at anchor in a Cuban harbor, provoking an official protest from Moscow.

There was an immediate consensus among the Ex Comm members, who included Secretary of State Rusk, that the United States should do all it could to stop the exile raids. "If anyone is shooting Russians," Rusk was quoted as saying, "we ought to be doing it. Not Cubans who are acting beyond our control." The Kennedy brothers, who knew better than anyone else that the exiles in question had likely been "shooting at the Russians" with the secret support of U.S. intelligence and arms, seemed almost to be enjoying the discussion. The official notes of the meeting paraphrased the president's comment that "these in-and-out raids were probably exciting and rather pleasant for those who engage in them. They were in danger for less than an hour. This exciting activity was more fun than living in the hills pursued by Castro's military forces." Even Robert McNamara, one of the president's closest confidants, seemed to be out of the loop. He pointed out that the administration could "stop the raiders if we use the Navy. If we don't want to stop the raids," the secretary of defense shrewdly added, "we can modify them, making it difficult for the raiders to attack targets not of our choosing." The president then suggested, said the notes, "that we first tell the British and then, on a background basis, tell the press that the raiders are staging out of the Bahama Islands." Washington reporters, the president clearly believed, would print anything his White House told them.

Kennedy eventually got around to the serious issue underlying American support for the ad hoc raids: the exiles were creating unneeded tensions in the U.S.-Soviet relationship. The president seemed not fully to understand, as did his brother, the extent to which some exile groups were out of control. They were being given intelligence, weapons, and money by the CIA — but not instructions. JFK "suggested," nonetheless, the notes showed, "that we tell the raiders that they must not attack Soviet ships — but could attack purely Cuban targets." The whole point of financing and supplying some of the more extreme exile groups, as no one at the meeting said, was their lack of control — and their ability to hurt Castro in ways that, so the CIA believed, had always gratified the president and his brother. The president made it clear that he wanted continued guerrilla action against Cuba, telling the Ex Comm that he wanted to "handle this problem [restraining the exile raiders] in such a way as to avoid the appearance of prosecuting Cuban patriots." Smith's notes of the meeting end with Kennedy's suggestion that the group meet the next day to discuss its recommendations. State Department historians reported in 1996 that they were unable to locate any record of the next day's meeting, if one did take place. Ex Comm's role in the Kennedy administration was over: it never met again.

In June 1963 Jack Kennedy, fully aware of all the negatives involved, formally approved the CIA's covert support for the ad hoc raids: the hit-and-run exile teams were blandly depicted in CIA working papers, according to declassified documents, as the "autonomous groups."

By early spring 1963, Operation Mongoose was out of business, Bill Harvey was drinking his martinis and taking his naps in Rome, and Desmond FitzGerald's Task Force W had been renamed the Special Activities Staff (SAS). Johnny Rosselli and his Mafia colleagues were no longer involved in assassination plotting; Rosselli's role ended when Bill Harvey, his CIA handler, left. But the Kennedy brothers still wanted Castro dead. That job, too, fell to the ill-equipped FitzGerald. Two of FitzGerald's assassination schemes were made public by the Church Committee in its 1975 report. Castro was known to enjoy skin diving, and, Halpern told the committee, "Mr. FitzGerald came in the office one morning with a book on seashells. I asked him why the seashells and he said he thought . . . if we can develop an exotic-looking shell, Castro . . . might go for a shell which might be rigged up to explode. I thought the idea had no merit and said so. Despite that," Halpern testified, "he asked me to check it out with our technical people. . . . As far as I know, nothing ever came of it." The second scheme, equally dubious, called for a contaminated diving suit to be manufactured and somehow given to Castro as a gift. The agency bought a diving suit and began experimenting with it, but the suit apparently never left the laboratory.

Halpern, in one of his interviews for this book, expressed sympathy for his former boss. "He was trying to be a good soldier," he said. FitzGerald would soldier on, even after Jack Kennedy's death, in his effort to assassinate Fidel Castro.

On June 10, 1963, with the world increasingly concerned over fallout from nuclear weapons tests, Kennedy gave what historians consider to be the best speech of his presidency, telling a commencement audience at American University in Washington that the time had come for Americans to reconsider their views about the Soviet Union and the Cold War. It was a speech unlike any he had given before, with no threats and no promises of instant retaliation. "Most Americans felt he had proven his mettle by facing down the Russians over Cuba," Michael Beschloss noted in *The Crisis Years,* his study of the Kennedy-Khrushchev relationship. "Now he could advocate better relations without fear of being branded 'a weak sister'"— or, as Kennedy might have put it, an Adlai Stevenson.

In the speech, Kennedy called for world peace and asked, "What kind of peace do I mean? . . . Not a Pax Americana enforced on the world by American weapons of war. Not the peace of the grave or the security of the slave. I am talking about genuine peace, the kind of peace that makes life on earth worth living, the kind that enables men and nations to grow and to hope and to build a better life for their children — not merely peace for Americans but peace for all men and women — not merely peace in our time but peace for all time."

The president treated the Soviet Union as a superpower of equal status and bearing. The leaders in Washington and Moscow, Kennedy said, have "a mutually deep interest in a just and genuine peace and in halting the arms race. . . . If we cannot now end our differences, at least we can help make the world safe for diversity. For, in the final analysis, our most basic common link is that we all inhabit this small planet. We all breathe the same air. We all cherish our children's future. And we are all mortal."

"Among the many traits the peoples of our two countries have in common," Kennedy said, "none is stronger than our mutual abhorrence of war. Almost unique among major powers, we have never been at war with each other. . . . We are not here distributing blame or pointing the finger of judgment. We must deal with the world as it is, and not as it might have been had the history of the last eighteen years been different." Those conciliatory words echoed around the world.

Other sections of the speech perhaps had a special meaning for the president, given what really took place during the missile crisis. "Above all," he said, "while defending our own vital interests, nuclear powers must avert those confrontations which bring an adversary to a choice of either a humiliating retreat or a nuclear war. To adopt that kind of course in the nuclear age would be evidence only of the bankruptcy of our policy — or of a collective death wish for the world. . . . We can seek a relaxation of tensions without relaxing our guard. And, for our part, we do not need to use threats to prove that we are resolute."

Nikita Khrushchev told Averell Harriman, the president's special emissary in Moscow for ongoing test ban talks, that it was "the best speech by any president since Roosevelt." Within two months the Soviet Union ended two years of haggling over on-site inspections and other issues of verification, by signing a treaty with the Kennedy administration that banned the testing of nuclear weapons in the atmosphere and underwater. The nuclear weapons of the future could now only be tested underground.

Did the president's passionate speech indicate that he had learned from his manipulation and lies about the missile crisis? The evidence is that it did not. The nation was terrorized in the summer of 1963 by fear of strontium 90 — radioactive fallout from American and Soviet nuclear tests, which was found at heightened levels in cow's milk and human bone structure. A partial test ban treaty was good politics. Michael Beschloss concluded in *The Crisis Years* that the speech "was as much the product of political calculation as any address Kennedy ever gave. It was designed to build public support for the test ban treaty he hoped to achieve, to mollify Khrushchev, . . . and overcome any Soviet skepticism that he was willing to jeopardize his domestic position in order to push a controversial agreement through the Senate."

Khrushchev had his political needs, too. The Soviet economy was stagnant, and Khrushchev believed some respite from the extravagant cost of the nuclear arms race was essential in order to meet the growing demand for consumer goods. The premier was also facing a series of difficult meetings in Moscow in June with the leaders of the Chinese Communist Party, who were vitriolic in denouncing his retreat in the Cuban missile crisis.

Pushing for the test ban was not all politics for Kennedy. He had a carefully conceived strategic agenda reaching back to his days in the Senate: he was convinced that a test ban treaty would freeze the huge American advantage over the Soviet Union in weapons research and deployment. A treaty would also prevent the spread of the bomb to nations that he viewed as especially dangerous — most notably Communist China. What Kennedy knew in 1963, and Nikita Khrushchev did not, was the extent to which the Pentagon's nuclear scientists were prepared to continue their work underground. The test ban treaty would not slow the arms race.

It became clear during Senate ratification hearings on the treaty that Kennedy was willing to bargain to get what he wanted. He

assured the skeptical members of the Joint Chiefs of Staff that in
return for their endorsement of the test ban they could significantly
increase underground nuclear weapons testing and development.
The funds budgeted for such weapons development increased
steadily over the next few years, and so did the sophistication of the
research. By 1968 the Pentagon's weapons manufacturers began to
conduct underground tests of nuclear warheads in the megaton
range — fifty times greater than the weapons detonated at
Hiroshima and Nagasaki. A new generation of offensive weapon, the
multiple independently targeted reentry vehicle, or MIRV, was successfully developed in underground testing by the late 1960s. A MIRV
is a hydra-headed missile that can thrust as many as fourteen nuclear
warheads into outer space, where, with the aid of complex electronics, each warhead can reenter the atmosphere and strike a target with
precision. MIRV was not just an improved weapon but a qualitative
leap forward in the ability to wage nuclear war. The antiballistic missile defense system (ABM) was also successfully tested and developed
by the late 1960s in underground testing.

Despite Kennedy's stirring words at American University, during
Senate hearings on the test ban treaty in the summer of 1963 there
was no talk of the recklessness and wastefulness of an uncontrolled
arms race. The test ban treaty was described to senators hostile to
arms control not as a victory against the arms race but as a victory in
it. In his memoir *Kennedy*, Ted Sorensen, who wrote the first draft of
the American University speech, recalled that Kennedy's essential
skepticism was not about Senate ratification, but about obtaining
Moscow's acceptance of the treaty. "Inasmuch as even a limited test-
ban treaty required a Soviet acceptance of a *permanent American
superiority* in nuclear weapons [emphasis added]," Sorensen wrote,
"[Kennedy] refused to count too heavily on the success" of negotiations with Moscow.

Khrushchev would immediately have broken off the test ban talks
had he been able to anticipate Robert McNamara's testimony to the
Senate Foreign Relations Committee in support of the treaty. On
August 13, 1963 — eight days after the Soviets signed the treaty —
McNamara, wary of criticism from the right, outlined an exponential
increase in the arms race. America would triple its fleet of ICBMs,

from 500 to 1,700, by 1966. This new push would also triple the total of available submarine-launched missiles by the same year. As for America's missile defense system, McNamara told the Senate that the ABM warhead designs "we now have or can develop through underground testing will provide a high probability of killing Soviet warheads even if [the Soviet warheads] incorporate advanced technology far beyond what now exists." The journalist I. F. Stone, in a 1970 essay on the test ban treaty for the *New York Review of Books,* caustically wrote that when McNamara's testimony was read in Moscow, Khrushchev's opposition within the Kremlin — which had steadily grown since the missile crisis —"must have felt Khrushchev had lost his mind in believing that the treaty was a step toward lightening the burden and danger of the arms race."

Khrushchev, perhaps as much dazzled by Jack Kennedy as the reporters who covered him and the aides who worked in the White House, was ousted as premier and stripped of all his government and party posts in October 1964.

22

ELLEN

Jack Kennedy's luck began running out in the fall of 1963, well before November 22. He was confronted with a no-win situation in South Vietnam, where President Ngo Dinh Diem, the despot he had armed and supported, was increasingly taking the war to his political opponents instead of the communist-backed armed opposition. There was a crisis at home, too, as had been foreseen by Larry Newman and Tony Sherman of the Secret Service — one of the president's pool-party women turned out to be an East German. That fact was uncovered not by Kennedy or an aide but by a group of Republican senators investigating a graft-and-sex scandal on Capitol Hill. The president's womanizing was on the verge of being exposed as a national security issue.

The woman's name was Ellen Rometsch. She was a Washington party girl with a quality that made her a natural for Jack Kennedy: she was stunningly attractive, an Elizabeth Taylor look-alike. That was all that mattered in late spring of 1963. The president did not know that Rometsch was born in 1936 in Kleinitz, Germany, a village that became part of East Germany after World War II. He did not know that, as a child growing up in Kleinitz, Rometsch was a member of a Communist Party youth group and that, as a young adult, she joined a second Communist Party group. He did not know that she fled with her family to West Germany in 1955 and, after a failed first marriage, moved in 1961 to the United States with her second husband, a sergeant in the West German air force who was assigned to the German Embassy in Washington. Kennedy also did not seem to realize — or care — that if his sexual relationship with Ellen Rometsch somehow became known, she would be thought by many to be a communist spy.

Rometsch, twenty-seven when they met, fulfilled another essential criterion for the president: she was a professional, a prostitute who would take her money, do what was wanted, and keep silent. Kennedy stumbled upon Rometsch in the usual way, through one of his many procurers in Washington, this time Bill Thompson, the railroad executive.

Rometsch had become one of Bobby Baker's girls by early 1963, and she spent many evenings with Baker and his friends at the Quorum Club, a private hideaway for legislators and lobbyists on Capitol Hill. Baker, the secretary to the Senate Democrats, was known as the man who made the legislative process work. He was a parliamentary expert and brilliant vote counter. He was also the man who did what the Democratic senators needed done, and discreetly got them what they wanted, including women.

Baker arrived in Washington from Pickens, South Carolina, as a fourteen-year-old congressional page in 1943 and rose through the ranks with his mentor, Lyndon Johnson, of Texas. He became, as he put it in his memoir, *Wheeling and Dealing,* "a Capitol Hill operator" who in mid-1963 was accused of influence peddling — taking payoffs in return for steering federal contracts to his friends in business. Baker resigned from the Senate, under pressure, on October 7; he was being investigated by the Justice Department and also the Senate Rules Committee, whose Republican minority was eager to turn the case into an issue in the 1964 presidential campaign. Baker eventually served eighteen months in a federal penitentiary after being convicted on nine counts of fraud and tax evasion.

None of that had yet happened when Baker was approached one evening in the spring of 1963 by Bill Thompson in the Quorum Club, and asked, Baker recalled in an interview for this book, a typical question: "'Baker,' he said, 'who is that good-looking girl? That woman looks like Elizabeth Taylor.' And I said, 'She's a German, and her husband is a sergeant who works for the German Embassy. And she's a real pro as far as I'm concerned. I mean, everybody who has had a date with her has really enjoyed her company.'

"So he said, 'Bakes, do you think that if I invited her to the White House that she would go with me to meet President Kennedy?' I said, 'Gee, she's a Nazi. She'll do anything I tell her.' And so I asked her, and she said she would be delighted." It was arranged, Baker told me, for Thompson to pick Rometsch up at her apartment in northwest Washington and take her to the White House. Rometsch later told Baker, he told me, that "the president was really a fun guy and how delighted she was to be with him." When he next went to the White House, Baker added, "the president told me that she was the most exciting woman that he had been with."

Rometsch was very much in demand that spring. "She was a very lovely, beautiful party girl . . . who always wore beautiful clothes," Baker told me. "She had good manners and she was very accommodating. I must have had fifty friends who went with her, and not one of them ever complained. She was a real joy to be with."

Kennedy knew, Baker said, that Rometsch was there to service him and would have to be paid: "President Kennedy did not want a date with somebody for social purposes. It was clearly understood when [Thompson] took girls to the White House they were going to be party girls." Baker said he had first supplied women to Kennedy "in my official position in the Senate. When a good-looking girl would send a card in to Senator Kennedy, the doorman would come to me and say, 'Mr. Baker, what shall I do?'" It happened all the time, Baker said. Once, he recalled with a laugh, a woman sent a note to Kennedy saying, "Senator, you can put your shoes under my bed any time you want."

"A lot of celebrities are chased by beautiful people," Baker said, and Jack Kennedy "loved it." Baker told of one meeting early in the presidency when he was invited to the Oval Office to meet with Kennedy. "He really didn't want to talk about the Senate," Baker told me. "He just said, 'You know, I get a migraine headache if I don't get a strange piece of ass every day.'"

Over the next few months, Ellen Rometsch helped Kennedy ward off headaches. And she gossiped to Baker about it. She described pool parties in the White House, Baker told me, where "everybody's running around there naked." There was one occasion, Baker told me, without naming his source, "when Jackie came home and Bill Thompson had all these people" in the pool.* On May 18, 1963, Baker said, Rometsch joined a group of legislators and friends on a bus outing to the Preakness, the annual stakes race at the Pimlico Race Course, near Baltimore. "We were talking because we were seatmates," Baker told me, "and she had gone to the White House two nights before for a naked party in the swimming pool. I think there was like five guys and twelve girls in the White House indoor pool." In all, Baker estimated, Rometsch visited Kennedy at least ten times that spring and summer.

Those visits eventually triggered what became a nightmare for the hard-to-rattle president — the one scandal, had he lived, that he and Bobby Kennedy might not have been able to continue to cover up.

In June the Harold Macmillan government was rocked by a sex scandal that led to the resignation of John Profumo, the British minister of war, after he admitted that he had lied to the House of Commons. The Profumo scandal, as it was quickly dubbed by London's tabloid press, revolved around a prostitute named Christine Keeler, who was having simultaneous affairs with Profumo and Yevgeny Ivanov, a Soviet naval attaché. The story was made poignant by the fact that Profumo had an unblemished record: he had served valiantly as a brigadier general in World War II and was married to Valerie Hobson, a prominent English actress who had just played the

---

* The first lady did her best, apparently, to avoid such surprises. Gerry McCabe was assigned as a presidential navy aide in 1963 to the communications room in the basement of the White House, where the government's most sensitive dispatches arrived. Jacqueline Kennedy, when on vacations in Europe or elsewhere, always wired the president in advance of her return, McCabe told me in a 1995 interview for this book, pointedly saying on one occasion that she was "coming back a day earlier than planned." The young navy officer said he and everyone else in the communications room understood the first lady's real message: "You'd better get your friends out of the White House."

lead role in *The King and I*. There were fears, the press breathlessly reported, that Profumo, while cavorting poolside with Keeler and at least four other prostitutes, including a Chinese beauty named Suzy Chang and a bleached-blond Czech named Maria Novotny, was spending his weekends answering the girls' questions — planted by Ivanov — about British nuclear policy. The significance of Profumo's national security transgressions, if there were any, paled beside the overwhelming appearance of his impropriety. The fact that a married senior defense official was frolicking with prostitutes proved lethal to Macmillan's leadership. He resigned in October, and a badly tarnished Tory government was voted out of office in 1964.

The president, needless to say, was fascinated by the scandal. "Kennedy had devoured every word written about the Profumo case," Ben Bradlee reported in *Conversations with Kennedy*. "It combined so many of the things that interested him: low doings in high places, the British nobility, sex, and spying. Someone in the State Department had apparently sent him an early cable on the Profumo case from David Bruce, the American ambassador to Great Britain. Kennedy . . . ordered all further cables from Bruce on that subject sent to him immediately."

The president's interest was far from academic. Maria Novotny and Suzy Chang worked as high-class prostitutes in New York as well as London, and, as Novotny would tell reporters later, she and Chang had serviced Jack Kennedy before and after the 1960 presidential election. As a senator, Kennedy had taken Suzy Chang to dinner at 21, the very public New York restaurant. He, too, with a wife as lovely as Profumo's, could be drawn into the scandal.

Once again the president turned to his brother, who took action within days of the first published newspaper reports on Profumo's pending resignation, in early June of 1963. On June 11, the day after Kennedy's speech at American University calling for a "just and genuine peace" with the Soviet Union, Charles Bates, the FBI's legal attaché in London, was cabled by J. Edgar Hoover and ordered to "stay on top of this case and . . . keep bureau fully and promptly informed of all developments with particular emphasis on any allegation that U.S. nationals are or have been involved in any way." A heavily censored copy of Hoover's cable was declassified in 1986.

The same demand was forwarded by Director John McCone to the CIA station in London. "When the business broke about Profumo," Cleveland Cram, the deputy chief of station, said in a 1997 interview for this book, "we suddenly got an 'Operation Immediate' from John McCone" asking the station to determine whether any Americans were involved. Cram and Charles Bates, the senior FBI man in London, "gossiped together a lot, as you can imagine," Cram told me, "and we immediately assumed it had something to do with the Kennedys." The CIA officer was ordered to make contact with Sir Roger Hollis, the director general of Britain's MI5, and explain that he needed full cooperation. To Cram's surprise, he got it. Cram spent the next "three or four" weeks at MI5 headquarters, poring over the Profumo files. "It was like getting access to a spider's web," Cram told me. "It was a lot of fun." He also got a glimpse into MI5's ability to pry — learning, for example, that one of his neighbors was a secret informer for MI5.

He had "no question" at the time what the unusual assignment was all about, Cram told me: to learn whether "one of the Kennedys" was dealing with the Profumo girls. "They wanted to be forewarned if [the American names] became public, and forewarned is forearmed." Charles Bates informed him, Cram said, that he had checked with FBI colleagues in Washington and learned that his order from Hoover originated at the White House. Cram said he snooped around, too, and learned that he was sent to MI5 to look for American involvement because of a "specific request from [President] Kennedy.

"That's, you know, pretty electrical," Cram added. When he did not immediately report to CIA headquarters on his findings from the MI5 files, he said, "we got a blast from McCone. 'What are you guys doing? Get busy and find something. Aren't the British cooperating?' We had to write back and say, 'Yes, they're cooperating one hundred percent, but we just haven't turned up anything.' They kept niggling at us every other day. It was terrible. We had never received a request like this before and, to my knowledge, we never received a similar one afterward."

Cram said that he found nothing in his research indicating that any high-level Americans were involved in the British scandal. Nor did he find any evidence that the Profumo-Keeler relationship posed a serious national security threat to Britain. Christine Keeler did ask Profumo questions, Cram said, "like, 'Are you going to move nuclear warheads in Germany?' and things like that. I doubt that he answered anything." The scandal resulted from the mere fact that Ivanov was working for Soviet intelligence. "He was, through this source, Miss Keeler, in touch actually with John Profumo," Cram said. "It was a very important case for MI5, I can tell you. They had this woman who was sleeping with John Profumo and was also sleeping with Ivanov."

On June 23 Kennedy arrived in Bonn to begin his first trip to Europe since the Vienna summit, and on June 26 he got his first look at the Berlin Wall. His speech was a triumph; a million people jammed a plaza, now named after Kennedy, and broke into prolonged and emotional cheering when the president said in German, *"Ich bin ein Berliner."* It was one of the memorable scenes of his presidency. "There are many people in the world who really don't understand, or say they don't, what is the great issue between the free world and the communist world," Kennedy said. He paused a beat, then said, *"Lassen sie nach Berlin kommen!"* ("Let them come to Berlin!")*

The presidential entourage went on to Ireland, where Kennedy, greeted everywhere like a rock star, spent a few days paying homage to his family roots. On Saturday, June 29, Kennedy flew to England for a lonely dinner with the battered Harold Macmillan. England was the last place Kennedy wanted to be during the Profumo scandal, and his closest ally among the European leaders, whose government was on the run, was the last person he wanted to spend time with. The British Foreign Office had been told earlier that the president, after

---

* Kennedy's ringingly defiant Cold War speech in West Berlin, which came less than three weeks after the American University speech, did not faze Khrushchev. In *The Crisis Years,* Beschloss quoted the Soviet premier as responding, "If one reads what he said in West Germany, and especially in West Berlin, and compares this with the speech at the American University, one would think the speeches were made by two different presidents." Khrushchev added that the American president was wasting his time "courting the old West German widow."

spending three days touring in Ireland, would visit England for only one. The British were further told that Kennedy wished to visit the prime minister at his country home in Surrey, and not in the more public London.*

While Kennedy faced a gloomy Saturday-night meal with Macmillan, Bobby Kennedy was facing his own gloom: the result of a copyrighted story in the *New York Journal-American,* part of the Hearst chain, linking "a man who holds a 'very high' elective office" in the Kennedy administration to "a Chinese girl" in the Profumo scandal. The article, published Saturday afternoon, was written by two solid investigative reporters, James D. Horan and Dom Frasca, and splashed on page one under a three-line headline that said: "High U.S. Aide Implicated in V-Girl Scandal." It quoted Maria Novotny as saying that a Chinese-American woman — identified by Horan and Frasca as Suzy Chang — was the "former paramour of the American government official."

The story was pulled after one edition. Horan and Frasca both died in the 1980s. Before his death, Horan told his sons, Brian and Gary, that Bobby Kennedy had done everything possible to yank the story. "Bobby was putting the arm on Dad and saying this isn't going to happen," Brian Horan told me in a 1997 interview for this book. "It went up to Bill Hearst and it was spiked." Hearst, son of William Randolph Hearst, was chairman and director of the Hearst Corporation, publishers of the *Journal-American.*†

That afternoon, the attorney general telephoned Warren Rogers, a trusted reporter who was a Washington correspondent for *Look* mag-

---

* Kenny O'Donnell and Dave Powers were scheduled to stay with the president at Macmillan's country home, but slipped away to join a press party at Brighton with the crew of *Air Force One.* Kennedy telephoned O'Donnell just as he checked into his hotel, O'Donnell wrote in *"Johnny, We Hardly Knew Ye,"* and complained: "Thanks for leaving me stranded. I suppose you've been cooking up this little party for a week or more. Who's there? What's going on? I suppose you've got a big drink in your hand."

† The Kennedys had enormous, and hard-earned, clout with the Hearst family by 1963. In January 1962 a few of the young attorneys in the Justice Department antitrust division began agitating for a possible investigation into the simultaneous suspension of publication earlier in the month of the unprofitable *Los Angeles Mirror,* an afternoon newspaper owned by the Otis Chandler family, publishers of the flagship *Los Angeles Times,* and what was said to be the equally unprofitable *Los Angeles Examiner,*

azine, and urged him to call anyone he knew at the *Journal-American* to get the name of the unidentified American official in the Horan-Frasca article. Kennedy's plea for help was memorable, Rogers said in a 1997 interview for this book, because he and his wife were having a backyard party that afternoon. "My guests never saw me," Rogers told me. "Bob [Kennedy] was persistent, and I kept getting called to the telephone." As usual, "there was no chitchat," Rogers said. "Bob was all business. He asked me if I'd seen the story. I had not. He wanted to know who it was." Rogers had no luck; the one senior editor he knew at the *Journal-American* would not say.

Jack Kennedy carried on as usual, while his brother struggled to keep the lid on at home. The last stop was Italy, where the president was to meet with government leaders and the newly elected Pope, Paul VI. The president had worked hard to arrange a long-planned

a morning newspaper owned by the Hearst empire. The chains would each retain a monopoly in, respectively, the morning and afternoon daily newspaper market in the Los Angeles area. The Justice Department lawyers quickly scheduled a meeting with their boss, Lee Loevinger, the assistant attorney general in charge of the antitrust division. "We took it to Loevinger," George Miron, one of the attorneys, recalled in a 1996 interview for this book, "and he said, 'Oh yeah, I know about it.' It stunned us. He said, 'There was a guy who came to see me and told me about it.'"

The "guy" turned out to be James McInerney, who since the early 1950s had handled personal and legal problems for Joe Kennedy and his sons — Florence Kater among them (see Chapter Eight). McInerney, a former assistant attorney general who had no experience in newspaper issues, had nonetheless been retained by the Hearst Corporation as its Washington adviser for the closure. Otis Chandler also relied on McInerney. Miron and his colleagues quickly summoned McInerney to a meeting; he told them that he had discussed the closing of the two newspapers with Bobby Kennedy, who gave his oral blessing. Kennedy's action precluded any significant criminal investigation into possible collusion. If the attorney general had investigated, a subsequent congressional hearing showed, he would have discovered that the *Examiner* was in the black in the early 1960s; the Hearst Corporation was shutting down a profitable newspaper to get an afternoon monopoly in Los Angeles. "We were a bunch of punks who didn't like to be pushed around," Miron told me, "so we pressured Loevinger to try and open an investigation — not a criminal investigation," but a civil inquiry into what clearly seemed to be a prearranged decision to shut down the two newspapers at the same time. The civil investigation did not happen, Miron said, and he and his colleagues "were not considered team players," because of their persistence. McInerney's brilliant lobbying became a focal point of a 1963 hearing by the House Subcommittee on Antitrust and Monopoly; the hearing record, not printed until 1968, for reasons that are still not clear, included evidence of the profitability of the *Examiner* in the years before it was closed.

dalliance at Lake Como with Marella Agnelli, the wife of Gianni Agnelli, a prominent Italian businessman. He had been forced to ask Dean Rusk, not one of his usual go-betweens, to arrange the perfect hideaway. Years later, Rusk described the painful incident to Pat Holt, a senior staff member of the Senate Foreign Relations Committee. While planning the trip, Holt told me in a 1994 interview for this book, "Jack said to Rusk, 'Mr. Secretary'— he never called him anything else —'can you find a place that's sort of quiet and restful where we could stop on the way home?'" Rusk was conflicted about recommending a villa at Lake Como that was owned by the Rockefeller Foundation. As a former president of the foundation, Rusk knew that there were long-standing rules against the use of its facilities by public figures. "Nonetheless," Holt recounted, "they made it available, and Rusk was looking forward to it. He hadn't been in office very long and he hoped to spend a day or two with the president, letting his hair down. The plane stops in Milan and Rusk is thinking they're going to Lake Como. Instead, the president says, 'Thank you, Mr. Secretary, for arranging this. I'll see you back in Washington.' And he goes off."*

On Monday, with his brother still in Italy, Bobby Kennedy summoned Horan and Frasca to the Justice Department. A summary of the meeting, written by Courtney Evans, the FBI liaison officer to the attorney general, emphasized the reluctance of the two reporters "to volunteer information." Kennedy was forced to ask for the name of the American official. "It was the President of the United States," Frasca told the attorney general, according to Evans's memorandum, made public under the Freedom of Information Act. The two journalists added, under questioning, that the source of their information was a conversation on June 28 between Frasca and a London journalist named Peter Earle of *News of the World,* a popular tabloid. *News of the World* had earlier signed a contract with Novotny for her story of the Profumo affair, and Earle had been assigned by his newspaper to write it for her. Novotny listened in on an extension telephone as Frasca and Earle talked, the Evans memorandum said, and

---

* In their memoir, Kenny O'Donnell and Dave Powers described the president's retreat in bucolic terms: "We arranged for him to land at Milan and to spend the rest of the day at Lake Como, killing some time and getting a bit of relaxation before going on to Rome on Monday."

spoke "very briefly." Most of the information came from Peter Earle, Evans wrote. Frasca and Horan had tape-recorded the conversation, Evans added. Kennedy asked the journalists, Evans wrote, if they had written a story involving the president of the United States "without any further check being made to get to the truth of the matter." At that point, Evans reported, "Frasca contended that he had other sources of a confidential nature."

The meeting must have been very difficult for Robert Kennedy. Initially he asked Evans not to put anything in writing, but he changed his mind after learning that Evans later discussed the meeting with J. Edgar Hoover. In a note to Hoover two days later, July 3, made public under the Freedom of Information Act, Evans tried to put the best light on Kennedy's initial request for silence by reporting that the attorney general, upon learning that Hoover had been told of the meeting, "was glad that this had been done and . . . he hoped I had not misunderstood his earlier admonition not to write a memorandum. He just wanted to be assured that you had been informed." Evans further noted that Kennedy "treated the newspaper representatives at arms' length and the conference ended most coolly and, in fact, there was almost an air of hostility between the Attorney General and the reporters."

Horan, discussing the meeting with his sons years later, recalled the attorney general's intensity. "Bobby was just sitting there, looking at him," Gary Horan said in a 1997 interview. "'I'll never forget those steel blue eyes,' [Dad] said."

The one-edition Horan and Frasca story slipped quickly into obscurity. Over the next few weeks, with prodding from Bobby Kennedy, the FBI was able to document, according to files made available under the Freedom of Information Act, that Suzy Chang had flown from London to New York many times, allegedly to visit her ailing mother in Elizabeth, New Jersey. Now married and living under a different name on Long Island, Suzy Chang politely told me in two 1997 telephone conversations that she had nothing to say. In 1987, however, she was quoted by the journalist Anthony Summers, in *Official and Confidential,* his biography of Hoover, as admitting that she knew Jack Kennedy. "We'd meet in the 21 Club," she told Summers. "Everybody saw me eating with him. I think he was a nice guy, very charming. What else am I going to say?" Other FBI files provided to Bobby Kennedy showed that Maria Novotny, who died in the 1970s in London, had been arrested for prostitution in New York in 1961. Before her death, Novotny wrote an unpublished manuscript, made available for this book, in which she claimed to have been recruited by Peter Lawford, Kennedy's brother-in-law, to engage in group sex with Jack Kennedy a few weeks before his inauguration. She and another prostitute, Novotny said, pretended to be nurse and doctor; the president-elect was their patient.

Bobby Kennedy soon had more on his mind than the *Journal-American* and its uncooperative reporters. On July 3 Hoover informed him of yet another allegation about his brother — one involving Ellen Rometsch. Hoover reported, according to a summary written by Courtney Evans to an assistant FBI director, that a sometime bureau informant had spent time with Rometsch and been told that she was having "illicit relations with highly placed governmental officials." That phrase, Evans and Bobby Kennedy had to assume, included the president. There was an ominous new factor in Hoover's revelation, however: "Rometsch is alleged," Evans quoted Hoover as saying, "to be from East Germany and to have formerly worked for Walter Ulbricht," the communist leader of East Germany. The Profumo affair had arrived in Washington.

Bobby Kennedy quickly sought to minimize the report, telling Evans that "he was appreciative of the Director's sending this information to him on a confidential basis, and there always are allegations about prominent people that they are either homosexuals or promiscuous." But the attorney general was anything but casual about Hoover's allegation. "It was noted," Evans said in a memorandum to Hoover, "that the AG made particular note of Rometsch's name." Bobby Kennedy also expressed "his appreciation," Evans said, for the FBI's discretion in handling the matter.*

---

* Evans, now retired as a practicing attorney in Washington, remains a model of discretion. He was interviewed three times during the preparation of this book, and managed to be voluble while saying very little. Always amiable, Evans usually said he did not remember a specific incident, or did not remember handling a specific docu-

That summer, the FBI's counterintelligence division opened an investigation into Rometsch as a possible spy. "I knew the allegations," Raymond Wannell, head of FBI counterintelligence, said in a 1997 interview for this book. "I knew it was a serious matter. I didn't know if they were proved" or disproved.

The Kennedy brothers did not wait for the FBI's report. On August 21, 1963, Rometsch was abruptly deported to Germany, at the official request of the State Department. She was escorted home by LaVern Duffy, one of Bobby Kennedy's associates from his days on the Senate Rackets Committee; the two flew to Germany on a U.S. Air Force transport plane. There are no known records documenting her departure, according to the State Department. Rolf Rometsch left the country a few days later; he was granted a divorce in late September on grounds of his wife's "relations with other men."

Duffy, a lifelong bachelor who died in 1992, had been dating Rometsch for months before she was deported; he was seen having drinks with her in the summer of 1963 at the Quorum Club. It was that connection, apparently, that prompted Bobby Kennedy to ask for Duffy's help in getting Rometsch out of Washington and in keeping her quiet. There is much evidence that Rometsch and Duffy were in love. Over the next few months, Rometsch sent Duffy a series of passionate letters, expressing her deep feelings about him — and also thanking him for sending her money. One of Rometsch's letters, dated April 8, 1964, and made available for this book, urged Duffy to send her money by personal check rather than by money order. "Which way you send it is up to you," Rometsch wrote in her fractured English. "The bank is telling me that it would be more easy for them and the money would be fester in my hands if you should make up a check payable to me. you ask your Bank about it." It was not clear whether Rometsch was referring to a token gift from Duffy or a substantial transfer of funds.

In interviews for this book, Duffy's brother and one of his close

ment. Asked about Jack Kennedy's dealings with Sam Giancana and Judith Exner, he said, "The rich are different." Was Jack Kennedy vulnerable to blackmail? "I don't doubt it," Evans said. Did Jack Kennedy know about the Castro assassination plotting? "Of course." Evans also claimed not to have much recall of the Ellen Rometsch matter. "You know more about it than I do," he told me with a smile.

friends both said that Duffy gave money — lots of it — to Rometsch on behalf of the Kennedys.

Wayne A. Duffy, a retired California banker, told me that he had been close to his brother LaVern and, after his death, found Rometsch's letters to him while sorting through his personal papers. "The letters show she was getting paid," Wayne told me. "You don't send a gal out of the country and tell her to keep quiet and not pay her." Asked if the money given to Rometsch had been his brother's, Wayne Duffy said, "Absolutely not." The money that was sent, in deutsche marks, came from the Kennedys, he said. The amount, he added, in response to questioning, "could have been five thousand dollars or fifty thousand."

Wayne Duffy told me that he had always assumed that Ellen Rometsch was a spy for East Germany. "Most people thought she was for a long time," he said, adding that he had no direct knowledge of such matters. The fact is, Duffy said, "she could have" been a spy. "It would have been very easy for her to be one." He and LaVern had often discussed the Rometsch matter, Wayne Duffy said, and his brother told him of Rometsch's relationship with the president. "Obviously, [the White House] was scared because they didn't want it to become public," Duffy told me. "But everybody on the inside knew it." Duffy added that his brother had been offered a White House job by Jack Kennedy early in the administration, but turned it down to continue his investigative work in the rackets for the Senate.

Georgia Liakakis, who worked as a secretary and girl Friday for a number of Washington lobbyists and power brokers in the 1960s, including Bobby Baker, was one of LaVern Duffy's close friends in 1963. Liakakis told me in a 1997 interview for this book that "the Kennedys gave [Rometsch] a lot of money." Her source for that information, Liakakis told me, was LaVern Duffy: "He told me the Kennedys put him up to it. . . . Bobby Kennedy was pushing him to keep her away and to keep her mouth shut," Liakakis added. "They [the Kennedys] were afraid. There was a lot of money changing hands."

LaVern Duffy and Kennedy money may have combined to get Ellen Rometsch out of Washington and keep her quiet, but there was one event even a Kennedy could not control in 1963: the political demise of Bobby Baker, secretary to the Senate Democrats. In September newspapers and magazines began unraveling a seamy story of Baker's financial ties to a fast-growing vending machine company. Baker and a group of investors, it turned out, had been awarded many contracts while the new company was still being organized, and had also received instant credit from a bank controlled by Democratic senator Robert Kerr, of Oklahoma, and his family. By October the Baker scandal had turned into a newspaper tempest, and reporters were beginning to dig up dirt on a number of present and past senators — including Baker's mentor, Vice President Johnson. A Maryland insurance broker named Donald Reynolds met privately with Senator John Williams of Delaware, a Republican, and complained to him about advertising he had been forced to buy on the vice president's radio and television stations in Austin, Texas, as a condition of writing Johnson's life insurance policy. Johnson also demanded, and got, a television set and a new stereo from Reynolds as a cost of doing business. John Williams's best friend in the Senate was Carl Curtis of Nebraska, the senior Republican on the Rules Committee. As the scandal spread in the newspapers, alarming other Democrats — including senators who had received many thousands of dollars in campaign contributions through Baker — the Rules Committee announced an all-out investigation. Baker's personal life was soon thrust into the limelight, along with the mysterious goings-on at the Quorum Club. It took only days for the Republicans on the committee to find out all they needed to know about Ellen Rometsch.

The next step was inevitable. On October 26, 1963, the investigative reporter Clark Mollenhoff published a dispatch in the *Des Moines Register* revealing that the Rules Committee was planning to hear testimony about Ellen Rometsch and her abrupt August expulsion from the United States. Mollenhoff's story, like the one on the Profumo scandal published four months earlier by Horan and Frasca, did not name names, but it noted that the committee was "in the process of examining allegations regarding the conduct of Senate employees as well as members of the Senate" with Rometsch. The committee's interest went beyond the Senate: "The evidence also is likely to include identification of several high executive branch officials as friends and associates of the part-time model and party girl," Mollenhoff wrote.

Mollenhoff, who died in 1991, obviously had good sources, one of them being John Williams of the Senate. His story noted that Senator Williams "has obtained an account of the woman's life in Washington over a period of more than two years." Rometsch was born and raised in East Germany, Mollenhoff wrote, and "still has relatives on the other side of the iron curtain. The possibility that her activity might be connected with espionage was of some concern to security investigators because of the high rank of her male companions."

"Last summer," Mollenhoff added, "the FBI started an investigation of the girl. With less than a week's notice, she and her husband were sent back to Germany . . . at the request of the State Department."

Mollenhoff had written widely on labor corruption in the 1950s and had been an enthusiastic supporter of Bobby Kennedy's work as general counsel of the Senate Rackets Committee. The two men had grown apart — the specifics of their dispute could not be learned for this book — and the increasingly conservative Mollenhoff wrote extensively, and critically, of the Kennedy administration's decision in late 1962 to bypass Boeing and award the TFX contract to General Dynamics. His reporting was taken most seriously by Bobby Kennedy.

The reason for the attorney general's concern was obvious. The mere fact that a Senate committee and the FBI were investigating espionage charges against a foreign-born prostitute who undoubtedly would talk, if compelled to do so, about partying with the president in the White House pool could cripple Jack Kennedy as similar accusations had crippled Harold Macmillan's government. The Republicans on the Senate Rules Committee would soon begin demanding in public that they needed to interview Ellen Rometsch, and insisting that she be given a visa to return to Washington. The Democrats controlled the Senate, but any attempt to forestall the Republicans with parliamentary tactics would produce nothing but negative press.

Bobby Kennedy needed help, and he needed it right away — from J. Edgar Hoover. Two days after the Mollenhoff story, the attorney general summoned Courtney Evans to his office at 9:30 A.M. to talk about the Rometsch case, and gave him a message for Hoover that played on the FBI director's strong feelings of patriotism and respect for the presidency. "He said that he was greatly concerned, as was the

President, with the possible harm which will come to the United States if irresponsible action is taken on the Hill in connection with the Ellen Rometsch allegations," Evans noted in a memorandum made available under the Freedom of Information Act. Kennedy added, Evans wrote, that he had "talked with the President on the telephone" and Jack Kennedy was thinking of personally telephoning Senate leaders Mike Mansfield and Everett Dirksen to ask them to meet with Hoover. "This would be for the purpose of insuring that the Senate leadership in both political parties was aware of the facts," recorded Evans, "and to place on them responsibility in an effort to prevent irresponsible action."

At 9:45, having laid the groundwork with Evans, Kennedy telephoned Hoover, and made clear why he and his brother were running scared. "The Attorney General called," Hoover reported in a memorandum of their conversation, made available under the Freedom of Information Act, "and advised that he had talked with [Courtney] Evans and the President about the whole situation regarding the Rometsch girl; that he could visualize Senator Williams talking about this and [the] fact [that the] girl was from East Germany and the security angle." Hoover added to the attorney general's fears when he told him that, according to an FBI informant's report in July, "Rometsch said she was sent to this country to get information."

Rometsch had been contacted the day before by FBI agents at her home in Germany, Hoover told Kennedy, but was refusing to be interviewed. The FBI director then gave Bobby Kennedy what he was looking for. "I advised the Attorney General we should see something is done that she does not get a visa to come back and the Attorney General agreed." Kennedy told Hoover that "he was going to talk to the President and give him a brief summary." He would tell the president that Hoover had come through. Ellen Rometsch would remain in Germany — and remain silent. Without Rometsch, the Republicans had no witnesses and no hearing.

Hoover's promise to try to keep Rometsch out of the country was not enough. Within hours of their phone call, Bobby Kennedy was forced to walk over to the FBI director's office — a walk he rarely took. There, invoking his brother, the president of the United States, he asked for an extraordinary favor: Would Hoover do what the president wanted and meet with Mike Mansfield of Montana, the Senate majority leader, and Everett Dirksen of Illinois, the minority leader, to "brief them" about Rometsch before the Rules Committee began its hearings? In other words, the Kennedys wanted Hoover to kill the Rules Committee investigation.

Hoover tried to fight off the request. "I told the Attorney General," he wrote in an account of the meeting, "that he already had a complete memorandum upon this matter which he, himself, could read to the Senators if he so desired, rather than have me personally meet with them." But Kennedy pushed ahead, telling him, the FBI director wrote, that "he felt I should see the Senators as they were primarily interested in any breach of security which might have occurred in the Rometsch case and they would give more credence to what I had to say than any statement he might make." The attorney general was laying it on a bit thick, but his appeal was effective.

Hoover was driven that afternoon to meet with Mansfield and Dirksen at Mansfield's home in northwest Washington. There was no need to discuss any of the indelicate details. Mike Mansfield, interviewed by telephone in 1997 for this book — he was ninety-four years old and very acute — said he distinctly remembered meeting with Hoover, because it was the only time he and Dirksen, the two Senate leaders, were brought together by the FBI director. "I really don't recall" what the meeting was about, he added. "I'm afraid I can't be very helpful, except to say that Dirksen and I did meet with Hoover." Everett Dirksen died in 1969, and archivists at the Dirksen Congressional Center, in Pekin, Illinois, where Dirksen's papers are on file, told me that they were unable to find any mention of Ellen Rometsch or the October 28 meeting with Hoover and Mansfield.

A few days later, Hoover was invited to lunch with the president at the White House, his first such meeting since March 1962, when the subject was Judith Exner and Sam Giancana. No memoranda of the lunch are known to exist.

It seems clear that the president still felt that he was just a newspaper story or two away from the fate of Profumo and Macmillan. On November 5, less than three weeks before his assassination, Kennedy summoned the Ben Bradlees at the last minute for a private dinner. Bradlee, who had other plans, tried to beg off, he wrote in

Conversations with Kennedy, but the president was persistent. At dinner, Bradlee wrote, JFK was full of talk about his lunch with Hoover a few days earlier.

> He told us how FDR used to have Hoover over regularly, and said he felt it was wise for him to start doing the same thing, with rumors flying and every indication of a dirty campaign coming. "Boy, the dirt he has on those senators," Kennedy said, shaking his head. "You wouldn't believe it." He described a picture of Elly Rometsch that Hoover had brought with him. Her name had popped up and in and out of print as one of the women who frequented the Quorum Club, Bobby Baker's relaxing emporium on Capitol Hill. . . . Kennedy said the picture showed her to be a "really beautiful woman." Hoover told Kennedy at lunch that his agents had obtained an affidavit from Elly Rometsch in West Germany stating that she wanted to return to the United States, not to go back in business, but to marry the chief investigator of a Senate committee, whom Kennedy knew. This man, Kennedy quoted Hoover as saying, "was getting for free what Elly was charging others a couple of hundred dollars a night." . . . There is something incredible about the picture of the president of the United States and the director of the Federal Bureau of Investigation looking at photographs of call girls over lunch in the White House living quarters.

The president could have been living dangerously once again, and recklessly shooting the breeze about Ellen Rometsch with his pal Ben Bradlee. But it is far more likely that Kennedy was setting Bradlee up to write a story, if needed, knocking down any public hint of a presidential relationship with Rometsch. Bradlee had performed that service the year before, in the *Newsweek* story that curbed speculation in the establishment press about the president's marriage to Durie Malcolm.

The final lie about Rometsch — and the Senate — fell to Bobby Kennedy, in his 1964 interview with the Kennedy Library. "Clark Mollenhoff wrote an article that she had been tied up with people at the White House, which was, in fact, incorrect," Kennedy said. "I looked into the files," he added, with obvious indignation, "and she *had* been tied up with a lot of people at the Capitol! [Emphasis in original.] I got all the information she had . . . and it got to large numbers on both ways"— Democrats and Republicans. His concern, Bobby Kennedy added, was for the reputation of the United States. "I thought it was very damaging and . . . I spoke to the President about it. It didn't involve anybody at the White House, but I thought it would just destroy the confidence that people in the United States had in their government. . . . Some of the Senators had Negro girl-friends and all kinds of things which were not very helpful." Those concerns, Bobby Kennedy said, led him to urge a meeting between Hoover and the two Senate leaders, Mansfield and Dirksen, "to ex-plain what was in the files and what information [the FBI] had. I guess it was a shock to both of them.

"From then on," Kennedy added, "there was less attention [in the Senate] on that aspect of the situation."

Robert Kennedy, in rewriting the Ellen Rometsch story for the Kennedy Library, was doing more than protecting his brother. He was also shielding his own role in the Bobby Baker scandal. The at-torney general had his own business with the Senate Rules Commit-tee in the fall of 1963, dealing not with Baker but with the despised Lyndon Johnson. The vice president stood between the attorney gen-eral and any realistic chance of his succeeding his brother as the Democratic Party's presidential nominee in 1968. Johnson had to be knocked off the ticket in 1964 to make way for the president's younger brother.

In a series of interviews for this book, Burkett Van Kirk, who was chief counsel in 1963 for the Republican minority on the Rules Com-mittee, told me of his personal knowledge of Bobby Kennedy's direct intervention. "Bobby was feeding information to 'whispering Willie'"— the nickname for Senator John Williams. "They"— the Kennedy brothers, Van Kirk said — "were dumping Johnson." Williams, as he did earlier with Donald Reynolds's information about Lyndon Johnson, relayed the Kennedy materials to the senior Republican on the Rules Committee, Carl Curtis. The attorney gen-eral thus was dealing secretly with Williams, and Williams was deal-ing secretly with Curtis and Van Kirk. The scheming was necessary,

Van Kirk told me, because he and his fellow Republicans understood that a full-fledged investigation into Bobby Baker could lead to the vice president. They also understood, he said, that the chances of getting such an investigation were slim at best. The Democrats had an overwhelming advantage in the Senate — sixty-seven to thirty-three — and in every committee. The three Republicans on the ten-member Rules Committee, Van Kirk said, had little power. "We never won one vote to even call a witness," he told me. The investigation into Bobby Baker and Lyndon Johnson would have to be done in a traditional manner — by newspaper leak.

Van Kirk, who was named after his grandfather Senator E. J. Burkett of Nebraska, said that Bobby Kennedy eventually designated a Justice Department lawyer that fall to serve as an intermediary to the minority staff; he began supplying the Republicans with documents about Johnson and his financial dealings. The lawyer, Van Kirk told me, "used to come up to the Senate and hang around me like a dark cloud. It took him about a week or ten days to, one, find out what I didn't know, and two, give it to me." Some of the Kennedy-supplied documents were kept in Williams's office safe, Van Kirk said, and never shown to him. There was no doubt of Bobby Kennedy's purpose in dealing with the Republicans, Van Kirk said: "To get rid of Johnson. To dump him. I am as sure of that as I am that the sun comes up in the east."

The Kennedy brothers repeatedly denied that they had any intention of dropping Johnson from the 1964 ticket. On October 31, 1963, at his next-to-last news conference, the president reaffirmed that he wanted and expected Johnson to be on the ticket. A year later, Bobby Kennedy told the Kennedy Library that "there was no plan to dump Lyndon Johnson" in 1964. "There was a lot of stories that my brother and I . . . [had] started the Bobby Baker case in order to give us a handle to dump Lyndon Johnson. . . . There was never any intention of dropping him. There was never even any discussion about dropping him."

Charles Spalding, Kennedy's old friend, may not have known the president's plans for 1964, but he did know Jack Kennedy. "Jack didn't like Lyndon," Spalding told me in a 1997 interview. "I know. He was just awful — so jealous, so disagreeable and ugly." What's worse,

Spalding said, he and the president knew that Johnson wasn't loyal —"he really was anti-him [Kennedy]."*

The most specific contradiction of the Kennedy brothers' denial came from Evelyn Lincoln, the president's loyal secretary, in her 1968 memoir, *Kennedy and Johnson*. She described a conversation on November 19, 1963, two days before the president left for Texas, in which Kennedy expressed his dissatisfaction with Johnson and said, "I will need as a running mate a man who believes as I do." Asked by Lincoln whom he was considering, he told her, Lincoln wrote, "At this time I am thinking about Governor Terry Sanford of North Carolina, but it will not be Lyndon."

Lincoln's papers were donated to the Kennedy Library after her death. Those documents were opened, in part, to researchers in mid-1997; among the documents, library officials say, are contemporaneous stenography notes corroborating her 1968 claim that Kennedy had told her he was planning to pick a new running mate in 1964.

Evelyn Lincoln may also have had irrefutable evidence of the president's thinking about the vice presidency. Until this book it has not been known that for at least five years, Lincoln had access to all of the office and telephone tape recordings that were removed from the White House after Kennedy's death and retained by the Kennedy family, and she took some of those recordings to her home — to Bobby's consternation.

Sometime after Kennedy's death, Lincoln, as the keeper of the president's office records, was put on the payroll of the National Archives and Records Administration, the federal office responsible for presidential records. She worked there with Frank Harrington, who, he explained in a series of interviews for this book, was the first archivist to be hired by the Kennedy Library. Harrington recalled that he was quickly reassigned by the library to Washington to help Evelyn Lincoln process the millions of pages of Kennedy administration papers. There were deep conflicts over the tapes between Lincoln and then-Senator Robert Kennedy, Harrington told me. "It drove Bobby batshit," he said, "because she took some of them home.

---

* Years later, when he was in the Senate, Robert Kennedy described Lyndon Johnson to Adam Walinsky, one of his aides, as someone who "panicked and couldn't function" in crises. "Kennedy told me," Walinsky, a New York attorney, said in a 1993 interview for this book, "that Johnson had been a physical coward during the Cuban missile crisis."

She was working on them for her own book"— *Kennedy and John-son*. Bobby Kennedy was then doing research for *Thirteen Days*, his study of the Cuban missile crisis. "I remember Bobby coming to the archives looking for a certain tape," Harrington said. "Evelyn couldn't produce it. She said, 'I'll get it for you tomorrow.' She produced it on the next day and said she'd found it in the archives. But she hadn't. I knew she'd taken it home. She lied. Bobby was a little bit afraid of her, because he didn't do anything to her." Instead, Harrington said, "he'd storm up to me to complain, but not to her."*

With Lyndon Johnson on his way out, Jack Kennedy had every reason to look forward to the 1964 campaign and his reelection. There was some talk from inside the family of having a Kennedy-Kennedy ticket in 1964, most of it, Gore Vidal told me in an interview, coming from Ethel Kennedy, Bobby's wife. The only trouble spot, besides the growing difficulties in South Vietnam, was Ellen Rometsch and her desire — as Hoover told Kennedy over lunch, and Kennedy later confided to Ben Bradlee — of returning to the United States to marry a Senate investigator (LaVern Duffy). The initial Kennedy pay-ments to Rometsch hadn't done the trick, and now a way had to be found to keep her in West Germany — and happy to keep quiet.

Sometime early in November, Kennedy summoned Grant Stock-dale, a friend from his early days in the House of Representatives, to the Oval Office. Stockdale, a real estate broker in Miami, had stayed friendly with Kennedy through the 1950s, and helped him in his po-litical campaigns. There were many visits to the Kennedy compound at Palm Beach. By 1960 Stockdale was serving as the Democratic Na-tional Committee's fund-raising chairman for the southern states, and he raised a great deal of money for the Kennedy-Johnson ticket.

---

* Harrington, a professional archivist, said it was clear that "there was sensitive stuff" on the presidential tape recordings, "because of how carefully they [family members and friends] worked with them. The thing that was disillusioning for me was the fact that no transcripts were made" in real time, that is, within a few weeks or months of the initial tape recordings. "The thing that could justify the tapings was to use them to refresh [Kennedy's] memory" before various meetings. "I had a hunch it was bad," Harrington added. "They were so secretive about it. Why were they so secretive? The machine was set up, after all, in the Oval Office. There shouldn't be any hanky-panky there."

His reward was to be appointed in 1961 as ambassador to Ireland. The post had obvious sentimental value for Kennedy, and Stockdale was flattered. Once in Ireland, he went all out to represent the new administration and lavishly spent his personal money on embassy entertaining. Eighteen months later, he told Kennedy he was broke and had to go back to his real estate business in Miami.

The president understood. Stockdale appealed to Kennedy, perhaps, because he was all the things Kennedy was not: a self-made man who was precisely what he seemed to be. He had been a football star in college before serving in the war as a marine intelligence officer in the Pacific. "His life was an open book," Stockdale's son, also named Grant, told me in a 1996 interview. "When he got back to Miami, he told his friends he was broke. He was happy to have served, but happy to get back to his business."

Stockdale also knew how to keep his mouth shut. He had joined Kennedy in 1962 at one of his private parties in the Carlyle Hotel in New York, and later told his son that "there were women, beautiful women there." It was a world, Grant said of his father, "that was too fast for him. He was completely out of his league." He did not go back.

But now it was November 1963 and Stockdale was in the Oval Office. Grant told me the story his mother, Adie, had told him. "Kennedy said, 'I need you to raise some dough — fifty thousand dollars.' 'Why me?' 'Because I need it and I can count on you to keep it quiet.' 'What's it for?' 'It's for personal use.'"

The president's request made his father very uneasy, Grant said. "He raised money," Grant told me. "That's what he did for the Democratic National Committee. But not for personal use." Stockdale asked the president, his son said, "'How are you going to acknowledge this money [to donors]?' Kennedy said, 'It's never going to be acknowledged.'" His father returned to Miami and did what Kennedy asked — he raised $50,000 in cash, telling contributors that the money was for Jack Kennedy. "He hated it," Grant told me, "but he felt, 'Shit, it's the president.' He was very distressed about being asked to raise cash for the president's personal use when he's got his own money problems. The clincher was the part about no acknowledgment. There was something wrong with the whole thing. He knew he was being used, and my mother knew he was being used. She really resented it. 'It's the craziest thing I've ever heard,' she said. 'Don't do it. Turn it down.' But he felt he couldn't.

"So," Grant continued, "my father went around and collected money. I think he did it not believing that Kennedy wouldn't acknowledge it [as a loan or contribution] in some way. He couldn't believe it was so underhanded." There was no secret in Miami about Stockdale's money needs. "All of his buddies knew he was broke," Grant said, "because he was open about it: 'Hey guys, I'm broke.'" He had trouble raising the $50,000 in cash, Grant told me. "Some of the people he approached were as incredulous as my mother was. They were simply disbelieving, and turned down the request." Word began spreading in Miami, Grant added, that Stockdale was really raising the money for himself — that there was no Kennedy connection. "My father was devastated when he heard that story," Grant told me. "It got to his core. My father was still trying to figure out how he could get Kennedy to acknowledge the contributors when November twenty-second came."

A family friend had gone with his father, Grant said, to the Kennedy compound to deliver the money. "Kennedy said, 'Thank you,' opened a nearby closet door, and threw the briefcase in there," Grant was told. "The closet was full of briefcases."

Kennedy's assassination devastated the Stockdale family, and left Stockdale with a serious problem, his son recalled. "He told everyone that the money he had collected was for Kennedy, but now he had no proof." Grant said that his father "was very worried about Bobby Baker. Why would my father be worried about Bobby Baker?"

Edward Grant Stockdale committed suicide by jumping from his office window in downtown Miami ten days after the president's murder. He was forty-eight years old. His son still wants to know why Kennedy needed the money.

23

VIETNAM

John Kennedy's enduring legacy as the thirty-fifth president of the United States was not the myth of Camelot or the tragic image of an attractive young leader struck down at the peak of his career. It was the war in Vietnam, a war that in the decade after his death would kill many thousands of the young Americans he had inspired and propel many others to the edge of insurrection.

Kennedy's personal responsibility for the November 2, 1963, overthrow and murder of Ngo Dinh Diem, the president of South Vietnam, has been obscured by the lies of the men who worked for him, and the lies of his ever-loyal brother Bobby. Diem's fall is now considered by many historians to be a turning point in what suddenly became no longer a Vietnamese but an American war. The men and women around the president, in their eagerness to shape the truth, have also obscured one of the reasons Kennedy decided Diem had to go: in the months before his murder, the South Vietnamese president had begun to talk settlement secretly with North Vietnam. Diem was looking for a way to get the Americans out — before the Kennedy administration took him out.

Little of this can be found in the official records or newspaper reports of the time.

In the fall of 1963, the war was still seen as a Vietnamese conflict. The repressive Diem and his brother and political counselor Ngo Dinh Nhu were viewed by Henry Cabot Lodge, Jr., the new American ambassador to Vietnam, and by the Saigon press corps as the main obstacles to progress in the war against the National Liberation Front (NLF). The NLF (known to the U.S. government and the Saigon press corps as the Viet Cong) was the political arm of both communist and noncommunist opposition in the South. Most Americans knew nothing of the NLF, and the few who were aware of it saw it as indistinguishable from North Vietnam, rather than as an internal South Vietnamese resistance force with grievances of its own. There was no challenge on the editorial pages or in the universities to the Kennedy administration's avowed policy of saving South Vietnam from communism. The debate was over how best to do it.

The United States had 16,500 soldiers in South Vietnam in 1963, most of them in administrative and intelligence jobs. But — unknown to those back home — a steadily increasing number of air force and army pilots were attacking suspected Viet Cong targets, dropping bombs from South Vietnamese aircraft and firing rockets from South Vietnamese helicopters. American infantrymen were advising Vietnamese army units going into battle and, in some cases, dying in combat alongside them. Seventy-eight American soldiers were killed fighting in South Vietnam during the Kennedy presidency. More than 58,000 American deaths were still to come. The low number of American casualties in 1963 made it difficult for most Americans to understand the intensity of the war; at the time, Vietnamese soldiers and civilians were dying by the thousands. The president understood how tough it was.

"The thing that bothered [Kennedy] most," Michael V. Forrestal, the National Security Council's expert on Vietnam at the time, told a congressional research team in 1978, "was that we were . . . helping Diem fight a war with massive military means in a situation which was essentially a civil war — an elephant trying to kill a fly sort of thing. We were killing lots of other people at the same time we were trying to kill Viet Cong. . . . We were assisting the Vietnamese in undertaking search-and-destroy, and [there were] great waves of battalions and regiments running all over the country pillaging and burning, doing all the things that soldiers do." Forrestal, whose interview was published in a 1984 Library of Congress history of the war (he died in 1989), claimed that Kennedy tried to cut back on the heavy use of napalm, herbicides, and land mines, but was unable to get his way. "Our army supported all those activities," Forrestal said, "and thought they were necessary and militarily justified."

The story as reported at the time by journalists had Diem's final crisis beginning in the spring of 1963. The war in Vietnam did not become a serious foreign policy concern — and thus a political concern — for Jack Kennedy until May, when South Vietnamese troops at Hue fired into a crowd of Buddhist monks who were protesting lack of religious freedom, killing nine. Nhu pushed his brother to take a hard line against the Buddhist opposition. Diem and Nhu rejected demands for reparations and a public apology; the protests escalated, and government troops smashed their way into Buddhist pagodas, ostensibly looking for hidden weapons. Amidst the furor, a monk set himself on fire in Saigon, while Malcolm Brown of the Associated Press — one of many journalists who had been alerted in advance — looked on. Brown's stunning photograph of the self-immolation, published on every front page the next morning, horrified America; it also got the president's attention. The situation worsened when Nhu's wife, the outspoken Madame Nhu, ridiculed the suicide as a "barbecue."

In late August, with the Buddhists stubbornly continuing to protest and the American public getting its first exposure to the depth of the disaffection the South Vietnamese had for their government, the Kennedy administration gave tacit approval to a military coup d'état against Diem that was to take place in the last days of the month. It didn't come off. Meanwhile, the demoralized South Vietnamese army's efforts against the Viet Cong came to a standstill, as Diem and Nhu resisted demands to ease up on the Buddhists and other dissenters; the South Vietnamese president and his brother saw American pressure for reform as infringing on their sovereignty.

In late October, Ambassador Lodge encouraged a renewed attempt by the same plotters, who were headed by General Duong Van Minh ("Big Minh"), chief of the South Vietnamese army's general staff. Lodge told the generals that Washington would not oppose

Diem's overthrow. This time the coup took place as expected, and early in the morning of November 2 it succeeded. But what was not expected in Washington, according to histories of the time, took place after the coup: Diem and Nhu were seized by General Minh's troops in a Roman Catholic church, blindfolded, and executed by gunshots to the back of the head. There were press reports that the brothers had refused an American offer of sanctuary before the coup.

Americans who followed the newspaper accounts were pleased by the coup, which was seen as giving the South Vietnamese government a chance to fight the communists with more vigor and more internal cohesion. The American press corps also cheered Diem's demise. "Americans are gratified by a sense of joy that they find in Saigon," the *New York Times* commented in an editorial on November 4. The unnamed and perhaps imaginary Americans cited by the editorialists were also said to be hoping "that the repressive political climate that weighed heavily on the population and the army has been lifted for good."

President Kennedy was said to be shocked and distraught by the murder of Diem, a fellow Catholic. His dismay seemed logical. Diem was a Vietnamese nationalist who in 1950 had been sentenced to death in absentia by Ho Chi Minh, the communist leader of North Vietnam. Diem fled to a seminary in suburban New York, where he became friendly with many Americans, among them Joseph P. Kennedy and his son the senator from Massachusetts. Both Kennedys admired the young leader's patriotism, fervid anticommunism, and devotion to the Catholic church. Diem's brother Ngo Dinh Thuc was a Roman Catholic bishop, and Diem was a lay celibate — a level of religious conviction that could not fail to impress the Kennedy family. In the mid-1950s the Kennedys joined with other prominent Americans, including Supreme Court Justice William O. Douglas; Henry Luce, the publisher of *Time* magazine; and Arthur Schlesinger, Jr., the Harvard historian, to help finance the American Friends of Vietnam (AFV), a lobbying group. Senator John Kennedy was the principal speaker at the group's symposium in 1956, and was listed on the AFV's membership roster in 1961, as president.

Over the next three decades, with the unauthorized publication in 1971 of the so-called Pentagon Papers and the occasional release of classified documents under the Freedom of Information Act, a more nuanced picture of the Kennedy administration's complicity in both the coup and the executions emerged. It was learned that Ambassador Lodge and the CIA station in Saigon had worked closely with General Minh and his plotters before the coup, and had supplied weapons and cash on demand. President Diem had clearly received advance word of the time and place of the coup. "I want to know," Diem asked, in a chilling last-minute telephone conversation with Lodge, according to a transcript, "what is the attitude of U.S.?" Lodge's answer was classic: "I do not feel well enough informed to be able to tell you."

Thus the essential account has remained — until a series of interviews for this book revealed that Jack Kennedy, as he had in the plotting against Fidel Castro, both actively sought Diem's ouster and knew that the Vietnamese president would be murdered in the coup. The most telling new information was supplied by Lucien Conein, a longtime clandestine operative for the CIA, who in October 1963 served as a middleman between Henry Cabot Lodge and the Vietnamese coup plotters. Conein told me in a 1996 interview that there was never any doubt that General Minh, leader of the military plotting, was going to have Diem and his brother killed. "I discussed this with Lodge," Conein said. "I'd been told by Big Minh a month before [that] they were going to knock off Diem. I said, 'Don't do it, because there could be trouble.' Big Minh said, 'We will not discuss it.' I reported this to Lodge."*

The president's distress upon hearing of the death of Diem may certainly have been real. And there is new evidence that he tried to

---

* Conein gave a slightly different account in 1975 to the overburdened Church Committee, which was able to conduct only a perfunctory investigation into the Diem assassination. Conein testified that he learned of the pending assassinations of Diem and Nhu in early October 1963 and relayed the word to Ambassador Lodge. Three weeks later, Conein testified, Lodge informed him that John McCone, the CIA director, after consulting with the president, had sent a cable instructing the embassy that "we cannot be in position actively condoning such course of action and thereby engaging our responsibility therefore [sic]." Conein told the Church Committee that he followed the CIA's instruction from the president, informing one of the Vietnamese plotters, an army general, that the United States opposed assassination. The general responded, Conein testified, "All right, you don't like it. We won't talk about it anymore." In its final report the committee noted that Conein's "detailed after-action report" did not mention his conversation with the general.

stop it; in the days immediately before the coup, Kennedy, once again operating through the back channel, sent a trusted personal emissary, a friend who had nothing to do with his administration, to meet privately with Diem. The message for Diem, who was still an ally of the United States, was a blunt warning: Get rid of your brother and accept sanctuary in the American Embassy, or face certain death in the coup. Diem ignored it.

An important development in South Vietnam in the late summer and fall of 1963 was all but ignored by the American press correspondents in Saigon: persistent intelligence that Diem and Nhu were conducting informal talks with North Vietnam aimed, ultimately, at establishing a neutral regime in the South. The American pilots and military advisers, who were in the South purportedly at the express invitation of Diem's government, would be asked to leave.

Rumors about such preliminary negotiations were rife in Saigon but were considered little more than idle talk. Diem was known to be an ardent nationalist, but he was also seen as an anticommunist and patriot who shared the American view of better dead than red. "In my contacts here," General Paul D. Harkins, chief of the U.S. military mission in Saigon, wrote Maxwell Taylor in October 1963, "I have seen no one with the strength of character of Diem, at least in fighting communists." Not one of the dozens of memoirs written after Kennedy's assassination by senior officials of his administration deals at any length with rumors of the North-South talks. Arthur Schlesinger did not mention the negotiations in *A Thousand Days,* but described them in detail in *Robert Kennedy and His Times,* published in 1978. He wrote then that the talks, which he said took place "without Kennedy's knowledge," were a possible "means of an American exit from Vietnam in 1963."

The fact is that at least two important officials took the rumored talks most seriously: Jack Kennedy and Henry Cabot Lodge.

That fall, the president vented his frustration — and his fear — about Vietnam to a good friend, the journalist Charles Bartlett. "Toward the end of his life," Bartlett told me in an interview for this book, "he was very negative about the whole thing. He said, 'Charlie, I can't let Vietnam go to the communists and then go and ask these people'— the voters of America —'to reelect me. Somehow we've got to hold that territory through the 1964 election. We've already given up Laos to the communists, and if I give up Vietnam I won't really be able to go to the people.* But we've got no future there. [The South Vietnamese] hate us. They want us out of there. At one point they'll kick our asses out of there.'"† In a similarly worried conversation that fall with the writer William Manchester, Kennedy mentioned the "possibility," Manchester said in a 1995 interview for this book, that Diem would enter into peace talks with the North Vietnamese. "He had a problem with Diem," Manchester told me. "He didn't trust Diem."‡ Manchester chose never to publish an account of the conversation.

* Kennedy inherited a crumbling situation in early 1961 in Laos, where the United States and Soviet Union had supported competing factions since the 1950s. Phoumi Nosavan, the general who was supported by the United States, was no match for the more competent communist troops of the Pathet Lao, who were aided by North Vietnam as well as by the Soviets. Kennedy's only option, other than the commitment of untold thousands of American troops — an impossible stand after the Bay of Pigs — was to discard the Eisenhower administration's insistence on a noncommunist Laos and work privately for a neutrality that, as all involved understood, would not hold. The new president masked his policy retreat in the spring of 1961 by issuing a series of public threats — taken at face value by the Washington press — about his determination to face down the communists in Laos. "The security of Laos," he declared, "runs with the safety of us all." There were ostentatious military deployments to back his bluster: the Seventh Fleet at Okinawa, with a detachment of 1,400 marines, was put on alert and ordered to be ready to steam to Southeast Asia; another group of 150 combat-ready marines was sent by helicopter to the Thai-Lao border. Kennedy's moves were seen in Moscow, correctly, as bluffs. The president settled for a weak coalition government in Laos and the understanding that Washington and Moscow would continue clandestinely to resupply their supporters with men and arms. His limited options in Laos rankled Kennedy, and made him all the more leery of neutralism in South Vietnam.

† Bartlett was distressed, he told me, by the president's linking the war in South Vietnam to his political fortunes. "This made me a champion of the single six-year [presidential] term," he commented.

‡ In early 1964 Manchester was asked by Jacqueline Kennedy to write about the events of November 1963; the result was *The Death of a President,* published in 1967. The writer told me that he had befriended Jack Kennedy in 1946, as a fellow veteran of the war in the Pacific, and had remained his friend. After Kennedy's election, Manchester decided to write a book on his first year in office and, he told me, began what became

The published memoirs of Henry Cabot Lodge, who died in 1985, did not tell the whole story about his experiences in 1963. Among his personal papers, Lodge left an unpublished account of his time in Vietnam, which he marked "Top Secret," with instructions that the pages dealing with the days before the November 1–2 coup were to be published "only after submission to a representative of President Kennedy." In the unpublished memoir, made available for this book, Lodge said that he had been sent to Saigon with orders from Kennedy to report to him through a CIA back-channel link. "I was instructed to send my telegrams directly to [President Kennedy]," Lodge wrote, "and he would decide how to distribute them." The patrician Lodge, who was a major general in the army reserve, was unfazed by the White House belief that what was good for America was good for South Vietnam. "I had nothing to do with the origination of the policy," Lodge wrote, "but I thought it was correct. I think we have an absolute right frankly to use legitimate pressure and influence as part of a bargain with another government. . . . When people accept our help, we have a right to make stipulations if we want to." In his initial meetings with Diem after arriving in Saigon in late August, Lodge wrote, Diem would

> look at the ceiling and talk about his childhood or talk about Vietnamese history and would absolutely refuse to discuss the matters with me that President Kennedy wanted me to discuss with him. I thought this was not a proper way to treat the representative of the President of the United States. . . . I believe that continuance of the Diem regime . . . might have led to a communist takeover. Either the communists would have come in because of the public revulsion against what was going on, or Mr. Nhu [Diem's brother] would have made a deal with them.

The president said as much in public, telling a news conference on September 12, "What helps to win the war, we support; what interferes with the war effort, we oppose. . . . We are not there to see a war

a series of informal interviews with the president. "I'd see Jack at the end of his last appointment for the day," Manchester said. "We'd have a daiquiri and sit on the Truman balcony. He'd smoke a cigar and I'd have a Heineken. He'd let loose — things he couldn't discuss with anyone else."

lost, and will follow the policy which I have indicated today of advancing those causes and issues which help win the war." A few days earlier, in a television interview with Walter Cronkite, of CBS, Kennedy was asked whether he believed that the South Vietnamese government could still regain the support of the people. "I do," he responded. "With changes in policy and perhaps with personnel I think it can. If it doesn't make those changes, I would think that the chances of winning it would not be very good."

By mid-September there was much talk in the United Nations and around the world about a political settlement between the rival factions in the South, but there was little such talk in the American press. On September 11 the National Liberation Front sent a three-point peace plan to the United Nations that called for an end to American military assistance to the Diem government, withdrawal of all U.S. forces, and the formation of a coalition government in the South. Two days later U Thant, the UN secretary-general, harshly criticized the Diem regime at a press conference, depicting it as one of the most corrupt governments in the world. Echoing the NLF proposal, U Thant called for a coalition government in South Vietnam. Later in the month, President Charles de Gaulle of France enraged the White House by announcing his support for neutralization of the South and the eventual reunification of Vietnam. The American intelligence community began reporting that Roger Lalouette, the French ambassador in Saigon, was attempting to broker talks between Diem and North Vietnam. There was outrage in Washington over de Gaulle's intervention, which was viewed as malicious meddling and an attempt to make sure that America would fail in Vietnam — as the French had a decade earlier. The president, asked about de Gaulle's suggestion, said crossly, "It doesn't do us any good to say, 'Well, why don't we all just go home and leave the world to those who are our enemies.'"

The intelligence about the talks — initially disregarded by many Americans in Saigon and Washington as impossible to credit — turned out to be superb. Twelve years after the fact, in early 1975, when the collapse of South Vietnam was imminent, Mieczyslaw Maneli, a Polish diplomat who had been posted to the International

Control Commission (ICC) in Saigon in the early 1960s, published a revelatory essay in the *New York Times* about what might have been.* "In the spring of 1963," he wrote,

> I was secretly asked by President Ngo Dinh Diem and his brother . . . through Roger Lalouette to approach the Government in Hanoi in order to explore the possibilities for a peaceful resolution of the struggle. During the subsequent months, I had many wide-ranging discussions with the highest North Vietnamese officials, including President Ho Chi Minh and Premier Pham Van Dong. . . . The North Vietnamese leaders were slowly developing plans, which I discussed with a group of Western ambassadors. Under the plans, North and South Vietnam could slowly develop postal, economic and cultural relations. Northern industrial goods would be paid for by the South with its rice. Also, the North would not press for a speedy reunification, but instead a coalition government would be set up in the South. I asked if such a government could be headed by Mr. Diem. In the summer of 1963 the answer was finally yes. . . . Neither Soviet nor Chinese [nor American] troops would under any conditions be allowed on Vietnamese soil. I pursued the matter further: What guarantees could be offered to the West that Hanoi would keep its word? I stressed that the West would not be amused by a new game called "the international commission." The answer was that in case of a United States withdrawal, the North would be prepared to give all kinds of substantial guarantees and American participation in the supervisory process was not excluded. At the time, I knew about strained relations between Hanoi and both Moscow and Peking;† further,

* The ICC was created by the Geneva Accords of 1954, which formally divided North and South Vietnam. Its three members — one each from communist Poland, anti-communist Canada, and neutralist India — were theoretically in place to prevent third-party nations like the United States and Soviet Union from violating the accords by supplying military equipment to either the North or South. Few inspections took place, but Maneli and the two other ICC members had the privilege of being able to commute between Hanoi and Saigon on a special aircraft; ICC members had living quarters and offices in both cities. The ICC commissioners were rarely available to the Saigon press corps, but their activities were closely monitored by the American and South Vietnamese intelligence services — and presumably by North Vietnam.

† Even in 1975, these ideological strains were not fully understood in Washington, and would not be for another decade.

Hanoi's leaders wanted to preserve and widen their small margin of independence from their powerful allies, whom they hated and feared. They were willing to accept a negotiated agreement whose result would not have been worse for the West than the one in 1973: Vietnam would have been divided into two parts, with free commercial and cultural intercommunication between them.

Maneli, an intellectual who taught law at the University of Warsaw, had by 1970 emigrated to the United States, and he began teaching political science at Queens College. He offered a first-person account of the talks between North and South Vietnam in a 1971 memoir, *War of the Vanquished*, published by Harper and Row. Astonishingly, the American press ignored it: the book was not reviewed by any major newspaper or magazine. Still prosecuting the war, the America of 1971 was not ready to be told that the war did not have to be. In one prescient cable to Warsaw and Moscow, quoted in his memoir, Maneli made a point that no American, apparently, considered in the fall of 1963.

How does it happen that the National Liberation Front is . . . less active now than during the period before the [present] crisis in the Diem regime? At the present time, the Diem-Nhu regime is so weak that a larger partisan offensive could end up in the liquidation of the South Vietnamese administration, leaving only American units on the battlefield. Hanoi must also be aware of this, as are many outside observers. If the government in Hanoi does not undertake an offensive designed to remove Diem and Nhu from Saigon, this is certainly because it wishes them to survive for a time yet — long enough to come to an agreement with them behind the Americans' backs.

In interviews for this book, American officials involved in Vietnam policy in the fall of 1963 confirmed that there was widespread reporting in the intelligence community about the North-South talks. But the officials differed on the importance of those talks. Richard R. Smyser, a State Department officer who arrived in Saigon in early 1964 and worked closely with Ambassador Lodge, told me that it was his understanding that a major motive for U.S. support of the coup d'état was the fact that "Diem was trying to make a deal" to establish a neutral South Vietnam. "Remember what neutralism was in 1963" for most Americans, Smyser said — "a new word for communism. If Diem made a deal, the deal was that the U.S. would leave and South Vietnam would become a neutral country. Vietnam would still be divided. For Kennedy, this was anathema, because they [his political opponents in the 1964 elections] would say, 'He lost Vietnam because he let it go neutral.' So that meant you had to get rid of Diem."

Allen Whiting, a China scholar who was a State Department intelligence officer in 1963, told me that he and most of his colleagues "all thought that this Nhu-Diem tie with the North was a very live possibility." The talks posed risks to the senior officials making policy, he added: "You don't want Diem and Nhu to cut a deal with the North and tell us to get the hell out." Tom Hughes, who in 1963 was the State Department's director of intelligence, said in a 1997 interview for this book that "there was a lot of talk about neutralism in the cable traffic from Saigon. It wasn't all that secret" to the people inside the U.S. government, he added. "Some of us thought it [an agreement between North and South] was a very good idea," Hughes said, "because it'd get us out of the place."

Other government Asia experts saw the talks as posturing by Diem and Nhu. The brothers were seen as deliberately leaking word of the negotiations in an effort to gain leverage over the Kennedy administration and curtail the acute American pressure for political reform. In September, Kennedy sent Defense Secretary Robert McNamara and Joint Chiefs chairman Maxwell Taylor on another of what had become their many missions to South Vietnam. Their report to the president, which included only a cursory mention of the North-South talks, focused on Nhu, who was viewed in Washington as a dark influence on Diem: "A further disturbing feature of Nhu is his flirtation with the idea of negotiating with North Vietnam, whether or not he is serious in this at present. This deeply disturbs responsible Vietnamese and, more basically, suggests a possible basic incompatibility with U.S. objectives."

On September 18, the first — and only — major American newspaper account of the secret talks between Saigon and Hanoi was published in a column in the *Washington Post*. Joseph Alsop, Jack Kennedy's favorite reporter, mounted a scathing attack on the French and their behind-the-scenes maneuvering with Ho Chi Minh and Ngo

Dinh Nhu. Alsop's column, entitled "Very Ugly Stuff," cited Roger Lalouette and Mieczyslaw Maneli by name and said that both diplomats were playing intermediary roles between Saigon and Hanoi. Alsop quoted Nhu as telling him in an interview that the North Vietnamese "begged him to open negotiations." He had not told Diem about the approach from Hanoi, Nhu said to Alsop, because it "would have caused a stir." In a subsequent interview with Diem, Alsop wrote, the Vietnamese president assured him that he knew nothing of such approaches — an "astounding detail," noted Alsop, "revealing so much about the real relation between the two brothers."*

The Alsop column was a perfect reflection of the attitude in the White House — the notoriously anti-American Ngo Dinh Nhu now stood accused in print of plotting behind his brother's back against U.S. interests. The Pentagon Papers quote Michael Forrestal of the National Security Council as writing the president late in the summer, "It is now quite certain that Brother Nhu is the mastermind behind the whole operation against the Buddhists and is calling the shots." No one in Washington seemed to consider that Nhu might have been saying what his brother wanted said — just as Bobby Kennedy often had done his brother's bidding, and had taken the public heat for so doing. The intellectual Nhu, an ardent nationalist, had enraged the Americans throughout the summer and fall of 1963 by repeatedly calling for a limit to the American role and American influence in South Vietnam. In an interview with the *Washington Post* in May, for example, Nhu said there were too many Americans assigned to Vietnam and that their presence was making the war look like an American war. "Half the Americans in Vietnam should leave and the other half should not expose themselves to enemy fire," Nhu was quoted as saying. He told other journalists that he and his brother had always opposed American military intervention; the Americans, he said, were an obstacle to the transformation of Vietnamese society which was necessary for victory.

---

* Anne E. Blair, an Australian historian who studied Lodge's tenure as ambassador, reported in *Lodge in Vietnam*, her 1995 book, that Alsop had shared a private dinner with Lodge four days before publication of the column. The column caused surprisingly little comment in Saigon, and no other journalist attempted to match or better Alsop's reporting.

Jack Kennedy agreed in September that Nhu had to go. Advice to that effect was pouring into the Oval Office from Saigon and Washington. But how to do it? Kennedy, if anyone, understood the difficulty of separating brother from brother. In early September a U.S. civilian official stationed in Vietnam named Rufus Phillips was invited by Michael Forrestal to attend a National Security Council meeting with the president. Phillips had arrived in Saigon as an army officer in 1954 and gone to work for the American military mission; its director at the time had been Edward Lansdale, then an air force colonel on assignment with the CIA. Phillips was awed by Lansdale and his willingness "to stick his neck out," he told me in a 1995 interview for this book. Lansdale, unlike others, reported the facts as he saw them to his superiors. Phillips returned to Washington in 1959, but by the fall of 1962 he was back in South Vietnam to serve, at Lansdale's urging, as director of the Rural Assistance Program. Phillips was thus the American expert on the Vietnamese government's controversial Strategic Hamlet Program, which was theoretically meant to provide centralized protection for peasants. Instead, the program often resulted in the forced resettlement of peasants to miserable huts in areas that were left unprotected at night from the Viet Cong. Phillips, who worked for the CIA in the late 1950s after leaving the army, was deeply committed to an American victory in the war. He was also convinced, as Forrestal knew, that it was still possible to separate Nhu from Diem. And Phillips was convinced that Ed Lansdale was the only one who could perform that delicate task.

In an unpublished memoir made available for this book, Phillips wrote of sitting quietly through a National Security Council meeting on September 10, 1963, while a marine general, just back from a visit to the combat zone, reeled off a set of optimistic statistics. A State Department official then described what he said was widespread hatred of the Diem regime and urged the ouster of Nhu. The official's implication, Phillips wrote, "was that Diem and Nhu were inseparable and that both must go."

At that point Forrestal, knowing what Phillips felt, invited him to speak up. (It seems likely that both the invitation to Phillips and his presentation at the meeting were agreed upon in advance by Kennedy.) "The problem is Nhu," Phillips told the president, according to his memoir. "He has lost the respect of the majority of the civilian and military leadership. . . . Nhu must leave the country or there will be chaos. I still believe that Nhu can be split from Diem, but there is only one American who has Diem's confidence and who could persuade Diem to let Nhu go. That man is General Lansdale," Phillips said. "No one would be more qualified to help [Diem] to put together a new government. I recommend you send him there as soon as possible."

Phillips's unpublished account is supported, in close detail, by the top-secret minutes of the meeting, which were declassified in 1995. The minutes further quote Phillips as telling the president what Forrestal, and perhaps Kennedy, wanted everyone at the meeting to hear: "We could keep Diem, but we could not win the war with Nhu in control." What was needed, Phillips added, was "a U.S. campaign and a U.S. campaign manager." Phillips, according to the minutes, said Lansdale "was the most competent person to become a campaign manager. . . . He believed we could win with General Lansdale." Kennedy responded that "Nhu was capable of seriously weakening the existing government, and then leaving for France. We would then be blamed for the resulting collapse of the country."

Phillips, in a 1995 interview for this book, remembered that the president had taken notes during his presentation —"the only notes he took. At the end he said, 'I want to thank you, Mr. Phillips, particularly for your recommendation of Mr. Lansdale.'"

What happened next is Edward Lansdale's story, as he told it in the mid-1960s to Daniel Ellsberg in Saigon, where the two men, survivors from Kennedy's Washington and McNamara's Pentagon, worked as special advisers for pacification — the war for "the hearts and minds" of the Vietnamese peasants. "While working for Lansdale," Ellsberg told me in a series of interviews for this book, "I spent one and a half years in the evening listening to war stories of his past CIA career. He talked about covert operations in the Philippines and in Vietnam in the fifties. One night when the two of us were talking alone in [Lansdale's] house in Saigon, Lansdale told me stories about his relationship with Robert McNamara — and how it had ended."

Lansdale and McNamara had not gotten along for years; Lansdale was pleased that Ellsberg, a brilliant McNamara "whiz kid" who had in the early 1960s written speeches for the secretary of defense and consulted on nuclear war planning, had left the Pentagon to work on his team. Lansdale's final break with McNamara had come in the fall of 1963, after Lansdale was passed over for promotion from brigadier general to major general. His work on Operation Mongoose had ended eight months earlier, and in the interim Lansdale had had little contact with the White House. He planned to retire.

Then a call came from McNamara, Lansdale told Ellsberg, instructing him to accompany the secretary of defense to the White House for a meeting with the president. The three men met alone. "The president said to Ed," Ellsberg recounted, "'I am prepared to send you back to Vietnam to work with Diem and see if you could get Diem to separate himself from Nhu.' Nhu was seen as the guy who'd caused the crisis — the evil genius." The president asked Lansdale if he was willing to go.

Lansdale said yes. Then the president told Lansdale, Ellsberg recounted, "But if that didn't work out"— getting Nhu to leave —"or if I changed my mind and decided that we had to get rid of Diem himself, could you go along with that?" In telling him the story, Ellsberg said, Lansdale "relived the incident. He hesitated, his face got troubled. He looked kind of abashed, almost shamefaced and regretful — exactly the way a man would look if he's reliving how reluctant he was to give up a role he wanted. He shook his head slowly and sadly as he said, 'No, Mr. President, I couldn't do that. Diem is a friend of mine and I couldn't do that.'"

Kennedy did not show any anger when Lansdale said he could not or would not go along with eliminating Diem, Ellsberg continued. But he was quickly dismissive. "It was clear to [Lansdale]," Ellsberg said, "that he would not be going to Vietnam. He was saying no to the job, and it was a job he desperately wanted. He wasn't presenting his refusal as a matter of high principle, and he was not being critical of the president. He made it clear that Kennedy had the right to ask him." The president, Ellsberg said, had turned to "the one man who couldn't possibly have killed Diem."

On the drive back to the Pentagon, Ellsberg continued, McNamara was "furious" at Lansdale. "He had never expressed such direct fury before. 'You can't talk to a president that way.'" The secretary of defense's caustic message was, Lansdale told Ellsberg, "When the president wants you to do something, you just don't say to him, no, you won't do it." McNamara never spoke to him again, Lansdale told Ellsberg; Lansdale left the Pentagon one month later. "I was packing up my desk in the Pentagon," Lansdale told Ellsberg many times, "when I got word that Diem had been killed."

In Lansdale's telling of the story, Ellsberg said, "Kennedy did not use the words 'kill' or 'assassinate' in connection with Diem. But Lansdale told me he was in no doubt that this was what was being discussed."

Lansdale, a believer in the principle of plausible denial, is not known to have talked to anyone else about his meeting with Kennedy and McNamara. Rufus Phillips recalls hearing Lansdale, who died in 1987, admit his ambivalence. "I remember him telling me that people [in the Kennedy administration] were being put in an impossible situation and being asked to do some things," Phillips said in an interview. Lansdale said he "felt the need" to get proper authority for any planned action "on a piece of paper. He didn't want to be the fall guy."*

Phillips returned to Saigon in late September, about three weeks after attending the National Security Council meeting. Within a week or so of his return, he said, Diem told him that he had learned about the meeting — and what Phillips had said to the president. There was one more important detail, Phillips told me. During a subsequent meeting late in October at the presidential palace, Diem asked Phillips whether a coup was coming. "I said yes," Phillips confessed. He told Diem nothing more, he said.

---

* The talk with Lansdale of impossible situations arose, Phillips told me, during a conversation about McNamara. "He distrusted McNamara," Phillips added. "He thought he was strange — all facts and figures. People trying to get up the career ladder learned to feed him what he wanted." Lansdale's view, said Phillips, was that McNamara "set the framework. He was talking about what seemed to be tangibles, but they were unreal tangibles. He made you play in his ballpark."

By the end of October, it was clear that Diem had no intention of turning away from his brother. He would stay in Saigon and so would Nhu. Shortly before the coup, Lodge offered Diem safe conduct by airplane to a neutral country, but the proud Diem rejected the offer as apparently was expected. There is no evidence that Lodge or any embassy official made a serious effort to save Diem. No American, for example, urged General Minh and his fellow plotters to spare Diem's life. In his 1975 testimony to the Church Committee, Lucien Conein claimed that at about six o'clock on the morning of the coup he was asked by General Minh to procure an aircraft to evacuate Diem. He checked with the CIA station in Saigon, Conein said, and was told that it would be impossible to get a plane to Saigon within twenty-four hours. The aircraft had to be capable of flying Diem to a suitable neutral country without being forced to land for refueling — no one in the Kennedy administration wanted Diem to hold a planeside news conference. The only plane available, Conein said he was told, would have to be flown from Guam. By eight o'clock that morning, as Conein surely knew, Diem was in the hands of the military men who would murder him. In any case, a suitable aircraft could easily have been provided in advance but was not. Jack Kennedy had written off Diem, and everyone in Saigon knew it.

In the course of reporting for this book, it was learned that Jack Kennedy made a second effort in the fall of 1963 to separate Nhu from Diem. This time, he did not use someone who, like Lansdale, had special rapport with the South Vietnamese president; he sent instead a personal emissary who represented the power of the American presidency. This was to be Diem's last chance to save himself, and retain his office. By early October, Ambassador Lodge knew from Lucien Conein that the Vietnamese army plotters were planning Diem's murder. Although no paper trail exists, it is difficult to believe that Lodge did not directly relay such important information to the president.

After Kennedy's assassination, many of his aides began telling reporters that the president — as Kennedy himself told Charles Bartlett — did not believe the United States had a future in South Vietnam, but had to remain there through the 1964 elections. The most detailed account of Kennedy's withdrawal plan was provided by

Kenny O'Donnell in *"Johnny, We Hardly Knew Ye."* O'Donnell quoted the president as privately telling Senator Mike Mansfield in the spring of 1963, after Mansfield had publicly criticized American involvement in the war, that he would order a complete military withdrawal in 1965. "But I can't do it until 1965 — after I'm reelected," Kennedy told the senator. "After Mansfield left the office," O'Donnell's account continued, "the President told me, 'In 1965, I'll become one of the most unpopular Presidents in history. I'll be damned everywhere as a Communist appeaser. But I don't care. If I tried to pull out completely now from Vietnam, we would have another Joe McCarthy red scare on our hands, but I can do it after I'm reelected. So we had better make damned sure that I *am* reelected.'" In later interviews, Mansfield confirmed the O'Donnell account.

The O'Donnell passage has become the centerpiece of an ongoing debate about Kennedy's responsibility for the war in Vietnam, which is increasingly seen as one of America's most tragic foreign policy entanglements. O'Donnell, at the time he wrote, may not have known the full story of the plotting against Diem; he surely could not have foreseen that Jack Kennedy's probable advance knowledge of the death of Diem would be made public.

If O'Donnell, Mansfield, and Bartlett are right, the president always planned to disengage from Vietnam. Yet he chose not to act in the fall of 1963, when Diem's unpopularity and pending overthrow gave him the perfect opportunity. Again, assuming that O'Donnell, Mansfield, and Bartlett have it right, Kennedy's policy was not to save South Vietnam but merely to postpone the inevitable until after his reelection. Ngo Dinh Diem was killed because he wanted to do something in 1963 — get the Americans out of Vietnam — that Kennedy wanted to do only after the election. Kennedy thus kept up the American involvement in the war for the most expedient of reasons — to ensure his reelection in 1964. He also chose to stand aside and, at the minimum, acquiesce in the murder of a fellow Catholic and fellow anticommunist. For all of his faults, and they were many, Ngo Dinh Diem was not a political threat to the United States. He was not a Fidel Castro. He was, in fact, much more vulnerable than Castro.

It's also possible that Kennedy believed that General Minh and his military colleagues would rally the Vietnamese army and revive the nation's democratic institutions, thus keeping South Vietnam safe from communism — at least through the election. On November 7, 1963, five days after the coup, the United States formally recognized a token new civilian government headed by Nguyen Ngoc Tho, the former vice president under Diem. At his news conference on November 14 — his last as president — John Kennedy was asked only three perfunctory questions about the events in South Vietnam, none of them suggesting that the Washington press corps had any insight into the extent of presidential involvement in Diem's overthrow. The American objectives now, Kennedy told the reporters, were "to bring Americans home, permit the South Vietnamese to maintain themselves as a free and independent country, and permit democratic forces within the country to operate." None of those objectives would be met in the coming years.

The final player in the Diem saga in the fall of 1963 was Torbert Macdonald, Jack Kennedy's roommate from college and one of his closest friends. Macdonald, a member of Congress from Massachusetts, died in 1976; he is one of those mystery men who played a major role in Kennedy's life about whom very little can be learned. He was not mentioned in Arthur Schlesinger's memoir, and was mentioned only casually by Ted Sorensen. Macdonald's oral interview with the Kennedy Library was originally sealed; upon being opened in 1995 it turned out to be innocuous. His collected papers from his ten terms in Congress say nothing about his relationship with Jack Kennedy. Bobby Kennedy, in his oral history for the Kennedy Library, did not mention Macdonald.

What could be learned during reporting for this book was that Macdonald was one of Jack Kennedy's playpals — a regular at the afternoon White House pool parties and a partner in many of Kennedy's escapades, especially in Hollywood. He was trusted, a trust that he validated after Kennedy's assassination. Macdonald remained in the Congress until his death — he became an increasingly effective legislator — and he never talked. Joe Croken, a Boston politician who long worked as Macdonald's administrative assistant, told me in a 1997 interview for this book that there were many secrets between Macdonald and Jack Kennedy — "certain things they didn't talk to anybody about." By anybody, Croken said, he meant Bobby Kennedy. "Bobby was straight," Croken explained.

One of the things Macdonald would not discuss, Croken told me, was a secret trip he made to Saigon for Jack Kennedy. "He was the last American of any significance to visit Diem," Croken told me, adding, "It was the only trip he took" for the president. Croken said Macdonald told him of the trip, though he never discussed the message he was carrying.

But Macdonald's longtime mistress, Eleanore Carney, did know what the message was. In his talk with me, Joe Croken confirmed that Carney's closeness to Macdonald put her in a position to know at least some of those "certain things" that only Macdonald and Kennedy knew. After Macdonald's death, Carney, who worked at the National Institutes of Health, briefly considered writing a memoir in collaboration with Herbert Parmet, a history professor at the City University of New York. In 1977 she provided Parmet with four hours of revelations, all of which he tape-recorded. The memoir was never written, but Parmet used some of the information, without identifying Carney by name in his 1983 biography, *JFK: The Presidency of John F. Kennedy.*

In her taped interview, Carney — described by Parmet as a "confidential" source — quoted Kennedy as explaining to Macdonald that he had learned that General Minh and his group were planning to assassinate Diem. (That information could have come from Lodge, who, as we have seen earlier, had been warned by Conein of the general's determination to do away with Diem.) President Kennedy, Carney told Parmet, "wanted to make a direct contact [with Diem]. He was hesitant about using the embassy in Saigon because he could not trust his own people there. Nor did he have enough confidence in Lodge. . . . Finally, there was no South Vietnamese he could trust. So he called on Torby, who then carried the President's personal plea [to Diem], which was to get rid of his brother and take refuge in the American Embassy." It was at that meeting, Carney told Parmet, that Macdonald warned Diem: "They're going to kill you. You've got to get out of there temporarily to seek sanctuary in the American Embassy." But Diem refused. "He just won't do it," Macdonald reported to the president, according to Carney. "He's too stubborn; just refuses to."

In a series of interviews for this book, Macdonald's son, Torbert Macdonald, Jr., recalled learning about his father's extraordinary involvement in Vietnam during their "endless arguments" in the late 1960s about the morality of the war. Macdonald told his son, then a student at Harvard University, that Kennedy had relied on him to warn Diem because "he didn't trust the official channels." Torbert Jr. further quoted his father as saying that "Diem was unwilling to give up his brother." Macdonald reported directly to Kennedy after the mission, his son said, and made it a point to fly in and out of Saigon on military rather than civilian transport, to maintain secrecy.

"He didn't keep records on anything," Macdonald's son told me. When the family retrieved Macdonald's personal effects after his death, they found his congressional passport in shreds. "Sections were sliced out with a razor," his son said.

Jack Kennedy's warning to Diem, as depicted in Eleanore Carney's account, seems contradictory on its face. Why would the president allow his men to plot against the South Vietnamese president, and then tip him off about his fate? But Kennedy had perhaps taken a similar step before, in the spring of 1961. As we have seen (Chapter Thirteen), according to testimony heard by the Church Committee, the president asked George Smathers to meet privately with Rafael Trujillo, the dictator of the Dominican Republic, and raise "the possibility of relinquishing his power and moving out." Trujillo ignored the advice and was assassinated, with American complicity, within weeks. There was also a personal reason for Kennedy's decision to seek a last-minute reprieve for Diem: he was an old friend and fellow Catholic who years before had won the respect of Joseph Kennedy.

Ngo Dinh Diem and his brother knew what was coming, and accepted their fate. On October 26, only days before the coup, Diem ordered Tran Van Dinh, his trusted chargé d'affaires in Washington, to return to Saigon. "I arrived on the thirtieth," Dinh said in a 1995 interview for this book, "and immediately saw Diem, who had just met with Lodge. He asked me to go back to the United States and say"— in an effort to buy time —"that 'Diem is surrendering to you.'" After stalling the Americans, Dinh was "to go to India to negotiate with the

North." It remains his belief, Dinh told me, that Diem, who knew the coup was near, "was in the process of telling the United States to get out" when he was assassinated. Diem had told him, Dinh added, "I cannot talk to the Americans anymore." He never made the trip to New Delhi, Dinh said, and remained in Washington after the coup and assassination. He eventually became a U.S. citizen and retired in 1985 as professor emeritus of international affairs at Temple University.

To this day, Dinh told me, he does not understand the Kennedy administration's policy toward his country. "They were the most amazing years of my life," he said. "I couldn't figure out what the Kennedy administration's goal was. You had a group of people who pursued personal and political ambitions. It was like the Mafia. No disloyalty was permitted. 'Anybody who is not part of my plan is out.'"

The South Vietnamese government never considered the American demand that Diem oust his brother, Dinh added. "What right does the United States have to tell Diem" whom to discard or take on? "Can they come to my house and tell me to get a new wife?"*

* * *

* Dinh, who was technically the acting ambassador in 1963, would have been fascinated by a White House tape recording of Kennedy's telephone conversation shortly after the coup with Roger Hilsman, the assistant secretary of state for the Far East. The issue, as explained by Hilsman, was the suspicion of Prince Norodom Sihanouk, the ruler of Cambodia, that the U.S. was plotting his overthrow.

Hilsman: "Behind all this is fear of what's happened to Diem and Nhu. Fear of his own military. This is bothering Sihanouk; he's a highly emotional fellow. And also, as the [American] ambassador [in Cambodia] is frank to say, there's a history during the administration of President Eisenhower where the Agency did play footsie with opposition groups there."

Kennedy: "Did they? Was that a true story about '59 or something?"

Hilsman: "It really is true."

Kennedy: "CIA did it?"

Hilsman: "Sure. They supplied the money and they were involved in the plot against Sihanouk back before this administration."

Kennedy: "Christ! They did it in Indonesia, they did it in Laos, they did it in Cambodia."

Hilsman: "We're paying for it all over Asia for ineptitude. . . . The Agency in those days wasn't responsible to the State Department. . . . Every time I go on Capitol Hill I get this thrown in my face: 'Are you in control?'"

Kennedy (laughing): "Well, in any case, there's some talk about sending [Dean] Acheson out, is there?"

In his 1964 interviews for the Kennedy Library, Bobby Kennedy blamed everyone else in the government in his effort to protect his brother. It was an especially ugly performance.

"Nobody liked Diem particularly," Kennedy said. "But how to get rid of him and get somebody who would continue the war . . . was the great problem. . . . It was difficult to deal with all of these things. Perhaps it should have been watched more carefully or closer. . . . Bob McNamara and Maxwell Taylor [were] so involved with the military . . . that they didn't see things correctly. Dean Rusk [was] not helping at all. . . . He was for a coup and then he was against. He was all over the lot. There wasn't anybody. And Mac Bundy wasn't particularly helpful."

"We were going to try to get rid of Henry Cabot Lodge," Kennedy said. "He was supposed to come home [for consultations] if that coup hadn't taken place, . . . and we were trying to work out how he could be fired, how we could get rid of him. . . . He didn't have answers to questions. It was a difficult business. . . .

"If you lost Vietnam," Kennedy added, "I think everybody was quite clear that the rest of Southeast Asia would fall. . . . It would have profound effects on our position throughout the world. . . . It

Hilsman: ". . . I'm afraid it's past that. If it were just the Khmer Serei . . ."

Kennedy: "What's the Khmer Serei? What do you mean by that?"

Hilsman: "Well, this Khmer Serei is an opposition movement. An exile group. . . ."

Kennedy: "Well, what are we going to do? What's our public position going to be?"

Hilsman: ". . . Two things. One is the categorical denials that we have anything to do with the Khmer Serei and their opposition or any plots to topple Sihanouk. And our second public opinion is, as you've so often said, our aid is because people want us there. If they don't want us there, we are happy to get out."

Kennedy: "Yeah. Are you going to withdraw [or] are we going to say we're going to get out?"

Hilsman: "I wouldn't say that publicly just yet. . . ."

Sihanouk was one of the first world leaders to publicly accuse the Kennedy administration of direct involvement in the Diem coup. Journalist Elizabeth Becker, in her 1986 study of Cambodian politics, When the War Was Over (Simon and Schuster), reported that Sihanouk responded to Diem's murder by immediately renouncing all American aid to Cambodia. He wanted, she wrote, "to keep the United States out of Cambodian affairs altogether and reduce the possibility that Americans would plot his overthrow or death."

would affect what happened in India. . . . It would have an effect on Indonesia. . . . All of these countries would be affected by the fall of Vietnam."

Robert Kennedy, who knew the most, did not tell the library that his brother had privately been more of a dove than a hawk and planned to end the war after his reelection. That piece of the legacy, if true, would come from O'Donnell, Mansfield, and the many who mourned Kennedy as a peace-loving and wise president. Perhaps getting out of Vietnam was not Jack's real intention. Or perhaps Bobby did not talk of future peace in South Vietnam because he himself could not deal with the truth about Diem's downfall, and wanted no journalist or future historian to be able to tell the full story — that John F. Kennedy had put his reelection ahead of the well-being of the soldiers and civilians in Vietnam, and the life of a former ally.

Lyndon Johnson, Kennedy's successor, chose to believe what all of the men around Jack Kennedy believed — that prosecuting the war was essential to American national security. If President Kennedy privately held a different view, he did not share it with his vice president.

His brother, Bobby Kennedy told the library, "felt he had a strong, overwhelming reason for being in Vietnam and that we should win the war in Vietnam." Jack Kennedy did not want to put American troops on the ground in Vietnam, Bobby Kennedy added, "because everybody, including General [Douglas] MacArthur, felt that land conflict between our troops — white troops and Asian — would only end in disaster. So we went in as advisers to try to get the Vietnamese to fight, because we couldn't win the war for them. They had to win the war for themselves."

Kennedy then had this exchange with his interviewer, John Barlow Martin:

Martin: "But the president was convinced that we had to stay in there?"

Kennedy: "Yes."

Martin: "And we couldn't lose it?"

Kennedy: "Yes."

Martin: "And if the Vietnamese were about to lose it, would he propose to go in on land if he had to?"

Kennedy: "We'd face that when we came to it."

Bobby Kennedy was justifying his brother's continued prosecution of the war by falling back on the domino theory, which drove so much of America's foreign policy in the Vietnam War. History has shown that the only dominoes that fell were the eight successive military governments in South Vietnam that collapsed, corrupt regime after corrupt regime, after Ngo Dinh Diem's murder in November 1963. Whatever Jack Kennedy's intentions were, Vietnam was his war, even after his death.

24

LAST DAYS

The old and the new came together in the last days of John F. Kennedy's life, as his reelection campaign took him to Texas. The usual Kennedy glamour was heightened by the presence of the first lady, who accompanied her husband on a political trip for the first time since the 1960 campaign. Behind the glamour was a level of scheming that no one in the public or the press could imagine. The CIA was trying, once again, to murder Fidel Castro. Lyndon Johnson was still targeted for political demise. One new undertaking involved Kennedy's fear of Communist China and its development of the bomb, and his eagerness to destroy — perhaps with the aid of the Soviet Union — China's nuclear facilities. There were also new charges, presented to Bobby Kennedy on Thursday, November 21, as his brother left the Oval Office for the last time, that Kenny O'Donnell, the president's most trusted aide, and others in his administration were diverting 1964 campaign money for their own use.

Any of the old and new secrets, if made public, would raise questions about the president's judgment — and open a Pandora's box of potential scandals.

Some of the new was welcome. White House aides could see that the president had moved closer to the first lady in the months since the death of Patrick, their newborn son. One immediate result was her agreement to go with him to Texas. She and the president sat together on the *Air Force One* flight, "talking and just chitchatting together," Malcolm Kilduff, the deputy press secretary, told me in a 1996 interview for this book. "It was different than I had seen them before — you know, they were laughing and being like husband and wife. It was very nice." Sometime earlier, Kilduff said, Kennedy had abruptly canceled a press trip to the new presidential retreat in the countryside near Atoka, Virginia. "'I don't want that done,' he said. 'You go and cancel it. That's just for Jackie and me. That's our place.' I thought to myself how protective he was being of her," Kilduff told me.

There was the usual other side, too, of Kennedy's private life. Even aboard *Air Force One,* the president was forced to wear a stiff brace that stretched from his shoulders to his crotch — the aftermath of an errant poolside grab while he was on a campaign trip to the West Coast. Two months before the end, Hugh Sidey, *Time* magazine's White House correspondent, recalled in an interview for this book, a woman acquaintance of Sidey's "came to me and told me how Kennedy tried to put the make on her at the pool. She wrenched away and [the president] fell into the pool, hurting his back."* The brace would keep the president upright for the bullets of Lee Harvey Oswald.

On November 16, Jack Kennedy made his first visit since December 1962 to the family home at Palm Beach, Florida. Two days later he

---

* In a column published in *Time* magazine on May 18, 1987, Sidey gave a slightly different version, moving the scene of the action from a pool to a bedroom. "One insider," he wrote, "claimed that Kennedy reinjured his weakened back during a bedroom tussle at a party in Bing Crosby's Palm Springs, Calif., house, which the President was using in September, 1963, thus forcing him to return to a rigid back brace. That brace held him erect in the limousine two months later in Dallas after the first gunshot struck him. The second shot killed the still upright President." Sidey wrote the column after Senator Gary Hart of Colorado, a Democratic candidate, was forced to withdraw from the 1988 presidential campaign upon being publicly linked to a woman who was not his wife. Sidey's account attracted little attention.

made what seemed to be a routine speech to the Inter-American Press Association, calling for social justice and economic welfare in Latin America. The speech included a reference to Fidel Castro as a "barrier" to be removed.

The address was unremarkable on its surface — full of praise for the Alliance for Progress, the president's initiative for Latin American progress that had been announced, to much fanfare, two years earlier.* There were some especially harsh words about Castro. Twelve years later, investigators for the Church Committee would be told that the tough language was drafted not by Kennedy's speechwriters but by the CIA, as a message of presidential support for a skittish Cuban operative code-named AMLASH. The operative, Rolando Cubela, was the agency's best hope in the fall of 1963 in its continuing effort to assassinate Castro. The CIA was finally going to get done what Jack Kennedy had wanted since the Bay of Pigs.†

After returning to Washington and cheerfully accepting a fifty-five-pound Thanksgiving turkey in the Oval Office (the photographs were winning), Kennedy turned to what had become another of his obsessions: destroying China's nuclear weapons facilities. The president had been concerned since his days in the Senate about the danger of a China armed with nuclear weapons; in his televised

---

* "The hope," Kennedy declared in the 1961 speech, "is for a hemisphere where every man has enough to eat and a chance to work, where every child can learn, and every family can find decent shelter." The president did not say that military aid to Latin America, under the Alliance, had risen by 50 percent over the Eisenhower-era levels, with increasing emphasis on internal security and police training. For many Latin Americans, the Alliance was little more than a cynical means of providing arms for a regional war against communism, domestic opposition — and Fidel Castro.

† James Johnston, a lawyer on the Church Committee, said in a 1995 interview for this book that he had been told of the president's signal of support for Cubela by Seymour Bolton, a senior CIA officer who was assigned as liaison to the Church Committee in 1975. Bolton's revelation came after Johnston and a colleague presented him with a prepublication draft of the committee's final report on assassinations for review. "Bolton had no objections about classification," Johnston said, "but he went into orbit over the implication that the CIA was a rogue elephant." It was at that point that Bolton told Johnston that in 1963 he had "carried a paragraph [to the White House] to be inserted into Kennedy's November 18 speech" to the Inter-American Press Association. At their meeting, Johnston told me, Bolton (who died in 1985) was incensed at the implication that there was "any difference between Kennedy's policy and the CIA policy."

interview with three network correspondents at the end of 1962, Kennedy said that the Chinese, unlike the Soviets, believed "in war as the means of bringing about the communist world." China also believed, the president added, that it could survive a nuclear war because its population numbered 750 million.* In a 1966 essay in the *Saturday Evening Post,* the journalist Stewart Alsop revealed that the president had convened a meeting on the Chinese bomb just before his assassination. Alsop re-created an exchange between the president and a leading government expert on the Far East in which the expert, asked for a recommendation by Kennedy, proposed "a surgical operation" to bomb the Chinese nuclear reactor at Lanchow, located near the test site at Lop Nor. "We could have plans for you," Alsop quoted the expert as telling the president, "with various optional means of taking out the plants, in the near future."

Kennedy, in fact, was by then much more advanced in his planning. William C. Foster, who was director of the Arms Control and Disarmament Agency in 1963, told the Kennedy Library in 1965 that the president had "deep personal feelings about . . . the necessity of doing something about ostracizing or containing China." Foster's remarks on China, declassified by the library in 1994 but not made public until this book, depict what he said was the president's "willingness to consider politically dangerous" actions. "You know," Foster quoted the president as saying, "it wouldn't be too hard if we could somehow get kind of an anonymous airplane to go over there, take out the Chinese facilities — they've only got a couple — and maybe we could do it, or maybe the Soviet Union could do it, rather than face the threat of a China with nuclear weapons."

In July 1963 Kennedy asked Averell Harriman, the chief negotiator in Moscow for the nuclear test ban treaty, to secretly raise the issue of

---

* In March 1988 historian Gordon H. Chang published "JFK, China, and the Bomb" in the *Journal of American History,* arguing that "it is doubtful" that Kennedy's policies toward China "were consistent with the interests of international peace." In the article, Chang quoted a State Department official as revealing that the president, during a White House dinner with André Malraux, the French minister of culture, stated that the Chinese "would be perfectly prepared to sacrifice hundreds of millions of their own lives" to carry out their aggressive foreign policies. The State Department official, William R. Tyler, an assistant secretary of state, was further quoted in Chang's article as recalling, in an oral history for the Kennedy Library, that the president said he believed that the Chinese attached a "lower value" to human life.

a joint strike against China with Nikita Khrushchev. The official record of Kennedy's instructions to Harriman is still sealed. But Chester Cooper, a CIA official who was one of Harriman's former advisers for the test ban, told me in a 1994 interview for this book that "the proposition was not to fly a joint mission" with the Soviets, but to "work it out so the Russians wouldn't protest" if American planes bombed the Chinese facilities. A slightly different account comes from Karl Kaysen, who was deeply involved in the test ban talks as the deputy White House science adviser in 1963. Kaysen, in a 1994 interview for this book, said that the issue of destroying China's nuclear facilities did come up in the secret talks with Khrushchev. "There was talk of hitting Lop Nor," Kaysen told me. "The substance of Harriman's brief was to get the Soviets to tell the Chinese to knock it off," Kaysen said. One reason for the continued secrecy over the Harriman meeting may have been Khrushchev's response to Kennedy's joint bombing proposal. "Khrushchev was very angry" at the American approach, Kaysen said, "and told Harriman, 'I don't run a post office.'" The message for John F. Kennedy was clear: any bombs meant for China could be sent directly, without Soviet intervention.

The question of how to destroy the Chinese nuclear facilities was still being studied at Kennedy's death.

During his last days in Washington, Kennedy was confronted with a serious allegation against Kenny O'Donnell, the appointments secretary who, along with Dave Powers, was indispensable to his way of life. O'Donnell's accuser was a professional politician named Paul Corbin, a hardworking campaigner in 1960 who was assigned to the Democratic National Committee after Kennedy's election; since then he had maintained a close personal relationship with Bobby Kennedy. Corbin, a former marine who served in World War II, provoked something close to fear among the senior aides in the Justice Department and White House. He was conspiratorial and full of swagger, but he was also a fiercely independent whistle-blower who saw himself as a Galahad among the political hacks who surrounded the president and his brother. Corbin was barely tolerated by Jack Kennedy, who did not trust him. But he had superb access to Bobby

Kennedy, and used the attorney general's private entrance and private elevator in the Justice Department.

"Everybody hated Corbin," Joseph Dolan, one of Bobby Kennedy's deputies, told me in an interview, "except Bobby, John Seigenthaler [another aide], and Steve Smith," a Kennedy brother-in-law. "Steve sheltered him." Dolan told of a meeting at Bobby Kennedy's house in Hickory Hill on a Justice Department issue when Corbin walked in unannounced. "Bobby whispered," Dolan said, "'I told him not to come.' It was one of the few times I saw Bobby blush from head to toe."*

Although he had an excellent relationship with Bobby, Corbin was someone who apparently made no assumptions about anyone. He attempted in 1963 to get his information about O'Donnell and the others — information he realized no one wanted to hear — directly to the president. He did so by sharing his story with Charles Bartlett, the journalist who could, as Corbin understood, relay word directly to his good friend Jack Kennedy. Corbin and Bartlett had met during the difficult 1960 Wisconsin primary campaign, Bartlett told me in an interview for this book. "He was a good friend of mine." Bartlett learned that Corbin, on his own, had been keeping track of the handling of campaign money at the Democratic Party headquarters in Washington. In the late spring of 1963, Corbin concluded that he had solid evidence of the skimming of campaign contributions by O'Donnell and two others, and he went to Bartlett to have him warn the president. The process was simple, as Corbin explained to Bartlett.

---

* Corbin had contempt for many of the old Kennedy pals, and did not let up after the assassinations of Jack and Robert Kennedy. Sometime in late 1968, after the death in June of Robert Kennedy, Dolan told me, there was a reunion of Kennedy aides. Dolan approached Corbin with a plea for peace, saying, in essence, "We may have had our differences, but we worked for a great man." The two men threw their arms around each other in a bear hug. As they did so, Dolan told me with a laugh, Corbin whispered, "Bobby never trusted you." When Corbin himself died in early 1990, John Seigenthaler eulogized him as "sharing one abiding, dominating trait of character" with Bobby Kennedy: loyalty. "Loyalty was a bond of trust," Seigenthaler said, according to a copy of his remarks, "a first tenet of faith. I think all of us in the room knew and felt and benefited from that loyalty of Paul Corbin. Between Bob [Kennedy] and Paul, the loyalty grew to a shared love."

In one specific case, Corbin said, a senior executive of a California oil company with a merger proposal pending in the Justice Department was told to give $100,000 to the reelection campaign in $100 bills. The quid pro quo was an age-old Washington tradition: a promise to try to resolve, or "fix," the problem. Only $50,000 of the oilman's cash was recorded as having been contributed to the campaign; the other $50,000 ended up, Corbin told Bartlett, in the pockets of Kenny O'Donnell and his cohorts.

Bartlett eventually did Corbin's bidding, and in July 1963 began writing memoranda to the president warning him of corruption inside his White House. It was a courageous act. No president likes to be told that his closest aide, who knows the most about him, has to go. After a series of interviews, Bartlett provided me with startling evidence of his own warnings, as well as support for Corbin's allegations: carbon copies of some of the letters he sent the president.

On July 19, Bartlett told the president in a typewritten note relayed by Evelyn Lincoln, "I know well how you dislike bearers of bad news but I am passing these memos along under a deep conviction that they deal with an area which urgently requires your personal scrutiny. An aura of scandal is building up — someone as remote as John Sherman Cooper [the Republican senator from Kentucky] observed to me the other evening that . . . it would be a terrible thing if your record as President were to be impaired by disloyalty on the part of your associates." Bartlett then named O'Donnell and two other aides who, he said, were "performing legitimate political functions in a way that is breeding resentment and suspicion. At worst they are the heart of an extensive corruption which is reaching into many of the government agencies. No books are kept, everything is cash, and the potential for a rich harvest is clear. . . . I am fearful that unless you put a personal priority on learning more about what is going on, the thing may slip suddenly beyond your control."

Bartlett told me that he was alarmed by O'Donnell, who was doing little to hide his newfound wealth. The presidential aide had offered a large sum of money for an elegant house in Georgetown, Bartlett learned, only to lose it to a higher bidder. Later that summer Bartlett wrote Kennedy another memorandum, reporting that O'Donnell, while drinking at a bar in Hyannis Port, had been overheard by a Secret Service agent making derogatory remarks about the president. "The purport of O'Donnell's remarks," Bartlett wrote, "was that the President was in fact rather stupid and that if it were not for [O'Donnell's] assistance, he would fall flat on his face. O'Donnell said he had had a great many offers from industry but that he was afraid to leave because he knew that the administration would fall apart." Kennedy's response was to give the note to O'Donnell, who had the Secret Service agent immediately removed from the White House presidential detail, disrupting his career. The agent did not learn the facts behind his reassignment until he was interviewed in 1995 for this book.

The possibility exists that Bartlett and Corbin misunderstood O'Donnell's role. Some of the political cash that he was allegedly skimming may have been taken for the president himself, who had problems — with Ellen Rometsch, for example — that Charles Bartlett could not envision; problems that only cash could solve. The president responded very coolly to the July 19 letter, Bartlett told me, calling him one day to say, "Charlie, there are a lot of people over here mad at you." Kennedy's view, Bartlett said, was patrician: "He made his money. Other people should make theirs."

Jack Kennedy's obvious lack of concern about O'Donnell's behavior did not stop Paul Corbin. He returned to his inquiry with renewed determination, Bartlett told me, and, after months of preparation, "brought Bobby the stuff. He had affidavits proving that it was still going on" as of November 1963. "He was a good sleuth," Bartlett said. "He told me he got it all together, signed statements, with Kenny O'Donnell being the bagman. He took it to Bobby and Bobby went through it and said, 'This is it.' He called Jack" in front of Corbin. Evelyn Lincoln told the attorney general that his brother had just left for Texas. "Bobby said," Corbin told Bartlett, "'We'll do it Monday. First thing.'" After the assassination, the distraught attorney general told Corbin to let the issue rest. "Lyndon wouldn't believe me," Kennedy said, according to Corbin.

Bartlett never wrote a newspaper story about the scandal, which died with the murder of his good friend. Like Ben Bradlee and others who covered the White House, he found himself trapped in the gray area between friendship and professionalism. Bartlett remained troubled enough by what he knew and, perhaps, by what he did not do at the time, to make his letters to the president available for this book.

There were two brutal ironies on November 22.

That Friday started as a great day for Bobby Kennedy, and a potentially ruinous one for Vice President Lyndon Johnson. At ten o'clock in the morning, Donald Reynolds, a Washington insurance broker, walked with his lawyer into a small hearing room on Capitol Hill and began providing Burkett Van Kirk, the minority counsel of the Senate Rules Committee, with eagerly awaited evidence of unreported gift-giving to Johnson. Van Kirk had learned about Reynolds independently, but he and Bobby Kennedy had been secretly working together for weeks, through intermediaries, to accumulate evidence of payola against Johnson and Bobby Baker, Johnson's former Senate aide. Reynolds told Van Kirk and a Democratic staff member of the Rules Committee how he had listed Bobby Baker as a vice president of his insurance agency, and he claimed to have funneled off-the-books cash to Baker — subsequently written off as a "business expense." Reynolds told of making payoffs to Democratic Party officials, arranged through Baker's office in the Senate, in return for being allowed to handle the insurance on a large federal construction project. He told what little he knew of Ellen Rometsch and her associations at Baker's Quorum Club, the private club on Capitol Hill where senators and lobbyists shared drinks and other pleasures. And, finally, he told of selling life insurance to the vice president and being pressured in return to buy unnecessary advertisements on Johnson's television station in Austin, Texas — no one in Texas would be interested in buying insurance from a broker in suburban Maryland, 1,500 miles away. Reynolds also told of being compelled to provide Johnson with a stereo record player, as a kind of bonus. Bobby Baker had given the Johnson family a catalog, Reynolds testified, and Lady Bird Johnson had picked out the stereo she wanted. Reynolds was still being questioned at 2:30 P.M. when a secretary burst into the hearing room with the news from Dallas. Lyndon Johnson was now president of the United States, and no one was going to challenge his legitimacy because of a stereo set and a few thousand dollars' worth of television ads.

Burkett Van Kirk remains convinced that Johnson would have been fighting for political survival had he remained vice president. "There's no doubt in my mind," Van Kirk told me in an interview, "that Reynolds's testimony would have gotten Johnson out of the vice presidency." The outnumbered Republicans on the Rules Committee tried to continue an investigation into Reynolds's charges, but the effort petered out after President Johnson told a news conference in January 1964 that the stereo set his family received had been a gift from Bobby Baker.

As the deadly volley of shots was being fired in Dallas, an essential step in another murder — one sanctioned by the Kennedy administration — was taking place in a Paris hotel room. An undercover CIA agent from Washington met with Rolando Cubela and gave him a specially prepared assassination device — a syringe full of poison designed to look and act like a fountain pen. The poison was meant for Fidel Castro. Cubela, a former student radical who had joined Castro's revolution in the mid-1950s, had become disaffected by 1959, and had talked since then of killing Castro. His recruitment, which took years to accomplish, was the best thing that happened to Desmond FitzGerald's Cuba task force all year, Sam Halpern, then of the CIA, told me in an interview. "Des thought [Cubela] was going to do it — get to Castro," Halpern explained. "Believe me, he thought he was going to do it."*

Three weeks earlier, FitzGerald himself had flown to Paris to meet with the jittery Cubela, who was demanding a meeting with Bobby

---

* Halpern told me that a CIA scientist spent a weekend turning the fountain pen given to Cubela into, in effect, a hypodermic needle. The pen was filled, in the end, with Black Flag 40 — a commercially sold insecticide — as the poison. The contrast between the James Bond image of CIA technicians devising elaborate weapons of murder and the reality, Halpern added, was often unclear even to the men at the top of the agency. He noted that Vice Admiral William Raborn, who replaced McCone as CIA director in 1965, was fond of watching *Get Smart,* a television sitcom that featured an intelligence operative who took off his shoe and talked into it to reach another agent hundreds of miles away. One morning, Halpern said, Raborn telephoned and asked a senior CIA scientist "to get some of those gadgets for the men in the field." He was told that the devices did not exist.

Kennedy before carrying out an assassination attempt. According to the CIA's 1967 Inspector General's Report on the planned assassination of Castro, the documents on file in FitzGerald's office showed that he had been authorized by his superior, Richard Helms, the director of clandestine operations, to tell Cubela that he was the "personal representative of Robert F. Kennedy." FitzGerald was further authorized to give Cubela "assurance of full U.S. support [for a coup] if there is change of the present government in Cuba." The IG Report quoted FitzGerald as explaining that he and Helms had discussed the question of going to Kennedy, and Helms told him that "it was not necessary to seek approval from Robert Kennedy for FitzGerald to speak in his name."

Cubela, less jittery after FitzGerald's visit and the words inserted by the CIA at the last minute into the president's speech to the Inter-American Press Association, was all business at the meeting with the CIA's operative on November 22, according to the IG Report. At the moment the two men learned of Jack Kennedy's assassination, they were talking about delivering a large arms cache to Cuba in subsequent weeks. Cubela was visibly upset, according to the IG Report, asking the agent, "Why do such things happen to good people?"

The Church Committee, confronted in 1975 with a strong possibility of the direct involvement of a Kennedy in the Castro assassination plotting, turned away. The committee dealt with the FitzGerald visit to Paris as it did with the telephone calls and visits from Judith Exner to Jack Kennedy at the White House — it accepted every denial at face value. Richard Helms, asked by the committee in 1975 whether FitzGerald could use Bobby Kennedy's name without Kennedy's personal approval, said yes. "I felt so sure," Helms testified, "that if I went to see [Robert] Kennedy that he would have said yes, that I don't think there was any need to." In its final report, the Church Committee made no judgment about Bobby Kennedy's role in the Cubela matter, noting that the evidence "falls into a pattern similar to that described in the discussion of post–Bay of Pigs activity in the Kennedy Administration." Former Kennedy administration officials consistently testified, the report said, that they knew nothing of assassination, and Richard Helms repeatedly testified that he believed "assassination was permissible in view of the continued press to overthrow the Castro regime."

Sam Halpern had his own views, he told me in a 1997 interview. "I can't imagine either Dick [Helms] or Des [FitzGerald] going off and using Bobby Kennedy's name without checking. But that's the way it's written," he said with a shrug, as if to say, Of course the files would reveal nothing explicitly of a Kennedy role — to put in writing that the president's brother knew of assassination plotting was against every rule in the CIA book.

The Inspector General's Report included, perhaps unintentionally, an epitaph for a slain American president who had stalked Fidel Castro for nearly three years: "It is likely that at the very moment President Kennedy was shot a CIA officer was meeting with a Cuban agent in Paris and giving him an assassination device for use against Castro."

EPILOGUE

Robert F. Kennedy's despair over the murder of his brother was heightened by the fact that he could do nothing to avenge it.

He and Jacqueline Kennedy were convinced that the president had been struck down not by communists, as J. Edgar Hoover and many others believed, but by a domestic conspiracy. Even if they had no clear idea of who ran it or the motives behind it, one immediate suspect was Sam Giancana, who had been overheard by the FBI since early 1961 claiming again and again that he had been double-crossed by Jack Kennedy after helping to elect him in 1960.

Thus the private telephone call was made on the evening of November 22 to Julius Draznin, the Chicago expert on labor racketeering for the National Labor Relations Board. "We need help on this," Bobby Kennedy said. "Maybe you can open some doors [with] the mob. Anything you pick up, let me know directly." Draznin was instructed to stay in contact through Angie Novello, Kennedy's faithful secretary at the Justice Department. Draznin told me in a 1994 interview for this book that he understood Kennedy's reference to the mob: "He meant Sam Giancana." Two days later, on Sunday, November 24, Jack Ruby, a Dallas barkeeper with ties to organized crime in

Chicago, shot and killed Lee Harvey Oswald, as the world watched on television.

Draznin recruited a few friends who were also in law enforcement, and over the next few weeks the ad hoc group looked for ties between Oswald and the Chicago mob and also pulled together an enormous dossier on Ruby. But the group could find no evidence that Sam Giancana's henchmen had anything to do with Kennedy's assassination. "I said, 'Bobby, I'm drawing a blank,'" Draznin told me. "'Nothing here.'"

His inquiry, Draznin went on, continued "on and off for over a year" — longer, ironically, than the work of the Warren Commission, the august group established by President Johnson to investigate the assassination. Draznin spoke once a week or so to Walter Sheridan, a Justice Department expert on organized crime. By early 1964, Draznin said, "we talked much less," and he fell out of touch with his Justice Department contact. Eventually, Draznin met privately in Chicago with Bobby Kennedy and told him, he said, that Jack Ruby had acted alone in killing Oswald. "Ruby thought [killing Oswald] was a patriotic act," Draznin told me. "I believe it to this day. I picked up nothing at all tying it to Chicago mob men."

Over the next thirty-five years, the nation would remain obsessed with the Kennedy assassination. Hundreds of books would be written, full of feverish speculation about Oswald and Ruby and their possible links to organized crime or Soviet intelligence. In five years of reporting for this book, I found nothing that would change the instinctive conclusions of Julius Draznin, or the much more detailed findings of the Warren Commission — Oswald and Ruby acted alone.

Bobby Kennedy seems to have kept his deepest fears about his brother's murderers to himself. In interviews for this book, his closest aides offered differing opinions, based on their conversations with Kennedy, about the possibility of conspiracy. Kennedy told some friends that he accepted the Warren Commission's conclusions; to others, he suggested that the full story might never be known.

Kennedy was much more forthcoming with Georgi Bolshakov, his old back-channel colleague, who had been sent home to Moscow after the Kennedy brothers thought he had betrayed them during the Cuban missile crisis and stopped talking to him. Soviet files made available in the mid-1990s to Aleksandr Fursenko and Timothy Naftali for their book *"One Hell of a Gamble"* revealed that Bobby Kennedy sent an emissary to Moscow in late November of 1963. The emissary was William Walton, an abstract painter and former journalist who was a family insider and had stayed close to Jack Kennedy after he got to the White House. Walton, who died in 1994, had been scheduled to fly to Moscow on November 22 to meet with Soviet artists. But he flew a week later, with a different mission: to find Bolshakov and urge him to advise the Soviet leadership to remain resolute during the regime of Lyndon Johnson. Bobby Kennedy would one day return as president.

Walton told Bolshakov, according to the Soviet files, that the Kennedys believed that a major political conspiracy was behind Jack Kennedy's murder. Walton also dramatically described how the crime devastated the Kennedy circle and threw Washington into confusion; only McGeorge Bundy, the national security adviser, had the presence of mind to run the affairs of state. When the grief-stricken Bobby Kennedy finally got to bed on the night of November 22, Walton told Bolshakov, he spent the next few hours weeping, unable to sleep. According to Walton, wrote Fursenko and Naftali, "the Kennedy clan considered the selection of Johnson [as vice president] a dreadful mistake. 'He is a clever timeserver,' Walton explained, who would be 'incapable of realizing Kennedy's unfinished plans.'" The one hope for the future of U.S.-Soviet relations was Robert McNamara, who would remain in the Johnson cabinet as secretary of defense. Bobby Kennedy, Walton told Bolshakov, would stay on as attorney general through the end of 1964 and then run for governor of Massachusetts before beginning a campaign for the presidency. "Walton, and presumably Kennedy," Fursenko and Naftali wrote, "wanted Khrushchev to know that only RFK could implement John Kennedy's vision and that the cooling that might occur in U.S.-Soviet relations because of Johnson would not last forever." It was explained that, contrary to what some in the Kremlin might think, Robert

Kennedy shared all his brother's progressive views. "If Robert differed from Jack," the Soviet files said, "it was only in that he is a harder man; but as for his views, Robert agreed completely with his brother and, more important, actively sought to bring John F. Kennedy's ideas to fruition."*

By early Saturday, November 23, John F. Kennedy's most important papers — official and unofficial — had been moved intact by the Secret Service to the most secure room in the White House complex: suite 300 of the Executive Office Building, in a hallway that housed offices of the National Security Council staff. The hallway was under twenty-four-hour armed guard.

The office was a fitting place for the president's papers: its previous occupant had been General Maxwell Taylor and the top-secret files of his Special Group for Counterinsurgency. The president's papers would remain in locked files and under armed guard in the Executive Office Building until they were moved for safekeeping to the National Archives. "I secured the place," James R. Dingeman, an army major who was then executive secretary of the Special Group, told me in a 1993 interview for this book. "Nobody came in except one Saturday morning" in early 1964, he said, "when Mrs. Kennedy and Bobby came."

---

* Over the next few months, Jack Kennedy's grieving admirers continued to undercut Lyndon Johnson with the Soviet Union, according to Fursenko and Naftali. In early 1964, they wrote, Charles Bartlett approached a Soviet intelligence source in New York and warned him that Johnson was not to be trusted. Soviet intelligence files quoted Bartlett as saying that Johnson was "a pragmatic and experienced politician who would change Kennedy's course with regard to the achievement of agreements with the USSR if it seemed advantageous to him." The new president, Bartlett added, "would never equal Kennedy in terms of the consistency and sincerity of his thinking on relations with the USSR." The Soviet fears about the new man in the White House turned out to be unfounded, as Johnson quickly reassured Moscow that he would continue Kennedy's open-door policy. The Soviets were further informed, however, according to their intelligence files, that the new president would no longer pass messages through Ambassador Dobrynin. Even the most sensitive of communications were now to be relayed, as they had been prior to the Kennedy administration, through the American ambassador in Moscow and Secretary of State Dean Rusk. The back channel was over.

Sometime early in the year, said Dingeman, a navy yeoman named George E. Dalton, who had demonstrated his loyalty to the family while on assignment at Hyannis Port, was transferred to Washington and put in charge of the documents. "He used to call me down to read some of Kennedy's writing, because I write as badly as Kennedy did. [Dalton] was going through all the papers." The papers were still in room 300, Dingeman said, when he was reassigned to Europe in the summer of 1964.

Dalton, who later would join Senator Ted Kennedy's personal staff after retiring from the navy, stayed on, culling and removing documents from the Kennedy papers. He also did a preliminary review of the Oval Office tape recordings and prepared transcripts. There was nothing subtle about Dalton's mission: to screen the tapes and papers for sensitive materials that were to be erased or removed. Dalton bragged in the mid-1970s to Richard Burke, a colleague in Ted Kennedy's office, that his mission with the tape recordings was to edit out "anything that would reflect badly on the family." Burke, who spent ten years as a personal aide to Senator Kennedy (and wrote a controversial and bestselling book in 1992 about those years), told me in a 1994 interview that he had read some of the Oval Office transcripts prepared by Dalton, which had been left on file in Ted Kennedy's office safe. The transcripts included a series of Oval Office telephone conversations between Jack Kennedy and two important women in his life, Judith Exner and Marilyn Monroe. There was much explicit talk of a sexual nature with Monroe, Burke said. The transcripts also revealed presidential talk of "cash payments" to various people and discussions of "federal grants and payments." Dalton told him, Burke said, that he had erased all of the references to cash payments from the tapes.

John F. Kennedy's papers and tapes were eventually transferred to the Federal Archives and Records Center in Waltham, Massachusetts, where the fledgling Kennedy Library began a custodial and processing activity. The Kennedy family formally deeded the president's papers and the White House tape recordings to the federal government in May 1976, and the Kennedy Library assumed physical control of the materials. By then, George Dalton and other Kennedy family insiders had had nearly thirteen years to do what they wished with the documents and recordings.

Dalton's transcripts, as a Kennedy Library archivist told me in 1994, were "ineptly done — riddled with errors and omissions — and hence useless for content research." Some of the tapes included what the archivist, who wished not to be named, depicted as "puzzling anomalies," with sections apparently spliced and removed. The library acknowledged to a reporter for the *Boston Globe* in 1993 that other tapes had been wound backwards, and at least nine tape boxes, as numbered by the Secret Service at the time of the recordings, were empty. In a history of its collection of presidential recordings, published in 1985, the library acknowledged that it could not be doubted "that at least some items were removed." The history also said that a preliminary survey of the tapes, made at the time the library took possession, "did not reveal tampering." George Dalton, who according to the *Globe* is today the owner of a string of gas stations in the Washington area, moved in the late 1980s to a home in a luxury area in Palm Beach Gardens, Florida. He has refused all interview requests in the past five years.

Over the next few weeks, as the reality set in — and the reality included the fact that Lyndon Johnson was president — the toll it took on Robert Kennedy began to show. In early 1964 Frank Mankiewicz, then working for the Peace Corps, was ordered by his superiors to discuss the pending War on Poverty with the attorney general, who had championed the legislation. "I must say," Mankiewicz told me in a 1994 interview, "I have never been as appalled at the sight of a human being since seeing a concentration camp as a nineteen-year-old infantryman. He was so wasted, like he disappeared into his shirt." Kennedy was "haunted" and "thin-wristed," Mankiewicz added. "He seemed out of it. The only thing he said was, 'Is this the program President Kennedy had in mind?' My thought was that this guy is not going to be a figure in American life again. He was going to get smaller and smaller and disappear. I've always thought that may be the reason he didn't talk about it [his brother's murder]. He knew talking could not bring him back to life, so why talk? I felt so sad." Kennedy recovered in time to win a tough campaign in the fall of

1964 for a seat in the Senate from New York, and Mankiewicz eventually became his press secretary.

Robert Kennedy did nothing to pursue the truth behind his brother's death in 1964. He would have done nothing even if he had won the Democratic nomination in 1968 and the presidency. The price of a full investigation was much too high: making public the truth about President Kennedy and the Kennedy family. It was this fear, certainly, that kept Robert Kennedy from testifying before the Warren Commission.

In a letter dated June 11, 1964, Earl Warren, the head of the commission, who was also Chief Justice of the Supreme Court, asked Kennedy whether he was "aware of any additional information relating to the assassination . . . which has not been sent to the Commission." Two months later Kennedy sent Warren a reply stating that he knew of no evidence suggesting that his brother had been murdered by "a domestic or foreign conspiracy." He added, "I have no suggestions to make at this time regarding any additional investigation which should be undertaken by the Commission prior to the publication of its report." He was not asked to testify.

CHAPTER NOTES

1. November 22

The best account of November 22 remains William Manchester's *The Death of a President,* published in 1967 by Harper and Row. Charles Spalding was interviewed by telephone and then at his home in Hillsborough, California, in May 1997. Martin E. Underwood was interviewed in Baltimore in July 1996 and January 1997. Charles Bartlett provided the author with some of his memoranda to John F. Kennedy and other documents during an interview at his Washington office in March 1994; other documents were provided in many subsequent interviews. Bartlett was interviewed on camera for Lancer Productions at his office in June 1997. Robert Bouck was interviewed at his home in suburban Virginia in December 1995. The John F. Kennedy Library at Columbia Point in Boston published a detailed memorandum on the White House taping system in April 1985; copies are available from the library. Philip Bennett of the *Boston Globe* wrote a series of penetrating articles on the taping system in March and April of 1993. Julius Draznin was interviewed four times for this book, beginning in April 1994 in Los Angeles and continuing in Chicago, where he moved, through the fall of 1997. He was interviewed at his home for Lancer Productions in June 1997. Evelyn Lincoln was interviewed three times in her suburban Maryland apartment, beginning in March of 1994. Tony Sherman of the Secret Service was interviewed twice, in March 1995 in Green Valley, Arizona, and again in

March 1997 at his new home in Salt Lake City. Sidney Mickelson was interviewed by telephone and over lunch near his art gallery in downtown Washington in April 1996.

2. Jack

The most compelling biography of John F. Kennedy is Nigel Hamilton's *JFK: Reckless Youth,* published by Random House in 1992. Hamilton did not write a planned second volume. *The Fitzgeralds and the Kennedys,* by Doris Kearns Goodwin, published by Simon and Schuster in 1987, also was invaluable. Other useful studies include *President Kennedy,* by Richard Reeves, published in 1993 by Simon and Schuster; *Front Runner, Dark Horse,* by Ralph G. Martin and Ed Plaut, published in 1960 by Doubleday; and two volumes by historian Herbert S. Parmet, *Jack: The Struggles of John F. Kennedy* (Dial, 1980), and *JFK: The Presidency of John F. Kennedy* (Dial, 1983). Jewel Reed was interviewed by telephone in December 1994, and for Lancer Productions at her home in Longmeadow, Massachusetts, in June 1997. Joseph Kennedy's fatalistic comments about his son were cited by William Manchester in *Portrait of a President,* published by Little, Brown in 1962. Marcus Raskin was interviewed in Washington twice, in December 1993 and April 1994, for this book, and in September 1996 for Lancer Productions. Larry Newman of the Secret Service was interviewed many times by telephone and at home in Fort Collins, Colorado, beginning in February 1995. He was interviewed in February and again in March of 1997 for Lancer Productions. Gloria Emerson was interviewed for this book and for Lancer Productions in New York City in June 1997. Hugh Sidey was interviewed in his offices at *Time* magazine in January 1995, and for Lancer Productions in May 1997. Joe Naar was interviewed at his home in Brentwood, California, for this book and for Lancer Productions in March 1997. Mrs. Betty Spalding was interviewed many times by telephone, beginning in January 1995, and at her home in Hartford, Connecticut, in May 1997. Dominick Dunne was interviewed by telephone from his home in Connecticut in December 1994. Bobby Baker was interviewed many times by telephone and at his home in Washington, beginning in February 1995. He was interviewed by Lancer Productions in Washington in September 1996 and May 1997. Richard Goodwin was interviewed by telephone many times, beginning in March 1994, and by Lancer Productions at his home in Concord, Massachusetts, in June 1997. Ralph Dungan kindly interceded with the Kennedy Library to allow me access to his closed oral history interview. Ben Bradlee was interviewed for this book and for Lancer Productions in Washington in September 1997. Jerry Bruno was interviewed three times by telephone, beginning in March 1994, and at his home in Portland, Maine, in May 1995.

3. Honey Fitz

The most detailed biography of John F. Fitzgerald is *"Honey Fitz": Three Steps to the White House,* by John Henry Cutler, published in 1962 by Bobbs-Merrill. See also "Honey Fitz," by Richard Russell, in *American Heritage* magazine, August 1968. The House debate that led to Fitzgerald's ouster from Congress can be found in the *Congressional Record* for October 23, 1919, beginning at page 7391. Fitzgerald's demise was headline news: see the *Boston Herald* for October 24, "House Votes to Oust Fitzgerald; Tague Then Takes His Seat." Chester Cooper was interviewed in Washington in December 1994.

4. Joe

There are two excellent biographies of Joseph Kennedy: *The Founding Father,* a pathbreaking book by Richard J. Whalen, published in 1964 by New American Library, and *Joseph P. Kennedy: A Life and Times,* by David E. Koskoff, published by Prentice-Hall in 1974 (many of Koskoff's interviews were done a decade earlier). Ronald Kessler's *The Sins of the Father,* published by Warner Books in 1996, contains much new information. Cartha DeLoach was interviewed for this book and for Lancer Productions at his home in Hilton Head, South Carolina, in June 1997. Harold E. Clancy was interviewed at his home in Boston in May 1995 and April 1997. Q. Byrum Hurst was interviewed by telephone by researcher Michael Ewing in February 1996. Judge Abraham Lincoln Marovitz was interviewed for this book and for Lancer Productions in his chambers in Chicago in June 1997. Mark Stuart's biography, *Gangster #2: Longy Zwillman, the Man Who Invented Organized Crime,* was published in 1985 by Lyle Stuart. The cited biography by Dennis Eisenberg, Uri Dan, and Eli Landau is entitled *Meyer Lansky: Mogul of the Mob,* published in 1979 by Paddington Press. The testimony of Thomas J. Cassara can be found in Part I of the Senate Hearings Before a Special Committee to Investigate Organized Crime in Interstate Commerce, known as the Kefauver hearings, that took place between May and September 1950. Daniel P. Sullivan and Charles "Joey" Fusco also testified before Kefauver. The Cassara link to Kennedy has received little attention, but was cited by the journalist Stephen Fox in *Blood and Power: Organized Crime in Twentieth-Century America,* published in 1989 by Morrow. Sandy Smith provided excellent guidance on organized crime in Chicago in many interviews, beginning in December 1993, on the telephone and at his home in Seeley Lake, Montana. He was interviewed for Lancer Productions in March 1997. Richard Rosenthal was interviewed in his office in Stamford, Connecticut, in April 1995. Milton Gould was interviewed in his New York office in April 1995. Edward K. Linen was interviewed by telephone in May 1995.

5. The Ambassador

The best account of Jimmy Roosevelt's questionable business dealings was published by Alva Johnston in the July 2, 1938, *Saturday Evening Post*, "Jimmy's Got It." For the Roosevelt tie to the National Grain Yeast Corporation, see "James Roosevelt Quits Jersey Firm," *New York Times*, November 21, 1935, page 9. Harvey Klemmer died in Eustis, Florida, in 1992. Phillip Whitehead, a London television producer, kindly provided me with a transcription, totaling 134 pages, of his interviews with Klemmer. For a good obit of Klemmer, see the London *Independent* of July 31, 1992. For Winston Churchill's shaving comment to his son, Randolph, see *Winston S. Churchill,* by Martin Gilbert, volume VI, Houghton Mifflin, 1983, at page 358. The Ickes diary citation can be found in volume III of *The Secret Diary of Harold L. Ickes,* Simon and Schuster, 1954. For an account of the anti-Hitler plotting, see *To Kill the Devil,* by Herbert Molloy Mason, Jr., published by Norton, 1978. The most direct of many planted stories promoting a Kennedy presidency in 1940 was "Will Kennedy Run for President?" by Ernest K. Lindley, in *Liberty* magazine, May 21, 1938. Walter Trohan was interviewed for this book and for Lancer Productions in Washington in August 1997. The disputed German foreign office documents cited in the footnote were the lead story in the *New York Times* for March 30, 1940, "U.S. Brands as False Nazi Documents Charging We Fostered War in Europe and Promised to Join Allies if Needed."

6. Taking On FDR

The Tyler Kent case, although little known, has been described in many books and articles. One full account, including interviews with Kent, can be found in the late John Costello's *Ten Days to Destiny,* published in 1991 by Morrow. One of the first accounts published in the United States to raise questions about Kennedy's role was written by Richard Whalen, "The Strange Case of Tyler Kent," in *Diplomat* magazine, November 1965. A much more sympathetic view of Kennedy's actions can be found in "Roosevelt and Prewar Commitment to Churchill: The Tyler Kent Affair," by Warren F. Kimball and Bruce Bartlett, *Diplomatic History,* Fall 1981. In England, see *Some Were Spies,* by the Earl of Jowitt, Hodder and Stoughton, 1954, and *The Man Who Was M,* by Anthony Masters, published in 1984 by Basil Blackwell (at chapter six). Robert Crowley was interviewed many times at his home in Washington, beginning in February 1995. He also kindly shared his file of thousands of declassified U.S. and British documents on the Kent case. Joe Kennedy's fight with Franklin Delano Roosevelt is described in much of the daily press reporting in late 1940; the Whalen and Koskoff biographies also tell the story. The cited British Foreign Ministry documents have been declassified by the British Foreign Office and are publicly available; a full set is in the author's possession. Gore Vidal's anecdote was published in "Eleanor," in the *New York Review of Books,* November 8, 1971. J. Edgar Hoover's file on Joe Kennedy and "Ben" Smith is included in Kennedy's declassified FBI files. Frank Waldrop provided some of his unpublished writings on Jack Kennedy and Inga Arvad in an interview at his home in Washington in February 1995. The Arvad affair is most fully reported in the Nigel Hamilton biography of John Kennedy.

7. Nomination for Sale

Rumors about corruption in the West Virginia primary election have been rampant since 1960, but the first book-length study on the election is *Kennedy vs. Humphrey, West Virginia, 1960,* by political scientist Dan B. Fleming, Jr.; it was published in 1992 by McFarland and Company. Ed Plaut, who now lives in Ridgefield, Connecticut, kindly provided the author with the original notes of interviews conducted with Jack and Joe Kennedy while he was researching *Front Runner, Dark Horse.* Hyman B. Raskin's unpublished memoir was made available for this book by his widow, Frances. Before his death, Raskin was interviewed twice at his home in Rancho Mirage, California, in November 1994 and March 1995. Alan Otten was interviewed by telephone in December 1994. Roscoe Born was interviewed three times by telephone, beginning in December 1994. Robert Novak was interviewed by telephone in September 1995. Max Kampelman was interviewed by telephone in October 1994 and again in January 1995. James McCahey was interviewed in his home in Bratenahl, Ohio, a suburb of Cleveland, in November 1996. Victor Gabriel was interviewed by telephone from his home in Clarksburg in November 1996. Bonn Brown of Elkins, West Virginia, was interviewed at his daughter's home in suburban Washington in June 1995. Curtis Trent was interviewed by telephone from Charleston, West Virginia, in June 1995. Rein Vander Zee was interviewed many times by telephone from his home in Bandera, Texas, beginning in November 1994. He was interviewed for Lancer Productions in Los Angeles in August 1997. Milton Rudin was interviewed twice at his home in Bel Air, California, and once in New York City, beginning in March 1994.

8. Threatened Candidacy

Former Senator George Smathers was interviewed in his Washington office in October 1994 and March 1995. He was interviewed for Lancer Productions in Washington in September 1996. Patricia Newcomb was interviewed in Los Angeles in June 1996 and January 1997. Vernon Scott was interviewed for this book and for Lancer Productions at his home in Studio City, California, in March 1997. John Miner was interviewed in Los Angeles in January 1997, and by Lancer Productions in March 1997. Michael Selsman was interviewed in his Los Angeles apartment in March 1995, and interviewed again in January 1997. He was interviewed by Lancer Productions in March 1997. James Bacon was interviewed for this book and for Lancer Productions at his home in Simi Valley, California, in March 1997. Florence Kater's FBI file, available under the Freedom of Information Act, includes copies of her letters to various public officials. Bob Clark was interviewed by telephone from his office in Washington in August 1997. Alicia Darr Clark's stormy marriage to Edmond Purdom was widely reported in gossip columns in the late 1950s and in the *New York Daily News*. See, for example, "Babs Coldly Foots It To Court; Purdom Sick," by Eleanor Packard in the *Daily News* for December 30, 1959, and "Marry-Go-Round Turns Into a Quad-Wrangle," by Henry Lee in the *Daily News* for September 10, 1961. Metrik and Friedman's travails also were reported in the *Daily News* for June 5, 1963, "2 Lawyers Censured for Their Particulars," by Alfred Albelli. The Appellate Division's disciplinary proceedings are cited as In Re Metrik, 240 N.Y.S.2d 443. Clark Clifford was interviewed twice for this book in his suburban Maryland home, in December 1994 and January 1996. H. Edward Munden was interviewed by telephone from his office in suburban Virginia in February 1995. Alicia Darr Clark was interviewed three times by telephone from her apartment in New York City, beginning in November 1996. Edmond Purdom was interviewed from his home in Rome by telephone in June 1997. Maxwell Rabb was interviewed in Washington in January 1995.

9. Lyndon

Robert Kennedy's many interviews with the Kennedy Library were collected in one volume and published by Bantam Books in 1988, entitled *Robert Kennedy: In His Own Words*. Bobby Baker's memoir, *Wheeling and Dealing*, written with Larry L. King, was published in 1978 by Norton. Pierre Salinger was interviewed in his Washington office three times, beginning in February 1994. Joseph Dolan was interviewed in Denver twice, in February 1995 and January 1997. Kennedy's quote to Kenny O'Donnell appears in *"Johnny, We Hardly Knew Ye,"* written with Dave Powers, published by Little, Brown in 1972.

10. The Stolen Election

There are a number of excellent books that describe Chicago, its politics, and its long-standing ties to organized crime figures such as Sam Giancana and Murray Humphreys. See *Secrecy and Power: The Life of J. Edgar Hoover*, by Richard Gid Powers, published in 1987 by the Free Press; *Roemer: Man Against the Mob*, by William F. Roemer, Jr., published in 1989 by Donald I. Fine; *Clout: Mayor Daley and His City*, by Len O'Connor, published in 1975 by Avon; *Captive City: Chicago in Chains*, by Ovid Demaris, published in 1969 by Lyle Stuart; *Boss: Richard J. Daley of Chicago*, by Mike Royko, published in 1971 by Dutton; and *The Legacy of Al Capone*, by George Murray, published by Putnam's, 1975. Benjamin Bradlee's quote about Mayor Daley and the 1960 election is in his revealing *Conversations with Kennedy*, published in 1975 by Norton. Robert McDonnell was interviewed for this book and for Lancer Productions in his suburban Chicago home in June 1997. Patrick Tuohy and his brother, John, were interviewed by telephone from Chicago in July 1997. Thomas King was interviewed in Chicago in September 1995. Tina Sinatra was interviewed in her offices in Burbank, California, for this book and for Lancer Productions in July 1997. *My Story*, by Judith Exner with Ovid Demaris, was published in 1977 by Grove Press. Robert Blakey was interviewed for this book and for Lancer Productions in New York in May 1997. Bill Woodfield was interviewed in Los Angeles in July 1995. Jeanne Humphreys was interviewed for this book and for Lancer Productions in Atlanta in February 1997. J. Edgar Hoover has been the subject of dozens of books. Some of the more recent include *Official and Confidential: The Secret Life of J. Edgar Hoover*, by Anthony Summers, published in 1993 by Putnam's; *Hoover's FBI*, by William W. Turner, published in 1993 by Thunder's Mouth Press; *J. Edgar Hoover: The Man and the Secrets*, by Curt Gentry, published in 1991 by Norton; and *Hoover's FBI: The Inside Story by Hoover's Trusted Lieutenant*, by Cartha D. "Deke" DeLoach, published in 1995 by Regnery. Thomas McCoy was interviewed by telephone from Washington in February 1995. William Colby was interviewed in Washington in February 1995. Hoover's conversation with Philip Hochstein was reported in *Official and Confidential*. Oscar Wyatt was interviewed by telephone in Houston in April 1995.

11. Campaign Secret

Lionel Krisel was interviewed many times by telephone and at his home in Bel Air, California, beginning in April 1995. He very kindly supplied many documents from his own research into the Bay of Pigs. The Nicolae Malaxa saga received more attention from the Congress than from the Washington press corps, with the exception of the columnist Drew Pearson. For one of many colloquies in the House, see the *Congressional Record* for October 5, 1962, at page 22672. For accounts of the Malaxa-Nixon relationship, see *Drew Pearson: Diaries 1949–59*, edited by Tyler Abell, published in 1974 by Holt, Rinehart and Winston; *The Secret War Against the Jews*, by John Loftus and Mark Aarons, published in 1994 by St. Martin's; *Richard Milhous Nixon*, by Roger Morris, published in 1990 by Henry Holt; and *Wanted! The Search for Nazis in America*, by Howard Blum, published in 1989 by Simon and Schuster. Gordon Mason was interviewed in his suburban Washington home in May and September 1996. His role in the Malaxa affair first surfaced in *Cold War Crucible: United States Foreign Policy and the Conflict in Romania, 1943–1953*, a doctoral thesis by Elizabeth W. Hazard published in 1996 by East European Monographs, distributed by Columbia University Press. Kenneth Crosby was interviewed in Washington in July 1996. The most important government document on the assassination plot against Fidel Castro is the report *Alleged Assassination Plots Involving Foreign Leaders*, published in November 1975 by the Senate Select Committee to Study Governmental Operation with Respect to Intelligence Activities (the Church Report). The most informative and nuanced book on the CIA published in recent years is *The Man Who Kept the Secrets: Richard Helms and the CIA*, by Thomas Powers, published in 1979 by Knopf. Robert Maheu was interviewed at his home in Las Vegas in November 1994, and many times thereafter by telephone. He was interviewed by Lancer Productions in Las Vegas in May 1997. Cuba's seizure of David Christ and his CIA colleagues was described in "Our Men in Havana," by Nathan Nielsen, an internal CIA study that was declassified in 1994 after its publication in *Studies in Intelligence,* the CIA's in-house journal. The study is in the author's possession. Thornton Anderson, one of the agents arrested, was interviewed by telephone in February 1995. Peter Wyden's study *Bay of Pigs: The Untold Story,* published in 1979 by Simon and Schuster, is by far the most detailed account of the failed invasion. The CIA's Inspector General's Report was declassified, without significant deletions, in 1993 and released to the public under the Freedom of Information Act. The IG Report was heavily relied upon by the Church Committee during its investigation in 1975.

12. Trapping Nixon

Richard Bissell's posthumous memoir, *Reflections of a Cold Warrior,* written with Jonathan E. Lewis and Frances T. Pudlo, was published in 1996 by Yale University Press. Clarence Sprouse was interviewed by telephone from Converse, Texas, in April 1995. Bissell's oral history interview with the Kennedy Library took place on April 25, 1967. R. Harris Smith was interviewed by telephone from the San Jose area of California in April 1995. Grayston Lynch was interviewed three times by telephone from Tampa, Florida, beginning in April 1995; in 1998 Brassey will publish his memoir, *Decision for Disaster: Betrayal at the Bay of Pigs.* Allen Dulles's oral history interview with the Kennedy Library was taped on December 5 and 6, 1964. The Kennedy din-ner with Ian Fleming was also described by John Pearson in his 1966 book, *The Life of Ian Fleming,* published by McGraw-Hill. John Patterson was interviewed by tele-phone from Montgomery, Alabama, in January 1997; the cited newspaper article was "Patterson Told Secret Cuban Invasion Plans to Candidate JFK," by Andrew Kil-patrick, *Birmingham News,* October 24, 1982. For more on the Nixon-Kennedy polit-ical skirmishing around the final television debate in October 1960, see *Remember-ing America: A Voice from the Sixties,* by Richard N. Goodwin, published by Little, Brown in 1988; *Nixon: The Education of a Politician 1913–62,* by Stephen E. Ambrose, published in 1987 by Simon and Schuster; *Kennedy and Nixon,* by Christopher Matthews, published in 1996 by Simon and Schuster; and "Necessary Lies, Hidden Truths: Cuba in the 1960 Campaign," by Kent M. Beck, in *Diplomatic History,* Winter 1984. Richard Nixon's much-cited memoir, *RN: The Memoirs of Richard Nixon,* was published in 1978 by Grosset and Dunlap.

13. Executive Action

During the course of research into this book, the author was provided with a copy of William Harvey's personnel file; it includes many documents not made public by the CIA and the Church Committee. There are extensive discussions of executive action in the Church Report and in the CIA Inspector General's Report. The CIA has declassified thousands of documents on executive action in recent years; they should be available through the Freedom of Information Act. For more on the CIA and Guatemala, see "CIA Plotting Killing of 58 in Guatemala," by Tim Weiner, *New York Times,* May 28, 1997; and *Harper's* magazine for August 1997, at page 22. Doris Mirage, whose married name is Doris Kitzmiller, was interviewed by telephone from her home in North Carolina in December 1995. McGeorge Bundy's testimony before the Rockefeller Commission was declassified in 1996. David Belin was interviewed in Washington in April 1997. Lawrence Devlin was interviewed by telephone for his book in May 1994. Dr. Sidney Gottlieb was interviewed at his farm in rural Virginia in November 1994. Samuel Halpern was interviewed many times for this book, in Washington and at his home in suburban Virginia, beginning in November 1993. He was interviewed in February 1997 for Lancer Productions. Michael R. Beschloss's *The Crisis Years: Kennedy and Khrushchev, 1960–1963* (HarperCollins, 1991) consistently provided comprehensive and judicious reportage. The best account of the CIA's role in the Congo can be found in *The Congo Cables: The Cold War in Africa, from Eisenhower to Kennedy,* by Madeleine G. Kalb, published in 1982 by Macmillan. Igor Cassini's self-serving, although fascinating, account of his involvement with the Kennedy family and the Dominican Republic is in *I'd Do It All Over Again,* a memoir written with Jeanne Molli, published in 1977 by Putnam's. The best account of the early 1961 diplomacy involving Joseph Kennedy is "Diplomat Made a Secret Visit to Trujillo for Kennedy in '61," by Tad Szulc, *New York Times,* July 22, 1962. Tom Powers shared his notes on Tofte with me in an interview in April 1994 and in a subsequent written recollection.

14. Bay of Pigs

Three other useful studies of the Bay of Pigs are *The Cuban Invasion,* by Karl E. Meyer and Tad Szulc, published in 1962 by Praeger; "Ships in the Night: The CIA, the White House and the Bay of Pigs," by Piero Gleijeses, in the *Journal of Latin American Studies* for February 1995; and "Cuba: The Record Set Straight," by Charles J. V. Murphy, in the September 1961 *Fortune* magazine. Apparently only one political scientist, H. Bradford Westerfield of Yale University, has made any systematic attempt to connect the ongoing assassination plotting against Castro to the Bay of Pigs. In a letter published in the *New York Review of Books* for October 23, 1997, Westerfield suggested that Bissell's willingness to accept the constant White House cutbacks in the invasion stemmed from his belief that Castro would be dead by the time the exiles hit the beach. "Indeed," Westerfield wrote, "Kennedy's own insistence on the cutbacks may well have been buoyed by the same closely held secret knowledge, but for this surmise there is less evidence." Jacob Esterline was interviewed at his home in Henderson, North Carolina, in March 1995, and many times thereafter by telephone. Thomas Polgar was interviewed at his home in Orlando, Florida, in May 1994. Ernest Betancourt was interviewed in Washington in March 1994. Hedley Donovan's cited memoir is *Roosevelt to Reagan: A Reporter's Encounters with Nine Presidents,* published in 1987 by Harper and Row. The cited White House documents have been declassified and are available in the Department of State's history series known as the *Foreign Relations of the United States, 1961–1963,* published by the Government Printing Office in Washington. The reminiscences of Admiral Robert L. Dennison are available from the U.S. Naval Institute in Annapolis, Maryland; the interviews were conducted between November 1972 and July 1973. Janet Weininger was interviewed by telephone many times from her home in Florida beginning in April 1997; she kindly supplied me with notes and other documents dealing with her father and the CIA. For an account of her father's death, see "The Mission," by Candace M. Turtle, in *Tropic,* the *Miami Herald Sunday Magazine,* for June 21, 1987. Rose Kennedy's memoir is *Times to Remember,* published in 1974 by Doubleday.

15. Secret Service

Along with Tony Sherman and Larry Newman (see notes for Chapters One and Two, respectively), two other Secret Service agents agreed to be extensively interviewed for this book. William "Tim" McIntyre was interviewed in Phoenix, Arizona, in March 1995, and interviewed again by Lancer Productions at his home in May 1997. Joseph Paolella was interviewed in Los Angeles in May 1995, and by Lancer Productions in Los Angeles in March 1997. Hugh Sidey's account of Kennedy's speed-reading appeared in *Life* magazine, March 17, 1961, "The President's Voracious Reading Habits." Blair Clark was interviewed by telephone from New York in October 1994; he was interviewed by Lancer Productions in New York in June 1997. Fred Holborn was interviewed in Washington in January 1995. Some of Jack Kennedy's medical files, including the notes taken by Dr. William P. Herbst, Jr., were kindly shared with me by Richard Reeves, the author of *President Kennedy.* Dr. Sidney Wolf was interviewed in his Washington office in April 1995. For an excellent newspaper discussion of chlamydia and its implications for women, see "It's Called Chlamydia," by Susan Okie, in the health supplement to the *Washington Post,* June 24, 1997. Dr. Manfred Wasserman was interviewed by telephone from his home in New Mexico in April 1995. Dr. Max Jacobson's unpublished manuscript was supplied through the courtesy of Richard Reeves. A thorough account of Jacobson's high-risk treatment was written by Boyce Rensberger in the *New York Times* on December 4, 1972, "Amphetamines Used by a Physician to Lift Moods of Famous Patients." The writer Gore Vidal, cited in a footnote, was interviewed many times for this book beginning in December 1994. Judge William Orrick of the U.S. District Court in San Francisco was interviewed in his chambers in June 1996. For a review of the General Aniline & Film Corporation dispute, see *Robert A. Schmitz v. Société Internationale et al.,* case number 85-47 on the civil docket of the U.S. District Court for the District of Columbia. Mary Gallagher's *My Life with Jacqueline Kennedy* was published by Van Rees in 1969. The upgrading and remodeling of the White House pool was innocently reported in *Time* magazine on December 7, 1962.

16. Crisis in Berlin

Morton Halperin was interviewed in Washington in July 1995. The cited Joseph Alsop comment can be found in *The Kennedy Crises: The Press, the Presidency and Foreign Policy,* by Montague Kern, Patricia W. Levering, and Ralph B. Levering, published in 1983 by the University of North Carolina Press. David Herbert Donald was interviewed from Boston by telephone in June 1996. The CIA's David E. Murphy was interviewed by telephone in July 1997; his book, *Battleground Berlin: CIA vs. KGB in the Cold War,* written with Sergei A. Kondrashev and George Bailey, was published by Yale University Press in 1997. Raymond Garthoff's important article on Checkpoint Charlie, "Berlin 1961: The Record Corrected," appeared in the Fall 1991 issue of *Foreign Policy.* Bobby Kennedy's tough television talk was reported on September 25, 1961, in the *New York Times,* "Robert Kennedy Says U.S. Would Use A-Bombs," by Robert F. Whitney. Jack Kennedy's policies are fully described in the *New York Times* edition of the Pentagon Papers, published in 1971 by Bantam. Tim Weiner's *New York Times* dispatch on Cheddi Jagan appeared on October 30, 1994, "A Kennedy-C.I.A. Plot Returns to Haunt Clinton."

17. Target Castro

Peter Wright's memoir, *Spycatcher,* was published by Viking in 1987. For a good account of the Taylor study group and its recommendations, see *Operation Zapata,* edited by Paul L. Desaris and published in 1981 by University Publications of America, Inc. Gerry McCabe described life in the White House in an interview in Washington in September 1995. The transcript of the Burke-Lemnitzer conversation was provided for this book by Lionel Krisel.

(Admiral Burke, and his unflinching integrity, was a source of concern for the president. On February 15, 1961, dozens of newspapers in America and around the world published a tough-talking interview in which Burke asserted that the U.S. Navy had the right to "go where we please in international waters"— including the Black Sea. It seemed to be a direct violation of an early administration directive barring such interviews, but, as it turned out, the interview, by prominent Greek journalist Elias Demetracopoulos of the *Athens Daily Post,* had been conducted on January 12, 1961, and cleared for publication by the outgoing Eisenhower administration. Kennedy got a big laugh, nonetheless, at a news conference on February 15 when he remarked that Burke's interview "makes me happier than ever that such a directive has gone out." The public rebuke of the admiral, who became famed as "Thirty-One-Knot Burke" while commanding a successful destroyer flotilla in the Pacific during World War II, created instant enmity among the Pentagon's senior officer corps and also led to extensive hearings by a Senate Armed Services subcommittee into what became known as Kennedy's "muzzling" of the military. The hearings received significant press attention at the time but little since then from the many Kennedy biographers, although the enmity between the military men in the Pentagon and the

White House may have played a role in the military's docile acceptance of the poorly planned, and thus doomed, Bay of Pigs invasion. Kennedy's distrust of the military became clear during the Bay of Pigs, as reported earlier in this book, when the White House overrode the normal chain of command and gave direct orders to the Atlantic Fleet. Demetracopoulos suffered for publishing his interview with Burke: a State Department notice eventually was sent to all American embassies in NATO countries cautioning senior officials against the granting of any interviews to him. He also was investigated for years by the CIA, at the request of Pierre Salinger, the White House press secretary.)

Walter N. Elder was interviewed twice at his suburban Virginia home, in November 1993 and October 1994; he was interviewed by Lancer Productions in June 1997. Thomas Parrott was interviewed in Washington in June 1995. Robert Hurwitch was interviewed many times by telephone from Santo Domingo in the Dominican Republic, beginning in November 1993; his privately published memoir is entitled *Most of Myself.* For more on Edward Lansdale (but not Cuba), see his autobiography, *In the Midst of Wars: An American's Mission to Southeast Asia,* published in 1972 by Harper and Row. For more on Maxwell Taylor, see his *The Uncertain Trumpet,* published in 1959 by Harper and Row. The vast majority of Mongoose documents have been declassified and are available in the State Department's *Foreign Relations of the United States, 1961* series. Tad Szulc was interviewed in Washington in March and May 1994. Angie Novello's brief telephone conversation with me took place in December 1994. The quotation from John Lewis Gaddis appears in *We Now Know: Rethinking Cold War History,* published in 1997 by Clarendon Press-Oxford.

18. Judy

Judith Campbell Exner was interviewed at length at her home in Newport, California, in July 1994; there were many subsequent telephone calls. She was interviewed in nearby Newport Beach for Lancer Productions in August 1997. The most important published works on her, along with *My Story* (Grove Press, 1977), include "The Dark Side of Camelot," by Kitty Kelley, *People* magazine, February 29, 1988; "Kennedy, the Mafia and Me," London *Sunday Times* magazine, by Anthony Summers, October 6, 1991; and "The Exner Files," by Liz Smith, *Vanity Fair* magazine, January 1997. For a typical mid-1950s movie magazine spread on Judy Campbell and her husband, see "New Men in Town," *Movie Stars* magazine, August 1955. Gail Laird, the daughter of Bill Thompson, was interviewed in Miami, Florida, in January 1995. William R. Carter was interviewed in Oklahoma City, Oklahoma, in February 1997. Jane Leahy was interviewed by telephone from her home on Cape Cod in November 1995. The FBI communications about the August 1962 break-in at Exner's apartment were released under the Freedom of Information Act. For a good account of the TFX issue, as known at the time, see *The TFX Decision: McNamara and the Military,* by Robert J. Art, published in 1968 by Little, Brown; see also *The Pentagon: Politics, Profits, and Plunder,* by Clark R. Mollenhoff, published in 1967 by Putnam's. Tommy Hale was interviewed by telephone from his home in Fort Worth, Texas, in June 1996. George Spangenberg was interviewed in his suburban Virginia home in March 1997. Johnny Grant was interviewed in Los Angeles in November 1994; he was interviewed for Lancer Productions in Los Angeles in July 1997.

19. First Marriage

The British press has written widely in recent years about Durie Malcolm and her alleged marriage to John F. Kennedy. See "JFK's EX File," by Tim Carroll, London *Sunday Times* magazine, January 26, 1997. Father James J. O'Rourke was interviewed by telephone from his parish in Boston in June 1997; he was interviewed in Boston by Lancer Productions later that month. Frances Howe was interviewed by telephone in June 1997. Morton Downey, Jr., was interviewed by telephone in August 1997. Clark Clifford's memoir, *Counsel to the President,* with Richard Holbrooke, was published by Random House in 1991. Sue Waite was interviewed by telephone for this book from her home in Marietta, Georgia, by Ed Gray of Lancer Productions in December 1996. Maxine Cheshire was interviewed by telephone from Houston, Texas, in February 1995.

20. Missile Crisis

Of the many books on the missile crisis, a few stand out: *"One Hell of a Gamble": Khrushchev, Castro, and Kennedy, 1958–1964,* by Fursenko and Naftali, published in 1997 by Norton; *The Crisis Years: Kennedy and Khrushchev, 1960–1963,* by Beschloss, published in 1991 by HarperCollins; *Eyeball to Eyeball,* by Dino A. Brugioni, published in 1991 by Random House; *In Confidence,* by Anatoly Dobrynin, published in 1995 by Times Books; *Reflections on the Cuban Missile Crisis,* by Raymond L. Garthoff, published in 1989 by the Brookings Institution; *The Cuban Missile Crisis Revisited,* edited by James A. Nathan, published in 1992 by St. Martin's (see especially the chapter "Reconsidering the Missile Crisis," by Barton J. Bernstein); and *Thirteen Days,* by Robert F. Kennedy, published in 1969 by Norton. Arthur Schlesinger's *A Thousand Days* and Theodore Sorensen's *Kennedy* also include long sections on the missile crisis. The view from the Soviet and American military is presented in *Operation Anadyr,* by General Anatoli I. Gribkov and General William Y. Smith, published in 1994 by Edition Q. The account of DEFCON 2 comes from Brugioni. The first details about Project Mongoose and its implications for the Soviet planning for Cuba were declassified in early 1989, just as an international conference in Moscow on the missile crisis was scheduled to get under way. See "Document Details '62 Plan on Cuba," by Michael Dobbs in the *Washington Post* for January 27, 1989. Two days later came the first detailed reports of Soviet nuclear preparations in 1962. See "Missiles Aimed at U.S. in '62," by Dobbs, in the *Washington Post* for January 29, 1989. For an excellent account of the deployment of the Jupiter missiles, see *The Other Missiles of Octo-*

ber, by Philip Nash, published in 1997 by the University of North Carolina Press. The first volume fo Nikita Khrushchev's memoirs, *Khrushchev Remembers,* was edited and translated by Strobe Talbott, and published by Little, Brown in 1970. The CIA's extensive intelligence reporting on the extent of the Soviet missile deployment can be found in volume XI of the State Department's *Foreign Relations of the United States* series, *Cuban Missile Crisis and Aftermath.* Walter Lippmann's problems with Jack Kennedy and his later capitulation is described in *Walter Lippmann and the American Century,* by Ronald Steel, published in 1980 by Atlantic-Little, Brown. Kennedy's role in the public attacks on Adlai Stevenson after the crisis is described in *The Papers of Adlai E. Stevenson,* volume VIII, edited by Walter Johnson et al. (Little, Brown, 1979).

21. Deceptions

Alexander Haig's memoir, *Inner Circles,* was published by Warner Books in 1992. The testimony from Dean Rusk and Robert McNamara, and the letter to Bundy from Raymond Aron, were cited in Philip Nash's *The Other Missiles of October.* Elie Abel's *The Missile Crisis* was published in 1966 by Lippincott. General Charles Johnson's interview with the Church Committee was obtained under the Freedom of Information Act; it was not published in the committee's report. Jack Kennedy's meeting in Miami with the exiles can be found in *The Bay of Pigs,* by Haynes Johnson, published in 1964 by Norton. *The Very Best Men,* by Evan Thomas, was published in 1995 by Simon and Schuster. Some documents describing the ad hoc exile group were declassified in late 1996 and published as part of the ongoing series *Foreign Relations of the United States: Cuban Missile Crisis and Aftermath,* volume XI. The best account of the Kennedy administration's secret maneuverings behind the 1963 test ban treaty can be found in the cited I. F. Stone essay, "The Test Ban Comedy," published on May 7, 1970, by the *New York Review of Books.* Stone's essay was the third of a four-part series on the arms race since the early 1800s.

22. Ellen

Ellen Rometsch has been ignored by the media since the mid-1960s, when she briefly came into prominence as part of the Bobby Baker scandal. The final report on the Baker case was filed on July 8, 1964, in the Senate: *Financial or Business Interests of Officers or Employees of the Senate,* published by the Committee on Rules and Administration. A good early article on the Baker scandal was published on November 22, 1963, by *Life* magazine, "The Bobby Baker Scandal," by Keith Wheeler; also see Baker's 1978 memoir, *Wheeling and Dealing,* for a self-serving but very readable account. The Profumo affair caused a sensation in the United States as well as Great Britain in mid-1963; see "The Crisis over Christine," by Edward Behr, in the *Saturday Evening Post* for July 13, 1963, for a sense of the story. Beschloss and Reeves have good summary accounts of the scandal and its impact on the Macmillan government and British diplomacy. Two books have been published on the Profumo affair: *Honey Trap*, by Anthony Summers and Stephen Dorril, published in 1987 by Coronet, and *An Affair of State: The Profumo Case and the Framing of Stephen Ward*, by Phillip Knightley and Caroline Kennedy, published in 1987 by Atheneum. Cleveland Cram was interviewed in Washington in July 1997 and for Lancer Productions in Washington a month later. Brian Horan was interviewed by telephone from his home in New Jersey in August 1997; his brother, Gary, was interviewed by telephone from his office in Brooklyn a few days later. Warren Rogers was interviewed by telephone in February 1994 and again in August 1997. The footnoted intervention of James McInerney in the Los Angeles newspaper suspensions was not publicly known at the time. George Miron was interviewed in his Washington office in February 1996. The delayed publication of the Congressional hearings on the newspaper closings can be found as *The Failing Newspaper Act*, before the House Subcommittee on Antitrust and Monopoly, March and April 1963, published in 1968 by the Senate Judiciary Committee's Subcommittee on Antitrust and Monopoly. Pat Holt was interviewed in his suburban Maryland home in October 1994. Courtney Evans was interviewed at his office in Washington in May 1994, May 1995, and April 1997. Evans's FOIA document was made public in the 1980s, as were other Justice Department memoranda relied upon in this chapter. The full import of those documents, in terms of the direct concern of President Kennedy, was not clear until this book. Raymond Wannell was interviewed at his home in suburban Maryland in March 1994, and by telephone in August 1997. Wayne Duffy was interviewed four times by telephone from his home in southern California in July and August 1997. Georgia Liakakis was interviewed by telephone from her home in suburban Maryland in April 1997. The cited Mollenhoff article was "U.S. Expels Girls Linked to Officials," October 26, 1963, in the *Des Moines Register*. Mike Mansfield was interviewed by telephone from his Washington office in September 1997. Burkett Van Kirk was interviewed many times in Washington for this book, beginning in December 1993; he was interviewed in his home in Sea Pines, Georgia, by Lancer Productions in June 1997. Adam Walinsky was interviewed in his New York office in May 1993. Frank Harrington was interviewed three times by telephone from his home on Cape Cod, beginning in February 1994. Grant Stockdale was interviewed in Washington in April 1996.

23. Vietnam

The best account of the events leading up to Diem's murder can be found in *A Death in November*, by Ellen J. Hammer, published in 1987 by Dutton. The book attracted much less attention than it deserved. For a good overview of the Kennedy administration's policies in South Vietnam, see *The Best and the Brightest*, David Halberstam's classic, published in 1972 by Random House; *The Irony of Vietnam: The System Worked*, by Leslie H. Gelb with Richard K. Betts, published in 1979 by the Brookings Institution; and *An International History of the Vietnam War: The Kennedy Strategy*, by R. B. Smith, published in 1987 by St. Martin's. Also see Noam Chomsky's brilliant essay on the Kennedy impact in Vietnam, *Rethinking Camelot*, published in 1993 by Verso. Michael Forrestal's testimony was cited (at page 138) in *The U.S. Government and the Vietnam War, Part II, 1961–1964*, published in 1984 by Congressional Research Service of the Library of Congress for the Senate Committee on Foreign Relations. The volumes were written by Dr. William Conrad Gibbons of the Research Service. For a critical review of Henry Cabot Lodge's service in Vietnam, see *Lodge in Vietnam: A Patriot Abroad*, by Anne E. Blair, published in 1995 by Yale University Press. The Kennedy family's early history with Ngo Dinh Diem was reported in Part I, published in April 1984, of the previously cited Library of Congress history of American involvement in Vietnam. Lucien Conein was interviewed at his suburban Virginia home in January 1996. General Paul Harkins's praise for Diem can be found in the Pentagon Papers. William Manchester was interviewed in his office in Middletown, Connecticut, in July 1995, and by telephone thereafter. Henry Cabot Lodge's papers and unpublished memoir are on file at the Massachusetts Historical Society in Boston. Mieczyslaw Maneli's cited op-ed article in the *New York Times* was "Vietnam, '63 and Now," January 27, 1975. One American scholar who has extensively researched the issue of neutralism in South Vietnam in the early 1960s is Robert K. Brigham of Vassar College. His forthcoming book is *The NLF's Foreign Relations and the Viet Nam War*, to be published by Cornell University Press. Richard Smyser was interviewed in Washington in July 1995. Allen Whiting was interviewed in Washington in September 1995. Tom Hughes was interviewed in Washington in December 1994, and by telephone from New Delhi, India, in September 1997. Rufus Phillips was interviewed in his suburban Virginia home in December 1995; he provided the author with a copy of an unpublished memoir of his service in Vietnam. Daniel Ellsberg was initially interviewed in December 1995 about his conversations with Edward Lansdale; he wrote a detailed summary of those talks for this book in April 1997. Senator Mike Mansfield's recollection about Kennedy's plan for a pullout in South Vietnam has been widely quoted; see "LBJ and the Kennedys," by Kenneth O'Donnell, *Life* magazine, August 7, 1970. Joe Croken was interviewed by telephone from Boston in September 1997. Herbert Parmet kindly supplied the author with tape recordings of his 1977 interviews with Eleanore Carney. Torbert Macdonald, Jr., was interviewed by telephone from his home in Cape Neddick, Maine, in December 1994 and September 1997. Tran Van Dinh was interviewed at his home in Washington in June 1995.

24. Last Days

Malcolm Kilduff was interviewed three times by telephone from his home in Kentucky, beginning in February 1995; he was interviewed in Washington for Lancer Productions in September 1996. Hugh Sidey's cited column on Kennedy, "Upstairs at the White House," was published in *Time* magazine on May 18, 1987. James Johnston was interviewed in Washington in March 1994 and May 1995. The cited Stewart Alsop column was "A Conversation with President Kennedy," in the *Saturday Evening Post* for

January 1, 1966. Karl Kaysen was interviewed in Boston in May 1994. Donald Reynolds's testimony before Burkett Van Kirk and the Senate Rules Committee was described in Clark Mollenhoff's *Despoilers of Democracy,* published in 1965 by Doubleday.

Epilogue

James Dingeman was interviewed by telephone from his suburban Virginia home in November 1993 and May 1995. Richard Burke was interviewed in Washington in March 1994 and in Los Angeles in January 1997. His much-criticized book on Senator Ted Kennedy, which became a bestseller nonetheless, is *The Senator: My Ten Years with Ted Kennedy,* published in 1992 by St. Martin's. Frank Mankiewicz was interviewed in his Washington office in April 1994. Bobby Kennedy's exchange of letters with Earl Warren is included among the records of the Warren Commission.

ACKNOWLEDGMENTS

In the five years I worked on this book, I was constantly amazed by the number of former Kennedy administration officials who agreed to be interviewed, and agreed to have their interviews put on the record. Many of Kennedy's personal friends and associates also talked openly and honestly to me. Their purpose in talking was merely to try to set the record straight. I hope I've done them justice.

This book owes its being to Jim Silberman, senior editor at Little, Brown and Company, who began urging me a decade ago to write about the presidency and the Cold War. His sense of what may be out there is uncanny, and his constant support and encouragement were essential to getting it done. My editor, Corby Kummer, of Boston, has his fingerprints on every page, every paragraph, every comma. His unyielding standards and sense of how to tell a story, and how to tell it grammatically, were crucial to this book. Peggy Leith Anderson, developmental editor at Little, Brown, was relentless in the search for facts and readability; her sensible queries were a delight (usually). Sarah Crichton, the publisher of Little, Brown, was formidable in her enthusiasm and support for this project. My agent, Heather Schroder of International Creative Management, provided expert counsel at the right time.

I was blessed with the services of Max Friedman, now a graduate student at the University of California. Max is a brilliant researcher, fact-checker, collaborator, and rewrite man, and a wonderful friend. Jock Friedly, of Washington, also did inspired research for this book, and I thank him, too.

Beginning in the fall of 1996, much of the reporting for this book was done in collaboration with Lancer Productions, an independent television production company owned by Mark Obenhaus, a New York filmmaker. Obenhaus bought the television rights to *The Dark Side of Camelot* in July 1996. In my thirty-five years as a journalist, I have never worked with a more dedicated and more committed group of reporters and researchers. Mark Obenhaus is a superb journalist, as is his fellow producer, Edward Gray, and their associate producer, Richard E. Robbins. Gus Russo did an outstanding job as a researcher, especially on organized crime issues. Sally Rosenthal was consistently cheerful and helpful, and a marvelous fact-checker.

S.M.H.

INDEX